About This Book

Why is this topic important?

Organizations and managers are facing unforeseen technological, labor force, economic, environmental, political, and social issues and changes. They are increasingly operating in international and world settings. The organization development (OD) profession and field is extending its range of knowledge and methodologies to be responsive, relevant, and effective in assisting organizations and managers with these issues and changes. New OD practitioners, students in academic and certificate OD programs, and even experienced practitioners are faced with understanding and integrating an evolving profession and field with many schools of thought and an extensive body of knowledge, theory, and methodology. *The NTL Handbook of Organization Development and Change* supports the effectiveness and development of OD practitioners and consultants by providing a description of the organization development profession and field and in-depth explorations of key OD approaches and applications. The book presents a framework for thinking about and understanding the variety and range of OD work in organizations. Core OD methods and approaches are described, along with new knowledge and innovations.

What can you achieve with this book?

The NTL Handbook of Organization Development and Change is a resource for OD practitioners and others interested in OD as they enter the field, participate in professional development and degree programs, and seek to gain information and understanding about OD as a profession and field, or aspects of the practice of OD. Based on the thinking and experiences of a range of academicians, researchers, and seasoned practitioners, many perspectives and approaches are discussed, explored, and examined, making this a useful and comprehensive handbook. The integrative perspective in *The NTL Handbook of Organization Development and Change* reflects the current state of the field and the complexity of organizations and the world; it offers working models for the development of OD consultants.

How is this book organized?

The book has seven parts. The first three parts describe the core elements of the OD field: the field and profession itself and its values and history, core theories and methods, and the phases of the OD process. The next three parts focus on the evolving nature and practice of organization development: working from different levels of systems perspectives, the practice of OD in international and world settings, and new and emerging applications. Part Seven addresses the future of the field and profession. The book is designed so that each chapter can be read separately, and sections and chapters are organized in a way that recognizes the evolving nature of the field. The content flows generally from core methodology and practice to innovation and from historical to present to future perspectives.

About Pfeiffer

Pfeiffer serves the professional development and hands-on resource needs of training and human resource practitioners and gives them products to do their jobs better. We deliver proven ideas and solutions from experts in HR development and HR management, and we offer effective and customizable tools to improve workplace performance. From novice to seasoned professional, Pfeiffer is the source you can trust to make yourself and your organization more successful.

Essential Knowledge Pfeiffer produces insightful, practical, and comprehensive materials on topics that matter the most to training and HR professionals. Our Essential Knowledge resources translate the expertise of seasoned professionals into practical, how-to guidance on critical workplace issues and problems. These resources are supported by case studies, worksheets, and job aids and are frequently supplemented with CD-ROMs, Web sites, and other means of making the content easier to read, understand, and use.

Essential Tools Pfeiffer's Essential Tools resources save time and expense by offering proven, ready-to-use materials—including exercises, activities, games, instruments, and assessments—for use during a training or team-learning event. These resources are frequently offered in looseleaf or CD-ROM format to facilitate copying and customization of the material.

Pfeiffer also recognizes the remarkable power of new technologies in expanding the reach and effectiveness of training. While e-hype has often created whizbang solutions in search of a problem, we are dedicated to bringing convenience and enhancements to proven training solutions. All our e-tools comply with rigorous functionality standards. The most appropriate technology wrapped around essential content yields the perfect solution for today's on-the-go trainers and human resource professionals.

www.pfeiffer.com

Essential resources for training and HR professionals

THE NTL HANDBOOK OF ORGANIZATION DEVELOPMENT AND CHANGE

THE NTL HANDBOOK OF ORGANIZATION DEVELOPMENT AND CHANGE

Principles, Practices, and Perspectives

Brenda B. Jones and Michael Brazzel, Editors

Pfeiffer
A Wiley Imprint
www.pfeiffer.com

Published by Pfeiffer
An Imprint of Wiley
989 Market Street, San Francisco, CA 94103-1741
www.pfeiffer.com

Library of Congress Cataloging-in-Publication Data

The NTL handbook of organization development and change: principles, practices, and perspectives /
　　Brenda B. Jones and Michael Brazzel, editors.
　　　　p. cm.
　　Includes bibliographical references and index.
　　ISBN-13: 978-0-7879-7773-3 (alk. paper)
　　ISBN-10: 0-7879-7773-X (alk. paper)
　　1. Organizational change—Management. 2. Business consultants—Handbooks, manuals, etc. I. Title: Handbook of organization development and change. II. Jones, Brenda B. III. Brazzel, Michael. IV. NTL Institute for Applied Behavioral Science.
　　HD58.8.N78 2006
　　658.4'06—dc22

Acquiring Editor: Matt Davis
Director of Development: Kathleen Dolan Davies
Developmental Editor: Susan Rachmeler
Production Editor: Andrea Flint

Editor: Thomas Finnegan
Manufacturing Supervisor: Becky Carreño
Illustrations: Lotus Art

Printed in the United States of America
Printing　10　9　8　7　6　5

CONTENTS

Contents

PART FIVE: ORGANIZATION DEVELOPMENT IN AN INTERNATIONAL AND WORLD SETTING

PART SIX: ORGANIZATION DEVELOPMENT APPLICATIONS AND PRACTICES

PART SEVEN: THE FUTURE OF ORGANIZATION DEVELOPMENT

FIGURES, TABLES, AND EXHIBITS

Figures

Tables

Exhibits

FOREWORD

We are writing this from the Bingham House in Bethel, Maine, a few hundred feet from the Founders House of the NTL Institute. It seems like an appropriate setting since our own experience, and that of most if not all, of the contributing authors of this volume has been deeply influenced by the founders and pioneers of what began as the National Training Laboratory in Group Development in 1946. This early name actually has a great deal of meaning, and the chapters of this book consistently mirror the underlying concerns, values, and dreams of those who led the way for NTL to become a major force in the field of organization development.

National is the word that seems to represent the tentative or conservative nature of the original group and a reluctance to assert that the methods and practices might somehow reach around the globe. There had always been broad interest in the work of international colleagues, even though the membership and programs focused in the main on domestic audiences. *Training*, by contrast, was a strong word that came from the work of Ronald Lippitt in his counterinsurgency training in Indochina during World War II. It was descriptive of the positive outcome of the process of learning by doing through skill exercises that involved feedback and reflection. *Laboratory* captured the essence of the work of Kurt Lewin, Lee Bradford, Ron Lippitt, and Ken Benne, the four founders of NTL, who articulated the need for action research through experiential learning.

Groups, however, was the one thing the founders were sure about. Small group process was the major focus in the early years of NTL: group dynamics, group development, and group research. Basic skill training groups (the name was soon shortened to T-groups) were viewed as the center of the learning laboratory. Learning objectives focused on the link between individual contributions in the dynamics of the group and the processes of the larger community; groups became the building blocks in applying democratic principles of participation in decision making and the world of action. Groups were seen as having the same critical elements for members working in a variety of settings: communities, industry, education, and voluntary organizations. Specifically, distributed power, influence, and leadership were key elements in managing groups and organizations in the aftermath of World War II.

All of the key words in the original name find their way into the chapters of this book and represent the base from which our particular branch of organization development has evolved.

The role of the founders of NTL was critical in grounding all of these ideas and skills in an action research format. They outlined and evolved a process of reflective learning that changed adult education in general and constituted the base for the future of training and organization development. They brought their experience in role playing, simulations, and skill practice in cross-cultural scenarios together with the creative techniques for wide participation in the precursors of Future Search and Whole System Change. They combined the educational philosophy of John Dewey with a concern for ethics and democratic values, which was a compass that is still used to assess the values and ethics of planned change. The wide participation of all levels and functions in organization change led to the evolution of organizational culture change methodologies.

Democratic process was the key to all of these pioneers who conceived of the early programs in Bethel. This place was chosen because it met the requirements of Lewin for a cultural island: an island devoted to research and laboratory training; an island that looked and felt a lot like Brigadoon; an island hard to get to and even harder to leave; an island where people could explore new ideas for changing their own behavior and their visions of change outside of the constraints of their everyday environments.

As NTL members working with group development began to realize that groups were microcosms of organizations, they began to realize that the work being focused in improving the functioning of groups could be expanded to include the improved processes of organizations. Thus, in the 1960s, NTL added organization development to its programs and research studies; changed its name to the NTL Institute; and became a separate organization, leaving the protective umbrella of the Adult Education Division of the National Education Association.

A new era had begun, in which organization development would blossom and flourish and gradually distinguish itself from the focus on individual and group development.

We were fortunate to be early second-generation members of NTL. Edie arrived in Bethel in 1950 and Charlie showed up in 1957 as a research assistant. We met when Charlie participated in a T-group where Edie was cotraining, and our relationship with each other and Bethel has continued to this day. Our combined hundred-plus summers in Bethel and twenty-five years as faculty with the American University/NTL Master's Program in OD have spanned much of the history of the field of organization development as we know it. Our exposure to many of the pioneers in the field has given us a perspective that we want to share on the occasion of publication of this notable and important book connecting group development, participative leadership, experiential learning, and organization development.

Six decades ago, seeds were planted here in Bethel that became significant roots for the field of organization development. Those roots included not only well-known theorists and practitioners but also those people who have extended leadership to the organizations that embraced, expanded, and shaped the current state of the field of organization development. Among them are the Organization Development Network (ODN); the Organization Development Institute (ODI); and significant divisions of many other professional organizations: the American Society for Training and Development (ASTD), the Academy of Management (AOM), and the many universities that developed OD master's and doctoral programs.

The taproot of OD that influenced the formation of NTL, and virtually all of the chapters in this book, goes back to Kurt Lewin. His work charted the way for much of what is widely shared by the many practitioners of our field. It also laid the groundwork for the differences and some of the uniqueness that characterize each scholar-practitioner's approach to our work. Philosophically and pragmatically, Lewin and his colleagues contributed the conception of individuals and their social relationships existing within a field of forces rather than the Aristotelian and Newtonian conceptions of simple cause and effect. This was an adaptation that Lewin made from field theory in physics. It served to open up the possibilities of action research and intervention in creating planned social change at all levels of systems. Lewin's basic formula of $B = f\ [P,E]$ was shorthand for "behavior is a function of personal characteristics and the environment." This highlighted the importance of understanding how creating changes in the environment of a relationship, a group, or an organization could be an extremely powerful force in determining an individual's behavior, the outcome of group processes, and larger systems dynamics.

As a pioneer social psychologist, Lewin came to the United States in reaction to Hitler's persecution of Jews. His work was at the heart of the interdisciplinary movement in the pursuit of meaningful social change. World War II also heightened the deep hunger for structures and processes that would give hope to the idea of world peace. Shortly after the armistice, Lewin's Research Center for Group Dynamics was established at MIT and then moved to the University of Michigan following his death in early 1947. Rensis Likert brought leadership to the Survey Research Center and the umbrella organization, called the Institute for Social Research. Meanwhile, in other developments on the group process front, sociodrama and sociometry were flourishing under Jacob and Zerka Moreno, and the Tavistock Institute in London was exploring the relevance of psychoanalytic theory to group process and social change. Revolutionary ideas were simultaneously being explored in the fields of adult education, leadership, psychiatry, management, and community development.

Experiential learning was in the spirit of many of these innovations, as was the use of systematic data gathering as part of action research and the field of strategic planning. Social scientists who had been active in the war effort in both the military and the civilian sectors were fired up with the opportunity to reinvent democracy, put a new take on social justice, and experiment with applying scientific methods to human affairs, especially individual development and social relationships that form the backbone for exercising leadership in small groups, organizations, and communities. The concept of feedback, informed by the work of Norbert Weiner and colleagues in the field of cybernetics, became an integral part of the exercise of leadership and the processes of the management of change. The implications of new technology were additional challenges to the understanding of process management in successful task achievement. The foundations of sociotechnical systems work flowed out of the wartime experiences of Bion and others in the Tavistock Institute in London. All of this work is still relevant to the issues that have arisen in the approaches to improved efficiency and effectiveness promised in change management strategies.

The critical values underlying that work still inform the world of organization development. It is the expression of those values that you see in the chapters of this book. First and foremost is the idea that people have a right to participate in the processes that control their lives. Active participation, meaningful involvement, and an opportunity to make one's voice heard can unleash the creative forces and collaborative activity that help groups and organizations thrive and flourish. Functional leadership, the flexibility in structures and process that reduce dependency and oppressive hierarchical control of one set of persons by another, challenged the prevailing models of autocratic position-based exercise of power. Sound and current data that could be assembled, analyzed, and put to use in open and transparent processes could amount to the basis for high trust and collaboration at all levels of organization. Feedback and the free flow of information and communication among individuals, groups, and larger units of organization became the focus of interventions and change processes. Most important, social justice and the appreciation of differences and diversity could be integrated into the goals and visions of organizations to build a foundation for sustainable change.

These values had a high degree of resonance with those who chose to see the importance of managing change at all levels of society. The core assumptions about effective leadership were challenged and reassessed. The search was on for more effective processes and procedures for managing conflict, engaging the full potential of all members of groups and organizations, and looking at leadership in radically different ways. The tradition of power being associated with the position of the leader began to give way to wide distribution of leader functions among group members. There were powerful implications for the development of high individual involvement, commitment, satisfaction, and competence as parallel outcomes to effective task management in achieving organization goals and visions. The conception of change management and the managing of change were related to the idea of continuous learning and growth and lead to the current interest areas of organization learning and planned change in organization culture.

Doug McGregor, one of the early shapers of organization development, gave us a simple language to explore the impact of individual processes on people and organizations. Doug's classic *The Human Side of Enterprise* spoke to the belief systems we have around process and people. Theory X and Theory Y symbolized the beliefs we hold in working with people. This theory was one of the key underpinnings of "OD = People, Process, and Organization." He focused on the powerful connection between one's beliefs about human nature and the effects of the self-fulfilling prophecy. If leaders using Theory X conceived of people as lazy, avoiding work, and reluctant to work together without coercion, they were likely to generate exactly that behavior on the part of the worker. If, on the other hand, leaders operated out of Theory Y beliefs, they would see individuals as creative and eager to join in challenging tasks for achieving group goals. That would then be the behavior more likely to be elicited in the interaction of leaders and group members.

At the time that Edie encountered Doug, she was a student at Antioch College and he was the college's newly appointed president. In his inaugural speech, he expounded on the concept of process and the role it played in all of our activities. It was an astonishing eye-opener to those who had always concentrated on task, never acknowledging that no task could be accomplished without an accompanying process and that the process often molded the shape of the task. That principle, once in focus, became essential to the practice of organization development.

Our field is based on an appreciation and understanding of process at all levels of social systems. Process underlies everything that is going on—individually, interpersonally, in and among groups. As Bob Blake and Jane Mouton demonstrated in the Managerial Grid process, process could be integrated with the focus of attention that had historically been on task. The profound realization that process could be observed and refined to enhance use of self, development of highly productive relationships and procedures, and creation of powerful organization cultures has been articulated in the work of Ed Schein, a colleague heavily influenced by his association with McGregor at MIT.

NTL's concern and understanding for the dynamics of groups became an international phenomenon. In the early 1960s, many European countries sent teams of group researchers to NTL to take part in building processes and structures that would help foster peaceful resolution for conflictual situations. These European teams returned to their countries and started institutes similar to NTL, many of which are still active today, in Austria, Germany, Holland, Denmark, the Scandinavian countries, Hungary, and England. Many of these institutes are also moving their research and consulting from group development to organization development. Following right along with Europe came India, China, South America, and Asia, all of which started their own action and research training and consulting programs designed to focus on change projects in their cultures. In the late 1960s and early 1970s, as the civil rights and women's movements emerged as major forces in the United States, NTL reorganized by deliberate design from an organization whose members and leaders were predominantly white male to a diverse organization. At that time, the leadership and membership of NTL became much more balanced in the proportions of women and people of color. Inclusion and diversity became powerful forces in the practice of organization development. This included the founding of firms specializing in diversity, such as Kaleel Jamison Associates and Elsie Y. Cross Associates. Diversity also became a strong program emphasis of individual OD consultants.

As the field of organization development matured, it moved more and more heavily into a focusing on work flow, organization models and structures, and use of increasingly sophisticated technology, all of which have the potential to squeeze out the values-based concern of the early years. Recently, these values are being slowly reintroduced into organizations through leadership and management training programs, and increasingly the demand for executive coaching for leaders and managers. Now the shift in the field of OD is more than ever on how executives use themselves to affect the organization and set the tone for a productive organization culture.

The focus on leadership continues to swing between the charismatic leader at the pinnacle of the organization and development of leadership competencies throughout the organization, empowering more distributive decision-making capacity and building a culture of accountability. It is here that the values of organization development become a foundation for advocacy, challenge, and constructive engagement so as to maintain the "human side of enterprise." Corporate organizations are driven to produce profit margins that ensure survival and satisfy customers and shareholders. Nonprofits and governmental organizations are challenged to demonstrate their worth. All organizations share the challenges and opportunities of integrating values when balancing the underlying importance of people with the achievement of their goals.

Challenges that lie ahead for the field of OD and NTL's continued involvement are to continue its foundation of action research and concern for social justice in a diverse, international world that increasingly needs peaceful approaches to resolving conflict over major cultural differences. The underlying values that NTL and OD have brought to groups and organizations need to find a voice in the increasing complexity of today's virtual groups and global organizations.

The array of authors and editors in this book reads like a diagonal slice through the generations of OD over the last fifty years. Brenda Jones and Michael Brazzel have brought the wisdom and experience of the third generation. They have both been at the forefront of organization development and change as well as the diversity and inclusion movements as an integral part of NTL. Brenda moved from graduate student at Johns Hopkins University to part of the faculty in the American University/NTL Institute Master's Program in OD and at the Gestalt Institute of Cleveland, as well as chair of the ODN board of directors. Michael was a student in the first class of the AU/NTL program, has been on the OD faculty there, and is a cofounder and codeveloper of the NTL Diversity Certificate Program. Both have been active practitioners over the past twenty-five years. Brenda and Michael have carefully selected authors to bring a fresh eye, a new perspective, and imaginative thinking on the current state of organization development to produce this creatively designed book.

The book takes its place alongside the state-of-the-art publications of the NTL Institute. Together with the other major professional organizations in our field, NTL has regularly amounted to a reference point or compass heading for our practice world. Together with the ODN, the NTL Institute has served as an incubator and major support system to generate a large and diverse assembly of scholar-practitioners. This volume is a direct outcome of the sustained energy, trust, and cohesion characteristic of a strong, healthy, collaborative group of colleagues along with the inclusion of significant differences that ensure the vitality and growth of new ideas and practices.

We believe this book can make a significant contribution to the evolution of our field through integrating new practices and challenging opportunities while continuing to articulate those underlying values of social justice, individual respect, and high internal collaboration. As the next decade unfolds, the discipline that we have known as organization development may change in form, or even in name. However, it is the consistent spotlight on human values that has given the field of OD as we know it the definition that will continue to shape our discipline. These values will always be our signature.

Bethel, Maine, and Columbia, Maryland   Edith Whitfield Seashore and Charles Seashore
February 2006

ACKNOWLEDGMENTS

It is our pleasure to acknowledge and thank the many people who helped to make this book possible. *The NTL Handbook of Organization Development and Change* is a testament to NTL being a major resource for and supporter of the field of OD. We appreciate the many current, former, and late NTL members who are architects of the field of organization development—those who are well known and less known in the field, including Dick Beckhard, W. Warner Burke, Bob Chin, Elsie Cross, Kathleen D. Dannemiller, Darya Funches, Kaleel Jamison, Ron Lippitt, W. Brendan Reddy, Herb Shepard, Robert Tannenbaum, Marv Weisbord, Leroy Wells Jr., and those who have been constant supporters of the emerging field and of current and future generations. They include as well many of the authors who have contributed chapters to this book.

We want to express our thanks to a number of NTL colleagues who supported this book in various ways, those who served as a sounding board to us at all times of the day and night, those who considered writing a chapter for the book, those whose chapters were omitted because the book was too big, and those who encouraged us in our project. They are Clay Alderfer, Frances Baldwin, Earl Braxton, Nancy Brown-Jamison, John D. Carter, Jack Gant, Pauline Frederick Hicks, Evangelina Holvino, Mary Ann Huckabay, Lennox Joseph, Judith H. Katz, Frederick A. Miller, Jane Moosbruker, Mikki Ritvo, Arty Trost, Morley Segal, and Judy Vogel.

We thank the thirty-eight contributors in this book who for the past three years believed in its publication. It has been our privilege to work with John D. Adams,

Billie T. Alban, Rebecca Chan Allen, Barbara Benedict Bunker, Anthony J. DiBella, Katherine Farquhar, Arthur M. Freedman, Seán Gaffney, Susan M. Gallant, William Gellermann, Jonno Hanafin, Stanley R. Hinckley Jr., Bailey W. Jackson, David Jamieson, Frances Johnston, Mark Leach, Roland E. Livingston, Carolyn J. Lukensmeyer, Robert J. Marshak, Rick Maurer, Ed Mayhew, Anne McCloskey, Annie McKee, Matt Minahan, Edwin C. Nevis, Julie A. C. Noolan, Edwin E. Olson, Daisy Ríos, Cathy L. Royal, Edgar H. Schein, Charles Seashore, Edith Whitfield Seashore, Juliann Spoth, Daniel Stone, Tojo Thatchenkery, Mary Ann Rainey Tolbert, Ted Tschudy, and Chistopher G. Worley. We appreciate their time and effort.

Thank you to all at Pfeiffer who have been so affirming of *The NTL Handbook* and have done the important work of making its publication possible: Kathleen Dolan Davies, Matt Davis, Thomas Finnegan, Andrea Flint, Susan Rachmeler, Jeanenne Ray, Laura Reizman, and Nina Kreiden. We want to thank the incredible reviewers of the book: Alan S. Davenport, Nancy M. Haus, and Peter F. Norlin; and thanks to Marilyn E. Blair, editor-in-chief of the *OD Practitioner.*

We especially would like to thank the past president of the NTL Institute, Diane Porter, and its current president, Margaret Tyndall. Their interest and general support for the book enabled us to work on this project and create a book for practitioners in the field of OD. Our special thanks to Irene V. Jackson-Brown, who worked tirelessly at the beginning of this project to obtain a publisher who would bring momentum and excitement for this book. We owe a large debt to Mary Blum Rusk, who joined us as our administrative support partner on the project. Her dedication to our partnership, providing insights and perspectives about the work and administrative support for the book, has been enjoyable and invaluable.

Final Thoughts

From Michael: Thank you to Susan Carton Brazzel, my love, my partner in life, and my friend. You have supported and encouraged me to follow my passion with this book . . . and reminded me gently whenever it began having too large a presence in our lives. I am blessed that you are in my life.

From Brenda: I am very grateful to my family for their continuous encouragement and enthusiasm for my work and this book; I want to thank Bill, Brian, and Robyn, who—with their wonderful hearts—respect and care about the things that matter to me and offer inspiration and hope.

February 2006   BBJ
                                                                                      MB

INTRODUCTION: GETTING
THE MOST FROM THIS BOOK

The NTL Handbook of Organization Development and Change began life as an idea that we, the editors, had from working together for NTL Institute's introductory workshop with its OD certificate program. We partnered, off and on, for twenty years in numerous projects and as faculty for the workshop. Over time, we wanted a more comprehensive, current resource to support workshops as well as certificate and degree programs. We stated this idea, with the offer to edit the book, to the then-president of NTL, Diane Porter, who gave her enthusiastic support and encouragement to the project. The current president, Margaret Tyndall, has continued the support and encouragement through to publication. Several years have passed and this book is the result of our partnership based in years of working together as colleagues and as friends. It is a contribution and celebration of the passion we feel for organization development as our profession and as a field of practice.

Purpose

The NTL Handbook of Organization Development and Change is created to reflect views regarding the current state of the field, the complexity of organizations and the world, and the need to support development of OD practitioners and consultants. Chapters are written from an OD practitioner's perspective, fostering breadth of information about the field of organization development, working models of OD, and OD applications, describing what OD is, how to do it, and the competencies required. This perspective includes themes of having a multiple-levels-of-systems viewpoint, a social justice and diversity stance, and an international and world context. These themes are integrated in chapters throughout the book. Individually, they highlight aspects of OD that are useful and beneficial to a practitioner's work in organizations. Together, they promote layers of thinking, principles, and practices that create a broad capability for addressing organizational issues and dilemmas.

Organization development is an evolving practice and involves multiple bodies of knowledge, theories, methodologies, and practices from many schools of thinking about OD and a variety of professional organizations. This book describes organization development in a time of ferment involving specialization, fragmentation, integration, challenge, and competition—a time of concerns that are relevant to clients, customers, suppliers, boards, and stakeholders, and a time when there are questions about the value of OD. Its practitioners will need to support organizations in considering broad economic, environmental, and social justice implications, change and continuity, and operation in an interconnected international and world setting.

The NTL Handbook is designed as a functional resource for practitioners and others as they enter the field and grow in it over time. It describes an OD with core elements, an OD that is evolving and changing. Among the core elements are use of self, action research, change and resistance theory and practice, multicultural OD, the OD map, phases of the OD process, and OD values and ethics.

Increasingly, organizations (and OD itself) must understand globalization strategies and cross-cultural transformation, unravel theoretical foundations, and link them to effective OD practices. Organization change must be supported while working at multiple levels of systems: with individuals, groups, large groups, and large social systems, and by changing organizations from the outside. New approaches to OD practice are being developed and expanded: appreciative inquiry, complexity science, developing organizations as learning systems, cultural assessment, working with energy and emotion, and building sustainable organizations. A well-trained and educated OD practitioner is competent to consult to groups and organizations. *The NTL Handbook of Organization Development and Change* supports the effectiveness and development of practitioners and consultants with its range of in-depth exploration of key theoretical models, methodologies, and applications as they apply to individuals, groups, and organizations.

The book has been designed so that each chapter stands on its own and can be read separately. The sections and chapters can also be read in sequence. The overall book is organized so that the content flows generally from core OD methodology and practice to new and innovative OD applications, and from historical to present to future perspectives.

Audience

This book is written for OD practitioners; people who are just entering the OD field; people beginning an OD certificate, graduate, or other educational program; human resource professionals; managers; leaders; and others who are interested in what OD is about and how it might apply to what they do. It describes OD foundations and current and emerging OD practices, and it is a resource for OD workshops, OD certificate programs, and master's and Ph.D. graduate OD programs.

About the Editors, Authors, and NTL Institute

The NTL Handbook of Organization Development and Change presents an NTL perspective about the OD field and profession. It builds on the assumptions, skills, knowledge, thinking, and values from research, debates taking place in the field, papers and presentations in OD conferences, workshops, certificate programs, graduate programs, and working with clients. The editors of the book are members of the institute. The contributing authors are current and former NTL members and distinguished colleagues in the field of organization development and applied behavior science. They are theorists, educators, and practitioners representing a fairly large and diverse group. They are well-known OD consultants in the field, OD practitioners with internal and external experience in the public and private sectors and in a variety of nations, and faculty members in graduate programs in OD and other fields. They come from varying backgrounds: organization development, organization behavior, management, psychology, organizational learning, education, diversity and social justice, economics, and engineering.

NTL and its members were central in founding the OD field and in creating an OD professional association, the OD Network. NTL has published a leading professional journal, *The Journal of Applied Behavioral Science,* for many years. It offers a range of professional development workshops and certificate programs in OD and has partnered with American University since 1980 in offering the AU/NTL master's degree program in OD, which has graduated more than fifteen hundred OD practitioners, researchers, and academicians. NTL Institute continues to influence the contemporary field of OD.

Contents of the Handbook

The NTL Handbook of Organization Development and Change is organized with seven primary parts:

• Part One: Organization Development as a Profession and a Field is a comprehensive overview of the field with definitions, context, and a perspective on the history, values, and ethics of organization development and change.

• Part Two: Core Theories and Methods covers several underpinning theories, concepts, and methods from the field of organization development and change. Chapters in this part address use of self, action research, change processes, resistance, and multiculturalism as essential information of organization development.

• Part Three: Organization Development and the OD Process describes a visual and cognitive map representing many aspects of organization development; four chapters then elaborate on the phases of OD and include a list of tasks and actions for each phase.

• Part Four: Working from Levels of Systems Perspectives: Individuals to Environment offers unique lenses that describe an OD practitioner's work with important phenomena operating within and about organizations. Each chapter characterizes working at a level, or multiple levels, of systems as well as some considerations for the practice of organization development.

• Part Five: Organization Development in an International and World Setting has several contributions about perspectives, current thinking, and models from a global, international, and world view. Each chapter opens the door to new insights, ways of understanding the practice of working cross-culturally, and the broad realm of diversity and multiculturalism.

• Part Six: Organization Development Applications and Practices includes specialized bodies of knowledge about innovation in the field of organization development. Themes in this part support numerous theories and practices that are evolving over time, with topics about emotions, energy, appreciative inquiry, culture assessment, complexity science, and learning organizations.

• Part Seven: The Future of Organization Development explores future perspectives in the field. The final chapter in the book addresses the evolution, challenges, and scope of changes and offers a scenario that examines the multiple frames that exist as the future of organization development and change emerges.

The Foreword, written by Edie and Charlie Seashore, reflects on the NTL Institute's early and continuing role in developing and shaping the field and profession of OD. They share insights and perspectives about NTL and OD from their experience as long-term members with NTL and work as leaders, academicians, and practitioners in the field of OD.

Part One begins with Chapter One, "Organization Development as a Profession and a Field." Organization development is both simple and complex. This chapter begins to shape the understanding of organization development and presents definition, context, a value system or philosophy, and multiple perspectives about the field, in particular a number of knowledge areas and roles and skills required for professional practice.

Chapter Two: "A History of Organization Development." OD practitioners need to understand the conceptual and practice history of the OD field as it came into being and has changed and developed. This chapter describes the people, events, developments, traditions, challenges, organizations, and trends that are instrumental in what OD is today.

Chapter Three: "Values, Ethics, and OD Practice." The values of organization development practitioners affect both what they do and how they do it. This chapter defines values and ethics, examines the importance of values and ethics for OD practitioners, and offers a current view of the value base of OD and its differentiation from other approaches to change.

Part Two begins with Chapter Four: "Use of Self in OD Consulting: What Matters Is Presence." From its earliest years, the OD profession maintained the importance of the practitioner to the change process. The practitioner must have an understanding of self along with understanding self in relation to clients and others. This chapter explores the significance of understanding self and the relationship between use of self and presence.

Chapter Five: "Action Research: Origins and Applications for ODC Practitioners." Action research is at the core of the practice of organization development and change (ODC) practitioners and of action researchers. The origins of action research and ODC and some contemporary approaches to conducting action research are discussed in this chapter.

Chapter Six: "Organizational Change Processes." Understanding planned organizational change and change processes means considering systems thinking, change dynamics, planning change, leading change, and implementing change. This chapter explores these key aspects and lays out a step-by-step approach to complex organizational change.

Chapter Seven: "Resistance and Change in Organizations." Resistance is the most important factor in managing change, and probably the most neglected. This chapter presents a model of the cycle of change and resistance in organizations and offers ways to either avoid resistance or create the conditions that minimize its devastating effects.

Chapter Eight: "Theory and Practice of Multicultural Organization Development." Multicultural organization development emerged from the work of diversity practitioners and OD practitioners who share a commitment to social justice and social diversity in systems and in society. This chapter describes the history of multicultural organization development (MCOD) and MCOD practice, including the MCOD goal, development stages, and process for fostering change in organizations.

Part Three begins with Chapter Nine: "An OD Map: The Essence of Organization Development." Most people coming into the field of organization development struggle to understand, "What is OD?" The OD Map was developed in an attempt to answer questions that a group of newcomers to OD asked in an NTL learning program. The map outlines foundational aspects of the current theory and practice of OD.

Chapter Ten: "Entry and Contracting Phase." The consultation begins the entry and contracting phase in an organization or with a group within it. This chapter describes the stages of the entry and contracting process: preentry, entry, contracting, and transition.

Chapter Eleven: "Organization Diagnosis Phase." Organization diagnosis is critical to the organization development process. This chapter outlines aspects of organization diagnosis: planning to collect data, data collection, analysis, and feedback to the organization. Organization diagnosis forms the basis for determining subsequent interventions through action planning and action taking.

Chapter Twelve: "Intervention Phase." The intervention phase of the OD process has four stages: defining the present state and framing a desired future, designing the actions to bring about change, implementing these actions, and following up. This chapter describes how the practitioner develops and directs this data-guided program of actions and experiences designed to change the organization's current habits of thought and action.

Chapter Thirteen: "Evaluation and Termination Phase." This chapter discusses what the evaluation phase is, why it is an important part of the OD process, specific evaluation tasks and actions, and an evaluation checklist. The examination of this phase incorporates termination of the OD process as an intervention; the OD practitioner and the client must both know when it is time to end the relationship and the OD process.

Part Four begins with Chapter Fourteen: "Working with Individuals in an Organizational Context." Many practitioners are spending more and more time with executives and managers in an advisory capacity, in contrast to being a consultant in the traditional sense. This chapter examines a systematic perspective of the possibilities and issues involved in various ways of working with individuals in an organizational context.

Chapter Fifteen: "Working with Groups in Organizations." One of the major challenges of being and working in groups is to understand the variety and complexity of group dynamics. This chapter outlines some of the foundational thinking and knowledge of groups, identifies tools that help in working with and understanding groups, lists some factors that affect group performance, and presents an integrated group development theory and model.

Chapter Sixteen: "Large Group Methods: Developments and Trends." OD practitioners working with systemic problems in an organization developed methods for bringing together all the concerned parties in a system in one place to make decisions about the issues facing them. This chapter covers large group methods in three periods of development: early invention and development, adoption of new methods, and incorporation of these methods into a variety of situations.

Chapter Seventeen: "Working in Very Large Social Systems: The 21st Century Town Meeting." This chapter describes an OD approach for supporting deliberative democracy in very large social systems. Characteristics of large social systems, key components of the 21st Century Town Meeting, staffing requirements, OD practitioner roles and competencies, and future directions are explored.

Chapter Eighteen: "Changing Organizations and Systems from the Outside: OD Practitioners as Agents of Social Change." Many OD practitioners work at the boundary, both inside and outside the organization. OD practitioners involved in social change work often work to change organizations from the outside. This chapter is addressed to both new and experienced practitioners who would like to use their skills as external change agents in the service of progressive social change.

Chapter Nineteen: "Building a Sustainable World: A Challenging OD Opportunity." Practitioners of OD need to make working with the mental models of their clients a priority whenever possible, especially in coaching, mentoring, and strategy planning arenas. This newly emerging community of practice will draw on OD skills and knowledge with transorganizational and transformational perspectives.

Part Five begins with Chapter Twenty: "Borders and Boundaries: Cross-Cultural Perspectives for OD Practitioners." This chapter explores some core constructs in cross-cultural studies, both well known and lesser known, and applies them to the work of international organization development practitioners. The implications of national culture, individual identity, and boundaries for cross-cultural work of OD practitioners are examined.

Chapter Twenty-One: "Working Effectively as a Global OD Practitioner: The Whole World in One Room." The array of challenges facing global organizations can be overwhelming. By using whole-world perspectives, tools, and competencies, global OD practitioners can feel more empowered to make a difference. The challenges facing practitioners are explored and the whole-world approach and applications are described.

Chapter Twenty-Two: "Organization Development in Asia: Globalization, Homogenization, and the End of Culture-Specific Practices." Asian culture is typically framed as distinctly different from Western culture. One goal of this chapter is to help OD practitioners avoid such stereotypical traps in their understanding of Asian organizations and people.

Part Six begins with Chapter Twenty-Three: "The Impact and Opportunity of Emotion in Organizations." This chapter reviews existing knowledge about the power of emotions in driving individual behavior; examines the impact of emotional intelligence on effective leadership; and discusses how practitioners can use emotions (their own and others') for professional development and refinement of OD practice.

Chapter Twenty-Four: "Working with Energy in Organizations." OD has sought to understand the interconnectedness among people, systems, and the environment. Increasing understanding of energetic forces and how to alter them gives practitioners more options for shaping interventions. This chapter embraces the fascinating world of energy, understanding its impact on all levels of systems and how to effectively intervene.

Chapter Twenty-Five: "Appreciative Inquiry as an Organization Development and Diversity Process." This chapter examines appreciative inquiry as an organization development change process and a diversity intervention. Emphasis is placed on what is needed to create an environment where the inquiry is organization-driven and the OD practitioner is the inquiry guide. The chapter has information that the OD practitioner needs when using AI as an OD and diversity change process in a system, community, or organization.

Chapter Twenty-Six: "Culture Assessment as an OD Intervention." This chapter explores how OD practitioners can work with organizations on cultural issues to enable members of the organization to identify important cultural assumptions and evaluate the degree to which those assumptions aid or hinder changes that the organization is trying to make.

Chapter Twenty-Seven: "A Complexity Science Approach to Organization Development." This chapter applies a complexity science perspective to current OD diagnostic and intervention methods in unpredictable environments and examines use of a complexity approach for intervening in organizations and the roles of the OD practitioner in this approach.

Chapter Twenty-Eight: "Developing Organizations as Learning Systems." OD practitioners help clients learn from their own experience and that of others to more effectively and more efficiently realize their mission and stated goals. This chapter explains the overlap and relationship between OD and learning and offers a framework to intervene in organizational systems to promote learning in a manner consistent with traditional OD principles.

Part Seven has a single chapter, Twenty-Nine: "A Positive Vision of OD's Future." A critical question facing the field at this crossroads is, What does the future of OD look like, and how will it get there? This chapter proposes one answer by describing a positive, possible, and hopefully provocative future scenario. The trends in the economic, social, political, and technological environment of organizations—and trends within OD itself—all contain the seeds of an integrative and influential force capable of shaping a positive world future.

PART ONE

ORGANIZATION
DEVELOPMENT
AS A PROFESSION
AND A FIELD

CHAPTER ONE

ORGANIZATION DEVELOPMENT AS A PROFESSION AND A FIELD

Robert J. Marshak

Organization development (OD) has been around since the late 1950s and early 1960s, but it still proves difficult to explain what it is, what it does, and why you might want it or need it. The reasons for this seem twofold. First, it is still an evolving field of practice and is therefore difficult to pin down. Second, it requires an understanding of a synthesis or integration of several sets of knowledge united by an underlying philosophical belief and value system(s). Consequently, the range of definitions offered over the years all sound somewhat similar, and they also seem to miss the mark in explaining to outsiders, "So, what exactly is OD?"

Consider these definitions:

> Organization development is an effort (1) *planned*, (2) *organization-wide*, and (3) managed *from the top*, to (4) *increase organization effectiveness* and *health*, through (5) planned *interventions* in the organization's "processes," using behavioral science knowledge [Beckhard, 1969, p. 9].

> Organization development refers to a long-range effort to improve an organization's problem-solving capabilities and its ability to cope with changes in its external environment with the help of external or internal behavioral-scientist practitioners, or change agents, as they are sometimes called [French, 1969, p. 24].

Organization development is a planned process of change in an organization's culture through the utilization of behavioral science technology, research, and theory [Burke, 1982, p. 10].

Organization development is a systemwide application of behavioral science knowledge to the planned development and reinforcement of organizational strategies, structures, and processes for improving an organization's effectiveness [Cummings and Worley, 1997, p. 2].

Now, at this point in most discussions of "what is OD?" the author offers his or her or their definition of OD, intended to make clearer what it is and what it does. No such effort is expended here. Instead, the intention of this discussion is to go behind the words to the underlying ideas and values that not only give definition to organization development but make it both a field and a profession distinct from other forms of management and organizational consulting or training. First, the underlying knowledge and philosophical systems that help define what is and is not the field of OD are described. Next, some of the implications for the professional practice of OD are explored. Finally, some of the current and emerging issues confronting OD are enumerated.

The Field of Organization Development

There are some who would not describe OD as a field, partly because it draws from many academic fields and disciplines and partly because it is a field of practice more than a field of academic inquiry. Nevertheless, OD practice is informed and defined by a more or less integrated set or sets of theories, ideas, practices, and values and therefore qualifies as a field of applied knowledge. Consequently, to understand what OD is and what it does, we must first understand the dimensions of knowledge, ideas, and values that in combination produce practices that are labeled as organization development.

There are three primary sets of knowledge and an underlying value system that lead to what is called organization development. The discussion that follows errs on the side of attempting to simplify and present essential characteristics. No attempt is being made to elucidate the full characteristics and nuances involved. In this sense, the discussion aspires to make clear some of the fundamentals for understanding organization development at the risk perhaps of appearing to be too simplistic or leaving some important dimension(s) out of the discussion. Finally, in this discussion the reader is reminded that the focus of the field follows its name: the development of organizations. Diagnostic and intervention activities may involve individuals, pairs, and teams, but these efforts are presumed to be part of a systemic effort to enhance the functioning of an organizational system.

Understanding Social Systems

The first set of knowledge, at its simplest level, is understanding the potential subject(s) of an intended development or change effort. Because OD seeks to foster the improved effectiveness of organizations and other social systems, a range of knowledge pertaining to the functioning of individuals, groups, organizations, and communities—separately and as integrated systems—is required. Thus organization development draws on a number of theories and ideas predominantly from the behavioral or social sciences (psychology, social psychology, sociology, anthropology, political science) but also to a lesser extent from economics, religion, and even the hard sciences of physics and biology. However, as is explained in more detail later, OD does not draw equally from all types of theories and ideas about human behavior in organized social settings. Instead it tends to be based in those theories and ideas that are consistent with its underlying, and sometimes unarticulated, philosophical value system. So, for example, most organization development practices are predicated on the assumption that people are motivated by factors beyond purely economic incentives.

Understanding the Hows and Whys of Change

A central aspect of OD is fostering planned development and change in social systems. This means that the bodies of knowledge that help explain how individuals, groups, organizations, communities, and even societies change are all pertinent to organization development. How do we go about inducing, supporting, or facilitating change in a manager, in a team, in an organization, in a network of organizations? The range of ideas about change and development coming from, for example, education, training, economics, psychology, social psychology, sociology, and anthropology is all potentially relevant to OD practice. Again, however, not all ideas about change are embraced by the underlying OD value system. For example, we might be able to force or coerce people to make certain changes, but this would not be considered organization development (and would in fact be refuted by OD practitioners).

Understanding the Role of a Third-Party Change Agent

The final set or sets of knowledge helping define OD pertain to the role of the OD practitioner. When working with an organization to help bring about a desired change, the OD practitioner is not the person in charge. Instead the OD practitioner is a third-party change agent aiding the person or persons in charge as well as the system itself to bring about the desired changes. An OD practitioner, whether internal or external to the subject system, must understand the issues, politics, psychological processes, and other dynamics associated with being a third-party change agent or practitioner working with people called clients in complex social systems. Here too, not all theories and ideas about the third-party role are endorsed or embraced by organization development. Once again, it is those ideas and practices that are consistent with or congruent with the underlying values and philosophy of OD that become part of the theories and practices associated with the proper role and responsibilities of an OD practitioner. For example, a third-party role wherein an expert tells people what they should do is an accepted if not essential part of a great deal of management and other types of consulting but is rejected in organization development as a general mode of practice.

These three sets of knowledge about (1) social systems, (2) how to change social systems, and (3) third-party change agent roles are the essential areas of expertise for an effective organization development practitioner. They are also insufficient to fully understand the theory and practice of OD as distinct, for example, from other forms of consulting and training intended to foster or induce development or change in organizations or other social systems. To make this distinction requires understanding the underlying philosophy of organization development and how it links and integrates selective aspects of each of the main bodies of knowledge making up OD practice.

Understanding the Underlying Values and Philosophy of Organization Development

Organization development is often referred to as a values-based or normative field of practice. This is true, although not always fully understood. Furthermore, it is difficult to precisely enumerate the exact values that are the essential ingredients making OD more or less uniquely OD. It is, however, possible to describe some of the defining characteristics of the underlying value system and some of the ways in which this value system is evolving over time. At some considerable risk of oversimplifying or leaving out something important, four key value orientations help form the underlying philosophy of organization development:

1. A humanistic philosophy
2. Democratic principles
3. Client-centered consulting
4. An evolving social-ecological systems orientation

A Humanistic Philosophy. Organization development not only accepts but also promotes a humanistic orientation to social systems. This includes beliefs that people are inherently good, not evil; that they have the capacity to change and develop; and that through the exercise of reason and judgment they, not outside forces or inner drives and emotions, are capable of empowered action in the best interests of the enterprise. This orientation also affirms the value and dignity of each person. Furthermore, to be effective, social systems should not restrict, limit, or oppress people regardless of their role in the organization or their demographic background. In organization development the human side of enterprise is always a central consideration, along with other aspects such as economics, technology, and management practices and principles. Historically, this orientation in OD has been expressed by the assertion that an organization that empowers its people is also a more effective organization.

Democratic Principles. Partly because of its humanistic philosophy and the roots in World War II of many of its founders, organization development also advocates democratic principles—meaning, involvement in decision making and direction setting should be broadly rather than narrowly delineated. Another way of saying this is that OD tends to reject the notion that there are elites who possess superior knowledge and who alone should make decisions on behalf of others. Instead, OD believes and advocates that important and relevant knowledge is more broadly distributed and that more rather than fewer people are capable of and should be involved in making inputs or in the actual process of decision making. In this regard, organization development is in the tradition of the British philosopher John Locke (1632–1704) and Anglo-American liberalism in general, rather than that of Thomas Hobbes (1588–1679), who justified autocracy and an absolute monarchy as required to protect people from their baser instincts. In practice therefore organization development advocates more democratic processes not simply as a way to get buy-in (although buy-in is famously associated with involvement) but because there is a belief that the resulting decisions are also superior, implementable, and more relevant to important audiences and stakeholders.

Client-Centered Consulting. Consistent with humanistic and democratic values, organization development believes that change efforts should be client-centered, not practitioner-centered. This expands on humanistic and democratic values and assumptions and asserts that human systems are capable of self-initiated change and development when provided with appropriate processes and supportive conditions. The role of the OD practitioner is therefore to partner with the client system in self-directed change efforts operating from a third-party change agent role. In carrying out this role, the practitioner uses knowledge and skills about how social systems function and change in order to support, educate, facilitate, and guide the client system in its work. The role of the practitioner in client-centered consulting is neither to impose or enforce an unwanted change agenda on the client system nor to furnish "expert" answers to the client's issues. It is, however, acceptable and appropriate for an OD practitioner to constructively confront blind spots in a client system and to engage in education or awareness-raising interventions should a client system be operating from incorrect or incomplete information. Therefore a primary intervention by an OD practitioner is often to suggest and facilitate participative processes for diagnostic data gathering, informed decision making, and building client-system commitment for change.

An Evolving Social-Ecological Systems Orientation. A social-ecological systems orientation is, perhaps, a more recent or emerging aspect of the underlying organization development values and beliefs. In its simplest form, it means that ends should not be defined in terms of an individual, group, or organization alone. Rather, a perspective of the much larger and broader social, economic, and environmental system(s) must be held, and ends should be considered in terms of their impact on the broader, even global, system—not, for example, on a specific organization. Thus, if maximizing the profits of a specific organization might threaten the environment or negatively affect a community or country on the other side of the planet, it should be avoided in favor of outcomes that take into account the broader global or ecological system of which everyone is a part. On the basis of this orientation, it could therefore be a legitimate role for an OD practitioner to help an organization understand the full range of impacts of its choices, beyond perhaps what was considered in the past. This orientation might also lead an OD practitioner to seek to help a client system rethink or reposition projects or endeavors that are intended to contribute to a specific organization's success but could ultimately be harmful from a broader social, economic, or ecological perspective. A summary depiction of the three core knowledge areas and the underlying values and philosophy of OD are in Figure 1.1.

FIGURE 1.1. CORE KNOWLEDGE SETS AND UNDERLYING PHILOSOPHY OF ORGANIZATION DEVELOPMENT.

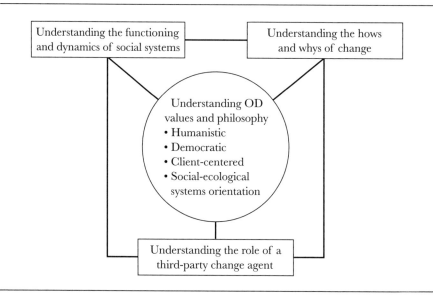

Organization Development Results from an Integration of Ideas and Ideals

What is called organization development results from putting into practice these three sets of knowledge and skills, integrated by the underlying normative value system(s) and intended to enhance an organizational system. This integration defines what OD is and also what is not OD. Thus change activities aimed at, for example, individual performance alone, or based on prescriptive methods, may be important forms of coaching, training, and consulting but are not considered to be organization development. To help illustrate these important points, a few simple examples will be given as stand-ins for a more thorough and complex discussion.

OD and Social Systems

First, let us consider that there are numerous theories and ideas about human nature. In psychology, for example, psychoanalytic theories such as those advanced by Freud and his followers postulate that individual behavior is influenced, if not controlled, by basic inner drives and that individual behavior can be controlled by unconscious and nonrational processes. In contrast, behavioral theories such as those associated with B. F. Skinner consider the positive and negative reinforcements coming from an individual's environment to be the determinants of behavior. Partly in response to the more limited or limiting view of human nature advanced by these two schools of psychology, a third school, called humanistic psychology, emerged in the 1950s and suggested that individuals were inherently capable of higher-order functioning, that they could determine for themselves how to develop and behave, and that individuals were capable of transcending narrow self-interest in service to themselves or others.

In general, it was the ideas of the pioneering humanistic psychologists, notably Abraham Maslow (hierarchy of needs), Douglas McGregor (Theory X and Theory Y), Carl Rodgers (unconditional positive regard), and Chris Argyris (congruence of individual and organizational needs), that helped define the field of organization development by implicitly contributing to its strong, underlying humanistic value system. Consequently, in practice humanistic theories of human behavior have a central or prominent role in how OD practitioners think about and diagnose human systems, even though they augment those theories with an eclectic array of other theories and belief systems, including, at times, those of Freud and Skinner. Similarly, given the range of theories about groups and organizational behavior, OD tends to reject, for example, those theories and ideas that postulate the need to provide economic incentives (alone) or closely monitor and control people. The need for more autocratic management based on Theory X assumptions is rejected as unwarranted and ultimately counterproductive.

OD and Change in Social Systems

Just as there is an array of theories about individual, group, and organizational behavior, there are also theories about how individuals, groups, and organizations change and develop. Staying at the individual level of behavior and again contrasting psychoanalytic, behaviorist, and humanist schools, one confronts varying ideas and emphases about how change and development occur. For example, from a behavioral orientation one would seek to condition new behavior through manipulation of the environment of rewards and punishments resulting from an individual's behavioral choices. From a more humanistic perspective, one might assume instead that people are capable of rational, self-directed learning and growth, especially in a supportive environment that treats them with dignity and respect. Thus change theories and practices that might suggest or support the notion that people must be forced, coerced, manipulated, or ordered to change tend to be rejected in favor of theories and practices that assume people can, on their own, rationally assess the need to change and are capable of changing, especially when given the appropriate data or feedback information.

Although OD draws on a variety of theories and ideas about individual, group, and organizational change and has a range of methodologies and practices, all or almost all OD practices are predicated on more positive and humanistic ideas about change in human systems. For example, action research, which is one of the fundamentals of organization development, is based on the assumption that people can and will change when involved in a process of rational inquiry into their present situation to determine new courses of action. This orientation is so strong in organization development that some would include an action research orientation as part of its core values. Others include it as one of OD's preferred theories of change along with others supported by rational, humanistic, democratic, and client-centered assumptions and values. These theories of change and supporting values and assumptions about change lead to OD practices that tend to emphasize giving the involved or affected people supportive processes wherein they can rationally assess their situation and develop new actions, behaviors, and directions. Theories and practices predicated on somehow forcing people to change, or developing answers for them because they are somehow incapable of doing so themselves, are not part of the accepted change philosophy and practices in organization development.

OD and Third-Party Roles

In organization development, the third-party role of the practitioner is defined, in many respects, by its underlying values and supporting theories about the nature of change in social systems. If we assume that most people are capable of self-directed growth and development, especially when given appropriate feedback or information in a supportive environment, then the role of the third-party OD practitioner becomes clear.

Specifically, the role of the OD practitioner is to collaborate or partner with the subject system by facilitating, coaching, or otherwise supporting self-directed change. This is done by suggesting and facilitating processes that encourage and support inquiry, discovery, and motivation to change, while establishing and reinforcing new behaviors, actions, or directions. An assortment of skills, interventions, and practices are required to successfully carry out this role, but the first and most essential ingredient is to operate from a client-centered, collaborative, and facilitative mind-set. If instead one were to assume that people were not capable of changing on their own, or were totally governed by narrow self-interest, or were lacking somehow in intelligence or capability, then quite different third-party roles could be justified as necessary and appropriate. After all, why would you want to involve people in working on a change initiative if you think they are somehow incapable of developing a good or appropriate answer to whatever the situation is under consideration? Might you not instead be more helpful by offering them the right answer to implement based on your neutrality or your superior knowledge or information? Because organization development tends to reject this set of assumptions and resulting reasoning, it also tends to reject the expert third-party role in favor of a more collaborative or facilitative one—recognizing, of course, that within an overall collaborative or facilitative role OD practitioners can and should suggest to ("tell") clients what are considered to be successful practices and processes on the basis of their knowledge and expertise in facilitating change.

In sum, then, organization development is an applied field whose practitioners draw on knowledge about how social systems function and change while working from a third-party collaborative and consultative role based on and integrated by humanistic, democratic, client-centered, and more recently, social-ecological values and principles. Organization development practices are applied in organizational and community settings where the responsible managers, executives, and leaders wish to enhance the functioning and effectiveness of their organizational unit or enterprise. Organization development is usually more successful when applied in a setting where the responsible parties are in at least minimum agreement with, or ideally wish to advance, its underlying normative values and principles. Thus settings where leaders and managers are more in agreement with Theory Y versus Theory X assumptions, or believe most people are willing and able to develop new organizational practices and behaviors if given a supportive, data-based, facilitated process of inquiry, may be more conducive for organization development than others.

The Professional Practice of Organization Development

In the early days, developing and advocating application of sound humanistic and social science theories and principles to help improve organizations was at least partly an *avocation* or calling of the early pioneer practitioners of what became known as organization development. Many, but not all, were university-based or university-trained, and most or all believed that the World War II triumph of democratic values combined with advances in the social sciences could improve the functioning of the highly bureaucratic organizations typical of that era. They also believed they could improve and enhance the human condition in organizations (and in general) by incorporating into organizational functioning the latest humanistic and democratic theories, principles, and values. Over time, the ideas and practices of the often part-time and usually externally based OD advocates became accepted in varying degrees and incorporated into a range of full-time, internally and externally based OD practitioner roles. There has also developed a number of OD-related professional associations or divisions of associations; a substantial and still-evolving practitioner and academic literature; and certificate, master's, and doctoral degree programs. From an avocation of the pioneers, organization development in the twenty-first century is now an established—although not licensed—*vocation* or profession.

Professional Roles

The discussion of the three knowledge bases and underlying philosophy of organization development suggests the range of knowledge and skills required for the professional practice of OD. This is compounded by the multiple roles an OD practitioner may need to play in engaging with a client system. Various descriptions of OD practitioner roles have been advanced over the years emphasizing the need to be proficient in many skills and practices. Several of the most critical roles are highlighted here. For example, an OD practitioner needs to be:

• A skilled *professional practitioner* able to initiate, negotiate, and maintain a collaborative consulting relationship with managers, executives, and leaders over the life of an engagement. This also includes knowledge of and ability to manage or facilitate the phases and processes associated with an organizational change effort.

• A skilled *diagnostician* capable of reading and understanding the behavioral dynamics of individuals, teams, organizations, and even larger social systems.

• A skilled *social scientist researcher* capable of designing and conducting various data-gathering and data-analysis methodologies, including interviews, questionnaires, focus groups, and so on.

• A skilled *interventionist* knowledgeable of a range of participative methods and processes that enable and encourage people to collectively engage or explore important issues and opportunities.

• A skilled *educator or trainer* able to communicate new ideas and skills to system members to better prepare them to address their issues, opportunities, and concerns.

• A skilled *facilitator* of small and large group participative processes capable of dealing with such difficult dynamics as those associated with issues of power, authority, leadership, conflict, diversity, resistance, and the like, as well as able to keep participants engaged and on track.

• A skilled *coach* able to advise, support, and when appropriate constructively confront client system mangers, executives, and members to encourage and help develop the skills, behaviors, and attitudes necessary for their success and that of the overall change effort.

Each role requires in itself a depth of knowledge and skills, but successful OD practice demands integration and appropriate application of all of these roles. The ability to effectively perform some or a subset of these roles using OD practices can be valuable, but it should not be mistaken for full professional practice of organization development.

Professional Values and Ethics

Finally, although organization development has neither a governing body nor an officially recognized and enforced code of conduct, it does have a set of generally recognized values and ethics that are based on its underlying philosophy and principles. (See for example, Gellermann, Frankel, and Landenson, 1990.) In this sense, organization development practitioners form a values-based community of practice. In a way, what helps define someone as an organization development practitioner, as opposed to another type of change practitioner, is belief in and adherence to a significant portion of the underlying humanistic, democratic, client-centered, and social-ecological values and principles.

Tensions Within Organization Development

Primarily because of its strong values-based orientation, there are a number of tensions and ongoing discussions within the field of organization development. This includes whether or not OD focuses too much on "soft" people issues; whether it should address diversity and multicultural dynamics, including considerations of the degree of applicability in all countries and cultures; and issues related to dealing with lack of readiness for change.

OD Is Too Touchy-Feely

Almost from its inception, OD was labeled by some as too touchy-feely. This reflects its strong humanistic and developmental orientations, as well as the psychological and social-psychological knowledge and methodology bases. Balancing humanistic values with more technological or business-oriented goals, such as economic efficiency, can be difficult. Holding humanistic values and assumptions while addressing challenges from "pessimistic" economic assumptions about human nature and motivation can also be difficult without coming across as too strident or doctrinaire. If the balance struck appears too rooted in human development or humanistic values, perhaps as opposed to economic values and objectives, then organization development or the OD practitioner can be labeled too touch-feely. On the other hand, if the core values of organization development are ignored or subjugated to a great degree, the practitioner is likely to be accused of not practicing OD. This is made especially difficult by the absence of clear criteria about what is too much or too little. These tensions are also revealed in the ongoing discussion within the field about the importance of "our values" as well as among those who on the one hand wish to adopt a more pragmatic values orientation and those who by contrast wish to remain strongly centered in the traditional orientation (Worley and Feyerherm, 2003). These discussions and periodic challenges to the field raised in journals, at conferences, and by clients are inherent in a strongly values-oriented field, especially if the values are not taken for granted by everyone or by all managers and organizations. The challenges also become an opportunity for the OD profession and individual practitioner to periodically reassess, rebalance, and rededicate themselves to a set of core values and principles that define the field of practice.

Addressing Multiculturalism and Diversity

Organization development promotes a range of values (for example, respect, inclusion, democratic principles, and empowerment) as core aspects required for effective functioning of groups, organizations, and communities. Since perhaps the early 1980s, if not earlier, this has led to a number of challenges and tensions within the profession, notably whether organization development is applicable in all countries and cultures and whether addressing issues of diversity or social justice should be a central aspect of the professional practice of OD.

First, in terms of multiculturalism, there has been continuing commentary over the years questioning whether a field of practice based so strongly on Western, liberal-democratic, and humanistic values can be equally applicable in all countries and cultures (see, for example, Jaeger, 1986). Others assert that with multicultural sensitivity and some adaptation OD is applicable in all cultures and contexts. This is a discussion fueled in recent years by globalization and the increasing number of OD practitioners working in multinational or transnational organizations. Although sensitivity, balance, and flexibility are called for, OD is also predicated on a core set of values; the choice therefore, in some settings, may be whether to use OD premises and methods at all, rather than trying to adapt or downplay some dimensions or practices.

Since the 1980s, intervention to help organizations deal with and effectively incorporate an increasingly diverse workforce located in many cases around the world has become commonplace. Interventions range from multicultural awareness training to transforming organizations with the intent of ridding them of hidden but institutionalized barriers to the full inclusion of all people. This set of practices, in the United States, is often called dealing with diversity, and its practitioners diversity practitioners. Many but not all might also consider themselves to be organization development practitioners. The tension within the field and among practitioners is whether or not diversity is a separate or semiseparate field of practice or an inherent aspect of organization development. If the latter, then it would be expected of all professional practitioners to be knowledgeable, adept, and required to deal with diversity and social justice dynamics and issues. If it is not an inherent aspect of the field, then although OD practitioners should of course be sensitive and aware the requirement to address such issues in some fashion would be optional as a matter of professional practice and responsibility.

At this point, whether organization development practitioners should address the multicultural dynamics of groups, organizations, and communities seems no longer open to serious question or debate. Given the core values of OD and the increasingly diverse and multicultural organizational settings for its practice, it is clear that all professional practitioners need to fully understand and as appropriate address multicultural and diversity issues and dynamics as they present themselves, just as they would need to address any other set of issues and dynamics central to the theory and values orientation of OD. Exactly what this means in practice, as well as divergent views about how to best address these issues, will remain ongoing areas of discussion and reflection among practitioners.

Change and Readiness for Change

Organization development is about change in human systems, but not just any change under any circumstances. Instead, OD theory and practice assumes and even promotes several key criteria related to change efforts:

- Change(s) should be directed toward enhancing or developing individual, group, and organizational capabilities, as well as the conditions under which people work and contribute. It is assumed that this is a primary determinate of higher performance in organizations.
- Change(s) should be carried out in a way consistent with social science knowledge about human systems and how they change, as well as a generally optimistic set of values and assumptions about human capability and potential.
- Change(s) should be initiated and led, to the greatest extent possible, by the people involved; it should also be based on their assessment and concurrence with the need to change.
- Change efforts should not only lead to the desired change but also leave a client system with increased capabilities and skills to address future situations and needs.

A dilemma and discussion in organization development is what to do when one or more of these criteria are absent. Consider, for example, corporate downsizing, which has been going on since the late 1970s. In its early days, many OD practitioners felt it was inappropriate or even unethical to be involved in downsizing change efforts that did not seem to match any (or very many) of the implicit criteria needed for an OD change effort. In later years, as downsizing was redefined as "rightsizing" to enhance corporate competitive capabilities, more—but not all—OD practitioners felt using OD technology in rightsizing redesign efforts was workable and acceptable.

Another aspect of this ongoing tension relates to the concept of readiness for change. In organization development it is not simply a matter of there being a call or demand for change; there must also be readiness for change in the system. Because of the values, assumptions, and criteria guiding OD change efforts, unless there is a felt need or readiness for change in the system OD interventions may not work. Simply put, it would not be possible to enter into a client-centered, collaborative change effort intended to enhance the capabilities of the organization on the basis of social science theories and practices and guided by humanistic and democratic values if the client system were not ready and willing to do so at some level. Instead, initial interventions such as education or diagnostic action research would be needed to develop readiness for change, particularly readiness for OD change methods. In many contemporary organizations, however, OD practitioners (especially internal practitioners) are asked to conduct change interventions whether the target system is ready or not, and with little or no time to create readiness. This sometimes places the OD practitioner in the position of trying to carry out interventions under conditions where the premises for success are not fully met or else risk appearing to be unresponsive or unable to help.

Exactly how to handle such dilemmas is an important discussion within the professional practice of organization development, because of its philosophy and values about change. As new situations present themselves, the field and individual practitioners must adapt and adjust to be responsive within the broad framework of the principles and practices of the profession.

Conclusion

Organization development is at once a simple and complex field of professional practice. Initially learning the many knowledge bases, roles, and skills required for professional practice and then integrating and internalizing how they all fit together according to an extensive, but sometimes only implied, value system or philosophy can be both challenging and confusing to would-be practitioners and clients alike. Once the sets of values, knowledge, and skills are understood and mastered, the practice of OD becomes much simpler and more straightforward. It is indeed the requirement to know an extensive range of knowledge and methodologies integrated by a philosophical system that makes organization development a worthy field of professional practice.

References

Beckhard, R. (1969). *Organization development: Strategies and models.* Reading, MA: Addison-Wesley.

Burke, W. W. (1982). *Organization development: Principles and practices.* Boston, MA: Little, Brown.

Cummings, T. G., & Worley, C. G. (1997). *Organization development and change,* 6th ed. Cincinnati, OH: South-Western College Publishing.

French, W. (1969). Organization development: Objectives, assumptions and strategies. *California Management Review, 12*(2), 23–34.

Gellermann, W., Frankel, M. S., & Ladenson, R. F. (1990). *Values and ethics in organization and human systems development.* San Francisco: Jossey-Bass.

Jaeger, A. M. (1986). Organization development and national culture: Where's the fit? *Academy of Management Review, 11*(1), 178–190.

Worley, C. G., & Feyerherm, A. E. (2003). Reflections on the future of organization development. *Journal of Applied Behavioral Science, 39*(1), 97–115.

CHAPTER TWO

A HISTORY OF
ORGANIZATION DEVELOPMENT

Stanley R. Hinckley Jr.

This chapter is an attempt to present a concise history of the field and profession of organization development (OD), from its beginning in the late 1940s to the early 2000s. There are so many people who created, explored, adapted, and applied theories, ideas, and interventions in creating this history that it is not possible to name all of the significant individuals and their contributions. Consequently, two criteria have been applied to select the people and the theories, ideas, and practices mentioned in this chapter: (1) those who are remembered and still described as important by the figures who began the practice of OD in the 1960s, and (2) those known as essential contributors to the current description of what OD people are doing and learning.

The Foundations of Organization Development

In the aftermath of World War II, there was a massive need to rebuild countries, economies, and industries, especially in Europe, Japan, the USSR, and the United

---

Note: The research required for this chapter was greatly enhanced by the detailed histories of organization development found in the enjoyable rereading of works by Marvin R. Weisbord (2004) and Eric L. Trist (1981).

States. Confidence in the power of civilization to control man's ability to do evil was shaken. As stories and photographs of the damage done by the massive bombing of cities, the atomic bomb, the Holocaust, and the many cruelties to human beings spread around the world, everyone reacted to these misuses of power. Visions and hope for a better world grew, a world where ordinary people had more control over their lives, where democracy was spread widely in countries and businesses, and where families could live and grow in safety.

Around the world, people's need for an improved standard of living meant increasing productivity. Challenges included using returning military personnel, many of whom had had enough with command-and-control management, and providing higher education for the new business world. In the United States the GI Bill extended valuable support to the need for education.

These challenges meant that historical thinking about how to organize and manage a company needed to change. Fortunately, many executives and managers recognized this need and began proposing new ideas about how to do this. Some important concepts were developed prior to and during World War II:

• *Action research* was developed by Kurt Lewin in Germany in the 1920s and brought to the United States when he moved to Iowa in 1935. It is a process that involves people in describing and learning from their own behavior as they work and collaboratively making decisions (usually of higher quality than those made by a manager), thus enhancing their commitment to implementing those decisions and their satisfaction with them.

• *A change model,* also developed by Lewin, describes the process of changing individual behavior through the three steps of unfreezing, changing, and refreezing. This model was soon applied to changing organizations.

• *Force field analysis,* another Lewin creation, pictures the forces in any situation that are causing the individual or the system to behave the way it does. The restraining and driving forces are in equilibrium; change can occur only if the field is disturbed, creating an imbalance. Successful planned change can occur only as the restraining forces are reduced or the driving forces are increased.

• *Resistance to change* is a term that also sprang from an understanding of Lewin's force fields. Each driving force and each restraining force involves human action and behavior. Driving forces are those promoting change in the current situation. Restraining forces keep things as they are—that is, forces representing resistance to change.

• *Group dynamics,* a term coined by Lewin and Ron Lippitt in 1939, identifies the interactions between how a group is managed (autocratic, democratic, laissez-faire) and how it behaves, including the group climate it creates and the work results the group produces.

- *Open systems,* a concept of the relationship between all living systems and their environment, was adapted by social scientists in the United States and the United Kingdom after publication of an article by Ludwig von Bertalanffy (1950). As this idea was applied to organizations, early practitioners realized that the study of organizations and management had historically assumed that the organization was a closed system. The focus was always internal (on managerial and individual behavior and on teams and groups) and ignored the fact that each organization exists in its own unique environment, an environment of other groups and organizations (competitors, suppliers, customers, employees' families, government, and other aspects of the organization's environment) that have a stake in what the organization does and how it does it. Further, open systems emphasize that the needs and desires of these environmental domains determine the fate of the organization in the long run. In other words, the fit between the organization and its environment must be optimized, and this is a challenge since the environment is continuously changing. The open systems concept grew useful for understanding the internal processes and the external relations of workgroups and organizations and the relationships and fit between them.

These fertile experiments and learnings about people in groups and people in organizations—and many others, some now lost in history—constituted the foundation for what was to become the field of organization development.

The Birth of OD

OD practice and theories have come, and continue to come, from the gradual integration of the applications of anthropology, biology, psychology, sociology, physics, industrial engineering, and management science. These fields, singly and in various combinations, were the basis of experiments in organizations beginning, for the most part, in the aftermath of World War II. Three important integrations occurred in the early days. Two somewhat different sociological or psychological orientations involved a focus on individuals and workgroups in the United States and a focus on workgroups and larger systems in the United Kingdom. A third area of focus on management began in the 1930s, mostly concerned about labor problems and how managers handled them.

Focus on Individuals and Groups

In the aftermath of World War II, the Connecticut State Inter-Racial Commission created a conference in 1946 to address racial and religious prejudice. They asked Lewin, with Leland P. Bradford, Ronald Lippitt, and Kenneth D. Benne, to lead the conference. Staff meetings were held at the end of each day to debrief and plan the next day's agenda. As a few participants joined this meeting, they provided data on their own experiences during the day; the feedback greatly enhanced everyone's understanding of what was going on in the small groups. As more participants joined in the daily debriefings, the learnings were greatly enhanced for everyone and were applied in the next day's conference sessions. This process became the basic design of learning groups, soon to be called T-groups ("training groups").

These four colleagues founded the National Training Labs (later changed to the NTL Institute) in 1947, with support from the National Education Association. Under a grant from the Office of Naval Research, NTL established a summer site, a "cultural island," for its programs in Bethel, Maine, and became the developer and promulgator of T-groups for learning about individual and group behavior and also for developing competent T-group trainers. T-groups, eight to twelve people meeting for an extended period with no agenda except to learn about groups, were initially based on the use of sociology to understand individual behavior in interaction with others and to understand the behavior of the group itself. The purpose was soon expanded by the use of psychology to learn in more depth about interpersonal and intrapersonal processes. Action research was used to learn from what happened in the group, focusing only on interaction among the participants and on the development of the group itself.

Soon after, colleagues on the West Coast, primarily at UCLA, also offered T-groups to the public, using a resort in Ojai as their cultural island. The use of T-groups for intrapersonal development fit in well with the emerging human potential movement and supported formation of the Esalen Institute in 1962, a center for research and experimentation that continues its work today.

Learnings from T-groups were rapidly conceptualized and shared, in the form of models of the stages of group development; studies of leader-follower dynamics; exploration of many varieties of conflict and ways to resolve or work through it; and identification of the skills of observation, intervention, expression of feelings, giving and receiving feedback, and improving interpersonal relationships. Among the group development theories that are still used today are Jack Gibb's model of trust formation that identifies four "concerns" (acceptance, data flow, goal, and control); Will Schutz's ICA model (inclusion, control, and affection); and Tuckman's well-known model of four phases: forming, storming, norming, and performing. Another early model, developed by Joe Luft and Harry Ingham, was the "Johari Window," which is still used today to explore how two people interact and can become more open and better known to each other, in order to develop an improved relationship.

Early attempts to spread T-groups, sometimes called "sensitivity training" or "the laboratory approach," into the world of organizations produced many case studies that encouraged further research. T-groups for managers from the same organization were intended as an intervention to improve the functioning of a company by reaching for a better balance between the hard side of business and the soft side of human beings working in the organization's structure and management systems. However, participants returned to work and experienced a major conflict between (1) their desire to apply their learnings about social processes and human feelings and (2) the expectations of others that they would continue to fit in their (unchanged) rational and mechanistic organization cultures.

Search for more effective intervention led to focusing on workgroups with a more structured approach, especially team building and the Managerial Grid. Team building usually followed a model of interviewing individual members of the workgroup; summarizing those data in some organized way; presenting the data back to the team at the beginning of a two-day off-site meeting; and facilitating the team's work on the data to understand, analyze, and plan what and how to change. UCLA faculty, among others (especially Robert Tannenbaum and James V. Clark), developed this model. Robert R. Blake and Jane W. Mouton (1964) developed the Managerial Grid. Their program consisted of a step-by-step agenda for team building for workgroups, followed by intergroup meetings, and then moving analysis and planning of change up the hierarchy to the top.

An unexpected effect of work teams trying to change to become more effective, applying their learnings from team building and the Managerial Grid, was the resistance of other groups and individuals in the team's environment to their attempt to change the behavior of a team and its members. This learning created an urgent need to explore the internal interfaces in an organization and began shifting the focus of these change efforts toward the whole system.

Focus on Work Teams and Larger Systems

The Tavistock Institute of Human Relations in London was formed in 1947 to meet Britain's need to rebuild its economy and infrastructure. The initial work was in the coalmines. Trist and others led the way to the discovery of the possibilities for redesigning workgroups to permit greater self-direction, more flexibility in worker roles and redundancy of skills, and opportunities for workgroups to choose how to organize. The early results were increased productivity, reduced turnover, and much more satisfied people.

Over the next few years, members of Tavistock engaged in numerous action research projects on the social system of workgroups, including projects by Elliott Jaques at the Glacier Metal Company in the United Kingdom, A. K. Rice at the Calico Mills in India, and Fred E. Emery at UK coal mines and at the Norwegian Industrial Democracy Project (with Trist). As they worked with more and more workgroups, a significant area for their learning was the processes and dynamics of those groups. The Tavistock Institute already had a foundation in this area, begun years earlier with Wilfred R. Bion's theories about the psychic issues in groups and developed further by their work with the British army, beginning in 1942, to select leaders. Finding a need to train members of industry in these group dynamics, they developed a training event, called a "large group conference" (later called "Tavi group"), that provided learning about issues of authority and power in groups, between groups, and in larger systems. Naturally, individuals also learned in these conferences about their own response to authority and power.

The Tavistock group realized, through their experience on the early projects, that separate approaches to the social and technical systems of an organization did not make sense because of the interdependency between the two. They also recognized that people at work live in a sociotechnical system that can be designed consciously for higher productivity and greater individual job satisfaction. This learning shifted the focus of much current research from human relations—studying people's relationships in organizations, especially between managers and employees—to research on the interdependency of the social (human) system and the technical (business or work) system.

Focus on Management and Labor

Work on military leadership that began during World War II in the United Kingdom, Canada, and the United States became relevant to studies of management, also prompted by the need to improve the performance of industrial companies. Managers' difficulties were largely due to the understanding of the term *management* that had been inherited from Frederick Taylor's work on "scientific management" (1915). Taylor located all planning, organizing, and decision making in the hands of the manager and treated employees as units of physical capability. Among those intrigued by the difficulties, especially in labor-management relations, was Douglas McGregor, a social psychologist who graduated from Harvard in 1935. Two years later he went to Massachusetts Institute of Technology and helped found its Industrial Relations Section. While teaching, doing research, and consulting with various companies, he met Lewin and Trist, among others. McGregor helped Lewin found the MIT Research Center for Group Dynamics; he recruited Richard Beckhard, Warren G. Bennis, Edgar H. Schein, and other early OD people to MIT.

McGregor practiced what he had learned as president of Antioch College from 1948 to 1954. He published an important book (1960) explaining the two sets of assumptions that a manager might hold: Theory X (autocratic management or Taylorism) and Theory Y (participative or more democratic management). Theory X and Theory Y became an important link between the people of NTL and

Tavistock and the students and teachers of management. It was also a way for those consulting with businesses to talk with executives and managers in a language that they understood. McGregor and Beckhard, consulting together in the 1950s at General Mills, coined the term *organization development* and defined it to mean a bottom-up organization change effort (Weisbord, 2004).

Early OD Consulting

Beginning in the late 1950s, some of the first OD practitioners were McGregor working with Union Carbide; Beckhard working with Procter & Gamble and ICI (United Kingdom); Herbert A. Shepard working with Esso; Sheldon Davis and Shepard working with TRW; Tannenbaum, Clark, and others from UCLA working with Non-Linear Systems, and many others. Some were external consultants from universities; others were internal managers becoming interested in this field. Many of the internal people were not educated formally in the behavioral sciences. They became involved and energized by attending "laboratories" at NTL, UCLA, the Tavistock Institute, and those sponsored by the Episcopal Church in the United States. NTL and the Episcopal Church soon offered a sequence of laboratories in human relations; group process; experiential learning; and the design of such learning events, consulting skills, and community change. Managers also learned on the job by coleading OD events and interventions in one or another part of their organization, especially team building, with an external professional taking the lead role.

For everyone, there emerged the need for learning a new kind of consulting because, in the prevalent model of consultants, they were experts in some technology who analyzed some aspect of an organization and presented written recommendations for improvements. OD consulting was recognized as being quite different from that. Success requires joining with people in the organization to help them identify, analyze, and solve problems, bringing expertise in these *processes* and in human behavior, but little in-depth knowledge of the *content* of this work. NTL led the way by developing consultation models, theories, and skills and establishing ways to learn experientially how to be an effective OD consultant.

The question then for everyone who wanted to get involved in OD was, "What do I need to learn?" The professionals needed to learn how to plan, design, and carry out effective consulting and training interventions in the business world. In addition to these tools, the managers needed to learn the basics of the behavioral sciences, primarily by participating in labs and seminars offered by the professionals. Those wanting to become OD practitioners experience the dichotomy between academic learning in the behavioral sciences and practical learning in the business world. Since many societies place considerable value on an academic degree, younger people tend to choose obtaining an advanced degree; but then they may find that they lack enough business experience to qualify for an internal OD position. Many have to settle for beginning positions in training or human resource functions. Experienced managers are sometimes reluctant to spend the time and money to acquire an advanced degree and so struggle to find ways to learn how to be an effective OD consultant. Many in both groups struggle to understand how necessary it is for successful OD efforts to *integrate* knowledge and understanding of behavioral sciences with knowledge and understanding of business and management.

OD Competence and Ethics

The unintended result of this struggle, as the profession grew, was wide variation in the capabilities of people identifying themselves as OD consultants.

As concern grew about the less competent practitioners giving OD a bad name and potentially causing harm to some of their clients, leaders in the field began talking about some kind of a certification process that would ensure quality OD work. In the late 1960s, those concerns led to development of a peer review process by some members of NTL Institute and some members of church systems (mostly Episcopal and Presbyterian). In 1968, the professionals working in church systems formed a new organization: the Association for Religion and Applied Behavioral Science (ARABS), later renamed the Association for Creative Change (ACC). The purpose of ACC was to support dialogue and learning among people promoting human development and planned system change. Only some of their members were professionals who engaged in periodic peer review and were "certified."

After some NTL members were unsuccessful in influencing NTL leadership to institute a certification process, they formed a new organization in 1970, the International Association of Applied Social Scientists (IAASS), later renamed Certified Consultants International (CCI). IAASS intended to have all of its members certified in one or more types of OD consulting. Although the development efforts were separate, ACC and CCI shared their learning about their experience with setting up their certification processes. The peer review processes that emerged were effective and rewarding. The key idea was that the practitioner took responsibility for demonstrating to a small group of peers (other certified professionals) that she or he was working from a solid conceptual and knowledge base, was using the best proven approaches to changing human systems, was successful in developing effective relationships with her or his clients, was continuing his or her professional development, and was consciously facing and resolving ethical and professional dilemmas. These criteria were soon enhanced by the addition of awareness and skills required to handle diversity, specifically the oppression of people of color and women in organizations.

By 1980, the combined membership of ACC and CCI had grown to a total of about seven hundred people from a variety of countries. CCI had members in the United States, Canada, South Africa, Germany, France, and a few other countries. ACC members were primarily in the United States and Canada. The original incentive to form both organizations included a concern that some governments, responding to rumors of negative effects on some individuals, were going to pass laws requiring licensing of OD consultants and trainers. But this did not come to pass, and it became difficult to offer enough benefits to members for the annual dues needed to sustain the association. In 1989, the CCI board decided to end the association, although area groups in Germany and around Seattle and Toronto (Canadian IAASS) continued for several more years. The ACC board made the same decision in 1995, but again an area group around Toronto continued for a while longer. In 1995, the two Canadian groups (CIAASS and ACC) merged and formed a new organization, the Association for Creative Change in Organizational Renewal and Development (ACCORD). It continues today.

A vitally important element of competence in OD is the individual's commitment to ethical behavior. In 1981, Donald W. Cole and the OD Institute began work on an "OD Code of Ethics"; William Gellermann became leader of this project. At the 1982 annual conference of the Academy of Management, the "Interorganization Group" was created through the efforts of Cole and Shepard, the latter at the time chair of CCI, to bring together the leaders of several OD associations—CCI, the OD Institute, ACC, and the American Society for Training and Development OD Division—for the purpose of growing OD as a profession. Renamed the Human Systems Development Consortium and led by Shepard and Jeanne Cherbeneau, it took on sponsorship of the work on ethics. This project was funded by a grant from the National Science Foundation, coordinating with the Center for Study of Ethics in the Professions at the Illinois Institute of Technology and later hosted by the American Association for the Advancement of Science. The result was a statement of ethics (Gellermann, Frankel, and Ladenson, 1990, found in Appendix B of that work).

Even with all of these efforts to define, elaborate, and develop the professionalism of the practitioners of organization development and human systems development, and many other sincere and competent efforts that continue today, the goal remains elusive. It is still difficult for many OD practitioners to really grasp Tannenbaum's understanding that "OD is not about a kit of tools. OD is about the way we live our lives" (Robert Tannenbaum, personal conversation, Mar. 1970).

Professional OD Associations and Networks

Under the leadership of Warner Burke, NTL established the Industrial Trainers Network in 1964 for the purpose of sharing experiences and promoting mutual learning among practitioners. The name was subsequently changed to OD Network. Following Burke, Tony Petrella guided the OD Network through its early years. The first annual conference was held in 1967, with members presenting their best experiences and theories. These annual conferences continue today. The membership grew very quickly, many of them line managers moving into an OD role in their organization who welcomed the opportunity to share with their academic and business colleagues. The selection of presentations for the conferences grew difficult as more newcomers wanted to gain visibility, while the older pros were more likely to attract participants to the conferences. An informal hierarchy of renown developed that caused some frustration for the less well-known members.

Cole founded the OD Institute in the 1970s to meet a need for a more participative professional association that would foster opportunity for newcomers to share their learnings and experiences. In 1978, he initiated an annual "World Congress" where OD practitioners in many countries meet for mutual sharing and learning.

Between 1970 and the mid-1990s, many OD associations were formed in other countries. Through the efforts of Rolf Lynton (the first leader of IAASS) in India, he and Uday Pareek formed the Indian Society for Applied Behavioral Science in 1971; today it includes members in India, the United States, Canada, Singapore, Malaysia, Spain, and Cyprus. Other examples are OD associations in Hungary, Russia, Southeast Europe (Bulgaria), the Philippines, Poland, and Mexico.

In 1986, the International Organization Development Association (IODA) was formed after the seed was planted at an OD Institute World Congress in Israel in 1984. Some attendees were unhappy about the U.S. influence in the OD Institute. The small group that created IODA included Marc Silverman, K. C. Soares, Walter Galloway, Marvin Egbert, and a few others. Initially the leadership was from the United States but soon spread around the world. Rita Aloni of Israel and Joske Diesfeldt of Belgium lead IODA today. The source of IODA's energy was a strong desire for a collegial organization with a flat structure that operated according to OD principles in its design and in the processes used for planning, communicating, and conducting its business. A volunteer in each country serves as liaison between IODA and its local members. IODA continues today with annual conferences on several continents. There are 226 members in twenty-seven countries. Those with the largest number of members are the United States (48), Hungary (23), Germany (22), the Netherlands (21), and Israel (12). Almost half of the membership lives in Europe, including Russia.

In 1980, Saul Eisen created the first use of the Internet for sharing OD knowledge and experiences at Sonoma State University. His Fulcrum Network was a bulletin board where people typed commands and messages over telephone lines at 300 baud. Fortunately, Eisen found a succession of host systems available at no cost. He presented a session on Fulcrum at the 1981 OD Network conference and generated a lot of interest, encouraging him to continue, and the OD Network Board decided to provide support.

In 1994, OD Network members Barbara Bunker, Billie Alban, Donald Klein, and others decided that the OD Network should sponsor a listserv for members, and Eisen shut down Fulcrum. Frank Burns had started an OD listserv on MetaNet. A small group, including Marti Kaplan, Alan Klein, Matt Minahan, and Robin Reid, picked up the MetaNet listserv and created the ODNet listserv in January 1995. Since then thirteen sublists on special subjects have been added, among the subjects people of color, health care, and coaching, with about three thousand people now subscribing on all lists.

Sharing OD Knowledge

As interest in the practice of OD grew, the marketplace responded by collecting and publishing the "tools" of OD. Many professionals were upset by the availability of such tools to anyone, regardless of their ability to use the materials knowledgeably and ethically. Others, especially those new to the field, were pleased at the opportunity to gain recognition by having their materials published, and many newcomers were delighted to have a toolkit available. The most prominent publisher over the years has been University Associates, founded in 1971 by William Pfeiffer and John Jones (now published by the Pfeiffer imprint of Wiley). From practitioners they collect structured experiences, instruments, lecturettes, theory pieces, and resources for the practitioners of human relations training, organization development, and human resource development and publish them annually.

To meet the need for conceptual and theoretical knowledge, some publishing houses began producing books in the OD field. Perhaps the best known is Addison-Wesley, which initiated a series of books on OD under the editorship of Beckhard and Schein. The first six books were published in 1969. By 1991, there were twenty-seven titles in this series.

Additionally, several journals were founded to spread the knowledge being developed. In 1946, Lewin and Trist at Tavistock established a new journal, *Human Relations.* NTL sponsored the *Journal of Applied Behavioral Science* in 1964 (now published by Sage). Other journals were started later: in 1968, the OD Network's *OD Practitioner*; in 1971, the American Management Association's *Organizational Dynamics* (now published by Elsevier); in 1975, Sage's *Group and Organization Studies*; in 1979, *Leadership and Organization Development* in the United Kingdom (now published by Emerald). Since then many others have been created, notably the Academy of Management's *Executive* and *Learning and Education*.

Educating OD Professionals

By 1965, recognizing that there was a growing need to supply programs that integrated academic learning and experiential learning, a number of institutions began offering short-term and part-time learning programs, as well as academic degree programs.

Learning Programs

UCLA developed a six-week course, Learning Community in Organization Development, beginning in 1969 and designed by Tannenbaum and Arthur Shedlin with the involvement of Charles K. Ferguson and other faculty. This was intended for managers and consultants in business, educational, and religious institutions who were filling internal OD roles.

In the early 1970s, NTL added laboratories in organization development, large system change, conflict, process consultation, diversity, group and team development, and others more narrowly focused. They also established a connection with Tavistock, especially through the efforts of Harold Bridger of Tavistock, and began offering Tavistock conferences in Bethel.

In the mid-1970s, the Gestalt Institute of Cleveland, under the leadership of Ed Nevis, John Carter, Elaine Kepner, Carolyn Lukensmeyer, and Leonard Hirsch, developed certificate programs in organization and system development, ranging in length from one to three years. These programs include an international program with sessions variously held in the United States, Sweden, Israel, the Netherlands, Italy, Canada, Singapore, Ireland, and South Africa.

Beginning in 1978, Columbia University's Teachers College offered the Advanced OD and HRD Program, consisting of three one-week seminars over a nine-month period for internal OD people. David Nadler, Noel Tichy, and Warner Burke led development of the program; the staff is drawn from a short list of well-known and experienced OD practitioners. It continues today as a two-week program with a new class each fall.

Degree Programs

Case Western Reserve University began offering a Ph.D. program in organizational behavior in 1965 under the leadership of Herb Shepard. Later, a master's in organizational development program was added. Their students usually come from the business world and spend three or more years full-time in the program. In 1980, NTL joined with American University to offer an OD master's program. Pepperdine University, Bowling Green State University, and many others in the United States, Canada, United Kingdom, Switzerland, and France added graduate programs in organization development or organization behavior or began to include courses in organization behavior and development in their graduate business programs.

The Expanding Field of OD

By about 1970, the number of people working on numerous "OD projects" was growing so rapidly that it is difficult to trace what was created and when. From then until now, there have evolved several major themes in the continuing development of OD, including the broader definition of human systems development (HSD). The themes are discussed in this section:

- Open systems approaches
- Diversity and social justice
- Manager's needs
- Globalization and culture
- Quality and excellence
- Leadership and emotional competence
- Appreciative inquiry
- Whole systems and searching
- Learning organizations

Open Systems Approaches

The open systems model affords great insight into the processes critical to organization health and success. Internally, three processes are identified. The producing process gathers inputs and transforms them into outputs by doing work that adds value in the eyes of the customer. The social process describes how individuals and groups interact with each other to create norms that might support effectiveness or might foster a negative, hostile climate. The individual fulfillment process causes people either to be satisfied, growing, and committed or to be un-happy, frustrated, and doing as little as possible. Most importantly, the open sys-tems model emphasizes the relationship between the organization and its environment. It recognizes that each of the relevant external groups places de-mands on the organization that, if ignored, reduce drastically the chances that the organization will be successful for long. The specific domain of the customer of the organization's products or services becomes of primary importance be-cause it is feedback from the customer that tells the organization the value of what it produces.

Diversity and Social Justice

By 1970, the civil rights movement and the women's movement had influenced U.S. society and its institutions. Companies and universities were feeling pressure from black men and black and white women, within and outside organizations. Organizations were being asked to assess their own cultures and systems to de-termine the extent to which the various forms of racism, sexism, and classism were present. The women's movement also had an impact on many other countries in the Western world.

This new emphasis affected the field of OD in two ways. Once it became ob-vious to organizations that U.S. governmental agencies were paying attention to their compliance with new laws and regulations dealing with racism and sexism, many turned to internal and external OD professionals (who were mostly white men) for help in figuring out how to uncover and deal with these dynamics. Ad-ditionally, professionals of color and female professionals in OD and related fields became a scarce resource; there arose strong incentives to develop training and educational approaches for managers, staff, and employees in those organizations. In the 1970s and 1980s, some OD practitioners began integrating diversity and social justice into their OD work. Some of these early practitioners were Elsie Y. Cross, Bailey Jackson, Rita Hardiman, Kaleel Jamison, Frederick Miller, Judith Katz, Edith Seashore, and others.

Rather quickly, professional associations (especially NTL, CCI, and ACC) took action to create policies and procedures that would encourage fair and equal treatment of all peoples. CCI may have been the first to define this as "sociopo-litical competence" and emphasize the importance to its members as a part of the certification process. Although personal development was always important for OD practitioners, the newly required learning about racism and sexism inevitably required self-examination. A deeper understanding of oneself was essential to un-cover one's biases and to learn how to cope with the ever-present possibility that one's words and actions might be inappropriate and unethical if those biases were operative. The focus on prejudice was uncomfortable for most OD people—often those most passionate about justice and humaneness in organizations—leading some to avoid involvement in this new field of OD work; but over the years the field has benefited tremendously. Today, the effective OD practitioner is much better equipped to see and deal with all forms of oppression in human systems, but there is still a vital need to continue to learn and develop in this area.

Managers' Needs

By the 1990s, managers were facing more competition and financial challenges. This fact, combined with their discomfort with the OD emphasis on people and their needs, caused managers and executives to prefer more "business-oriented" help. OD people talked about this as meeting managers "where they are." Over time, this reality caused many people to develop such additional theories and tools as strategy development, visioning, reengineering, the balanced scorecard, and others.

Globalization and Culture

The growth of international companies and global business also had a major impact on OD. As issues in multinational organizations surfaced, the subjects of culture and diversity became popular. Initially, the focus was on national culture; the beginning of understanding cultural differences was aided greatly by Geert Hofstede's research on IBM employees in many countries (1980). Research and learning about national cultures and organizational cultures grew rapidly, with quite useful work by Terrence Deal, Allan Kennedy, Edgar Schein, Fons Trompenaars, and Nancy Adler. Understanding and working with an organization's culture has become a significant part of the OD professional's competencies and practice, especially with the growing presence of organizations and teams that are diverse in employee nationality, race, gender, and socioeconomic background.

Quality and Excellence

As Japanese companies became world leaders in automobiles and electronics, Western companies faced shrinking markets. They welcomed W. Edwards Deming, whose understanding and convictions about quality and the importance of the customer had contributed so much to Japanese management and helped them produce higher-quality products at lower costs. Importing "quality circles" from Japan to the United States was attempted but did not work well because the required changes in upper management thinking and behavior were not understood or implemented. However, the Americans found "Total Quality Management" a more useful approach, and its implementation has been more successful, gradually becoming integrated in general management thinking and practice. More recently, an approach called "Six Sigma" has gained widespread attention, thanks largely to its development and application at General Electric.

Then Tom Peters and Robert Waterman published *In Search of Excellence*, a book that had a huge impact on the awareness of American and European managers regarding different ways of thinking about organizations, management, and leadership (1982).

Leadership and Emotional Competence

It seems inevitable that a focus on leadership would emerge from all that has become the field of OD. Years of curiosity and study about effective leadership have created a large body of knowledge, some of it quite contradictory, about the personality, thinking, style, and behavior of effective leaders. The important competencies and behaviors for leaders have been enhanced by more recent work on "emotional competence" (Goleman, 1995).

Appreciative Inquiry

The appreciative inquiry approach to changing organizations was developed by David Cooperrider at Case Western Reserve in the mid-1980s. Historically, OD had focused primarily on identifying problems in and barriers to more effective and humanistic organizations. Inevitably, the focus on problems produces a negative effect and highlights areas of incompetence and inadequacy. Appreciative inquiry emphasizes discovering what is best about an organization and unleashing the "life-giving" possibilities, the hopes and dreams of its members, and the implicit knowledge people have about how to make the organization healthier and more successful. A much more positive effect is generated as well as positive energy.

Whole Systems and Searching

Beginning with the idea that people from all parts of an organization could work together to plan the future, the "search conference" was developed by Emery and Trist in the 1960s. Adaptation to community groups came from the work of Lippitt and Eva Schindler-Rainman in the 1970s. Over the ensuing years, better concepts, theories, and practices were developed by many others, notably Marvin Weisbord and Sandra Janoff, Kathy Dannemiller, Dick Axelrod, Barbara Bunker, and Billie Alban. The scope of such conferences expanded to getting the whole organization in the room, including representatives of customers, suppliers, and local communities.

Learning Organizations

As awareness of the rapidly changing global environment comes to the forefront for everyone, so does the necessity for people to learn and cope successfully with what is happening right now in organizations. This need for flexibility may risk losing or downplaying the importance of the expertise that an organization has created from its past experience. Thus, creating a learning organization (Peter Senge) has become an important way to move toward longer-term organizational success.

Conclusion

Although one might be tempted to visualize the field of OD from its birth to today as a tree having an original seed and then a trunk and many branches, this analogy does not fit well. There are too many branches and threads that start out disconnected from this tree. Grasping both where OD came from and where it is today requires more the eye of a Picasso. The picture depends on where the viewer stands and what the viewer already knows.

The reader of this chapter may well find some parts of what is described here irrelevant, others simply curious, and hopefully sees many as new and important. The goal has been to create a better understanding of the history of OD. More important, this understanding should encourage practitioners to preserve the key ideas and values of OD's origins, rather than ignoring or discarding them. As described in the previous section, and as explored in greater detail in other chapters, the field of organization development continues to include other elements, many created by the interaction between OD and other areas of new and growing knowledge about the world. This pattern is consistent with OD's history and has always been the greatest strength of the OD field.

References

Blake, R. R., & Mouton, J. S. (1964). *The managerial grid.* Houston, TX: Gulf.

Gellermann, W., Frankel, M. S., & Ladenson, R. F. (1990). *Values and ethics in organization and human systems development.* San Francisco: Jossey-Bass.

Goleman, D. (1995). *Emotional intelligence.* New York: Bantam Books.

Hofstede, G. (1980). *Culture's consequences: International differences in work-related values.* Thousand Oaks, CA: Sage.

McGregor, D. (1960). *The human side of enterprise.* New York: McGraw-Hill.

Peters, T. J., & Waterman, R. H. (1982). *In search of excellence.* New York: HarperCollins.

Taylor, F. W. (1915). *The principles of scientific management.* New York: HarperCollins.

Trist, E. L. (1981). *The evolution of socio-technical systems* (Occasional Paper no. 2). Ontario, Canada: Ontario Quality of Work Life Centre.

von Bertalanffy, L. (1950). The theory of open systems in physics and biology. *Science, 3,* 23–29.

Weisbord, M. R. (2004). *Productive workplaces revisited: Dignity, meaning and community in the 21st century.* San Francisco: Pfeiffer.

CHAPTER THREE

VALUES, ETHICS, AND OD PRACTICE

David Jamieson and William Gellermann

The values of organization development (OD) practitioners affect both what they do and how they do it. Their values can either align with or clash with the values of client organizations.

This chapter examines the importance of values for OD practitioners: in their work with human systems, in the means and the ends of change, in the philosophy and methods of OD, and in establishing ethics for practice. The historical roots and evolution of OD values are discussed, as well as their erosion and subsequent renewal. The chapter closes with a current view of the value base of OD and its differentiation from many other approaches to change.

Throughout this chapter, *values* are defined as standards of importance, such as integrity, honesty, effectiveness, efficiency, productivity, profitability, service, and quality of life, while *ethics* are defined as standards of good and bad behavior based on values. *Organization development* refers to a values-based process of improving individuals, relationships, and alignment among organizational components to enhance the effectiveness of the organization and the quality of life for its members, to better serve the organization's purpose and its fit with the larger system of which the organization is itself a subsystem. *OD practice* refers to the strategies and methods used in facilitating the OD process.

Values and OD Practice

Values are fundamental to OD practice because they determine the degree to which OD practitioners are aligned with the purpose and values of client organizations and how they work with clients. Practitioner values shape individual purpose and meaning, personal conduct, and the means of working with clients. People's value bases guide them toward wealth or service, power or helping, achievement or contribution, personal gain or social responsibility. Individual values shape personal conduct in such areas as integrity, authenticity, honesty, compassion, trustworthiness, roles and boundaries, human dignity, and personal growth. Finally, practitioner values are embedded in the means used to work with systems affecting such things as collaboration, community, inclusion, learning, participation, empowerment, equality, justice, choice, responsibility, differences, and spirituality.

Client systems also operate with value bases. An organization's values are related to its outcomes (what it accomplishes), conduct, and means of working (the culture). If the client's values differ significantly from a practitioner's values, the decision to work together comes into question. If they are working together, serious problems with motivation, commitment, and integrity are likely and conflict is inevitable.

Awareness of practitioner and client values is an important first step, but the reality is more complex. There can be multiple values, with different priorities at different times under different conditions. There can also be a lack of clarity among *actual values, espoused values, and desired values,* which highlights the importance of being clear about which values are operating (Hultman and Gellermann, 2001).

Values Conflicts and Dilemmas

Values can come into conflict, and conflicting values (the practitioner's own or between practitioner and client) lead to dilemmas about what to do. Sometimes a value is so central and strong that the choice between values is clear and unambiguous, and there is no dilemma. More often shades of gray pervade and the challenge is to balance priorities (personal or combined with others') while the self (who we are) is operating to help or hinder thoughts, choices, and actions. Here are illustrations of situations in which value conflict and dilemmas are at the core of the OD practitioner's worldview and practice:

> Tom, an independent consultant, has not been selected for the last few
> projects for which he submitted proposals. Now there is the possibility of

work for which he does not have the requested background. He is sure he can do the work, and he knows he will never be selected if he says he does not have that background.

Tom's dilemma highlights values conflicts. Within the context of recent proposal rejections (which may or may not be affecting him economically or in terms of self-confidence), he is weighing the importance of authenticity and honesty in representing himself, his belief in his competence, what the client is requesting, what is lost if he does not get this contract, and what is gained if it is acquired under false pretenses.

> Mary is feeling a bind. She has uncovered some information that would help her primary client, but if she uses it she will have to violate her promise of confidentiality to others in the client system.

Mary's case is quite a common dilemma: the need to use information discovered in confidence to help her client. Contracts with her client and with others in the organization are in question as well as the values of trust, confidentiality, openness, and being helpful.

> Juan is working with a poor community in another culture, on a grant for the World Bank. He knows OD and how to help a client improve processes at all levels, become more effective, and develop potential. However, openness and authenticity are not valued in this culture, and self-sufficiency has become a way of life. It is clear to Juan that the people in this community need to be able to air differences and learn to work together. He is caught between respecting existing values and intervening to create new behavior. He has built good relations with his key clients in the community and is responsible to the World Bank for results.

Juan's situation highlights the complexity of value dilemmas in a global context. Here a balance must be found among how people generally operate in this culture, what Juan believes will make a difference, and his courage and strength in confronting his clients. In addition, his funding is dependent on showing that the community is making progress toward becoming viable.

> Nancy, an internal consultant with a large government department, has increasing tension with one manager with whom she works. He is controlling, quite hard on his staff, and under pressure from higher management to improve the performance of his section. Nancy has tried to talk to him about

new ways of respecting, involving, and developing his people, but he is resistant. She knows his staff is often angry and alienated from him, and she is sure his style and methods are contributing to the problems.

Nancy's situation pits her values and beliefs about management style, performance, and effectiveness against the manager's. It also surfaces a dilemma about being internal, pushing against resistance, and feeling concern for employees in a hostile and alienating environment. Nancy has to resolve questions about her independence and security as an internal practitioner in this organization and her responsibility to her direct client, the people in his department, the larger organization, and herself.

> Steve is facing a difficult situation. He is being offered an opportunity to work on a highly visible project with a major company doing his favorite type of work. However, this company was recently involved in a sexual harassment lawsuit that ended in a large settlement and was also investigated and fined by a federal agency for improper waste disposal. Steve cares deeply about the environment and human dignity. What kind of company would he be helping?

Steve is an advocate for human rights and environmental preservation, and this company has violated both of these values. Should he help them? Can he influence the organization's stance about human rights and the environment? How will Steve and his work be affected by his decisions?

These and other scenarios are commonplace and represent the many ways in which values, value dilemmas, and choices affect the practice of OD.

Values as Guides

Some argue that values are "shoulds" that must be universally adhered to. This chapter takes the perspective that values are *standards* that every practitioner is responsible to achieve on the basis of his or her own experiences, choices, and reflection.

Values can be thought of as guides, developed over a lifetime of influences, experiences, and reflection. Core values serve as a rudder to steer through varied situations. Values can be adapted and changed over time, on the basis of reflection about life's influences and experiences. Some values are deeply held and a part of one's core identity, while others are relatively less important, central, or fundamental.

The relativity of values shows up in a corporation when the greed of a few wins over the satisfaction of many, such as when the CEO and others increase their own wealth while stockholders lose money and employees are laid off. It shows up when individuals value justice but often feel unfairly treated. Or when a practitioner believes in equality with the client yet puts up with being treated like a hired hand.

Understanding one's own value hierarchy helps the practitioner make decisions, resolve dilemmas, compromise, and stand firm. Values are guides about what to pursue or prefer. Values have an impact on what a practitioner wants from life (as reflected in purpose or desired outcomes) and how to live life and engage with others (conduct, means). Yet the reality of the world, circumstances of the moment, and the self—who one is—can interfere with, modify, or even change how practitioners live their values.

Values and Self

The self—who one is and one's core identity—plays an important role in the work of OD practitioners in terms of their use of *self as instrument*. Values are part of the OD practitioner's self; they interact with other parts of the self in their expression. This interaction can support and strengthen a value, hinder and weaken its expression, or even change the importance the practitioner gives to it (Jamieson, 2003). For example, a practitioner may truly value openness and be able to live that value with most people. But then with some people the practitioner may have an overriding fear of losing their affection or approval; the interaction becomes less direct and open. Or consider the OD practitioner who has a hard time confronting authority figures and keeps compromising values as the higher-ups push for outcomes or methods that reflect differing values.

From another perspective, in a prior study several practitioners were interviewed about downsizing in the organizations where they worked. Generally, they tended to resist downsizing when it was done in response to a short-term drop in demand, though most went along with it reluctantly. In two cases, practitioners held values so strongly that they protested. They were unsuccessful and resigned because they believed that downsizing would do harm to the organization by destroying the trust, loyalty, and motivation of workers. Practitioners' responses to higher management seeking to downsize employees are an example of how practitioner values can conflict with those of the organizations that employ them.

OD Values: Then and Now

Values have always been central to the development and practice of OD. They brought the founding practitioners together and lent focus and identity to early OD work. Values have continued, with varied strength and emphasis, to differentiate OD practice from many other approaches to change, management, consultation, and facilitation.

The early values of OD were central to its identity as a profession because they were so different from prevailing values in operation in many organizations. Prior to the early days of OD, organizations operated on principles of mechanistic and bureaucratic systems, including authority obedience, division of labor, hierarchical supervision, formalized procedures and rules, chain of command, top-down directives, and impersonality. In contrast, the field of OD brought distinctly different values that were a counterforce to the prevailing organizational environment. OD offered a more holistic view of people and organizations and the belief that this approach was better not only for people but also for the performance of the organization.

OD values are traced in this section from the formative days of OD to today. A sampling of views of OD values and themes over this time period is in Table 3.1. Values are loosely organized along common themes and similarities: humanistic behavior, diversity and justice, performance improvement, life and spirituality, collaboration and community, democracy, human development, and process effectiveness.

Values and the Formative Years of OD: 1950s and 1960s

The early espoused values of OD were humanistic, democratic, and developmental in nature. The emphasis was clearly on human-social aspects as opposed to a technical-production focus. Yet the early OD pioneers had not lost sight of effectiveness, performance, productivity, and efficiency. As Bennis (1969, p. 13) stated, "More often than not, change agents believe that realization of these values will ultimately lead not only to a more humane and democratic system, but to a more efficient one." Argyris (1962) further emphasized that without interpersonal competence to help create a psychologically safe environment, organizations tend to develop defensiveness, mistrust, intergroup conflict, conformity, and rigidity which in turn decrease success in decision making and problem solving. In their historical view of the state of organization development at the time, French and Bell (1999) said, "We think most organization development practitioners held these humanistic and democratic values with their implications for different and 'better' ways to run organizations and deal with people" (p. 67).

The earliest values, philosophy, and methods were influenced by findings from the behavioral sciences and leading management researchers who brought the whole person, social systems, democracy, and development to center stage, highlighting the impact on behavior and performance in organizations (French and Bell, 1999). The threads being woven together by early OD pioneers formed the

TABLE 3.1. OD VALUES AND VALUE THEMES OVER TIME.

Bennis (1969)	Tannenbaum and Davis (1969)	Gellermann, Frankel, and Ladenson (1990)	Burke (1997)	2001 ODN Conference (Griffin and Minors, 2002)	ODN Principles of Practice (Church, 2003)
Humanistic Behavior					
	Authentic behavior, appropriate expression and use of feelings, willingness to risk	Authenticity, congruence, honesty, openness, understanding, acceptance, responsibility, self-control	Openness	Authenticity, honesty, presence, compassion, courage	Authenticity, openness
Diversity and Justice					
	Accepting and using individual differences	Respect, dignity, integrity, worth, fundamental rights of human systems, justice, freedom, diversity	Fairness	Respect (diversity), integrity, inclusivity	Respect, diversity, inclusiveness, integrity, ethics, empowerment
Performance Improvement					
		Effectiveness, efficiency, alignment			
Life and Spirituality					
		Life and the quest for happiness		Live large, faith	
Collaboration and Community					
Interpersonal competence	Collaboration, trusting people	Community, whole-win attitudes, cooperation-collaboration, trust		Community	Collaboration

Democracy					
Choice		Widespread, meaningful participation in system affairs, democracy, appropriate decision making	Choice		Democratic processes
Human Development					
Development of organic systems	Learning, growth, balance	Confirming people as human beings, individual as whole person, individuals being in process, people as basically good	Learning, development, growth, transformation, human potential, empowerment, flexibility, change, proaction	Human development, balance of autonomy and constraint	Self-awareness
Process Effectiveness					
More competent team management, group and inter-group understanding, improved conflict resolution		Appropriate confrontation, process work essential to task accomplishment, use of status for organizationally relevant purposes			Confidentiality

fabric for a new value set and view of organizations. These threads are represented by:

- The early work of Follett (1924, 1942), advocating participative leadership and joint problem solving by labor and management.
- The later work of Lewin, Lippitt, and White (1939), demonstrating that democratic leadership was superior to authoritarian or laissez-faire leadership in affecting group climate and performance, and Likert's later research (1961) showing the superiority of democratic leadership.
- The Hawthorne studies and their profound effect on people's beliefs about organizational behavior: that social factors held primacy on productivity and morale, that whole people come to work with feelings and attitudes that influence their performance, and that group norms have a powerful effect on productivity (Mayo, 1933, 1945; Roethlisberger and Dickson, 1939; Homans, 1950). The human relations movement grew out of this work, bringing greater attention to participative management, workers' social needs, and training in interpersonal skills.
- Lewin's and others' work on group dynamics (Lewin, 1947a, 1947b; Cartwright and Zander, 1953).
- The laboratory training movement, spearheaded by Bradford, Gibb, and Benne (1964), teaching people how to improve interpersonal relations, increase self-awareness, and understand group dynamics (Schein and Bennis, 1965).
- Rogers's work advocating self-responsibility for behavior and growth; supportive, caring social climates; and effective interpersonal communications (Rogers, 1951).
- The later work depicting a range of leadership styles, from authoritative to participative, with varying uses, pros and cons (Tannenbaum and Schmidt, 1973).
- The early work by Trist and Bamforth (1951) demonstrating the sociotechnical nature of organizations.
- The new views of the person articulated by Maslow (1954), McGregor (1960), and Argyris (1957), which shifted thinking about the nature of the person/worker, motivation, and the inherent conflict between worker needs and organization needs.
- Burns and Stalker's work (1961) on differentiating mechanistic and organic structures and their relevance in various environments.
- The influence of Katz and Kahn (1966), who first presented the organization as an open system.

From these research and theory contributions, the early values and philosophy of the field were created, leading to radical strategies and methods for improving or-

ganizations and people's lives in the organization (with, for example, sensitivity training, T-groups, team building, sociotechnical work design, and survey feedback).

Bennis (1969) and Tannenbaum and Davis (1969) published some of the earliest descriptions of OD values. Bennis identified a set of OD values and concluded that *choice* is the central value of OD. Tannenbaum and Davis focused on
the shift in values represented by the new field of OD and offered a more extensive list of values. Both lists of OD values are in Table 3.1.

Values and the Expanding View of OD: 1970s and 1980s

Although the earliest efforts focused heavily on the individual and interpersonal relations, by the 1980s OD was squarely focused in larger systems, from teams to organizations, communities, and societies. Tannenbaum, Margulies, Massarik, and
Associates (1985) captured this view of OD expanding from individuals to organizations to human systems. Experience with T-groups and sensitivity training showed
that individuals can learn about themselves and group dynamics directly from their
experience in a group. From this came the recognition that to improve workgroup
functioning practitioners needed to help people who work together learn together
as a group, hence team building. From this in turn, it followed that the focus had to
expand to include the entire organization, hence organization development. Then,
beyond organizations, it must include all the human systems of which societies are
made up, and ultimately our entire global community.

Even though OD is not considered by most to be a formal profession—with
clear standards of practice, competencies, agreed values, and code of ethics—many
concur, as first suggested by Dick Beckhard, that OD is a "field of practice" and
that OD practitioners operate as a "community of professionals." There was a sense
in the early 1980s that the community of OD practitioners could function more effectively with clarified values and ethics, and shared knowledge and principles of
practice. So a project was started to develop a statement of values and ethics for
professionals in organization and human systems development (OD/HSD).

This project to develop "A Statement of Values and Ethics by Professionals
in Organization and Human Systems Development" was approached not as a set
of "shoulds" to be imposed on practitioners but as a resource for practitioners to
use to clarify their own values and ethics. The process was initiated by the Organization Development Institute in 1982. Most of the leading OD-oriented networks, associations, and societies and more than one thousand OD practitioners
from around the world gave support. The project involved drafting a "statement";
distributing it for comment; revising it on the basis of the comments; and repeating the cycle of drafting, distributing, and revising more than twenty-five times.

It has been endorsed as a "working statement" by approximately fifty leaders in the OD community.

Since 1990, the statement has changed little and has been published in *Values and Ethics in Organization and Human Systems Development* (Gellermann, Frankel, and Ladenson, 1990) and the *Handbook of Organizational Consultation* (Golembiewski, 2000). It stands today as the most comprehensive, widely accepted set of values in the OD field and continues to serve as the foundation of the OD Institute's Code of Ethics. The statement and background material are available from the Clearinghouse for Information on Values and Ethics in Organization and Human Systems Development (www.odethicsclearinghouse.org).

These are the values identified through this project:

1. Fundamental values
    A. *Life and the quest for happiness:* people respecting, appreciating, and loving the experience of their own and others' being while engaging in the search for and the process of cocreating good life
    B. *Freedom, responsibility, and self-control:* people experiencing their freedom, exercising it responsibly, and being in charge of themselves
    C. *Justice:* people living lives whose results are fair and equitable
2. Personal and interpersonal values (may also be larger system values)
    A. *Human potential and empowerment:* people being healthy and aware of the fullness of their potential, realizing their power to bring that potential into being, growing into it, living it, and generally doing the best they can, both individually and collectively
    B. *Respect, dignity, integrity, worth, and fundamental rights of individuals and other human systems:* people appreciating one another and their rights as human beings, including life, liberty, and the quest for happiness
    C. *Authenticity, congruence, honesty and openness, understanding, and acceptance:* people being true to themselves, acting consistently with their feelings, being honest and appropriately open with one another (including expressing feelings and constructively confronting differences), and both understanding and accepting others who do the same
    D. *Flexibility, change, and proaction:* people changing themselves on the one hand and acting assertively on the other, in a continuing process whose aim is to maintain or achieve a good fit between themselves and the external reality within which they live
3. System values (may also be values at personal and interpersonal levels)
    A. *Learning, development, growth, and transformation:* people growing in ways that bring into being greater realization of their potential, individually and collectively

B. *Whole-win attitudes, cooperation-collaboration, trust, community, an*
people caring about one another and working together to/
that are good for everyone (individually and collectively), experiencing
the spirit of community and honoring the diversity that exists within
community

C. *Widespread, meaningful participation in system affairs, democracy, and appropriate decision making:* people participating as fully as possible in making the decisions that affect their lives

D. *Effectiveness, efficiency, and alignment:* people achieving desired results with an optimal balance between results and costs, and doing so in ways that coordinate the energies of systems, subsystems, and macrosystems—particularly the energies, needs, and desires of the human beings who comprise [sic] those systems [Gellermann, Frankel, and Ladenson, 1990, pp. 375–376].

The values from Gellermann, Frankel, and Ladenson are also listed in Table 3.1, together with another version of OD values that Burke (1997) suggested: human development, fairness, openness, choice, and balance of autonomy and constraint.

The Erosion of Core Values? 1990s

From a strong showing in the formative years (1950s and 1960s) and growth into the 1970s and 1980s, many have expressed concern over the past ten to fifteen years that "OD has lost its way" (Burke, 1998, p. 3) or that "practitioners [have] apparent amnesia regarding the values that underlie the field" (p. 4). As the number of practitioners has grown and approaches have proliferated, some new values are coming to guide OD practice. Some contradict and conflict, some undermine, and some just distract from earlier OD values. For example, certain values that have proliferated in organizations contradict and undermine humanistic, democratic, and developmental values: profit over people; dehumanizing practices in downsizing and layoffs as opposed to humane treatment; "doing to" instead of "doing with"; efficiency at all costs; withholding information; manipulation; and coercion instead of sharing, involving, or offering free choice.

There is no one universally correct set of values, so it becomes even more important for OD practitioners to be clear about the value bases of various alternatives for difficult problems, changes, and decisions and for conscious and considerate decision making about the values that are chosen in the inherent tradeoff of any dilemma. Church (1996) suggested that a duality has emerged in OD and that only two primary value constraints underlie OD practitioners' work with organizations: (1) fostering humanistic concerns and (2) focusing on more traditional business issues (effectiveness, efficiency, the bottom line). He concludes that economic pressures and issues are driving clients and the consultants they hire toward economic values, often at the expense of humanistic, democratic, developmental values. In fact, many major corporations (including about three hundred of the Fortune 500) are required by their charter of incorporation to maximize value for shareholders. Similar dynamics exist even without an economic motive. Leaders can place higher priority on self-enhancing values over the welfare of stakeholders. Power, prestige, control, reputation, promotion, and competition for funding can create the same value conflicts and dilemmas as the drive for profit.

This duality of value themes was present in the beginning of organization development and continues today. Balancing both sets of values is what made OD a significant improvement over prevailing thinking fifty years ago. Perhaps the humanistic, individual focus was overemphasized. Perhaps others pushed business issues and short-term economic results to an eager audience pressured for such results. As a consequence, the duality became an unrealistic dichotomy—an either-or choice, rather than both-and.

OD practitioners can resolve many of the differences inherent in the dichotomous, short-term thinking involved in the question of economic interests versus humanistic and democratic interests. The renewed concern about corporate social responsibility, the development of new economic models that include a triple bottom line (Willard, 2002), and the radically optimistic notion that business can be an agent of world change suggest that economic and humanistic perspectives are not fundamentally incompatible. Resolution is essential for grounding organizational effectiveness in authentic human commitment rather than coerced compliance. True value conflicts will always exist as long as people and situations continue to differ. Yet better results can be produced by not creating dichotomous thinking out of competing values.

A Renewed Interest in Values: 2000s

A resurgence of interest in values has emerged in recent years, in much the same way OD formed: as a response to prevailing undesirable trends. People are being right-sized and reengineered; short-term economic indicators have become the Holy Grail; optimizing one organization at the expense of others has become common practice; short-term success and profit are overshadowing environmental deterioration and resource depletion. In contrast, values such as spirituality and community are gaining voice, sustainability is being raised, and human potential and personal development values are reemerging. Many in OD are reasserting core values or yearning for their return. OD is a field that must struggle for balance among often-conflicting values and manage inevitable pendulum swings.

Participants at the 2001 OD Network Conference joined in a values identification exercise about what they thought was the most important value to focus on in the coming year. The results are reported in Table 3.1. Participants identified authenticity, respect and diversity, honesty and integrity, balance, presence, learning and growth, community and inclusivity, compassion, living large, faith, and courage (Griffin and Minors, 2002).

Subsequently, a project was launched by the ODN to identify current values operating in the field through the use of scenarios with focus groups across the United States. This effort resulted in an extensive summary of values and principles (Griffin and Minors, 2002) and a draft statement of principles of practice (Church, 2003). Extracting the value statements from this work produced a number of values seen as important to the participants in this project: authenticity and openness, respect and diversity and inclusiveness, integrity and ethics, collaboration, democratic processes, empowerment, self-awareness, and confidentiality (Church, 2003). These values are also listed in Table 3.1, along with the other lists of OD values described earlier in this chapter.

The statements of OD values shown in the table were developed over more than a forty-year time period. There are some differences among the lists, but the high degree of similarity is striking. These similarities suggest that there have always been central values differentiating OD from other ways of managing and changing. This does not mean these values always operate; individual practitioners make choices that support or undermine them. As years of OD practice and changing organizational environments unfolded, many of the original values have eroded for some practitioners and been strengthened for others.

Ethics, Ethical Dilemmas, and Ethical Competence

Values, which are standards of importance, have been emphasized up to this point. *Ethics* are also important. They are standards of good and bad behavior based on values. Metaphorically, ethics are like a compass that gives us direction, while values are like magnetic north, drawing the compass needle in that direction. Ethics, based on values, help OD practitioners guide themselves as they move along the paths of their work and lives. An example of a statement of OD ethics can be found in "A Statement of Values and Ethics by Professionals in Organization and Human Systems Development" (Gellermann, Frankel, and Ladenson, 1990, pp. 378–388). The OD ethics in this statement are:

1. Responsibility to ourselves
   A. Acting with integrity and authenticity
   B. Striving for self-knowledge and personal growth
   C. Asserting individual interests in ways that are fair and equitable
2. Responsibility for professional development and competence
   A. Accepting responsibility for the consequences of our acts
   B. Developing and maintaining individual competence and establishing cooperative relations with other professionals
   C. Recognizing our own needs and desires, and dealing with them responsibly in the performance of our professional roles
3. Responsibility to clients and significant others
   A. Serving the long-term well-being of our client systems and their stakeholders
   B. Conducting ourselves honestly, responsibly, and with appropriate openness
   C. Establishing mutual agreement on a fair contract
4. Responsibility to the OD-HSD community
   A. Contributing to the continuing professional development of other practitioners and the field of practice
   B. Promoting the sharing of professional knowledge and skill
   C. Working with other professionals in ways that exemplify what the profession stands for
5. Social responsibility
   A. Acting with sensitivity to the consequences of our recommendations for our client systems and the larger systems within which they are subsystems
   B. Acting with awareness of our cultural filters and with sensitivity to multinational and multicultural differences and their implications
   C. Promoting justice and serving the well-being of all life on earth [adapted from Gellermann, Frankel, and Ladenson, 1990, pp. 378–388].

OD work involves confronting many situations that pose ethical dilemmas. Egan and Gellermann (2005) suggest that ethical dilemmas in OD are created through the conflict among competing rights, obligations, and interests. White and Wooten (1983); Gellermann, Frankel, and Ladenson (1990); DeVogel (1992); and Page (1998) have identified ethical dilemmas experienced by most OD practitioners:

• *Misrepresentation and collusion,* including the illusion of participation, client presenting a partial picture, or adopting the client's bias

- *Misuse of data*, including sharing confidential information or presenting partial data to support a prior conclusion
- *Manipulation and coercion*, including using undue practitioner influence, a client misleading a practitioner, or incorporating inappropriate threats and rewards to reach certain outcomes
- *Values and goals conflicts*, including differences on means or ends with clients or differences with a copractitioner
- *Technical ineptness*, including inappropriate intervention, shortchanging diagnosis, or working beyond one's competence
- *Client dependency*, including clients needing too much of the practitioner's help or the practitioner not helping the client learn and develop capabilities

In the past decade, another ethical issue has emerged involving *intellectual honesty*. Concepts, ideas, models, and tools with lineage to founders and other practitioners are showing up in various forms in presentations, handouts, PowerPoint documents, and even books, with no reference to the creators and the presumption that they were created by the current author. Another variation, in highly commercial enterprises, involves slight changes to someone's previous work with a new author's copyright. These practices are unethical and disrespectful to the community of OD practitioners.

Being aware of these ethical issues helps OD practitioners recognize and respond to them. A recent article on the future of OD suggests that it is experiencing a period of confusion and ambiguity about values (Worley and Feyerherm, 2003). Practitioners are in the position of having to rely on their own value bases and individual ethical framework instead of generally agreed on ethical standards. In these circumstances, ethical behavior depends on the decision making of each OD practitioner and the values used in conflicting situations. It is therefore critically important that practitioners develop ethical competence, which DeVogel believes is a function of the extent to which practitioners have:

- "Informed their intuition" with a clear understanding of their own beliefs, values, ethics, and potential ethical challenges
- Reflected on their experiences to create a knowledge base for future action
- Practiced the use of values and ethics in a way that makes them available when they are needed—that is, developed and implemented a model of ethical decision making (DeVogel, 1992).

In the absence of such development and personal clarity, a practitioner runs the risk of drifting toward a form of unexamined self-interest (Egan and Gellermann, 2005).

Ethical competence and capacity is developed through reflective practice (Schön, 1983). Because there are never right-or-wrong choices, the ability of OD practitioners to know what to do depends on how well they learn from experience and build a knowledge base and decision-making competence through continued reflection and personal conclusion. One way of developing ethical competence is to review the situations cited in the references listed in this section and reflect on one's own response to them.

Evolving Values in a Continuously Changing Future

Values and ethics and how they relate to the practice of OD have been discussed in this chapter. They are continuously evolving, just as organizations, environments, and practitioners all keep changing. Hopefully, consciously chosen values and ethics consistent with Bennis's notion (1969) that choice is the central value of OD will guide this evolution.

Because OD is based in particular values, the field is not for everyone. Practitioners need to assess who they are, their alignment with the set of values generally seen as the foundation of OD, and their commitment to working with processes, principles, and methods that are consistent with those values.

The central requirements for being an OD practitioner are described in this section; they are based on the key value themes from this chapter. A practitioner's purpose needs to focus on service to others. One must care about the well-being of all human systems and strive for their growth and development of potential. Even though the field may work with larger and larger systems—and ultimately the global system—there will always have to be concern for the individual and for quality of life. Additionally, one must believe in the use of self as the instrument of change in helping others. What OD practitioners bring of themselves in engaging with clients plays an enormous role in what actually transpires in the practice of OD.

Most OD values involve personal conduct and how practitioners work with others. It is important to strive for authenticity, congruence, openness, and wholeness—to be who we really are and not a set of personas. To acknowledge the whole person—intellectual, emotional, spiritual, physical—and this complexity. To model open exchange between people that leads to deeper understanding. To strive for integrity and to operate in a fair and just manner. To be accountable and trustworthy. To keep all stakeholders in mind and ensure equitable treatment and unbiased justice. Further, practitioners must include differences with respect and dignity and believe in the value and rights of diversity. Being an OD practitioner requires constantly seeking the balance required for being a whole person, between individual and organizational needs, between performance and humanness, and between content and process. More than most fields, OD looks for the common ground, the balance, the both-and, the win-win solution.

In OD work there has to be a context of democracy, empowering people to participate with free choice and responsibility, developing processes and structures that build people's involvement in their destiny and hold people accountable for their actions and decisions. To work in OD is also to use the power of the group and facilitate interpersonal competence, cooperation, collaboration, and synergy; and to build jointness—collective and community—into the mind-set of the human system.

These purposes and values are the *desired intention* and require serious commitment. They are the foundation for OD practice and the hope for clients and all levels of human system. They represent desired outcomes of work with others, and they constitute the rudder for navigating through the practitioner's life. Values and ethical behavior are so central for OD that all practitioners must look inside; get clear about their purpose, values, and ethics; and translate this understanding into practice.

References

Argyris, C. (1957). *Personality and organization.* New York: HarperCollins.

Argyris, C. (1962). *Interpersonal competence and organizational effectiveness.* Homewood, IL: Irwin-Dorsey Press.

Bennis, W. (1969). *Organization development: Its nature, origins and prospects.* Reading, MA: Addison-Wesley.

Bradford, L., Gibb, J., & Benne, K. (1964). *T-group theory and laboratory method: Innovation in re-education.* New York: Wiley.

Burke, W. (1997). The new agenda for organization development. *Organizational Dynamics, 26*(1), 7–20.

Burke, W. (1998). Living OD values in today's changing world of organization consulting. *Vision/Action, 17*(1).

Burns, T., & Stalker, G. (1961). *The management of innovation.* London: Tavistock.

Cartwright, D., & Zander, A. (1953). *Group dynamics: Research and theory.* Evanston, IL: Row, Peterson.

Church, A. (1996, Winter). Values and the wayward profession: An exploration of the changing nature of OD. *Vision/Action, 15*(4), 3–6.

Church, A. (2003). *Principles of practice of OD.* Unpublished document, Organization Development Network.

DeVogel, S. (1992). *Ethical decision making in organization development: Current theory and practice.* Unpublished dissertation, University of Minnesota.

Egan, T., & Gellermann, W. (2005). The ethical practitioner. In W. Rothwell, R. Sullivan, & G. McLean (Eds.), *Practicing organization development,* 2nd ed. San Francisco: Pfeiffer.

Follett, M. (1924). *Creative experience.* New York: Longmans, Green.

Follett, M. (1942). *Dynamic administration: The collected papers of Mary Parker Follett* (H. Metcalf & L. Urwick, Eds.). New York: HarperCollins.

French, W., & Bell, C. (1999). *Organization development: Behavioral science interventions for organization improvement* (6th ed.). Upper Saddle River, NJ: Prentice Hall.

Gellermann, W., Frankel, M., & Ladenson, R. (1990). *Values and ethics in organization and human systems development.* San Francisco: Jossey-Bass.

Golembiewski, R. (ed.). (2000). *Handbook of organizational consultation, 2nd ed.* New York: Marcel Dekker.

Griffin, P., & Minors, A. (2002). *Values in practice in organization development: An interim report.* Unpublished document, Organization Development Network.

Homans, G. (1950). *The human group.* Orlando: Harcourt, Brace.

Hultman, K., & Gellermann, W. (2001). *Balancing individual and organizational values: Walking the tightrope of success.* San Francisco: Pfeiffer.

Jamieson, D. (2003). The heart and mind of the practitioner: Remembering Bob Tannenbaum. *OD Practitioner, 35*(4), 3–8.

Katz, D., & Kahn, R. (1966). *The social psychology of organizations, 2nd ed.* New York: Wiley.

Lewin, K. (1947a). Frontiers in group dynamics, Part I: Concept, method and reality in social science: Social equilibria and social change. *Human Relations, 1,* 5–41.

Lewin, K. (1947b). Frontiers in group dynamics, Part II: Channels of group life: Social planning and action research. *Human Relations, 1,* 143–153.

Lewin, K., Lippitt, R., & White, R. (1939). Patterns of aggressive behavior in experimentally-created social climates. *Journal of Social Psychology, 10,* 271–299.

Likert, R. (1961). *New patterns of management.* New York: McGraw-Hill.

Maslow, A. (1954). *Motivation and personality.* New York: HarperCollins.

Mayo, E. (1933). *The human problems of an industrial civilization.* New York: Macmillan.

Mayo, E. (1945). *The social problems of an industrial civilization.* Boston: School of Business Administration, Harvard University.

McGregor, D. (1960). *The human side of enterprise.* New York: McGraw-Hill.

Page, M. (1998). *Ethical dilemmas in organization development consulting practice.* Unpublished master's thesis, Pepperdine University.

Roethlisberger, F., & Dickson, W. (1939). *Management and the worker.* Cambridge, MA: Harvard University Press.

Rogers, C. (1951). *Client-centered therapy.* Boston: Houghton Mifflin.

Schein, E., & Bennis, W. (1965). *Personal and organizational change through group methods: The laboratory approach.* New York: Wiley.

Schön, D. (1983). *The reflective practitioner: How professionals think in action.* New York: Basic Books.

Tannenbaum, R., & Davis, S. (1969). Values, man, and organizations. *Industrial Management Review, 10*(2), 67–86.

Tannenbaum, R., Margulies, N., Massarik, F., & Associates. (1985). *Human systems development: Perspectives on people and organizations.* San Francisco: Jossey-Bass.

Tannenbaum, R., & Schmidt, W. (1973). How to choose a leadership pattern. *Harvard Business Review, 51,* 95–102.

Trist, E., & Bamforth, K. (1951). Some social psychological consequences of the longwall method of coal-getting. *Human Relations, 4*(1), 3–38.

White, L., & Wooten, K. (1983). Ethical dilemmas in various stages of organization development. *Academy of Management Review, 8,* 690–697.

Willard, B. (2002). *The sustainability advantage: Seven business case benefits of the triple bottom line.* Gabriola, BC, Canada: New Society.

Worley, C., & Feyerherm, A. (2003). Reflections on the future of organization development. *Journal of Applied Behavioral Science, 39*(1), 97–115.

PART TWO

CORE THEORIES
AND METHODS

CHAPTER FOUR

USE OF SELF IN OD CONSULTING: WHAT MATTERS IS PRESENCE

Mary Ann Rainey Tolbert and Jonno Hanafin

Use of self and presence in organization development (OD) consulting are explored in this chapter. Even though the two concepts are often used interchangeably, an important distinction is made. Presence is represented as an extension and higher-order use of self. The field of psychotherapy serves as the context for tracing the epistemological assumptions that support use of self. The aim is to create a better understanding of presence by defining it, explaining its significance, and sharing insights on how to cultivate and sustain it. In particular, the notion that presence can be calibrated is discussed using a construct known as the "Perceived Weirdness Index" (Hanafin, 1976).

Shifting the Paradigm

Sigmund Freud paved the way for much of what is done today in psychology, psychiatry, therapy, and other areas of behavioral science, on the basis of what he did or else did not do. It is known that Freud would sit behind his clients in therapy

Note: Many of the principles of Gestalt OD consulting are used in this discussion. Gestalt OD, or "OSD," is an approach to organizational consulting developed in 1977 at the Gestalt Institute in Cleveland and represents an integration of Gestalt principles, organization development, and general systems theory. (See Nevis, 1987; Rainey and Stratford, 2001; Tolbert, 2004.)

sessions. To him, this practice ensured that he would maintain the most detached and objective stance when working with patients. He believed that, if not sufficiently controlled, the personal experience of the therapist would negatively influence the work. His thinking was consistent with positivist epistemology, which dominated the natural sciences at the time (Burrell and Morgan, 1979). The non-positivist perspective is an alternative paradigm, one that underscores the value of subjective information. This stance views the social world as relative and best understood from the vantage point of the individuals involved in a given activity. These assumptions are similar to those that guide OD.

Riding the wave of the human relations movement and sensitivity training in the 1960s, OD entered the consciousness of Western society against a backdrop of openness, love, and fairness. The goal of OD is to enhance organizational effectiveness by attending to both human and organizational needs. Organization development has always prided itself on being a values-driven profession with a unique set of assumptions about people and work.

The OD practitioner's relationship with the client can be distinguished from that of the expert or technical practitioner. Task issues are addressed less through *what* the task is (a new technology system, job redesign, restructuring) and more through *how* the task is accomplished (goals, roles, interpersonal relationships). The work involves helping organizations define and clarify values and goals, manage and solve problems, make informed decisions, and develop and effectively use human resources.

Benne (1975) emphasizes three important tenets of OD: (1) scientific inquiry, (2) the democratic process, and (3) the helping relationship. Guided by concepts, theories, and technologies of behavioral science, the OD practitioner maintains a collaborative relationship of relative equality with the client. They "labor" together, each possessing knowledge and skills that differ but are needed by the other. This suggests another important aspect of the OD client and practitioner relationship: the practitioner as an engaged and active participant.

Understanding Self

All practitioners want to do their best. They go to great lengths to enhance their skills and performance through education, using the most extensively tested theories and refined models, and investing in the most up-to-date technology. Even with these efforts, the ultimate success of an intervention rests with the practitioner and what one brings to the process. In other words, self is the most important tool of the practitioner.

Jung ([1921] 1971) called the total personality, known and unknown, the self. He would go on to structure the self in various ways. Many of the delineations are based on mythical images, which he called archetypes. Two archetypes important to a better understanding of self are *persona* and *shadow*.

Persona is the public self that Goffman (1959) speaks of as a presentation of self in everyday society. The persona is the compromise between self and society as to what one should appear to be. It is an aspect of the self that could very well belong to someone else but is often mistaken as individuality. In some ways, it is a mask that many people wear. A good example is the bell-bottomed hippie of the 1960s, who was perceived to be a unique individual. In fact, every hippie was embracing the trends, habits, and dress of every other hippie.

The persona is a necessity, because through it people connect with their world. The persona makes life pleasant, just as clean teeth make for a nice smile. Too rigid a persona means too complete a denial of the rest of the personality. The key is proper management of the persona; many people lose themselves in playing a role for those around them.

Jung called the hidden side of the self the shadow. The shadow is the private self. It represents that inferior being hidden deep inside the personality. It causes shame and is all that is undesired. Like the persona, the shadow is a collective phenomenon; everyone possesses a shadow side. According to Jung, the shadow rests outside the awareness of the individual but not within the deepest level of the unconscious. Therefore, with deliberate attention, the shadow can be accessed and assimilated into a healthy persona. The shadow is where much of an individual's personal development work is found. The more the practitioner learns about self, whether it is persona or shadow, the more effective the self as an instrument of change.

Use of Self in OD Practice

From its earliest beginnings, the OD profession maintained the practitioner's importance to the change process. The field gives legitimacy to the practitioner tapping into and acting on personal data and observations in an effort to influence the client, whether the client is an individual, a group, or an organization. Use of self creates a more powerful and compelling engagement. This stance is based on the work of Fritz Perls: "And rather than leave the therapist half-hidden in the wings in order to encourage regression and transference in the patient, the heart of the psychoanalytic method brought therapist and patient onto center stage together in order to illuminate their actual relationship as clearly as possible" (Perls, 1969, p. viii).

Edwin Nevis goes on to say:

> The practitioner is not only to stand for and express certain values, attitudes, and skills, but to use these in a way to stimulate, and perhaps *evoke* from the client, action necessary for movement on its problems. This means that the practitioner is generally more open and revealing about the thoughts and feelings than might be true in other forms of process consultation. The aim is to take advantage of the issues of difference, marginality, and attraction by the client so as to use oneself in the most powerful way possible. Thus the Gestalt-oriented organization practitioner primarily focuses on *interaction with the client* as a means through which movement toward improved organizational functioning will occur. Specifically, the practitioner models a way of approaching problems and, through interest in the attractiveness of this way of being, hopes to mobilize the energy of the client [Nevis, 1987, p. 54].

Presence: The Practitioner's DNA

Taken to its zenith, use of self involves making a difference, giving and risking, and providing a force not usually seen or experienced by the client. What really matters is the practitioner's personal style. Consequently, use of self is elevated to a level referred to as presence, which requires a more holistic and deliberate engagement with the client.

There are two primary goals of OD practice: to improve the functioning of the client system by understanding and using OD concepts, theory, and methods; and to give a presence that is otherwise missing in the client system.

Presence represents the translation of personal appearance, manner, values, knowledge, reputation, and other characteristics into interest and impact. Presence is not manufactured. Everyone possesses presence, regardless of the level of awareness of the impact of that presence. Princess Diana and Dr. Martin Luther King Jr., had presence. Deepak Chopra and former U.S. President Bill Clinton also come to mind. President Clinton is known for his ability to make whomever he is talking to feel like the only person in the world at that moment. When it comes to presence, there are no duplicates, only originals. In this sense, presence can be understood as "practitioner DNA," a composite of unique qualities.

Presence is use of self with intent. It requires the practitioner to be constantly aware of self and others, and to selectively use that awareness to advance the work with the client. Over time, intent becomes second nature. By noticing internal experience and paying attention to the reaction and response of others, the practitioner is on the path to expanded presence. Exhibit 4.1 identifies principles of presence: be honorable, be an effective agent of change, and be curious.

EXHIBIT 4.1. PRINCIPLES OF PRESENCE.

Be Honorable

Align personal assumptions, values, beliefs, behavior

Stand for something; take a position

Dare to be different (or similar)

State the obvious

Speak the unspeakable

Be an Effective Agent of Change

Be an awareness expert

Facilitate enhanced interaction among members of the client system and with self

Teach basic behavioral skills

Model a methodology for solving problems and for dealing with life in general

Cultivate conditions for the client to experiment with new behavior

Help the client complete work and achieve closure on unfinished business

Be Curious

Stay in a space of perpetual wonderment

Show genuine interest in the client

Be interested in self

Explore the nature of relationships between self and client and among individuals in the client system

Presence: Past, Present, Future

Another way to look at presence is through the lens of time: past, present, and future—that is, in terms of what the individual has done, is doing, and will do. These three elements influence the public's perception of the practitioner and the level of esteem that will be extended.

Past Presence

The "past presence" consists of characteristics that contribute to credibility and authority. This includes credentials, work and life experience, whom one knows, where one has been. It is the "been there, done that" factor. Being able to point to ten other mergers and acquisitions gives the practitioner a platform on which to stand at the beginning of a new merger and acquisition opportunity. One's past experience can set the level of gravitas perceived by others. A good example is former South African President Nelson Mandela, who generates respect and deference that are based on his life's accomplishments, history of leadership, and ability to persevere in the face of insurmountable odds. His reputation moves him to a place of high regard on the part of the public.

Present Presence

The more explicit characteristics of a person are found in "present presence." They include attire, posture, voice tone, content of conversation, gender, race and ethnicity, and physical ability. Many of these characteristics are already evident as the practitioner shows up. The practitioner who dresses casually in a conservative environment may not be regarded as highly as one who dresses in a dark suit and white shirt. It can be difficult to determine the degree to which these qualities influence how a person is perceived. Many practitioners do not know what they evoke. It is important to become self aware and interested in the impact one has on others.

Future Presence

Impact is what drives "future presence." It involves the client's interest in the practitioner and one's work beyond the present moment. Future presence is a lingering presence that often leads to follow-up engagement for the practitioner. Clients want to experience a repeat performance with the practitioner who makes a difference. Another aspect of future presence is the ability to catalyze shifts in the client system in the moment that will have an impact in the future. An example here is a practitioner influencing a client, John, to examine a deeply held belief that he must be prepared with a highly polished, electronic presentation or "deck" in his first meeting with his potential client. Future presence happens when the client begins to consider attending the meeting without a deck and simply having a conversation. The shift in the client's thinking begins during the interaction between the client and the practitioner. Additional impact could be reflected in the client's future behavior. Effective future presence suggests several questions regarding the impact of the practitioner:

- Did the practitioner spark a shift in the client's assumptions, thoughts, and behaviors?
- What did the practitioner teach?
- What new learning occurred for the client?
- Did the practitioner exceed expectations?
- Did the practitioner evoke curiosity about what he would do next?
- Did the practitioner make lasting positive impressions?

Modes of Presence: Evocative and Provocative, Being and Doing

Working with intent implies that the practitioner has an objective in mind when intervening. One objective is to influence the client in a manner that advances the work. Nevis (1987) describes two ways practitioners can be influential: by assuming either an "evocative" or a "provocative" stance.

If the goal of the intervention is to raise client awareness or interest in a particular topic or situation, the practitioner assumes the evocative mode. This usually occurs in the early stages of a new issue, problem, or engagement. Evocative mode helps the client assess the situation, understand implications, and brainstorm options about the direction that should be taken. Here, the agenda is still emerging. The evocative mode creates a climate that allows the practitioner to track the interest and energy of the client. The job of the intervener is to actively listen and elicit responses in an effort to shape and structure the client's thoughts and feelings.

This does not mean that *self as evocateur* is a passive presence, void of challenge. The goal is to stimulate but not unnerve the client. Consider a white male practitioner who shares his feelings about the absence of multiculturalism in an all-white-male client group. Multiculturalism is a personal value of the practitioner. By speaking to the issue, the practitioner is not making a demand on anyone to do anything but is simply using his presence to give voice to data that sit in the room. Someone may be interested and moved to act as a result. The extent to which the group is influenced is information for the practitioner.

Once the direction of the work has been determined, the task is to formulate a plan of action and then move to implement it. A more assertive presence is required. Action is behind the provocative mode. The practitioner uses presence to support the client in getting things done. *Self as provocateur* is an action-driven and directed intervention style that demands a response. Saying to a CEO that his behavior is inconsistent with behavior that he publicly advocates for his firm is provocative. It is probably difficult for the CEO to resist reacting to the comment. Provocative connotes a range of impact on the client, from slight irritation to infuriation. The idea is not to incite a riot but to stir things up. The provocative practitioner lives on the edge of certainty and uncertainty, never knowing what the response or reaction might be.

Another way of looking at evocative and provocative modes is along the continuum of *being* and *doing*. As with the evocative mode, the strength of the practitioner in a being orientation is the ability to help the client examine situations, gain perspective, generate ideas, and explore implications. The practitioner holds a diffuse and open awareness that is easy and unencumbered. Understanding people and their feelings is important in the being orientation.

Conversely, a doing orientation is best supported by focused and structured awareness. The value of the doing orientation rests in implementing plans and tasks. Reaching the goal line is a key driver. Experimenting with new behavior and experience is involved. As with the provocative mode, the practitioner assumes more of a leadership role in a doing orientation. The intervener is active, risk-taking, and opportunistic.

Cultivating Presence

Even though presence is not manufactured, it can be cultivated. Seeing self as the most powerful tool the practitioner possesses calls for constant maintenance of equipment. Cultivating presence requires more than downloading the latest organizational change models, attending conferences and workshops, or perusing the current leadership bestseller. These things may be necessary, but they are insufficient. Cultivating presence requires a commitment to lifelong learning and development. Figure 4.1 identifies the six elements of cultivating presence:

1. *Continuing to work unresolved issues and unfinished business.* Therapy, personal growth experiences, and support groups are avenues to consider. Unresolved issues of power, authority, intimacy, and inclusion distort the relationship between client and practitioner.

2. *Committing time and energy to active reflection.* This helps to go beyond simply having an experience, to understanding the experience. Personal insight is the goal. No matter how similar engagements and situations may seem, each one is unique and offers learning.

3. *Actively seeking feedback from colleagues, clients, and friends.* The OD practitioner needs to understand what kind of impact one is having, including what one evokes. What one evokes in others can be the most difficult feedback to capture; yet it is critical to using one's presence.

4. *Living life fully.* This means creating a rich ground of experience of all kinds. The richer the field of life experience (family, relationships, travel, hobbies, spirituality), the more the practitioner has to draw from, and the more likely a lively part of self will emerge in the relationship with clients. Personal development is professional development.

5. *Investing in a broad worldview.* Traveling the world to explore new cultures and keeping current on world events help create a fertile context and enhance the opportunity to connect to people and issues.

6. *Experimenting with new ways of being.* The familiar can be comforting and numbing. Taking a different route home, ordering a new entrée, acting on a repressed impulse unveil fresh parts of the self, as does trying on new styles, postures, and behaviors in the interest of expanding one's range.

FIGURE 4.1. SIX ELEMENTS OF CULTIVATING PRESENCE.

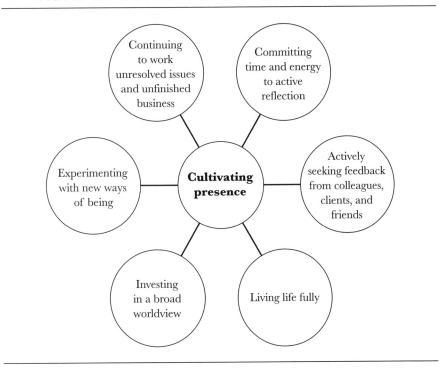

Marginality and Boundary Management

By definition, presence means being different. The marginality of the practitioner is a major asset in creating presence. What is meant by marginality is maintaining a distance from the client or client system in order to keep a healthy perspective on what is happening. Distance encompasses the spiritual, emotional, cognitive, and physical.

In the initial stages of consulting, when the practitioner is entering the system, lack of knowledge about the client in some ways supports marginality. Neither practitioner nor client tends to be eager to reveal all at this point. As the relationship builds, caution gives way to comfort, and the marginality of the practitioner begins to suffer. The act of maintaining marginality is often referred to in OD as "boundary management." It is an essential component of presence.

Boundaries are lines of demarcation that are visible and invisible. In establishing boundaries, one chooses what or who is in bounds and what or who is out of bounds. Boundaries are perceptual and are constructed through a process of choice. Suppose, for example, a practitioner decides to begin a major change initiative with the global executive team rather than with just executives based in the United States. The decision to expand the boundary of inclusion to all executives is strategic, and intended to realize maximum impact. Boundaries can extend from rigid and closed to flexible and open. Change made to a boundary or in the bounding process always causes resistance. Furthermore, anytime a system opens its boundaries, it risks being influenced, co-opted, drained, or irreversibly changed. The practitioner must anticipate and plan to deal with these realities of change. Understanding the concept of boundary and the bounding process helps practitioners better define and guide the work.

Boundaries also involve the extent to which a practitioner uses self in the work. A practitioner who is "underbounded" is apt to share more experience than is practical and is likely to be perceived as too familiar. On the other hand, the practitioner who is overbounded will be less forthcoming in talking about personal experience and thus perceived as distant. Either extreme has an impact on presence. The practitioner does not want to be too present or not present enough. There are ways for practitioners to manage and calibrate personal boundaries.

Calibrating Presence with the Perceived Weirdness Index (PWI)

Change takes place at the boundary, at the intersection of what is familiar and what is different. The OD practitioner usually chooses to position himself or herself on or outside the boundary, using interaction with the client from this position as a central part of the work. To have a practitioner maintain a presence at the boundary is unusual for most clients. However, it is the give-and-take, the negotiation of differences between the client and the practitioner that generates excitement, learning, and solutions.

Difference is also necessary for synergy, but it does not guarantee it. Difference is a prerequisite and a peril of presence; one can have too much or too little presence. The Perceived Weirdness Index (PWI) is a guide to how different (weird) one is in relation to a system (see Figure 4.2). Agents of change must model a different way of being, thinking, and behaving. Otherwise, what value do they bring? Winston Churchill said, "Show me two men who think exactly alike and I'll show you one man I don't need." Churchill is an example of low PWI. At the same time, if the practitioner is too different (a high PWI), effectiveness is jeopardized. The client focuses on the practitioner's difference rather than the work. Practitioners must manage the dilemma of furnishing a presence that is missing in the system while keeping PWI at a palatable level.

FIGURE 4.2. PERCEIVED WEIRDNESS INDEX (PWI) AND RANGE OF EFFECTIVENESS.

Managing PWI requires awareness, intent, and timing. At the beginning of a new engagement, the practitioner must be seen as similar enough to establish credibility. This comes from demonstrating familiarity with the situation, experience in working related issues, understanding the corporate terminology, and having a comfortable but relaxed demeanor. It serves the practitioner well to emphasize being on the same wavelength as the client by expressing appreciation for the client's situation. This is achieved by asking informed questions, offering examples, and affirming the client's perspectives when there is agreement.

Being too different too soon can convey lack of understanding of the client and the problem. Once a connection is made and the intervener has passed the test of admission, the opportunity for greater differentiation is there. The practitioner can reframe the situation as first presented by the client, challenge some of the client's underlying assumptions, ponder aloud how the client may be contributing to the problem, or suggest unconsidered paths and processes in addressing issues.

The underlying principle is to first create a platform of credibility in the client relationship. This is done primarily through joining and connecting with the client. From this platform, the intervener is then able to launch ways of interacting that challenge, provoke, and unsettle the system.

In terms of PWI, the degree of difference in one's presence that the client is able to tolerate is often a function of what the practitioner has accomplished. This competence-eccentricity continuum (or the Dennis Rodman principle) asserts that the better one is at what one does, the more leeway one will be allowed to be different. Because Rodman was one of the best defensive players in the National Basketball Association, his nightly hair color changes and other unconventional behavior were accepted. Most firms have quite another code of conduct (such as dress and work schedules) for their award-winning researchers than they do for the rest of their workforce. Competence breeds tolerance for the eccentric. Furthermore, the practitioner with name recognition, a proven track record, or a compelling presence is often expected to exhibit behavior that is a bit weird.

Consider the PWI Range of Effectiveness in Figure 4.2. When PWI is too low, the practitioner runs the risk of being absorbed into the system. This disappearance or lack of presence can severely limit the ability of the practitioner to get the attention and buy-in necessary to influence the client. After a practitioner has been in an organization for years, it is a great challenge to sustain a compelling presence. This is a particular struggle for internal practitioners or external practitioners who have developed an intimate relationship with the client. Some clients issue identification badges to external practitioners. Employees are sometimes surprised when they discover that these individuals are not employees.

If PWI is too high, the client is unable to extend the boundaries to include the practitioner's differences. The client system, like the human body, finds a way to isolate and expel the foreign matter. Issues of inclusion, autonomy, and standing out are activated in choosing a stance that is different. In his "Rules of Thumb for Change Agents," Herb Shepard (1985) suggests that the practitioner start where the system is.

The primary challenge for the OD practitioner is to locate and operate in the "PWI sweet spot." This means a presence that is similar enough yet sufficiently different to compel the interest of the client to test some of its assumptions, thoughts, and behaviors. The best interventions are those made at the high end of the PWI sweet spot. Searching for the sweet spot is ongoing work because it changes with the client. The objective is to influence systems and stay alive while doing so, which is Shepard's first point of advice to change agents (1985; see also Hanafin, 2004).

Skills and Abilities of Presence

Being fully present means intervening with conviction. It involves having an attractive aura, without being charismatic. Even though the practitioner does play to the audience in some ways, it is achieved with the right mix of spontaneity and intent. There are specific skills and abilities associated with presence:

- Tolerating confusion and ambiguity without rushing to organize it, allowing something to emerge naturally rather than forcing it.
- Separating data from interpretation and emphasizing nonjudgmental observations. The closer to actual data, the less distortion of the client's experience.
- Stating things succinctly, clearly, and directly.
- Seeing and being respectful of where the client is at all times; scanning for clues and asking when unsure.
- Attending, observing, and selectively sharing observations of what is seen, heard, felt, and so forth.

- Attending to one's own experience of feelings, sensations, and thoughts, and selectively sharing them.
- Being aware of one's intentions at any moment; being clear about the priorities of the work.
- Focusing on what is most interesting to the client; being aware of the emergence or lack of emergence of themes for which there is excitement; supporting joining so that something happens.
- Making good connections with others and helping others do the same; modeling clear and permeable boundaries, influencing dialogue, and letting go of being in control.
- Stating observations in a way that can be heard and considered.
- Using the client's language to heighten the capacity to be heard; using metaphors to paint a verbal picture.
- Staying in the power of the here-and-now and focusing on the ongoing process.
- Appreciating the quality of good breathing and body centering to support self and other.
- Stating observations in a way that can be heard and considered.

These skills and abilities require a personal appetite for the excitement of the unknown and confidence that one can handle what emerges. Self-awareness minimizes the OD practitioner's projections as well as fixed patterns that might get in the way of effectiveness. One's ability to care for self influences the ability to sense, create, and choose openness over defensiveness.

Summary

This chapter has explored the relationship between use of self and presence and offered suggestions for cultivating and effectively using presence to have greater impact when intervening in organizations. In the industrial age, employees were seen as little more than a pair of hands, executing assigned tasks. The postindustrial era ushered in a shift to viewing employees as complete human beings capable of participating more fully in the work process. This change in worldview was consistent with the field of OD. The one thing that is distinctive about OD is the significance it places not only on the client as individual but also on the practitioner as individual. The personal experience of the practitioner has always been regarded as a valued and valid source of data and information in the change process. Use of self is a primary consideration of the OD practitioner and even more critical when viewed through the lens of presence.

References

Benne, K. D. (1975). Conceptual and moral foundations of laboratory method. In K. D. Benne, L. P. Bradford, J. R. Gibb, & R. O. Lippitt (Eds.), *The laboratory method of changing and learning: Theory and application* (pp. 24–55). Palo Alto, CA: Science and Behavior Books.

Burrell, G., & Morgan, G. (1979). *Sociological paradigms and organizational analysis*. Portsmouth, NH: Heinemann.

Goffman, E. (1959). *The presentation of self in everyday society*. Garden City, NY: Doubleday.

Hanafin, J. (1976). PWI—Perceived weirdness index. (Educational document). Cleveland: Gestalt Institute of Cleveland.

Hanafin, J. (2004). Rules of thumb for awareness agents. *Organization Development Practitioner, 36*(4), 24–28.

Jung, C. G. (1971). The collected works of C. G. Jung. In J. Campbell (Ed.), *The portable Jung*. New York: Viking Press. (Original work published, 1921; original translation, 1923)

Nevis, E. C. (1987). *Organizational consulting: A Gestalt approach*. New York: Gardner Press.

Perls, F. S. (1969). *Ego, hunger and aggression*. New York: Vintage Books.

Rainey, M. A., & Stratford, C. (2001). Reframing resistance to change: A Gestalt perspective. In G. Bergmann & G. Meurer (Eds.), *Best Patterns—Erfolgsmuster für Zukunftsfahiges Management* (pp. 327–336). Neuwied, Germany: Hermann Luchterhand Verlag.

Shepard, H. A. (1985). Rules of thumb for change agents. In D. A. Kolb, I. M. Rubin, & J. S. Osland (Eds.), *The organizational behavior reader* (5th ed., pp. 682–689). Upper Saddle River, NJ: Prentice Hall.

Tolbert, M.A.R. (2004). What is organization & systems development? All about the O, the S, and the D . . . and of course, Gestalt. *Organization Development Practitioner, 36*(4), 6–10.

CHAPTER FIVE

ACTION RESEARCH: ORIGINS AND APPLICATIONS FOR ODC PRACTITIONERS

Arthur M. Freedman

The action research method is at the core of the practice of both organization development and change (ODC) and action researchers. In the defined scope of this chapter, the origins of action research and ODC are briefly discussed, as are some contemporary approaches to conducting action research. The conceptual confusion related to the distinction between the phases of consultation and action research is demystified in a detailed case study used to illuminate the action research method in the context of a multidisciplinary consultation project. A brief description of the operational values of action research and some approaches of ODC practitioners and action researchers can only suggest the historical depth of influence of action research on OD practice as well as possibilities for future practice collaborations. There are many descriptions of action research; this chapter offers a contemporary working definition of method and purpose.

The action research method is a reiterative, cyclical four-step process: diagnosing, planning, action taking, and evaluating action. ODC practitioners and action researchers employ action research when collaboratively consulting with leaders and members of an organization or community in a joint democratic inquiry (local parties) for the purpose of creating and executing effective plans that result in systemic changes to deal with issues important to those leaders and members and their stakeholders in a given context. The action research method empowers involved local parties by enabling them to gain the competencies needed to apply action research method on their own and in their own behalf. Thus local parties become increasingly self-reliant and less dependent upon technical expert, or "techspert," consultants and authority structures. The action research method generates new knowledge about the subject matter or content of a change process as well as about the change process itself.

The Origins of Action Research

The founders of NTL (Ken Benne in particular) and the pioneers of the organization development and change (ODC) field of practice identified themselves as the intellectual descendents of John Dewey (Freedman, 1988); "Dewey translated the scientific method of problem solving into terms understandable by practitioners and laypersons" (French and Bell, 1995, p. 144). In so doing, Dewey spelled out the basic phases of what became the standard for virtually all forms of the consultation processes. Management consultants of all kinds and types, ODC scholar practitioners, and action researchers follow Dewey's version of the scientific method in their respective practice areas. Lewin's concept of action research was philosophically compatible with Dewey's work and the phases of the consulting process as described, with minor variations, by such ODC scholar practitioners as Blake and Mouton (1976), Block (1999), Cummings and Worley (2001), Lippitt, Watson, and Westley (1958), and Lippitt and Lippitt (1986).

Action research evolved from the perceived need to pair research with action in order to solve real-world issues, especially social problems. Lewin realized that those affected by such problems, or "local partners" such as community residents and organizational employees, must be actively involved in diagnosing, planning, taking, and evaluating the effects of action to ensure their emotional investment in and commitment to supporting planned change. The results of action research–driven systems change efforts contributed to generation and dissemination of new knowledge pertaining to the social and organizational issues as well as to the dynamics of planned change. Further, action research was used to train and otherwise enable local partners to master the action research process, thus empowering themselves to plan and take effective action for and by themselves in the future.

Lewin conceived of action research as *a reiterative cyclical process* (Figure 5.1). Recognizing that traditional social science research may study current situations but generally fail to contribute to creating and executing solutions for real-world social issues, Lewin was committed to research that both guided action and assessed the effects of that action. According to his biographer, Al Marrow (1969), Lewin advised *no action without research; no research without action.* Emphasizing the utilitarian aspects of action research, Lewin pointed out that "in a field that lacks objective standards of achievement, no learning can take place. If we cannot judge whether an action has led forward or backward, if we have no criteria for evaluating the relation between effort and achievement, there is nothing to prevent us from making the wrong conclusions and [encouraging] the wrong work habits. Realistic fact-finding and evaluation is a prerequisite for any learning" (Lewin, 1946, p. 35).

FIGURE 5.1. LEWIN'S CONCEPT OF ACTION RESEARCH.

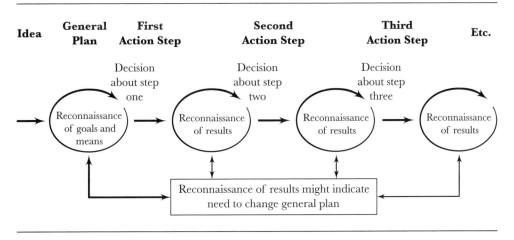

Lewin may not have been the first person to name or begin to define action research. John Collier (1945), the U.S. Commissioner of Indian Affairs from 1933 to 1945, implied the utilitarian and moral requirement that researchers must actively collaborate with local community members if the research was to be used to create social change.

Lewin's action research concepts and methods were exported to and adopted by a number of European action researchers. According to Gustavsen (1992), interactions among Lewin, Eric Trist, and Fred Emery in the mid-1940s influenced the Tavistock Institute's practices of sociotechnical systems (STS) work redesign. The first well-known example of STS in action was the application of action research to problems encountered during mechanization of coal-mining operations (Trist and Bamforth, 1951). At around the same time, Einar Thorsrud collaborated with Emery in developing the concept of industrial democracy in

Norway and subsequently in many other western European societies (Emery and Thorsrud, 1976).

Contemporary Action Research

Virtually all ODC scholars agree that action research is a reiterative cycle of diagnosis; planning; action taking; reconnaissance or research on the effects of the actions that are taken; and reevaluation of the underlying assumptions, goals, and plans in light of what was discovered (Argyris, Putnam, and Smith, 1985; Collier, 1945; Cummings and Worley, 2001; Shepard, 1960; Israel, Schurman, and Hugentobler, 1992; French and Bell, 1995; Greenwood and Levin, 1998; and Reason and Bradbury, 2001).

Purposes

The purposes of an action research–based consultation by ODC practitioners and action researchers generally include enabling all involved parties to actively participate in performing two functions:

1. Client system leaders and members learn about and acquire the competencies needed to perform these action research functions.
2. Generation and dissemination of new knowledge. All involved parties, including the ODC practitioners or action researchers, test the validity of existing social science and organizational behavior theory and methods that pertain either to the subject matter or to the change strategies and methods employed in the change effort. Further, all involved parties cogenerate new theory, knowledge, and methods as they innovate, using the action research method, to cope with the emergent and predictable surprises they encounter. The involved parties are obligated to contribute these lessons learned to both the client system's organizational learning (Argyris and Schön, 1996) and the relevant areas of consulting practice.

Four Steps of Action Research

Coghlan and Brannick (2001) offer a practical conceptualization of action research. Their notion of a single cycle in an action research project (Figure 5.2) incorporates the *purpose* of the project, the *context* in which it takes place, and the *process* that is employed.

FIGURE 5.2. A SINGLE CYCLE IN AN ACTION RESEARCH PROJECT.

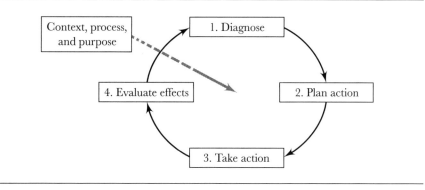

Step One: Diagnosis. On the basis of collected and organized (often categorized) data, ODC practitioners or action researchers collaborate with involved local partners to identify and prioritize issues of concern to the leaders and members of the organizational or community client system. *Issues* include problems to solve, opportunities to exploit, and dilemmas to manage.

Step Two: Plan Action. ODC practitioners or action researchers and involved local partners cocreate a change strategy and comprehensive action plan that consists of a series of sequential or parallel action steps. Each step of the implementation or action plan includes who has overall responsibility, which party will play which role, the schedule, and required resources. The plan may consist of a single action step or just a few steps. All involved parties must explicitly understand and accept the idea that the complete plan will *emerge* and *evolve* as the first steps of the action plan are executed and that action research is in part a process of exploration and discovery. All involved parties must (learn to) *trust the process (TTP)*.

Step Three: Take Action. The responsible parties execute each action step.

Step Four: Evaluate Effects. All involved parties pay close attention to the manner in which each action step unfolds during implementation to determine if the actual progress and effects or results match what was expected. Attention is paid to intended and unintended outcomes, the content or subject matter involved, the processes used, and whether or not the underlying premises or assumptions prove to have been valid and reliable. The evaluation process assesses whether the original diagnosis was correct, if the correct action was taken, if the action was taken appropriately, and what was learned from taking the step that should feed into the next cycle of diagnosis, planning, action, and evaluation.

The Planning and Implementation Processes

The processes required to realize these purposes depend upon the *clarity or ambiguity of the desired state* and the *specificity or uncertainty of the pathway* to the desired state, from the perspective of those who must guide or contribute to the planning and implementation processes. Where both the desired state and the pathway to that desired state are specific, clear, and well known, the client system may require only techspert consultants (Freedman and Zackrison, 2001). When either the desired state or the pathway is uncertain, ambiguous, unprecedented, or discontinuous, the ODC practitioner or action researcher serves an essential function. Having the participatory action research–based processes of exploration and discovery as their particular area of competence, ODC practitioners and action researchers are expert at enabling client system leaders and members to clarify, establish, and modify (as needed) their own desired states and the pathways (strategies and methods or processes) needed to realize these desired states.

Context of the Consultation

Consideration of two variables has proven useful when client systems need to employ consultants. The first is the number and variety of involved parties. The term *involved party* refers to two distinct populations. First, it refers to all individuals and groups who—by virtue of their knowledge, experience, or capacity—can (and should) contribute to both the planning and the implementing processes. Second, involved parties include those individuals and groups whose work is likely to be affected either by execution of the implementation plans or by the intended or unintended results of the change. Members of both classes have personal interests at stake in the organizational change. Open systems planning or stakeholder analysis (Jayaram, 1976) and impact analysis (Freedman, 1999) can identify these two classes of involved parties. The larger the number and variety of involved parties, the greater the probability that ODC practitioners or action researchers will be required to facilitate their meaningful participation in planning and implementation processes even if the organizational change is driven, top-down, by a technological or structural (technostructural) innovation that is guided by techspert consultants (Freedman and Zackrison, 2001).

The second contextual consideration is defined by the interaction of two variables. The first is the extent to which it is important to gain the *commitment* of all involved parties to support the change effort. The second is the extent to which it is important to achieve a high-quality *solution* that enables the involved parties to achieve or realize their desired state. There are four possibilities:

1. If both the solution quality and the involved parties' commitment are considered important, then:
   A. An action research approach is essential.
   B. Both techspert consultants and ODC scholar practitioners are essential.
   C. Local knowledge and wisdom must be supplemented by external expertise.
   D. A high level of involvement and participation of all significant involved parties is required.
   E. Diversity of knowledge, experience, capability, perspective, interests, values, beliefs, and so forth is required.
2. If involved parties' commitment is considered important but the solution quality is not, then:
   A. An action research approach is essential.
   B. ODC scholar practitioners are essential to facilitate cocreation of high involvement and participation processes.
   C. The collective local knowledge and wisdom of the involved parties must be acknowledged and accessed in order to contribute to creating goals (desired states) and pathways (implementation plans) that all involved parties are willing to support.
   D. A high level of involvement and participation of all relevant involved parties is essential.
   E. Techsperts may not be essential.
3. If involved parties' commitment is not considered important but the solution quality is thought to be important, then:
   A. The action research approach may be useful to ensure that the desired state and the implementation plans do not conflict with the vested interests of the significant involved parties.
   B. Relevant techspert or SME (subject matter expert) consultants must make recommendations or develop and execute implementation plans.
   C. ODC practitioners may not be essential.
4. If neither the involved parties' commitment nor the solution quality is considered important, then:
   A. Virtually any arbitrary management decision and expedient implementation process will probably suffice.
   B. The action research approach is probably not necessary.
   C. Neither techsperts nor ODC practitioners may be needed.

Coghlan and Brannick (2001) speak to the issue of knowledge generation when they point out that ODC practitioners or action researchers and their client system leaders and members must make adequate time available to reflect upon and learn from their emerging experience with each iteration of the action research cycle. There are three areas from which significant learnings can be derived through research on the effects of action and reflection on those results:

1. *The content*—*what* is diagnosed, *what* is planned, *what* is acted upon, and *what* is monitored and evaluated
2. *The process*—*how* diagnosis is undertaken, *how* the planning of action flows from that diagnosis, *how* action plans are implemented, and *how* monitoring and evaluation are conducted
3. *The premise*—the unstated underlying assumptions or mental models, which influence *perception* (what was seen and heard), *meaning attribution* (what sense was made of what was perceived), *feelings* (emotions related to the meaning attributed to perception), *behavior* (what was said and done), and *results* (what effects were brought about by the behavior)

Greenwood and Levin (1998) add that action research has specific characteristics:

• Action research is bound by the situational and cultural contexts in which the real-life issues manifest themselves.
• Participants and researchers collaborate in cogenerating knowledge.
• Recognizing and using the diversity of experience and capacities among the local participants enriches the action research process.
• The action research process leads to action and change.
• Reflection on action leads to creation of new knowledge.
• The credibility and validity of action research is tested by measuring whether the process resulted in viable solutions and increased participants' control over their own situation.

Relationship of Action Research to the Phases of the Consultation Process

The phases of the consulting process (Block, 1999; Lippitt and Lippitt, 1986; and Lippitt, Watson, and Westley, 1958) are not the same as in action research (Argyris, Putnam, and Smith, 1985; Coghlan and Brannick, 2001; Lewin, 1946). Rather, whether practiced by techsperts, action researchers, or ODC practitioners, the typical *phases of consultation* follow the fundamental guidelines originally established by John Dewey (1991a, 1991b). Briefly, as illustrated in Figure 5.3, these are (1) preentry, contact, entry, and negotiating consulting agreements; (2) data collection; (3) data organization and preparation for data feedback; (4) data feedback, identification of issues, establishing priorities among issues, and setting goals for high-priority issues; (5) developing implementation or action plans; (6) executing the implementation plans; (7) evaluating results; (8) terminating or recycling the change effort; and (9) using feedback loops throughout the consultation process to identify and analyze any variance between expected and actual progress at each phase and from one phase to another to identify and deal with *predictable surprises* (the unanticipated side effects and emerging nascent issues).

FIGURE 5.3. PHASES OF THE CONSULTING PROCESS.

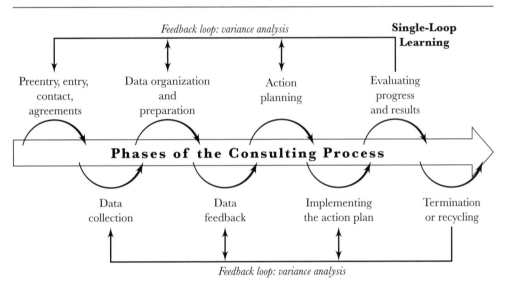

Source: Lippitt, Watson, and Westley (1958), Lippitt and Lippitt (1986), and Block (1999).

What establishes both areas of practice—those of ODC practitioners and action researchers—as unique and contributes to their power in effectively mobilizing essential systemic resources to achieve meaningful objectives is systematic, reiterative application of action research to each and every one of the phases of the traditional consultation process (Coghlan and Brannick, 2001; see Figure 5.4).

FIGURE 5.4. APPLICATION OF THE AR CYCLE
TO EACH PHASE OF THE CONSULTATION PROCESS.

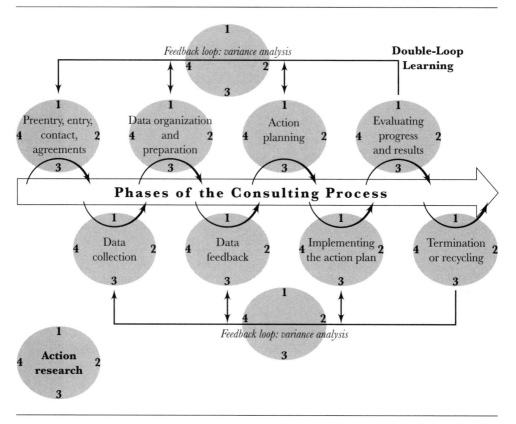

For descriptive purposes, each phase of the consulting process is treated as having a beginning, middle, and end. For example, consider the implementation phase of the consulting process. The *current state* is the beginning of the implementation phase—that is, the entire data feedback process, including identifying issues, setting change objectives, establishing priorities, and developing implementation plans, has been completed. The transition state is the *middle* of the implementation phase—that is, execution of the implementation plans. The *desired state* is the end of the implementation phase. When achieved, the desired end state for one phase becomes the current state for the next phase; for example, the end of the implementation phase is the beginning of the phase during which the effects of executing the implementation plans are fully evaluated.

The implementation phase begins as the ODC practitioners or action researchers assist their local partners in executing their cogenerated implementation plans (often by providing process facilitation, procedural guidance, coaching, conceptual education, or behavioral skill training). The implementation phase includes monitoring the effects of executing each step of each implementation or action plan. These effects may encompass unanticipated side effects of the action step that was taken or uncovering previously unrecognized nascent organizational issues. As Lewin said, *the best way to understand an organization is to try to change it* (Marrow, 1969). As any of these predictable surprises occur, the ODC practitioners or action researchers guide their local partners through the four-step action research process to enable them to understand what happened, why it happened, and what they might do about it.

As illustrated in Figure 5.5, these reiterative action research cycles are unplanned but essential side trips. They invariably generate greater understanding of the organization and the effectiveness of the strategies and methods being used to try to change it. However, the reiterative action research cycles also may appear to be irrelevant or wasteful to naïve, linear-thinking techsperts, or cost-and-schedule-conscious project managers.

FIGURE 5.5. REITERATIVE AR CYCLES APPLIED TO THE IMPLEMENTATION PHASE OF THE CONSULTATION PROCESS.

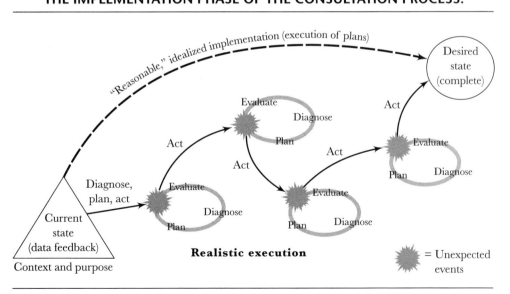

All relevant involved parties participate in each of the four steps of the action research process—with the ODC practitioners or action researchers acting as partners in the process with relevant client system or community leaders and members and external stakeholders. The focus is not only on *what* was done but also *how* it was done, as well as the operational *premises* that guided the parties in constructing their particular content and process decisions.

As a consequence of participating in this process, the involved local parties acquire knowledge and skill in applying the action research–based ODC consultation process for and by themselves in the future. With all of their collective wisdom, diverse interests, concerns, priorities, and preferences, the involved local parties learn how to collectively participate in and influence the entire change process. The results are (1) a critical mass of internal and external stakeholders becoming committed to supporting execution of the implementation plans; (2) a higher-quality process and "solution" likely to result in realizing the desired end state; and (3) the local partners acquiring sufficient competence, confidence (in themselves and in the action research method), and comfort in applying the action research process for them to become increasingly self-reliant, freeing themselves from dependency on experts. In addition, local partners usually gain an enhanced sense of self-esteem as they build their capacity for self-determination. This is Dewey's learning from experience (1991a, 1991b) and Lewin's action research (1946), resulting in Argyris and Schön's double-loop learning process (1996; Argyris, Putnam, and Smith, 1985).

Without the action research method as an integral component, the consultation process remains a simple single-loop trial-and-error learning process (Argyris and Schön, 1996). This is the typical techspert consultant approach (Block, 1999; Freedman and Zackrison, 2001).

An Example of Action Research in an ERP Project

There are many variations of action research philosophy, values, and methods practiced in various multinational and global settings (see Reason and Bradbury, 2001). The case study presented here illustrates one and one-half cycles of the action research process. This took place within one subphase of a considerably larger and longer ODC consultation that was an element of a still larger multidisciplinary technostructural consultation.

Context

This was an ERP (enterprise resource planning) design and implementation project within a global research and development company that generates upward of US$3.5 billion a year in revenues.

Purpose

The intent was to determine the degree to which, and how, managers and staff from end-user groups should be involved in the design and implementation process.

History

Initially, design and implementation projects of these integrative software platform systems were staffed and driven almost exclusively by external management consultant firms' information technology (IT) and project management (PM) techsperts who are employed by management consulting firms. These techsperts specialize in determining user groups' needs, designing the ERP system to satisfy these needs, and then implementing the designed features of however many modules the particular ERP system contained. ERP systems are composed of a number of modules, each pertaining to a particular function (inventory management, human resource information, sales). Each module affects the operations of one or more functional subsystems within the larger organization. Consultants and the client organization's decision makers determine which modules are required for a given project.

Such projects are expensive and complex. End to end, an ERP project could go on for two, three, or more years and cost upward of $120 million. Software development firms such as SAP, PeopleSoft, Oracle, and Baan often place their IT techspert advisors on these projects.

As experience unfolded within this particular project, the ERP project management team (PMT) encountered considerable resistance from the managers of the user groups who were to become responsible for making the ERP system work in their respective settings. In this project, the user groups were regionalized around the globe; each regional group was configured with its own functional groups to accommodate the nature of the business that it conducted within its own host countries. The ERP system was being designed to ensure, if not enforce, uniformity and consistency across all groups. Although the design of each model may have been "elegant" from the perspective of the IT techsperts, the user group managers felt the designs were imposed on them and were, for the most part, unresponsive to their unique circumstances. The PMT and the user group managers were continuously engaging in contentious and annoying but fruitless "e-mail wars" and "lobbing grenades over the wall." Each involved party tried, unsuccessfully, to invalidate the other's position.

The PMT initially believed that the sheer elegance and power of the ERP software platform system would force all involved parties to accept and support the changes during and subsequent to its design and implementation. This belief was now being tested and disconfirmed. The PMT gradually came to believe that, to reduce resistance, they had to find some way to get the user groups more actively involved in the design and implementation process so as to induce them to buy into (become emotionally invested and committed in) the project. Therefore, since the original premise was proven unrealistic and had to be modified, a new tactic had to be introduced. This was the first example of single-loop trial-and-error learning.

The PMT brought on several "change management" specialists whose primary function was to increase the quality and frequency of information flowing out from the PMT to the user groups. The implicit assumption was that if user groups knew what was going on in the project group, what progress was being made, and what technical difficulties were being encountered, their concerns would be satisfied. This turned out to be a positive step but was insufficient. The resistance continued. A team of experienced, senior ODC practitioners replaced the change management specialists. This was a second example of single-loop learning.

Subsequently, the PMT took an incremental step toward involvement and participation and asked each user group manager to identify and redeploy to the ERP project a few of the best and brightest employees to serve as full-time but temporary members of those design and implementation teams whose modules would have an impact on the operations of each user group. This structural modification was imported from the ERP industry's best practices. This was the third example of single-loop learning. The intent was to satisfy the user groups' concerns by having these individuals fully involved from beginning to end to represent their back-home groups. However, many user group managers saw that this would constitute a brain drain in their operations and therefore substituted "expendable" for best and brightest. This was an unexpected side effect of the modified plan.

First Action Research Step: Diagnosis

The ODC team inquired as to how the PMT understood the nature and underlying sources of the user groups' resistance. The operative assumption was that each user group was addicted to its familiar but isolated legacy computer systems and was trying to prove that the consistency and discipline to be imposed by ERP would be counterproductive or even dysfunctional in the local setting. The ODC team requested and was granted permission to test these assumptions by contacting the managers of the various globalized user groups.

Using phone calls and e-mails, the ODC team members contacted the user group managers and confirmed some of the PMT's assumptions. At a more comprehensive level, the managers and members of the user groups were confounded by the uncertainty and ambiguity of the ERP project's progress and the strategy that would be employed to roll out the modules once their design was completed. They did not know how the ERP system would affect their staffing patterns or the job requirements of the local staff members who would have to operate the system. The user group managers felt excluded from the process and did not know how to respond to their employees' concerns ("When will this project get out of the design phase and begin to be implemented?" "Will we be the test case for these modules, or will another global or domestic regional group serve as the guinea pigs?" "Who will lose their jobs as a result of this?"). The managers wanted meaningful reassurance that their doubts, concerns, and reservations would be addressed, and that there would be viable mechanisms through which they could influence the process going forward.

They were also upset by what they perceived as the ERP techsperts' arrogance and patronizing attitude. When asked, they explained that the ERP techsperts spoke and wrote in acronyms and did not respond to e-mails and phone calls requesting definition and explanation of the significance of these acronyms. They were further annoyed that no one in the project seemed to know or understand, or care about, local language and customs. In general, the user group managers were extremely appreciative about being asked about their concerns. Of course, as a result of being asked, they now expected to get precisely what they wanted.

Second Action Research Step: Plan Actions

On the basis of our interviews, the ODC staff made a recommendation to the PMT: design, schedule, and conduct an interactive event with all of the PMT, ERP techsperts, user group representatives, and user group managers and their key staff members. Let the user group managers and staff see and hear from their own representatives on each of the design and implementation teams. Have these representatives present the progress that their ERP design and implementation teams were achieving. Also, have them discuss the issues they were encountering while working on their respective modules. Give the user group managers and staff opportunities to express their doubts, concerns, and reservations, making sure that their representatives (backed up by the ERP techsperts) respond in a way that is comprehensible to those managers. In short, make the event a series of meaningful, two-way, interactive dialogues.

The PMT agreed that, though extremely expensive, a one-day event should be designed and scheduled. The PMT assigned the details to a couple of their more experienced ERP techsperts. The ODC staff was not invited to participate in the design process. However, we were allowed to review and comment on the results.

The proposed design and schedule for the event were to start at 8:00 A.M., after a welcome by the project manager; a progress review from each module's design and implementation team would be presented by an end-user group representative. ERP techsperts would stand by to furnish informational support, as needed. Each spokesperson was allocated *seven minutes* to present his or her progress report. There would be eight minutes during which the user group managers could ask and get answers to their questions. There were thirteen modules. The elapsed time for the presentations and Q&As, excluding comfort breaks, would be three hours and fifteen minutes.

The afternoon would consist of a tour through the ERP project's rather elegant open office environment. Each module's team would have a display of both the completed and the open items layout with Gantt charts indicating whether they were ahead of or behind schedule. The representatives and ERP techsperts would answer any questions that might be asked. The ODC team would also have a display of our scheduled activities and commitments. The user group managers and staff members could start their tour anywhere and end anywhere; they could spend as long as they wanted at any displays of their choice, so long as we wrapped up the process by 6:00 P.M.

The ODC team agreed with the overall intent and design but expressed deep concern that the user group managers would require more Q&A and discussion time. We recommended that the event be planned for two days instead of squeezing so much into one day. The PMT leader and her senior managing partner from the management consulting firm both disagreed. We predicted that they would have trouble getting through the morning schedule. If for no other reason, this was because each module's design and implementation team representative would have to resort to using acronyms to save time and would then lose time by responding to questions from the audience as to the meaning of the acronyms. The project team leader again disagreed.

During the period leading up to the great interactive event, all the teams devoted some time each day to designing and preparing, the ODC team included. This work was added on to the routine work for which we were responsible. The stress and tension levels grew as everyone put in twelve-to-sixteen-hour days, six and sometimes seven days a week. In addition to listing our functions and creating displays of our planned activities and schedule, the ODC team devoted some time to creating a glossary of ERP terms and tested it out on the ERP techsperts and representatives. We anticipated that the user group managers would create a major issue around the ERP acronyms.

Third Action Research Step: Take Action

The planned event began as scheduled. During the first representative's presentation of the first module, several user group managers interrupted the speakers (a user group representative and her IT techspert consultant). The managers had some issues they believed were not being addressed, and they were going to talk about those doubts, concerns, and reservations come hell or high water. The schedule for delivering the presentations was disrupted and had to be modified. Ultimately, the entire event was extended for a second day; this was an *in situ* recycling of the steps of diagnosis, plan action, take action, and evaluate the impacts of the action taken.

The first day was then allowed to be completely occupied by one discussion after another—module by module. The glossary of ERP terms was distributed—though only after several episodes of confusion and anger about who meant what when she or he used one or the other acronym. The PMT reluctantly acted on the end-user group managers' demands. The second (unscheduled) day of the interactive event consisted of an extended, more relaxed, and casual tour through all of the modules' display stations on the part of the user group managers and their staff members.

Fourth Action Research Step: Evaluate Effects of Taking Action

Exit interviews revealed that several learnings were derived from the event; in general, the user group managers left the project site feeling rather more gratified than they had expected. The glossary of ERP terms was seen by the managers as a serious effort by the PMT to help them understand the arcane ERP nomenclature. They believed they were finally heard and understood by the PMT. They believed they had made a difference in the design and implementation process and had improved the relationship between the user groups and the PMT.

Second Iteration of First AR Step

The second iteration was to diagnose to reevaluate and modify original goals and plans. In a debriefing meeting, the PMT expressed their annoyance with the ODC team but acknowledged that the unscheduled, expanded design salvaged what might have been a disaster and was "productive." They were disturbed because of the "unbudgeted time" required to involve the user group managers and their staff members. It seemed that all involved parties were now significantly closer to agreeing upon the design and implementation process and strategy. This was considered by all involved parties to be a marked improvement from prior conditions.

Second iteration of Second AR Step

Next was reiteration of planning action. In consultation with the client organization's executive management team, similar expanded interactive events would now be scheduled quarterly. Mechanisms to maintain contact and exchange information between the design and implementation teams and the user groups would be explored, developed, and installed.

Operational Values of Action Research

Action research is a values-driven approach to planning and achieving social and organizational change. From Dewey and Lewin, a consensus is apparent that five primary values drive the practice of action research in all of its various forms:

1. Action research enables *local parties* or *local partners* (employees or community residents) to set and achieve change goals that are meaningful to them. They identify and deal effectively with their own important real-life issues. Thus they take control over their community or organizational lives and participate in shaping their own future.

2. Action research creates practical knowledge. Action research tests the validity of traditional social and behavioral science theory and also generates new theory about the issues that are addressed, the dynamics of planned change, and the process methodologies used to achieve change.

3. Action research enables local partners to learn to master action research theory and become proficient in applying action research methods and, consequently, building their capacity to identify and deal with future issues. Thus action research is *emancipatory*, enabling involved parties to free themselves from dependence on experts and authority structures. This is a *democratizing* process in that power is redistributed such that *all* involved parties gain a meaningful voice in identifying issues, setting change goals, creating change strategies, planning, and achieving results that are meaningful to all of them.

4. Action research is a highly *inclusive* process that encourages active involvement and participation of all parties who have an interest in a given organizational or community issue. This includes persons and groups (stakeholders) who are likely to be affected by either the implementation of action plans or the results brought about by the change effort.

5. Action research recognizes that "even in the most homogeneous-appearing groups, there are wide differences in knowledge, interests, experience, and capabilities [that are] a rich social resource that, when effectively mobilized, gives a group or an organization a much greater capacity to transform itself" (Greenwood and Levin, 1998, p. 12). Thus action research values surfacing, acknowledging, and making productive use of diversity in all forms.

ODC Practitioners and Action Researchers: A Question of Nomenclature

Collier's observations (1945) illuminate significant differences between ODC practitioners and action researchers. Both areas of practice share common origins (the work of Dewey, Lewin, Collier, Emery, Trist, and A. Kenneth Rice). In fact, action research is a participative, democratizing process that results in action and change. Action research is common to the work of both ODC practitioners and action researchers. It is the source and the purpose of any planned change that differentiates between the two areas of practice. Over the past four or five decades, what was originally a unified area of practice or discipline has diverged in a rather dramatic fashion.

The most significant distinction is that ODC practitioners employ action research primarily to enable their organizational client systems to achieve technostructural change objectives that are established by the leaders of the client systems. Thus ODC practitioners assist their client organizations in becoming increasingly effective and efficient. However, the researchers employ action research to enable local parties or partners such as members or residents of their organizational or community client systems to set, plan for, and achieve their own goals for social change focusing on issues relating to the local parties' concerns about social justice (and, more recently, environmental sustainability).

Need for a Partnership

Collective experience over the past twenty-five years or so strongly indicates that when organizational or community client system leaders consider making substantive, consequential organizational changes, recruiting ODC practitioners or action researchers is definitely not the first priority the leaders consider. They seek out and employ techsperts as project managers, IT systems analysts, financial analysts, lawyers, or various types of engineers. Yet by themselves these techsperts tend to fail to achieve the value propositions they initially claimed would be realized. It appears that their *technostructural* talents, though essential, are not sufficient to facilitate large-scale organizational changes by themselves. Techsperts need ODC scholar practitioners to anticipate and facilitate maintenance and enhancement of the organization's *sociotechnical* system and subsystems to support the technostructural changes. As one ODC scholar put it (confidentially), "They [the techsperts or leaders] call us in only after there's blood on the floor." Until blood is spilled, action research–based ODC theory and methods seem irrelevant and wasteful of scarce resources.

It seems reasonable to conclude that there is great potential for action researchers and ODC practitioners to invest the time and energy necessary to gain visibility and earn credibility from the perspective of techspert consultants. In fact, Freedman and Zackrison (2001) believe that the historical role of ODC practitioners as stand-alone consultants is rapidly coming to an end. The same may be true for action researchers. A more viable alternative is that OD practitioners and action researchers create or discover effective strategies that enable them to become visible, credible, and respected members of *multidisciplinary consulting teams.*

References

Argyris, C., Putnam, R., & Smith, D. M. (1985). *Action science.* San Francisco: Jossey-Bass.

Argyris, C., & Schön, D. (1996). *Organizational learning II.* Reading, MA: Addison-Wesley.

Blake, R. R., & Mouton, J. S. (1976). *Consultation.* Reading, MA: Addison-Wesley.

Block, P. (1999). *Flawless consulting: A guide to getting your expertise used* (2nd ed.). San Francisco: Jossey-Bass/Pfeiffer.

Coghlan, D., & Brannick, T. (2001). *Doing action research in your own organization.* London: Sage.

Collier, J. (1945, May). United States Indian Administration as a laboratory of ethnic relations. *Social Research, 12,* 275–276.

Cummings, T. G., & Worley, C. G. (2001). *Organization development and change* (7th ed.). Cincinnati, OH: South-Western.

Dewey, J. (1991a). *Logic: The theory of inquiry.* Carbondale: Southern Illinois University Press. (Original work published 1938)

Dewey, J. (1991b). *The public and its problems.* Athens: Ohio State University. (Original work published 1927)

Emery, F., & Thorsrud, E. (1976). *Democracy at work.* Leiden, Neth.: Martinus Nijhoff.

Freedman, A. M. (1988). *NTL founders: An interview with Kenneth D. Benne.* (Videotape). Alexandria, VA: NTL Institute. (Transcript of videotape interview published in *Journal of Applied Behavioral Science.*)

Freedman, A. M. (August, 1999). *An example of complex system change: An enterprise resource planning (ERP) design and implementation.* Fellows address, American Psychological Association, Boston.

Freedman, A. M., & Zackrison, R. E. (2001). *Finding your way in the consulting jungle.* San Francisco: Jossey-Bass.

French, W. L., & Bell, C. (1995). *Organization development and transformation: Managing effective change.* New York: McGraw-Hill.

Greenwood, D. J., & Levin, M. (1998). *Introduction to action research: Social research for social change.* Thousand Oaks, CA: Sage.

Gustavsen, B. (1992). *Dialogue and development.* Assen-Maastricht, Neth.: Van Gorcum.

Israel, B. A., Schurman, S. J., & Hugentobler, M. K. (1992). Conducting action research: Relationships between organization members and researchers. *Journal of Applied Behavioral Science, 28*(1), 74–101.

Jayaram, G. K. (1976). Open systems planning. In W. G. Bennis, K. D. Benne, R. Chin, & K. E. Corey (Eds.), *The planning of change* (3rd ed.), pp. 275–283. Austin, TX: Holt, Rinehart and Winston.

Lewin, K. (1946). Action research and minority problems. *Journal of Social Issues, 2*(4), 34–46.

Lippitt, G., & Lippitt, R. (1986). *The consulting process in action* (2nd ed.). San Francisco: Jossey-Bass/Pfeiffer.

Lippitt, R., Watson, J., and Westley, B. (1958). *The dynamics of planned change: A comparative study of principles and techniques.* Orlando: Harcourt, Brace.

Marrow, A. J. (1969). *The practical theorist: The life and work of Kurt Lewin.* New York: Basic Books.

Reason, P., & Bradbury, H. (Eds.). (2001). *Handbook of action research: Participatory inquiry and practice.* London: Sage.

Shepard, H. A. (1960). An action research model. In *An Action Research Program for Organization Improvement.* Ann Arbor, MI: Foundation for Research on Human Behavior, University of Michigan.

Trist, E., & Bamforth, K. W. (1951). Some social and psychological consequences of the longwall method of coal getting. *Human Relations, 4,* 3–38.

CHAPTER SIX

ORGANIZATIONAL CHANGE PROCESSES

Ed Mayhew

The pace of change in today's organizations is increasing. Organizations are dealing with change from many directions: new chief executive officers, new technology, demands from shareholders, managing suppliers. Organization leaders and organization development practitioners need to understand organization change and have models for approaching change. Key aspects of organization change are systems thinking, change dynamics, planning change, leading change, and implementing change. This chapter explores these key aspects and presents a step-by-step approach to complex organizational change.

Complex organizational change begins with systems thinking. All organizations are social systems, meaning they are networks of structures, customs, and relationships intertwined in ways that are difficult to understand. Systems thinking involves examining events and looking for underlying patterns and structures. Change dynamics is what happens to organizations and the people in them when change occurs. Because cause and effect can be connected and reactions of people and organizations to change can be anticipated, strategies and activities can be designed to increase the likelihood of desired results.

Planning change includes finding a compelling reason for change, having an idea of what the future will look like, knowing how to build commitment to change, navigating the difficulty of transition, and having strategies to institutionalize change. Leading change entails being clear about the roles and responsibilities of change leaders and about characteristics of leadership that ensure successful change. Successful organizational change depends on implementing change well. Implementation involves creating the structures, strategies, and organizational conditions necessary to accomplish organizational change objectives, as well as understanding and addressing the impact of change on organization members.

Systems Thinking

Systems thinking begins by recognizing patterns of events, considering why the patterns exist, and finding the structures that underlie them. For example, a pattern of slowed traffic could be caused by lots of people going to the same destinations at the same time, or perhaps by many new people moving into an area with limited mass transit and narrow roads. Considering ways to change a traffic pattern requires exploration of structures. In this example, one set of structures could be aimed at reducing traffic volume and another at increasing capacity.

Events, Patterns, and Structures

Systems thinking means analyzing a situation on three levels: events, patterns, and structures (see Figure 6.1).

FIGURE 6.1. LEVELS OF SYSTEMS THINKING.

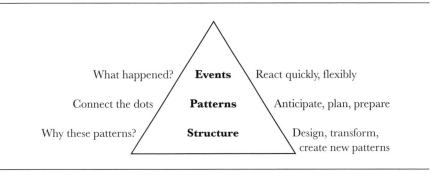

Events are single occurrences. Seeing events permits reacting quickly and flexibly to changes in the moment. Focusing only on events can lead to doing the same thing again and again, caught up in a cycle that cannot be broken because of limited perspectives.

Patterns are connections among events. Seeing patterns permits anticipating, planning, and preparing for change over a longer period of time. Changing a pattern can change future events. In the traffic example, drivers can choose to go on the road earlier in the morning and later in the evening, or take another route to avoid congestion.

Structure is identified by asking why patterns occur. Structure permits designing and creating new patterns that last for a long time. Traffic volume can be reduced by adding highway tolls and encouraging carpooling. Traffic capacity can be increased by adding commuter buses and other mass transit options or by adding more highway lanes. Structural changes are more complex and take longer to develop than pattern changes, but they are comprehensive and long-lasting.

Thinking in systems terms considers the whole picture—events, patterns, and structure—to decide where to focus activity. Changing a pattern may be all an organization can do when it is in crisis. This lets the organization buy time to look for structural answers. The point is to be able to see and think on all three levels in order to expand options for actions that are taken.

Closed and Open System Thinking

Closed and open system thinking is another dimension of systems thinking. Organizations can be described as relatively closed or relatively open systems in relation to their external environment. Table 6.1, based on the work of Harold Bridger (1980), illustrates differences between closed and open system thinking.

TABLE 6.1. CLOSED VERSUS OPEN SYSTEM THINKING.

	Closed System	Open System
Leadership style	Directive	Collaborative
Decision making	Hierarchically determined	Where problem and information reside
Conflict management	Eliminate or suppress	Engage and use as information
Managing arena	Within a supervisory unit	Within and at the supervisory unit boundary

Source: Bridger (1980).

Closed system thinking assumes that organizations are self-contained entities with no connection to their outside world. A closed-system organization's focus is on internal structures and dynamics. When closed system thinking is present, an organization places great value on its organization charts, division of labor, superior-subordinate relations, policies, procedures, controls, and stability, rather than customers, suppliers, markets, technologies, or community. This insular way of thinking makes it difficult for an organization to see change coming and to change when the need becomes apparent.

Open-system-thinking organizations see themselves embedded in a web of external relationships. When open-system thinking is present an organization still has its charts, division of labor, superior-subordinate relations, policies, procedures, and controls, but the emphasis is much different. These structures are seen as flexible, adaptable, and able to respond to new or changing conditions. Emphasis is given to external stakeholders such as customers, suppliers, shareholders, governmental agencies, unions, and competitors. Open-system thinking makes change easier because the organization has a comprehensive picture of its dynamic environment, and its internal structures are limber.

A system becomes more open and more complex during change. So many things are going on that leadership does not have enough information to make good decisions. Decision making has to be passed to people who have the information needed to make good decisions. Conflict increases as the boundaries between organizational units change. Conflict management and negotiation skills are needed to resolve unit differences and create new unit boundaries.

Systems thinking paints an increasingly comprehensive picture of an organization's environment. An environment is always changing, and organizations must change to maintain harmony with their environment. Most organizational change is driven by changes in the external environment: a competitor comes up with better technology, or customers become more demanding because they have more choices. Events of this kind ripple inward to organizations, creating need for organizational change.

Dynamics of Change

This section examines key aspects of organizational change dynamics: the three-stage cycle of organization change, boundaries, effects of change on people, and resistance to change.

Present, Transition, and Future States

Organizational change occurs in a three-stage cycle: present state, transition state, and future state (Beckhard and Harris, 1987). The cycle repeats again and again as an organization adjusts to maintain harmony with its external environment and among its internal units. Each state has unique characteristics and dilemmas.

The *present state* is the here-and-now situation of an organization. It is an organization's structure, processes and people, and current internal and external environment. When a present state is stable, tranquil, or comfortable, an organization may not be interested in changing. When a present state is unstable, turbulent, or uncomfortable, an organization may be very interested in changing but not have much agreement or idea about the direction of change.

The *transition state* refers to the structure, processes, people, and environment of an organization as it undergoes change. The structures and processes of the transition state are quite different from those of the present state. A transition state is nearly always a turbulent and uncomfortable place where old structures and processes that worked well in the past do not work well anymore. New structures and processes intended to operate in the future are not in place yet.

The *future state* is a destination. It is the structure, processes, people, and environments that will be in place once an organizational change is completed. In a future state most, perhaps all, of the problems besetting a present state are gone. Because change is a cycle, a future state then becomes a present state for the next round of change.

Planning for complex system change requires thinking about all three states and being prepared to meet their inherent challenges. The major challenge in a present state is beginning change. In a transition state it is maintaining an environment that facilitates change. In a future state it is getting change to stick. Each state requires its own leadership structure and its own plan. Linked together, these plans become a comprehensive plan for a whole, complex system organizational change.

Organizational Boundaries

Boundaries serve two major purposes: they define what is in and what is out, and they regulate transactions across boundaries. Boundaries are easy to cross, or they are a substantial barrier. When a boundary is thick, things inside are tightly held and it is difficult to cross in either direction. When a boundary is thin, things inside are loosely held and it is easy to cross the boundary—sometimes so easy the boundary does not seem to exist.

When organizational boundaries are *tight*, an organization is substantially walled off from its outside world. Think of prisons, research labs, secret societies, or intelligence organizations. Internal boundaries can be tight too, as when finance, marketing, engineering, and manufacturing act like independent entities with no relationship to each other or the larger organization. When boundaries are *loose*, an organization does not have much of a wall between itself and the environment. Think of community service or volunteer organizations, or moving from one municipality to another. Movement is easy and boundaries may not be noticeable.

Boundaries in organizations are such things as organizational units, goals, roles, processes, authority, and time. When change occurs, boundaries may change. For example, roles and structures change as workgroups combine or new tasks are assigned, and when separate business units replace functional departments.

The tightness and looseness of boundaries creates conditions that support or get in the way of organizational change (Alderfer, 1980). This continuum of boundary conditions is described in Table 6.2, with tight boundaries on one end, loose boundaries on the other, and optimum boundary conditions in between. Using the information in Table 6.2, one can identify the state of specific organizational boundaries.

TABLE 6.2. ORGANIZATIONAL BOUNDARY CONDITIONS.

Organizational Boundaries	Tight	Optimum	Loose
Goals	Clear, immutable	Clear, contemporary	Unclear, conflicting
Roles	Well defined, constrictive	Well defined, adaptable	Ill defined, conflicting
Authority	Clear, centralized, autocratic	Clear, located where information resides	Unclear, diffuse, conflicting
Information	Clear, propaganda	Clear, factual, reliable	Unclear, rumors, unreliable
Human energy	Low, channeled, underused	High, diffuse, highly used	High or low, overused
Affect	Positive expressed, negative suppressed	Positive and negative expressed as data	Negative expressed, positive expressed
Time horizon	Long-term, multiyear	Medium-term, years, months	Short-term, months, days, hours
Conflict	Suppressed	Managed	Eruptive

Source: Alderfer (1980).

Tight boundaries lead to conditions where change is difficult. Loose boundaries may indicate that the effects of change are already present. Optimum boundaries indicate ideal open-system conditions. Rarely does an organization have all the boundaries in one category; an organization will often have enough boundaries in one category to indicate that the organization is leaning toward tight or loose boundary conditions.

In a diagnostic mode, when boundaries are too tight, interventions are needed that will loosen them so change can begin. When boundaries are too loose, interventions are needed that will tighten them so change can proceed under more orderly conditions. Organizational boundaries drift toward a loose condition during change, requiring tightening of boundaries to ensure that enough structure is present to hold change.

Effects of Change on People

The effect of change on people has been studied for years. Barrie Hopson and John Adams (1977) found that when change occurs in organizations the self-esteem of people in an organization increases, diminishes, and then recovers, affecting how people feel and behave. They concluded that as change occurs self-esteem travels through a seven-step cycle, whether the perceived impact of change is positive or negative (see Figure 6.2).

FIGURE 6.2. PEOPLE AND CHANGE.

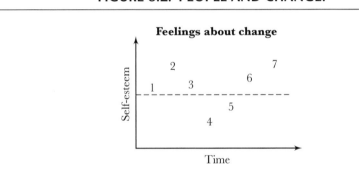

Source: Based on the work of Hopson and Adams (1977). Used with permission.

In the beginning, step one, people cannot grasp the implications of the change they are beginning to experience. In step two, people believe they are immune from the impact of change, and their self-esteem rises on false hope. In step three, there is a realization that change will involve loss. When loss is experienced, self-esteem begins to dip. Self-esteem continues downward until step four, when people begin to accept their losses, decide to let go, and leave some old ways behind. In step five, people begin trying new approaches, perhaps a new way of working or beginning a new relationship. Self-esteem begins to rise as confidence grows. People become reflective in step six, trying to find meaning and lessons in both past and present experience. In step seven, they come to terms with their new, changed reality. Self-esteem rises to a new level as people understand they have changed.

The reaction of people to change has implications for those who aspire to guide organizational change, whether as a leader or an OD practitioner.

- Guides experience this cycle themselves, so it is important for them to be aware of their own emotions and reactions.
- Communication and patience are essential since people do not instantly understand the implications of change and often have good reasons not to like change.
- Guides must regularly engage with people who are being asked to change. Presence and proximity are essential.

Resistance to Change

Resistance is a usual and predictable companion of organizational change. As people resist change, they make a statement about who they are and what they stand for. Resistance is always rational, though it can be expressed emotionally or irrationally. Resistance can be active, as when someone says, "I won't do what you're asking. Period." Or resistance can be passive, as when someone regularly chooses not to hear, understand, or remember. Reducing resistance means identifying how to alter the nature of change and the process of change.

Changing resistance by changing the nature of change means changing the structure of change. Here are some examples.

- The greater the magnitude and impact of a change, the more resistance there will be. Scaling down the scope of change and introducing change in phases reduces potential resistance.
- Less resistance is likely when an organizational change is reversible, meaning it is possible for things to go back to the way they were if change does not work out. Making a change reversible can dampen resistance.
- Loss of power, authority, or resources encourages resistance. Taking win-lose situations and winners and losers out of a change process can reduce resistance.
- People resist change that threatens their sense of competence and makes them feel vulnerable. Helping people acquire needed future competencies obligated by an organizational change reduces resistance to that change.
- People resist changes that break up or significantly change relationships with coworkers. Creating ways to continue important organizational relationships and finding ways to facilitate new relationships can reduce resistance to change.

Resistance can also be reduced by changing the process of change or how change comes about:

- Resistance is avoided when change leaders are credible and respected by the organization.
- Leaving groups out of the change process or giving them a diminished role in it creates resistance. Resistance is reduced when people and groups have meaningful roles in the change process.
- Resistance increases when the pace of change is too slow, or when change is so rapid that an organization cannot keep up and people are burning out from too much change, too fast.
- Resistance is reduced when a change plan is thoughtful and credible enough that people believe it will work and are willing to follow it.
- Resistance is dampened by frequent, reliable, and understandable communication, which reduces uncertainty and anxiety, manages rumors, and informs people about progress.

These potential sources of resistance can be used as a checklist to tweak the nature and process of change. The idea is to design out as much resistance as possible and create strategies for working with the resistance that remains.

Planning Change

Change always goes better when it is thoughtfully planned—even when changes, crises, or golden opportunities happen quickly and unexpectedly. Planning complex system organizational change means completing five tasks: finding a compelling reason for change; evaluating readiness, capability, and commitment for change; defining a recognizable and achievable future; navigating transition; and ensuring that change sticks.

Finding a Compelling Reason for Change

The first planning task is to find a compelling reason for change, a reason strong enough to pull people out of their inertia. Change must be seen as essential and unavoidable. If change is optional, too many will choose the option of not doing so.

The ingredients of a compelling reason are usually found in an organization's external environment. Sometimes it is necessary to meet a competitive threat or to satisfy new customer expectations. Changes in the political domain create new priorities or threats and opportunities that ripple inward, causing organizational change; new people are elected, large nations break up into smaller ones, or trade agreements are signed. Change in the economic domain has far-reaching effect, as foreign currency changes its relative value, offshore outsourcing becomes attractive, or Alan Greenspan, the chairman of the U.S. Federal Reserve Board, speaks about interest rates. Changes in the world economy affect markets, the ability to manufacture and sell, and employment.

Imagine an organization as a tree and the people in it as birds sitting on the branches. Branches are neighborhoods, just as organizational units are neighborhoods. Each neighborhood will support a compelling reason for change that serves neighborhood interests. Although a common reason for change may be to maintain competitive advantage, birds on the top branches translate that into stock options and earnings per share; birds on middle branches translate it into bonuses and opportunity for promotion; and birds on the lower branches are looking for wage increases, continued employment, and a better quality of life. The gold standard for a compelling reason is something an organization must do to ensure its survival, given unavoidable current or future changes that are beyond the organization's control.

Evaluating Readiness, Capability, and Commitment for Change

Beckhard and Harris (1987) suggest evaluating the readiness, capability, and commitment of each stakeholder group. Stakeholders are the people and groups who are involved in and affected by change. Readiness for change means a favorable attitude or motivation toward change and is about willingness and interests. Capability is the physical, financial, or organizational capacity to change. It is concerned with power, influence, and authority to allocate resources.

Listing all stakeholder groups and grading each of them as low, medium, or high both for readiness and for capability can assess readiness and capability for change. This involves making an educated guess about where stakeholders stand. One more level of analysis is necessary to identify those stakeholders who must be committed to change for change to occur. All organizations have influence leaders, people whose credibility and respect is well known throughout the organization. The credibility and influence of these leaders often exceeds the status of any organizational position they hold. When they get behind something, it usually happens.

Commitment to change is assessed by looking at the most important and influential stakeholders from the readiness and capability list and identifying the five or six who must support change if it is to happen. Commitment can be assessed on a four-point scale:

1. *Opposed* to change
2. Willing to *let change happen*—people who do not oppose change but will not support it either
3. *Supportive*—people who will take initiative and provide resources for change
4. *Make it happen*—people who will lead and do whatever it takes to bring change about

Ideally, commitment to change has at least two key stakeholder groups making change happen, two or three supporting, and few or none opposing or letting it happen. The objective is to create a critical mass of influential stakeholders who lead and actively support change.

Once the stakeholder groups are identified, the next step is to contact each group to acquire firsthand a sense of their readiness, capability, and commitment to change. Building commitment is a political process that involves engaging stakeholders, discovering their interests, and designing change responsive to their interests. Engagement and dialogue usually increase commitment. Remember: it is possible for people to agree to do something as long as they do not all have to do it for the same reasons. Sometimes the best that can be done is to get a stakeholder group to move from a position of opposing change to letting it happen. The shift turns negative energy neutral and greatly increases the chance of achieving change.

Defining a Recognizable and Achievable Future

The third task in planning organizational change is to define a recognizable and achievable future, which Beckhard and Harris (1987) call a future state. A compelling reason gets an organization going, and a recognizable and achievable future gives an organization a place to go.

When organizations focus on their present condition, they usually move into problem solving. Today's problems should be fully addressed, but this will not be enough to take an organization into the future. A better future occurs when the future takes on its own definition and the organization purposefully directs activities and resources to achieve it. Defining a future tends to create optimism. It also creates tension that encourages change. As an organization compares a favorable future to an unpleasant present, dynamic tension between the two creates energy in support of change.

A future state is a statement of leadership's intentions, priorities, and commitments. It is an overall picture of an organization in the future, after change has been completed. It describes the work of the organization, performance objectives, organizational structure, organizational processes, major aspects of the organization's culture, and how employees achieve a sense of meaning by working there. Describing the future is the responsibility of an organization's leadership. It is not something everybody in an organization has to vote on or agree with; it is something people must support and follow if they plan to remain with an organization.

Navigating Transition: Organizational Boundaries

The fourth planning task is navigating transition. Transition is an in-between state. During transition, change is beginning to occur, old ways of doing things no longer work well, and new ways of doing things are not fully in place. Organizational boundaries become unstable during transition, and self-esteem begins to erode. The two main tasks in guiding transition are creating necessary boundaries and aiding recovery of self-esteem.

Certain organizational boundaries are needed during transition.

A Leadership Structure to Manage Transition. An organization must change itself while it continues doing business, creating a conflict of priorities between managing day-to-day-business and managing change. A leadership structure devoted to managing transition ensures maximum attention to the complexities of organizational change. Ongoing leadership can manage small-scale change by partitioning their time so they are clearly focused on both priorities. Larger-scale change may require dedicated leadership such as a project manager or transition leadership team. Really large-scale change may require parallel leadership structures, one managing ongoing business and another managing transition.

A Master Plan for Managing the Total Change Effort. A master plan contains key activities that advance change, responsibilities for each activity, a timetable, metrics, and progress reports. A master plan ensures a thoughtful approach to change and provides structure that guides activity during transition. The master plan needs to be publicized to communicate that change is coming and should be taken seriously. Publication of progress lets an organization know change is advancing. Publication of changes in a plan lets an organization know the plan is being adapted to experience and demonstrates leadership's ability to lead change.

A Widely Publicized Future State Scenario. Disseminating a future state scenario tells an organization what is in the defined future. A well-written future state lets people find themselves in it, which can inspire them during difficult times.

Navigating Transition: Help for Individuals

Some things can be done to ease the difficulty of transition for individuals.

Encourage the Presence and Proximity of Leadership. When transition leadership regularly engages the people in an organization, people have more confidence in leadership's ability to lead during difficult times. When leadership engages in authentic two-way communication about the rationale for change and progress toward change goals, the rumor mill is dampened and confidence in leadership is reinforced. When leadership listens well and offers support and reassurance, people tend to become supportive in return. When leadership shows respect for the values people hold and treats everyone with dignity—even those who disagree with them—confidence rises.

Create and Maintain a Flow of Reliable Information. Communication and understanding are stressed during transition. Rumors fly, and a lot of energy is expended trying to separate truth from fiction. Frequent communication about the progress of change, what is being learned, and changes in plans is important.

Avoid Simplifying Complexities. Change is difficult, messy, and stressful. Not everyone boards the Change Express at the same time. Some hold on to old ways too long, mistakenly believing change is temporary and the good old days will return. Others become too busy to be involved in change, mistakenly believing it will not affect them if they do not acknowledge it. The expression "get over it and get on with it" does not usually facilitate change. People will when they can, but it takes awhile. Effective change leadership listens carefully to understand the complexities change brings and does not dismiss or gloss over them. Leadership must be patient and understanding—but also demanding, expecting people to engage in action and behavior that support change.

Ensuring That Change Sticks

The final planning task is ensuring that change sticks. Since change is a recurring cycle, and a dynamic external environment is bringing new demands for change all the time, getting change to stick is a relative matter. In the early years, organizational change was thought to have three phases: *unfreezing,* to get an organization ready for change; *change,* in which desired changes were installed; and *refreezing,* in which change was solidified and institutionalized. It is a little different these days. Many organizations are in such a dynamic environment that they are far from frozen. Environments are often so turbulent that the shelf life of any change is not very long. What we have today is more like *slush-change-slush.*

Still, there are three actions that help solidify change and should be included in any change plan.

Check to See That Change Has Actually Occurred. Frequently the people guiding change assume if everything seems to be going according to plan change is actually taking place. Trust and verify. Trust people are doing the right thing, but verify that they are. This allows recognition and reinforcement when change has occurred and provides valuable feedback when change does not happen, or results turn out differently than intended.

Make Sure Key Organizational Processes and Structures Reinforce Change. Once an organization begins doing things differently, underlying infrastructure is usually affected. New reports are required to track performance, changes in ac-

counting classification must reflect changes in the use of organizati
budgets require revision, reporting relationships and liaison structi
new job titles and classifications appear, and so on. This requires a gɪɑ....
at infrastructure that is worth the effort. If infrastructure does not support change,
it will not stick.

Make Sure Reward Systems Support the Change. It is difficult to solidify change
when reward systems do not reward people for behavior that supports change. In
the worst cases, reward systems can discourage change. Involving the human resources department early in planning any change ensures that issues of this kind
will be addressed upstream.

Leading Change

Leadership is a space many people occupy as change unfolds. Sometimes leadership is held by an executive who describes a future that pulls change. Or a manager who figures out how to get people enthusiastic about change holds it.
Sometimes a senior worker who is passing on knowledge about how to do a new
task holds it. Or a consultant advising about change processes or gathering information about how change is progressing holds leadership. Sometimes leadership
is held by teams of people from varying organizational units working out new
ways to interact.

There are two key change leadership roles: *champion* and *change agent*. A champion's responsibility is to make change happen. Champions make decisions, assign work, check to ensure change is progressing, administer rewards, and do all
the things usually associated with leadership. They are members of the organization being changed and stay in an organization after it has taken place. Champions have to be tough-minded and relentless in extracting performance that
produces change.

A change agent's responsibility is to support a champion. Change agents are
often OD practitioners who assist through their process and organization development expertise, or by offering emotional support to a champion. Sometimes
change agents are members of an organization who counsel a champion in areas
where the champion is not knowledgeable. Change agents are often not members
of an organization being changed and probably will not continue in it after change
has taken place.

Change agents operate with a softer edge than champions do. A champion
acts like a police officer, enforcing the "law" of a change plan. A change agent
acts more like a social worker, advising a champion and others on the basis of

knowledge of change dynamics and underlying conditions in an organization. Conventional wisdom suggests one cannot be a cop and a social worker at the same time. This is especially true when it comes to organizational change.

Champions are mostly focused on moving the tasks of organizational change along. Change agents mostly concentrate on the processes of change. Working together, both see a wider and more complete picture of what is happening than either can alone. The toughness of champions tends to distance them from important information, particularly when things are not going as expected. The accessibility and nonevaluative nature of change agents opens them to information because people know they can confide safely. Effectiveness is lost when the roles are blurred or combined.

Sometimes change agents take on tasks that belong to champions—perhaps because a champion is overloaded and the change agent wants to help. Or because a change agent feels strongly about some aspect of change and wants to champion it, or wants to be a champion instead of a change agent. These adventures always end badly. The change agents do not have organizational authority or experience to champion well, and they lose credibility because people begin to mistrust them. It is important to establish and hold clear boundaries when it comes to these change leadership roles.

Effective change leaders are aware of their emotions and understand how emotions affect behavior. A strong and positive sense of self-worth helps get through the doubts and uncertainty inherent in change. Effective leaders keep their more disruptive impulses and emotions under control; no yelling or throwing cell phones or sending flaming e-mail.

Empathy is sensing other people's emotions, understanding their perspectives, and taking an active interest in their concerns. It is the most important emotional intelligence skill for change leaders (Goleman, Boyatzis, and McKee, 2002). Empathy helps soften the hard edge leaders often have to use. Empathy connects with people in ways intellect cannot.

Leadership is always a process of mutual influence. Leaders influence and are influenced by the people they lead. Being able to use a range of influencing strategies is essential when leading change.

Implementing Strategies

Implementation is the last link in the change process. Many failed change initiatives turn out to be failure of implementation. Imagining a new future, getting people enthusiastic about it, and setting up the structures and processes to make change happen are challenging and exciting tasks. Implementing change requires attention to some pretty mundane things, and for a long time.

A list of implementation activities and strategies follows. The first two were mentioned earlier in the section on navigating transition and are repeated here for emphasis.

- Leadership structures that support change through all three states must be carefully constructed. Leadership tasks differ in the present, transition, and future states. This often means leadership must change as change evolves through the various states. If leaders who begin change know they will not be around at the end, leadership must change to ensure continuity. It takes comprehensive knowledge to implement change, so implementation teams are usually differently constituted and often larger than planning teams.
- A master plan for managing the total change effort should be carefully crafted and publicized as widely as possible. "Carefully crafted" means a change plan should be held to the same standard as any strategic plan, financial plan, marketing plan, or human resource plan. "Widely publicized" means communicating within the constraints of prudent organizational confidentiality and providing enough information to let the organization know what change is about and that progress is being made. It does not mean publicizing all the organization's competitive strategies.
- Screen implementation activities to ensure they contain both educational and power strategies. Educational strategies offer information about why change is necessary and what the future will be. Education alone is not enough to ensure change. Power strategies yield consequences that reinforce action supporting change, such as choice assignments, promotion, or increased compensation, and they discourage actions that do not support change. People resist when only power strategies are used, so both strategies are necessary. The idea is to make sure implementation activities inform people about change and foster incentives for them to actually change.
- Build commitment to change one step at a time. Divide implementation into several sequential steps so it does not look like one grand leap. Divide the commitment to implement into several sequential steps so confidence builds as progress is experienced. Divide commitment of assets into several sequential steps so those funding change do not feel they are writing a blank check. Sequence implementation tasks so that costly, less reversible decisions appear later in the process, to reduce resistance and increase commitment.

Conclusion

Guiding complex organizational change functions somewhat like sailing. Sailors cannot fully understand and control all the combinations of weather, wind, and tide they face. One can never fully understand and control everything that is going on in an organization either. Sailors prepare by making sure boat and crew are fit and ready, are well provisioned, and have a plan for the voyage. Readiness and capability are needed in an organization on the brink of change. Leadership prepares a plan, assigns resources, and commits to the business of change. Once under way, sailors do not control wind, weather, and tide, so they steer, trim the sails, and regularly adjust their course to reach a destination. Organizations do not control their environment either, so they adjust strategies and shuffle resources to achieve organizational change objectives.

Complex organizational change behaves more like a sailboat than an automobile. An auto changes direction instantly with even a slight turn of the wheel, without much loss of momentum. Sailboats do not respond to a turn of the helm right away. It takes a few seconds before a boat begins to change course. People new at sailing often jerk the helm from side to side because they think their boat is not responding. It is, but more subtly and more slowly than they are used to. The effects of organizational change develop gradually too. It is wise to stay alert, look for slight indications of change, be patient, and go easy on the helm.

References

Alderfer, C. P. (1980). Consulting to underbounded systems. In C. P. Alderfer & C. L. Cooper (Eds.), *Advances in experiential social processes* (pp. 267–284). New York: Wiley.

Beckhard, R., & Harris, R. (1987). *Organizational transitions: Managing complex system change* (2nd ed.). Reading, MA: Addison-Wesley.

Bridger, H. (1980). The contribution of O.D. at the level of the whole organization. In K. P. Trebesch (Ed.), *Organizational development in Europe: Papers of the first European forum of organization development, Aachen, West Germany, 1978.* Bern, Switz.: Paul Haupt Verlag.

Goleman, D., Boyatzis, R., & McKee, A. (2002). *Primal leadership: Realizing the power of emotional intelligence.* Boston: Harvard Business School.

Hopson, B., & Adams, J. D. (1977). Towards an understanding of transition dynamics. In J. D. Adams, J. Hayes, and B. Hopson (Eds.), *Understanding and managing personal change.* London: Universe Books.

CHAPTER SEVEN

RESISTANCE AND CHANGE IN ORGANIZATIONS

Rick Maurer

If you want to truly understand something, try to change it.
KURT LEWIN

Resistance is the most important factor in change, and the most neglected. Failure to understand the impact of resistance can kill otherwise worthy ideas. Research suggests that resistance is often the primary reason change fails (J. Johnson, 1995; Fisher, 1994; Schiemann, 1992).

Since the field of organization development (OD) is so concerned with the human aspects of organizational life, you might expect OD texts and journals to put a heavy emphasis on this topic. Sadly, much of the literature about organization development gives it only a passing glance. One major text devotes half a page to resistance.

Folger and Skarlicki (1999) define it as "employee behavior that seeks to challenge, disrupt, or invert prevailing assumptions, discourses, and power relations." If their definition is correct, it seems as though the topic might be worth more than a couple of paragraphs.

Whenever resistance is addressed, the discussion is often misguided. Freud's earliest thinking suggested resistance was something that got in the way of treatment and that persuasion was the means to overcome it. Freud later believed that resistance (and transference) were "important sources of data to be studied carefully rather than merely obstacles . . . of the treatment proper" (Michels, 1985). Those are wildly differing views. Sadly, Freud's early thinking transferred directly to the thinking of many who worked in organizational change. Today, many in organizations simply desire to see people get over resistance.

Try this experiment. Ask a client to quickly express the words that come to mind as you say "resistance." You are likely to hear words that describe resistance as negative and something to be overcome.

Experience teaches that when people attempt to overcome resistance to change, they simply encounter even more reluctance or opposition and actually create more of the very thing they are trying to eliminate.

The desire to overcome someone else's resistance reveals arrogance. It assumes that you—the one with the oh-so-brilliant idea—are right and know best. The so-called resisters are the benighted, misguided, or recalcitrant ones who are getting in your way. This position allows no room to be influenced. To overcome, you must get those other people to come around to your way of thinking. To overcome suggests strategies such as overpowering, manipulating, cajoling, or overwhelming them with sheer force of reason. None of those approaches require that you allow yourself to be influenced by their thinking and feelings (Maurer, 1996).

In the popular book *Influence: the Psychology of Persuasion*, Robert Cialdini uses research in social psychology to show readers how to get past people's reluctance to buy or go along by evoking "fixed pattern responses" to stimuli such as reciprocity, creating scarcity, and authority (Cialdini, 1998). These tactics can work as long as you don't have to live with the people after you've used these approaches on them. Deal making can cause people to respond with a fixed pattern. It is based on the notion that if you scratch my back, I'll scratch yours. In *Overcoming Resistance to Change*, Jellison (1993) devotes most of the book to exploring this approach. Deal making is all right for little things—it is a significant part of just getting along—but major changes such as merger, reorganization, downsizing, enterprise resource planning (software systems that cut across the entire organization), quality and service programs, and diversity initiatives need something not served by a tit-for-tat trade.

These "overcoming resistance" approaches never demand that the change agent think about how he or she might be creating opposition. Nor does this stance demand that the change agent be influenced by those he or she is attempting to influence. That creates a problem.

The literature on change is mixed. Some see resistance as the lifeblood of change since it is where energy is currently focused; others see it as something to be gotten past on the road to nirvana. This chapter argues strongly in favor of the former position. Resistance can be understood as feedback or expression of a differing point of view. Individuals in systems that resist do so for very good reasons, all of which are legitimate and necessary.

Even though the writing doesn't support us well in this more expansive and respectful approach, our body of practice can. Fortunately, the field of organization development is filled with techniques that support effective change. Through intuition and experience, OD practitioners are often quite savvy about the techniques of working effectively with resistance.

Sometimes OD practitioners suggest replacing the term *resistance* with *multiple realities*. This is based on the premise that reality is in the mind of the beholder. Since people work toward their own self-interest, what looks like resistance to one is purposeful activity to another. There is great merit to this view, which is the product of a rich philosophical stew of phenomenology, pragmatism, and existentialism, flavored with a dollop of the new sciences. However, the term *resistance* still has great utility. Clients know what it means. They feel it in their gut. It gives them headaches. Other terms take non-OD types away from their own felt experience and into a specialized language.

Using the notion of multiple realities as the base, this chapter attempts to explain why people resist and suggest alternatives to the intuitive, knee-jerk desire to overcome it.

A Way of Thinking About Resistance, and Support for Change

Discussion inside organizations about change is often limited to exploration of the financial and the technical aspects of what needs to be done. Of course these are important considerations. But they are not sufficient to address the challenges of most large organizational changes. When resistance does come up, leaders usually ask, "How can we overcome it?"

This question bypasses a more important one: Why do people resist? Literature on change has come up with various explanations. For example, Argyris and Schön suggest that resistance to change is a defense mechanism to protect against frustration and anxiety (Piderit, 2000). Let's assume the definition is accurate; then the next question should be, Why do people get frustrated and anxious? You might respond that it is part of their character to be a resister. If so, this lets us off the hook. We bear no responsibility; it's their problem.

The "resister" notion is popular but wrong. With millions of copies sold, *Who Moved My Cheese?* (S. Johnson, 1998) has been a hugely popular book on change. The story suggests that some people (or rats) can't get with the program and are left behind and starve. If only they could summon up the gumption to accept change, how much better life would be. In this story, leaders bear no responsibility for contributing to conditions that might cause resistance. Of course, no one suggests that people might resist simply because the change is a bad idea.

Resistance is often defined as something residing within an individual. All these definitions fail to address the relational aspects. Resistance occurs in the relationship between people; there is cause and effect.

It can stem from realities colliding. If a practitioner can help individuals and subsystems see resistance and support for change as simply different realities, contact is possible. (Hence the popularity of the term *multiple realities*.) If you can help the organization see that resistance is protective and not necessarily a negative thing, it gives people more options for engaging others. If the client can understand this, sometimes resistance is the message they should hear. It can be the voice of reason warning them of danger. So instead of attempting to overcome resistance, they might choose to engage it.

Sticking with multiple realities, it is easy to see how the actions of a leader working from one set of beliefs and expectations ("we are hemorrhaging money and our plant may be forced to close") versus the hourly workers' reality ("management routinely cries wolf to get concessions from us") come into conflict with each other.

But the resistance itself is no single thing. Like the word *love*, *resistance* is too small a word to cover its broad range of meanings. In meetings, it is common for the word to get tossed about, with each player meaning something different. Rather than using the term as an umbrella to cover all possible reasons people might be reluctant or oppose you, it is helpful to be able to distinguish among the various types of resistance.

Consider this: resistance occurs in three arenas. Level one is the simplest and easiest to work with; level two is more difficult, and level three can be extremely demanding. All of these levels are at play at all times (Maurer, 1996).

Level One: I Don't Get It (Information)

Level one resistance is based on the content of the idea: facts, figures, and data. People who exhibit level one resistance may simply need more information or may be confused. Perhaps they need time to *think* about the proposition. Level one resistance involves the world of thinking and rational action. Level one resistance may also come from a strong disagreement over interpretation of what the data could mean.

Newsletters, open forums, e-mails, videos, and PowerPoint are the tools commonly used to address level one issues. They can work just fine, provided the issue is limited to ensuring that people understand. Many organizations limit their response to resistance to level one exclusively. They give people data, and if that doesn't work they offer even more data. Although explaining things is important, the real resistance often lies in the other levels, and level one strategies do little to address those concerns.

Too often a focus on facts and figures causes people to miss seeing that resistance may be residing on level two or three, and PowerPoint cannot adequately address these emotional and more highly charged levels. Peter Norvig, a former engineer at NASA, got tired of suffering through endless mind-numbing Power-Point presentations. He worked at NASA, an agency with an inspiring mission, and yet people sapped all passion from their presentations. He wondered: What if Abraham Lincoln had had access to PowerPoint at Gettysburg? Tongue planted firmly in check, Norvig reduced one of the most influential speeches in American history to bullet points and bar graphs. (You can see his presentation at http://www.norvig.com/Gettysburg.) The slide show takes all the heart and soul out of Lincoln's message. If Lincoln had had access to PowerPoint, the stirring 266-word speech would surely be little remembered today.

OD professionals can help clients offer more comprehensive messages that capture information and emotional content, and build trust and confidence in the process. Sometimes it is as easy as drawing attention to the three levels and inviting clients to consider strategies that address levels two and three as well as level one.

Level Two: I Don't Like It (Emotional Reaction)

Unlike level one resistance, which is limited to rational and fact-based concerns, level two resistance is an emotional reaction to what people perceive the change will mean to them. Bodies react: heart rate increases, pumping more blood to large muscles, and adrenaline rushes through the body. People are getting ready for what has historically been called the fight-or-flight response. They are exhibiting what brain researcher Joseph LeDoux calls, in *The Emotional Brain* (1998), "the fear response."

Think about when you've reacted negatively to some news that suggests a change. You are afraid. Perhaps you could lose your job, reputation, control, or face in front of colleagues. Make no mistake, level two is not some soft, touchy-feely reaction that a little motivational pep talk will cure. When you experience this level of resistance, your body believes that your survival is at stake.

John Gottman works with couples headed toward divorce. He found that as they argue with each other their pulse rate goes up. The higher the pulse rate, the less able they are to take in what the other person is saying (Gottman, 1994). This same thing can happen when a leader mentions a change that could result in lay-offs. The pulse rate of the members of the audience increases and their ability to hear the rest of the presentation declines.

But the emotional aspects of change can work in your favor. Major change needs positive emotional response. When a leader says, "I need you to give 100 percent," "I need their commitment," "Who will volunteer?" he or she is referring to emotions. Level two (as with the other levels) has a plus side and a negative side. People lean in or they lean away. They either emotionally support the change or feel some fear about it. The OD practitioner can support clients by helping them assess where stakeholders are on this sliding scale between support and resistance.

Tools such as dialogue are especially helpful in working with this level. When it works well, dialogue allows people to explore their own beliefs, feelings, and points of view deeply. If so-called negative reactions are allowed to be voiced, it often allows the person to experience the situation differently. Dialogue itself can sometimes shift negative level two reactions to support.

In addition, the OD professional can help people learn more about the reasons and assumptions behind their fears. If face-to-face conversation is too threatening—if there is no support for this type of contact—then surveys, focus groups, and the like can help begin to provide critical information that speaks to the emotional level.

Level Three: I Don't Like You (Trust and Confidence)

In level one and two resistance, the person is reacting to a specific idea or proposal. Level three resistance works independently of the issue at hand. People may not be resisting the idea; in fact, they may understand it fully and even love what this suggestion could offer. Their opposition is in reaction to the person or people leading the change. Level three is the domain of deeply entrenched beliefs, experiences, and biases. (Once again, dialogue can be an effective way to support work at this level as well.)

Level three can be based on the leader's relationship with the people resisting. For example, suppose the other people were burned in the past. The leader let them down. Lied to them. Didn't follow through. Withheld information. None of these things have to be objectively true; all it required is that people believe those bad things happened.

Level three resistance may also stem from whom you represent. Union versus management; region versus headquarters; and differences in age, gender, race, and culture can all create level three suspicion.

This level of resistance is seldom discussed in literature on change. Leaders often consider strategies for introducing a change with little regard for the relationship they have with those who need to go along. That's a mistake. If level three is present, it must be dealt with first. A bad relationship can kill an otherwise decent idea. A major task is to support clients in seeing the world through the eyes of others, and then help clients find a way to begin to change perceptions. This can be a long process. Trust is difficult to build and easy to destroy.

This is the most difficult type of resistance; that's why it is referred to as level three, the last. Many wish to avoid looking at themselves. They'd prefer to think they couldn't possibly be part of the problem. Yet if they fail to clearly see how others see them, they put their ideas at risk.

As a practitioner, people may have strong level three reactions toward you as well. Sometimes they work in your favor, but the more common reaction to a practitioner is negative. Many people don't trust the profession. They think practitioners are condescending, arrogant, and peddling canned solutions. Assuming that you don't fit that description, you would be well served to anticipate level three reactions wherever you are working inside the organization and be prepared to do things that dispel their suspicion and mistrust.

Just as the three levels can work against a change, they can also work in its favor. The polar opposites of those three levels—understanding, emotional reaction, and trust—are precisely what you and your clients need in order to build support for ideas.

The levels are always at play; the question is whether they are working in your favor or against you. Do people get it or not? Do they like it or dislike it? Do they have trust and confidence in your clients, or do they harbor fear and suspicion? The more leaders and their practitioners can see these levels at play—and the subtle moves from resistance to support and back again—the more they will be able to develop strategies that can build support for change.

You can create a quick diagnostic for your clients. You can help them identify if people understand their idea or not (level one). Do they react favorably to the idea or not (level two)? Do they have trust and confidence in the person or people leading the change, or don't they (level three)? If all three of the levels fall on the support side, you have a much higher chance of being successful.

The Stages of Change

Practitioners find the work they are asked to do to support change usually falls into four areas: making a compelling case for change, getting the change started, sustaining commitment, and getting back on track. Table 7.1 shows the key issues to be addressed in each of these areas for the three levels of resistance.

TABLE 7.1. LEVELS OF RESISTANCE: PUTTING IT ALL TOGETHER.

	Level One Resistance (Information)	Level Two Resistance (Emotional Reaction)	Level Three Resistance (Trust and Confidence)
Making a compelling case for change: people know why a change is needed	• Provide understandable information • Define internal strengths and weaknesses • Define external opportunities and threats	• Respond to the emotional connection and reactions to the information	• Address issues of distrust, dislike, or lack of confidence in the leaders of the change effort
Getting started: "How will the work get done?"	• Create and articulate a clear and compelling direction or vision • People need to know what is expected of them	• Create ways for people to feel engaged in the process • People are not fearful of what is to come	• Issues with leaders are addressed • People feel confident they can follow the leaders • Cross-organization trust is built
Sustaining commitment: integration of change as the new status quo	• Implementation strategies are known by all • Clear contract gives priority to changing the status quo • Adequate resources are allocated	• Leaders continue to make the case for change throughout the integration phase • Ownership of the initiative is the norm • There are rewards for this work	• Major changes demand committed senior leadership • Beware of unintended events that could diminish trust in the leaders
Getting back on track: when things begin to fall apart	• Messages may be garbled or slowly communicated • People are confused • Try dialogue, surveys, and focus group interviews	• People are afraid of something • Changes are causing bad feelings or anxieties • Try exploring dilemmas as they are revealed	• Leaders do not seem to be acting in good faith • Leaders seem to have lost interest in process and moved on to other projects • Leaders must work persistently to reestablish trust and confidence in them

Making a Compelling Case for Change

According to one study, making the case compelling is the most important part of a major change (Maurer, 2003). Some 90 percent of successful changes in organizations attended to this area in ways that ensured people saw the need for some change. This phase creates the urgency. Without it, leaders will find that they are constantly trying to motivate others and overcome resistance. The good news is that it is often relatively easy to make a compelling case.

Making a case is a combination of level one and level two. People need to know what's going on, and they need information in a way they can understand. They require the type of information generated during a SWOT analysis: internal *strengths* and *weaknesses*, and external *opportunities* and *threats*. This often demands that the stakeholders understand the financial implications of choices, market and other global trends, and so forth. That, of course, is the domain of level one.

But they must also understand it in their gut. This is the world of level two emotional reactions. Some describe change as seeing the burning platform. That's not good enough. You can see a burning oil-drilling platform out in the harbor and feel compelled to do something about it—anything except call 911. But if you are standing on the platform, you now feel a great deal of urgency to do something right away.

This phase has nothing to do with the new idea but everything to do with the context that surrounds it. Making a case deals with potential. Once people see *why* a change is needed, they can open up to exploring options for dealing with the opportunity or threat, creating visions, and developing plans. It places *why* before *how*.

Jeff was a plant manager. During a planning meeting, he blurted out, "Don't you realize that our plant is idle 40 percent of the time?" His management team was shocked. Someone asked, "Why didn't you ever tell us?"

He replied, "I've been telling you for the past six months."

His team disagreed. What Jeff had done was give them page after page of spreadsheet data. He had never given them such a clear picture of the problem. The simple sentence—"Our plant is idle 40 percent of the time"—got his team to recognize that they had to do something differently to stay economically viable.

Level three can enter into the picture as well. If people don't trust the person or group delivering the data, they will dismiss it.

Another common problem is ignoring or rushing through this stage. Many people leading change in organizations are under immense pressure to show results quickly. With the best of intentions, they reckon they can move to action quickly. They skip addressing *why* this is critical and move directly to *how* they'll get things done.

An important role for practitioners is to find how to support clients staying with the uncertainty and confusion of this stage.

One example of making a compelling case comes from Future Search (Weisbord and Janoff, 2000). During these very active planning sessions, multiple groups engage in dialogue and creating on-the-spot visual displays of data (mind maps) regarding the multiple forces that create the current conditions for the organization.

James Collins identifies companies in which new projects are built on such a solid foundation that the organization doesn't need to "manage change" or ramp up each time someone comes up with a new idea. In these organizations, they make a case for change every day. Therefore people are already on board and don't need to be motivated or led. For them, change occurs to support a direction in which they are already headed (Collins, 2001). If leaders truly understood the power of making a compelling case for change, there would be little need for so many change management practitioners roaming their halls.

Getting Started

After people see why something is important, the getting-started phase deals with *how* the work will be done. This includes identifying where they want to go (direction, vision), ways to get there, and determining who needs to be part of the planning and implementation.

Issues of resistance and support at this stage often center on:

• Level one, information: creating and articulating a clear and compelling direction or vision, and making sure people know what's expected of them.
• Level two, emotional reaction: creating ways for people to feel engaged in the process.
• Level three, trust and confidence: making sure that any mistrust or lack of confidence in leaders is addressed such that stakeholders can feel confident they can follow those who are leading. Trust and confidence extend across the organization as well. Warring departments, old management-labor quarrels, and issues between the organization and its customers and suppliers all need to be addressed so that people can move ahead with some degree of confidence that others can be counted on.

The field of organization development is particularly adept at coming up with strategies for supporting work at this stage. Meetings that get individuals and groups working together are at the core of OD practice.

One such example is Whole-Scale Change (Dannemiller, 2000), also known as Real Time Strategic Change (Jacobs, 1997). By putting people in "max-mix" groups (groups that represent a cross-section of the organization), the design supports people exploring why something is important and then gets them working together on how to begin moving ahead. These small max-mix groups are the heart of the process. People are actively involved in making decisions that affect them, and they are building relationships across the organization (level three) that can support their work together throughout the change process. (These approaches do a fine job of making a compelling case as well.)

Sustaining Commitment

The sustaining phase is often neglected by practitioners. Once the analysis is done, plans are made, new systems are in place, and people receive training, the contract ends and you get paid and leave town. But that only gets the change implemented. Lots of work was done, but there is still little to show for it. The organization has not seen any real benefit from all that effort. Implementation guarantees only that someone has spent a lot of time and money. Organizations must find how to sustain commitment so that the change becomes part of the new way of working and is now reaping benefits.

On major changes that take months or even years to see any significant results, it is easy to lose momentum. It is tempting for OD practitioners in particular to contract for work that has more pizzazz to it, such as creating a vision, building a team, or inventing a new process. (The early stages of the cycle can be energized, full of visioning and creating new teams.) Yet the sustaining-commitment phase is where all too many changes fail. For example, think of Total Quality Management's dismal success rate in many organizations. TQM often served up the low-hanging fruit but failed to deliver the bountiful harvest that the methodology promised. It wasn't the process that was bad; the problem often came from never attending to the issues that allow an organization to move from rollout to results.

It's important to attend to several things at this phase:

- Level one, information: people need accurate information regarding implementation strategies. They require access to those who can debug systems and solve those nagging small problems that will bog down an otherwise good change.
- Level two, emotional reaction: leaders have to do a lot to keep the importance of the change alive in people's minds and hearts. Eighteen months into a major new software installation, it is easy to forget why the journey was once so important.
- Level three, trust and confidence: people need to see that leaders still care deeply about this project. They must know that this is still critical to the success of their organization. If there has been a change in leadership since the change was begun, they have to believe that the new leaders are firmly behind this initiative.

In a survey of practitioners and people who have led successful change, they identified a number of things that must be attended to at this stage (Maurer, 2005). Here is a summary of that report (for more details you can access the full report at www.beyondresistance.com).

Strong Leadership. Respondents said that leaders needed to be champions for the change. Support creation of symbolic acts that capture people's attention. Find places to embed the change in the business plan. Protect the process to ensure that this project remains a high priority. Make sure that the people responsible for making this happen have a clear contract so they know what is required of them.

Communication. One person referred to the importance of "vision painting"— that is, creating a compelling and attractive picture of where you are headed. Give updates frequently and in digestible form. Leaders of the change need to allow themselves to take in information; communication is two-way. Find means of celebrating wins along the way.

New Structures. Respondents recommended encouraging creation of a new structure and culture that supported the intent of the change. This must include dealing with disruptions in power and not being undone by inevitable power struggles. The new structure needs to lock in the new way of working.

Project Management Office and Process Management Organization. Special formal and permanent groups are established to support this process. They become command central, where everyone knows they can go with questions and suggestions.

Resources. People should be assured they will have sufficient time and money to complete implementation and carry out new ways of working once the change is operational.

Support the People. The need to be supported can manifest itself in many ways. Leaders must be attentive to places where motivation and attention wane and points where people begin to grow frightened of the change. One clear form of support that is almost always essential is education.

Clear Measures of Success. In addition to having clear, understandable, and accessible ways to measure success, those targets need to be used in enhancing performance. Therefore there must be a commitment to monitor the process.

Getting Back on Track

There is no magic in addressing these issues that can help sustain commitment. Just about any decent process for getting people talking and making good decisions can support work on these issues, provided the right people are involved. And who are the right people? At the very least, they are the men and women who have the power to get things done.

Even the best-laid plans can derail. Helping an organization spot resistance early and develop strategies for keeping the train on track is critical. Key things to consider:

- Level one, information: sometimes people are confused. Messages are garbled or slow in coming. These are the easier problems to fix.
- Level two, emotional reaction: this is a common reason for projects going off the tracks. People get scared. They see what they are changing is doing to others (for example, downsizing), or they fear the worst.
- Level three, trust and confidence: it seems that leaders have not acted in good faith and people resist the change. Or it appears that leaders have turned their attention to some other project, and people feel they are left holding an empty bag.

Fortunately, getting back on track is an area where OD traditionally has shown great insight and competency. Interventions such as third-party consultation, dialogue, and focus groups can be helpful in getting things back on track.

Two approaches can be particularly helpful in this stage: GE's Workout, and exploring dilemmas.

Workout. General Electric developed a process known as Workout that can be quite helpful when things begin to derail. Workout lends itself to the types of skills used by OD practitioners. Although Workout can take various forms, here is what a typical process involves:

1. *Choose a specific business challenge.* It's important that the issue be one that is vital to the business. Holding a Workout on secondary issues not only is a waste of time but breeds cynicism.

2. *You invite a lot of people.* Not only do you have more people tackling a problem, but you get greater word of mouth or buzz throughout the organization.

3. *Find a problem with a solution attached.* Anyone can identify a problem with regard to the challenge, but each problem must have a solution attached. This helps keep the focus on solving problems rather than on complaining.

4. *The person in charge must react to the suggestions in real time.* He or she can accept, reject with an explanation, or accept portions of the suggestion. If the leader needs time to think about it, he or she must make a commitment to get back to people with the answer within forty-eight hours.

5. *Choose a champion.* A champion is assigned to make sure the suggestion gets implemented.

In GE, Workout has become part of how things get done, so when someone calls for one people already know what's expected. This tool fits within the scope of the types of intervention OD practitioners should be adept at planning and facilitating (Ulrich and Lake, 1990).

To intervene, leaders need to know when things are beginning to get off track. Here's where surveys, interviews, and focus groups can come in handy.

Exploring Dilemmas. Exploring dilemmas can be a good way to turn resistance into a force that can be used productively—a great method to get back on track. As I've already suggested, consider reframing the term *resistance* into *multiple realities*. Edwin Nevis (1996) describes multiple realities like this: "individuals living in an apparently common reality often construct different versions of this reality, influenced by the differential forces that create their sub-unit, referent group, or individual role."

Barry Johnson talks about managing polarities (B. Johnson, 1997). He suggests that all organizations are filled with things that pull people in opposite directions, such as low cost and high quality, or centralized versus decentralized. These ideals become polar opposites, and the battle begins. One side wins for a while and then the pendulum swings to the other side, until it swings back again. He suggests embracing both ends of the polarity and finding what's powerful and good about both ends. It is a way to embrace the multiple realities.

These views of reality have a significant impact on how people view any change that is facing them. Since most people assume that their view of reality is not just one point of view among many but truth itself, helping clients recognize and grapple with these varying "truths" can be important.

Identifying the dilemmas that emerge from fully understanding the depth of the various realities can be a helpful way to engage an organization in exploring important issues that can either support or block change. For example, if the executive group wants to cut costs dramatically and quickly, but others fear this will mean their jobs, posing it as a dilemma can be a helpful intervention ("Is there a way we can cut costs while saving jobs?").

Dilemmas are often a combination of opposing forces that first appear as resistance. For example, leaders want to cut costs and workers fear that this may result in downsizing.

Moving on: Another Stage

There is another stage, the transition away from the new status quo. Once a change becomes routine and is no longer looked at as something novel, it is easy to ignore the fact that nothing lasts forever. People often hang onto an old idea far too long. It's not that the idea is bad; it is simply time for the cycle to move on. Today's award-winning idea can become tomorrow's joke. No stage lasts forever. It is this stage that William Bridges identifies in his 1980 book *Transitions*. He speaks of the difficulty of recognizing that it is time to let go and move on. Yet that is exactly what organizations must do if they are going to fully embrace new ideas.

(This chapter does not address the fifth phase but refers readers to Bridges's fine work in this area.)

The Limits and Value of Thinking in Terms of Stages

As much as you might want progress to be linear—one thing building on another in an inexorable rise toward perfection—it is most often much sloppier. Steps overlap, work moves forward, then back. At times, the cycle seems more like a Möbius strip. Nevertheless, these four areas make good reference points to help you see where people are and what we might do to support their work.

Each stage of the cycle has in it the seeds of its own destruction. For example, implementation won't last forever; it inevitably leads to integration or failure. Waning activity leads to either renewal or an ending. And on it goes.

The Biggest Mistake

Getting out ahead of others on the cycle is the biggest mistake clients and practitioners can make. Imagine this scenario: as the CEO reads financial reports and sees the challenges competitors are mounting, she recognizes that the company must do something. She considers the initial action of hiring a practitioner to help develop a plan for addressing these threats. As she gets ready to implement the plans developed along with the practitioner, the CEO realizes that she needs to tell others about the new plans. She calls everyone together to tell them why the company needs to make dramatic changes. They assume that this meeting will make the compelling case for change and allow them to get started working on plans. That seldom happens.

Instead of rising in applause at the brilliance of their thinking, people begin to resist. The CEO and the practitioner expected the group's arrows to move from one to six o'clock; but instead they dive into the center of the cycle. They go directly into resistance. The more they push, the more they embed the resistance. If this persists, both sides become locked into their positions.

The Paradoxical Theory of Change can be a helpful reminder to not get ahead of others on the change.

Paradoxical Theory of Change

In his paper "The Paradoxical Theory of Change," Arnold Beisser (1970) writes that "change occurs when one becomes what one is, not when one tries to be what one is not." Most important, he states, "Change does not take place through a coercive attempt by the individual or by another person to change him, but it does take place if one takes the time and effort to be what he is—to be fully invested in his current positions. *By rejecting the role of change agent,* we make meaningful and orderly change possible" (italics added).

OD interventions that get people to tell their stories to each other ("What do you gain and what do you lose from this change?" "What's it like to work here?") heighten awareness of people's perspectives and feelings. During these exchanges people often begin to see things differently. The paradox of spending time examining the picture as it is today often frees people to move on. It is not uncommon for people to begin to see others and their needs more clearly. You may hear pronouns shift, from "their idea" to "our idea." You may hear people begin to take ownership in getting the change started.

Time devoted to heightening awareness of the business conditions that prompted this change can be well spent. Too many changes move from "Why is this important?" to "How are we going to do it?" very quickly. This shift to action fails to adhere to Beisser's advice: better to spend time expanding people's views of the current state of affairs.

The Paradoxical Theory of Change is especially important as a governor to regulate the pace of change. Keeping the theory in mind can keep both practitioners and clients from attempting to push people around the cycle. Sometimes people act as if it were possible to predict when they were ready to move and schedule things accordingly. Life doesn't work so neatly. Too often, changes build in some time for buy in, assuming that an event will automatically create the needed support and nothing further will have to be done. Beisser suggests otherwise. If people aren't ready to move, they aren't ready to move; you can't force individuals or large groups to work in the next phase just because that's what the timeline says.

The Second Biggest Mistake

Once people start thinking about a change and get interested in and then excited about it, everything else fades into the background. The idea takes over, and the context surrounding the change is ignored.

When the space shuttle *Challenger* crashed in 1986, the press picked up on the commission's investigation of the disaster by saying the problem was with faulty o-rings. The distinguished panel looked for the reasons the shuttle exploded. They found it and made their report. They were right in that the o-rings were a critical factor, but there was more to it.

When a similar commission was convened to investigate the explosion of the shuttle *Columbia* in 2002, they took a much broader perspective. They found that indeed there were specific problems with the heat shield, but they also found that the organizational culture, budgets, and pressures from the U.S. Congress all played a part in the disaster.

It would be possible to use any problem-solving model to address the o-ring problem. You could identify the challenge, initiate remedies, implement solutions, and integrate these new procedures into how shuttles are designed and maintained. All of that could be quite helpful. However, the limited view would miss all of those other factors that the *Columbia* commission picked up on. They attended to field conditions as well as to the specific technical problem.

The field is broad. Ask what the varied conditions are that have an impact on what's going on in an organization. Organizations often fail to look expansively at many forces; consequently they "solve" problems and make changes in a partial manner that ends up having unintended consequences, or never really addressing the underlying problem. The *Columbia* commission looked not only at faulty heat shields but also at structural and environmental pressures that contributed to the tragedy.

Interventions must help people see the field conditions. What are the forces that influence this organization? What impact does the organization's history and culture have on its ability to do productive work today? Because organizations often look for blame, they may narrow in on a single cause to a problem, while that issue—say, an o-ring—is only one part of the field. We do our clients a disservice if we are seduced by the single smoking gun and help them solve just that problem.

Moving Ahead

There is no one-size-fits-all set of techniques, but using the ideas described in this chapter can help you adapt and create interventions that build support for change in organizations by:

- Honoring the tenets of the Paradoxical Theory of Change by helping parts of the system stay focused on heightening awareness of where they are right now. Ask, What is the work right now? Make a case? Get started? Sustain commitment? Get back on track?
- Helping people stay aligned in the work.
- Treating resistance as something important that gives people the opportunity to give voice to their multiple realities, which facilitates their hearing what they say and remaining in contact with various individuals and groups.
- Allowing people to come into greater and deeper contact with each other around critical issues. (As an added benefit, attending to this tenet helps organizations build capacity for change in the future.)

The key to everything described in this chapter is listening—but not just the textbook techniques of listening. It takes more. It takes clear intention. Leaders of change (and practitioners) must ask themselves, *Why do we want to listen to those people?* Actor Alan Alda said it best: we "need to listen with a willingness to be changed" (Maurer, 2002). If people in organizations can be supported to listen with the intent of being influenced or having their opinions changed, there is hope. The organization development profession is in a perfect position to help people listen with profound interest and curiosity.

References

Beisser, A. (1970). "The paradoxical theory of change." Originally published in *Gestalt Therapy Now*. New York: HarperCollins (now available from www.gestalt.org).

Bridges, W. (1980). *Transitions: Making sense of life's changes*. Boulder: Perseus.

Cialdini, R. (1998). *Influence: The psychology of persuasion*. New York: Perennial Currents.

Collins, J. (2001). *Good to great*. New York: HarperCollins.

Dannemiller, K., et al. (2000). *Whole-scale change*. San Francisco: Berrett-Koehler.

Fisher, A. (1994, January 24). How to make a merger work. *Fortune*, Vol. 129n2, pp. 66–70.

Folger, R., & Skarlicki, D. (1999). Unfairness and resistance to change: Hardship as mistreatment. *Journal of Organizational Change Management, 12*(1), 35–50.

Gottman, J. (1994). *What predicts divorce?* Hillsdale, NJ: Erlbaum.

Jacobs, R. (1997). *Real Time Strategic Change*. San Francisco: Berrett-Koehler.

Jellison, J. (1993). *Overcoming resistance*. New York: Simon and Schuster.

Johnson, B. (1997). *Polarity management*. Amherst, MA: HRD Press.

Johnson, J. (1995, January). Chaos: The dollar drain of IT projects. *Application Development Trends*, 41–47.

Johnson, S. (1998). *Who moved my cheese?* New York: Penguin.

LeDoux, J. (1998). *The emotional brain*. Carmichael, CA: Touchstone.

Maurer, R. (1996). *Beyond the wall of resistance*. Austin, TX: Bard Press.

Maurer, R. (2002). *Why don't you want what I want?* Austin, TX: Bard Press.

Maurer, R. (2003). *Leading change effectiveness survey* (www.beyondresistance.com).

Maurer, R. (2005). *Building capacity for change sourcebook* (rev. ed.). Arlington, VA: Maurer and Associates.

Michels, R. (1985). *The evolution of psychodynamic psychotherapy*. Strecker Monograph Series, Institute of Pennsylvania Hospital.

Nevis, E. (1996). *Intentional revolutions: A seven point strategy for transforming organizations*. San Francisco: Jossey-Bass.

Piderit, S. (2000, October). Rethinking resistance and recognizing ambivalence. *Academy of Management, 25*(4), 783–795.

Schiemann, W. (1992, April). Why change fails. *Across the Board. 29*(4), 53–54.

Ulrich, D. & Lake, D. (1990). *Organization capability: Competing from the inside out*. New York: John Wiley.

Weisbord, M., & Janoff, S. (2000). *Future search*. San Francisco: Berrett-Koehler.

CHAPTER EIGHT

THEORY AND PRACTICE OF MULTICULTURAL ORGANIZATION DEVELOPMENT

Bailey W. Jackson

This chapter describes multicultural organization development (MCOD). MCOD refers to building organizations and organizational cultures that include people from multiple socially defined group identities: race, ethnicity, gender, sexual orientation, nationality, class, religion, and other human differences. The chapter begins with a history of this approach to organization development (OD). Then the theoretical tenets of MCOD are examined. This is followed by a discussion of MCOD practice, including the MCOD goal, development stages, and process for fostering change in organizations.

Historical Overview

More than twenty years ago, practitioners in the field of organization development and systems change joined with those who focused on diversity issues in the workplace to explore how to address diversity and change in organizations. This union, though seemingly natural and obvious today, was slow to develop. Prior to this connection of OD with diversity, internal and external organization change agents typically addressed diversity issues in the workplace only as a module in a larger system change initiative. Diversity issues were not an integrated part of the overall change effort.

In actuality, even those diversity modules focused only on issues pertaining to what is more commonly referred to as "social justice" rather than "diversity." The terms *social justice* and *social diversity* are often used interchangeably. In MCOD terminology, the terms are meant to describe aspects of the social or organizational change agenda. Organizational change interventions focused on social diversity tend to address issues related to "group inclusion." The goals of social diversity interventions focus on building an organizational culture that includes people from various social identity groups that are based on such human differences as race, ethnicity, gender, sexual orientation, social or economic class, religion, nationality, age, and other socially defined group identities. A change effort focused on social justice would emphasize elimination of racism, sexism, heterosexism, classism, anti-Semitism, and other manifestations of social oppression or social injustice. These forms of social injustice are also based in human differences. Although MCOD acknowledges the difference between the justice and diversity agendas, many practitioners use the term *diversity* to refer to both social justice and social diversity concerns.

Those diversity practitioners who saw their work as assisting organizations to become more just, inclusive, and humane places to work described themselves as working toward and managing diversity in the workplace. This was typically approached through use of seminars and training sessions focused on an individual's exclusionary behaviors, attitudes, and limited awareness of the nature of discriminatory practices. Their goal was to change individuals, with the hope that this change would establish a supportive workplace climate in organizations that was conducive to appreciating individual differences and capitalizing on the strengths of a diverse workforce.

Practitioners who were grounded in both OD and diversity were the first to consider integration of these two change agendas, notably Kaleel Jamison (1978), Bailey Jackson and Rita Hardiman (1994), Roosevelt Thomas (1992, 1996), Elsie Cross (2000), Taylor Cox (2001), and Frederick Miller and Judith Katz (2002). Jamison was one of the first to write about the possibility of justice or affirmative action work in organizations as having a positive effect on organizational health throughout the organization. Jackson and Holvino (1988) first presented the eventual work of Jackson and Hardiman (1994), who were among the first to bring OD, social justice, and diversity together as multicultural organization development (Jackson, 1994).

Jackson and Hardiman recognized that their work in organizations to address behaviors and attitudes related to various forms of discrimination manifested by individual managers and workers was indeed necessary. But it was not sufficient to produce the kind of organizational change that would result in a socially just organization, or to move the organization to becoming a multicultural organization (MCO). Grounded in both OD and diversity or social justice in the workplace, they theorized that to achieve the vision of an MCO it would be necessary to view the organization or system as the target of change. In other words, the organization is the client, rather than the individuals in the organization. Since this fusion of approaches to organizational change in the area of diversity and social justice some twenty years ago, MCOD has developed and evolved into a practice that continues to show promise and grow as an approach for change agents who are working with organizations seeking to become multicultural organizations.

Assumptions Behind the Theory and Practice of MCOD

Certain key assumptions are imbedded in MCOD theory and practice:

• *Individual consciousness raising and training activities for individuals in organizations may be necessary but are not sufficient to produce organizational change.* Organizations must also change the policies and practices that support the status quo around diversity issues.

• *Organizations are not either "good" (multicultural) or "bad" (monocultural).* They exist on a developmental continuum with multicultural and monocultural on opposite ends. It is important to understand what the other points on the continuum are and where the client organization is on that continuum. Then, and only then, can MCOD practitioners help organizations operate from an accurate diagnosis when developing change goals and intervention plans.

• *The change process needs to be pursued with a clear vision of the "ideal" end state, or the multicultural organization, in mind.* A well-articulated and owned vision of the ideal organization, one that is a manifestation of the ideal MCO, must inform all aspects of the change process. Only with a clear sense of the ideal can the data that describe the current or real situation have any meaning. It is only when one juxtaposes the ideal with the real and considers the discrepancy that the problems and issues to be addressed emerge.

• *The picture of the real should be derived from an internal assessment process.* A structured assessment that can be used to identify and describe the current state of diversity and social justice in the organization should be used to establish the baseline or current state of what "is" in the organization.

• *Ownership of the MCOD process is a key to success.* A significant majority of the members of the organization must own the data that describe what is, the vision that describes the ideal or the *ought,* and the problems that have emerged from comparing the real to the ideal. For an MCOD initiative to be a success, organization members must also own the change goals and any sense of priority in working to remove those problems.

• *Significant organizational change in social justice and diversity will occur only if there is someone monitoring and facilitating the process.* The health of the organization is served when there is a commitment to stay with the change effort over time and where the goals are linked to and facilitate the overall success of the organization's mission.

The Practice of MCOD

The practice of multicultural organization development is based in MCOD assumptions and involves three major elements: (1) the MCOD goal, (2) the MCOD development stages, and (3) the MCOD process. These three elements of MCOD practice are described in the next subsections of this chapter.

The MCOD Goal

The first element focuses on the goal of any MCOD effort. Typically, an organization enters into an MCOD process because it is understood or believed that a system that manages its human resources well has a greater chance of gaining and maintaining a competitive advantage or achieving its overall mission. A system that is invested in its human resources also recognizes that to develop and maintain a strong, productive, and high-performing human resource system there must be effective management of social justice and social diversity in the organization. Organizations invest in becoming an MCO for other reasons as well. Some believe that it is the right thing to do. Others believe they have evidence that an organization with a diverse workforce and a socially just workplace will enhance the quality of the product or service that is produced.

The MCO is an organization that seeks to improve itself or enhance its competitive advantage by advocating and practicing social justice and social diversity internally and external to the organization. Specifically:

• The MCO is an organization that has within its mission, goals, values, and operating system explicit policies and practices that prohibit anyone from being excluded or unjustly treated because of social identity or status. A multicultural organization not only supports social justice within the organization; it advocates these values in interactions within the local, regional, national, and global communities, with its vendors, customers, and peer organizations.

- The MCO is an organization that has within its mission, goals, values, and operating system explicit policies and practices that are intended to ensure that all members of the diverse workforce feel fully included and have every opportunity to contribute to achieving the mission of the organization. This organization also appreciates all forms of social diversity and understands the strengths and advantages that social diversity brings to the local, regional, national, and global communities.

When applying this two-part goal to an MCOD effort, it is important for MCOD practitioners to recognize that a level of social justice must be achieved before social diversity can be pursued. Many have tried unsuccessfully to move directly to social diversity objectives—for example, building a climate of inclusion in the workplace—without adequately attending to the absence of social justice (the existence of sexism, racism, classism, anti-Semitism, heterosexism, and other manifestations of social injustice). The goal of becoming an MCO involves achievement of social justice (an antiexclusionary objective) and social diversity (an inclusionary objective).

The MCOD process can begin when there is evidence of a significant investment on the part of the leadership and key parts of the organization's workforce in becoming an MCO, or at least in exploring the possible benefits of becoming such an organization. The first steps are often to engage the leadership and as many of the workforce-at-large as possible in developing the MCO goal in their own words and then owning it.

MCOD Development Stages

One of the core assumptions of MCOD is that most organizations are neither all good nor all bad. In the language of multicultural organization development, organizations are neither purely multicultural nor purely monocultural. Organizations are in various places on the continuum that has these two points at the ends. They generally are not simply stuck on the "embracing diversity side" of the continuum, nor are they stuck on the "rejecting diversity side." In most large organizations, divisions, departments, groups, or other organizational units will be in differing places from each other and from the larger organization on this developmental continuum with respect to the strength of their affinity for (or against) the MCO goals of the organization. The MCOD Developmental Stage Model is a significant element of MCOD theory and practice (1) because it is essential in MCOD theory and practice to be able to assess the developmental issues, opportunities, and challenges of an organization as it attempts to move toward becoming an MCO; and (2) because it is also essential that the change process be guided by a conceptual framework that helps in identifying change strategies that are consistent with the developmental readiness of the organization.

Bailey Jackson and Rita Hardiman developed the MCOD Development Stage Model (Figure 8.1) on the basis of their work in social identity development theory (Jackson and Hardiman, 1997) and racial identity development theory (Jackson and Hardiman, 1983; Wijeyesinghe and Jackson, 2001). They coupled their research and writing on individual development with their work and observations as OD practitioners. The MCOD Development Stage Model identifies six points on a developmental continuum, each describing the consciousness and culture of an organization with regard to issues of social justice and diversity and where the organization is relative to becoming an MCO.

FIGURE 8.1. CONTINUUM OF MULTICULTURAL ORGANIZATION DEVELOPMENT.

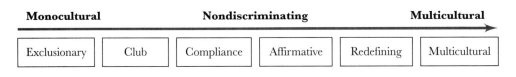

Monocultural		Nondiscriminating			Multicultural
Exclusionary	Club	Compliance	Affirmative	Redefining	Multicultural

Stage One: The Exclusionary Organization. The exclusionary organization is openly devoted to maintaining the majority group's dominance and privilege. These values are typically manifested in the organization's mission and membership criteria. It is usually openly hostile to anything that might be seen as a concern for social justice or social diversity. An organization that is rooted in this stage of development is unlikely to entertain anything like an MCOD process. Most large organizations can identify a department, group, or some other unit that embraces this developmental perspective even within a more enlightened organization.

Stage Two: "The Club." The organization or organizational unit that is at the "club" stage can be thought of as stopping short of explicitly advocating anything like the majority group's supremacy, but seeking to maintain privileges for those who have traditionally held social power. This is done by developing and maintaining missions, policies, norms, and procedures seen as "correct" from their perspective. The club allows a limited number of people from other social identity groups into the organization if they have the "right" perspective and credentials.

The club is seen as more "liberal" with regard to social justice issues, compared to the exclusionary organization. It engages with social justice issues only when they can be approached with comfort and on club members' terms.

Stage Three: The Compliance Organization. The compliance organization is committed to removing some of the discrimination inherent in the club by permitting access to members of social identity groups that were previously excluded. It seeks to accomplish this objective without disturbing the structure, mission, and culture of the organization. The organization is careful not to create too many waves or offend or challenge its majority employees' or customers' bigoted attitudes or behaviors.

The compliance organization usually attempts to change its social diversity profile by actively recruiting and hiring more nonmajority people at the bottom of the organization. On occasion, the organization will hire or promote tokens into management positions (usually staff). When the exception is made to place a nonmajority person in a line position, it is important that this person be a "team player" and "qualified" applicant. A qualified team player does not openly challenge the organization's mission and practices, and is usually 150 percent competent to do the job.

Stage Four: The Affirming Organization. The affirming organization is also committed to eliminating the discriminatory practices and inherent advantage given members of the majority group in the club by actively recruiting and promoting members of those social groups typically denied access to the organization. The affirming organization takes an active role in supporting the growth and development of these new employees and initiating programs that increase their chances of success and mobility. All employees are encouraged to think and behave in a nonoppressive manner, and the organization may conduct awareness programs toward this end.

Stage Five: The Redefining Organization. The redefining organization is a system in transition. It is not satisfied with merely being socially just or nonoppressive. It is committed to working toward an environment that goes beyond managing diversity to one that "values and capitalizes on diversity." This organization is committed to finding ways to ensure full inclusion of all social identity group perspectives as a method of enhancing the growth and success potential of the organization.

The redefining organization begins to question the limitations of relying solely on one cultural perspective as a basis for the organization's mission, operations, and product development. It seeks to explore the significance and potential benefits of a multicultural workforce. This organization actively engages in visioning, planning, and problem-solving activities directed toward realization of a multicultural organization.

The redefining organization is committed to developing and implementing policies and practices that distribute power among all of the diverse groups in the organization. In summary, the redefining organization searches for alternative modes of organizing that guarantee the inclusion, participation, and empowerment of all its members.

Stage Six: The Multicultural Organization. The multicultural organization reflects the contributions and interests of diverse cultural and social groups in its mission, operations, products, and services. It acts on a commitment to eradicate social oppression in all forms within the organization. The MCO includes members of diverse cultural and social groups as full participants, especially in decisions that shape the organization. It follows through on broader external social responsibilities, including support of efforts to eliminate all forms of social oppression and to educate others in multicultural perspectives.

This description of the multicultural organization represents the vision for an MCO. It must remain a vision and a statement of the ideal, because *there are no known MCOs*. This is a vision for the organization to reach for. When MCOD practitioners see parts of this vision manifest in an organization or organizational unit, it is important for that organization to be recognized and celebrated, even if it is not a perfect representation of the vision. Organizations need to know they can get there.

Using the Developmental Stages

The MCOD developmental stages are most useful in the assessment and planning phases of the MCOD process. The stage model presents a framework for designing assessment instruments and techniques, which can help the organization identify its stage of development and construct a beginning benchmark for the organization's diversity and social justice initiative. MCOD assessment instruments have been developed by most of the MCOD practitioners mentioned in this chapter. Generally these instruments are proprietary, have been adapted for use in specific organizations, and are not available for broad use.

Once an organization has determined where it is on the continuum with the help of MCOD practitioners, the next task is to develop a change plan. The change plan addresses specific aspects of that stage as demonstrated by this organization and guides strategies to help the organization move to the next stage on the developmental continuum. The overall MCOD process is described next.

The assessment and change planning process needs to be understood in the context of the overall MCOD process.

The MCOD Process

Once the organization has made the decision to pursue the goal of becoming multicultural, the MCOD change process begins. The change process has four components (with a number of subcomponents): (1) identification of the change agents, (2) determination of the readiness of the system for a diversity and social justice change initiative, (3) assessment or benchmarking of the organization, and (4) change planning and implementation.

Identification of the Change Agents. There are three primary actors or change agents involved in the change process: the internal change team, external MCOD practitioner consultants, and the leadership team.

The Internal Change Team. The internal change team is a group of people from within the organization who agree to take on the responsibility of managing the MCOD process for the organization. Managing the process can take a number of forms. For some change teams, it means hiring an outside MCOD practitioner consultant who comes into the organization and runs the process for the change team. The team's role at this level of involvement is to hire the consultant, monitor the consultant's activities, offer input to the consultant when necessary regarding the best way to negotiate the organizational culture, and report on the progress of the initiative to the leadership. In other organizations, the change team may take a more involved or high level of responsibility for the MCOD change process. In this case, the team may have the internal competence to conduct its own assessment, develop its own change plans, and implement those change plans with only minimal technical assistance or guidance from outside sources.

Once the team is formed, a first task is to determine how involved it wants to be or feels capable of being. The level of involvement of the change team should also influence the level of involvement of the outside consultant team.

The internal change team should:

• *Be of a manageable size,* usually no more than twelve members. They should understand that all team members will come to every meeting, except in case of emergency.

• Understand that *this is now part of their job.* This is regular work. Team members should be released from some other task assignments so that their team membership is not an overload. Because this is part of their regular job, team members can and should be evaluated on their performance and rewarded consistent with the regular merit and recognition system in the organization.

• *Have good connections with as many constituencies as possible* within the organization. Because the size of the group is limited, not all constituencies can be represented on the team, but it is possible to have the voices of all constituencies heard through those who are chosen to serve on the team. The team should represent a horizontal and vertical cut of the organization as much as possible.

• *Comprise people who are opinion leaders* in the organization. Opinion leaders are not always in a position of authority. Their legitimacy comes from the trust their peers have in them.

• Understand that the diversity and social justice effort *involves at least a two-year commitment* from each member. Supervisors need to be supportive of team member assignments.

• *Be supportive of the organization's intention and commitment* about engaging in this MCOD process and becoming a multicultural organization. The voices of those who are opposed to this effort need to be heard and their concerns addressed, but it will not help the process if they are on the change team.

Once assembled, the change team and external consultants meet to review the MCOD process. The external consultants can also carry out some of the team-building work with the change team. It is often helpful if the leadership announces formation of the change team, expresses gratitude for team member contributions, and uses this moment to proclaim the beginning of the MCOD initiative.

The External MCOD Practitioner Consultant Team. The external consultant team brings an outside perspective about the MCOD change process. It is imperative that the external consultants be familiar with MCOD or MCOD-type change processes. In addition to extending guidance on the best way to conduct an MCOD change effort, the external MCOD practitioners:

• Assist with development of assessment instrument(s) for the assessment phase, conduct interviews and focus groups, and collect sensitive data where it might be difficult for change team members to do so.

• Act as a buffer between the leadership of the organization and members of the change team. The external consultant is often better able to deal with the leadership of the organization than are the members of the change team who more than likely report to people on the leadership team.

• Help facilitate team building among change team members. The external consultant should be able to help the change team with its own team building and group dynamics. MCOD change teams typically need outside consultant help with their own group process. Social justice and social diversity issues bring their particular tension to any group. It is difficult for a group to manage these issues for itself. Having an external consultant as a resource that can help the group work through these issues as they arise benefits the change team and the overall change effort.

• Understand that part of their charge is to build internal capacity for the organization. This means internal change team members and consultants understand that the MCOD process will need to go on for a long time, and it is not the intention of the organization to have the external practitioners become part of the organization. The external MCOD consultants guide the change team through the change process. They also furnish the skills and knowledge necessary so that on the next round the change team has the capacity to manage the change for the organization. At that point, the change effort will require external resources for only those tasks where an external presence or perspective is required.

One of the keys to being an effective external practitioner is to stay clear of the organization's internal politics. The apolitical perspective of the external consultant can be both an asset and a liability. Because external consultants are not part of the power politics that exists in any organization, their credibility is not questioned in the same way as the credibility of internal change team members. However, external consultants can lack understanding of all the organization's history and internal politics; this can cause blind spots that could hurt the change effort if not recognized. Missing historical and political cues and nuances can negatively affect any MCOD effort. It is therefore imperative that both internal and external perspectives be available to this effort at all times.

The Leadership Team. The third primary agent in the MCOD change process is the *leadership team.* This term is used rather than *leader* because in most organizations, especially larger systems, the leadership is typically made up of a group of individuals. These organizational leaders (president, CEO, CFO, chancellor, vice president, and so forth) usually have primary responsibility for and authority over all internal policies and procedures. They are responsible for their own area and collectively responsible for leading the organization as a whole. For an intervention like MCOD, it is important that this leadership team knows what is going on and has direct involvement in the manner in which the initiative is carried out.

The leadership team must be involved in the initial decision to engage in an MCOD initiative. Although one key officer often brings a process like MCOD to the organization, this person must receive the approval of the leadership team before going too far with the process. This is one place where an outside consultant can be a significant help to the organization by helping the leadership team understand the MCOD change process and what its role will be. The leadership team must decide what level of involvement it wants to have in the process. Like the change team, the leadership team can decide to be highly involved in conceptualizing the initiative and the activities of the MCOD process, or it can decide to bless the process and charge the change team with moving forward and reporting to the leadership team from time to time. The more direct the involvement of the leadership team in this initiative, the faster it will move and the greater the chance of success.

Organization Readiness. One important component of the MCOD process is a test of the readiness of the organization for a change initiative that focuses on an area as volatile as social justice and diversity. This test asks critical questions about the level of awareness and support in the workforce for an MCOD initiative and the leadership's readiness to support and engage in this process.

The purpose of the MCOD readiness inventory is to assess at the very beginning of the process how best to enter into an organization with an intervention of this kind, since it ultimately calls for an intensive data-collection phase. The readiness inventory is given to a sample of the organization, and to all of the change team and leadership team. The typical MCOD readiness inventory asks six basic questions:

1. How are manifestations of social oppression (sexism, heterosexism, classism, and so forth) handled when discovered or reported?
2. Is support for diversity a core value in this organization?
3. Is there a clearly expressed commitment to social justice in this organization?
4. Does the leadership express or demonstrate its support for social justice?
5. How well does the leadership model a value for diversity and social justice?
6. Is the commitment to diversity and social justice clearly stated in the mission and values of the organization?

These and other questions help the change agents get a sense of the organization's readiness to move forward. No organization at this point is going to score very well on a readiness inventory, but a minimum score (equivalent to a 50 percent positive response) should be attained to assume readiness. Less than a 50 percent positive response indicates that a stronger base for an MCOD initiative is required before moving forward.

This type of readiness inventory can also provide beginning data about existing organizational issues. On rare occasions, work may be needed to bring the leadership or the workforce up to another level of awareness before trying to fully engage in the MCOD process. This might require awareness seminars as well as clarification and enforcement of existing policies and procedures that support social justice pronouncements from the leadership about their commitment and intent for the organization to become a multicultural organization. The organization could address long-standing social justice issues in the organization that, when taken on, send a message throughout the organization that something serious is happening. The additional work might involve conducting harassment-training sessions for the workforce. As soon as the organization is sufficiently ready to begin the MCOD change initiative, the next step is assessment and benchmarking.

Assessment and Benchmarking. MCOD is a data-driven process. Establishing a benchmark for where the organization begins its journey to becoming an MCO is critical to the MCOD process. It is essential to understanding how far the organization has to move to become an MCO and how the organization is progressing as it implements the action or change plans.

The initial assessment accomplishes a number of objectives. It establishes the benchmark and engages the system in naming and owning the current developmental stage of the organization. Data are needed to yield a detailed description of how the organization manifests its stage of development. This detailed description assists the change team in identifying issues and problems that need to be addressed, determining the priority for each issue and problem, and developing a focused set of strategies and criteria for measuring success.

The assessment methodology used in most MCOD initiatives is based on survey feedback. The MCOD assessment process involves collection of three types of data: (1) survey data, (2) interview data, and (3) audit data.

Survey Data. An MCOD assessment questionnaire is used to inform construction of a change plan and is administered to everyone in the organization. The assessment survey is keyed to the MCOD developmental stages, which makes organizing the data less difficult and developing a change plan easier.

Interview Data. Interviews help flesh out quantitative data from the survey and provide a backdrop or context for data that can sometimes appear confusing or contradictory. Because there is rarely enough time or resources to collect individual interview data, focus groups are typically used at this stage. Focus groups are formed from the various social groupings in the organization (gender, race or ethnicity, sexual orientation, class) and from organizational groupings (secretaries and administrative staff, managers, engineers, part-time workers, instructors, counselors, and so forth).

Two types of data are usually collected in these focus groups. First, the group is asked to talk about their perception of the organization relative to social justice and diversity. The data collected from these discussions help flesh out what is known from the survey instrument. Second, the focus groups are presented with survey data that are not clear, or that seem to contradict other data; they are asked to give their perspective on the apparent contradictions.

Audit Data. Finally, the MCOD assessment process includes audit data. Audit data are information gleaned from a review of the organization's records. Specific sets of questions are asked about the organization records, particularly records of the organization's personnel and budget offices. Audit data are collected about hires, terminations, resignations, grievances, promotions, and performance evaluations. These data are aggregated by race, gender, physical or developmental ability, sexual orientation (when available), religion (when available), and other social identity groups. The data are also aggregated by organizational unit (division, department, workgroup) and by job grade or classification. The survey and focus group data are impressionistic. Audit data either support those impressions or highlight serious questions about the organization's performance around social justice and diversity issues.

After the assessment data are collected, the data are "sanitized" and compiled for presentation to the organization. Sanitizing involves removing any language or names that might compromise the anonymity of respondents. In some cases this can eliminate a group from the data; for example, if there is only one African American woman in a unit, this person's identity cannot be protected and will need to be included with responses from "people of color," or removed altogether.

The change agents compile and organize the data for presentation to the organization. They do not analyze the data, and the data are organized in a format that all organization members can understand. The primary purpose for the presentation of the data is to give organization members an opportunity to hear what was said in the assessment, offer any major adjustments or corrections, and ultimately own the data. Once the data are owned and the group has indicated that "yes, the data represent our organization," the next step is to identify those things that must be changed so that the organization can become an MCO. Involving organization members in exploring the data and defining the MCOD initiative differentiates the MCOD approach to systems change from others that tend to be either top-down or bottom-up. This process is all-inclusive.

Change Planning and Implementation

After the assessment is completed and the data have been presented and owned, the change agents and MCOD practitioner consultants assist each organizational unit in building change plans and goals. The units are encouraged to identify those issues and problems that when addressed will be affected in an observable and measurable way. Change goals are based on the issues and problems that have been identified. Issues are prioritized by focusing on those that can be addressed and significantly affected within eighteen months to two years. It is critical that results of the MCOD initiative be seen and measured and that the organization and those responsible for the initiative are accountable for its success.

When the change plan has been implemented and the results evaluated, it is time to redo the assessment, renew the organization's commitment to becoming an MCO, develop the next change plan, and implement it. With successive completion of these rounds of assessment, commitment, change plan development, and change plan implementation, the MCOD process becomes internalized within the organization; its culture and the internal capacity of the organization to run and monitor its own MCOD process develops and takes root (see Figure 8.2).

FIGURE 8.2. MCOD PROCESS.

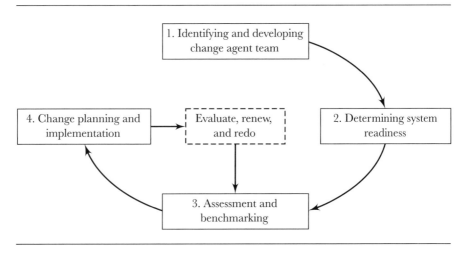

Conclusion

Multicultural organization development has been in practice for more than two decades. How it is practiced and the theory behind the practice continue to grow and evolve. Some of that growth is represented in this description of MCOD. MCOD emerged from the work of diversity practitioners and OD practitioners who share a commitment to social justice and social diversity in systems and in society. Because this is a commitment to the health of human systems, both the theory and the practice of MCOD will necessarily evolve over time. What remains to be seen is the long-term effect of MCOD as a change model. Will systems that use this model indeed become MCOs and therefore come significantly closer not only to achieving their social justice and diversity vision but also to enhancing their ability to realize the bottom-line mission for the organization?

Understanding the impact of MCOD on the organization's bottom line is only the first question to be answered. Transforming what looks like the obvious answer to "Will it work?" to the statement "It does work" will take some long and rigorous study. While this type of inquiry is conducted, we should also pay attention to how the practice of MCOD changes MCOD theory, and the theory and practice of OD. Since MCOD was in part an invention intended to fill a perceived gap in the theory and practice of OD, it might seem that as MCOD continues to evolve not only will that gap be filled but the theory and practice of OD and MCOD will be thought of as one rather than two separate or overlapping fields.

References

Cox Jr., T. (2001). *Creating the multicultural organization: A strategy for capturing the power of diversity.* San Francisco: Jossey-Bass.

Cross, E. Y. (2000). *Managing diversity: The courage to lead.* Westport, CT: Quorum Books.

Jackson, B. W. (1994). Coming to a vision of a multicultural system. In E. Y. Cross, J. H. Katz, F. A. Miller, & E. W. Seashore (Eds.), *The promise of diversity: Over 40 voices discuss strategies for eliminating discrimination in organizations* (pp. 116–117). Arlington, VA: NTL Institute.

Jackson, B. W., & Hardiman, R. (1983). Racial identity development: Implications for managing the multi-racial workforce. In A. G. Sargent & R. Ritvo (Eds.), *NTL manager's handbook* (pp. 107–119). Arlington, VA: NTL Institute.

Jackson, B. W., & Hardiman, R. (1994). Multicultural organization development. In E. Y. Cross, J. H. Katz, F. A. Miller, & E. W. Seashore (Eds.), *The promise of diversity: Over 40 voices discuss strategies for eliminating discrimination in organizations* (pp. 231–239). Arlington, VA: NTL Institute.

Jackson, B. W., & Hardiman, R. (1997). Conceptual foundations for social justice courses. In M. Adams, L. A. Bell, & P. Griffin (Eds.), *Teaching for diversity and social justice: A sourcebook* (pp. 16–29). New York and London: Routledge.

Jackson, B. W., & Holvino, E. (1988, Fall). Developing multicultural organizations. *Journal of Religion and Applied Behavioral Science* (Association for Creative Change), 14–19.

Jamison, K. (1978, December). Affirmative action program: Springboard for a total organizational change effort. *OD Practitioner, 10*(4).

Miller, F. A., & Katz, J. H. (2002). *The inclusion breakthrough: Unleashing the real power of diversity.* San Francisco: Berrett-Koehler.

Thomas, R. (1992). *Beyond race and gender: Unleashing the power of your total work force by managing diversity.* New York: AMACOM.

Thomas, R. (1996). *Redefining diversity.* New York: AMACOM.

Wijeyesinghe, C. L., & Jackson, B. W. (Eds.). (2001). *New perspectives on racial identity development: A theoretical and practical anthology.* New York: University Press.

PART THREE

ORGANIZATION DEVELOPMENT AND THE OD PROCESS

CHAPTER NINE

AN OD MAP: THE ESSENCE
OF ORGANIZATION DEVELOPMENT

Ted Tschudy

The practice of organization development (OD) has grown from its early roots in small-group dynamics, survey research, and laboratory learning to become an accepted function in contemporary organizations. First named by early practitioners in the late 1950s, OD, or derivative terminology such as organizational improvement or organizational effectiveness, is now commonly found on the organization charts of business, government, and not-for-profit organizations around the globe. Although early pioneers of the work were often derided as practitioners of mysterious "touchy-feely" exercises unrelated to the bottom line, leaders of contemporary organizations acknowledge—and often champion—the critical importance of effective human systems and OD support in today's competitive business environment.

The founders of OD were masterful general practitioners who, on the basis of their small-group, laboratory-education, and planned-change experiences, invented applications to organization and worklives. Today, OD is (1) a matured practice, characterized by a focus on individuals, groups, and organizations; (2) a multitude of subspecialties and varied change targets with names such as culture

Note: The original creators of the OD map were Pauline Frederick Hicks, Mikki Ritvo, Leroy Wells, and me. Thank you and appreciation to NTL members who have commented on the map, and to a roomful of colleagues who offered comments and suggestions at a Sunrise Seminar Session presented during the 2003 Organization Development Network National Conference.

change, large system change, team building, process consultation, coaching, socio-technical systems, diversity, leadership development, quality management, Gestalt approaches, large group interventions, appreciative inquiry, and organizational transformation; (3) a number of professional associations; (4) a diverse and segmented community of service providers; (5) and a vast, growing theory-and-practice literature. Aspects of OD have been adapted to countless organizational change and improvement initiatives, among them leadership development, quality management, process reengineering, reorganization, organizational learning, and strategy development.

Unlike more formalized "helping" practices such as law, psychology, or social work, which have defined professional boundaries, OD has been characterized by open boundaries. It has been a welcoming host in its practice house, entertaining practitioners and thinkers from many behavioral sciences. OD has fostered an explosion of innovative applications derived from the transforming process and human development insights first realized by the pioneers. On the other hand, OD's porous boundaries and its "spread" to other human system change practices have resulted in a diffuse picture of what OD is (and what it is not).

Newcomers to the study and practice of OD often find the variety of terms, approaches, and foci confusing, or understandably see their particular area of practice or experience as a definition of OD. Some experienced OD practitioners, believing that it has devolved into a batch of unrelated techniques and processes, find themselves asking a basic question: "Is OD still a viable, coherent practice?" Others take an opposite, more encompassing view of OD, seeing almost all attempts to change organizations as potential components of an OD effort. The concept of OD described by the OD Map falls closer to the view of the latter camp, seeing OD as a *systems-focused architecture for organizational change and transformation*. The OD Map attempts to describe the core components of this OD architecture that provide coherence and definition to the field and to the work.

The Map as Territorial Guide

The OD Map was originally developed in 1993 to answer questions that a group of newcomers to OD asked in an NTL learning program held in Washington, D.C. Frustrated by a confusing array of terms and practices (OK: it was a revolt!), they asked the staff to put together a summary that answered a number of questions, among them:

- What do OD practitioners do?
- What kinds of skills do you need to do it?
- How does it all fit together?

These newcomers to OD wanted a "picture" of OD practice that could help them place their learning in context. Knowing the potential of such uprisings to spark creativity and learning, the staff (Pauline Hicks, Mikki Ritvo, Leroy Wells, and me) worked through the night to create the first visual presentation of "OD: A Map of What to Know and What to Do." The map is not meant to be static. It has been refined in minor ways, including some revisions I made in the course of writing this chapter. As presented, the OD Map is scaled to present a whole picture. However, like all maps, it invites you to look closer at its parts, drilling down into the details that are revealed by zooming in on a specific location. Figure 9.1 presents the complete map.

There are seven primary parts of the OD Map.

1. *Core and supplemental theories.* OD is theory-based. Its conceptual lenses guide what OD practitioners look at, what they make of what they see, and how they intervene. The map identifies three core theories that underlie OD practice, and it holds a place for the countless number of supplemental theories that support the varieties of OD work.

2. *Values, ethics, and practice theories.* Values are the stated and unstated "goods" and "bads" that influence the practitioner's choice of clients, work, and action stances. Ethics are behaviors that are prescribed and proscribed by a profession or discipline. Practice theories are the assumptions and practical rules of thumb that practitioners use in the moment to direct their work with a client in a specific situation. Much as a prism bends light, each of these shapes the work of the individual OD practitioner.

3. *OD as "the big I."* The OD Map presents the OD process as a whole process. It is *intervention writ large.* "Big I" intervention is portrayed as the ongoing work that differentiates OD. It is distinct from the multitude of designs, workshops, and other OD events that are characterized as "little i's" in the action-taking phase of the map.

4. *Phases of OD practice.* In its classic form, OD is carried out in a consulting sequence with the client. In actuality, practitioners may work backward, forward, and concurrently in these phases. In some instances, phases may be merged such that it is difficult to distinguish when one phase begins and another ends.

5. *Consulting tasks associated with each phase of practice.* The OD Map portrays the primary tasks that practitioners carry out in each phase of the OD consulting process.

6. *Competencies.* Each phase of the OD consulting process requires competencies that OD practitioners develop and refine over the course of their training and practice careers. Of course, competencies listed for each phase are not exclusive to those phases but are emphasized because of their relationship to the primary tasks of that phase.

FIGURE 9.1. OD: A MAP OF WHAT TO KNOW AND WHAT TO DO.

Core theories: (NTL Institute)
- Action Research
- Systems Theory
- Change Theory
- Supplemental Theories

Values · Ethics · Practice theories

"Big 'I' Intervention (Consultant-Client System Interaction)"
What? Where? When? Who? How?

OD phases:

Entry/contracting	Data collection	Data analysis	Feedback	Action planning	Action taking	Evaluation	Termination

Consultation tasks:

Entry/contracting	Data collection	Data analysis	Feedback	Action planning	Action taking	Evaluation	Termination
Initial contact	Prepare for data collection	Analyze data	Plan feedback	Assess problems/gaps/opportunities	Carry out action plan(s)	Review goals	Assess need to continue
Define problem/need/client	Collect data	Prepare report/summary	Produce feedback materials	Prioritize opportunities	Interventions (Small "i")	Assess progress	Decide to end
Explore readiness for change			Do feedback	Plan actions	Individual	Identify new learnings	Phase out
Agree on contract outcomes			Provide frameworks		Interpersonal	Redirect (as needed)	Stay open to be called
Who, what, when, where			Diagnosis and planning		Group		
					Intergroup		
					Organization		
					Organization-Environment		
					Global		

Competencies:

Entry/contracting	Data collection	Data analysis	Feedback	Action planning	Action taking	Evaluation	Termination
Communicate	Constructing questions	Knowing concepts and theories	Giving and receiving feedback	Using theory and concepts	Managing conflict	Understanding evaluation methods	Bringing closure
Listen	Interviewing	• Group dynamics		Identifying system leverage points	Managing diversity	Connecting outcomes and objectives	
Negotiate	Observation	• Systems theory		Knowing small "i" interventions	Managing resistance		
		• Change theory			Training		
		Identifying themes			Managing transitions		
		Summarizing			Learning theory		

Use of self:

Awareness	Integration of mind and body	Self as rational or intuitive instrument	Self as empathic, evocative, provocative	Ethics, values, insight, multiple frames	Authentic commitment / Nonreactive presence	Self-learning risk	Experiment

Source: NTL Institute, Alexandria, VA.

7. *The use of self.* OD differs from other forms of consulting in its emphasis on the *use of self* as an instrument in the multiple aspects of OD practice. As with most helping professions, OD is an *artful craft.* It cannot be effectively practiced without a *strong commitment* to *personal* as well as *professional* development.

Core Theories

The OD Map identifies three conceptual foundations for OD. They are, like most theories in social science, sets of often loosely connected propositions and models that are held together by a few primary assumptions. Why is theory important to OD practice? Because in its most basic form theory is one's assumptions about how things work. Formal or informal, cogently articulated or operating beneath one's awareness, these assumptions are what guide actions as practitioners.

Action Research: The Heart of the OD Process

Action research is the "process" theory lens through which OD is practiced (Clark, 1972). (See Figure 9.2 for a simple representation of the action research process.) It underlies the core of OD practice portrayed in the phases portion of the map and the nature of the evolving practitioner-client relationship. Action research is

FIGURE 9.2. ACTION RESEARCH.

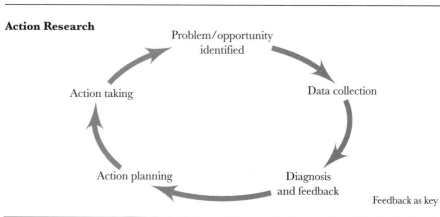

Action Research

Problem/opportunity identified

Data collection

Action taking

Diagnosis and feedback

Action planning

Feedback as key

results-focused; it attempts to help clients envision and move toward a desired future. Unlike most other kinds of research, action research is an intentionally collaborative effort that values the client's contribution. It assumes that participation will enhance the final result, as well as the client's acceptance of and competence to manage the change effort. Rather than taking the distant or objective stance traditionally associated with academic research, the action researcher engages the client in mutual problem solving.

Like academic research, action research is actively involved in creating theory. Theory is the ongoing *why* conversation; it happens as a natural part of OD work. Theory emerges in its simplest form from the interaction of practitioner and client as they pursue a more systematic understanding of why things are the way they are and what needs to change. More elegant theory is developed as practitioners use action research to refine their assumptions and propositions about how organizations work, and then contribute to the larger body of formal theory that is shared in journals and practice publications. (See Figure 9.3.)

FIGURE 9.3. THEORY HAPPENS.

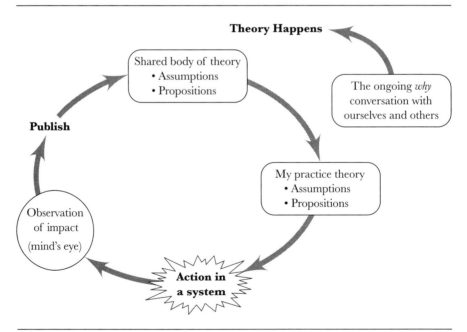

Systems Theory: The OD Framework for "Seeing" Organizations

Systems theory originated as an attempt to develop a general theory of system behavior (Von Bertalanffy, 1976). Applied to organizations, systems theory gives OD practitioners a language to identify important parts of organizations and how they relate to each other (see Figure 9.4). OD practitioners see organizations as constantly changing open systems, which have important internal components (such as goals, tasks, technologies, structures, people, coordinating mechanisms, rewards, leadership, and culture) but also interact with their environments, influencing them and being influenced by them (French and Bell, 1998). Practitioners use contemporary systems principles to diagnose and map dynamic system changes over time and the characteristics of organizations that allow them to respond to today's rapidly changing organization environments (Senge, 1990; Oshry, 1995). Basic components of an open systems view of organizations are described here.

FIGURE 9.4. ORGANIZATIONS AS OPEN SYSTEMS.

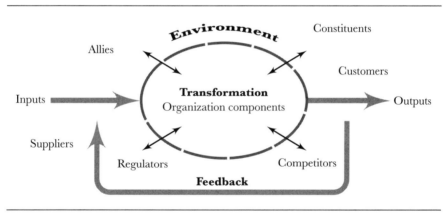

Inputs, Transformation, Outputs. Organizations, like other systems, are entities that have inputs (such as raw resources, employee capabilities, and funding) and outputs (products, information, services) that are created by a transformation process carried out by the organization.

Environments and Boundaries. Organizations have boundaries that can be relatively closed or open. They exist in environments (customers, allies, competitors, trends) that can be hostile or friendly, sparse or resource-rich, slow-moving or fast-changing. Systems are affected by their environments, and they in turn have an impact on the environments they inhabit.

All Parts Related. All parts of a system are related. If any part changes, the others are changed as well. OD practitioners understand that what happens in an organization is multi-causal, the result of numerous forces acting in and on the organization. In any change effort, OD practitioners consider that when one part of the organization is changed, others will be impacted, and those parts, in turn, will impact the part being changed.

Feedback. Organizations get information from their environments about how their outputs are received. The information comes in many forms: dollars received for products or services, increased interaction with the other organizations, customer feedback, competitor countermeasures, and others.

Systems Within Systems. OD practitioners see at least five levels of a system active in organizations: individual, group, intergroup, organization, and organization-environment. Other subsystems may be conceived around organizational processes such as product development, manufacturing, human resources, accounting, and numerous other functions and processes, or informal aspects of organization such as group affiliations, politics, and leadership. Changes in one part of a system are seen as having an impact on other levels and subsystems.

Change Theory

OD practitioners need a set of assumptions and propositions about how systems change. Kurt Lewin, the social scientist most identified with planned organizational change, used his field theory to understand how forces in a system could be "unfrozen" and shifted to bring about system change and a new system "equilibrium" (Lewin, 1951). Since Lewin's original work, other theories of change have been incorporated into OD practice—theories centered around loss (Tannenbaum, 1976); large system change (Beckhard and Harris, 1977); transformation (Adams, 1984); learning organizations (Senge, 1990); "new sciences" of quantum physics, self-organizing systems, and chaos (Wheatley, 1994); the social construction of reality (Watkins and Mohr, 2001; Srivastva and Cooperrider, 1990); and complex adaptive systems (Olson and Eoyang, 2001), to name some of the most well known. Each shift in perspective has led to innovations in OD practice.

Supplemental Theories

Contemporary OD work is multidisciplined and multifocused. Not surprisingly, in specific aspects of their work OD practitioners draw upon theories from such behavioral sciences as psychology (Segal, 1996), social psychology (Katz and Kahn, 1978), organization theory and design (Morgan, 1997; Bolman and Deal, 1997; Galbraith, 1977; Grenier and Metes, 1995), and the variety of research and concepts within them as well as other related behavioral science disciplines. In addition, OD consultants practicing in specific practice areas, such as executive coaching (Goldsmith, Lyons, and Freas, 2000), team building (Katzenbach and Smith, 1993; Lipnack and Stamps, 2000), diversity (Cross, Katz, Miller, and Seashore, 1994), process consultation (Schein, 1998), large group interventions (Bunker and Alban, 1997), sociotechnical redesign (Passmore and Sherwood, 1978), and large systems change (Beckhard and Harris, 1977)—to cite examples from various levels of systems in organizations—have generated theory and concepts that support the work in their areas of practice.

Values, Ethics, and Practice Theories

When OD practitioners put theory into practice, their actions are moderated by the values they hold, ethical guidelines they understand to be commonly held by practitioners of their craft, and those practice theories that the practitioner has learned to rely on over time.

Values. With its strong roots in social change, the human potential movement, and organizational participation, OD espouses values related to human development, social justice, and participation (Gellermann, Frankel, and Ladenson, 1990). OD practitioners generally believe these values to be in harmony with optimal organization performance, but they sometimes find them in conflict with forces at work in contemporary organizations.

Ethics. Ethics, as used in the map, differ from values and attitudes. They are publicly agreed on, and publicly stated, guidelines for practice in a profession. There have been significant efforts to formulate statements of ethics for OD (Gellermann, Frankel, and Ladenson, 1990). Yet because OD has resisted the impulse to formalize its practice as a profession, there is no generally accepted statement of ethics for OD. Nevertheless, in any roomful of OD practitioners, it is likely that one would find many shared practice guidelines. They follow from the roots of OD honoring the quality of relationship between client and practitioner, authenticity, healthy human development, healthy human system behavior, and the imperative to do no harm.

Practice Theories. Practice theories are those sets of beliefs and assumptions that practitioners actually use to make decisions about the *what* and *why* of human systems and what should be done to bring about change. Distinct from the more formal core and supplemental theories that are taught and shared through the literature of OD, practice theories may be within or outside one's awareness. Indeed, practitioners often rely on assumptions and principles that are acted on out of "gut intuition." Regardless, when push comes to shove these are the maxims, large and small, that guide one's behavior. Some examples offered by colleagues are "Always have an appropriate level of sponsorship for an intervention," "Understand the business drivers for change," and "A certain level of pain or dissatisfaction with the status quo is necessary for change to occur."

OD: The "Big I" Intervention

OD is often characterized by its events. Organization development has evolved a wonderfully diverse array of technologies: team-building exercises, self-assessment instruments, approaches to process consultation, large- and small-group processes for problem solving, data-gathering methods, visioning and coaching methodologies, and more. These tools, often included in OD text chapters titled "interventions," have been developed by OD practitioners over the past fifty years. Unfortunately, OD's increasing focus on these interventions, the fact that participation in them is often the only contact that clients have with OD, and practitioner specialization have led to a widely held misperception of OD as a toolbox of techniques and events.

The OD Map distinguishes these tools of OD from the larger meaning of OD intervention by introducing the concept of the "big I." The big I represents OD intervention as *artful interaction with the client system in which the organization moves from its current state to some desired state*. It is at once system, process, and outcome-focused. From the first client contact, throughout the consultation to the last contact, the practitioner is constantly aware that she or he is intervening in the client system. The action research process operates between the client and practitioner *within* each phase as well as *across* the phases.

Careful attention is given to building a trusting and effective relationship with members of the client system and to building an organizational environment in which collaborative work can take place. Conscious choices are made about where and when to take next steps. Client system concerns are anticipated and efforts are made to get behind them. Opportunities for increased awareness and issue clarification are engaged in the moment. Each individual and group interaction is conducted with a view toward building trust and readiness for subsequent work. The OD practitioner is always looking forward and backward in the OD process, asking questions: "How does this work contribute to the overall goals?" "What do we think we can accomplish at this time?" "What can we achieve?" "Where is there a need for involvement?" "What data would be helpful in the moment?" "What voices need to be heard?" "When should they be involved?" "How should they be involved?" This constant, purposeful attention to developing the client-practitioner relationship and to systemic change is the power of the OD process.

OD Phases, Phase Tasks, and Competencies

The OD consulting phases follow an action research sequence and process. Although they are presented serially in the map, in practice these activities and consulting functions may be recycled and revisited many times in an OD consulting engagement. There are also times when the work may play out as phases within phases, as when a practitioner collects preliminary data to help define a more specific contract with a client, or when a specific intervention is being designed as part of a larger change effort and this intervention requires its own contracting and data-collection process. In other instances, such as use of large-group interventions, most of the phases may be carried out in association with a single event (Bunker and Alban, 1997). The map describes consulting work associated with each major phase of the OD process. Obviously, the listed tasks, though characteristic of each phase, are not exclusive to that phase; many of them are also operative in other phases of the consulting process.

Entry and Contracting

Entry and contracting begins with the initial contact between client and practitioner and is completed when there is a contract: an agreement about the desired outcomes for the consultation, the work that will be done to accomplish the outcomes, the role each party will play in completing the work, and the financial and other business terms of the consulting relationship. Believed by most practitioners to be critical to success in the OD process, contracting establishes both the task and the relationship foundation for the consultation. This is critical because the OD process is one in which client and practitioner must discover, learn, and act together to bring about desired changes. Important questions are answered: "What is the problem that the client is experiencing or the opportunity to be pursued?" "What would the client like to have changed?" "Who is, or should be, the actual client for this work?" "Who needs to support it?" "What is the level of readiness for change in the client system?" "What is the level of commitment of the client and the practitioner to this work?" "Who will do what, where, and when in the course of the consultation?" "What are the business arrangements: fees, support to be provided by the client, and so on?" Answers to these questions may shift during the consultation, and it is not unusual for practitioner and client to recontract a number of times over its course.

Practitioner competencies in the entry-and-contracting phase support his or her capacity to listen to and understand client concerns, elicit important aspects of the client's situation that will affect how the OD work is accomplished, articulate practitioner needs in the relationship, negotiate a satisfactory agreement, and build a solid relational foundation with the client. As such, these competencies help build the level of trust between client and practitioner that is necessary to support information sharing and ownership of change goals and tasks.

Data Collection

True to its action research roots, OD practice is data-based. With a few arguable exceptions, all OD work has at its core generating data that become the catalyst for change in the client system. Chris Argyris has described the essence of intervention as (1) providing valid information, (2) presenting it to the client in such a way as to foster free and informed choice, and (3) conducting the process in a way that builds and maintains commitment (Argyris, 1970). Purposeful choices are made in data collection: What information to collect? Who and how many to involve? Data collection instruments (surveys, interviews, focus groups, workshops) and processes are crafted to get good information *and* build trust in the practitioner(s) and the process. To build trust, the practitioner demystifies the data-collection process, assures participants of anonymity in reports of their data, and helps them receive feedback on the results.

Two key capabilities are required of the practitioner in the data-collection phase. The first is technical skill in data-gathering methods and processes (for example, constructing open- and closed-ended questionnaires, developing interview or focus group protocols; and participant observation). Second, the OD practitioner must get good information while at the same time build commitment to the OD effort. Conducting meaningful and engaging interviews with individuals and groups, facilitating workshop data-collection methods, and masterfully introducing questionnaires to a large population of responders ensures that quality information is collected and the OD effort has credibility with those who produce and use the data.

Data Analysis

In the data-analysis phase information is summarized in ways that are useful to the OD change effort. Where quantitative data have been collected, there may be a need for number crunching. In other instances (for example, a team-building engagement), data are often collected and analyzed qualitatively in open-ended interviews and then summarized by themes. Some workshop designs engage participants in analyzing their own data as part of their workshop process. OD data analysis is constructed with an awareness of how it will affect the client (Nadler, 1977; Block, 2000). Information is summarized to act as a catalyst for choice and action. Themes are highlighted. Differences between the ideal and current situations and across groups are compared and contrasted. Recently, informed by postmodern insights into the power of language and research on the energizing impact of envisioning the future, OD has developed ways of helping clients focus on their aspirations, designing data-collection processes such as those found in search conferences that rely heavily on intuition and heart (Weisbord and Janoff, 2000). Similarly, appreciative inquiry helps organization members explore the "life giving energy" in their best work and life experiences (Watkins and Mohr, 2001).

Data analysis is supported by the practitioner's theoretical and analytic capacities. The content and process of the data collection and analysis are largely guided by one's assumptions about how systems work and how change takes place, as well as those supplemental theories practitioners carry in their practice theory repertoire.

Feedback

Feedback is the spark plug for the OD change engine. Beginning with its early roots in T-group learning and survey feedback, feedback processes have served as a catalyst for collaborative change. Because feedback is viewed as such a powerful process in OD, it is choreographed. The feedback event, most often a face-to-face gathering of client system members, is carefully planned to support the important conversations that follow from the client's engagement with their data. The OD practitioner attempts to provide a nondefensive, nonreactive environment in which participants can take in (own) the data, hear each others' views about them, and move toward understanding and action.

Action Planning

Action planning follows from feedback, and the two processes are often combined. Action planning is a collaborative effort between practitioner and client. It may be done on the spot in large group meetings, by a planning group in follow-up, or by responsible managers who are the primary clients for the consultation. In this phase, clients and practitioner plan action steps that will promote progress toward change goals.

OD practitioners rely upon their theory base to guide action planning. They also rely upon their client's understanding of the organization and its readiness for change. OD practitioners bring to the action-planning process an expert understanding of collaborative processes for action in organizations (the little i's that make up the action-taking phase).

Action Taking

Action steps are implemented in the action-taking phase. These steps may be as simple as carrying out problem-solving measures developed in the action-planning process or as complex as concurrently implementing a multitude of small-i OD technologies. These small i's (which have such names as training, coaching, team building, conflict resolution, quality circles, third-party consultation, and sociotechnical work redesign, to cite just a few) are generally bounded in time, space, and participation (Cummings and Worley, 2004).

Action taking calls upon the practitioner to conduct collaborative learning and problem-solving events. This requires design skills to create small group and large group collaborative structures and processes, facilitation skills to manage conflict and consensus with small and large groups, and up-front platform skills to present data and concepts. Masterful OD work in the action-taking phase is supported by solid knowledge of process in small and large groups, how change is resisted by individuals and groups, and learning theory.

Evaluation

Typically, evaluation receives less attention in OD than do other phases of the process. Some regard this as evidence of OD's unwillingness to look objectively at the effectiveness of its consulting engagements—the bottom-line impact on customer or stakeholder satisfaction, profitability, and quality of work life. This is a legitimate criticism. Sometimes, OD fads have been promoted without a careful look at their effectiveness. Nonetheless, some OD efforts do include evaluation components. Evaluation procedures and protocols are established early in the consultation and carried out independently of other consulting activities.

However, evaluation in OD is typically more nuanced than in other settings. Evaluation protocols may be difficult to maintain in OD work. The ongoing OD process often reveals problems, issues, or factors not seen early on that shift desired outcomes. Occasionally the benefits of an OD effort are not realized until some time after it is completed. Furthermore, even when standard measures of organizational performance are improved in conjunction with an OD effort, it may be difficult to prove a direct connection, given the multivariant nature of cause and effect in most human systems. Finally, effective big I work implies that evaluation is ongoing and results from effective collaboration between practitioner and client(s). Desired outcomes are made clear in the beginning of the relationship and revisited as necessary as the process proceeds. The practitioner and client reflect together on the effectiveness of their actions at all phases of the consultation, learning and making ongoing adjustments.

OD practitioners need an understanding of recognized evaluation practices. If they are not competent to carry them out, they must be able to work with those who *can* do this work. In service of their own learning and the client's, OD practitioners must be able to conduct backward-looking assessments of the OD effort. Most important, OD practitioners must have the capacity to develop trusting and open relationships with their clients that enable ongoing evaluation of the work and its effectiveness in achieving the consultation goals.

Termination

OD practitioners must pay attention to the beginning, middle, and end of their work with clients. Termination happens at the end of a project and at the end of a consulting relationship. In each case the client and practitioner finish their work together with a conscious attention to ending issues: attending to loose ends, clarifying work that may need to take place in the future, and resolving as much as possible any interpersonal issues that may remain from the work that has been done. Where new work emerges as one consulting effort is completed, that beginning is also recognized and clarified through a new contracting process.

Use of Self

Perhaps the most unique and exciting aspect of OD consulting is its intentional use of self as an instrument of change: "The use of self is defined as the way in which one acts upon one's observations, values, feelings, and so forth, in order to have an effect on the other" (Nevis, 1987, p. 125). The OD Map lists a number of important aspects of self (though certainly not all) that are used in effective OD practice. More than any other components of the map, these aspects of self operate as a whole, with the parts only slightly related to the consulting phase for which they are listed, as represented by the dotted-line boundary that surrounds them.

OD Practitioner as Awareness Expert

This concept, originally introduced by Gestalt-oriented OD practitioners, highlights the practitioner's "awareness creating" function (Nevis, 1987). The practitioner uses his or her own awareness of internal feelings (anxiety, joy, fear), body sensations, and shifts in attention to "get curious" about what might be going on in the client system and what they (the clients) are experiencing. The practitioner also looks outward to the client system for clues about what might be going on in it: body postures, who talks when to whom, the physical surroundings, and other less obvious data sources. Practitioners may structure opportunities for the client system to get curious about what it is experiencing with regard to the change process, using awareness to move the process forward. In each case, awareness is valued for its capacity to help clients (and practitioners) better understand their needs and act upon them.

Practitioner Style

OD consulting is a performance. Practitioners develop a style. Each style carries with it strengths and weaknesses. A good practitioner learns to use her or his strengths in ways that benefit the client–practitioner relationship and to manage those situations in which the style is less effective. Ed Nevis, a leading thinker in Gestalt approaches to OD, describes "evocative" and "provocative" uses of practitioner influence (Nevis, 1987). Evocative modes of influence seek to get the client system interested in its own behavior so that client action can emerge. In contrast to the emergent evocative approach, a provocative mode of influence is intended to make things happen; it ranges from behaviors designed to elicit specific responses from the client to more confrontational approaches to which "the client can hardly avoid responding" (Nevis, 1987, p. 128).

Practitioner Biases: Values, Insight, and the Value of Multiple Frames

OD practitioners see through their own worldview. They work within an OD value set that historically has prized personal growth and potential, individual freedom and responsibility, justice, participation, authenticity, honesty, openness in human relationships, and healthy human systems that serve both organizational and individual needs (Gellermann, Frankel, and Ladenson, 1990). OD practitioners also work out of their own unique value set, which may include personal stances on issues such as diversity, social justice, management versus labor interests, and myriad other value choices. OD practitioners seek to remain aware of their values and how they have an impact on their consulting work. In some instances where the practitioner's values feel incompatible with those of the client system, the practitioner may withdraw from consulting projects. Most OD practitioners seek to hold a number of conceptual lenses for their work, using these multiple frames to see a variety of ways to help the client system achieve its change goals.

The Integrated Practitioner

Masterful OD practitioners operate out of an integration of mind, body, and spirit. They work to develop both their thinking and feeling functions. They use their head to apply their knowledge of human and organizational behavior for analytical tasks in the consulting process; they use their emotions to respond with empathy and understanding when called on for emotional support or confrontation, rather than rational analysis.

The Practitioner as an Authentic, Nonreactive Presence

OD consulting done well can be emotionally risky. OD practitioners often find themselves in situations of conflict or strong emotionality. Clients may be unappreciative when confronted with information disconfirming their own views. They may project onto the practitioner issues and problems that are rightfully their own as they deal with anxiety that the process is evoking for them. OD practitioners need to maintain a nonreactive stance—that is, not get hooked by the emotional contagion that is sometimes played out in the systems in which they are working. Consequently, OD practitioners must do their own personal work, developing an understanding of their own hot buttons and a capability to remain emotionally neutral while staying authentically engaged with members of their client organizations.

The Practitioner as Learner

OD practitioners realize that they, like their clients, are in a growth process. Each engagement, whether successful or less than successful, brings its own learning opportunity. Learning adds to the practitioner's practice theories about organizations and change ("Now I see how leadership can be employed in this kind of situation!") and to the practitioner's understanding of his or her own capabilities as a practitioner ("Next time, I'll know not to give in so easily to the client's resistance!" and "What is it about this situation that caused me to give in so easily?").

The Future of OD: Essence out of Paradox

OD is living its future in paradox. Communication and data management technologies have produced information-rich environments for organizations, but people who use them are often on information overload. Information networks—voice, message, and data—link organization members instantly across the globe, but organizations often lack the trust to effectively take advantage of this capability. Today's competitive environment requires speed and flexibility, but organizations have difficulty engendering needed commitment from employees beleaguered by ever-changing structures, technologies, and work processes. Global corporations can leverage placing parts of their business anywhere in the world, but they must navigate significant cultural differences to get the whole to work with the parts. Knowledge management hardware and software put important information literally at the fingertips of organization members, but the human system interface lags far behind the capabilities of the technology. Merciless global competition forces organizations to reduce overhead and speed up work cycles, but as they do they lose the time and resources to reflect on their work processes and develop necessary human capital.

Like the organizations it serves, OD is also facing challenges from the contemporary organizational milieu. The sequential, linear process represented in the map, which can require extended data gathering, analysis, and feedback cycles and face-to-face meetings, is often too slow for today's fast-cycle organizations. Today's data are often tomorrow's old news. In response to these challenges, OD practitioners have developed large-group technologies, such as Search Conferences and Future Search, that bring the whole system into the room and carry out much of the data gathering, analysis, feedback, and problem solving at one place and time (Emery and Purser, 1996; Weisbord and Janoff, 2000; Bunker and Alban, 1997). Increasingly, organizations exist in virtual space. Global teams form, do their work, and never meet face to face; so OD practitioners have shifted attention to building teams in virtual, networked environments (Lipnack and Stamps, 2000). Supply chain software integrates development, manufacturing, and sales functions from around the world, and there is increased need to help members of distant, distinct organizations cross culture, distance, and workgroup boundaries.

Contemporary organizations require high trust, widely and freely shared information, and flexibility in work roles. These are all characteristics that OD has a proven capability to develop in organizations. The heart of the action research process—bringing forth information that increases the capability for free choice and commitment—remains a powerful vehicle for organizational learning and change, though it will more likely be carried out using new tools (such as electronic surveys, online performance indicators and feedback mechanisms, information databases, and knowledge management infrastructures). Future practitioners must deliver the core OD processes of relationship building, data creation, analysis, and feedback in alignment with contemporary organizational milieus and strategy. Consulting phases may be compressed or modified, but the essential OD functions will remain the critical value-added of the OD process. Although the range of internal and external practitioner contacts can be greatly expanded via the Internet, the need to build trusting, open relationships with clients will be as strong as ever. OD value stances regarding human development and social justice will be challenged anew in the face of global competition that creates new haves and have-nots, raises worldwide environmental issues, and calls for new understanding of differences across cultures and national boundaries. OD is entering an era as challenging and full of opportunities as when, early on, it was introduced in top-down, authority-driven organizations.

The future of OD lies with its ability to hold to its core legacies—taking a systems view, linking theory to practice, collaboration, experimentation, learning, dedication to human potential—*and* the capability of its practitioners to reinvent their organizational work in the context of today's human systems challenges.

References

Adams, J. (1984). *Transforming work: A collection of organizational transformation readings.* Alexandria, VA: Miles River Press.

Argyris, C. (1970). *Intervention theory and methods: A behavioral science view.* Reading, MA: Addison-Wesley.

Beckhard, R., & Harris, R. (1977). *Organizational transition: Managing complex change* (2nd ed.). Reading, MA: Addison-Wesley.

Block, P. (2000). *Flawless consulting: A guide to getting your expertise used* (2nd ed.). San Francisco: Jossey-Bass/Pfeiffer.

Bolman, L., and Deal, T. (1997). *Reframing organizations: Artistry, choice and leadership.* San Francisco: Jossey-Bass.

Bunker, B., & Alban, B. (1997). *Large group interventions: Engaging the whole system for rapid change.* San Francisco: Jossey-Bass.

Clark, P. (1972). *Action research and organizational change.* New York: HarperCollins.

Cross, E., Katz, J., Miller, F., & Seashore, E. (1994). *The promise of diversity: Over 40 voices discuss strategies for eliminating discrimination in organizations.* New York: Irwin.

Cummings, T., & Worley, C. (2004). *Organization development and change* (8th ed.). Florence, KY: South-Western Educational.

Emery, M., & Purser, R. (1996). *The Search Conference: A powerful method for planning organizational change and community action.* San Francisco: Jossey-Bass.

French, W. L., & Bell, C. H. (1998). *Organization development: Behavioral science interventions for organization improvement* (6th ed.). Upper Saddle River, NJ: Prentice Hall.

Galbraith, J. R. (1977). *Organization design.* Reading, MA: Addison-Wesley.

Gellermann, W., Frankel, M., & Ladenson, R. (1990). *Values and ethics in organization and human systems development: Responding to dilemmas in professional life.* San Francisco: Jossey-Bass.

Goldsmith, M., Lyons, L., & Freas, A. (Eds.). (2000). *Coaching for leadership: How the world's greatest coaches help leaders learn.* San Francisco: Jossey-Bass/Pfeiffer.

Grenier, R., & Metes, G. (1995). *Going virtual: Moving your organization into the 21st century.* Upper Saddle River, NJ: Prentice Hall.

Katz, D., & Kahn, R. (1978). *The social psychology of organizations.* New York: Wiley.

Katzenbach, J., & Smith, D. (1993). *The wisdom of teams.* Boston: Harvard Business School Press.

Lewin, K. (1951). *Field theory in social science.* New York: HarperCollins.

Lipnack, J., & Stamps, J. (2000). *Virtual teams: People working across boundaries with technology.* New York: Wiley.

Morgan, G. (1997). *Images of organization.* Thousand Oaks, CA: Sage.

Nadler, D. (1977). *Feedback and organization development: Using data-based methods.* Reading, MA: Addison-Wesley.

Nevis, E. (1987). *Organizational consulting: A Gestalt approach.* New York: Gardner Press.

Olson, E., & Eoyang, G. (2001). *Facilitating organization change: Lessons from complexity science.* San Francisco: Jossey-Bass.

Oshry, B. (1995). *Seeing systems: Unlocking the mysteries of organizational life.* San Francisco: Berrett-Koehler.

Passmore, W., & Sherwood, J. (1978). *Sociotechnical systems: A sourcebook.* San Diego: University Associates.

Schein, E. (1998). *Process consultation revisited: Building the helping relationship.* Reading, MA: Addison-Wesley.

Segal, M. (1996). *Points of influence: A guide to using personality theory at work.* San Francisco: Jossey-Bass.

Senge, P. (1990). *The fifth discipline: The art and practice of the learning organization.* New York: Doubleday/Currency.

Srivastva, S., & Cooperrider, D. (1990). *Appreciative management and leadership: The power of positive thought and action in organizations.* San Francisco: Jossey-Bass.

Tannenbaum, R. (1976). Some matters of life and death. *OD Practitioner, 8*(1), 1–7.

Von Bertalanffy, L. (1976). *General systems theory: Foundations, development, applications* (rev. ed.). New York: Braziller.

Watkins, J., & Mohr, B. (2001). *Appreciative inquiry: Change at the speed of imagination.* San Francisco: Jossey-Bass/Pfeiffer.

Weisbord, M., and Janoff, J. (2000). *Future search* (2nd ed.). San Francisco: Berrett-Koehler.

Wheatley, M. (1994). *Leadership and the new science: Learning about organization from an orderly universe.* San Francisco: Berrett-Koehler.

CHAPTER TEN

ENTRY AND CONTRACTING PHASE

Susan M. Gallant and Daisy Ríos

The entry and contracting phase of the organization development (OD) process sets the stage for the later phases of diagnosis, intervention, evaluation, and termination. During this first phase, there are many areas to be methodically and deliberately assessed. The client has a story to be told and a problem to be solved. Training, wisdom, and skill can establish a working relationship that blossoms into a successful and rewarding engagement.

The outcomes of the entry and contracting phase are to:

- Develop a solid working relationship between the client and the OD practitioner
- Make a joint decision about whether to go forward with the consultation
- Prepare a written contract for the consultation
- Build the foundation for the remaining phases of the OD process

Success in this phase is based on four assumptions:

1. There is a direct relationship between how well the OD practitioner completes the tasks of this phase of the OD process and the effectiveness of the overall consultation. It is the keystone for success of the entire OD process.

2. Clients, on some level, know what they need and how to go about getting it. The practitioner's job is to help them discover that, and liberate and transform energy in order to support the wisdom that resides with the client.

3. Energy is a critical element in creating the fuel needed for change. Consider it the oxygen that combines with heat and combustible materials to produce the fire. Concretely, energy can be seen as awareness, development, conflict, deflection, holding back, taking initiative, accountability, and simplified decision making.

4. The process of entry and contracting is the same for internal practitioners and external practitioners. What varies are specific strategies and tactical tasks based on the situation.

Creating an environment where honesty, inventiveness, inspired intellect, and decisiveness are honored and practiced facilitates discovery, purposeful action, and healthy relationships—all that is needed for a successful consulting engagement.

Overview

The entry and contracting phase of the consulting process comprises four stages—preentry, entry, contracting, and transition—as shown in Figure 10.1. Like the overall OD process, the entry and contracting phase is an iterative process of inquiry and action. At each stage, the OD practitioner decides whether to proceed, recycle through the previous stage(s), or say no to the work. The tasks of each stage must be sufficiently completed to move to the next stage. As new information emerges, there can be a cycling back to ensure that adjustments are made, highlighting the reality that contracting and recontracting is a process, not an event.

FIGURE 10.1. ENTRY AND CONTRACTING PHASE.

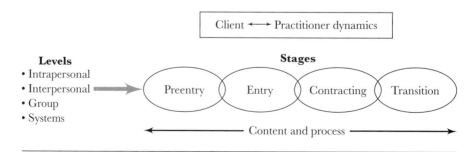

The work of the entry and contracting process takes place in one or more meetings with the client(s), whether face-to-face, by telephone, or by Internet. The process can happen in a thirty-minute meeting, or it can take several meetings over several days. The tasks for the entry and contracting meeting(s) and process are discussed in the next subsections; they are also outlined in Tables 10.1 and 10.2.

The four levels of system shown in Figure 10.1—intrapersonal, interpersonal, group, system and community—can be thought of as lenses that increase or decrease the understanding and the scope of the work. The practitioner and the client may choose to focus on one or more levels of system. All four levels can be operating in each stage of the consulting process. The intrapersonal level includes beliefs, values, principles, attitudes, feelings, preconceptions, perceptions, and assumptions of the organization members and the practitioner. The interpersonal level relates to organization members and the practitioner and who they are in relation to each other (and the practitioner), and to the dynamics among them. The group level relates to who organization members and the practitioner are as members of multiple groups, as well as the dynamics within and between various groups. The system and community level is concerned with the organization as a whole and its culture. It can be the entire community or some subgroup within a larger organizational culture.

Preentry

At preentry, the practitioner and the client are at a threshold, getting ready to step toward each other. At preentry the goal for OD practitioners is to prepare for the practitioner-client meeting(s) by:

- Conducting a practitioner self-assessment of such areas as skill sets, philosophical approach, mission, values, guiding principles, expertise, experience, strengths, style, energy, biases, fears, interests, focus of OD practice, consultant role, competence, traits, and development (Dillon, 2003), as well as assumptions, projections, and feelings about the work, the client, and the client organization.
- Gathering and reviewing available information about the client organization—for example, mission, values, philosophy, history, size, character, structure, products and services, market position, and reputation. Knowledge of the clients' industry and business is an important factor.

Thoughtful consideration of these areas on the part of the practitioner influences the form and nature of entry. If the practitioner does not systematically think through them, unnecessary confusion and ambiguity may result, in tandem with a less-than-effective consultative relationship (Cherniss, 1976).

The practitioner is ready to move from preentry to entry when:

- There is a clear, strong rationale for providing consultation
- The self-assessment has been completed
- Adequate information about the client organization has been gathered and reviewed, and the information indicates a likelihood that the consulting work identified by the client will match the practitioner's skill sets, philosophical approach, and value system.

Entry

The goals of the entry process are to begin building the client-practitioner relationship, identify the client(s), and explore the work to be achieved. This is accomplished by engaging in a process that allows the client to fully express what really matters, their desired client-practitioner relationship, and the outcomes for the work. Effectively managing the entry process and relationship issues helps create conditions for trust, credibility, and predictability that are essential to contracting and to the overall success of the engagement. During the entry stage, the practitioner's focus is on building an effective interpersonal relationship with the client.

The overall outcome of the entry process is a joint client-practitioner decision about whether the relationship is worth pursuing. OD practitioner tasks and actions involved in reaching this outcome are outlined in Table 10.1. They include tasks such as introductions; clarifying meeting boundaries; identifying who the client is; inviting clients to tell their story; inquiring about client wants, expectations, and hopes; examining diversity issues in the client-practitioner relationship and in the client organization; exploring values and ethics; surfacing resistance; and finally, assessing client-practitioner fit and deciding whether to proceed, recycle, or end the consultation. As the practitioner and client engage in these tasks of the entry process, both begin building patterns of relationship.

During entry the client will be looking for clues that the OD practitioner possesses characteristics, values, skills, and experience that support the work to be accomplished. The client observes and senses behaviors, physical presence, energy, confidence, and sense of self. How the practitioner "shows up" sends visible and invisible messages that either assure and comfort the client or potentially disturb the client.

TABLE 10.1. ENTRY PHASE TASKS AND ACTIONS.

Tasks	Actions
1. Do introductions.	Share and acknowledge personal and professional informa- tion for building client-practitioner relationship. Engage client with genuine interest and curiosity. Track what is being said and how information is being shared; attend to process and content; observe information about the culture, morale, and relationships.
2. Clarify meeting boundaries.	Model effective meeting management: time, pace, outcomes, who needs to be present, roles.
3. Identify client(s).	Identify contracting client(s), the client making use of the consultation, and the client with the authority to control the process and implement outcomes.
4. Invite client(s) to tell their story.	Ask questions and seek examples to understand concerns and issues, what the client system wants to change, the need be- hind the request for consultation, other change efforts, cur- rent and previous strategies, successes and failures. Actively listen and reflect back to the client understanding of issues and concerns. Learn, adapt to, and appropriately use the language of the organization.
5. Inquire about client wants, expectations, hopes.	Engage in dialogue about wants, expectations, hopes, fears, and risks for the work and client-practitioner relationship. Attend to feelings in client and in self (warmth, excitement, hostility, disinterest).
6. Explore diversity issues.	Explore client-practitioner differences and how they might affect the work and relationship. Inquire and share about or- ganizational patterns and impact on different groups; what is being tracked, heard, seen, and felt; and the meaning being made of it so far.
7. Explore values and ethics.	Share values and ethical boundaries, and inquire about those for the client. Foresee potential value conflicts or ethical di- lemmas embedded in the consultation, and explore them with the client.
8. Surface resistance.	Explore the forces that will help and hinder success. Identify, name, and explore resistance in self and the client. Inquire about what is not being discussed.
9. Assess client-practitioner fit and decide to pro- ceed, recycle, or tell the client no.	Assess fit between the client and practitioner needs, values, interests, time requirements, credibility, confidence, trust, readiness, and commitment to the work.

To have credibility with the client, the practitioner needs to be perceived as strong, knowledgeable, fair, wise, and ready to take action. Letting go of defensiveness and the need to be right and in control is critical. Curiosity, openness to a creative process, and willingness to access intuitive energy is valuable. Clients expect strength of character and solid knowledge, values, and ethics.

The practitioner's task here is to lead by openly disclosing and consistently telling the truth—simply, clearly, directly, and with optimism. Speaking the truth requires the practitioner to track patterns of behavior, feelings, and ideas and risk sharing with the client what is being observed and felt. Speaking the truth also means being authentic, fully expressing personal values, needs, and wants, not out of a sense of selfishness but from a desire to build a relationship and enhance the work.

During entry, the practitioner influences the client organization and in turn is influenced by it. The entry process is itself an intervention into the client organization. Guided by intellect and intuition, the practitioner's role is to help illuminate what is hidden from the client's awareness. This begins to happen as the client and practitioner engage in building a relationship with each other and in defining the work. The very act of preparing for a change creates heightened awareness and increases understanding of the issues, dilemmas, and concerns each holds, as well as a clearer picture of the work to be undertaken.

Through the process of building relationship, long-held patterns and beliefs that impede movement can be surfaced and explored. Consequently the client can begin to experience new self-awareness and efficacy. Old behavioral patterns or attitudes that get in the way of the work and relationships begin to be released so that more creative ideas and constructive behaviors may emerge.

At entry the client is looking for movement, for tools and ideas to move forward quickly. Clients just want things to work! They may want to rush the work, thinking that somehow things can be rearranged and quickly fixed. They may want to initiate change by starting with what is known, is comfortable, and has worked for them in the past. They desire quick results and change, while simultaneously they may be experiencing some level of ambivalence and confusion about taking real action. This is all to be expected. The practitioner must educate the client about the change process and exhibit a calm, reassuring, and confident stance.

Movement from entry to contracting happens when there is an emerging sense of commitment to change on the part of the client. There is a willingness to express and explore wants, desires, needs, fears, and hopes. There is also an emerging sense of deliberate purpose and a beginning maturity and knowledge of the problem to be solved, the work to be done, and what really matters. Clear intention and equilibrium between understanding and action begins to emerge and serves as an indicator that the practitioner can move into contracting. Clarity is found as to what is really needed and desired in order to develop clear objectives and outcomes to guide the work. Both client and practitioner confirm the assumption that the relationship and work desired by the client match the practitioner's skill sets, philosophical approach, and value system.

The practitioner and client are ready to move to contracting when the entry tasks have been sufficiently completed and the client and practitioner conclude that there is a fit between client and practitioner needs, values, interests, and time requirements; a sense of confidence, trust, and readiness; and strong commitment to the work that has been defined.

Contracting

The goal of the contracting process is to develop a clear, mutually agreed contract, either formal or informal. This contract is fundamental to the success of any change initiative. Through contracting, the energy in the client system is harnessed and brought into focus for the purpose of delineating a plan of action that will sustain the change that is sought. The contracting process brings needed form and structure to the relationship. It sets clear expectations and imparts a sense of assurance that the consultation is going somewhere solid and trustworthy.

The tasks and actions of the contracting process are outlined in Table 10.2. Contracting requires establishing and clarifying expectations, goals, and outcomes of the change effort, working relationship(s), roles, ground rules, consultant support needs, and financial arrangements; defining the scope, specifics, and success requirements of the consulting effort; establishing feedback, evaluation, and termination processes; and finally summarizing the contract and putting it into written form.

TABLE 10.2. CONTRACTING PHASE TASKS AND ACTIONS.

Tasks	Actions
1. Clarify client goals and outcomes.	Collaboratively develop clear statement of consultation goals and outcomes.
2. Describe consultation and requirements for success.	Collaboratively develop description of the consultation or change process; possibilities and dilemmas embedded in it; implications for individual, interpersonal, group, and organization levels of the system; and what is needed from the client, organization, and practitioner for a successful consultation.

TABLE 10.2. CONTRACTING PHASE TASKS AND ACTIONS, Cont'd.

Tasks	Actions
3. Clarify wants, needs, wishes.	Explore and share client and practitioner wants, needs, and wishes for contact, control, information, and involvement in the consultation. Make affirming statements and demonstrate understanding and empathy. Provide reassurance.
4. Clarify roles, responsibilities, commitment.	Clarify and define client and practitioner roles, responsibilities, and levels of commitment. Agree about joint client and practitioner responsibility for consultation outcomes.
5. Define scope of project or consultation.	Collaboratively define the scope of the project, including initial strategies, objectives, steps, critical success factors, stakeholders, participants, products (if any) and deliverable time lines, external factors that can affect the consultation, and who else needs to be involved in defining the details of the project.
6. Negotiate consultation resources.	Negotiate time, money, support services, and involvement of personnel required for successful project completion. Discuss costs openly, including practitioner fee structure, expenses, and payment schedule.
7. Establish process for feedback, evaluation, and termination.	Establish ongoing process for evaluating all aspects of the consultation, including outcomes, deliverables, client-practitioner relationship, and time lines. Provide for recontracting at appropriate intervals. Establish ground rules for terminating the consultation.
8. Summarize contract and put it in written form.	Collaboratively develop a written agreement summarizing the consultation, including client and practitioner expectations, process and scope, outcomes, deliverables, client-practitioner relationship, time lines, nature and frequency of client and practitioner communication, practitioner fee structure, expenses, and payment schedule. Determine next steps: who, what, when, where, how, how much, how long.

Documenting agreements in written form creates an opportunity for both parties to clarify expectations and internalize the level of commitment to the work and the client-practitioner relationship. The written contract creates a shared memory of the dialogue and decisions; it creates another opportunity to affirm the deliverables, roles, timetable, and approach (who, what, when, where, how, how much, and how long). Documentation can be in the form of a memo of understanding, a proposal letter, or a formal contract.

At this stage, the practitioner is required to tap into the knowledge and experience acquired over time, while also staying open to new and exciting possibilities inherent in every consulting relationship. The skill of discernment helps the practitioner integrate methodologies and tools that have worked in the past and create new processes as needed. Full use of self helps to model the competencies needed to continue building on the relationship(s) and formulating a solid contractual arrangement. As in entry, clarification and vigilant management of boundaries is essential.

Entwined within the procedural aspects of contracting are associated psychological aspects, which must also be considered. During contracting, hope and fear about the work and the relationship often coexist simultaneously. Therefore, trust and mutual respect are essential to the relationship and ultimately to the success of the engagement. It is important to remember that what occurred during preentry and entry has already established a complex structure for what is to follow, often predetermining certain consequences during contracting and in the ensuing consulting relationship. Keeping in mind the important events that emerged during preentry and entry facilitates tracking patterns and resolving issues that may emerge.

For contracting to be successful, the client must be determined, be highly committed, have personal involvement, and be invested in and feel ownership of the outcome. Contracts must be mutual, with all parties choosing to enter into them, fully informed. Without mutuality, client ownership and the success of the engagement are in jeopardy. Mutuality must be achieved, or there is no contract. If there is no contract, there is no client or work.

During the process of contracting, there are many areas that have to be methodically and deliberately assessed. The client has a story that wants to be told and a problem to be solved. As the story is elicited, observing, listening, clarifying, tracking patterns, and effective questioning help achieve an accurate assessment. Thoroughness requires time and patience. The client often becomes impatient and wants to move to action, to solve the problem. The practitioner must be careful not to get seduced into moving so fast that important elements affecting the situation are missed.

The client and OD practitioner have a good, solid contract when:

- There are shared expectations of each other, the relationship, and the work to include outcomes and deliverables, resources, participation, access and support, and communication.
- A structure is negotiated—who, what, when, where, how, how much, and for how long.

- Roles are clarified: Who does what? With whom?
- The client and the practitioner have defined how they will work together.
- There is mutual agreement on the proposed approach: how the objectives will be achieved; how the process for data collection and feedback will be determined; how the work will be measured and evaluated; how aspects of the contract can be renegotiated or terminated.
- There is an explicit discussion regarding confidentiality.
- There are clear expectations, and both the client and the practitioner know what actions are expected of them and how to proceed with the work.
- The decision-making process has been outlined and agreed to.
- There is clarity of purpose, confidence, and commitment.

If the practitioner and client have differing understandings, or if an area has not been addressed, they must go back and clarify and review gaps before proceeding to the transition stage. This review process helps guarantee that there is mutual understanding. Clarity and thoroughness are essential at this junction. There may be times when this review highlights areas where there are differences in understanding. In that case, it is important to determine how to bridge the differences. If this is not possible, it may be necessary to make a decision to terminate the consulting relationship.

Transition

Through the contracting process, many boundaries are clarified and agreed to, giving form, stability, and order to the client-practitioner relationship. Transitioning is an opportunity to summarize, reflect, analyze, document, and outline next steps while at the same time staying open to the creative energy, new opportunities, or concerns that sometimes emerge within the safety of the container that has been created.

The purpose of summarizing and reflecting is to be sure that communication has been clear, assumptions are explicit, expectations are shared, and all relevant information has been surfaced and explored. Most failures in OD change efforts occur during the detailed follow-through of the implementation phase. Therefore it is crucial that the practitioner engage as a partner with the client in outlining and making decisions about each step in the agreement, as well as creating mechanisms that support follow-through and successful implementation. These agreements should be part of the contract.

It takes acceptance, willingness, courage, caring, and honesty to engage in a change effort. To demonstrate empathy and build the client-practitioner relationship during the transition stage, it is important to acknowledge the courage involved in the client's risk taking. Both the OD practitioner and client have an opportunity to be transformed by creating trust and safety in the relationship, by being truly authentic with one another, while learning and achieving mutually satisfying goals.

The trail through the entry and contracting phase is replete with opportunities—or clutter, depending on how the terrain is defined and experienced. Areas that must be considered are highlighted in Figure 10.2.

FIGURE 10.2. FACTORS AFFECTING CLIENT-PRACTITIONER DYNAMICS.

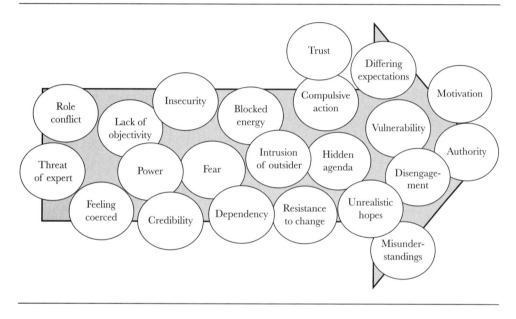

These are the factors that have an impact on client-practitioner dynamics. The factors carry energy and need to be understood within the context of the environment in which they are situated. The practitioner's job is to transform the energy by knowing whether to engage it, quiet it, illuminate it, or give it fire, all in service to the goals (work) and the relationship. This takes wisdom and skill.

Consultant Competencies

Managing the dynamics of the entry and contracting phase requires awareness of several basic theoretical principles and specific practitioner competencies, some of which are discussed here.

Boundaries

Entry and contracting (or reentry and recontracting) requires engagement across a boundary, the place where people meet each other. It is an invisible threshold that allows the consultant to enter the life space of the client and client system, while opening up to be of service. Entering with grace requires mindful, careful, responsible, and intentional behavior.

To effectively manage entry and contracting, the practitioner must maintain both a sense of separateness and a sense of connectedness. Doing this well necessitates vigilant attention to the concept of boundaries—the physical and psychological entities that establish beginning and ending points among people, tasks, time, and territory (adapted from Braxton, 1991). The ability to effectively identify, name, negotiate, influence, and hold boundaries is at the core of entry and contracting.

If a practitioner's own boundaries are too tight or rigid, others can experience the person as too separate, or aloof. This affects the ability to influence and may create difficulty in building one-on-one relationships. Boundaries that are too loose tend to invite being too personal or too involved, thereby creating loss of objectivity.

Resistance

Resistance is a healthy response to change. As such it is unavoidable. Resistance can be understood as feedback or expression of a differing point of view. Individuals and systems that resist do so for very good and varying reasons, all of which are legitimate and necessary precursors to change. The OD practitioner's job is to actively invite, allow space and time, and support open expression of resistance, which will be present in any OD change initiative and any client-practitioner relationship.

Resistance does not always announce itself. Although some aspects of resistance may be communicated directly, others are sometimes unconscious and expressed indirectly. Resistance may show up in the form of direct confrontation, disagreement or denial, questioning, lack of trust, lack of commitment or follow-through, helplessness, confusion, excuses, or blaming.

If a practitioner often views resistance as negative, something to be dreaded, avoided, or suppressed, it is time to reframe how to think about and support this energy, without which there is no change. The skills that are required include genuine curiosity and openness to the resistance in whatever form it emerges; willingness to explore and hang in through emerging conflict and misunderstanding in a respectful manner; communication of genuine interest in understanding; validation of the other's experience; and willingness to solve problems and negotiate. This is all in an effort to build trust, alignment, and commitment while using the energy of resistance to create movement, connection, and positive action.

Polarities

Throughout the entry and contracting process, there is constant tension between many polarities. Polarities are places where the energy and conceptual frameworks that the client and the practitioner bring are not initially aligned—where there seem to be points of disagreement and potential challenge. If explored, polarities can be harmonized or unified and serve as a launching pad for creative and expansive thinking. One of the skills required is the ability to explore and bring polarities into harmony. The client benefits by learning how to hold opposing polarities in right relationship.

Some polarities may become evident in the initial approach to the work. The client may want to focus on swift action. The practitioner, on the other hand, knows that the situation needs to be diagnosed and understood before taking action. As a consequence, the client and practitioner may feel impatient and perhaps at odds with each other, rather than aligned and connected in purpose. Both may begin to wonder if the relationship will benefit either party. It is important to note that both energies (polarities) are required. The practitioner's ability to be aware of and name the dynamic, as well as be inventive about how to harmonize the polarities as they emerge, is critical.

Other polarities include content and process, control and vulnerability, fear and hope, intuition and logic, thought and emotion, dependency and counterdependency, inner experience and outer world, feelings of competence and incompetence, self-focus and other-focus, and focus on different levels of system.

Diversity

Differences are imbedded in all our interactions. There is often a tendency to diminish the importance of differences, preferring instead to focus on similarities. In building relationships, similarities facilitate our ability to move to agreement quickly and easily. However, there is a cost. Whenever differences are ignored, relationships are built on a shaky foundation. Differences such as culture, ethnicity, race, age, class, gender, religion, sexual orientation, language, education, and nationality all have an impact on relationships among individuals. How these differences are valued and talked about either supports or hinders communication, the client-practitioner relationship, and the overall entry and contracting process.

Parallel Process

Attending to parallel processes can help inform and enrich the contracting process. This happens when the OD practitioner notices, observes, and selectively names what is happening in the moment between the practitioner and client (the interpersonal level). The practitioner then encourages, questions, and wonders with the client about how the same dynamic might be operating at the group and systems levels. The practitioner may also track patterns at the systems level and wonder how they are influencing the individual level. Skillfully done, this rooting around can broaden and deepen the mechanics of the contracting process, thus creating a sound assessment, a strong contract, and a healthy relationship.

Dialogue and Communication Skills

Good communication and dialogue skills are the foundation to success—especially the skills of actively listening, suspending judgment, empathizing, probing, clarifying, reflecting and summarizing, and giving and receiving feedback. Using effective communication skills cannot be overemphasized at this stage.

During entry and contracting, there is an opportunity to become familiar with the client's language by reading written materials or simply tracking patterns of verbal and nonverbal communication. Attention to words, tone, metaphors, and other linguistic differences that are peculiar to the client and the industry is essential. This is especially critical when working across cultural and national boundaries.

Effective communication skills are at the heart of competently expressing and working with conflict. Engaging conflict by steering toward it instead of deflecting or ignoring it requires an ability to actively listen while suspending judgment. The skill of bracketing—putting oneself aside for the moment—allows the practitioner to take in the experience of the other. Extending empathy, seeing the world from the other's point of view and acknowledging the person's experience, is a critical skill. Empathy can transform the emotional component of conflict into energy that facilitates productive movement toward shared goals. Being empathic does not necessarily mean agreeing with the other person—just understanding his or her experience and perspective.

Use of Self and Presence

Personal power and a strong sense of self are essential to success as an OD practitioner. Presence includes values, behavior, attitudes, ideas, attributes, emotions, and passion. Being present in any situation means showing up, fully grounded in the physical body, intellectual mind, and spiritual being. In this state, the practitioner is able to access the energy, intuition, and knowledge required to best serve the client. When truly present, practitioners have the ability to build relationship and make truly authentic connections, while at the same time differentiating and defining boundaries.

Strength comes through awareness. Awareness requires the ability to stay in a process of self-discovery in which the practitioner is consciously and continuously assessing his or her stance, and exploring judgments and biases about self and others. In the absence of this focused attention to self, others, and the context, the practitioner may become unable to clearly differentiate self from the client. As a result, the practitioner may lose perspective and clarity, and get hooked—which influences behaviors and is the product of assumptions that are consciously or unconsciously directing beliefs. If practitioners get hooked, they start to function from a reactive or defensive posture. When this happens, it is a sure sign that the practitioner has lost focus, grounding, and balance.

Building Trust

The practitioner must be seen as effective, dependable, and trustworthy. The client's perceptions of the consultant's competence, sincerity, reliability, openness, and concern for others are a few of the many variables that affect trust. The practitioner must be able to influence and negotiate while exhibiting patience, not pushing, pressuring, or manipulating. Trust is at the core of the client-practitioner relationship and is the foundation for meaningful work.

Conclusion

The outcomes of entry and contracting are a solid working relationship between the client and the OD practitioner, a joint decision about whether to go forward with the consultation, a written contract for the consultation, and a solid foundation for the remaining phases of the OD process.

It is relatively straightforward to describe and understand the stages of the entry and contracting process (preentry, entry, contracting, and transition) designed to achieve these outcomes. However, completing the tasks of each stage with the many dynamics (trust, fear, dependency, vulnerability, motivation, resistance, misunderstandings, and others) possibly at play creates a challenge for even the most experienced OD practitioner.

The dynamics all have their own energetic valence. The practitioner needs to be aware of the dynamics at all levels (intrapersonal, interpersonal, group, systems) and navigate the terrain with wisdom, energy, intention, and skill—all in service to the client's desired outcomes.

References

Braxton, E. T. (1991). *Effective management of work groups under conditions of conflict and stress.* Pittsburgh: Edge Associates.

Cherniss, C. (1976). Pre-entry issues in consultation. *American Journal of Community Psychology, 4*(1), 13–24.

Dillon, J. T. (2003, December). The use of questions in organizational consulting. *Journal of Applied Behavioral Science, 39*(4), 438–452.

CHAPTER ELEVEN

ORGANIZATION DIAGNOSIS PHASE

Julie A. C. Noolan

Having successfully navigated the entry and contracting phases, the next step is to conduct a diagnosis of the organization's current and desired states. The procedures used to do this may already have been specified in the contract letter or proposal—an example of how the organization development phases are not as linear as the OD Map. Today's faster-paced and global business environment pressures OD practitioners to minimize the diagnosis stage. However, the availability of newer telecommunications capabilities and real-time data-collection strategies means there are powerful tools for giving diagnosis the critical attention this phase requires.

Some OD practitioners prefer the word *assessment* to diagnosis because they believe that, from the medical field, the word *diagnosis* carries the connotation of disease. The medical field can in fact help make a clear delineation of the diagnostic process. One might go for a checkup to ensure that one is in good shape and needs to continue doing more of the good things, or to discover some areas to pay attention to; organization diagnosis is similar. Diagnosis is the point immediately before having a prescription filled. This chapter views the terms *organization diagnosis, assessment, discovery, analysis,* and *examination* as synonyms. Although each of the eight phases in the OD Map is a form of intervention, the *action-taking* phase is sometimes mistakenly viewed as the only form of intervention. However, the process of data collection, analysis, and feedback can also be a critical intervention (just as having information on one's cholesterol level can lead to a behavior-changing experience).

Here is the definition being used in this section: organization diagnosis is a collaborative process between organization members and the OD practitioner to collect relevant information, organize it, and feed the data back to the client system in such a way as to build commitment, energy, and direction for action planning.

Organization diagnosis determines "what is" and "what could be"; it seeks ways to bridge the gap. It consists of planning to collect data, data collection, analysis, and feedback to the organization, and it forms the basis for determining subsequent interventions (action planning and action taking). The diagnosis can focus on the organization overall or on specific aspects such as organizational culture (Rogers and Byham, 1994) or aspects of diversity (Harrison and Shirom, 1999). Harrison and Shirom suggest that one "start with a broad scan of an organization but then select core problems and organizational challenges for close up examination" (p. 18). Extensive discussion of the diagnostic process is in Levinson (2002), Nadler (1977), Burke (1992, 1994), Harrison (1994), Howard (1994) and Harrison and Shirom (1999).

Open Systems

Systems theory is one of the core theories underlying the OD process. The concept of open systems is particularly applicable in diagnosing an organization. Organizations are generally viewed as complex open systems; that is, their boundaries and environments influence them. Within the boundaries are *inputs* (such as suppliers, sources of funding, government regulations, shareholders), *throughputs* (transformational work processes), and *outputs* (customers, clients, investors), all within the constraints of the environment. All the parts or subsystems work together to achieve the purpose of the whole organization (Swanson and Holton, 1994). They are interdependent in such a way that anything happening to one part of the system can affect other parts of the system. As is explored further in the section discussing diagnostic models, "the open systems frame can help consultants and clients deal with the complexity of organization performance and change and thereby resist the temptation of management fads" (Harrison and Shirom, 1999, p. 42). An open systems model helps OD practitioners focus on all aspects of the organization, not just those parts with which they feel most comfortable. Wolf (1995) argues that most OD practitioners pay insufficient attention to the environment because they are not comfortable with assessing it. Yet if the environment is not conducive to an organization—for example, because the organization is too small to compete—looking at improving the transformational work processes is a futile endeavor.

Perceptual Bias

OD practitioners "play a crucial role in deciding what to study, how to look at chosen phenomena, how to account for them, and how to create images of them for use in diagnostic feedback" (Harrison and Shirom, 1999, p. 18). Particularly in diagnosis, where the practitioner's stance can influence data, self-knowledge is critical. For this reason, the adage *know thyself* is especially applicable. Where one stands often affects what one sees. Being aware of possible causes of bias is the first step in widening the lens to be able to take in more data. Just as it is easier to see things through a clean window rather than a dirty one, our goal as OD practitioners is to be aware of our own mental models, beliefs, heuristics, and other factors that can distort what we see, hear, or experience. The bottom line in dealing with perceptual bias is to try not to jump to assumptions but to keep our mind open, to be aware of what we may not be aware of naturally, and to pay attention to "what is not" as well as to "what is" as the organization diagnosis is conducted.

Diversity Issues in Organization Diagnosis

As new classes of employees (as examples, a more culturally diverse workforce; generational and gender differences) enter the workplace, they may challenge patterns of informal behavior that were once taken for granted, as in conducting business after hours and in all-white male-dominated settings such as bars and golf clubs. Assessment of informal behavior and structures requires more attention to patterns of interaction and interpretation among members of the client system than many open systems models promote (Harrison and Shirom, 1999). In interviewing employees, it is helpful to have interviewers who reflect the client system in gender, race, ethnicity, and so on, or to recognize and address the issue if this is not possible.

Because we operate in a global environment, recognition must be given to cross-national differences. In Asian and Middle Eastern cultures, face saving is a critical part of the culture. To suggest to the client system that its version of the presenting problem is a symptom and not the real root of the issue can be nearly impossible. The concept of feedback presents a similar dilemma. Demographic categories of exempt and nonexempt employees refer to U.S. labor law and are not used elsewhere. When considering using questionnaires or structured interviews in non-English-speaking countries, it is important to recognize that these should not be word-for-word translations but in the idiom of the country. Just as U.S. English is not always the same as Australian or British English, Latin American Spanish is not the same as European Spanish. The best check on ensuring intended meaning is to back-translate the same questions (for example, English translated to Canadian French and translated back to English to see if the real intent has been captured). Another pitfall to avoid is combining data from different countries. Country results are influenced to a great extent by culture; if combined, much of the individual richness will be "averaged" out (S. R. Johnson, 1996).

Diagnostic Models

Most OD practitioners have some implicit (if not explicit) model in their head when they conduct an organizational diagnosis. This section deals with published models that can be used directly, or studied as a way of enlarging the elements that might be included in one's own model. A model is a systematic approach to collecting data; it minimizes bias in what is collected, constitutes a mechanism for data analysis, and provides a common vocabulary for people to use. Lawler believes that survey results have more power if they can be presented through a model or conceptual framework rather than as a plain data readout (Lawler, Nadler, and Cammann, 1980).

There is no one best model. The model used depends on the situation and the practitioner's style and lenses. Burke lists three criteria for selecting a model. First, it should be one that the practitioner thoroughly understands and feels comfortable with. Second, it should fit the client organization as closely as possible—comprehensive enough to cover as many aspects of the organization as appropriate yet simple and clear enough for organization members to grasp fairly quickly. Third, it should be sufficiently comprehensive to enable data to be gathered about the organization according to the model's parameters but without missing key bits of information (adapted from Burke, 1992). Some of the best diagnostic models are quite old, but to paraphrase Mintzberg, sometimes, like good wine, some of the best models are the older ones (Mintzberg, Ahlstrand, and Lampel, 1998, pp. 8–9).

A 1999 survey of diagnostic models in use found that the Weisbord Six Box Model was the most frequently used (25 percent of respondents), followed by the McKinsey Seven S Model (19 percent), Galbraith's STAR Model (10 percent), and Nadler and Tushman's Congruence Model (10 percent). All are open systems models. OD practitioners rarely used the Malcolm Baldrige National Quality Award criteria (N. D. Samuels, personal communication, Jan. 20, 1999).

Here I present several models, each with its own advantages and disadvantages. The selection is on the basis of those most frequently used; the first three build on each other and are open systems models. The Four Frames Model looks at organizations from a very different perspective, and the final one, the Weisbord Six Box model, is older but is most frequently used. In teaching an Organization Diagnosis course for NTL Institute, where participants go through the experience of applying the range of models described here to a real-time client situation, all the models have been found to yield surprisingly consistent results.

The Nadler-Tushman Congruence Model (Nadler and Tushman, 1980) is a more traditionally represented open systems model with *inputs* (including the environment, resources, and history) that shape the *strategy*. The strategy then drives the *transformative work processes* box, which leads to the *outputs*, differentiated into organizational, group, and individual outputs. A *feedback* loop flows from the output box back to the input box. Four categories are included in the work transformation process: informal organization, formal organizational arrangements, individual (people), and task (work; see Figure 11.1). It is called the congruence model because it is built on the belief that, particularly in the work transformation area, the four categories should be congruent, or fit, with each other. In the short run, congruence can lead to improved effectiveness and performance, but in the longer run congruence can fuel resistance to change—a reality recognized by its authors in subsequent writings.

FIGURE 11.1. NADLER-TUSHMAN CONGRUENCE MODEL.

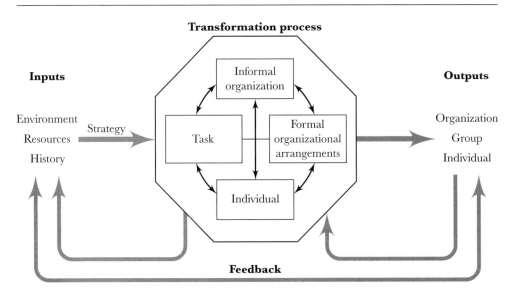

Source: Reprinted from *Organizational Dynamics,* Vol. 9, David A. Nadler and Michael L. Tushman, "A Model for Diagnosing Organizational Behavior," 1980, 35–51, with permission from Elsevier.

The Nadler-Tushman model is briefly presented here because it serves as a simple introduction to the next model, a very similar but more complex one.

The Freedman Swamp Model of Sociotechnical Systems (Freedman, 2003) looks complicated at first, because it makes explicit many of the categories, linkages, and boundaries that occur in an organization. At its center are the work transformation processes (*production*), including the services that support the work processes (human resources, structure, technology, finance). They are driven by the *strategic direction* of the organization and exist within a culture and an organizational climate. The strategic direction is derived from input stakeholders such as suppliers, regulators, investors, market information, and environmental trends. On the output side are clients, customers, investors, and regulators. Leadership manages both within the work transformation areas and the boundaries with the input and output stakeholders. A feedback loop reports variances not only to the inputs but also to each of the categories within the work transformation processes (see Figure 11.2).

FIGURE 11.2. FREEDMAN: SWAMP MODEL OF SOCIOTECHNICAL SYSTEMS.

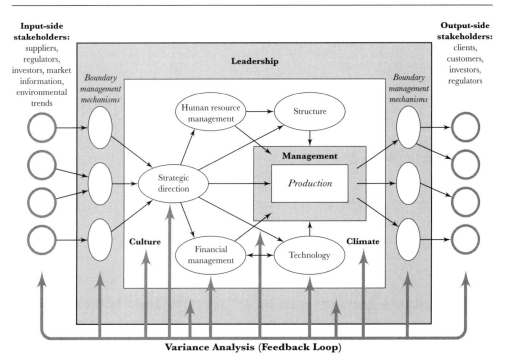

Source: Reprinted with permission of Arthur Freedman. Included in Noolan, J.A.C. (Compiler). (2003). *Diagnosing organizations with impact: Workbook,* section 2, p. 26. Alexandria, VA: NTL Institute.

Most people working with this model find that at first glance it is complicated, but once they start working with it, the comprehensiveness is attractive.

The Burke-Litwin Model (Burke, 1992) is also an open systems model, but unlike the Nadler-Tushman or Freedman models it is presented vertically in order to make a statement about how organizational change is effected (see Figure 11.3).

FIGURE 11.3. THE BURKE-LITWIN MODEL OF INDIVIDUAL AND ORGANIZATION PERFORMANCE.

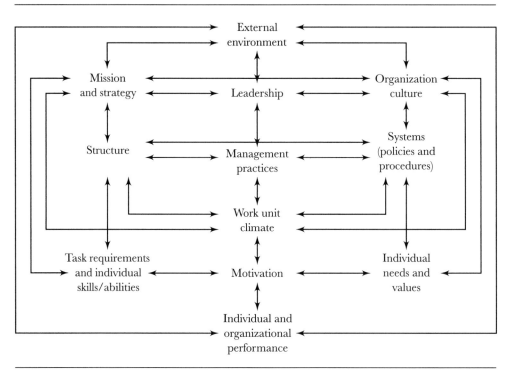

Source: Copyright 1992, W. Warner Burke Associates, Inc.

Burke believes that "organizational change stems more from environmental impact than from any other factor," which is why he puts it at the top of his model. Moreover, he sees the *external environment, mission and strategy, leadership,* and *organizational culture* as the primary levers for major organizational change, or transformational change. He sees the remaining elements in his model as levers for transactional change, for fine-tuning and improving the organization's existing behavior. Arrows connecting various elements in the model add to both its complexity and its richness and reinforce the open systems point that change in one part of the system may ultimately affect other parts of the system.

Human performance improvement models are also useful open systems diagnostic models, although the diagnosis is usually seen as preparatory to job or task analysis (Swanson and Holton, 1994; Rummler and Brache, 1995).

Weisbord's Six Box Model, although criticized by some as being too simplistic, is the one most frequently used because it is easily understood by practitioners and client organizations alike (Weisbord, 1976; see Figure 11.4).

FIGURE 11.4. WEISBORD SIX BOX MODEL.

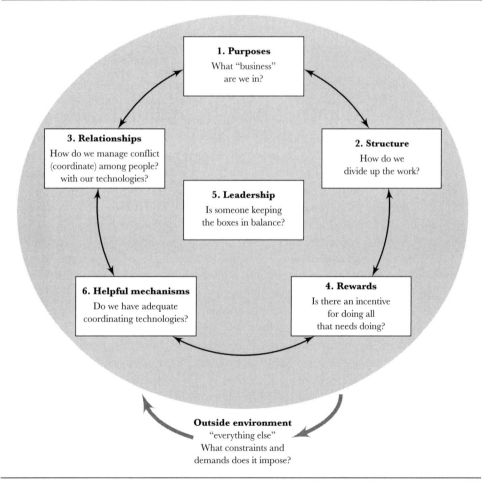

Source: Marvin R. Weisbord, *Organizational Diagnosis: A Workbook of Theory and Practice.* Copyright 1978 by Marvin R. Weisbord. Reprinted by permission of Perseus Books PLC, a member of Perseus Books, L.L.C.

Weisbord likens his model to a radar screen, where five categories of information are watched by the leadership (which is a separate category or box) for anomalies, within a boundary that is permeable to the *environment*. Each box is examined to determine what the formal system says should happen, and what actually happens (the informal system). In addition, the gaps between what is and what could or ought to be are identified. The first box to be examined is *purposes,* or mission. Is this clear and is it understood and bought into by the employees? Next he examines *structure*: how the work gets divided up, and whether it makes sense given the purpose. *Helpful mechanisms* asks if the organization has adequate coordinating technologies. The *rewards* box examines whether all the needed tasks have incentives. Rewards support or get in the way of achieving the task; for example, an organization that places high value on its service engineers contributing to a knowledge database but only rewards them on the basis of service calls made clearly does not have a fit between individual and institutional goals.

Relationships refers primarily to how units are coordinated, or not, and can give rise to conflict. It also refers to the role of technology in carrying out the work of the organization. The *leadership* box is addressed last, because Weisbord sees the role of leadership as watching for the blips in the other five boxes to ensure they are in balance, and if not then to take corrective action. For each of the six boxes, a series of key diagnostic questions are asked that supply the diagnostic data (Weisbord, 1978). The six-box model is well known and easy to explain to the client. Its disadvantages are that it is simple, does not show interdependencies clearly, and does not examine environmental influences explicitly (Mayhew, 2003).

Many of the popular models, such as the McKinsey Seven-S Model and the Galbraith STAR Model, are somewhat similar to the Weisbord model. That is, they have a series of categories, each connected to all the other categories.

Some organizational theorists agree that no single model or frame fully captures the complexity and multifaceted nature of organizational reality (Morgan, 1997; Bolman and Deal, 1991). The next two models take a different perspective on diagnosis from the open systems approach and may be used independently or as an overlay to other approaches.

The Bolman and Deal Four Frames Model looks at the world through four "frames," or windows (see Table 11.1). Frames filter out some things while allowing others to pass through easily. Frames help us order the world and decide what actions to take. Every manager has a personal frame, or image, of an organization to gather information, make judgments, and get things done. Bolman and Deal (1989) believe that managers who understand their own frame and who can adeptly rely on more than one limited perspective are equipped to understand and manage the complex everyday world of organizations instead of being unconsciously wed to a single, narrow perspective.

TABLE 11.1. BOLMAN AND DEAL FOUR FRAMES MODEL.

Structural	Human Resources
Roles, relationships, structures, rules, and policies	Tailoring the organization to meet human needs
Goal: coordination	Goal: individual job fulfillment
Political	**Symbolic**
Scarce resources, which leads to conflict, bargaining, and coalitions	Organization's shared values and culture as evidenced in rituals, myths, ceremonies, and beliefs
Goal: increase political skills	Goal: manage symbols, myths, traditions

Source: Designed by J.A.C. Noolan, based on material in L. G. Bolman and T. Deal, *Modern Approaches to Understanding and Managing Organizations.* San Francisco: Jossey-Bass, 1989.

The *structural* frame looks at organizations as rational, closed systems and examines whether the organization is structured in a way that meets goals and needs, given the environment and technology. The *human resource* frame looks at the interaction between people and the organization. This frame values people and the skills and insights they bring. It examines the strengths and weaknesses of current approaches to humanizing the workplace; problems occur when human needs are not met.

The *political* frame sees organizations as "arenas of scarce resources where power and influence are constantly affecting the allocation of resources among individuals or groups" (Bolman and Deal, 1989, p. 5). This is the darker side of organizations, where conflict, coalitions, and struggles for power and position are played out. The *symbolic* frame treats the organization as theater or carnival, not as rational organization (as in the other three frames). This frame explains the roles of myths, ritual, ceremonies, and plays at all levels of the organization. Organizations are viewed as held together more by shared values and culture than by goals and policies. Upset occurs when actors don't perform as expected, when symbols lose their meaning, and when ceremonies and rituals lose their power.

Each frame has its own vision of how the world is. Bolman and Deal believe that only when managers can look at organizations through all four frames are they likely to appreciate the depth and complexity of organizational life.

Although not designed as an organization diagnostic model, Beckhard's work on team building (1972) has been found to be a useful approach for diagnosing a range of groups and companies for alignment, when they are stuck or in conflict (Noolan, 2003b). It has been used successfully in conjunction with the Freedman Sociotechnical model (Noolan, 2003a). Adapting Beckhard's approach to organization diagnosis, one examines the organization and units of the organization according to their goals, roles, procedures, and interactions. The sequence of diagnostic questions is critical. As OD practitioners, we are often called in because there is a perceived problem among groups or individuals. Beckhard argues that there must first be clarity on mission or *goals*. Once there is clarity and commitment at that level, there must next be clarity on *roles*. After clarity on roles there must be clarity on *procedures* or how work gets done, and not until then should one look at *interactions*, either personally or intergroup. Without clarity on goals, roles, and procedures, there is little long-term benefit in diagnosing or working at the interaction level.

Planning to Collect Data

Stephen Covey's "begin with the end in mind" is a useful guide as data collection is being planned. Planning should work backwards from feedback, by determining what information is needed to make feedback effective. There should be an explicit plan on what data to collect, how to collect them, what will be done with the data, and why they are being collected (Nadler, 1977). These items, along with a statement about the confidentiality of the raw data, are likely to have been addressed during the contracting phase. Table 11.2 shows the tasks and actions associated with the diagnosis.

TABLE 11.2. ORGANIZATION DIAGNOSIS PHASE TASKS AND ACTIONS.

Tasks	Actions
1. Determine approach to be used.	Decide if an established diagnostic model will be used or not. Be clear about the purpose of the diagnosis. Collaboratively determine data-collection methods and restate confidentiality-of-data agreements.
2. Announce project.	Draft, and have management distribute, an announcement alerting staff to the organization diagnosis, time frames, and process that will be used. Meet with employees if possible to answer questions or concerns.

TABLE 11.2. ORGANIZATION DIAGNOSIS
PHASE TASKS AND ACTIONS, Cont'd.

Tasks	Actions
3. Prepare for data collection.	Maintain rapport with client system. Identify or develop interview guides, questionnaires, or other data-gathering methods. Request relevant internal records. Establish time frames. Be aware of one's own biases.
4. Collect data.	Carry out data collection using agreed-on approaches and ensuring confidentiality.
5. Do data analysis and presentation.	The goal is to make the data easy for the client to absorb, not to show how much data you collected. This can be done by using qualitative information such as themes, presenting the data according to a diagnostic model if used, or quantitative data such as averages and ranges if collected. Prepare a written report to the client if contracted for.

Other considerations in data collecting are the time frame involved, the financial resources available, and the geographic location of people from whom the data are collected. Decisions need to be made about whether to include the total population (census) or a sample of it. If sampling is chosen, a weighted sample may be needed to include sufficient underrepresented groups (Kraut describes sampling all of an organization's small number of African American employees and only a small fraction of the majority who were white employees; Kraut, 1996).

If the workforce is unionized, it may be helpful to include union representation in designing the survey. Companies that survey in an organized labor environment may choose to exclude questions such as compensation, which can influence contract negotiations. Further, doing a survey for the first time during a period of union organizing activity could be seen as an unfair labor practice (Kraut, 1996).

Interviews, though a rich source of data, are expensive to conduct and analyze because of the usually open-ended nature of the questions. An interview can take up to twice as long to write up as the interview itself took. A limited number of interviews can be used to help shape a subsequent questionnaire. If a questionnaire is used, it may be a standard off-the-shelf package such as the Mayflower Group's (R. H. Johnson, 1996; or Fields, 2002) or a customized questionnaire.

Standardized questionnaires have the advantage of being tested for reliability and validity. Customized questionnaires have the advantage of being more relevant to the specific organization. Most questionnaires use a Likert five-point rating scale with an agree-disagree format. For some questions, "Don't know" or "Don't have an opinion" should be offered as an option. Demographic questions should be asked toward the end, and at least two or three open-ended questions will add richness to the survey responses. Sometimes a "Please explain" added after a Likert scale rating yields important viewpoints. Questionnaires can be distributed individually or conducted in a group administration. If the latter approach is used, the respondents' managers or supervisors should not be in the room. Customized questionnaires should be pretested on a small group of people to ensure clarity in the questions.

Today's technology offers the possibility of telephony and teleconferencing for distance interviewing, e-mail, fax, and regular mail. Some data-gathering approaches blur the lines among data collection, analysis, and feedback. Examples of this are the use of groupware, Weisbord's Future Search conferences, and Dannemiller's large scale systems intervention.

Data Collection

The intent of data collection is to raise awareness of specific issues, create expectations that change is possible, and build relationships (Nadler, 1977). Data collection itself is an intervention. Just as a police car by the side of the road often causes motorists to slow down, the process of data collection causes people to think about their work and organization, and to raise expectations. More than one type of data-collection method should be used because each contributes to furnishing a fuller picture. Using more than one method of data collection also ensures greater confidence in the data obtained; this is known as "triangulating" the data.

There is no one best method of data collection. Using a diagnostic model orients the practitioner to cover key areas in that particular model. It also gives focus to the data collection by ensuring that it yields answers that fit into the categories demanded by the model. Avoid seeking information that does not serve your purpose; market research people call this "gee whiz" data (once you have it, all you can do with it is say, "Gee whiz!").

Interviews yield rich data and can help build rapport with people in the client system, but they can be expensive to document and analyze. Teleconferencing can be used for employees in distant locations. *Focus groups* or group discussions are an alternative, but some people may be reluctant to voice their opinions in a group setting where they lack anonymity in giving their responses. *Questionnaires,* particularly those using Likert-scale items, are less expensive to analyze, may make more people feel listened to because they can be widely distributed, and can be useful in gathering perceptual and attitudinal data. Remember to add two or three open-ended questions at the end, if open-ended questions have not been used elsewhere in the questionnaire. Also, be sure to pretest customized questionnaires. Through e-mail, questionnaires may be readily distributed to employees globally.

Observation of meetings, or of people doing their work, is another form of data collection. When practiced systematically, observing people at work yields a great deal of qualitative and quantitative information about the work, the worker, and the work environment (Swanson and Holton, 1994). Remember, though: the practitioner's presence, like the police car, can change behavior and affect the data collected. Analysis of *secondary data* such as a review of written company policies, handbooks, personnel or procedures manuals, or actual company records (such as attendance, absenteeism, personnel turnover, financial statements, and minutes of meetings) may be undertaken. *Metaphors, drawings,* and in some instances (depending on the client) *body sculptures* can produce rich information. Having people draw up *responsibility charts* or networks of people they work with (*sociograms)* is another form of data collection.

A whole new genre of data gathering, called *groupware* or *electronic meeting systems* (EMS), has emerged with advances in computer technology and software. Keypad tools, used initially by marketing firms to gather information on customer preferences for the past twenty years, can record multiple-choice question answers, calculate results, and project them onto a big video screen if desired. Groupware, using wireless computers, has been available for less than ten years. It allows both polling and text gathering. All the computers in the room are networked, and the overall results can be viewed either on each laptop or on a large video projection screen.

No matter which data-collection methods are used, it is important to introduce a personal element such as meetings to introduce and describe the project, and to answer questions and concerns (particularly about the confidentiality of the data). The OD practitioner may also need to coach management on its role in the process and support of the project. For further information on data collection, excellent sources are Swanson and Holton (1994) and Kraut (1996).

Data Analysis and Presentation

The goal in data analysis and data presentation is to make it easy for the client to absorb the data. This can be done by summarizing themes, employing diagrams to show relationships, presenting statistics, using color, or telling stories, to name just a few approaches. The intent is to be clear and focused rather than overwhelming. Data analysis is usually qualitative (such as the theming of open-ended responses) or quantitative (giving averages and ranges of scaled ratings, or using histograms to present data).

Qualitative techniques yield data that are often easy to take in; however they may be more subjective in their interpretation and more time consuming to organize than quantitative techniques. If a diagnostic model has been used for data collection, the themed data can be shown as a series of pluses (**+**) or minuses (**–**) directly in the boxes of the model (choosing, say, the three most important of each for each box). Even if the data were not originally collected using a model, a model can be used to display the information gathered. Another approach to displaying themed data is to present it as a force-field analysis, organizing the data into two main categories: forces for change and forces for maintaining the status quo (resistance to change). Sociograms of who interacts with whom, formally and informally, and responsibility charting are other means of displaying data.

Quantitative data are often easy to assemble but can make subjective choices in the data collection look more "scientific" in the reporting. An example of this approach is shown here, where themes have been coded into categories and the percentage of those responding to each category is given:

QUALITY PERFORMANCE 21%
JOB SATISFACTION 18%
COMPENSATION 11%

When displaying quantitative data, it is more effective to keep it simple: clear statistics (such as arithmetic means and ranges), charts, diagrams, frequency distributions in histogram formats, and scatter plots. More sophisticated statistical testing for significance or stepwise regression analysis can be used to analyze structured rating scale questionnaires (Burke, Coruzzi, and Church, 1996).

Data presentation should be calibrated to the culture of the organization. An important caution for many practitioners is to remember not to get ahead of the data, because once an assumption is made it is hard to see disconfirming data even when they are there (the perceptual bias issue again).

Feedback

Feedback affords an opportunity for the client's understanding of the change to become clearer. The intent of the feedback session is to create a heightened awareness of the issues confronting the client system, establish a space for the client system to validate or buy in to the information presented, and facilitate the client system in identifying and setting priorities to move the organization forward. Feedback at its best creates energy and direction for change. The various tasks of this phase are listed in Table 11.3.

TABLE 11.3. FEEDBACK PHASE TASKS AND ACTIONS.

Tasks	Actions
1. Have an agreed-on process for providing feedback.	This should have been agreed on in the contracting process and includes how feedback will be handled, whether management will get to see it first, who will be present, how information will get to others not present, where the feedback meeting(s) will be held, and how feedback will be shared.
2. Ensure that feedback mechanisms are in place.	Schedule feedback meetings(s) at the unit or organization level. Arrange for dissemination of feedback results, if appropriate, using newsletter, memo, or e-mail.
3. Design the feedback session.	The goals of the feedback session are to share the results of the diagnosis, build commitment to the validity of the data, increase awareness of the organization's reality, and create energy for change. Plan to use no more than one-third of the total meeting time for presentation, to allow adequate time for clarification and discussion. Plan to limit the number of themes being presented. Use color to underscore key points and lend visual interest. Design the session, prepare feedback materials, and ensure adequate space and room layout.
4. Give management a preview of the results.	The purpose is to ensure management is not caught off-guard. If there are "negative" data being presented, coach management on how to behave in the wider feedback sessions.
5. Arrange meeting room set-up and A-V requirements.	Arrange room to facilitate presentation of results and small and large group interactions. Ensure needed supplies are on hand.
6. Hold feedback meeting.	Maintain rapport with the client system. Restate the original contract. Describe the structure of the meeting. Describe how the information was obtained. Present the diagnosis information. Present information in such a way as to maintain interest and build commitment to the validity of the data. Ask for client reactions, possibly in small groups, to get the client to understand and validate the data. Heighten the system's awareness of the opportunities that are possible. Create energy and direction for future change, perhaps in small groups.
7. Determine next steps.	Move to prioritizing the data. Decide on follow-up actions, timelines, and responsibilities.

The issue of confidentiality of the raw data and who specifically contributed actual information would have been covered in the contracting phase. Also, an agreement may have been made up front to review the feedback with management prior to presenting it to those who contributed the information. Those involved in implementing any of the findings from the diagnosis, and those who were surveyed, would normally be included in a feedback session.

Feedback Affects Employee Perspective

Feedback has the most impact on an employee's perceptions, depending on how the feedback is given. Alper and Klein (1970, p. 56) report on the effectiveness of survey results when particular methods were used:

- Effectiveness was 39 percent when only written feedback was provided to employees.
- It was 57 percent when feedback was given to a large group (such as the whole plant).
- It was 70 percent when the feedback was given in departmental meetings.

A common pitfall in the feedback phase is to overwhelm the client system with all the data that have been collected, rather than presenting only the key pieces of data that help move the client forward. The admonition to keep it simple can be translated to giving five or six main themes with supporting data under each theme. As Nadler writes, "present only those data that are particularly meaningful. Data should be presented in a format that is easy for the layman to read and interpret" (Nadler, 1977, p. 149). Use of color can underscore key points and offer visual interest to the client. A good rule of thumb is to plan no more than one-third of the session to presenting the data. Block suggests an even smaller time frame of about 15 percent of the session, with the remainder being spent on discussion and action planning (Block, 2000). It is very important to plan adequate time for the client system to discuss and make meaning of the data.

Nadler believes that feedback is more effective if the data are based on some underlying model and the people receiving the feedback have some knowledge of that model (Nadler, 1977, p. 165). If a model has been used, the key points can be shown within the diagram of the model itself. The feedback is never of the raw data but rather organized within a conceptual model or themes. The culture of the organization will also influence how the data are organized and presented.

Nadler presents an interesting model on client reaction to feedback:

People go through a series of responses to unfavorable feedback that resembles the series of typical psychological responses to death or other losses. The cycle encompasses *denial,* where the validity of the feedback and data are questioned;

anger, towards those who supplied the data, those who responded to the survey; *flight*, where other causes for the unfavorable feedback are sought, such as the larger environment, to avoid personal responsibility; and finally *acceptance*. Only after acceptance can the individual move to the next stage, which is to use the data for finding problems, for understanding the real problems of which the data are symptomatic. After problem finding, the individual can engage in problem solving [Nadler, 1996, pp. 181–182].

Feedback Restates Original Contract

The feedback session should restate the original contract, declare the structure of the feedback meeting, describe what the practitioner did to obtain the information that forms the basis for the data analysis, present the diagnosis information, ask for client reactions, get the client to validate the data presented, and move to prioritizing the data and action planning. Block outlines in detail the steps one might go through in conducting a feedback session, and the time allocated to each step (Block, 2000, p. 239).

Feedback Opens Client to New Ideas

Feedback and discussion clarify issues, arouse awareness, generate feelings, and open up members of a unit to new ideas and plans. Once members of the organization have been motivated to become involved around the data, the feedback points out needs, suggests desirable outcome, and energizes employees to search for paths to attain those outcomes (Kraut, 1996).

As a result of an organization diagnosis, expectations are heightened, uncomfortable concerns are raised, and unresolved issues are surfaced. If no additional intervention is taken, there is a predictable increase in skepticism and reduction of trust (Fisher, 1994). Specific action items may be delegated to subgroups who meet on an ongoing basis to systematically tackle priority items that were identified in the diagnosis. Feedback without action planning or goal setting is unlikely to lead to change, and good action planning generally stems from a good diagnosis. If an OD practitioner struggles with action planning, it sometimes is reflective of the data-collection-and-analysis phase.

Conclusion

Organization diagnosis is critical to the organization development process. By gathering and organizing information, the practitioner is often able to help the client see the organization challenges in a new light. The diagnosis differentiates symptoms from underlying causes. There is no one best diagnostic model, but the practitioner who carries a clear open-systems-based model in his or her head is not likely to omit key data categories. To close, here are some useful admonitions to the practitioner in this phase of the OD process: create and maintain rapport with your client, be aware of your own perceptual biases, use a conceptual model even if it is your own, and collect data using more than one method. Do not collect more data than you can usefully analyze, do not get ahead of your data, and do not get in the way of the client system doing its work.

References

Alper, S. W., & Klein, S. M. (1970, November-December). Feedback following opinion surveys. *Personnel Administration*, pp. 54–56.

Beckhard, R. (1972). Optimizing team building effort. *Journal of Contemporary Business, 1*(3), 23–32.

Block, P. (2000). *Flawless consulting: A guide to getting your expertise used* (2nd ed.). San Francisco: Jossey-Bass/Pfeiffer.

Bolman, L. G., & Deal, T. (1989). *Modern approaches to understanding and managing organizations.* San Francisco: Jossey-Bass.

Bolman, L. G., & Deal, T. (1991). *Reframing organizations: Artistry, choice, and leadership.* San Francisco: Jossey-Bass.

Burke, W. W. (1992). *Organization development: A process of learning and changing* (2nd ed.). Reading, MA: Addison-Wesley.

Burke W. W. (1994). Diagnostic models for organization development. In A. Howard (Ed.), *Diagnosis for organizational change: methods and models.* New York: Guilford Press.

Burke, W. W., Coruzzi, C. A., & Church, A. H. (1996). The organizational survey as an intervention for change. In A. I. Kraut (Ed.), *Organizational surveys: Tools for assessment and change* (pp. 41–66). San Francisco: Jossey-Bass.

Fields, D. L. (2002). *Taking the measure of work: A guide to validated scales for organizational research and diagnosis.* Thousand Oaks, CA: Sage.

Fisher, K. (1994). Diagnostic issues for work teams. In A. Howard (Ed.), *Diagnosis for organizational change: methods and models.* New York: Guilford Press.

Freedman, A. M. (2003). Elements of socio-technical systems. In J.A.C. Noolan (Compiler), *Diagnosing organizations with impact: Workbook*, section 2, pp. 26–32. Alexandria, VA: NTL Institute.

Harrison, M. I. (1994). *Diagnosing organizations: methods, models and processes* (2nd ed.). Thousand Oaks, CA: Sage.

Harrison, M. I., & Shirom, A. (1999). *Organizational diagnosis and assessment.* Thousand Oaks, CA: Sage.

Howard, A. (Ed.). (1994). *Diagnosis for organizational change: methods and models.* New York: Guilford Press.

Johnson, R. H. (1996). Life in the consortium: The Mayflower Group. In A. I. Kraut (Ed.), *Organizational surveys: Tools for assessment and change* (pp. 285–309). San Francisco: Jossey-Bass.

Johnson, S. R. (1996). The multinational opinion survey. In A. I. Kraut (Ed.), *Organizational surveys: Tools for assessment and change* (pp. 310–329). San Francisco: Jossey-Bass.

Kraut, A. I. (Ed.). (1996). *Organizational surveys: Tools for assessment and change.* San Francisco: Jossey-Bass.

Lawler III, E. E., Nadler, D. A., & Cammann, C. (1980). *Organizational assessment: Perspectives on the measurement of organizational behavior and the quality of work life.* New York: Wiley.

Levinson, H. (2002). *Organizational assessment.* Washington, D.C.: American Psychological Association.

Mayhew, E. (2003). Comparing diagnostic models. In J.A.C. Noolan (Compiler), *Diagnosing organizations with impact: Workbook*, section 2, pp. 2–5. Alexandria, VA: NTL Institute.

Mintzberg, H., Ahlstrand, B., & Lampel, J. (1998). *Strategy safari: A guided tour through the wilds of strategic management.* New York: Free Press.

Morgan, G. (1997). *Images of organization* (2nd ed.). Thousand Oaks, CA: Sage.

Nadler, D. A. (1977). *Feedback and organization development: Using data-based methods.* Reading, MA: Addison-Wesley.

Nadler, D. A. (1996). Setting expectations and reporting results: Conversations with top management. In A. I. Kraut (Ed.), *Organizational surveys: Tools for assessment and change* (pp. 177–203). San Francisco: Jossey-Bass.

Nadler, D. A., & Tushman, M. L. (1980, Autumn). A model for diagnosing organizational behavior. *Organizational Dynamics.* Vol. 9, 35–51.

Noolan, J.A.C. (2003). Assessing the performance of a research organization: A case study. In J.A.C. Noolan (Compiler), *Diagnosing organizations with impact: Workbook*, section 7, pp. 9–12. Alexandria, VA: NTL Institute.

Rogers, R. W., & Byham, W. C. (1994). Diagnosing organization cultures for realignment. In A. Howard (ed.), *Diagnosis for organizational change: methods and models* (pp. 179–209). New York: Guilford Press.

Rummler, G. A., & Brache, A. P. (1995). *Improving performance: How to manage the white space on the organization chart* (2nd ed.). San Francisco: Jossey-Bass.

Swanson, R. A., & Holton III, E. F. (1994). *Results: How to assess performance, learning, and perceptions in organizations.* San Francisco: Berrett-Koehler.

Weisbord, M. R. (1976). Organizational diagnosis: Six places to look for trouble with or without a theory. *Group and Organization Studies, 1*(4), 430–447.

Weisbord, M. R. (1978). *Organizational diagnosis: A workbook of theory and practice.* Reading: Addison-Wesley.

Wolf, W. B. (1995). Reflections on organizational diagnosis in OD consulting. In F. Massarik (ed.), *Advances in organization development* (Vol. 3). Norwood, CT: Ablex.

CHAPTER TWELVE

INTERVENTION PHASE

Katherine Farquhar

Acts of intervention—the making of observations, the introduction of
learning experiences and other supportive procedures—are designed
or intended to affect the ongoing social processes.

NEVIS (1997/1998), P. 48

The definition of *intervene* is "to come between." When organization development (OD) practitioners intervene, they come between the organization's
past and its desired future. The intervention phase of the OD process has four
stages: defining the present state and framing a desired future, designing the actions to bring about change, implementing these actions, and following up. In
partnership with the client, the practitioner develops and directs this data-guided
program of actions and experiences designed to change the organization's current habits of thought and action.

Of the four phases of the OD process (entry and contracting, organization
diagnosis and analysis, intervention, and evaluation or termination), the intervention phase is often the most visible to the target population. Such visibility reflects the action orientation during this phase. Planning and taking action result
in events and activities that are seen or publicized throughout the unit or organization. Organization members often leave their usual duties to participate in such
activities as retreats, strategic planning sessions, data collection, feedback sessions,
business development processes, training sessions, open space forums, focus groups,
coaching, field trips, and others, designed to create the organization's future.

This chapter examines the basic concepts of the intervention phase and
illustrates how the OD perspective differs from management consulting. Four components of the intervention phase are presented, illustrated by the case of a multi-

year project in a religious organization, which describes intervention activities at various levels of organization life: intrapersonal, interpersonal, team, unit, inter-group, organizational, and organization-environment.

In addition, the chapter focuses on key skills and competencies needed during the intervention phase, illustrating them through a portrait of the OD practitioner as interventionist. OD practitioners are distinct among change agents because of their commitment to particulars of an ethical practice, and their emphasis on diversity and social justice. This chapter reviews the elements of such practice, presenting some typical challenges facing practitioners during this phase. The chapter concludes with a review of the outcomes of a successful intervention phase.

Understanding the Intervention Phase of the OD Process

Over time, OD practitioners have adapted the intervention phase to the changing needs in organizations. Although OD interventions may appear similar to change management programs, they are actually very different.

Overview of OD Interventions

OD pioneer Chris Argyris established three "basic requirements" for intervention activity: (1) valid information; (2) free, informed choice on the client's part; and (3) internal commitment by the client to learning and change (Argyris, 1970). Consistent with these principles, OD practitioners are guided in the intervention phase by the profession's ethics and an abiding commitment to values, which begin with the primacy of diversity, action research, and increased transparency in the workplace.

The OD practitioner is invited into the interventionist role during the transition between the organization's past and its desired future. He or she maintains an overall focus on process dynamics (the *how* in addition to the *what*) during the intervention phase, in roles such as partner, guide, coach, resource, sounding board, facilitator, designer, and trainer.

In a break from the pioneering years of OD, the phases of entry and contracting, data collection and analysis, and diagnosis are now often compressed into interventions that also incorporate processes for feedback and planning (Anderson, 1999). However, whether the time frame is serial (the traditional OD framework) or compressed, the intervention phase involves planning, implementing, and following up on actions targeted to planned change.

OD and Change Management

OD projects differ from change management programs, although both are targeted to bring about change in organizations. Table 12.1 suggests how inquiries from prospective clients might be handled differently by OD practitioners and change management consultants. The table demonstrates that clients who contract for an OD intervention want change that is deep, data-based, transparent, and more oriented to systems thinking and organizational learning than a change management solution.

Each inquiry in Table 12.1 is an opportunity for an OD intervention and a change management solution. However, interventions targeted to solving a problem might best be achieved through an "extra pair of hands," as described by Schein (in Block, 2000), or a techspert (Freedman and Zackrison, 2001). An OD practitioner approaches intervention as a process consultant with a systems perspective and action learning orientation. Table 12.1 illustrates four key distinctions between the OD interventions and change management:

1. The OD intervention builds the client's awareness and generates organizational learning through the process of resolving key issues. The change management approach applies reasonable solutions to achieve desired ends.
2. The OD approach to intervention targets system dynamics in the client organization, opening space for the organization to research, reflect, and revise its model of the situation. The change management approach is more focused on solutions.
3. The OD intervention builds on a partnership between the client and the practitioner and models an inclusive process. The change management approach emphasizes the roles of expert or pair of hands.
4. The OD intervention addresses covert processes such as the dynamics of power, race, gender, and social status, among other social forces that affect workplace behavior. The change management approach deals with the overt dynamics of the situation.

Such contrasts between the two approaches emphasize two key points: (1) each approach to implementing change has merit, depending on the preferences of the organization; and (2) in OD interventions, the practitioner brings a perspective that is client-focused, systemic, process-oriented, and attentive to covert dynamics. These themes emerge clearly in implementing OD interventions, as we shall see.

TABLE 12.1. OD APPROACHES VS. CHANGE MANAGEMENT.

Inquiry	OD Approach	Change Management
1. "Are you available to run a two-day retreat for us in August? We're ready to roll out the president's new priorities and need to get everyone on board."	Open a dialogue with client: What does "get everyone on board" mean? What mental models and values operate? Scan data on expectations, purposes, processes, possible effects, and outcomes; envision future state and what's needed to get there. Are diversity and workforce engaged? Develop contract. Work with design team if possible. Design and implement session and follow up per contract.	Check details for the retreat (dates, logistics). Accept assignment. Get copy of priorities. Do some research in organization to gather context. Design and run retreat. Assess satisfaction. Check back in thirty days to see that implementation is proceeding well.
2. "Our VP is ready to get going now, and I need an outsider to implement the Six Sigma process."	Certified in Six Sigma, you enter dialogue with VP to understand context and goals or program, and learn about employee involvement and commitment. Ensure that the Six Sigma technique is compatible with broad learning and nested within a broader awareness of organization development.	Certified in Six Sigma, you provide and evaluate the training, given an understanding that the conditions are favorable for success.
3. "They expect a strategic plan from us in three weeks. Can you help us edit the 1998 plan?"	Understand assignment, verify learning orientation, contract with client, and establish collaborative process to update the 1998 plan. Jointly rewrite and alter or expand as needed, with input.	Get the 1998 plan, gather some information about the organization, hold a meeting to solicit revisions, edit and amend as needed, and resubmit to them as a draft.
4. "The auditors beat us up again in their management letter. Our board's executive committee . . . wants to meet with you . . . about these problems; . . . they've committed the next year. . . ."	Obtain copy of the letter. Meet with chair and executive committee. Establish and carry out collaborative process to diagnose issues underlying the letter's "problems" and a roadmap for working with them over the year.	Obtain copy of the letter. Meet with chair and executive committee. Outline a proposal to help them deal with the problems raised in the letter.
5. "I'm over my head as executive director. The board is really conflicted, and I can't get clear direction from them."	Meet with executive. Who is client: board or executive? Establish contract for data collection, observation, analysis, feedback, coaching, training, mentoring, as needed.	Provide executive coaching, perhaps some mentoring for this new executive; set up board training.

OD Intervention Phase in Practice

The intervention phase can be understood in four parts: defining the present state and a desired future, planning and designing a program to bring about change, implementing actions to bring about change, and following up the actions. Table 12.2 presents the generic sequence of tasks and actions undertaken by the OD practitioner with the client during the intervention phase.

TABLE 12.2. INTERVENTION PHASE TASKS AND ACTIONS.

Tasks	Actions
1. Review contractual understanding relating to intervention.	Practitioner ensures that she or he and client(s) are up to date on the contract provisions regarding intervention. For outdated contract, jointly modify provisions to address responsibilities, activities, outcomes, and anticipated costs.
2. Clarify meeting purposes.	Mutually agree on the agenda for planning session. Ensure that appropriate parties are engaged and informed. Parties understand that intervention planning is forum to use newly desired behaviors.
3. Discuss and model implications of data collected.	Together, fully review and examine the data. Many practitioners work with client to model present operations and desired future scenarios for the organization. Practitioner works with client to isolate (1) what areas client feels are most appropriate for intervention and (2) what the desired outcomes of interventions in these critical areas are.
4. Brainstorm and examine options for action.	On the basis of this understanding, brainstorm intervention alternatives. Consider costs, benefits, consequences of the key alternatives.
5. Sketch intervention scenarios.	Explore several scenarios for intervention. Practitioner listens carefully to client's wishes and constraints so as to assist the client in evaluating the effects and systems dynamics associated with options. Support client in sustaining principled and ethical approach to intervention activity.
6. Usually in a second meeting: develop and assess a draft agenda for intervention activity, within available resources.	Usually in a second meeting: capture and reflect back to the client a draft agenda for intervention activity based on the scenarios discussed. Jointly consider the desired effects and undesired consequences, focusing on issues such as inclusion or exclusion of organization members; respect for diversity in this workplace; power dynamics (e.g., role of upper-level management vis-à-vis subordinates in public setting); disclosure and withholding of information; responsibility and authority

TABLE 12.2. INTERVENTION PHASE TASKS AND ACTIONS, Cont'd.

Tasks	Actions
	for outcomes; authenticity and honesty; realistic scope of what can be done. Ensure that a valid evaluation process is adopted for the intervention activity.
7. Secure feedback and input on the draft agenda; modify.	Engage and secure the understanding of parties with responsibilities within the agenda, and incorporate changes where needed.
8. Plan logistics for intervention activities.	Practitioner and client representative use event planning and management skills to ensure that every logistical detail is addressed.
9. Carry out intervention activities.	Put the intervention activities into play. Practitioner stays within agreed role.
10. Complete tabulation of evaluations and any follow-up assignments.	Practitioner and client ensure that the processes for tabulating and reporting evaluation and feedback are completed as agreed, along with any follow-up assignments.

Defining the Present State and a Desired Future

The OD practitioner and client review their contract and make necessary revisions. They then meet to review findings from the data collection and diagnosis. From this, they develop a model of the present state of the organization and a vision for the desired future state. This model might be as simple as a one-paragraph statement of what emerged from the diagnosis phase, or as complex as a graphic that portrays causal relationships and leverage points among key players, issues, and events.

Reaching agreement on a description of the present state of the organization is often more difficult than it sounds. Differing perspectives emerge and demonstrate where underlying assumptions diverge. The ensuing dialogue can yield a consensus about the starting point and direction for intervention action. As this phase progresses, the statement or model becomes part of the roadmap to guide the transition between the current state and desired future. Their joint focus on the model gives the OD practitioner and the organization client a tool to chart their explicit assumptions about the present, the transition state, and the desired future.

Designing Intervention Actions

The intervention phase builds on knowledge of a range of actions that facilitate change at various levels of organization life (individual, interpersonal, team or unit, organizational, and organization-environment). In designing interventions, the OD practitioner draws on this inventory of strategies for intervening at each level of the organization's system. Table 12.3 displays a simplified range of intervention formats. More extensive inventories of OD interventions are in Bunker and Alban (1997); Cummings and Worley (1991); Holman and Devane (1999); and Rothwell, Sullivan, and McLean (1995).

TABLE 12.3. EXAMPLES OF INTERVENTION ACTIVITIES AT INDIVIDUAL, TEAM, AND ORGANIZATION LEVELS.

Level	Activities
Individual	• Active listening • Coaching • Counseling • Instrumented feedback • Mentoring • Guided study • Observation and feedback • Reflection • T-groups and laboratory education • Educational programs • Personal development plans • Power Lab
Team	• Instrumented feedback • Team building • Action research • Visioning • Training • Benchmarking • Dialogue skills • Diversity awareness • Conflict management • Appreciative inquiry • Force field analysis • Retreats
Organization	• Open Space processes • Whole system events • Climate surveys and feedback • Strategic planning • Merger or acquisition • Executive transition • Culture auditors • Visioning • SWOT • Restructuring • Negotiation and contracting • Retreats

The role of the OD practitioner in the design phase is to help the organization consider options and make choices for intervention actions. A common hazard is the temptation to jump quickly to a specific design. For example, scheduling a two-day retreat sounds like a good idea to address strategic planning needs, but without extensive preliminary work it can waste time. Likewise, a management team feedback session to help a floundering manager is an efficient way to handle the problem—but in that format the good intentions might crush the manager.

The success of the organization's change efforts can hinge on decisions made in the design phase. Diagnosing and preparing an intervention strategy requires the practitioner to consider:

- The purpose(s) of the intervention
- The environment in which the organization functions
- The organization's culture, including its core technology, leadership, and professional identity(ies) (see Schein, 1997)
- The circumstances in which the strategy will be used
- The appropriate depth of the intervention (going only as deep as necessary to address the goal)
- The likelihood and consequences of collateral effects of the intervention
- The fit of the strategy within the available time frame and its flow inside the sequence of the intervention
- The client's response to the proposal

The process of planning and design may involve several meetings to consider alternative intervention strategies and sharpen the focus on a preferred approach. Repeated, revised drafts of the strategy document may be necessary to ensure that the organization's goals are clear and its commitment firm. Final documents may include an agenda or work plan that lists dates and times, goals, actions, presenters and resource persons, logistical information, and background work or materials.

Implementing the Intervention Actions

Effective interventions require meticulous planning and careful communication. This early preparation enables participants to focus comfortably on the activities. Since the participants are the critical mass for a successful intervention event, last-minute or sloppy planning for simple needs such as meals and appropriate surroundings can make people feel disrespected. Resistance to change often reflects frustration over how organization members are treated during the transition activities, as much as it does reluctance to confront necessary change.

One question nearly always arises in the intervention phase: "Is this event mandatory?" Removing barriers to participation and finding out what motivates this question is more effective than mandating compliance. For example, to many employees scheduling is a real hurdle, especially when change activities extend beyond regular work hours. Child care needs, other nonwork responsibilities, bus or carpool schedules, and fatigue are all burdens. The organization must encourage and facilitate participation, including compensating hourly employees for time beyond normal work hours (and supplemental child care, if possible). For reluctant participants, listening to their concerns can yield important information and reflects appreciation of their importance to the process. If the activity is seen as so important that no one wants to miss it, most participants will use the organization's support to be there.

The practitioner's use of event management and facilitation skills helps the intervention activities proceed according to plan. The experienced OD practitioner avoids getting drawn into any leadership or expert role during this phase. This potential pitfall is discussed later in the chapter.

Follow-up

Following the intervention event, it is exceedingly important to ensure that the group's work is captured and followed up. The OD practitioner can inquire about any recording that is needed to be certain that the output of the intervention activity is documented. He or she can make contact to follow up a summary or report that supports the client's ongoing work. The follow-up report can document what was done and decided, who committed to do what, and what happens next. Key materials generated in the session can be transcribed and distributed. Compiling this work helps to sustain the momentum and mark the progress of the OD strategy. In addition, the OD practitioner maintains communication with the organization and supports the process of ensuring that commitments made in intervention activities are honored.

"Build It and They Will Come" (Exhibit 12.1) is a minicase that describes a multiyear process in which a religious institution invested heavily to shift its vision, mission, structure, and management culture. This snapshot illustrates the four parts of an OD intervention and demonstrates typical activities involved. A map of the intervention phase in this project (Figure 12.1) shows how the activities at many levels during the transition state helped the client move between the present and its desired future state. This map also illustrates how a systems perspective looks in practice.

EXHIBIT 12.1. BUILD IT AND THEY WILL COME: CHANGING INSTITUTIONAL FOCUS.

Several years ago, the central church of a religious denomination was in crisis. Nearly a hundred years ago, the founding leaders had designed a massive building and worked to fund construction. They left the running of church activities pretty much to the staff. Now, as the long building process was finally ending, the current board and management were overwhelmed. How should they use this magnificent space? Beyond worship, what activities were fitting: arts center? choral development? tourist destination? continuing education? They reacted to ideas and proposals: accept this! reject that! The church was drifting. Its leaders saw the need to change the institutional focus from plans and construction to strategy and programming. This is where the overall OD intervention came in, as sketched here briefly.

Modeling

The board and top executive contacted a number of OD consultants, who contracted to work with the organization singly and in teams. After extensive contracting, data collection, and diagnostic activity, all in partnership with OD practitioners, the executive team developed a model of the current state (summarized as "bricks and mortar"). Their vision was a church that was strategically driven and focused on "people and programs." The model was clear enough, but what interventions would help them move from the present to this desired future?

Design

The OD practitioners coordinated their work through a long-term administrator who had excellent knowledge of the organization and was sensitive to its culture and politics. This partnership began by developing cross-functional and cross-level design teams who reviewed data, considered options, and gave feedback on proposals for intervention activities. For example, action research suggested a key blockage: the church's executives, though in theory operating as a team, had the habit of making an end run to the chief executive to get resources. These shortcuts caused conflict between departments, suspicions among managers, and frustration that the church's work wasn't being done well. With the facilitation of OD practitioners, the design teams and then the actual work teams talked about the root causes and interpersonal effects of such a pattern. The practitioners suggested interventions that could reduce the causes and negative effects of these behaviors, while clarifying reporting relationships and decision processes. Over several years, OD practitioners helped units to carry out interventions that opened such blockages, making change possible.

Implementation

The interventions during this lengthy project included sessions to clarify mission and vision; strategic planning by the board and executives; individual coaching with the top executive; practice in dialogue within the executive team; offsite retreats to promote teamwork, appreciation for diversity, and clearer vision; onsite work sessions to enable vision and mission development at all levels; workshops on management skills (such as running effective meetings); and facilitated planning to restructure units, reporting relationships, and management processes.

Follow-up

The OD practitioners followed up after the intervention activities. They issued summaries for virtually all sessions to keep track of agreements, changes, and next steps. This enabled the executive team to track commitments. As the project neared its end, the practitioners were sporadically invited to collect data, give feedback, and coach as the changes spread through the system. Clearly, the executive team was more self-reflective and better at making key decisions, managing huge programs, and working well together. Individual managers carried the changes into their units, often using OD processes (indeed, meetings now included time for units to reflect on their work together and their learning as a system). With its new work culture reinforced by OD interventions, the church became much better at thinking and acting strategically through its people and programs.

FIGURE 12.1. INTERVENTION MAP.

Intervention phase: Illustration of "Build It and They Will Come"

Present State

Future State

Intervention Activities:

Organization-environment
Presumed need: organization is seen as self-focused and removed from its environment; needs to be more networked and better serve its stakeholders. Tools/activities used: SWOT analysis, outreach to local and national entities, field visits, increased networking

Organizationwide
Presumed need: executive team must take on strategic leadership of the organization at this new stage of its evolution to provide strategy and mission-driven, flexible, professional management. Tools/activities used: visioning, strategic planning, restructuring of units, reporting relationships

Team
Presumed need: move beyond "spoke and wheel" management style that encouraged unit heads to compete and to strike individual deals with the executive, to a more collaborative, team-driven, transparent management style. Tools/activities used: leadership development, meeting management, action research, observation and feedback, diversity skills, appreciation and conflict skills

Interpersonal
Presumed need: impact of all this change and ambiguity on role definitions and people resulted in strained relationships and caused conflict and withholding of information. Tools/activities used: role clarification, practice in dialogue, conflict management, interpersonal contracting

Individual
Presumed need: new behaviors demanded of individual managers required increased self-awareness and new management behaviors and skills. Tools/activities used: coaching, MBTI/instrumented feedback, management development activities

Bricks and mortar
Long-term focus on managing the construction process and developing resources to complete the multidecade construction process

Presumed mission: provide leadership in worship and for the denomination

People and program

Develop a strategy-guided, well-managed, team-oriented, flexible, denominational leadership

Orient the organization to serve the denomination and the broader religious needs of the local community and visitors

Ensure the completed sanctuary has sufficient resources and is appropriately and fully used in ways consistent with overall stategy

Skills and Competencies for the Intervention Phase

Designing, carrying out, following up, and evaluating the intervention phase in a manner consistent with the ethics and values that guide OD practice requires certain skills and competencies. Over time, these skills and competencies enhance the practitioner's capacity to design effective interventions and implement them successfully. The two fundamental OD skills are listening and systems thinking.

These skills serve practitioners throughout all phases of the OD process. Asked to name the most important quality of an OD practitioner, former NTL President and veteran OD practitioner Edie Seashore said simply, "Curiosity." Strong interventions are shaped from capable diagnostic work and clear communication between organization and practitioner. An attitude of healthy, professional curiosity promotes the practitioner's most important tool: listening. As an active listener, the practitioner asks open-ended questions:

- "Can you say more about that? Let's understand that better."
- "What data led you to that conclusion?"
- "What would you like to accomplish?"
- "Who else has been involved in thinking about this?"
- "What do you hope this or that activity might accomplish? What do you expect will happen as a result? Have you considered . . . ?"

Beginning with such inquiry at the outset of designing an intervention, the practitioner models thoughtful listening and, through questions like these, encourages the discipline of systems thinking. The perspective of systems thinking is that the organization is a dynamic organism. Systems thinking is in effect a storyboarding of the organization's dynamics. Early in the intervention phase, client and practitioner examine the data, assumptions, and mental models that drive the organization's intentions and expectations in moving to action. Using the disciplines involved in systems thinking, they identify key elements at play in the organization's system, clarify patterns of cause and effect, examine hypotheses about chains of causality, and locate leverage points for making change. The practitioner uses knowledge of intervention options to support the client system to develop a vision for a desired future state, and a roadmap to move the system from here to there. A widely used resource on systems thinking is the *Fifth Discipline Fieldbook: Strategies and Tools for Building a Learning Organization* (Senge and others, 1994).

Competencies: Managing Conflict, Managing Diversity, Managing Resistance

Early in the OD cycle, collection and analysis of data brings to light the organization's concerns and challenges. Symptoms begin to emerge and often include issues around conflict, resistance, and diversity. Thus three of the competencies needed in the intervention phase focus on managing these areas that challenge social systems undergoing change. Each area may manifest at any level of the social system (a manager is accused of racism; conflict repeatedly arises in staff meetings; new procedures are ignored by the eastern sales division). OD practitioners are schooled in theory and practice related to conflict, diversity, and resistance. Effective practitioners develop their conflict management skills. In addition, they are aware of their personal issues around race, gender, sexual identity, social class, and power, and they are prepared to facilitate situations in which diversity is either an overt or a covert dynamic. Being sensitive to forms of resistance, the practitioner brings these issues to the organization's attention and facilitates actions that address resistance.

Competencies: Training, Managing Transitions, Learning Theory

The second set of competencies focus on how to build the organization's capabilities to cope with change: knowledge about transition theory, adult learning and development, and effective training strategies. The effective practitioner can design, modify, and deliver a group activity with good presentation skills, an effective feedback style, and the capacity to access various approaches to understanding a problem. The practitioner also understands how adults learn and respond to change, particularly during organizational transition. Building knowledge, skill, and awareness in these areas is a continuous process created through academic study, professional development activities, Internet research, shadow consulting, use of a coach or mentor, and networking.

An additional intervention skill required of OD practitioners is the ability to write effectively, specifically proposal development and report writing. The successful practitioner can write a concise, nonjudgmental, informative, accurately compiled document. Written work in the intervention phase may include the initial proposal for the intervention design, interim documents such as meeting notes and draft agendas, and a postintervention follow-up report. This skill can also be developed through academic study, coaching, and professional development.

The broader OD literature contains numerous inventories of the knowledge, competencies, and skills that characterize an effective OD practitioner. For this chapter, several senior OD practitioners (including NTL members Julie Noolan, Robert Marshak, and Judith Vogel) contributed to a composite two-hundred-word portrait of an OD interventionist (Exhibit 12.2).

EXHIBIT 12.2. THE EFFECTIVE OD INTERVENTIONIST (IN TWO HUNDRED WORDS).

The effective OD interventionist:

- . . . Is a systems thinker, thoughtful listener, versatile designer, credible presenter, effective facilitator, knowledgeable guide, insightful diagnostician, ethical practitioner, and appreciative and curious person who subordinates ego to the clients' needs.

- . . . Understands how an OD practitioner helps a client system move between present mental model and desired future; discerns clients' highest aspirations for themselves and supports movement to their goals; and creates a container of ambition, optimism, and kindness where clients work hard and learn from setbacks.

- . . . Models collaboration on diverse teams with clients and fellow consultants; handles conflict productively and without fear; and gives and receives feedback comfortably.

- . . . Knows and uses techniques and designs ranging from intrapersonal to whole-system interventions; understands cultural fit, pacing, and flow; and collaboratively builds designs based on clients' needs.

- . . . Takes intentional risks, handles setbacks and emergencies effectively, and decides wisely when to stick with or alter a design.

- . . . Knows supporting theory, including stages of individual, group, and organizational development; systems thinking; overt and covert processes; action research; change processes; resistance to change; and so forth.

- . . . Is ethical and self-aware; knows and respects own blind spots; is organized and prepared; brings gentle, appropriate humor; and attends to personal needs appropriately outside the consulting relationship.

In sum, the intervention phase requires ways of being—use of self—that support the organization during a vulnerable period of the change process. Through authentic commitment, the practitioner models stamina and true engagement with the organization's system. By maintaining a nonreactive presence, the practitioner sustains a safe container where members of the client system can take risks, be authentic, and be reasonably transparent.

The Primacy of Values and Ethics in the Intervention Phase

As the "onstage" segment of the OD process where much of the public activity takes place, the intervention phase showcases the values-driven and ethical behavior practiced by OD practitioners. As change actions are planned and implemented, important decisions and difficult choices are made, often in emotional circumstances. An OD practitioner specializing in environmental sustainability reflected: "My epiphany was realizing that . . . by making my clients more productive, I was showing them how to deplete the world's resources better, faster, cheaper. That wasn't the legacy I wanted to leave."

For this practitioner, the value of environmental sustainability became central to her future practice. Feeling her personal values incongruent with the outcomes she supported clients to achieve, she removed herself to a new specialization. In this case, the practitioner was sensitive to the values that were conflicting and used skills of observation and communication to enable ethical personal behavior in difficult circumstances.

The concepts of "authentic commitment" and "nonreactive presence" are principles of ethical practice in the intervention phase. The OD practitioner's modeling of commitment to the organization through difficult times in the process demonstrates the courage and persistence equally needed within the organization. The practitioner's ethical responsibility encompasses a broad area including readiness to (1) confront inauthentic behavior, (2) inquire into the nature of intolerance and resistance, and (3) examine evident breakdowns along racial lines. In using such practices, the practitioner opens the door for the organization to take similar actions and break through to new behaviors in difficult situations.

To be present with a nonreactive presence is a point of continuous learning. Sometimes the OD practitioner may begin to display personal reactions: taking sides, speaking out in frustration. If such a reaction occur, the practitioner has crossed an ethical boundary to become part of the problem. This is where nonreactive presence is a particular attribute of OD practitioners who have the commitment to remain disengaged from the debate or the action, while remaining present in the situation. They don't take sides, or step in for management or the union, or move to the role of expert or authority figure. Being present means exercising vigilance to ensure psychological and physical safety, and being ready to take steps that support the organization's efforts to move toward the desired future.

Ethics and Values Gone Awry

Given the central importance of ethics and values in OD practice, it is particularly toxic when an OD intervention contradicts espoused values. Because of the public face of the intervention phase, each decision and action receives public scrutiny. Observers and participants quickly perceive hypocrisy and contradictions. What happens when OD ethics and values are short-circuited or ignored at the intervention phase? Here are several examples:

• Violation of Argyris's *three criteria for intervention*: valid and useful information; free, informed choice; and internal commitment on the client's part. Example: the OD practitioner moves into the expert role or takes leadership of the process, thus shifting the power dynamic away from the client system. Outcome: the process backfires.

- *Failure to embed* in the OD intervention the *recognition of power dynamics and the central importance of workforce diversity* (race, gender, sexual preference, age, ability status, and other important factors). Example: the client organization proposes a planning group membership that is highly homogeneous and does not address demographic diversity. The OD practitioner does not bring this to their attention. People conclude, "This process is just like all the others around here." Second example: racial stereotyping occurs during an icebreaker exercise, and the facilitator's response is to move on with the topic at hand. Consequence: participants conclude that it is not safe to raise their concerns about being respected and heard.

- *Breaches of confidentiality throughout the intervention phase.* Examples abound: reporting of identifiable data from a "confidential" interview; overheard conversations in the elevator; cross-contamination of confidential data between interviews ("I heard the same thing from the last person I interviewed"); mishandling of raw data in a public presentation; restricting distribution of data from what was promised to those who provided it; retribution on the basis of release of confidential data. Impact: the OD process loses credibility, and resistance to OD mounts.

- *Inauthentic relationship* between OD practitioner and contact client, and *persistence of covert processes* during the intervention phase. Example: the OD practitioner engages in behind-the-back remarks about organization leaders or members during a three-day retreat. Conclusion: "Don't trust this consultant, who exhibits questionable behavior."

- OD practitioner *failing to practice and model the desired state* of the organization. Example: the OD practitioner is unable to participate in two scheduled meetings of the intervention design team before the delivery date and presents the team with a design proposal at the next meeting. Conclusion: "Is this process a sham? Why am I taking my time if the OD person can't be committed enough to go through with the process?"

- OD practitioners *working "solo" beyond their competency level or the demands of the situation.* Example: an OD practitioner guiding the intervention phase of a leadership transition from father to son in a family business continues as the solo consultant, despite sensing there are clinical issues arising that really require another trained professional. Worst case: a critical event occurs that evidences severe psychiatric trauma.

Sharpening one's sense of how to behave ethically and stay true to one's values continuously challenges OD practitioners. Seasoned pros and newcomers all take steps to ensure that they are working ethically: recognizing and examining feelings of unease; referring back to the contract to review ground rules, role definitions, desired outcomes; engaging in dialogue with the client about ethical challenges; reserving time to reflect on one's practice; contracting with a "shadow consultant" or backup resource whom one can consult confidentially. In sum, engage in continuous awareness and vigilance to ensure a safe container for work in the OD process.

Outcomes of a Successful OD Intervention Phase

The outcomes of a successful OD intervention phase fall into four categories: the organization's goals are met, the benefits of the OD intervention diffuse through the organization, the OD practitioner gains knowledge and experience, and the field grows by one more success.

Organization's Goals. The first harvest of a successful intervention phase is that the organization's goals are realized. Results of intervention actions are measured against the goals set for the project. In reflecting on the intervention phase, the organization sees the progression from beginning state toward desired future. In addition, members of the system have stronger knowledge of the tools and attitudes needed to continue momentum in this direction. Where the intervention phase has not yielded outcomes as hoped or planned, the OD practitioner has partnered with the client to reflect and learn.

Other Elements of the System. Just as news of conflict in an organizational unit diffuses rapidly across a system through word of mouth, the news of a successful OD process sparks attention. As the early detractors (or those in noninvolved areas of the organization) hear of the outcomes of a successful OD process, they may become curious and more open to the process. Such successes create data for the organization about its possibilities and what works. Frequently, OD interventions are staged so that they begin with a phase described as a "pilot" or "demonstration." The success of an OD project becomes a case for its own replication within the client system.

OD Practitioner. In successful OD interventions (and after the pain recedes from a less-than-successful intervention), the practitioner has had a close exchange with the client. The client gains from the practitioner's gifts in terms of skills, knowledge, perspective, and support. On the other side, the OD practitioner gains an additional relationship and one more intervention experience to reflect and build on, along with feedback about what worked and what didn't. This process of continuous learning by the practitioner benefits each succeeding organization.

The Field of OD. Each known story of an intervention, whether or not "success-ful," becomes a thread in the expanding tapestry of OD. This hybrid discipline is in its maturity and is now refining identity and practices. By accumulating case histories, the field learns more about how standard elements (action research, di-agnosis, intervention, evaluation, feedback, and the like) combine to create unique outcomes. Journals such as the *OD Practitioner, Journal of Applied Behavioral Science,* and *Human Relations* are examples of how this knowledge is diffused. The larger community of OD practice is a learning field where such accumulation of expe-rience is a key resource and a stimulus to continued learning. With disciplined dis-cussion and reflection, the community improves its ability to support clients. This occurs through exchanges at professional conferences, networking, journal arti-cles, and in books.

Conclusion

The four-stage intervention phase in organization development differs from the solution-driven approach to change often sought by organizations. OD practi-tioners develop their recommendations for action within a collaborative, values-guided, learning-oriented relationship with the organization. The diagnostic work and related discussion are framed into a model of the current and desired states. The practitioner and organization collaborate to build a roadmap for action based on this model. The practitioner proposes alternative intervention designs that are refined and focused into a final strategy derived from client responses to succes-sive drafts. The final strategy for intervention incorporates a set of actions that help the system through the transition from present to future state. Careful exe-cution of the strategy and thorough follow-up to all intervention activities ensure that the outcomes are met.

OD practitioners use certain competencies to manage the work of the inter-vention phase. Beyond the basics of listening skills and the discipline of systems thinking, practitioners need competencies to support clients through the challenges of change: managing conflict, diversity, and resistance. To develop and deliver ef-fective intervention activities, practitioners need strong capabilities in training, tran-sition management, and learning theory. A competency particularly important in the intervention phase is the ability to communicate effectively through writing.

The intervention phase presents particular challenges to OD practitioners in maintaining an ethical balance: holding a process orientation and avoiding the temptation to act as expert or pair of hands. Effective practitioners rely on the competencies of authentic commitment and a nonreactive presence to stay within an appropriate supporting role.

A successful OD intervention phase results in numerous outcomes at multiple levels of impact, from the process itself to the possibility of enhancing learning in the field of OD. At the end of a successful intervention, the practitioner can see that the organization's capacities for learning and future development are substantially enhanced. The practitioner and organization are prepared to enter the termination and evaluation phase of the OD process.

References

Anderson, M. (1999). *Fast-cycle organization development*. Cincinnati, OH: South-Western.

Argyris, C. (1970). *Intervention theory and method: A behavioral science view*. Reading, MA: Addison-Wesley.

Block, P. (2000). *Flawless consulting: A guide to getting your expertise used* (2nd ed.). San Francisco: Jossey-Bass/Pfeiffer.

Bunker, B., & Alban, B. (1997). *Large group interventions: Engaging the whole system for rapid change*. San Francisco: Jossey-Bass.

Cummings, T., & Worley, C. (1991). *Organization development and change* (7th ed.). Cincinnati, OH: South-Western.

Freedman, A., and Zackrison, R. (2001). *Finding your way in the consulting jungle*. San Francisco: Jossey-Bass/Pfeiffer.

Holman, P., & Devane, T. (1999). *The change handbook: Group methods for shaping the future*. San Francisco: Berrett-Koehler.

Nevis, E. C. (1997/1998). *Organizational consulting: A Gestalt approach*. Cambridge, MA: Gestalt Press.

Rothwell, W., Sullivan, R., & McLean, G. (Eds.). (1995). *Practicing organization development: A guide for consultants*. San Francisco: Jossey-Bass/Pfeiffer.

Schein, E. (1997). *Organizational culture and leadership* (2nd ed.). San Francisco: Jossey-Bass.

Senge, P., Kleiner, A., Roberts, C., Ross, R., & Smith, B. (1994). *The fifth discipline fieldbook: Strategies and tools for building a learning organization*. New York: Doubleday.

CHAPTER THIRTEEN

EVALUATION AND TERMINATION PHASE

Roland E. Livingston

It seems to me contracts have a natural life. Organizations eventually outgrow or tire of or cease needing a particular consultant, and vice versa. It's better for me and my client that we recognize explicitly when it's time to part.

WEISBORD (1977), P. 4

A wise friend once told me that in relationships it's a good idea to "start up as you would like to end up." The entry and contracting phase of the organization development (OD) process is the time to discuss how the parties would like to end up, which makes the discussion about evaluation and termination quite appropriate as the OD practitioner-client relationship begins.

In the entry and contracting phase of a planned change, the OD practitioner and the client discuss and explore the work to be done, decide upon what kind of data to collect, how to collect the data, and what each of them expects from the OD process. Lastly, they discuss what results they want and how the results will be evaluated.

Just as the entry and contracting process is an intervention into a client system, so too is the evaluation and termination process. A successful evaluation and termination phase is a great benefit to the client system, and it *can be* a great benefit to the OD practitioner as well. An effective evaluation process enables the client system to understand what was done, how it was done (and how well), and what impact the change process has had on the organization, on groups within the organization, and on individuals within the groups.

As for the OD practitioner, a well-planned and executed evaluation process makes it possible to assess the efficacy of the various interventions that were used throughout the change process within the client system. The OD practitioner is able to answer two key questions about their effort (Dillon, 2003): What are the results, and of what value are the results to the organization? Evaluative questions such as these are not only about the results. The OD practitioner should also be interested in the results in relation to what was planned and the intended outcome(s).

This chapter discusses what the evaluation phase is and why it is an important part of the OD process. It also discusses the specific evaluation tasks and actions to be attended to throughout the process, and it presents an evaluation checklist. Next is a discussion of the termination phase of the OD process as an intervention and how the OD practitioner and the client must both know when it is time to terminate the relationship and the OD process.

Evaluation

The word *evaluation* conjures up fear in the minds of many people. For the client leader of the OD process, evaluation may be seen as the time to reveal to the rest of the organization what difference, if any, the OD process has made in the way things were done in the past. For the OD practitioner, evaluation may be seen as a report card on the effectiveness of the interventions that were used throughout the OD process.

An effective way to mitigate these fears is to ensure that evaluation is included as part of the discussion of the OD process during the entry and contracting phase. When included as part of the overall effort, evaluation is not perceived at the end of the process as something to be dreaded. Rather, it is seen as an integral part of the change process, and through continuous ongoing feedback the client system has received many clear indicators of how things are going.

In the entry and contracting phase of a planned change, the OD practitioner and the client discuss and explore the work to be done. At this time, they also decide upon appropriate feedback mechanisms that will let them know how things are working as the OD process progresses. Others in the client system who have the responsibility for planning, development, and implementation of the change process should be involved in the discussion of feedback mechanisms. These are the people who will be asking themselves throughout the OD process, "How am *I* doing?" Their bosses will ask, "How are *we* doing?" At some prescribed end time, some key person in the organization or agency will ask, "How well did it go? Was it worth the effort?"

These are questions that ask for a judgment (and evaluation is, by definition, a judgmental process), so it is critical for the OD practitioner and the client to build in the mechanisms needed to answer them. If key members of the organization are involved in the process of deciding which indicators to look at along the way, the final outcome evaluation should not come as a surprise to any of the key participants in the process.

Evaluate Results, Not Activities

The final outcome evaluation of an OD process must focus on results, rather than activities. Activities that sound good, look good, and allow managers to feel good often contribute little or nothing to bottom-line performance (Schaffer and Thompson, 1992). Activities-driven changes tend to focus on fuzzy and vague outcomes and engage people in activities and experiential exercises that do little to make a lasting change or improve the bottom-line results. On the other hand, results-centered changes produce measurable improvement or change accomplished during a reasonable time frame.

There are several reasons for focusing on results in the evaluation phase of an OD process, and the OD practitioner should help the client system identify the key outcome measures that indicate success. One reason for evaluating the results, rather than the activities, of a planned organizational change is to improve implementation of the change. Depending on the size of the organization, a planned change may require several years to take hold. In small organizations, the change may take one year, while in larger organizations it might be up to five years.

A second reason for results-focused evaluation is that planned organizational change is never really complete; some workgroups might be readier to embrace the change than others. The results-focused evaluation process helps to identify areas of success and any barriers to the organizational change that still need attention. The OD practitioner should help the client system cycle through the entire change process two or three times. In this way, the organization is able to recognize, facilitate, and fine-tune an incremental change.

The third reason for results-focused evaluation is to determine whether the change process has achieved what it set out to accomplish. By looking at the predetermined key indicators of success, the OD practitioner and the client system are able to assess the effectiveness of what was attempted. It is also important to acknowledge what, if any, unintended consequences occurred during the change process and propose what to do about them.

Evaluate on Every Level

The evaluation phase of the OD process must track the effectiveness of the change process with a systems view (organization-level, group-level, and individual-level), because many change initiatives that begin at the organizational level fail at the individual level. What happens in between makes all the difference between success and failure. Many organizational change efforts fail or do not fully meet stated goals or objectives (Kotter, 1996). In fact, according to other researchers (Katz and Kahn, 1978; Marshak, 1993) major organizational change cannot occur without specific groups and individuals changing. Therefore, the evaluation phase will not succeed if it ignores any level of the system.

Evaluation Tasks and Actions

Interventions associated with a planned change are based on data collected within and around the client system. A key task in the evaluation phase is to shape goals and objectives so that they can be evaluated. Therefore, evaluation of a planned change must be grounded in data that reflect the degree of change from some previously noted state. The evaluation process looks at what was done (the various interventions) and how well they were done and assesses the outcomes (what has changed and in what direction) of the interventions.

The evaluation process should take place in the same sequence as implementation of the interventions. Trisko and League (1980) presented a five-level approach to evaluation of human service programs: at level one *tasks* should be *monitored*, at level two *activities* should be *assessed*, at level three *outcomes* (achievement of objectives) should be *enumerated*, at level four *goal attainment* should be *measured*, and at level five a judgment should be made as to whether the *problem* has been reduced. A similar approach may be used in evaluating an OD process. A list of key questions for each level of evaluation is in Table 13.1.

Members of the client system often state goals in vague or fuzzy terms to improve productivity or increase team or organizational effectiveness. Goals and objectives of a successful OD process must have end statements that are concrete and specific, realistic and attainable, measurable, and time-bound (Trisko and League, 1980). To have meaningful measures to evaluate, the OD practitioner and the client system identify measurable goals and objectives that are in the context of the day-to-day operation of the organization and can be translated into observable indicators of success.

It takes a group of highly motivated employees to accomplish successful organizational change. For the OD change process to be successful, the importance of realistic goal setting cannot be overemphasized. Without it, employees might suffer a "direction problem." Some years ago, for example, a football team defensive end picked up an opponent's fumble and—with obvious effort and delight—ran the ball into the wrong end zone! Clearly, the athlete didn't lack motivation. He did, however, fail to channel his energies toward the right goal. Such problems can be minimized if the OD practitioner and the

TABLE 13.1. QUESTIONS AT EACH LEVEL.

Process Evaluation		Outcome Evaluation	
Level One, Monitoring Tasks	Level Two, Assessing Change Activities	Level Three, Enumerating Outcome	Level Four, Measuring Effectiveness	Level Five, Assessing the Impact
Is the day-to-day work of the organization being handled?	What change activities are taking place?	What is the result of the change activities described in level two?	What would have happened at the organization level, the group level, or the individual level in the absence of the change process?	What changes are evident in the problem or opportunity that was the focus of the change activity?
Is the change in activity taking place where and when it should?	Who is the target of the change activity (number and type of people, with what problems or needs, from which areas, etc.)?	Should different activities be substituted?	What other factors may have contributed to the changes documented at level three?	What new knowledge has been generated for the organization about the problem or opportunity and how to go about addressing similar future challenges?
Are people in the organization working where and when they should?	How well is the change activity being implemented?	Have the change objectives been achieved?	How cost-effective is the change, compared to what preceded it?	
Are daily tasks being carried out efficiently?	How could it be done more efficiently?	What happened to the target population? How is it different from before?		How has the client system developed its capacity (knowledge, skills, and ability) to continue on its own?
Are employees adequately trained for their job, and ready to handle any new duties and responsibilities?	Were internal and external clients satisfied?	Have unanticipated outcomes also occurred, and are they desirable?		
	Does the change process have a favorable image?	What activities might be repeated to ensure their future occurrence?		

client system work together to set concrete, realistic, measurable, time-bound goals.

Most people like to have goals and measure themselves against a standard. They like to see who can run fastest, score the most, jump highest, and work best. They like to be measured by people whom they respect and who make a difference to them in life and at work. People are motivated when they have a say in how goals are set and measured, and they are likely to set goals at a realistically high level.

The tasks and activities associated with the evaluation process depend on the client system or section of the client system that is the target of the OD change process. Several key tasks and activities are outlined in Table 13.2. Among the tasks are (1) deciding on quantitative and qualitative measures, (2) determining what data to collect, (3) collecting the data, (4) measuring the outcomes, and (5) measuring effectiveness.

TABLE 13.2. EVALUATION PHASE TASKS AND ACTIONS.

Tasks	Actions
1. Determine what part of the evaluation is to be quantitative and what part is to be qualitative.	Write program goals and objectives that are concrete and specific, realistic and attainable, measurable, and time-bound. Decide collaboratively what amount of change in quantitative and qualitative measures equals success.
2. Determine what data should be collected that will indicate success in the OD process.	Work collaboratively with key members of the client system to identify which specific behaviors or events are to be observed, what items should be included in a survey questionnaire, what questions should be asked in individual or focus group interviews, etc.
3. Collect data to use in the evaluation process.	Decide how the data will be collected. Consider using the same data-collection methods as in the diagnosis process. Decide when and where the data will be collected.
4. Assess outcomes of the OD process.	Decide on the format being used to report the data. Collaboratively determine what indicators constitute success and what constitute failure.
5. Assess the effectiveness of the OD process.	Did the process accomplish the intended results? Compare the before and after quantitative measures and the percentage change on qualitative measures.

Quantitative and Qualitative Measures. Determine what part of the evaluation is to be quantitative and what part qualitative. From the viewpoint of stakeholders (consumers, stockholders, suppliers, federal agencies, the community) one can usually suggest some hard outcome measures, such as return on investment, earnings per share, profit, sales, number of clients served, market share, budget increases, number of patents and new products, new contracts and orders, productivity gains, and so on. Making a before-and-after comparison on any of these measures should produce an approximate impact, recognizing that other things could have happened.

Bottom-line, quantifiable measures certainly can be convincing but they have limitations and there is a time lag between decisions and actions on the one hand and performance on the other. Some of the bottom-line measures will not be affected until months or years after a key decision is made. Only if these measurements are made over a long enough period of time—in which one can expect to see true effects—can one take the results of such an "objective" evaluation seriously (Kilman, 1989). Other more subjective, qualitative measures should also be evaluated. Such an evaluation might reveal, for example, the need to improve the culture in one or more workgroups that have yet to get with the program. New managers or employees may have joined after the OD process began and may require additional skills training sessions to bring them up to speed with the rest of the membership. The OD practitioner can help the client system cycle through all the stages of planned change a second or third time to ensure that incremental change is taking place and to be certain that newer entries into the client system are brought on board.

Data to Be Collected. Determine what data will indicate success in the OD process. The answer to the question is determined by the operational definition of objectives. The OD practitioner and key members of the client system identify what specific behaviors or events are to be observed and what hard and soft data to collect. Hard data are quantitative: dollar amounts, scores on questionnaires, behavior indicators (such as rate of growth, days of absence from the workplace, either-or indicators, and so on). Soft data are qualitative: self-perceptions, attitudes, employee or customer satisfaction measures, changes in "climate," judgmental observations, and what questions should be asked in individual or focus group interviews. Using key members of the client system (including employees whose work is affected by the OD change process) ensures that the data are viewed as valid and reliable.

Collection of Data. Collect data to use in the evaluation process. Whoever is closest to the source collects the data. The more involvement the employees and key members of the client system have in the data-collection process, the more likely they are to acknowledge the resulting evaluation as being valid. However, the impact of bias must also be considered in data collection. The fact that employees of the organization know why data are being collected is likely to cause them, subconsciously or consciously, to present only the data that serve their "agenda." The OD practitioner or other trained person should therefore conduct interviews and focus groups to collect the qualitative data to minimize the impact of bias. Using the same data-collection methods that were employed in the diagnosis process brings consistency to the collection process. Focus groups and interviews should be scheduled carefully to create as little disruption as possible to the daily life of the organization.

Measuring Outcomes. Assess outcomes of the OD process. At this point in the OD process, the OD practitioner and the client system can agree upon the format used to report the data. It is a good idea to use the simplest format that serves the purpose of tracking all changes occurring from the start to the end of the process. This level of evaluation can determine whether the short-term objectives have been achieved. Long-term outcomes need to be assessed at a later date, using appropriate through-time measures.

Now is the time to determine what indicators constitute success and failure, and whether objectives are being met. If objectives are met, the OD practitioner can work with the client to identify activities to reinforce what is working well. If not, then more questions may be raised. For instance, have the wrong approaches been used to achieve this particular objective? Was the objective realistic and measurable in the first place?

Measuring Effectiveness. Assess the effectiveness of the OD process. Analyze the effectiveness of the OD process and consider whether it accomplished the intended results. The question the OD practitioner and the client need to address is, What would have happened in the absence of what was done? If the OD process is worthwhile and perfect in every way, there should be noticeable improvement in key quantitative measures and qualitative measures. The OD practitioner and the client now discuss jointly which next steps might be appropriate in the OD process, if any.

The results of the evaluation phase of an OD process should not come as a surprise to anyone; there will be no surprises if adequate attention to feedback is paid along the way. Throughout the implementation phase of a planned change, reliable feedback mechanisms make it easy to monitor and manage the change process and make necessary adjustments. Feedback can be obtained through questionnaires, interviews, focus groups, and conversations with reliable people who are involved with the change. In particular, department heads and a cross-section of employees at all levels must be polled to solicit their perceptions of the functional (what's working well) and dysfunctional (what's not working well) consequences of the OD effort. The key to feedback is to make it reliable, so that management can have confidence that the planned change is indeed moving in the desired direction. If the OD effort is moving in the right direction, people need to know it.

Evaluation Phase Checklist

An evaluation phase checklist to document the OD process is a useful tool. There are many variables that must be managed effectively throughout the phases of the OD process. All the key players must pay attention to these dimensions if the process is to be optimally effective. Careful evaluation takes time, and it is important not to shorten the process if one is to do justice to it. The contract that is agreed on during the entry and contracting stage should reflect the amount of time required to conduct an efficient and thorough evaluation phase of the OD process. The success criteria for the OD process should be established as a part of the entry and contracting discussion. Although some aspects of the contract may be agreed on verbally, it is a good idea to document the success criteria in writing. Having such a document makes the evaluation phase much easier for all parties involved in the OD process. The criteria can be included in a memo of understanding, a proposal letter, or a formal contract.

The evaluation checklist presented here includes qualitative and quantitative success criteria.

- *Use of resources.* To what extent were adequate resources available to ensure successful implementation of the change? Was there enough time, money, and materiel supplied to accomplish the goals and objectives of the OD process?
- *Participation.* Did all the right people in all of the right parts of the organization participate fully in the change process? In particular, did those who are most directly affected by the change have an opportunity to make their voices heard, and were they listened to?
- *Access and support.* To what extent was access to and support from the key decision makers in the client system available? What was the impact of their involvement on the outcome of the OD process?
- *Communication.* How were communications handled throughout the change process? What was the influence of verbal and nonverbal communications? What

was the impact of the words, tone, and metaphors used to draw people into the process? What about cultural differences? (This is especially important when working across geographic cultures, both domestically and internationally.)

• *Hard outcome measures.* What was the impact on quantifiable and other measures that were agreed to in the entry and contracting stage of the OD process?

• *Role integrity.* How well did the client and practitioner work together? What role-clarification problems developed, if any, and how were they handled?

• *Perspective.* What differences were there, if any, in how the outcomes are perceived—the client's perspective versus the OD practitioner's perspective?

• *Confidentiality.* Where it was important and appropriate, how was confidentiality handled throughout the OD process?

• *Conflict and decision making.* How were conflict and decision making handled throughout the OD process?

• *Speak truth to power.* Both the OD practitioner and the client operate with a certain amount of power, and it is important that both parties recognize each other's power position. The client holds the checkbook; the OD practitioner holds the knowledge of process. As Block (1981) writes, "Managers (and OD practitioners) avoid looking at their own behavior mostly because they feel helpless about changing it" (p. 193). It is important not to collude with the manager in this belief. It is also important to be willing to look at oneself and recognize when one's style or philosophy may be part of the problem, while trying to help the organization shift the way people work together.

In actual practice, evaluation of the OD process may be done through a combination of surveys, interviews, focus groups, and conversations with key people throughout the organization. In the interest of building capacity within the organization, the OD practitioner and members of the client system should plan to share the evaluation stage of the OD process. This means if interviews and focus groups are used to collect data in the evaluation stage, members of the client system should partner with the OD practitioner in conducting them. In that way, they get to hear firsthand what impact the OD process has had in various parts of the organization. At the same time, the client system is developing the skill required to conduct interviews and focus groups. Such skills can then be used later for other purposes within the organization after the OD practitioner has moved on to a new client.

The practitioner can also use this process to evaluate his or her own effectiveness in carrying out various interventions. In making the final assessment, the practitioner should seek to find out: Were the question(s) posed by the client system addressed adequately? The practitioner should also seek information that helps in assessing the appropriateness of how the work was done. What did it produce?

How did people feel about what was done and how it was done? This information is useful to the OD practitioner for use with future clients.

Termination

It is often tempting to continue with an OD process for as long as the client system is willing to pay for it, but the time does come when it is best to end the process. Ending an OD process is best done at a time and in a manner that is mutually agreeable. Sometimes, however, other events take over such that a clean ending is not possible. Weisbord ([1977] 1997) says he would rather see a clean ending than lingering agony.

A number of indicators may signal that it is time to end the OD process. If either the client or the practitioner makes and then forgets agreements, it is probably time to end. Also, if the practitioner has a feeling of being more heavily invested than the client is, it's time to find a way to end the process. Finally, if the client is truly doing better and no longer needs outside help, it's time for the practitioner to look for other work in a new client system.

Once the decision is made to terminate a successful OD process, to optimize the process to the fullest it is important to document what worked well and what the next steps are. In other words, how will the organization ensure that the benefits of the OD process are long-lived and become part of the fabric of the organization?

The practitioner and the client are responsible for ensuring the sustainability of the change process. It is imperative that enabling structures be aligned to support the changes that have occurred in the organization if they are expected to be maintained. This is an area of change management that is often overlooked.

A classic example of the importance of enabling structures is seen in the award-winning Total Quality Management (TQM) program at Florida Power and Light (FP&L). In 1989, FP&L was the first U.S. company to win the prestigious Deming Prize for quality control. James Broadhead, the chairman and CEO of FP&L, dismantled the TQM program in 1990. It was apparent that the program had become a bureaucratic maze with three large departments administering it; an emphasis on documentation, graphs, charts, and reports; and procedures and processes that made it more, rather than less, difficult for employees to do their job and serve customers (Broadhead, 1991).

Actually, it took the management of FP&L several years to recognize the reality of what was taking place, though there was a sense that something was not quite right. A few of the basics of change management, such as building in accurate feedback mechanisms, could have saved the company millions and made it possible to inject needed corrections into the program.

As was the case at FP&L, the ending of an OD process can usually be felt before it is actually over. It is a feeling that sometimes makes it hard for the practitioner (and sometimes the client) to come to grips with shutting it down. But the ending is a legitimate phase of the OD process (Block, 1981), an opportunity for the OD practitioner and the client to take stock of what each has learned through the process. Whether the project has been successful or not, at the very least the parties should discuss how they worked together and what they might want from each other in the future. The tasks associated with terminating the OD process are reflected in Table 13.3. They are (1) determining how to end the OD process, (2) giving feedback to the client, (3) getting feedback from the client, and (4) contracting with the client for any future relationship that may be mutually agreeable.

TABLE 13.3. TERMINATION PHASE TASKS AND ACTIONS.

Tasks	Actions
1. Determine how to end the OD process.	Discuss and decide with the client just what form the closing meeting will take. Clarify again the format (paper, PowerPoint, binding, etc.) of any reports you will present in the meeting. Discuss and clarify who will attend the closing meeting and what role, if any, each attendee will play.
2. Give feedback to the client.	Apart from the closing meeting, discuss with the client your perceptions of how they managed the OD process. Make sure your feedback is behaviorally focused, and be prepared to make suggestions for improvement if asked to do so.
3. Get feedback from the client.	Apart from the closing meeting, ask the client for feedback on how you worked with him or her and with others in the client system. Ask for specific examples of your behavior so you can know what you did well and what you might do differently.
4. Contract with the client for the future relationship you both wish to have.	Discuss with the client what each of you would like in terms of an ongoing relationship. Determine whether the client is open to regular check-ins from you.

Determine How to End the OD Process

Once it is clear that the OD process and relationship should come to an end, the OD practitioner and the client decide what form the closing meeting will take. Depending on the nature of the OD process, the closing meeting might be more or less formal in style and content. The important thing is to make sure the client's expectations for the meeting are known in advance so they can be met. The discussion should also clarify two other points: (1) the format (paper, PowerPoint, binding, among others) of any reports presented in the meeting and (2) who will attend the meeting and what role, if any, each person will have.

Give Feedback to the Client

A major benefit of the OD process is the learning that takes place on multiple levels for everyone actively involved in the process. Giving performance feedback to the client throughout the process builds capacity within the client system to handle future change initiatives more effectively. The feedback discussion with the client should take place soon after the closing meeting, if not on the same day— no longer than a week later. The timeliness of this feedback discussion is no less critical than for any other feedback session. The OD practitioner should discuss with the client any perceptions of how the client managed the OD process. It is important to make sure the feedback is behaviorally focused, so the client can re-call and relate to specific instances and to be better prepared to make suggestions for improvement, if asked to do so.

Get Feedback from the Client

Learning takes place on multiple levels in the process. To know more about how the OD practitioner's role was perceived and experienced, he or she solicits feedback from the client that is behaviorally focused and identifies specific instances regarding the impact of working with him or her and with others in the client system. Again, this feedback session should take place as close as possible to the formal ending of the OD change process, but not as part of the closing meeting. The OD practitioner should ask for specific examples of behavior, to know just what worked well and what might be done differently. This feedback is useful for future work not only with this client but also with any others.

Contract with the Client for the Future Relationship You Each Wish to Have

OD practitioners who are successful in their practice know that success stems primarily from the kind of relationship they build with a client and with members of the client system. Most successful practitioners recognize the power of partnering with their clients; they know that each partner must have something the other wants (Bellman, 1990). That said, it is important for the OD practitioner to discuss with the client what they both would like in terms of an ongoing relationship. The ongoing partnership requires that the parties be willing to discuss their expectations. For the practitioner, this may mean willingness to accept and respond to occasional phone calls that don't produce an invoice to the client. For the client, this may mean calling on the knowledge, skills, and abilities of the practitioner when there is a significant opportunity for using them or referring others to the practitioner when such needs are made known. For both parties, it means being completely open with each other and trusting in the power of the relationship.

Conclusion

"Start up as you would like to end up." Those wise words on interpersonal relationships are equally applicable to the kind of relationship an OD practitioner wants to have with a client system. The evaluation and termination phase of the OD process will work smoothly with no surprises as long as the entry and contracting phase includes discussion about what the end should look like. Along the way, it is important to give feedback on the process and on the key indicators of success, as movement toward the desired outcomes begins to occur. Buy-in to the process is more easily ensured when members of the client system are included in decisions about things that directly affect them. Ending the OD process with a strong assessment of the process and its impact in the organization provides understanding and support for the client's next steps.

References

Bellman, G. M. (1990). *The consultant's calling: Bringing who you are to what you do.* San Francisco: Jossey-Bass.

Block, P. (1981). *Flawless consulting.* San Diego: University Associates.

Broadhead, J. L. (1991). The post-Deming diet: Dismantling a quality bureaucracy. *Training, 2,* 41–43.

Dillon, J. T. (2003). The use of questions in organizational consulting. *Journal of Applied Behavioral Science, 39*(4), 438–452.

Katz, D., & Kahn, R. L. (1978). *The social psychology of organizations.* New York: Wiley.

Kilman, R. H. (1989). *Managing beyond the quick fix: A completely integrated program for creating and maintaining organizational success.* San Francisco: Jossey-Bass.

Kotter, J. P. (1996). *Leading change.* Boston: Harvard Business School.

Marshak, R. J. (1993). Lewin meets Confucius: A review of the OD model of change. *Journal of Applied Behavioral Science, 29*(4), 393–415.

Schaffer, R. H., & Thompson, H. A. (1992). Successful change programs begin with results. *Harvard Business Review, 70*(1), 80–89.

Trisko, K. S., & League, V. C. (1980). Evaluation of human service programs. In J. W. Pfeiffer & J. J. Jones (Eds.), *The 1980 annual handbook for group facilitators.* San Diego: University Associates.

Weisbord, M. (1997). The organization development contract. In D. F. Van Eynde, J. C. Hoy, & D. C. Van Eynde (Eds.), *Organization development classics: The theory and practice of change—the best of the OD practitioner.* San Francisco: Jossey-Bass.

PART FOUR

WORKING FROM LEVELS OF SYSTEMS PERSPECTIVES: INDIVIDUALS TO ENVIRONMENT

CHAPTER FOURTEEN

WORKING WITH INDIVIDUALS IN AN ORGANIZATIONAL CONTEXT

Edwin C. Nevis, Jonno Hanafin, and
Mary Ann Rainey Tolbert

The primary focus of organization development (OD) is to enhance the performance of an organization. The work is seen in the context of organizational mission and group targets. Yet organizations are structured so that individuals are responsible for groups of people or for coordination of effort of numerous employees. Thus no matter what a given consulting contract may entail, implementation of the work always involves various kinds of interaction between practitioners and individuals. Since these individuals play a critical role as "linking pins," the quality of interaction between them and practitioners can greatly influence the success or failure of an intervention.

Work at the individual level requires a set of distinct skills primarily focused on working at the margin, when the pull of one-on-one interaction is toward more intimate connection among the people involved. Boundary management becomes a more complex matter as the practitioner is drawn to reveal more of his or her own self. If the practitioner is too supportive and becomes too close to the individual, something is lost by way of clean observation and the ability to take a strong (potentially opposing) stance. The skill is in striking a balance between strategic and intimate interactions with the individual while keeping in mind the larger objective of enhancing organizational effectiveness. Strategic interactions are those designed to accomplish a task, and they often involve using hierarchical power. Intimate interactions are designed to bring people closer together and minimize power differences (see Nevis, Backman, and Nevis, 2003).

249

This chapter describes a model for characterizing and improving how working with individuals is carried out in the service of organization development. The model is an adaptation of a framework initially developed by the authors and Claire Stratford in 1997.

The need for a more complex framework for working with individuals in organizations is influenced by several developments. Almost all external consulting work involves partnering with internal specialists and managers on a range of initiatives, from planning events to supporting personal and professional development. Consulting that is geared to strategic planning, visioning, Total Quality Management, and other structural interventions represents a significant investment by organizations in executive coaching. There are new writings about leadership focusing on the importance of self-awareness and conversational skills. Many practitioners are spending more and more time with senior executives in an advisory capacity, as opposed to being a process practitioner in the traditional sense. These observations lead to the conclusion that it is time to examine a systematic perspective of the possibilities and issues involved in various ways of working with individuals in the organizational context.

The Three Faces of Individual Work

Although there are many roles in which working with an individual takes place, three major categories can be identified. They are referred to as "faces" to emphasize that these are stances, each driven by the intent of the practitioner or intervener. Something different is accomplished in each face, using one-on-one interaction as the method of operation. In so doing, the faces represent ways of intervening to support the particular objective. Exhibit 14.1 lists the three faces.

EXHIBIT 14.1. THREE FACES OF INDIVIDUAL WORK.

Coaching
- For improved performance; enhancement of skills
- For change in dysfunctional behavior
- For career development

Facilitating more effective interactions between people
- Enhancing individual readiness for third-party intervention
- Developing readiness for team building

Strategic advising
- Becoming highly involved in content issues
- Assuming some responsibility for action by the client

The original model presented four faces of individual work: (1) coaching, (2) facilitating more effective interactions between people, (3) strategic advising, and (4) planning large system interventions. The fourth face is well known to OD practitioners; much has been written about this perspective and the issues involved. However, the reader is reminded that many of the issues of working at the three faces presented here apply to working with the individual in planning large system interventions.

It follows from the differences in these stances that clear understanding of the intervener role is imperative. The sections in this chapter deal with each face, indicating special features and issues to consider:

- Even though being in a coaching role does not prohibit the practitioner from giving advice to an individual, responsibility for the actions taken by the client rests with the client.
- When acting as a strategic adviser, the practitioner is often asked to state unequivocally what course of action to take.
- If the practitioner is asked to implement a plan of action, she is clearly taking on responsibility for the outcome. If she is doing so in the position of an internal practitioner, she is even more responsible.
- To be effective as a coach, the practitioner must work to enhance the quality of the exchange or interaction between herself and the client.
- When acting as a third-party intervener, the practitioner's role is that of "stage manager" for the interaction between the two clients.

One way to better understand the contexts and intervention choices involved in organizational consulting is to pay attention to the complexity of each situation. Consulting involves entering often confusing and always-intricate organizational landscapes. It helps to sort out the presenting issues, the levels of system, and the choices available to the intervener in determining the location and nature of the actual work. This enables the intervener to be clear about the purposes for engaging in one-on-one work. Table 14.1 presents a matrix that was developed to assist in this analysis.

Using the matrix as a guide, it is possible to analyze the intent of one-on-one work in relation to important aspects of a given assignment. For example, a practitioner may be contracted by a two-person system (an executive and a human resource director) to coach another manager. Although the desired outcome may be expressed in terms of increased effectiveness of the person being coached, the extent and nature of the practitioner's interaction with the executive and HR director is often unclear. (More will be said later about this consulting

TABLE 14.1. MATRIX FOR WORKING WITH INDIVIDUALS IN AN ORGANIZATIONAL CONTEXT.

Levels Available	Point of Entry	Contracting Parties	Focus of Work	Scope of Desired Outcome
Individual, lower-level, midlevel, upper-level, CEO				
Two-person system				
Group				
Department or division				
Organization or firm				
Industry				

Source: Copyright © 1997 OSD Center, Gestalt Institute of Cleveland.

challenge.) Experience in training coaches suggests that the most common source of difficulty for practitioners is not poor work with the person being coached but failure to pay enough attention to the quality of the interaction with the other individuals involved.

In another case, one may be working with a CEO, but the focus of the work is on issues related to the whole system, with little attention paid to the CEO's management style or personality characteristics. Here, desired outcomes may be expressed in terms of new strategy or building a senior team. In some respects this looks like a coaching assignment, but it is more like acting as a strategic adviser.

In yet another case—an assignment of one of the authors—the contract was developed between the practitioners and the CEO. The work involved a culture change project with a major business unit of the firm, working with an internal practitioner. As the work progressed, it became clear that the internal practitioner did not like the executive in charge of the division and was avoiding him in the process of implementing the work. Since the internal practitioner was directing the project, it was necessary to confront him about the situation. This led to some tough conversation in which, at one point, the internal practitioner was challenged to change his attitude or give up this assignment. Eventually, the scope of work was expanded to include working one-on-one with the internal practitioner in the interest of doing good work at the organizational level. Secondarily, the internal practitioner was being helped to see the dysfunctional nature of his behavior—a frequent aspect of coaching work.

The First Face: Coaching

Coaching is first in this discussion because it is the first thing that comes to mind when practitioners talk about one-on-one work. It is also one of the first things raised by an organization that is interested in developing its leaders. Consider the development continuum in Figure 14.1.

FIGURE 14.1. HANAFIN AND KITSON DEVELOPMENT CONTINUUM.

Internal					**External**	
Manager's coaching on the job	External coaching on the job	Rotational assignments	Special projects and assignments	Company leadership development program	Company tailored skill/function training	Outside education
Assessment and feedback →						
Performance appraisal	External practitioner	Succession plan	Start-up	Assessments	Business skills	Advanced degree programs
Assessment			Turnaround	Core program	Function company forums	Courses
			Priority initiatives	Modules		Conferences
				Experiments	Organizational and people skills	Professional networks
				Learning groups		

Source: Copyright © 2002 Jonno Hanafin and Michael Kitson Associates, Inc.

The Hanafin and Kitson (H&K) Development Continuum offers a menu of development options ranging from completely internally resourced to completely externally resourced, with variations in between. When it comes to building development plans for individuals, most managers are inclined to look first at the organization's own catalogue of company-offered training and development programs. Internal programs may be of good quality, but they are usually generic in their design and appeal. However, special cases—for example, identified high potentials or interpersonally inept technical wizards—warrant something more tailored to the particular need.

One favored approach with the high-potential individual is sending him to an intensive and expensive general management program at a prestigious university. Programs of this sort offer a base of high-level and strategic perspective, but they still may not address the specific development needs of individuals. In the case of highly skilled individuals, these programs are not the answer.

Setting up Coaching

This is where the coaching option draws its appeal. An external coach is assigned to the individual with the objective of giving him or her focused and relevant guidance. Of course, all this assumes that the individual's manager is also actively coaching the individual. A number of issues must be addressed at the start of the coaching engagement.

Who Is the Client? The practitioner needs to be clear, and in the process make sure everyone else is clear, about whom the practitioner is working for and who will decide if the engagement is successful. Identifying the client has implications during the work for whether, how, and to whom progress is reported. Obviously a stronger relationship can be built with the person being coached if he is the client and has the responsibility for communicating progress to the rest of the organization. Realistically, the initiating manager or bill payer may want at least a periodic high-level update from the practitioner. The terms and boundaries of such reporting need to be established up front. It is often useful to schedule regular updates involving the coach, the individual being coached, and the individual's manager. This way everyone has access to the same information about the work. This also gives the practitioner an opportunity to hear how the individual describes progress to his manager.

Who Chooses the Practitioner? Even if the individual being coached has been "encouraged" to use a coach, the person being coached should have some say in the selection, perhaps being offered two or three coaches and choosing one with whom there is good chemistry. Influencing the selection of the coach helps reduce resistance and gives the individual some ownership of the process. Matching coach and person to be coached is a two-way process; the practitioner and the person being coached need to feel it is a good fit.

What Are the Coaching Goals? Being engaged to "help someone become a better manager" is an invitation to trouble. The contract needs to be precise: what are expected outcomes, and who will judge the results of the coaching assignment? The practitioner can support the organization by pushing for sharper definition of development goals. By asking probing questions and offering alternatives, the practitioner helps everyone develop a shared set of expectations.

What Are the Boundary Conditions of the Coaching Work? Are there things that are out of bounds in the work? Is it public knowledge that this individual is being coached? Can the practitioner speak with others in the organization? Who expects to be in the communications loop, and how will they be included? How long is the engagement projected to last? Involve everyone in determining the dimensions of the playing field.

The Context of Coaching: A Blessing or a Curse?

The context must be considered in any coaching assignment. Having a coach conveys very different meanings in different organizations. The practitioner needs to know whether coaching is primarily developmental or remedial. In some organizations, bringing in a coach for someone means the person is in trouble; a coach is a last-ditch effort to salvage a career or turn around sinking performance. In one multinational organization, it was even more specific: being assigned a coach meant you had ninety days to turn yourself around or face dismissal. These engagements are usually managed quite tightly, with rigorous performance criteria used to decide thumbs up or thumbs down at the end. Here, people being coached want to hide their coach, discussing the matter only with those who need to know. In other organizations, having a coach means you are one of the chosen few and have been designated for stardom. After all, the organization would not incur the considerable expense of a coach if it did not have some indication of a satisfactory return on investment. In this instance, a coach is a corporate seal of approval to be proudly discussed and displayed.

There is another consideration somewhere in between the blessing and the curse that requires attention: assessment. Is the coach being brought in to assess the potential, or to salvage the ability, of the individual? The distinction of purpose between development and assessment is critical to the work. Both tasks add value. The important thing is clarity of intent. It can confuse all involved if the roles of assessor and developer are combined. Organizations that use different resources for assessment and development tend to be more effective at developing their people. Individuals generally feel freer to open up to someone who is not influencing their career possibilities.

The Second Face: Facilitating More Effective Interactions Between People

The practitioner's second face includes two-person consulting and developing readiness for team building.

Two-Person System Consultation

In this work, the focus is on the interactions of the two people and the desired outcome is an enhanced working relationship. One application might be to support better coordination between a marketing director and the head of engineering. Another is to reduce conflict that has interfered with the effective functioning of either party or the two-person system as a whole. In dispute situations, the work is called third-party intervention. In each instance, the parties need to work together to accomplish some objective that is important to each but cannot be achieved by one of them alone. In his famous experiments on intergroup conflict, Sherif (1971) referred to this objective as a "superordinate goal." At some point, the work involves working with each individual in the dyad, both separately and when they are together. This allows each person to see and accept individual differences and get some insight into how they contribute to the dynamic that has been created. The importance of the individual work is that it supports the pair to engage in what is often a difficult conversation.

Individual work is generally needed to help bring the parties together. This is a bridging or gate-keeping role and may be seen as a variation of shuttle diplomacy. None of what is being said is new to the experienced practitioner. Often missed by both new and advanced practitioners is that a very particular stance is required:

- Focusing on readiness to engage—not rushing into meeting before each party is ready and conditions and ground rules are clarified.
- Balancing the attention paid to each person. This ranges from time spent with each party alone to allowing equal air time when they are together.

- Avoiding any semblance of bias or alignment with one party, or seeing one party as the needy one or the culprit.
- Maintaining a neutral stance. Focus on the collective behavior of the two-person system—that is, how they speak, respond, and react to each other.
- Avoiding involvement in the content or substantive issues. Heightening awareness of the individuals about the potential value of collaboration and the obstacles that impede it.
- Using self to establish trust in the process, to encourage a hopeful attitude in each individual and to teach the parties strategies for engaging with each other outside the session.

The role of the intervener is to improve the functioning of the pair as a system and support the interaction of the two. There are elements of individual work that support two-person work:

- Surfacing projections each has concerning the other
- Surfacing fantasies about what will happen if they get together
- Supporting each to feel more in control over what might happen
- Facilitating meetings, managing the logistics involved
- Acting to evoke a sense of hopefulness by soliciting from each person evidence of what the two do well together and what their strengths are

In a meeting with one of the individuals, the intervener might ask questions such as:

- How would you describe how the other behaves when with you?
- What would the other say about how you behave when the two of you are together?
- What are your objections to meeting with the other, to talking openly?
- What are the goals and values that the two of you share?
- What would it take to cooperate with the other?
- What do you think are the reasons the other doesn't cooperate with you?

Obviously, this work cannot be successful if both parties do not have some motivation to engage each other. One party is often more willing than the other. Dealing with this disparity requires great skill in working with each person alone in a way that avoids any sign of partiality. Any resistance on either side is to be respected.

There are also some critical moments in which individual work is useful when both are together. Here too the focus is on supporting the two individuals to engage each other.

Possible interventions include:

- Promoting the parties to talk to each other, not to the intervener
- Encouraging sharing of information on the part of both individuals; this includes facts, attitudes, feelings, projections, and fantasies about "What might happen if . . . ?"
- After the intervener addresses one party and gets a response, allowing the other party to comment on the first party's response
- Periodically checking in with each party
- Underscoring progress on the part of each person
- Allowing closure: what was accomplished by each, and work yet to be done

Developing Readiness for Team Building

These principles and suggestions apply equally well in preparing people to engage in team-building events, particularly in work to produce readiness for participation on a team. However, team development is a public event that usually involves hierarchical differences. Individuals tend to be more accepting of tough intervener statements made to them in a private setting, but the same statements made in front of others can provoke anger and defensiveness. It is important to recognize (as is more readily observed in Eastern cultures) that saving face is also important in the Western world. The last thing an intervener wants is to embarrass a leader or manager in front of her staff. For this reason, it is often necessary to do a considerable amount of work individually with the team leaders before team building occurs. Building readiness, creating ownership, clarifying objectives, and managing expectations increase the success of the endeavor.

The Third Face: Strategic Advising

This stance requires the intervener to shift the balance between process consultation and involvement in content. Both may be used in all three faces, but with this face there is much less concern with maintaining a neutral position. Opinions, points of view, information, even biases are expected from the intervener. If process consultation based on Gestalt or another orientation stresses the enhancement of client awareness, strategic advising or content consultation focuses more on client behavior and action. Interveners should feel free to support one alternative out of several that the client may be considering, or to attempt to convince the client not to take an action that is being contemplated. In so doing, the intervener assumes responsibility for the outcome. Experienced practitioners often shift between process consulting and content consulting for a period of time. The shift can be useful in supporting the client; it can have the effect of broadening awareness.

In one example, after hearing executives complain for years about their firm's incentive compensation plan, a practitioner convened a meeting of several executives and recommended that the program be changed. After partnering with the senior vice president of human resources and another executive and seeking the expertise of a compensation specialist, a new compensation plan was developed. It is worth noting that the initial contract had nothing to do with executive compensation. Rather, the purpose of the work was to conduct educational interventions and related consulting to help the firm function better as a knowledge-based network. Also of significance is that the practitioner had gained more than ten years of experience developing appraisal and compensation systems in an earlier career. The experience served to inform the practitioner about what was needed.

In another example, the vice president of marketing was advised for several years that he would not make his commercial marketing targets because he did not have enough marketing and sales personnel with the expertise required to do the job. The practitioner tells the executive what he needs and makes comments about certain individuals who are seen as failing in the job. What right does a practitioner have to do this? After all, the practitioner was not hired to give advice on commercial marketing. The answer is that the practitioner had worked with commercial marketing organizations in similar businesses and had many years of experience in assessing managerial talent. Of course, the practitioner might have been wrong to speak up; however, the willingness to take the risk in such instances is a trademark of the strategic adviser.

These examples can have a negative effect. A practitioner can give poor advice with detrimental results or can be told not to interfere. One important consideration for the practitioner is the nature of the relationship with the client organization—specifically, years of experience with a client. This constitutes a better base for opinion and enhances the possibility of being heard as a respected voice that is genuinely trying to help the organization achieve its desired goals.

On the other hand, giving advice can violate an expectation or a contract. For example, consider the impact of offering an opinion about the suitability of an individual for a promotion when your data about the person has been largely derived during training or through coaching that was deemed to be a private matter. This is a classic dilemma for internal practitioners, who have all kinds of opportunity to make observations about managers. If there is a presumed confidentiality in these encounters, how does the internal practitioner respond when an executive asks for an opinion about an individual? An internal or external practitioner asked to evaluate an individual has an obligation to let the individual know this may happen.

Practitioners who see themselves as strategic advisers will recognize that their struggle may be more around how to handle the familiarity and intimacy that develop with the client. Practitioners who have worked with an organization for many years and are held in high esteem often find that it is almost impossible to maintain a neutral stance or operate on the margin. They are now members of the client family. How is the work affected, and how does everyone involved adapt to this state of affairs? How does a practitioner maintain an external consulting role under these circumstances? This type of relationship clearly changes the nature of the interactions with the firm.

Distortions in Working at the Individual Level

Practitioners are faced with a unique set of dynamics when working with the individual, regardless of stance or role. In organizational consulting, the marginality of the practitioner is a major asset. In the initial stages of consulting, when the practitioner begins the work, the lack of knowledge about the system allows the practitioner to take in data and information with fresh eyes. This openness is a major strength and opportunity, although some practitioners pressure themselves to quickly draw conclusions in order to feel competent. As the work progresses, the practitioner builds a working relationship with the client and gradually loses some of the newness and marginality. This progression is natural. However, there are some pitfalls present, in the form of what is referred to as "distortions." Two distortions that are talked about in the clinical world are *transference* and *countertransference*. Transference is the distortion in attribution and expectation that the client has relative to the therapist. Countertransference is the distortion of perception and attitude that develops on the part of the therapist. Consulting distortions are discussed here from the perspective of the client and the practitioner.

Client Distortions That Affect the Work

Therapists need to be aware and attend to client transference and its impact on the therapist-client relationship. Similarly, practitioners have to be vigilant about how client distortions interfere with the contact between the individual members of the organization and the practitioner.

The Paradox of Engagement. One of the wonderful paradoxes of consulting is having a client contact a practitioner, contract for a major change initiative, and then immediately resist the change. The intent to change is real, but when it actually comes down to the *what* and *how* of the change, natural self-preservation mechanisms kick in.

Over There. Most people acknowledge that there are problems in the organization needing to be addressed. However, few problems are owned. Individuals or groups seldom see themselves as needing to change. Pointing to where the "real" problem is, we usually point "over there"—not with me or us. For example, leaders are eager to engage practitioners to fix cultural or systemic shortcomings but resist looking at how they contribute to sustaining the status quo through their own behavior and thinking.

Whatever You Say. Even though it is quite flattering to have a client willingly accept the influence of the practitioner, unconditional acceptance is questionable. A pattern of joining with others without consideration of one's own perspective is problematic. The job for the practitioner is to support the client in differentiating herself.

Consultants Are People Who Borrow Your Watch to Tell You What Time It Is. Individuals in organizations often lump practitioners into one group. If they have had a negative experience with any consultant or practitioner, then all practitioners are suspect. Practitioners who take the time to build relationships with members of the client system, showing their uniqueness, greatly decrease the chance of being viewed as "just another practitioner."

Practitioner Distortions That Affect the Work

In the world of organizational consulting, many potential distortions are also likely to occur and require the practitioner to become aware of his or her predisposition to skew the relationships and the work. Some of the distortions that are seen in practitioners are discussed here.

Let Me Show You How Good I Am. The urge to be perceived by a new client as capable and experienced can lead practitioners to end the scanning and assessment process too soon. This eagerness, driven by anxiety to be judged as an expert, causes major blind spots. The result can be loss of the most valuable asset that a practitioner has when entering a system: his or her ignorance or desire to learn. This ignorance should be used to maintain openness and curiosity rather than to shape premature certainties.

I've Seen This Before. This is the tendency to expect the next client to be the same as the last client. Work in the same industry obviously brings some similarities. However, the degree to which the practitioner can begin by searching out how the new client is unlike the last one will result in less distortion. This problem is caused not so much by anxiety but by overconfidence or sheer laziness.

Playing Favorites. The tendency is to form likes and dislikes about people or hold ingrained values about what is good or bad behavior. All practitioners have particular kinds of people with whom they prefer to work. When they work with a difficult manager or with someone whose style is different from their own, it becomes difficult to remain neutral. This can result in less patience or creativity in the client engagement. Likewise, practitioners often move closer to clients they like and fail to see less effective aspects of their behavior. Practitioners may arrange to avoid or seek some people and some parts of the organization. Biases such as these hinder the effectiveness of the work.

Getting Too Familiar. As the work progresses, practitioners are likely to either develop confidence in the client and begin to accept the perspective of the client without question or have less confidence in the client and become too doubtful and dismissive. Either tendency carried too far skews the work. Even the most competent client has errors in thinking and occasional miscues, and those with suspicious judgment will sometimes be correct in their appraisal.

Hooked on Power. Every human being has some behavioral pattern of dealing with issues of control, power, and authority. Most independent practitioners are highly autonomous people who possess a great deal of control, power, and authority about what they do. They also carry a lot of power in organizations by virtue of their role. The key for practitioners is to be mindful of how the work is affected by their personal issues of power.

Self-knowledge is necessary to effectively manage practitioner distortions. Some questions that can be asked include the following

- What are my values that I do not wish to compromise?
- Is this contract within my range of limits regarding use of myself?
- Who does this person remind me of? How is he or she different?
- Why am I irritated? What does this remind me of?
- What am I avoiding here? How would it help the situation to deal with it more directly?
- What is my stance in relation to authority? How did I become this way?

Conclusion

Working with the individual is an exciting and critical aspect of organization development. It allows the intervener to influence key members of the organization by creating opportunities that usually are not possible while working at larger levels of systems. On the other hand, it creates tension and dilemma, mismanagement of which can negatively affect an organizational intervention. By developing a heightened awareness of the issues involved, and through enhanced skills for working at the individual level within a range of contexts, interveners can significantly improve their work. This chapter offers a model to assist in this endeavor.

References

Nevis, S. M., Backman, S., & Nevis, E. C. (2003). Connecting strategic and intimate interactions: The need for balance. *Gestalt Review, 7*(2), 134–146.

Sherif, M. (1971). Superordinate goals in the reduction of intergroup conflict. In B. L. Hinton & H. J. Reitz (Eds.), *Groups and organizations.* Belmont, CA: Wadsworth.

CHAPTER FIFTEEN

WORKING WITH GROUPS IN ORGANIZATIONS

Matt Minahan

The history of human endeavor is full of great accomplishments that far exceed the capacity of any one person or group. They are often our most complex and demanding tasks, requiring interdependence among people and groups, leadership, communications, constructive norms, differentiated functions and roles, and perhaps most important the ability to understand and mobilize human behavior toward a common goal.

Whether the task is mapping the human genome, or printing and distributing twelve thousand copies of the 560-page *Report of the 9/11 Commission* within forty-eight hours, or determining the performance measures for a task team, the efforts and ideas and interests and egos of multiple people must be organized and aligned to produce a result that is greater than the sum of its parts. In fact, groups are simultaneously one of the most prolific yet profoundly puzzling elements of human and organizational life, which explains the push-pull, love-hate, approach-avoid reaction that people have about them.

One of the major challenges of being and working in groups is understanding the variety and complexity of the dynamics. There are complex issues happening within each person in the group, there are complex and often unspoken dynamics among pairs of people in the group, there are complex and difficult-to-observe phenomena occurring at the group level, and there is interaction between the group and its environment. It is vital for effective group members, facilitators, and OD consultants to be able to observe the several levels of interaction in order to intervene appropriately.

This chapter outlines some of the foundational thinking and knowledge of groups, identifies some tools that help in working with and understanding groups, lists some factors that affect group performance, points out some key differences between groups, and presents an integrated group development theory and model.

Foundational Thinkers and Thoughts

The earliest research on people and groups was conducted in the 1890s, when psychologist Norman Triplett was studying the results of bicycle races and discovered that cyclists' times were faster when they were racing against each other than when racing against the clock. Was it the presence of other people that stimulated better performance? Were there impacts other than just a faster time that resulted from having other people present? These were the first questions in our thirst for knowledge about our behavior in groups. Through the early twentieth century, researchers concluded that the presence of other people enhanced performance on simple tasks but impeded performance on more complex tasks.

Lewin

The first reference to "group dynamics" dates from 1939, when social scientist Kurt Lewin described the group as its own entity—different from, and more than just the aggregate of, its individual members, having its own "life" and underlying dynamics. Lewin (1939) also concluded that there is reciprocal influence between individual and group behavior, explaining that human behavior in groups is a function of both the personality of the individual person and the social or group situation in which the person exists. Neither the individual's personality nor the social circumstances alone could adequately explain what happens in groups; in his view, members influence what happens at the group level, and groups influence individual member behavior in groups.

He represented (Lewin, 1951) that dynamic in the "formula" $B = f(P, E)$, where behavior (B) is a function (f) of the interaction between the person (P) and the environment (E). In other words, how a person reacts or behaves in a given situation is a function of the needs and drives that are operative in them at the moment, and norms and social structures of the situation (Wheelan, 2005).

As a young Jewish man in Nazi Germany, Lewin developed an acute interest in the relationship between the individual and the collective, and he brought to his work a deep and abiding awareness of the power of the majority to isolate and victimize the minority—imperatives that still influence our field to this day. He found in the United States a laboratory for testing the principles of democracy and empowerment. OD's commitment to democracy, social justice, empowerment of the marginalized, and elimination of racism and oppression can be traced back to Lewin, Dorothy Day, and Paulo Freire, among others.

Through World War II, Lewin applied his theories on an even larger scale, researching the social principles of belonging, conformity, and the leadership styles that caused citizens in the United States to comply with voluntary rationing of commodities such as sugar, butter, and rubber, especially when there were no likely consequences for noncompliance.

Lewin's research was the setting for the discovery of a powerful form of group interaction, called the T-group, or training group. In working with three other behavioral scientists at a 1946 conference on race relations in New Britain, Connecticut, Lewin and his colleagues discovered that group participants were more interested in the private, end-of-the-day comments of the research observers than they were in what was happening in the open plenaries. Observations made in the evening discussions started to change behaviors that were occurring during the daytime sessions; gradually they were integrated into the work of the group, stimulating real-time feedback among participants and trainers and generating many of the rules of effective feedback that we still use today. This seminal conference was also the first time that newsprint (the antecedent of today's flipchart) was used for real-time illustration of spontaneous ideas that emerged from the group work (Weisbord, 1987).

Within a year, Lewin established a summer workshop in Bethel, Maine, where the T-group methodology was refined into what Carl Rogers called "perhaps the most significant social invention of this century" (Morrow, 1969). Lewin died prematurely of heart disease in 1947, but his research colleagues—Ken Benne, Leland Bradford, and Ron Lippett—went on to found NTL Institute. The institute carries on the T-group tradition in Bethel and at sites around the world, with a commitment to feedback and personal growth through laboratory education.

Bion

Meanwhile, in England, British psychoanalyst Wilfried Bion developed a structure for understanding group dynamics. Bion's theory is based in large part on his work managing a rehabilitation unit for psychiatric patients in the British Army during World War II and later with small groups at the Tavistock Clinic. The central concept in Bion's theory is that in every group, two groups exist: the "work group" and the "basic assumption group." It should be made clear that Bion was not referring to factions or subgroups within the group, but rather to two dimensions of behavior existing simultaneously within the group. The *work group* is that element of group functioning that is concerned with the primary task or work of the group. The mature work group is aware of its purpose and can define its task. Its members work cooperatively as separate and discrete members who willingly choose to belong to the group because they identify with interests of the group. This group tests its conclusions, seeks knowledge, and learns from its experience.

Bion's *basic assumption group* employs ineffective and self-contradicting behaviors that reduce the effectiveness of the group. The basic assumption group can be thought of as the "as if" group, meaning that the group behaves as if certain tacit assumptions were held by the members. These assumptions are hidden in the group subconscious, outside the awareness of group members. Bion identified three types of basic assumption group: the *dependency*, the *fight-flight,* and the *pairing* groups.

Bion noted that all three basic assumption groups offer instantaneous gratification, are resistant to learning from experience, interfere with work, fixate on leadership issues, ignore the consequences of their actions, are disoriented about time, display poor group memory, and behave as if their central assumptions are outside the group's awareness (Kass, 1996).

Because of the complexity of this theory and the hidden nature of the basic assumption group, it is often difficult for a practitioner to identify which basic assumption is at play, particularly in a highly structured group setting; it is easier to observe basic assumption behaviors in groups that lack structure and organization.

However, elements of basic assumption can be identified at different times within groups. The dependency basic assumption is often at play in the early stages of group life, before issues of leadership and structure have been resolved. It is particularly important for the practitioner to be aware of a group's dependent behaviors to avoid setting unrealistic expectations or presenting oneself as an omniscient expert figure.

When scapegoating occurs within a group dynamic, it is possible that the fight-flight assumption is at play. Members bond together to fight a common foe, the scapegoat, resulting in the majority of the group sharing a sense of purpose and "groupness" (often for the first time). The pairing modality can be suspected whenever two individuals within a group are looked upon as the sole hope of creating a solution to the group's problems, only to find that the solutions generated are immediately destroyed by the rest of the group (Minahan and Hutton, 2004).

Bion's work led to the establishment of the Tavistock Institute in London, which continues to conduct research, consulting, and professional development work to support change and learning.

Schutz's FIRO-B

From World War II's Manhattan Project came the nuclear-powered engine, which suddenly allowed submarines to remain at sea far longer than the thirty days of their combustion-engine predecessors. Missions of up to 180 days put enormous stress on crews, which sent psychologist Will Schutz looking for compatibility measures around which submarine crews could be commissioned. In 1958, he published the Fundamental Interpersonal Relationship theory, and its subsequent instrument, FIRO-B (for Behavior; see Table 15.1). The model explains interpersonal behavior in terms of the individual's orientation toward others with regard to three interpersonal needs—*inclusion, control,* and *affection*—and the individual's need to either *express* (demonstrate) that behavior to others or *want* (desire) to receive that behavior as expressed by others.

TABLE 15.1. THE FIRO-B SIX-CELL MODEL AND BEHAVIORS.

Inclusion	Control	Affection
Expressed Inclusion:	Expressed Control:	Expressed Affection:
• Talking and joking with others	• Assuming positions of leadership	• Reassuring and supporting
• Involving others in projects and meetings	• Advancing ideas within the group	• Giving gifts to show appreciation
• Recognizing others' accomplishments	• Taking a competitive stance	• Demonstrating concern about other members' personal lives
• Incorporating everyone's ideas and suggestions	• Managing the conversation	• Sharing personal feelings and opinions
	• Influencing others' opinions	
Wanted Inclusion:	Wanted Control:	Wanted Affection:
• Frequenting heavily trafficked areas	• Asking for help on the job	• Being flexible and accommodating
• Seeking recognition or responsibility	• Involving others in decision making	• Listening carefully to others
• Getting involved in high-priority projects	• Requesting specific instructions or clarification	• Sharing feelings of anxiety
• Going along with the majority	• Asking for permission	• Trying to please others
	• Deferring to others' wishes	• Giving others more than they want or need

Source: Adapted from Sweeney (1993). Reprinted with permission: *OD Practitioner,* 2002, *34*(3).

According to Schutz, groups develop in predictable stages, dealing first with the issues of inclusion, then control, and then affection, repeating the cycle each time the group convenes. The FIRO-B group remains one of the most validated, best-documented instruments for working with groups.

Bennis and Shepard's Theory of Group Development

During the same years, and from their work with T-groups, Warren Bennis and Herb Shepard (1956) incorporated concepts from Bion, Schutz, and others into their theory outlining six distinct stages of group development in which members must resolve two major areas of internal uncertainty: *dependence* (authority relations) and *interdependence* (personal relations; see Table 15.2).

TABLE 15.2. BENNIS AND SHEPARD'S THEORY OF GROUP DEVELOPMENT.

Phase One: Dependence (Authority Relations)	Phase Two: Interdependence (Personal Relations)
Subphase one: dependence—flight	Subphase four: enchantment—flight
• Members search fruitlessly for a common goal	• Members are happy, cohesive, and relaxed
• Members share harmless facts and information about selves, doodle, yawn, or intellectualize	• Coffee and cake may be served at meetings
• Group discusses interpersonal problems as if they are external to the group	• Group plans events such as group parties and outings
• Members look to trainer/leader for approval and direction	• Group may create poems or songs to commemorate important persons or events in the group
	• Disagreements and issues are misinterpreted or ignored
Subphase two: counterdependence—fight	Subphase five: disenchantment—fight
• Group splits into two opposing subgroups	• Group splits into two opposing subgroups
• Attempts to impose structure by electing a chairman, creating agendas, forming committees, etc., are thwarted	• Members go out of their way to join in a conversation with a subgroup rather than speak to the whole group
• Members frequently vote or suggest that group is too large and should split up	• Counterpersonals make disparaging remarks about the group, or demonstrate absenteeism or boredom
• Members openly question trainer/leader's competence	• Overpersonals insist they are happy and may speak in religious terms about "Christian love," consideration for others, etc.
• Members openly express hostility and dissatisfaction	

(Continued)

TABLE 15.2. BENNIS AND SHEPARD'S
THEORY OF GROUP DEVELOPMENT, Cont'd.

Phase One: Dependence (Authority Relations)	Phase Two: Interdependence (Personal Relations)
Subphase three: resolution—catharsis	Subphase six: consensual validation
• Group suggests trainer/leader leave group "as an experiment"	• External pressures and group-shared goals force group to examine itself
• Alertness and attention is heightened	• Unconflicted members provide a breakthrough by making a self-assessment, requesting an assessment of their own role, or expressing confidence in the group's ability
• Group discusses member roles and responsibilities	
• Group refers to removal of trainer as "the time we became a group" or "a turning point"	• Members enter into meaningful discussion and problem solving
	• Members demonstrate awareness of their own involvement and of the group's processes

Source: Reprinted with permission: OD Network 2004 Annual Conference Proceedings.

Phase one, dependence, refers to members' characteristics related to the leader, structure, or rules within the group. Members who are dependent are comforted by authority structures such as procedures, rules, agendas, and experts, whereas members who resist such structures are considered counterdependent. Members who are unconflicted with regard to leadership and power are considered independent and are responsible for the major movements of the group from one subphase to the next. The three subphases of dependence are flight, fight, and catharsis.

It is only after the group has resolved issues around authority, leadership, and structure that it can turn its attention to relationships among each other, which is phase two, interdependence, referring to members' need for interpersonal intimacy. Members who cannot feel comfortable until a high level of intimacy has been established within the group are termed "overpersonal," whereas members who avoid or withdraw from interpersonal intimacy are termed "counterpersonal." Those who are not conflicted in this area are called "personals." Resolution of the dependence phase signals the beginning of the group's struggle with issues of shared responsibility. The three subphases of interdependence are enchantment (another facet of flight), disenchantment (another facet of fight), and consensual validation.

Bennis and Shepard's Theory of Group Development was one of the first sequential, phased models for group development; it is the base on which dozens of others have been developed, including the model found later in this chapter.

An Eastern Perspective: Anthony Banet Jr.

The first attempt to integrate what had been mostly Anglo and Western research with Eastern philosophies was Anthony Banet Jr.'s "A Theory of Group Development Based on the I Ching" (1976). The concept of continuous change and dynamic phenomena goes back at least to 500 B.C., when the philosophers Heraclitus in Greece and Confucius in China separately compared the constant movement of experience to the ever-changing flow of a river. Where Western science tends to look for cause-and-effect and freeze-unfreeze-refreeze dynamics, Eastern philosophies acknowledge the continuous flow of experience in all things, called the Tao: "The energies of individual members and of the group are distributed," flowing between yin (passive, receptive, simple, docile) and yang (active, creative, exciting, firm; Banet, 1976, pp. 259–260).

What Schutz and Bennis and Shepard describe as stages or phases or group development Banet describes as "movements," or the changing arrangement of yin and yang forces; see Table 15.3).

Toward an Integrated Theory and Model

Almost all of the foundational concepts in group development and OD, especially from the 1940s through the 1960s, are based on research in psychology and sociology—many using T-groups and group therapy settings—where the focus is on the relationship between the individual and the group. In the 1950s through the 1990s, research in the field of management and organizations was established in its own right, bringing more of an organizational orientation to our knowledge and expanding the applicability of the foundation concepts to more everyday settings such as businesses and organizations.

Most of the group development models fall into two categories. The first, known as *linear-progressive* models, include those of Bennis and Shepard (1956), Mills (1964), Braaten (1974–75), Lacoursiere (1980), and Caple (1978) and are mainly sequential, one-directional, and operating on the assumption that groups advance by completing stages or periods of work (Smith, 2001); there's even one that rhymes (Tuckman, 1965). The second category, known as *cyclical and pendular* models, includes Schutz (1958); Napier and Gershenfeld (1973); Banet (1976);

TABLE 15.3. BANET'S THEORY OF
GROUP DEVELOPMENT BASED ON THE I CHING.

Movement	Governed by	Process Elements	Individual Elements	Facilitation
First: gathering together	Creative-receptive polarity	• Not a group • Many questions • Distrust • Wish for safety	• Self-identification • Focus on difference among members	• Clarify roles • Establish trust
Second: standstill	Thinking-feeling polarity	• Members bond with each other • Align against leader/facilitator	• Need to "let go" is frightening • Threat to internal norms, beliefs, values	• Challenge either-or thinking • Respect histories; reinforce letting go
Third: biting through	Confrontation-support polarity	• Group cohesion • Leadership distributed • Group is "safe haven" from outside world	• Experimentation • Intense feelings • Old way departed • New ways not yet arrived	• Strong reality orientation • Maintenance functions distributed
Fourth: the taming power of the great	Interaction-keeping still polarity	• Feelings of unity, nurturance, support • Affirm new behaviors	• Sense of newness, rebirth • Aware of moving into new territory	• Mostly not doing, letting change flower • Avoid fixation
Fifth: return	Cycle of movement temporarily ends	• Old is discarded; new is accepted • Upward movement, in harmony with heaven • Group terminates or reforms	• Transition from disorder to order not yet complete • Member may leave; new members may join	• Leading the group out of confusion and back to order

Bradford (1984); and Drexler, Sibbet, and Forrester (1988). They are based on the notion that groups revisit stages and phases repeatedly, addressing similar issues in multiple time periods and settings (Smith, 2001).

However, none of these models fully captures the shift in our OD knowledge base that has been occurring since the mid-1990s. New concepts from the physical sciences, such as mathematician Arthur M. Young's theory of process, physicist David Bohm's dialogue practice, and work by Chilean biologist and cybernetician Humberto Maturana; new science thinking from physicists such as Gregory Bateson, Ilya Prigogine, and Fritjof Capra; and philosopher Ken Wilber's integration of Eastern and Western thinking in "A Brief History of Everything," need to inform our models and perspectives on group life.

The Group Spiral

The Group Spiral (Figure 15.1 and Table 15.4) integrates some of the key concepts of early group research with the emerging principles of complex systems; it presents a useful tool for practitioners. The stages that are represented in the spiral appear more discrete and finite than they actually are; it's important to remember that groups work nonlinearly, that these stages are arbitrary markers in the life of a group, and that there is no clear boundary between the end of one stage and the beginning of another. The spiral is a useful metaphor for group life because it depicts the ever-increasing depth that group life can achieve, deepening our understanding and commitment to purpose, membership, goals, plans, processes, patterns, and relationships. The spiral also connotes the circularity of group life; working within bounded space and time; developing containers in which to join our own skills and best efforts with others; and deepening our knowledge of the task, the organization, the larger environment, each other, and ourselves. The spiral is also bidirectional, allowing movement both toward and away from depth and intimacy (Scheidel and Crowell, 1964) and infinite elasticity—rather like the children's Slinky toy (Fisher, 1974).

Entry

The overall *concerns* of entry center around the purpose of the group, and its membership. Every human's relationship with every system begins with a point of entry. The new entrant is preoccupied with *questions* about the purpose of the group and its alignment with her or his own goals and needs, whether or not to join the system, on what terms to join, and how fully to invest emotionally in the system and its members. "Am I willing to consider membership in this group, and if so, on

FIGURE 15.1. THE GROUP SPIRAL.

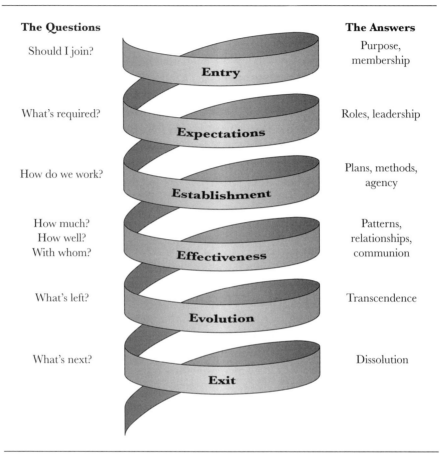

The Questions		The Answers
Should I join?	**Entry**	Purpose, membership
What's required?	**Expectations**	Roles, leadership
How do we work?	**Establishment**	Plans, methods, agency
How much? How well? With whom?	**Effectiveness**	Patterns, relationships, communion
What's left?	**Evolution**	Transcendence
What's next?	**Exit**	Dissolution

what terms? How much of my time, energy, and personhood am I willing to bring to this venture right now?" are right at the center of the individual's questions. The person actively collects data about the people and surroundings, compares the data to previous experience, and then makes a *judgment* about the worthiness of the group's purpose and leadership and the desirability or likeableness of the other members. In short, the new entrant sizes up the group's purpose, leadership, and people in these early moments and makes some decisions about whether to join.

One factor in that decision is a hunch or gut feeling about whether she or he will likely be included and accepted in the group. As the group works its way

TABLE 15.4. THREE LEVELS OF TASK WITHIN THE GROUP SPIRAL.

Phase	Concerns	Individual's Task	Group's Task	Facilitation Task
Entry	Purpose, membership	Explore own fit with purpose and other members	Establish purpose, membership	Assure all that they are welcome, introduced, and clear about the purpose
Expectations	Roles, leadership	Determine what's expected of one, and how one relates to the leadership	Establish obligations of members, formal and informal group leadership	Ensure roles and responsibilities are clear to all
Establishment	Goals, plans, measures, processes, agency	Establish own identity; position self as a contributor; tentatively build alliances	Establish plans, goals, measures, methods, and processes for production	Help articulate and re-inforce group's identity; guide consideration of communication and decision making
Effectiveness	Patterns, relationships, communion	Contribute efficiently and effectively; observe and comment on group process; look for ways to improve; deepen relationships	Establish and maintain norms and patterns; negotiate relationships and interdependencies with other entities	Examine routines, habits, and patterns; confront unspoken assumptions and unwritten rules; encourage dissent
Evolution	Transcendence	Growth; develop new skills and insights	Escape previous limitations; reach for higher forms	Ensure reflection occurs; integrate lessons learned
Exit	Dissolution	Integrate lessons learned; detach from this form; invent new ways to maintain key relationships	Assess contribution; celebrate success	Ensure acknowledgment and celebration

through later stages in the spiral, the new entrant's answers to some of these questions are likely to shift, but during this entry stage these questions need at least preliminary answers before the person is able and willing to commit to returning for the next meeting of the group. The group-level questions in entry have to do with establishing a worthy purpose for the group and determining its membership. The *facilitator's* job is to make sure that all members are introduced and feel welcome, that there is a clear statement about the purpose of the group, and that the purpose is discussed and openly debated, if appropriate.

Expectations

Expectations around leadership and roles are the concerns of this phase. With resolution to the questions of entry, the new member then wrestles with questions about what is required of the members of the group, how leadership in this group occurs, and specifically, "What will be required of me? Am I competent to deliver? How fully am I able or willing to commit?" There are several levels of expectations in play here, including the individual's expectations of the group, its members, the leaders, and self; also in play are the group's expectations of members in general and this person in particular. The individual is calibrating her or his own projections of the costs and benefits of membership against the actual expectations that the group holds and is able to enforce. Questions about individual contributions and accountability to the group are raised here for the first time, often within minutes of (and occasionally even simultaneously with) the entry questions about purpose and people. The individual makes several judgments, having to do with her or his own willingness to live up to the group's expectations around performance, productivity, and adherence to group norms as well as how to relate to the authority structure of the group.

Meanwhile, the group is working out the formal leadership structures and processes, with at least a tacit understanding that informal leadership is being established now and will continue to evolve through most of the future phases of the spiral. The group is also making a decision (most of the time tacitly) about whether the person is in fact worthy of membership and can be relied upon. The facilitator's job is to ensure that there is explicit understanding and agreement around roles and responsibilities, especially around leadership.

Establishment

The period of establishment is concerned with the plans, methods, processes, and the wholeness, or the agency, of the group. The individual's questions center around being established as a member in full standing, what can be contributed that would add value, and who can be trusted. The individual makes several judgments about her or his fit in the group, specifically about whether there is equity between effort contributed and satisfaction and other rewards returned, and how to calibrate both. As with other factors in the spiral, these questions may well be revisited later in the life of the group, but the individual must make an early first judgment about them now.

Meanwhile, the group establishes goals for the future, plans for achieving the goals, measures of progress, and processes or methods that enable it to reach the purpose. These structures also give the group its sense of agency, or identity, as a whole. Agency is the drive of all organic entities toward being autonomous; each has its own identity that captures its wholeness and makes it unique. Agency is often derived from the purpose, membership, and leadership of a group. Establishing agency is critical to some of the work that comes later in the spiral, and any entity that doesn't succeed at establishing agency will have serious difficulty in sustaining itself. Because the most difficult decisions to date are made in the establishment phase, it is likely that conflict will occur, forcing the group to discover a means—even if tacit—for dealing with conflict during this phase.

The facilitation task in establishment is to observe and confront the unspoken assumptions and unnoticed patterns.

Effectiveness

Internal patterns and relationships and relationships with other similar entities—or communion—are the concerns of the effectiveness stage. The individual is preoccupied with such questions as, "Am I being efficient? effective? with whom? why? What kinds of feedback do I get? give? should I get? give?" Similarly, the group is struggling with how it is going to manage the feedback process among members, or if it's even going to do so at all. The individual is making a judgment about the nature of her or his contribution, and deciding if or how to support the leadership. Formative relationships deepen during the effectiveness phase. When groups get to effectiveness, they have done just about everything at least once and are developing patterns that reduce uncertainty and anxiety, and that appear, at least on the surface, to improve performance. However, unexamined patterns can be suboptimal and detrimental to group performance. If the group has developed plans, methods, and processes well in the establishment phase and has clear and healthy mechanisms for dealing with conflict, this can be a period of consolidation and deep satisfaction for the group.

However, because this is often one of the longer phases in the spiral, it can also be turbulent, particularly if the group experiences any of the changes in mandate, membership, and leadership that generally mark a group's life. The establishment and effectiveness phases of group life are where conflict is frequently most evident. Resources are allocated, priorities are established, processes are defined, influence patterns are established, and leadership takes hold, each offering an opportunity for group members to disagree and conflict to arise. If the group experiences them as win-lose, the likelihood of conflict erupting is high. The probability and intensity of conflict are greatly reduced when decision processes are transparent, leadership is shared and consultative, and all members are clear and committed to a common goal. Meanwhile, the group builds on the agency developed in the establishment phase to reach out and relate to other, similar entities in its environment. This act of communion is necessary for the organic entity to calibrate itself with the environment and to establish interdependence with other related entities. If the group fails to figure out how to relate with the larger environment, it runs the risk of becoming isolated from, and irrelevant to, the broader context and authorizing environment, which could be a future-limiting failure in some settings.

The facilitator's task in effectiveness is to help the group examine its routines and patterns, and to encourage openness and dissent. The facilitator also works to confront and make discussable the assumptions and unwritten rules that may be hindering the group's performance.

Evolution

The concerns of this phase are around implementation of the group's work and transcending form. This is a pivot point for the group, offering choices about how to end, or in what form to continue. The individual is calculating the return on the effort investment, asking questions such as, "What have I given? gained? Has it been worth the effort? How did my contribution add value? What did I learn, and what can I take forward from this experience? Would I or should I ever do something like this again?" By this time, most relational issues have been worked out, people have figured out who to work with and how to accommodate each other, conflict is rare, accomplishment is in sight, celebration is nigh, and euphoria reigns. In this environment, it is almost impossible for an objective judgment to be made about the group or its effort, value, or contribution; the same is true about an individual's contributions as well. The downside of this euphoria is that it can distort stock taking and lesson learning. But the potential upside of this euphoria is that it can propel the group into new forms and structures, surfing the wave of energy and excitement that comes with success and transcending its former identity into new forms and structures.

The facilitation task revolves around structured exercises for assessment and reflection, integrating lessons learned, and maintaining a sense of balance and proportion in the face of the group's euphoria.

Exit

Confronting dissolution is the central concern of the exit phase on the spiral. The individual is trapped among competing questions. On the one hand, there is a sense of loss that the task is over, the goal has been met, the group is done, the form has expired, and relationships must come to an end. On the other hand, the individual is simultaneously likely to have a sense of relief that the job has been done and the pressure is now off, along with anticipation of the application of the group's work and the new forms that key relationships might take. These conflicting emotions can create tension in the group, which, if not well managed, can make the ending difficult and messy. The group task in the exit stage is to bring closure to the work, acknowledge the end of the group in its current form, and prepare for transitions to the future.

The facilitation task is to ensure that accomplishments and contributions are acknowledged and that the group's success is celebrated.

Factors That Affect Groups

Several factors significantly affect what happens in groups; the OD practitioner needs some familiarity with them and the skill to intervene.

Understanding Content and Process

In working with groups, it's important to distinguish between the content (or the *what*) of the group's work versus the process (or the *how*) of it. To leave aside for the moment the T-group, in which the content of the group's task is to learn about process, every group that's successful and sustains itself has a purpose to which members commit and most have a task to accomplish. When we look for how the task is being accomplished, we look for clear goals, adequate knowledge and other resources, and effective progress measures as typical variables affecting the content of the group's work (Schein, 1982).

When we look at the process variables (the *how* of the group's work), we look for how members join and leave the group, how leadership occurs, how decisions are made, how communication occurs, how the group remembers important things, who participates and how much, how norms and patterns are developed and enforced, how meetings are managed, how members participate, and a host of other variables.

Most times, members of groups have expertise in the task, content, or substance of the work; many times, group facilitators are retained for their knowledge about the process variables (the how). Knowing the difference, and being able to observe the variables separately, is a key skill need in working with groups.

Communications

Every interpersonal interaction depends on communication, which is a challenge even in the simplest, one-to-one relationship. The dynamics of group communication greatly increase the complexity and potential mishaps that can occur when communication goes awry. Some guidelines for good communication are to assume good intentions on the part of the other; listen with your head and your heart; verify your understanding of the speaker's message before responding; own your own perceptions, feelings, and messages; acknowledge that perceptions are facts (whether or not you believe they are accurate); and grant each other grace.

Goals

One powerful way to organize a group and make it productive is to orient members around a clear set of goals. Individuals will always have their own goals for any group, but when there is alignment and even overlap between the individuals' goals and the group's goals the prospect of high performance and satisfaction with the outcome increases dramatically. One of the most effective OD interventions is to conduct a strategic planning, or goal-setting or goal-clarification exercise, because the result is typically clarity and alignment around the desired outcomes for the group, which helps to manage out of the group process behaviors not supporting the goals and manage into the group process those behaviors that do so.

Norms

Norms are the unspoken rules and standards that groups adopt to define acceptable and unacceptable behavior (Napier and Gershenfeld, 1999). Early in group life, norms are often imported from the larger context in which the group is operating. As the group matures, however, it begins to base actions on meanings that have developed within the group; this is the point at which a norm has formed.

The norm is fully operative when there are sanctions on behaviors that violate the group's norms.

Norms can be extremely powerful at limiting members' behavior, which itself is constructive or destructive, depending on the norm and the situation. For example, a productive norm that contributes to the group's success might be that all deadlines are met on time. A destructive norm might be that members complain privately about group issues but do not raise them within the group or directly with the leader.

Because they are unwritten and unspoken, it is often difficult for group members to be aware of the existence of norms. One major asset that an OD consultant or group facilitator has is the distance and perspective to see routines and patterns in action in the group that seem puzzling or curious or counterproductive, and the ability to offer those observations to the group.

Leadership

The foundations of our leadership concepts began in the 1950s and 1960s. Douglas McGregor (1960) described two sets of leader beliefs about employees, and the two leadership styles that result. Theory X managers believe that people are reluctant to work, avoid responsibility, are self-interested, and would do nothing without managerial oversight. The Theory X leader directs, organizes, controls, and coerces. Theory Y managers believe that once our basic needs for survival are met, people will exercise self-direction and self-control and can do creative and imaginative work. The Theory Y leader creates challenges and opportunities that encourage employees to grow.

The Ohio State Leadership Studies (Yukl, 1989) synthesized eighteen hundred examples of leadership behaviors into two dimensions: *consideration,* or the degree to which a leader acts in a friendly and supportive manner, looking out for subordinates' welfare; and *initiating structure,* or the degree to which a leader defines and structures the work and roles of subordinates to accomplish the group's goals.

Conflict

No one likes conflict, but no one can avoid it in today's world of interaction and interdependence. Early models of conflict resolution were rooted in marriage and family systems work, encouraging parties first to *differentiate,* or describe all of the factors on which there is disagreement; and then *integrate,* which is to focus on factors that all can agree on. This methodology is based on the belief that the simple act of listening to each other as the parties describe the sides of the dispute furthers understanding and empathy, both of which are prerequisites for resolving conflict. In the mid-1960s, the field developed a specialization called "intergroup conflict," which specialized in union-management conflict; it quickly spread to conflict among race and gender groups. Today there are thousands of professional dispute resolution specialists whose job it is to resolve conflicts before they enter formal adjudication processes. Some are attached to the courts system, some work in law practices, some work in ombuds functions within organizations. Recent news reports indicate that dispute resolution will be one of the three fastest-growing professions in the twenty-first century.

But conflict is not all bad and need not be avoided as studiously in groups as it might be in the legal system. There is often heightened energy in a group experiencing conflict, which can be powerfully and constructively channeled for the growth of the group. The good news is that group conflict can be indicative of high interest and commitment of group members to the topic; when managed constructively, it can offer insights into the communication, leadership, and decision-making patterns that can support the group process. Conflict is also a good indicator about what's *really* important to group members, which is valuable information for a group facilitator.

Intervening in Groups

One early principle in OD is that if you want to change something or someone, you have to change the system around it. Our knowledge on this topic goes back to the bicycle racers of the nineteenth century, through the Hawthorne studies of the early 1930s, up to complexity theory of today. For the change agent, the implication is that even if the desired outcome is to change individual behaviors, the most effective, long-lasting changes are those that intervene at the level of the individual, the group, and the larger system.

The complexities of group and organizational life make it difficult to know exactly how and where to intervene to ensure success. The most effective group interventions are those accurately assessing the group, accounting for what's going on, and intervening narrowly and purposefully at the various levels within the system. Knowing whether an issue is related to leadership, or communications, or group norms, or conflict, or the current phase or stage of group life takes knowledge, skill, practice, and, to a certain extent, good instincts. Carter's Cube (Carter, 1980–2004) is a way to look at and work with groups at the various stages and phases of group life (see Figure 15.2).

FIGURE 15.2. CARTER'S CUBE.

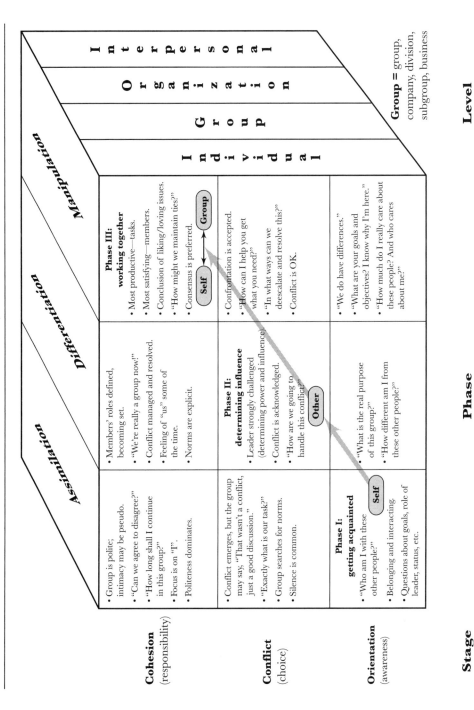

Assimilation — **Differentiation** — **Manipulation**

Interpersonal — **Organizational** — **Group** — **Individual**

Cohesion (responsibility)

- Group is polite; intimacy may be pseudo.
- "Can we agree to disagree?"
- "How long shall I continue in this group?"
- Focus is on "I".
- Politeness dominates.

- Members' roles defined, becoming set.
- "We're really a group now!"
- Conflict managed and resolved.
- Feeling of "us" some of the time.
- Norms are explicit.

Phase III: working together
- Most productive—tasks.
- Most satisfying—members.
- Conclusion of liking/loving issues.
- "How might we maintain ties?"
- Consensus is preferred.

[Self → Group]

Conflict (choice)

- Conflict emerges, but the group may say, "That wasn't a conflict, just a good discussion."
- "Exactly what is our task?"
- Group searches for norms.
- Silence is common.

Phase II: determining influence
- Leader strongly challenged (determining power and influence).
- Conflict is acknowledged.
- "How are we going to handle this conflict?"

- Confrontation is accepted.
- "How can I help you get what you need?"
- "In what ways can we deescalate and resolve this?"
- Conflict is OK.

[Other]

Orientation (awareness)

Phase I: getting acquainted
- "Who am I with these other people?"
- Belonging and interacting.
- Questions about goals, role of leader, status, etc.

[Self]

- "What is the real purpose of this group?"
- "How different am I from these other people?"

- "We do have differences."
- "What are your goals and objectives? I know why I'm here."
- "How much do I really care about these people? And who cares about me?"

Stage — **Phase** — **Level**

Group = group, company, division, subgroup, business

Source: Carter, J. D. (with Gestalt Institute of Cleveland Professional Staff). (1980–2004). *Organization & Systems Development Center: Gestalt Workbook.* Cleveland: Gestalt Institute. Reprinted with permission.

Carter's Cube identifies on the right side the four possible levels of intervention. An *individual*-level intervention might be a training course or coaching; a *group*-level intervention might be goal setting, developing performance measures, or a communication audit; an *organization*-level intervention might be strategy development or business process improvement; and an *interpersonal*-level intervention might be conflict resolution or mediation, among others.

The left side of Carter's Cube identifies the three *stages* of group development—orientation, conflict, and cohesion—which are cyclical and repetitive in that groups can move through them multiple times. Across the top are the three *phases* of group development, which are *not* cyclical or repetitive but rather developmental, similar to life stages. During *assimilation*, members are concerned about their "place" in the group and often find it hard to hear or understand group-level observations and interventions. During *differentiation*, members develop boundaries for themselves and their group, and there is much focus on shifting away from leadership dependency to independence; effective interventions help the group focus on its relationship with the outside environment and authority. During *manipulation* (for example, skillful handling), members are willing at times to subordinate individual needs and wants in favor of the group's; effective interventions encourage a healthy balance between "I want" issues and "we need" issues.

As interveners, we serve ourselves and our groups best by remaining constant students of group life and ourselves. The best group leaders and facilitators are always seeking to add to their knowledge and theory base about groups, the structure of group work and group life, and the best and most effective ways to shape a group's growth and development through interventions.

In the end, two major factors determine our success as an intervener in group life. The first is our ability to notice and understand what's going on at the various levels, stages, and phases of group life; Carter's Cube is a comprehensive tool for that. The second is our ability to notice and understand what's going on in our own inner life; our work as an intervener, leader, or member of a group is a function of our own self-awareness and ability to communicate about the complex factors and multiple motivations that make us human.

Competencies Needed

To be an effective member, leader, or facilitator of a group, it helps to have these perspectives and skills:

- Whole system perspective, with which to be able to observe action and interaction at the intrapersonal, interpersonal, group, intergroup, and systemic levels

- Knowledge and understanding about the life cycle (or spiral) of group life, including the dynamics that exist in specific stages and how to respond
- Capability to work with groups from multiple perspectives, seeing the psychological factors, the interpersonal relationships, the leadership dynamics, and the systemic patterns
- Knowledge and understanding about oneself and one's own reactions in group settings, in order to calibrate experiences, be mindful of impact on the group, and manage one's own reactions and interventions, both for one's own sake and the sake of the group.

Conclusion

It is hard to imagine a future in which we are in less contact, have less interaction, and less interdependence than we have now. As organizations and society become more complex, both will demand that we spend more time with more people, doing more complex and demanding work in groups. This only increases the premium put on our ability to work effectively in groups. To be effective as members, leaders, and facilitators, we need to have a few key tools and concepts at the ready, curiosity about group phenomena, and the willingness to reach beyond our comfort zone to where the real learning occurs.

References

Banet Jr., A. (1976). A theory of group development based on the I Ching. In *Creative psychotherapy* (pp. 258–282). San Francisco: Jossey-Bass/Pfeiffer.

Bennis, W., & Shepard, H. (1956). A theory of group development. *Human Relations, 9*(4), 415–437.

Braaten, L. J. (1974–75). Developmental phases of encounter groups: A critical review of models and a new proposal. *Interpersonal Development, 75,* 112–129.

Bradford, D. L. (1984). *Group dynamics.* Chicago: Science Research Associates.

Caple, R. B. (1978). The sequential stages of group development. *Small Group Behavior, 9,* 470–476.

Carter, J. D. (with Gestalt Institute of Cleveland professional staff). (1980–2004). *Organization and systems development center: Gestalt workbook.* Cleveland: Gestalt Institute.

Drexler, A., Sibbet, D., & Forrester, R. (1988). The Team Performance Model. In W. B. Reddy & K. Jamieson (Eds.), *Teambuilding: Blueprints for productivity and satisfaction* (pp. 45–61). Alexandria, VA: NTL Institute for Applied Behavioral Science; San Diego, Calif.: University Associates.

Fisher, B. A. (1974). *Small group decision making: Communication and group process.* New York: McGraw-Hill.

Kass, R. (1996). *Theories of small group development.* Montreal: Center for Human Relations and Community Studies, Concordia University.

Lacoursiere, R. B. (1980). *The life cycle of groups: Group development stage theory.* New York: Human Sciences Press.

Lewin, K. (1939). Field theory and experiment in social psychology. *American Journal of Sociology, 44,* 868–897.

Lewin, K. (1951). *Field theory in social science: selected theoretical papers* (D. Cartwright, Ed.). New York: HarperCollins.

McGregor, D. (1960). *The human side of enterprise.* New York: McGraw-Hill.

Mills, T. M. (1964). *Group transformation: An analysis of a learning group.* Upper Saddle River, NJ: Prentice Hall.

Minahan, M., & Hutton, C. (2004). *Group development: Meet the theorists.* 2004 OD Network Annual Conference Proceedings, San Juan, Puerto Rico, Oct. 2004.

Morrow, A. J. (1969). *The practical theorist: The life and work of Kurt Lewin.* New York: Basic Books.

Napier, R., & Gershenfeld, M. (1973). *Groups: Theory and experience.* Boston: Houghton Mifflin.

Napier, R., & Gershenfeld, M. (1999). *Groups: Theory and experience* (6th ed.). Boston: Houghton Mifflin.

Scheidel, T. M., & Crowell, L. (1964). Idea development in small discussion groups. *Quarterly Journal of Speech, 50,* 140–145.

Schein, E. (1982). What to observe in a group. *NTL reading book for human relations training.* Alexandria, VA: NTL Institute for the Applied Behavioral Sciences.

Schutz, W. C. (1958). *FIRO: A three dimensional theory of interpersonal behavior.* Austin, TX: Holt Rinehart and Winston.

Smith, G. (2001, Spring). Group development: A review of the literature and a commentary on future research directions. *Group Facilitation: A Research and Applications Journal,* no. 3.

Sweeney, N. (Ed.). (1993). *Introduction to the FIRO-B in organizations.* Palo Alto, CA: Consulting Psychologists Press.

Tuckman, B. W. (1965). Developmental sequence in small groups. *Psychological Bulletin, 63,* 384–399.

Weisbord, M. (1987). *Productive workplaces.* San Francisco: Jossey-Bass.

Wheelan, S. (2005). *Group processes: A developmental perspective.* Boston: Allyn and Bacon.

Yukl, G. (1989). *Leadership in organizations.* Upper Saddle River, NJ: Prentice Hall.

CHAPTER SIXTEEN

LARGE GROUP METHODS: DEVELOPMENTS AND TRENDS

Barbara Benedict Bunker and Billie T. Alban

One of the most interesting breakthroughs in organization development (OD) methods in recent history occurred in the 1980s and 1990s. OD practitioners working with systemic problems in organizations developed methods for bringing together "the system"—all the concerned parties or stakeholders—in one place to make decisions about the issues facing them.

Until the 1980s, change work often occurred within organizational departments or units. Team building was popular and effective for the group involved. At the same time, change processes led by top management that affected the direction of the whole organization usually occurred as a waterfall process; the plan or strategy began at the top and cascaded down the organization hierarchy. By the time it reached the floor of the organization, a rather watered-down version usually remained. To be sure, some change practitioners, particularly those whose practice is based in Gestalt theory or the Tavistock organizations-as-systems work, have always worked with the whole system. The ability to implement these ideas, however, was limited by lack of methods to bring all the stakeholders together to do the work of change.

The history of the development of large group methods can be understood in three periods of development: early invention and development, adoption of new methods, and incorporation of these methods into a variety of situations.

Invention and Early Development: Mid-1980s to About 1993

Three precursors made the invention of large group methods possible in the mid-1980s, all of them theory and practice developments in understanding organizational change that began in the 1950s. Large group methods could not have developed without these three strands. The first was the emphasis on systems in the organizational work of Eric Trist and Fred Emery in the 1950s, which developed from their study of new technology introduced into the British coal mining industry. Their theory, sociotechnical systems, showed how changes in technology can disrupt system functioning even when what is being introduced is a more efficient technology. They proposed a theory that requires attention to both the technological and the social systems for the best productivity (F. E. Emery and Trist, 1960). Their work helped practitioners understand that change in one part of the system affects the whole system. Thus sustainable change requires systemic intervention.

The second precursor was a shift from focusing on solving organizational problems that began in the past to more focus on the future and its potential. This occurred in both North America and the UK. In the United States, Herb Shepard, a creative early OD practitioner, began working with individuals in the late 1960s in "life planning" experiential exercises in which people created their own desired future. He found that "futuring" created positive energy for change at the individual level. About the same time, Ronald Lippitt at the University of Michigan noticed in his work with problem solving with organizational clients that dealing with problems is energy-draining. By contrast, he discovered that when you ask people to invent a future they would prefer and enjoy, energy is created in the people doing the planning. Lippitt began consulting with many cities in Michigan that were being devastated by the closing of automobile plants. He brought city stakeholders together in large group meetings—up to three thousand in one town—to create and plan their new future. The effects of this work focusing on the future are reported in *Choosing the Future You Prefer* (Lippitt, 1980). It is interesting that this work, which in retrospect is seen to be clearly groundbreaking, was viewed by many practitioners at the time as a kind of curiosity. Those were the days of growth in team-building methods, and many practitioners had practices in which this was their major business.

In the UK, emphasis on the future developed when Trist ran a conference with Emery working with the merger of two aerospace engineering organizations in the early 1960s. They asked the two merging companies to consider what kind of company they wanted to become in the future. This process of searching for a desired future eventually became the "Search Conference," which Fred and Merrelyn

Emery then further developed. Merrelyn Emery devoted more than thirty years of her practice in Australia to working with this method in organizations and communities and at the national level (M. Emery and Purser, 1996).

The third precursor was the work done by NTL Institute in the 1960s in large summer laboratories at Bethel, Maine. In the community lab and the college lab, trainers learned to work with large groups by creating small groups within a larger framework. This created a model for working with larger groups of people, which was fully developed only during the 1980s.

These early strands of work came together in the mid-1980s, when, almost simultaneously, the importance of working with the whole system became focal for OD practitioners. The first clear statement of this new approach appeared when Marvin Weisbord wrote a history of thinking about organizations, *Productive Workplaces* (1987). As he reflected on what had worked and not worked in his own change practice, he realized that when he was able to "get all the stakeholders in the room" he could effectively create changes that were desired and desirable. Out of the thinking in this book and a dialogue with Eric Trist and Merrelyn Emery about their Search Conference work, he developed a new method, which he called Future Search. One way it differed from the Search Conference was that it was intended for groups of seventy or more, which meant that many stakeholders could be present.

Also in the mid-1980s, Kathy Dannemiller, a student and colleague of Ron Lippitt, was asked to train Ford middle managers to be more proactive. Understanding that the Ford system was not encouraging this kind of behavior and that many hours of training would probably not be successful, she refused the quite extensive contract. The stunned potential clients at Ford asked her what she might do to reach the objective. After thinking about it, she proposed that they give her five hundred managers from three levels of management for a week in an offsite location if they really wanted change. This was the birth of Real Time Strategic Change, a method that involves stakeholders in planning and implementing changes for a better organization future. Real Time Strategic Change is now called Whole-Scale Change (Dannemiller Tyson Associates, 2000). The breakthrough that occurred in this work was the large number of people who could be involved at one time, so that literally a whole plant or organization could work on the same issue together and make decisions that would stick and could be immediately implemented.

About the same time, but in a quite different structure, Harrison Owen created a method of gathering people with passion and energy to discuss a topic in a method he called "Open Space" (Owen, 1992). Again, hundreds of people could participate in creating the agenda for the one- or two-day meeting and engage the topic as they wished.

A typical large group meeting is held in a spacious open room with many 5 or 5.5 foot round tables set up for working sessions. These are not the usual 6 foot banquet tables because they need to be small enough in diameter so that people can talk easily across them without shouting. There is a platform for the two facilitators located in a place optimal for viewing from all the tables. Flipcharts are stacked on the side walls to be available when needed. The logistics staff, usually wearing a distinctive color, circulate in their areas bringing printed instructions and materials to the tables, as well as microphones, in a period of report or discussion.

These breakthrough methods not only accommodate a large number of participants but do not require professional facilitators to be at every discussion table because leadership roles are rotated among table participants. This made use of these methods much more available to communities and organizations without big budgets. The composition of the table groups is heterogeneous for much of the work but in functional groups when appropriate to the task.

Adoption of the New Methods: 1993–2000

As the 1990s progressed, differences among the methods gradually became clearer. A number of publications and activities encouraged this development. A special issue of *The Journal of Applied Behavioral Science,* edited by Bunker and Alban (1992), gathered articles by originators of several large group interventions. They shared the idea of working with large groups of stakeholders. In addition to some of the methods already mentioned, Dick Axelrod was using a series of large group conferences to redesign work in a process he calls the Conference Model. Don Klein proposed that his 1970s SimuReal method was a systems model that could accommodate many stakeholders, and it was included. The Inter-Cultural Association (ICA) was using and further developing methods they had learned in the early days of OD from OD practitioners. Although associated with individual practitioners, all of these methods were being developed and refined in practice as ways of gathering stakeholders together to engage each other about issues of common concern. Interest was so intense that the special issue required five additional printings.

Beginning in 1993, two developments went hand in hand. First, developers of methods wrote books on how to use their methods, spoke at national conferences, and offered training workshops in the method. Practitioners were thirsty for this new knowledge. They wanted to understand in as much detail as possible what these methods were and how they worked. At the same time, Bunker and Alban developed and presented a framework for understanding all twelve of the original methods in training workshops and at conferences. There was so much interest that for four years (1995–1998) Tom Chase helped plan and sponsor a Large Group

Interventions conference in Dallas that was attended by method originators, practitioners, companies using the methods that offered a case describing their experience, CEOs talking about what it was like to involve the whole company, and organizations that were "shopping" (thinking about using these methods). Mobil, for example, brought a multilevel group of fourteen people to a conference just before they decided to use Real Time Strategic Change with one of their divisions.

The differences gradually became clear as methods were adopted and used. For example, some methods are easier to learn and adopt than others are. Methods with a structured flow of activities such as the Search Conference or Future Search are easy to grasp. This means they are easy to try out on an unsuspecting client. In any early period of innovation, there is always a certain amount of experimentation. Ethical practitioners keep this to a minimum and do not suggest methods when the issues are not appropriate for the method. Gathering stakeholders is expensive in time and resources. It should be reserved for issues that are worthy of this kind of commitment, such as future plans for the organization or important problems.

Some methods also take a longer time commitment to plan and implement than others. Work redesign takes months, with many large and small meetings. Open Space can be set up and run with very short lead time. Custom-designed methods such as Real Time Strategic Change require planning with an internal design team, so they need a longer lead time than prestructured methods.

Large Group Interventions (Bunker and Alban, 1997) was the first effort to describe and compare all large group methods. The authors organized the methods into three categories according to outcome: methods for the future, methods for work design, and flexible methods for discussion and decision making. Then they also compared them for degree of structure, size of group they could handle, and length of time for the event. This framework proved useful in helping people make good judgments in selecting a method. Several years later, Holman and Devane (1999) edited *The Change Handbook,* in which many of the methods included in Bunker and Alban (1997) were discussed by their originators and a few newer methods were added and compared.

Developers of methods have continued to publish new versions of their own work as they built experience and made changes in what they were doing. Table 16.1 is a comparison of the methods as they are currently practiced. In the work design section of the table, three methods that were originally developed separately, the Conference Model, Real Time Work Design, and Fast Cycle Full Participation, have blended with each other so as to be indistinguishable, though they are still practiced by those titles. The other work design method, Participative Design, is radically different in that it starts at the bottom of the organization and moves upward (Rehm, 1999).

TABLE 16.1. COMPARISON OF LARGE GROUP METHODS.

	Methods for the Future			Methods for Work Design	
Method	Search Conference	Future Search	Inter-Cultural Association	Conference Model, Real Time Work Design, Fast Cycle Full Participation	Participative Design
Optimal duration of meetings	2 days	2.5 days	2–3 days	Three to five 2-day conferences over six months	2–3 days
Meeting capacity	20–35	40–150	50–200	80–200	30–50
Time for preplan	Average	Average	Average	High	High
Design format*	1	1	1	2	2

Flexible Methods for Discussion and Decision Making

Method	Open Space	Real Time Strategic Change (Whole-Scale)	WorkOut	SimuReal	World Café	Appreciative Inquiry Summit	Participative Democracy (America*Speaks*)
Optimal duration of meetings	1–3 days	2–3 days	3 days plus 30-, 60-, 90-day follow-ups	1 day	2 hours; can be repeated	3 days	1–2 days
Meeting capacity	30–500	50–1,000+	20–200	50–150	12–1,200	80–1,000	500–5,000
Time for preplan	Low	High	High	Average	Low	High	High+
Design format*	1	3	2	2	1	2	3

Notes: 1 = Predetermined design, good written materials available; 2 = General guidelines and written material available, some consultant design skills necessary; 3 = Flexible design, written materials available but requires excellent design skills.

During the 1990s, practitioners were learning these methods and building an experience base. Some chose to define themselves as specializing in one of these methods. Others added competence in some of the methods because they needed it in a more general practice of organizational change. Because work redesign, which developed from sociotechnical design theory, usually occurs over months and even years, there are a group of practitioners who do mainly this work. Future planning consultants, on the other hand, often know several of the future methods. Future Search practitioners can join a network, Search Net; learn from each other; and offer Future Search expertise to communities and nonprofits with limited budgets. General Electric began offering clients training in its WorkOut process for solving organizational problems. The method was effective and widely adopted by companies, often with their own name for it.

After they learned the method and gained experience, practitioners began to modify methods to fit client requirements. Shorter versions of Search Conference and Future Search were tried. Open Space was planned with intervals between meetings. Simultaneous meetings in different parts of the country (or world) allowed global companies to use these methods more effectively. All kinds of innovation occurred in the late 1990s and continue today. Some of it worked well and added to our knowledge base. Some created problems and did a disservice to the method. Unfortunately, when people have a bad experience they tend to assume that the method does not work, not that it was used inappropriately.

By the end of the 1990s, these methods were established as a standard part of an OD repertoire in dealing with system-level issues.

Incorporation: 2000s

The twenty-first century marks the beginning of the third period of development. Large group methods were once new and intoxicating because there was both promise and the hope that a magic bullet for change had been found. Now large group methods have become part of the world of change practice. Bunker and Alban's work (1997) is now referred to as a "classic" text and is used in many OD courses. There have long been methods for change that are used at the personal, interpersonal, group, and intergroup levels. Now there are methods for the system or the organizational level. These methods fill a special niche where nothing like them was previously available. They have been accepted and incorporated into change practice.

Not only have these methods become part of the repertoire of human resource and OD practitioners but there has been fallout, into the general culture, of some of the basic ideas. For example:

- The idea that *stakeholders* need to be involved in decision making is not a new one, but using the word *stakeholder* connotes involvement. The word appears more frequently in the press and in spoken language than it used to.
- Rotating leadership in small groups is more common as a practice. Professional facilitation is often reserved for times that are expected to be difficult.
- Round tables are now commonly accepted for discussions. In the early days of this work, one had to do battle with hotels to get smaller-than-banquet-size tables. Now, most facilities know what is wanted and have them available.
- The idea of searching for common ground in situations of high divergence is common.

Recent Developments and Trends

In this section, some of the current uses of these methods in a number of venues are presented. They were selected because they show the diversity of use of large group methods.

In the Community

The National Education Association (NEA) is using these methods to hold community conversations about controversial issues in public education across the United States. First, a national research group identified seven key issues currently being debated (examples are funding, parental involvement, the purpose of education). All are issues where stakeholders hold widely divergent views. Communities that want to engage stakeholders in a conversation select the issue(s) with a planning committee of stakeholders that includes the school board, teachers and administrators, parents, students, and other relevant stakeholders. The planning committee picks an issue that is relevant to their particular community. Materials and a format are provided by the NEA, which also offers training for local facilitators.

These events are usually evening conferences that start with an informal meal. After dinner, there is a general introduction to the purpose and hoped-for outcomes for the meeting. Then participants go to assigned heterogeneous breakout groups. The groups are usually fifteen to twenty people and are facilitated by a trained facilitator. The conversation starts with a short professional video presenting quite credible but polarized views on the issue to be discussed. Rather than wait for the divergent views to emerge, the breakout group starts with the differences on the table. Participants then discuss the issues in a format that encourages each person to express a view and understand others. What participants tend to realize is that there is some truth on both sides. The group then lists those things they hold in common and those areas where there are differences. Each group comes up with some recommendations from their common-ground agreement. They are shared with the larger group at the end of the evening. These recommendations are transmitted to the school board or the planning committee, whichever is more appropriate. It is important to point out that the major purpose is to give people a better understanding of the issues that confront every school system. If positive actions also emerge, that is an added plus.

Another innovative use of these methods involved a modification of Future Search. In a community that was concerned about its youth, rather than having the adults conduct a future search with a few youths included, they decided to have the event run by young people. So young people were selected and trained to lead the event and facilitate it at the tables. The stakeholders included educators, police, parents, and representatives from social services, hospitals, and housing. One-third of the conference were youths of middle school and high school age. They were selected from public, religious, private, and alternative schools in the city. Recommendations about the need for a teen center, parenting classes in schools, and better transportation were sent on to the city commission on youth for action.

Communities in a number of states, among them Colorado, Vermont, and California, where there are environmental disputes between people concerned about jobs and those who want to protect the environment, have effectively engaged the issues using these methods.

In Business Organizations

Business organizations increasingly incorporate these methods with other change methods to help them do their regular business. Initially, the tendency was to try out these methods on big change projects, and indeed they are effective in that area. But as they have become more familiar, organizations are more and more using large group processes in day-to-day business. One health care system in Cincinnati held a series of large meetings of emergency room personnel across their hospitals to understand and solve problems they were having in their ERs. Toys-R-Us transformed their annual meeting for store managers from a "talking heads and golf" format to an imaginatively interactive event that rolled out a whole new store redesign and employee reorientation to the customer.

At the National Level

During the 1990s, Carolyn Lukensmeyer started an organization, America*Speaks,* devoted to creating conversation in the electorate about issues of national importance. She used large groups to hold conversations in major cities across the

United States about the dilemmas facing the Social Security system and how to address them. These large meetings (five hundred or more) were managed using innovative software technology developed by CoVision of San Francisco, which allowed people at roundtables to discuss a topic and input their ideas on a laptop to a central team that posted themes from all the tables on big overhead screens that everyone could see and react to. In addition, every participant at a table had a set of buttons to press that instantly recorded and summarized for the whole gathering the person's agreement or disagreement with issues presented. Thus each person's vote was recorded and seen.

America*Speaks* used this same technology in the July 2002 meeting of five thousand citizens at the Javits Center in New York City to react to proposals for the redevelopment of Ground Zero. This meeting changed the direction of thinking about the site as a result of the discussion at this large meeting. America*Speaks* has also held meetings for the mayor of Washington, D.C., every two years that allow three thousand citizens to react to his plans, comment on the progress the city has made, and generate new ideas about what city government should be doing. Using these methods with high-tech support, they are in the business of creating national conversations.

Technology Developments

The technology described here is becoming more widely available for meetings. A new software product, Unison, uses laptops and local area networks to allow meeting participants to communicate with each other, conduct polling, do brainstorming, hold group competition, and cover idea documentation (Hosford, 2004). Some activities, such as generating good ideas to solve specific problems, require a panel of experts who review what comes in from the laptops for similarities and create themes or generate the top ten suggestions from among hundreds. Firms such as Deloitte and J. P. Morgan Chase are using this process in large meetings to create more collaboration. At a Deloitte new partner meeting with partners from forty countries, the emphasis was on input from the new partners, not just one-way communication from the top. When an organization or a community truly wants to hear the views of all of the stakeholders, these processes allow individuals to have a voice to a much greater degree than any meeting innovations to date.

Costs of adding this type of technology to a meeting are described as about $30–40 per person per day, which includes laptops and plasma displays, onsite technical support and facilitation, and reports but does not include the $15 per person licensing fee (Hosford, 2004).

Another software program, Meetingworks, is now also available for smaller collaborative meetings and can include distant participants over the Web. This program offers templates for meetings, full documentation of decisions, opportunity for input, and prioritization.

Hosford (2004) comments on the change in social dynamics that accompanies using new technologies. For example, people are able to ask serious or difficult questions without being identified personally. This useful process was occurring before the introduction of technology. "Table questions" allow a group, not an individual, to pose a sensitive question and are a routine part of large group interventions. What is not discussed by Hosford is any potential dysfunction that can occur using this intensive level of technology. One danger for first-time users is that they get fascinated with the technology and are less engaged with the ideas of the meeting. However, these days most people use computers all the time, so this is less likely than overlooking the importance of good human conversation at the tables. At some of the early large meetings with technology, the group discussed and then agreed what to feed into the laptops. Groups got to know the people they were working with during the meeting, and the social group dynamics occurred naturally.

International Uses in Multicultural Settings

The use of large groups for system interventions has clearly become international. In Europe, the originators of these methods (Weisbord and Janoff, Dannemiller, Axelrod, and Owens) have been giving training seminars for OD practitioners since the latter part of the 1990s in England, Netherlands, Sweden, Germany, and other countries. Practitioners in those countries are actively using these methods. In Germany, a recent study (unpublished) documented more than a thousand large group events over a three-year period. Most frequently used are Open Space, Future Search, Whole-Scale Change, and more recently appreciative inquiry.

In Africa, Future Search has been used to take action to demobilize child soldiers and to work on problems of displaced children in the Sudan. Appreciative inquiry has been used in strategic planning in South Africa and Ethiopia. Many NGOs in developing countries are using these methods to involve their clients in decision making about how programs they administer go forward.

In Asia, there has been work in India and Indonesia. Future Search has also been extensively used in Indonesia, including the remote islands. Appreciative inquiry and Real Time Strategic Change have been used effectively in India. However, in the more formal Asian cultures such as Japan and Korea, where participation is less culturally part of management practice, we have not heard about much use of these methods. One of the authors of this chapter presented a seminar on these methods in Korea in the 1990s. She was well received and participants found the methods interesting, but when asked if they could be used in their companies there was general agreement that it would be difficult if not impossible!

Australia has held a Future Search about Aboriginal issues that included Aborigines in the meeting. Of course, Australia has thirty years of extensive experience with the Search Conference at both national and local levels. An Open Space about teenage suicide, an urgent problem within Maori culture, was held on Maori sacred ground in New Zealand.

Multiple methods have been used in Mexico (Manning and DelaCerda, 2003) to bring about change in business and government organizations. In 2004, the Parliament of World Religions met in Spain using these methods to bring two thousand delegates into conversation about critical issues facing the world and the role of faith communities in these issues.

This is only a sample of what has been occurring around the world. There is no mechanism for keeping track of all the work going on, so what is reported here is limited by these constraints.

Method Innovations

Since the late 1990s, practitioners who have learned these methods have been adapting them to new client situations. In the same period, many organizations are expecting more of employees who are experiencing greater and greater demands both to do more and to do it in less time. This means there is pressure on these methods to do the same thing in less time. This creates a dilemma for practitioners, who understand the methods well and have a good sense of the time it takes to get the full benefit from them. For example, Future Search is usually held for three days, beginning at noon on day one and ending at noon on day three. As a compromise, practitioners run a full Future Search over two days, beginning early the first morning and wrapping up on the second day with the end of the workday. Weisbord and Janoff now discuss what difficulties this can create and how to manage them. One-day programs using some of the modules from these methods can be implemented to great effect, but this work should probably not be labeled "Future Search." Practitioners are customizing their methods to meet their clients' needs, which creates confusion about how to label current practice.

Appreciative Inquiry

Some older methods have also changed their way of working by adopting large group methods into their methodology. *The Appreciative Inquiry Summit* (Ludema and others, 2003) is a clear example. Appreciative inquiry aims to capture and retain the best of the positive values and practices of an organization at the same time that changes are made for the future. In the first phase of appreciative inquiry, the *discovery phase*, employees are trained to interview other employees about positive experiences in the organization and what they see as the organization's values and strengths. The task of the interviewer is to tease out the core elements that help create these positive experiences. This phase may occur as part of a large group meeting called the *summit meeting*, or it may happen in advance of the meeting. The next phase, the *dream phase*, now uses large group methods to bring together the system and its stakeholders to plan how to build the positive elements from the interviews into a vision of the desired future state. The best stories from the interviews may be retold at the summit meeting; the core elements may be presented as "future possibilities." However it is done, the group comes to some common ground about what they want more of in their future. The final phase of the summit meeting is the *design phase*, in which participants plan actions to create and sustain the future they want. This involves examining leadership, infrastructure, policies, and systems that would support the proposed changes.

World Café

Another innovation in large group methods, called the World Café, was developed by Juanita Brown and is being used separately or in combination with other methods (Brown, 2002). The World Café is a process that fosters authentic conversation and takes about two hours. Each World Café activity is focused around a theme that engages the invited group of stakeholders. They sit at small tables covered with tablecloths of drawing paper and drawing pens. Each group is given about twenty to thirty minutes to both talk about and draw their conversation about the theme. After twenty minutes or so, the table host instructs them to leave one person at the table who will communicate to the next group the substance of the conversation that just occurred. Then everyone else separates and goes to another table, and the process repeats itself. There are at least three iterations of this process before the final groups post the ideas their table has developed. The entire group then engages in a town meeting discussion of what has occurred. If themes are identified, they can lead to whatever is appropriate: action, task force, or further discussion. This process is quite useful in settings where there are factions or where people come in with set ideas and need to engage with others and find out how they are viewing the situation; it mixes them up for a different conversational experience. Drawing opens a new dimension and assists the process. Critical to a productive experience is a focused theme that fully engages the participants. The World Café can be used in groups as small as twelve and as large as twelve hundred. It has been used internationally in many countries of the world.

Conclusion: Giving Voice, Managing Differences, and Finding Common Ground

There is some wonderful work going on using these methods, all involving two principles. The first underlying principle is that they all create interaction among diverse stakeholders and a process that allows stakeholders to participate and be heard. Essentially, these are democratic methods that encourage all voices to be heard. They foster input to decisions employees or citizens are asked to support. It is important to point out that this does not necessarily mean that five hundred stakeholders get together and make the decisions. They may be the decision makers, or their input may be incorporated by an executive group that is present at the event and responsible for the organization. Both methods work well if people know in advance what the ground rules are.

Practitioners who propose these methods need to understand that not all leaders and managers want to involve stakeholders in having their say or in mutual decision making. This means that sensitive negotiation and coaching are part of contracting with executives about use of these methods. There have been instances where practitioners, in their eagerness to help the client move into action, did not insist that the client really understand what these methods do in terms of stakeholder voice, involvement, commitment, new ideas, and what they require in terms of leadership participation, support, and follow-up. Taking enough time to fully educate clients during the contracting phase of the intervention is the key to realizing the true potential of these methods.

A second principle that underlies these methods is their process for managing differences (Bunker, 2000). None of these methods use conflict resolution strategies to deal with differences. In large groups with many stakeholders, there are bound to be differences, and many of them. This is not of great concern because there is no objective to resolve differences. The objective in most of these methods is *to find common ground*—that is, to understand what those present and representing the system *agree on*. The assumption is that once what is agreed on is clear, it is possible to move forward from that common ground even though differences remain. Differences are simply not the focus of the work. The theory is that when differences occur, the natural tendency is to focus on them and try to resolve them. In much of this work, differences and disagreements are acknowledged and dealt with if that can happen in a reasonable time period. But they are not allowed to stop the work of moving forward by crowding out awareness of areas of agreement. Merrelyn Emery proposes that there is usually far more agreement than most people are aware of in groups. If this becomes salient, the group can move forward. The search for common ground is a key principle.

There is great opportunity for use of these methods in communities where managing differences among diverse stakeholders is thwarting movement and holding up the progress that many urgently desire. Since these methods further a process that allows people to have a voice and manage differences, it is not surprising that they are being used in many community settings where stakeholders expect to have input into important decisions.

References

Brown, J. (2002). *The world café: A resource guide for hosting conversations that matter.* Mill Valley, CA: Whole-Systems Associates.

Bunker, B. B. (2000). Managing conflict through large group methods. In M. Deutsch & P. T. Coleman (Eds.), *The handbook of conflict resolution: Theory and practice* (pp. 546–567). San Francisco: Jossey-Bass.

Bunker, B. B., & Alban, B. T. (Eds.). (1992). Large group interventions. [Special Issue.] *Journal of Applied Behavioral Science, 28*(4).

Bunker, B. B., & Alban, B. T. (1997). *Large group interventions: Engaging the whole system for rapid change.* San Francisco: Jossey-Bass.

Dannemiller Tyson Associates. (2000). *Whole-scale change: Unleashing the magic in organizations.* San Francisco: Berrett-Koehler.

Emery, F. E., & Trist, E. L. (1960). Socio-Technical Systems. In C. W. Churchman and M. Verhurst (Eds.), *Management sciences, models and techniques, vol. 2* (pp. 83–97). London: Pergamon.

Emery, M., & Purser, R. E. (1996). *The Search Conference: Theory and practice.* San Francisco: Jossey-Bass.

Holman, P., & Devane, T. (1999). *The change handbook: Group methods for shaping the future.* San Francisco: Berrett-Koehler.

Hosford, C. (2004). Collaboration technology altering session dynamics. *Meeting News, 28*(1), 1/18–19.

Lippitt, R. (1980). *Choosing the future you prefer.* Washington, DC: Development.

Ludema, J. D., Whitney, D., Mohr, B. J., & Griffin, T. J. (2003). *The appreciative inquiry summit: A practitioner's guide for leading large-group change.* San Francisco: Berrett-Koehler.

Manning, M. R., & DelaCerda, J. (2003). Building organizational change in an emerging economy: Whole systems change using large group interventions in Mexico. *Research in Organizational Change and Development, 14,* 51–97.

Owen, H. (1992). *Open space technology: A user's guide.* Potomac, MD: Abbott.

Rehm, R. (1999). *People in charge: Creating self managing workplaces.* Stroud, Great Britain: Hawthorn.

Weisbord, M. R. (1987). *Productive workplaces: Organizing and managing for dignity, meaning, and community.* San Francisco: Jossey-Bass.

CHAPTER SEVENTEEN

WORKING IN VERY
LARGE SOCIAL SYSTEMS:
THE 21ST CENTURY TOWN MEETING

Carolyn J. Lukensmeyer and Daniel Stone

*Never doubt that a small group of thoughtful, committed citizens can
change the world; indeed, it's the only thing that ever has.*
MARGARET MEAD

Readers of the *New York Times* opened their newspapers on Sunday, July 21, 2002, to find on the front page (above the fold!) a full-color photograph of a meeting. Yes, a meeting—not an event, a rally, or a march. A meeting, with people sitting at tables, listening to speakers, reading materials, and talking with one another.

At first glance, it may not sound like something of great interest to the common person. Yet there was a great significance to this meeting. Called "Listening to the City," this was what is termed a 21st Century Town Meeting, a carefully designed and executed opportunity for a representative group of citizens who had been affected by the September 11, 2001, attacks from throughout the New York region to be in genuine dialogue—with one another and with those who held the power to make decisions—about the future of the World Trade Center site. By the end of the day, decision makers had heard the people's voices, and promises were made in keeping with those voices—promises that were kept.

Pete Hamill of the *New York Daily News* (one of about two hundred news organs in attendance) had this to say about the event: "From 10 a.m. to 4 p.m., they were presented with basic issues about the rebuilding of those 16 gutted acres in lower Manhattan. At each table, they debated in a sober, thoughtful, civil way. They voted, offered comments, and moved on to the next item on the agenda. We have a word for what they were doing. The word is democracy" (2002).

It was obvious to almost everyone who was there that this had been a demonstrably successful effort to get policy makers to listen to citizens on a vital issue. It was also clear to many that this had been an important experiment in what democracy could and should be in this age. What was understood by a few of the people was that the very core of the 21st Century Town Meeting was based on contributions that come directly from the field of organization development (OD).

This chapter describes the 21st Century Town Hall Meeting as an OD approach for supporting deliberative democracy in very large social systems. Characteristics of large social systems, key components of the 21st Century Town Meeting, staffing requirements, OD practitioner roles and competencies, and future directions are explored.

OD and Deliberative Democracy

Democratic processes are fundamentally about tapping into the wisdom of the collective as a basis for self-governance. In this modern technological age, there is a crying need for this kind of wisdom—wisdom that recognizes and accounts for the needs and perspectives of the whole, and not just a privileged few. The survival of humans as a species depends on recognizing this fundamental relatedness of all people—not just people, but all other species and facets of global life on the planet.

The United States is one of the oldest and most established democratic societies still functioning in the world. Yet today there is increasing evidence of a sense of a breakdown in this democracy. In response to what they feel is the imperviousness of public officials, continual broken promises, and the inordinate power of special interests, citizens believe their voices really do not count.

Among the most disturbing evidence of this breakdown is the extraordinary lack of participation by the electorate in the voting process itself. In the United States, participation in national elections generally hovers at around 50 percent of the electorate. People have simply opted out of the system. Citizens have lost confidence that their votes will make a difference. Democracy in its current form is viewed by many as inept at best, and insincere at worst.

There is thus a gap between the form and ideal of democracy and how it actually is implemented. This gap may partly be because those in power simply are not interested in generating a climate of genuine public participation in civic affairs. However, there is also an increasing number of politicians who want to meaningfully involve citizens in the important issues of their society but who simply lack the methods to make this happen.

It is to this latter group—one that seems to be growing in number and force—that the field of OD has something to offer. In recent years, OD practitioners—in collaboration with skilled professionals from other disciplines—have been forging new forms of democracy that can be brought to scale in helping to fulfill the promise of democracy.

OD practitioners are committed to fostering the development of better, more effective organizations. The roots of the OD profession come out of a fundamental concern with human values in the context of organizations, among its most fundamental values being a belief in democracy. Many understand democracy as being inextricably linked with the fulfillment of human potential at the individual and collective levels. The roots of OD grow out of Kurt Lewin's early research and theory about democratizing group processes.

As noted earlier, there is a small but growing body of experience with politicians who have a genuine commitment to democratic ideals, and who are willing to experiment with new forms of democratic processes. Many of these processes belong to the burgeoning field of deliberative democracy, which includes techniques such as deliberative polling, large-scale online dialogue, citizen juries, dynamic planning charrettes, national issues forums, constructive conversations, communitywide study circles, choicework dialogues, small group dialogue, as well as the 21st Century Town Meeting (Goldman and Torres, 2004).

The field of deliberative democracy is grounded in several core principles:

- Decisions that have an impact on people need to be informed by legitimate representation of those people being affected.
- Those people need to be sufficiently informed about the issues to participate in the democratic process.
- They need to be engaged in a genuinely dialogical manner to enable them to express their views, listen to others' views, and ultimately be able to render judgment about the issues under consideration.
- If citizens are given the opportunity to engage in this manner, and if they believe it makes a difference, they will in fact choose to engage.
- Having engaged and seen the results, they will be that much more willing to stay engaged in the democratic process.

Deliberative democracy has its roots in many fields of knowledge, notably political science, public administration, and philosophy. More recently, OD values and methods are being incorporated in these processes. Although the field of OD has been primarily focused on creating value-based change inside organizations, it has also evolved a range of human interactive methodologies for all levels of human social systems, including those that are usually much larger and less defined than the typical organization. The larger social system may be a community, a state, a nation, or even the world as a whole.

Characteristics of Large Social Systems

The OD practitioner who chooses to work in large social systems must understand the nature of this field and how it is similar to and different from the organizational environment. On one level, creating democratic processes in very large social systems is remarkably similar to the work done by many OD practitioners who work inside organizations, especially those who in more recent years have been engaged in the "large group intervention" movement. The difference is that democratic processes and values must be applied in a broad public context. Five core characteristics differentiate larger social systems from the typical organizational system.

Boundaries Are More Permeable

The boundaries between what is inside the system and what is outside are more permeable than is typically found in organizations. In reality, much of what takes place in the public arena occurs in the "white space" in between organizations; this is in loosely knit citizen groups, interorganizational groups, or simply among unfederated or unorganized citizenry. This lack of clear boundaries can create significant challenges for determining the scope of the issues under deliberation, and in determining who actually needs to participate as well as how to reach them.

Ensuring Participation Can Be More Difficult

Inside organizations, authority can mandate participation (the letter, if not the spirit). In most social systems, there is little basis for requiring people to actually engage and participate in democratic processes (one notable exception to this is in Australia, where citizens are actually penalized if they do not participate in their country's electoral system). Therefore, more extraordinary measures need to be taken to motivate people to commit their time and energy and invest their hope in actually taking part in such deliberations.

Decision Makers Are in Fact Accountable

Decision makers can be made more accountable to the participants. A battle cry among executives and managers in many organizations is "This is not a democracy." Organizational leaders often believe they owe their employees little accountability. However, there remains a genuinely felt belief by citizens within democracies— as battered and cynical as they may have become—that elected officials are supposed to be accountable to those who have elected them. This expectation can be used to help induce public figures to engage in democratic processes and actually behave in accordance with the guidance that comes out of them.

The Process Is Inherently Political

The deliberative democratic process itself can be used or subverted for political purposes.

There is a far more political context to the larger social system than in most organizational systems. What is done is communicated through a wide set of media prisms that are not under the direct control of those in power. In organizations, those in power do retain substantial control over many of the organs of communication. This therefore creates an imperative that the process be conducted in a way that can withstand extensive and careful scrutiny. Only in this way will the process and the outcomes be viewed by the public, and therefore by decision makers, as legitimate.

The Issues Are Complex

People face issues that represent the full range of the condition of human beings living in community. Inside organizations, the range of issues (and therefore of stakeholders) is usually significantly more limited and primarily bounded by the organization's mission. In the larger system, the stakeholder universe tends to be much larger and more diverse. A legitimate dialogue needs to include full representation of the key stakeholders to the issues. With such representation, the approach must be especially carefully designed to ensure the participation of many more groups and individuals than are usually involved in organizational contexts. Also, given the wider and more diverse context of the dialogue, there are often issues of language, disability, and other differences that must be effectively accommodated.

There are no doubt other differences; however, this list of characteristics highlights a perspective that OD practitioners must adopt if they hope to conduct a successful democratic deliberation. Accounting for these differences has implications for the methods that are used to create the democratic process and therefore the range of skills and capacities needed to carry out the process.

The 21st Century Town Meeting Model

Imagine a large space, perhaps a very large space. Convention centers have been used, as have other large open areas. There is a stage, sometimes at the center of the room, sometimes at one end. The floor is filled with round tables. At each round table are seated ten or eleven citizens, usually mixed on the basis of geography, race, age, or whatever other demographic seems important to ensure vigorous conversation at the tables. Many of them are individual citizens who were recruited and who volunteered to spend their day focusing on this issue. Some of them come from organized groups of citizens or other organizations interested in the issue. One of the people at the table is a trained facilitator, who is there not to participate but to help the others express themselves and have their voices captured. To capture those voices, there is a networked laptop computer on each table. These computers are used to register key comments from the tables; they are sent to another part of the room where a group of "themers" is gathered. Also, each participant has a handheld polling device that looks like a TV remote control unit.

One or two podiums for speakers are usually on the stage. There are also giant screens on which are projected images, themes that emerge from dialogue, and results of polling among participants. During the meeting, the participants are given basic information about the issues under deliberation. They also have written materials specially prepared for them that provide an unbiased definition of the issues and the options for addressing them. In addition, there are speakers well versed in the issues who speak to the assemblage to help them understand the importance of the issue and consider the options. The key decision maker in relation to the issue is also on the stage to state his or her commitment to listen to and weigh seriously the input that is received from the meeting.

Then the participants are led through a series of facilitated discussions about the issues, including questions such as:

- What are the most important values to be attended to in addressing the issues?
- What do they like about the options presented to them, and what concerns them?
- What additional options or considerations should be looked at?

The results of all of these conversations are sent, via computer, to the theme team, where they are quickly analyzed. A thematic analysis of the comments is then projected onto the giant screens, giving participants a chance to see how the room as a whole thought about the issue. Equipped with this perspective, participants are led through a process of polling about the various options, with the results being displayed instantaneously. Thus a collective voice is generated from the assemblage to which the decision maker is in a position to respond. On hearing the thoughts and reactions of the decision maker, participants walk out of the meeting knowing more about the issue, feeling their voice has been heard, and having a good idea about how their voice is going to be responded to.

In summary, the 21st Century Town Meeting is an electronic town meeting that incorporates facilitated small-group dialogue, networked computers, a theme team that identifies themes from small-group reports, electronic keypads for voting on issues, and large video screens for displaying real-time data, themes, and information. There is more. A huge amount of preparation leads up to such an event, and a significant amount of effort must take place after the event in order to make it all work. The prework and postwork involved in creating the 21st Century Town Meeting is described in the next section.

Core Components of the 21st Century Town Meeting Model

The key elements of conducting a 21st Century Town Meeting involve extensive preplanning, successful delivery of the event, and sustained follow-up. There are seven key components to the process. The discussion of these key components here is adapted from Lukensmeyer and Brigham (2002).

Selecting an Issue That Affects Policy and Resources for the Common Good. Citizens will engage with an issue if they believe it is important and will have a significant impact. Sometimes the 21st Century Town Meeting is focused initially on an identified issue, as was the case with the World Trade Center ("Listening to the City"). In other cases, the decision maker may primarily want to encourage a greater level of public participation and uses the preparation process to bring into focus those issues that citizens most care about. Before moving forward, the event must be focused on an issue of genuine vitality and concern to the larger community.

Developing the Strategy. Once the issue is known, a disciplined analysis must be done about the key social and political forces at play. Who are the key decision makers, stakeholders, and communities that care about the issue? What has already taken place relative to this issue that either informs the strategy or can be built on? When and under what circumstances would the deliberation have the most impact? Finally, what is the most effective communications strategy to get widespread awareness and participation?

Building Credibility with Citizens and Decision Makers. The true impact of the 21st Century Town Meeting is in its capacity to influence key decision makers. Those with power and influence relative to the issue must be brought into the process in such a way that they commit to participating, taking the input seriously, and being accountable back to the citizenry. It must be clear that there is no pre-set outcome or agenda to the deliberations, and there is a genuinely open field for citizens to influence.

Ensuring Large and Diverse Participation. The overall quality and credibility of the dialogue is largely dependent on the involvement of a legitimate representation of citizens affected by the issue. A major commitment is made to recruiting participants who represent the overall citizenry in whatever demographics are relevant to the issue under deliberation. This may include geography, age, race, income level, or other factors. In the case of the World Trade Center meeting, it was essential that there be a significant representation of victims' families. Other issues may require other unique constituencies to be well represented.

The number of participants required for success varies considerably with the issue and the overall context. A "statistically valid" number of people may simply not be sufficient for producing the face validity needed for the event to have public legitimacy. National polls may be based on as few as six hundred people. In contrast, the input process for a citywide issue may require two or three thousand people in attendance for the populace to grant credibility to the event.

Successful 21st Century Town Meetings have included as many as forty-five hundred people at a time in a single room. Other events have been conducted with significant numbers in several locations interacting with one another across space via interactive TV. To date, the upward limit has been set only by considerations of budget and the physical availability of the technology. The true ceiling on participation has never been tested.

Creating Safe Public Space. The core of the event is the dialogue that occurs at participant tables. A major effort is made to ensure that the table conversations are well facilitated so that all points of view are heard and respected, and that the input from the tables represents a fair and balanced synthesis of perspectives. The various technologies (computers, polling keypads) are also key factors in helping participants feel that their voice has been recorded and will count.

Supporting Informed Dialogue. The cornerstone of democracy is an informed electorate. A major effort is made to ensure that participants have sufficient and objective information about the issues. Participant materials are carefully crafted to be easily digested and to give a fair and balanced representation of the issues. Speakers are chosen for their ability, as a group, to stimulate thought in a balanced way. All facilitators are carefully chosen and trained to remain completely neutral to the issues, serving solely as honest brokers of dialogue.

Sustaining and Institutionalizing Citizen Voice. When the event is over, it is not over. There is a need to ensure that whatever is generated during the event is captured and made use of, and that citizens who have participated get genuine feedback as to how their input was used. Where possible citizens are given a way to continue their involvement in the issues they have just discussed. This might mean further public forums or providing them with materials, which they can use in their community to engage their neighbors in the dialogue. Internet Web chats have been designed as follow-on to some events, so participants with access to computers can continue to weigh in as ideas further develop. Additional strategies can be used to give participants the opportunity to be involved in other issues.

Staffing

A well-selected and well-trained staff is essential for a successful 21st Century Town Meeting. Even though there can be literally hundreds of people required to adequately staff such an event, several key roles deserve special attention. The key staff members include the project executive, producer, lead facilitator, project manager, area facilitators, table facilitators, theme team, and issue experts. Roles, responsibilities, and core competencies for the key staff people are described in Table 17.1.

TABLE 17.1. STAFFING REQUIREMENTS FOR A 21ST CENTURY TOWN MEETING.

Roles	Responsibilities	Core Competencies
Project executive	Overall responsibility for the managing relationship with the client and the overall project, including: • Overall contracting with client and ongoing liaison • Overall direction of project • Staffing the other key roles • Managing project budget	Team leadership Consulting skills Political acumen Project management Design Budget management
Producer	Overall program content, design, and delivery, including: • Overall leadership of design team • Design and scriptwriting • Development of participant materials • Coordination of design with production and project management • Training of table facilitators • Overall direction of program during event	Team leadership Design, including use of technologies Scriptwriting Narrative writing and graphics Training skills
Lead facilitator	Leading the event, including: • Working with producer on design • Facilitating the event	Large group facilitation

TABLE 17.1. STAFFING REQUIREMENTS FOR A 21ST CENTURY TOWN MEETING, Cont'd.

Roles	Responsibilities	Core Competencies
Project manager	Coordination of key logistics, including: • Creating overall project plan for the event • Hiring and supervising key project personnel • Tracking project plan and adjusting as needed	Team leadership Project planning Supervision Project management
Area facilitators	Providing support for a group of tables and table facilitators during the event	Coordination Facilitation Conflict resolution
Table facilitators	Leading dialogue and interactions during the event in keeping with the design	Group facilitation
Theme team	Reviewing data from tables as they are generated, developing key themes to be shared with the overall group of participants	Synthesizing large volumes of data and extracting themes (in a very short time period)
Issue experts	Providing input, either from the platform or on as-needed basis so participants have access to key information to knowledgeably discuss issues	Content knowledge Communication skills

Many OD practitioners have never experienced a large group event in a very large social system and are likely to need additional skills to be successful. Attention must be given both to selecting people for the roles who possess the right attributes and potential and to providing training and mentoring for people who are just learning those roles. The people in these roles must be able to demonstrate and maintain the required competencies in a high-visibility and high-demand environment.

Experiences with 21st Century Town Meetings

Over the last ten years, America*Speaks* has conducted more than forty 21st Century Town Meetings in thirty-some states across the country. At these events, citizens come out in large numbers and represent a full range of interests and perspectives. They are capable of dealing with complex public policy issues and of making balanced choices given a range of alternatives. Citizens are willing to commit their time and energy to participate in public dialogue when they feel safe and know that they will be heard and that they will have a genuine influence on the outcome. Examples of these town meetings are described in Table 17.2. They include three citizen summits and one youth summit in Washington, D.C., a regional planning event in northern Illinois, and the two Listening to the City events in New York City. These events involved a range of six hundred to forty-five hundred participants.

TABLE 17.2. 21ST CENTURY TOWN MEETINGS.

Event	Client	Participants	Purpose or Outcome
Citizen Summits I-III, 1999–2003	Mayor of Washington, D.C.	2,000–3,000 citizens from throughout the city	Generate citizen input into the City Strategic Plan and about key policy issues; rebuild trust between citizenry and government
Youth Summit, 2001	Mayor of Washington, D.C.	1,500 young people from throughout the city	Get youth input about what should be done to make Washington, D.C., a place where young people can thrive
Regional Planning, 2001	Northeast Illinois Planning Commission	800 participants	Identify most likely or preferred scenarios for planning the region's future and plan for how to address those scenarios
Listening to the City (LTC) I-II, 2002	Civic Alliance to Rebuild Downtown	600 participants (LTC I); 4,500 participants (LTC II)	Generate citizen input as to what should be done about the future of the World Trade Center site and Lower Manhattan overall

Future Directions: Institutionalizing Citizen Voice

A major challenge facing the United States is how to institutionalize citizen engagement. Sufficient experimentation and replication have been accomplished. Public policy decisions can be improved by using large-scale public engagement. The challenge is how to embed processes and structures of this kind at all levels of government (federal, state, local) so they can be used in a routine way to make decisions and allocate resources.

The methodology for institutionalizing citizen engagement will continue to evolve, especially as technology becomes more sophisticated. Polling devices and networked computers will become more affordable. Ever more citizens will be able to fully engage in such dialogues through the Internet.

The Organization for Economic Cooperation and Development (OECD) researches public participation around the globe. It has shown that institutions in the United States invest fewer resources in engaging the public than any other North American or European members. Canada, Britain, France, Germany, Denmark, and many other countries invest regularly in public participation. For example, each year the Danish Parliament determines the issues about which it wants public input, and the Danish Technology Board runs citizen dialogues about these issues. The results of these deliberations are then shared widely, and the outcomes of those dialogues are debated on the floor of Parliament.

The more central issue in the United States is one of policy—of creating a clear intention to truly democratize public policy decision making. A vision for the next decade is of the public engaged in genuinely meaningful ways on the central public policy decisions of the time and the results of those engagements being centrally placed within the deliberative decision-making processes.

For example, citizens are polled on a biannual cycle about the issues of greatest concern to the country at the time (for example, health care, environment, and foreign policy). A neutral or nonpartisan institute is established and funded by Congress, with the charge of implementing a nationwide discussion on that issue. The results of the dialogue are taken directly into the committee of jurisdiction in Congress for debate on the floor of Congress.

Comparable examples could be replicated at the state and local levels. There are no doubt many other ways to achieve the intention, variations that are appropriate and specific to various kinds of issues and contexts. What is clearly needed, however, is a major commitment on the part of this country's leadership about the importance of citizen involvement as a key to the future health of this democratic society.

Core Competencies

The core competencies for effectively implementing the 21st Century Town Meeting include many of the skills required for the practice of OD. Because of the public, political, size, and other characteristics of larger social systems, there are other key competencies that go beyond those traditionally taught to or learned by most OD practitioners. For this reason, OD practitioners need to join others who have these skills or develop these skills themselves.

Core OD Skills

Core skills, which are typical of the OD profession and are required for conducting large group meetings in very large social systems, are teamwork, diagnostic, design, presentation, facilitation, and large group platform skills. Included in required core OD skills are the ability to use groupware, polling keypads, interactive video, and other electronic supports for large group meetings.

Other Key Skills

There are other necessary skills not closely associated with the OD profession:

- *Communication and public relations:* ability to create strategies to recruit participants, craft messages for the public, and manage media interest and responses surrounding the event
- *Organizing and recruitment:* creating a target demographic for the event and then getting the word out at numerous venues to encourage participation that meets the target demographic
- *Project management:* establishing detailed project plans and budgets to ensure that all facets of the process are identified, sequenced, assigned out, and resourced; tracking the project plans at a sufficient level of detail to identify where there are any gaps, missed targets, or adjustments needed
- *Political acumen:* ability to identify the key stakeholders for the issues, understand their key motivations, and build sufficient confidence to encourage their genuine participation; ability to build confidence with decision makers so they commit to participating and being accountable to the results of the event

Personal Skills and Attributes

Finally, there are critical personal skills and attributes that practitioners of this form of democracy must embody:

- *Ability to establish and maintain a stance of neutrality and impartiality:* the role of the practitioner in the event is to safeguard the legitimacy of the process and trust that effective deliberation of the right people with the right process will produce the right results. Any evidence that practitioners are advocating a content agenda for the outcome of the process can create a perception of the event as an unsafe place for those of differing views.
- *Ability to operate on multiple levels of a system simultaneously:* the huge complexity of details can distract some OD practitioners from maintaining a focus on the

overall picture and process of what they are engaging in. For other practitioners, absorption in the overall process can hamper appreciation for managing all of the details—any one of which may turn out to be a critical factor in determining the success of the endeavor. OD practitioners must have the ability to keep the dots connected.

• *Ability to keep a large systems change perspective:* the very scale and visibility of the event can take a huge amount of attention and energy and lead to focusing solely on having a successful event. More important, the success of the event depends on two outcomes: the actual making and implementation of decisions in keeping with the voice of the people from the event, and ongoing engagement by politicians and citizens in the democratic process itself.

• *Ability to hold the ultimate intention of creating change:* practitioners must see the event as a key catalyst for promoting change, and they must foster and support receptivity and capacity for sustainable change.

• *Ability to sustain one's own energy:* the 21st Century Town Meeting is often conducted in an environment of tremendous demands—deadlines, glare of publicity, resource constraints, and other pressures. This can all test practitioners' capacity to maintain the requisite level of energy, focus, flexibility, and humor that supports their staying engaged and helping others stay engaged through what may feel sometimes like a gigantic marathon or relay race.

• *Ability to sustain hope:* one quality that every practitioner needs is the ability to hold the vision and hope, while at the same time dealing with the realities and disparities of power. Practitioners must believe that ordinary people, given the right opportunity, have the courage to stand up and be counted.

Conclusion

People in many professions take an oath as part of their rite of passage into their chosen field of endeavor: doctors take the Hippocratic oath, lawyers pledge to uphold and further the law, and so on. OD practitioners, who are not so uniformly credentialed, might also be seen as inheriting an important tradition and set of imperatives that make them worthy of their own oath. Perhaps what would figure prominently in such an oath is the responsibility of the OD practitioner to uphold the values of democracy.

OD practitioners have typically used OD skills to uphold these values in their families, in the groups they facilitate, in the organizations they serve. As the planet becomes more interconnected and issues become more compelling, there is an increasing need for OD practitioners to bring their abilities into a larger arena: into the societies in which they participate.

At this point in world history, there is an aching need for people who can create the conditions for ongoing development of genuinely democratic institutions. People's voices need to be heard to bring a balanced and whole view of the future they want to create. Skillful application of OD principles and methods, when combined with other key disciplines such as political science and public communications, can help create the conditions for truly open and honest dialogue.

When a group of well-meaning and informed people are able to share their individual truths, it results in a greater truth: a greater concern for the whole and less single-minded dedication to the interests of the isolated few. Those who have been gifted with the competencies and tools that can foster these core conditions of democracy have a unique privilege and responsibility to participate in making this contribution.

References

Goldman, J., & Torres, L. H. (2004). *Approaches to public engagement in the U.S.* (http://www.americaspeaks.org/library/del_methods_matrix_as.pdf).

Hamill, P. (2002, July 21). Thrilling show of people power. *New York Daily News* (http://www.nydailynews.com/news/col/phamill/story/4936p-4555c.html).

Lukensmeyer, C. J., & Brigham, S. (2002, Winter). Taking democracy to scale: Creating a town hall meeting for the twenty-first century. *National Civic Review, 91*(4), 351–366.

CHAPTER EIGHTEEN

CHANGING ORGANIZATIONS AND SYSTEMS FROM THE OUTSIDE: OD PRACTITIONERS AS AGENTS OF SOCIAL CHANGE

Mark Leach

M any OD practitioners work with organizations at the organizational boundary, both inside and outside the organization. OD practitioners involved in social change work often endeavor to change organizations from the outside. This chapter is addressed to both new and experienced organization development (OD) practitioners who would like to use their skills as external change agents in the service of progressive social change. For purposes of this discussion, *social change* is defined as "altering the structures, processes, and outcomes of domains larger than single organizations in ways that persist over time" (Brown, Leach, and Covey, 2005). More concretely, for an OD practitioner this could mean:

Note: This chapter is based on my experiences and those of my colleagues with the Institute for Development Research. Coming of age in the late 1960s and early 1970s, I grew up with the belief that I *could* and *should* use my life to advance social causes in which I believed. For me this began with issues of economic justice and social development, shaped in no small part by early exposure to people suffering the most grinding and dehumanizing kind of poverty in third-world countries. This expanded in later years to include environmental sustainability and public health. I feel fortunate to be able to spend my life consulting to organizations, and systems of organizations, whose missions I passionately support. Many of the things I find most intrinsically fascinating in life—the distribution of power and resources, group and intergroup dynamics, cultural differences, the role of leadership and the unconscious mind in group situations, and making sense of complex human puzzles—are some of the very things I have found most useful as a practitioner supporting progressive social change.

• Strengthening a nonprofit advocacy group whose mission is to change the practices of a target organization (such as the World Bank, Nike, or the Centers for Disease Control), whose activities have social, economic, or political consequences that extend far beyond the target organization's boundaries.

• Helping a small but innovative nonprofit literacy program drastically increase its impact by positioning its program model to be adopted as national policy by a developing country government.

• Helping create new coalitions, collaborations, or networks of organizations around a shared social change agenda (for example, to revitalize a depressed urban area, to change the political pressures on a company or a government, to change people's behavior on a massive scale to reduce the spreads of HIV-AIDS, or to ensure that the power of traditionally disenfranchised peoples is felt in the electoral process).

An OD practitioner engaged in such activities is involved in changing organizations and systems from the outside in at least two ways. First, immediate clients (the advocacy and policy nonprofits, the activist coalitions and networks, the sympathetic insiders in government or business) are themselves frequently outside the social change arena they are trying to influence. The executive director of a street persons' advocacy nonprofit is usually not herself homeless and is not part of the legislature whose policies her organization seeks to influence. The membership of a coalition to eliminate sweatshop labor does not typically include the corporate target of the coalition's work. The chief environmental officer of a polluting business is usually not a resident of the community where his corporation's effluent is dumped but may be part of a collaboration seeking to address the problem.

Second, OD practitioners involved in the kind of social change work described here are (like their counterparts in more conventional OD work) often not members of the organizations to which they are contributing their OD skills. Despite this distance from the actual impact of the social change work, the line between consultant and activist, OD practitioner, and social change agent can blur and in some cases dissolve entirely and appropriately.

This chapter begins with some information about social change organizations and the changing context of their work. A four-part typology is presented to help clarify the range of interventions, roles, and competencies needed to serve organizations whose mission is to make lasting social change in the world outside themselves. One of these types of intervention—creating new systems of organizations—is then explored in greater depth. This exploration includes an outline of the key factors in making these social change systems work, as well as a more detailed discussion of skills and approaches required of the OD practitioner.

Social Change Organizations, Systems, and Clients

Social change organizations and systems can involve such issue areas as international economic and social development, public health systems and policies, women's reproductive health and rights, environmental sustainability, human rights, and civil liberties. Since these issues are not amenable to solutions involving only one sector, the experience on which this chapter is based considers nonprofits, governments, and for-profit companies as legitimate organizational actors in the social change arena. In addition to these more conventional and well-bounded organizations, OD in the service of social change often requires working with multiple-organization systems (collaborations, consortia, partnerships) and also with more loosely bounded systems such as networks or social movements. The range of topics, sectors, organizational actors, and levels of intervention—local, regional, national, international, and global—where OD practitioners can apply and hone their skills in the service of social change is almost unlimited. Where the OD practitioner chooses to operate is likely to depend on the practitioner's substantive interests, values, life experience, political commitments, and personal theory of social change.

The nature of the issues and organizational actors in social change work also means that one's understanding of "client" must shift. In traditional OD, the client is usually the person or entity with whom the practitioner contracts and who pays the consultant's invoice. Social change work can require redefining the client as the mission of the organization (or organizations), and the intended beneficiaries of these organizations.

Current Context for Social Change Organizations

For many decades beginning in the 1940s, OD practitioners, especially in the private sector, could make a substantial contribution to the achievement of organizational mission while confining their work within the boundary of a single organization. Though somewhat more challenging, doing OD work within a single organization in the public and not-for-profit sectors could also yield serviceable results for a client organization. Conventional OD interventions (improving human and organizational processes, improving technology and structure, developing human resources, and intervening in the organization as a whole) and skills (intrapersonal and interpersonal skill development, consultation skills for entry, diagnosis, feedback, planned organizational change, and so on) were effective enough tools to usually meet client needs.

In the last fifteen or so years, however, things have become exponentially more complex and challenging. It is now a cliché to observe that the world is an increasingly interdependent place, linked together in the post–cold war era by the global economy, instant global communication via the Internet, relatively cheap international travel, global governance structures in the private and public spheres, and so on. But cliché or not, this interdependence has significant implications for the practice of OD in all sectors. However, the impact of this radical, global interdependence and increased complexity on OD in the service of social change is especially significant.

Specifically, leaders and staff of social change organizations are dealing *on a routine and widespread basis* with:

• Recognition that the scale and impact of their work in previous decades has not been nearly large enough to keep pace with the growth of the social problems their organization was designed to address.

• Recognition that no single organization has the resources, perspective, legitimacy, or skills needed to address the most pressing social problems of our time. To remain effective, this has required organizations to form a range of multiorganizational systems (collaborations, partnerships, networks, consortia, alliances, and so on). Competence in dealing with multiple-organizational systems will become a critical skill for the OD practitioner working in social change in the future.

• These multiorganizational systems require an organization to work with others that differ from it in numerous and challenging ways—frequently, differences in culture, perspectives, ideology, core mission, nature and amount of resources, political and economic power, geographic focus, stakeholder base, and so on.

• The sheer complexity and dizzying pace of change in the external situation leaves many organizational leaders feeling overwhelmed and in over their heads much of the time. External complexity exceeds the ability of many organizational leaders to take in, synthesize, and shape adequate organizational responses. Even when the leaders' complexity of mind *does* match the complexity of their external environment, they may find themselves saddled with organizational structures, habits, and skills suited for a much simpler time and task.

• Recognition that service delivery alone never solves problems that are rooted in deep-seated cultural and institutional arrangements that perpetuate inequalities in voice and resources. Having any real impact on the problems they are committed to addressing has prompted many organizations to lift *advocacy* of various kinds to the top of their organizational agenda.

• Younger staff members in many social change organizations are questioning the fundamental authority arrangements not only of the external world they are trying to influence but also of the organizations that employ them. Coming from social movement backgrounds themselves, many social change organization leaders lack a coherent, personal vision of leadership and organizational management that can deal simultaneously with internal challenges to authority and structure and with external demands of funders, boards of directors, collaborating organizations, and other external stakeholders.

So how does an OD practitioner find his or her bearings in this swirl of competing forces and changing contexts that is the world social change organizations inhabit daily? Clarifying the nature of the intervention task is a useful place to start, and the framework presented here can help.

Interventions for Changing Organizations from the Outside

Four types of intervention useful to OD practitioners working in the social change field are examined in this section: strengthening social change organizations, scaling up social change impacts, creating new systems of organizations, and reshaping the context of target institutions. The four interventions exist on a continuum. Moving along the continuum of intervention types, practitioners must be comfortable with and competent in a range of skills and roles that are increasingly unlike those of traditional OD. Practitioners must also face increasingly challenging issues of personal and professional development and boundary management—that is, the degree to which practitioners are inside or outside the system for which they are functioning as a change agent. These interventions, tasks, and OD practitioner roles are outlined in Exhibits 18.1 and 18.2. They are based on a framework developed by L. David Brown, Mark Leach, and Jane Covey (2005).

EXHIBIT 18.1. SUMMARY OF INTERVENTION TYPES AND TASKS.

Strengthen Social Change Organization
- Clarify linkages between the organization's mission and its activities.
- Manage conflicts over fundamental power and value differences.
- Design complex organizational architectures.
- Coach leaders.

Scale up Social Change Impacts
- Clarify social change theories that underlie organizational strategies.
- Design organizational architectures for expanded impact.
- Conceive and build external relationships.

(Continued)

EXHIBIT 18.1. SUMMARY OF
INTERVENTION TYPES AND TASKS, Cont'd.

Create New Systems of Organizations
- Convene a client system.
- Provide temporary leadership; gradually transfer leadership to system actors.
- Create formal and informal interface organizations.
- Create systems to enable multiple organization learning.

Reshape the Context of Target Institutions
- Articulate compelling visions.
- Build theories of contextual influence.
- Mobilize unorganized constituents for collective action.
- Create alliances to support reform.

Strengthening Social Change Organizations

At this point on the continuum, the OD practitioner is working to improve the functioning or capacity of a single organization. This work requires the most conventional OD skills and approaches and is the easiest type of social change work in which to maintain the external-internal boundary as a change agent. This said, it should not be assumed that private sector OD skills can be simply transferred to work with social change organizations.

These are typical tasks when working in this first type of intervention:

• *Clarifying linkages between the organization's mission and its activities.* Many social change organizations are clear about their mission and program activities but have a hard time describing the strategies and central goals that connect them. Given the complexity and rapidly changing environments in which these organizations exist, the OD practitioner's job is to help define and reframe the organization's activities around realistic yet challenging multiyear goals. The OD practitioner is frequently called on to manage significant internal conflict, often by reframing the inevitable internal tensions among program units in such organizations as the predictable, unavoidable consequences of the organization's mission.

• *Managing conflicts over fundamental power and value differences.* Participants in social change organizations frequently attribute strong ideological meaning to small differences, which can quickly escalate conflict. Conflict management is a key need in organizations mobilized around values and visions and organized to deal with constituencies whose interests are often in conflict with each other.

- *Designing complex organizational architectures.* Few social change organizations place high value on organization and management. This problem is compounded when staff members have roots in social movements that place high value on participatory decision making, flat hierarchy, low differentiation of tasks, roles and authority, and organic systems of accountability. The OD practitioner can bring knowledge and credibility to facilitate development of new organizational architectures and systems of decision making appropriate to the organization's mission, tasks, and membership.
- *Coaching leaders.* Many leaders of social change organizations are content experts or charismatic founders with little experience managing a growing and increasingly complex organization. Those with capacity and interest to learn can benefit greatly from dedicated, personal coaching. It is frequently useful to have this provided by a coach separate from the OD practitioner working on larger systems issues. Coaching requires a different skill set, focused on individual personality assessment and individual-level change. Having a separate coach also avoids conflict of interest in an instance where what is good for the leaders is in conflict with what is good for the organization. If coaching is insufficient to develop a leader whose organization has outgrown his or her capacity to manage it, then the leader may need to be coached to turn over significant management responsibilities to others or leave the organization.

In this typology of interventions and tasks, helping strengthen an individual social change organization requires the OD practitioner to play the roles of organizational strategist, mediator of conflict and authority relations, organizational designer and architect, and leadership coach for the chief executive and his or her top team. OD practitioner roles for this intervention type and others are summarized in Exhibit 18.2.

EXHIBIT 18.2. OD PRACTITIONER ROLES AND INTERVENTION TYPES.

Strengthen Social Change Organizations
- Organizational analyst
- Mediator of conflict and authority relations
- Organizational designer and architect
- Leadership coach

Scale up Social Change Impacts
- Social change theorist
- Network and partnership designer
- External relations facilitator

(Continued)

EXHIBIT 18.2. OD PRACTITIONER
ROLES AND INTERVENTION TYPES, Cont'd.

Create New Systems of Organizations
- Convener of multiple stakeholders
- Entrepreneur of new structures and systems
- Mediator of multiparty differences
- Catalyst of network learning processes

Reshape the Context of Target Institutions
- Activist visionary
- Policy analyst
- Movement-building leadership
- Influencer of public perceptions
- Conceptual-situational analyst of target institutions and external context
- Bridge builder with institutions and sectors

Scaling up Social Change Impacts

Organizations that are successful when small often find it difficult to increase the scale of their impact. They are unaware of alternatives to simply expanding their own operations through increased funding, increased number of direct beneficiaries, or growing the type of services or issues in their portfolio.

Other, more indirect approaches to scaling up are training others to do similar work, spinning off new organizations, or building temporary or long-term strategic alliances to influence the policies of other private, nonprofit, or government actors. Scaling up social change impact may require the OD practitioner to be involved in several tasks not commonly found in conventional OD. Each task pushes the practitioner to introduce ideas that are initially alien to insiders and to temporarily take an internal leadership role to shape the change project. This leadership is only useful if paired with the ability to bring other leaders and actors along who can assume this role for the long run. Here are some typical tasks for scaling up social change impacts:

   • *Clarifying social change theories that underlie organizational strategies.* Scaling up impacts by engaging and influencing other organizations requires that the OD practitioner accurately understand power dynamics in the external environment, the interests of all key players, and the nature of forces working for or against the desired impact. Organizational knowledge is not enough. The OD practitioner must know, or be able to quickly grasp, *how* social change related to the client's mission happens. For example, changing the way state supreme court judges are chosen requires a very different theory of social change from what is needed in increasing condom use among populations at high risk for contracting HIV-AIDS.

• *Designing organizational architectures for expanded impact.* Scaling-up strategies require their own organization designs. Conventional OD approaches to design are helpful for managing internal growth and increased complexity typical of direct approaches to scaling up. Indirect approaches to scaling up push the boundaries of most OD practitioners' training and require competence in organizational design intended to support diffusion of innovation outside the organization (for example, incubating and spinning off new organizations or building policy and advocacy coalitions to influence government policy).

• *Conceiving and building external relationships.* Indirect approaches to scaling up require social change organizations to become part of multiparty arrangements with such external actors as coalitions, partnerships, federations, alliances, subcontracts, and so on. OD support to these relationships can draw on conventional OD interventions such as conflict management, intergroup relations, and team building, but their application in multiorganizational settings is usually not part of most OD practitioners' experience or training.

OD practitioners who wish to help organizations scale up their social change impact must have capacities for several roles (Exhibit 18.2). They must be social change theorists (different from organizational change theorists), with expertise in large-scale political and social dynamics, coalition building, advocacy, and interorganizational relations. The practitioner should also be familiar with network and partnership design and be a capable facilitator of external relations. Overall this requires a shift in focus from dynamics and issues internal to a single OD client organization to those present in a larger constellation of organizations and social forces in the external world that one or more organizations seek to influence.

Creating New Systems of Organizations

The third type of intervention for changing organizations and systems from the outside is to assist in creating new systems of organizations, such as collaborations, strategic alliances, coalitions, or networks. This type of intervention is necessary when a problem cannot be addressed by a single organization and no organization, or system of organizations, exists as a focal point for collective action. Examples are when multiple, historically conflicting parties need to jointly manage a vital but scarce natural resource, or when an intractable social problem such as gang violence or racism is destroying communities and individual lives. Creating new systems of organizations is also necessary in many less overtly conflictual situations, as when multiple actors must cooperate to address a critical public health issue such as HIV-AIDS or reducing infant and maternal deaths.

Initially in these interventions the role and skills of the OD practitioner can look more like those of an organizational leader or movement organizer than those of a traditional OD consultant. It is at this point on our continuum of interventions that the OD practitioner role begins to blur into that of social change agent or activist.

Typical tasks in creating new systems of organization include:

- *Convening a client system.* Sometimes it takes a relatively uninvolved outsider such as an OD practitioner or action researcher to fill the need multiorganization systems have for a trusted, honest broker to bring disparate groups together. This might include working with existing community-based organizations and community organizers, or larger-scale movement leaders or network leaders to identify common ground, overcome old mistrust among actors, and explore possibilities for future joint action.

- *Creating temporary leadership and gradual empowerment of multiactor systems for social change.* After convening a group of organizations, the OD practitioner must gradually transfer the responsibility for multigroup convening and leadership to permanent members of the new system. This is a particularly sensitive time in the intervention and is a test of the degree to which participating groups are willing to trust one another with leadership and differentiated roles.

- *Creating formal and informal interface organizations.* If multiple organizations agree there is good reason for ongoing joint work, the OD practitioner can assist in designing and implementing a structure for managing the collective tasks. Depending on the nature of the groups' shared tasks and the political situation among and around them, such structures can include a leadership forum or council, a cooperative or collaborative board, or fairly traditional board of directors. Other basics of organizational infrastructure (staff, volunteer management, public relations systems, finance and accounting systems, and so on) often do not exist and need to be created, either anew or through collaboration with organizations with existing skills and infrastructure. The OD practitioner can help the multiorganization system identify and design ways to create this infrastructure.

- *Creating systems to enable multiple organization learning.* As single organizations have discovered, organizational learning is both valuable and challenging. The challenges of learning and adapting increase greatly when multiple organizations (often separated by hundreds or thousands of miles, contrasting worldviews, and vastly differing structures and resources) need to share their learning and coordinate joint action. OD practitioners with experience in action learning and the use of information technology in networks and collaboration can be useful in supporting learning, flexible adaptation, and the long-term effectiveness of multiple-organization systems for social change.

Fundamental OD practitioner roles for creating new systems of organizations are listed in Exhibit 18.2. They include convening multiple stakeholders, introducing new ideas about structuring, being a system entrepreneur, mediating multiparty differences, and being a catalyst of network learning processes.

Reshaping the Context of Target Institutions

This type of intervention is designed to bring external pressure to bear that will change the internal dynamics and policies of one or several target organizations that are critical to a particular social change. Examples are changing the lending and participation policies of the World Bank or influencing major commercial coffee buyers such as Starbucks to buy significant quantities of fair-trade coffee from producers.

Here the role of the change agent is almost unidentifiable as anything remotely resembling the typical external OD practitioner. In most cases there are multiple change agents, with change leadership shifting among people from various constituency and pressure groups, depending on the immediate task at hand and the phase of development of the work.

Here are typical tasks of the OD practitioner in this type of intervention:

• *Articulating compelling visions.* In this sort of situation, there is often no shortage of ideas about how the target organization should change. Examples are to close down the target organization, fundamentally change the composition and accountability of its governance body, reform its principles and practices, and so on. So the OD practitioner's challenge is often to help craft a common vision from multiple and competing visions of how the target organization should be changed.

• *Building theories of contextual influence.* Once the shared vision of change is established, there is the equally challenging task of building agreement on *how* best to influence the target organization to change. (The usual suspects are media campaigns, economic pressure, governmental pressure, public education campaigns, working with sympathetic insiders, and so on.) Again, one of the most valuable roles of the OD practitioner in this kind of intervention is to be a trusted, honest broker, preferably with experience and ideas from other similar situations that can help point the way.

• *Mobilizing unorganized constituents for collective action.* The role of actually mobilizing people to influence the context of a target institution is usually the purview of existing or newly formed advocacy or organizing groups. But the OD practitioner involved in this kind of intervention must have a firm grasp of the role and dynamics of social organizing and mobilization—if only to understand how these groups fit into the larger influence strategy and to recognize the limits of the OD practitioner's own specialization in organizational and interorganizational dynamics.

• *Creating alliances to support reform.* Occasionally a group of organizations with the common goal of influencing a target organization will request the OD practitioner to assist in crafting longer-term alliances or other structural relationships. This then requires the skills and roles already described in the section on creating new systems of organizations.

Reshaping the context of target institutions requires such OD practitioner roles as activist visionary; supporting movement-building leadership, policy analysis, and influencing public perceptions; conceptual and situational analyses of external context and target institutions; and bridge building with institutions and sectors (Exhibit 18.2). Rarely if ever will one person play all of these roles or have all these skills. So at a minimum the OD practitioner involved in this kind of intervention must know what is needed, know the limits of her or his own abilities, and be willing to use (and be skilled at) collaborative and shared leadership.

Creating Multiorganizational Systems

Because of the increasing complexity and interdependence of organizational environments, competence in multiparty situations is becoming increasingly important for OD practice. Creating multiorganizational systems may well shift from being a specialty of some OD practitioners to a necessary core competence for OD practitioners in many sectors—perhaps in the next ten to fifteen years. This section examines practices that are useful for creating multiorganizational systems and for working with existing multiorganizational systems in social change. This gives OD practitioners, who are considering working in this area, a glimpse into the kinds of issues that need to be addressed and the skills and competencies that are required.

From the perspective of the OD practitioner/change agent, four key areas require attention and skillful intervention: the design of the work itself, leadership for the system, governance for the system, and appropriate funding of the joint work. The practices and tasks for creating multiorganizational systems are outlined in Table 18.1.

TABLE 18.1. OD PRACTICES AND TASKS
FOR CREATING MULTIORGANIZATIONAL SYSTEMS.

Practices	Tasks
Design of the joint work	• Ensure adequate time during start-up to identify correct partners. • Define joint work as "close to the ground" as possible, and involve implementers early on. • Build trust early on by giving partners opportunities to deliver on small commitments. • Clarify each member's value added to the joint work. • Proceed only when shared overall goals, objectives, and priorities are agreed on.
Executive leadership of the multiorganizational system	• Make available technical and managerial skill. • Ensure skill and attentiveness to managing up to the governing body, down to the program implementers, and across to other governing body members. • Ensure skill in articulating a unifying vision, inspiring loyalty to the shared mission, and handling extraordinary levels of conceptual, technical, and relational complexity. • Provide for authority needed for key management responsibilities. • Clarify and hold the line between executive and governance responsibilities.
Governance of the multiorganizational system	• Build trusting relationships with and among governance group members and with key people in each of the members' home organizations. • Choose governance group members with strategic thinking skills and the ability to make decisions and commit resources on behalf of their home organizations. • Give a governance group the needed authority, training, and commitment to hold the line between governance and management. • Ensure that influence over policy and strategy is appropriately shared among governing body members. • Furnish a transparent and trusted system for financial accountability among members. • Buffer system operations from policy differences among member organizations. • Create an operations coordination group separate from the governing body when there are significant operations and programs.
Funding the multiorganizational system	• Ensure funders' support for implementer influence over design of the multiorganizational system and system program operations. • Establish flexible strategy as the multiparty system evolves, learns, and matures. • Provide adequate resources early on for high up-front costs of creating collaborative systems and for continuous joint learning. • Create formal and informal communication mechanisms to link funders and the governing body. • Promote transparency in funders' influence on strategy and policy.

Design of the Joint Work

Early on, development of multiorganizational systems requires attention to the design of the joint work that will be conducted by the multiorganizational partners in a social change effort. To support successful design of the joint work, the OD practitioner must help the architects of the multiorganizational partnership address a series of issues, described in Table 18.1.

Organizational partners need to be a good match for the work that is to be done by the multiorganizational system. Conversation about who should be involved and why should occur early on and be quite explicit. Too many partnerships and collaborations fail because organizations that should be included have not been, or organizations that should not have been included have been. This is sometimes because of pressure from funders, unwillingness to reach out to others with different but needed perspectives and skills, or time pressure to address an urgent social problem. The joint work should proceed only when fundamental purposes, goals, priorities, and outcomes are shared and agreed on by leaders and key implementers of partner organizations. They should never be fudged in the interest of getting on with the work or avoiding conflict in the organizational relationships.

Although organization leaders play a critical role in successful collaboration and partnership, the perspectives and concerns of operational staff and volunteers must be considered in relation to what is feasible and possible in the joint work, and what is needed—resources, systems, time to work out differences—to support effective work among people from the organizations. Small, short-term experiments in joint work, such as running a joint workshop or collaborating on a time-limited public information campaign, can be a good way to build trust and surface and resolve the inevitable difficulties when two or more organizations try to work together. Once these are worked out on a smaller scale, the organizations can take on higher-risk, longer-term joint work, such as joint fundraising or multiyear programs and campaigns.

Executive Leadership of the Multiorganizational System

Many, but not all, multiparty systems have an executive leadership role, held by an individual or small team (such as a lead manager, network coordinator, leadership council, or executive director) accountable to a larger governing body. Where this role exists, the skills and competencies of the executive leadership are critical; they must have the necessary authority for key management responsibilities. The OD practitioner can assist the multiorganizational partnership in this area by helping the partnership attend to necessary skills and competencies in selecting the executive leader(s) and supporting their development when selections have been made. Key skills and competencies are listed in Table 18.1. Executive leaders and leadership team members need technical and managerial skills. They must have the ability to articulate a unifying vision for the joint work of the partners, inspire loyalty to the shared mission, and handle an extraordinary level of conceptual, technical, and relational complexity. They must be clear about and hold the line between executive and governance responsibilities. They must be able to manage up to the governing body, down to program staff and volunteers, and across to leaders in partner organizations.

Governance of the Multiorganizational System

In creating the formal and informal interfaces where multiple parties come together, the change agent/OD practitioner must often take on temporary leadership roles that go well beyond the kind of facilitation and provision of expert opinion more common in traditional OD interventions. The OD practitioner involved in convening and shaping a multiparty governance group must build trusting relationships with each leader of the governance group and foster such relationships among the leaders. The practitioner must ensure that members of the governance group have strategic thinking skills, have the authority to make decisions and commit resources on behalf of their home organizations, are trained and committed to holding the line between governance and management, and engage in shared influence over policy and strategy. The multiparty governance group needs to be structured to have a transparent and trusted system for financial accountability among members and to buffer system operations from policy differences among member organizations. In a situation where there are significant operations and programs, an operations coordination group can be organized that is separate from the governing body, to reduce the tendency of the governing group to be overinvolved in operational detail.

Funding the Multiorganizational System

Multiparty systems designed to address social change agendas do not live on vision, commitment, and good will alone. The funding structures of these systems create powerful incentives in obvious and not-so-obvious ways. The OD practitioner has a responsibility and role very early on in creating a new, multiparty social change system to attend to the impacts and issues that can result from funders' agendas and interests. Funders, the governing body, and organizational partners have a legitimate stake in the outcomes of the collective work. Formal and informal communications mechanisms need to be created to link funders with the governing body. Staying in good communication is critical, and in most cases it should not be left to one or two individuals to manage this linkage. Funders' influence on strategy and policy, where it exists, should be transparent. They should be encouraged to foster operational staff and volunteer input and influence about the design of the system—network, consortia, alliance, partnership—and program operations. Strategy must remain flexible as the multiparty system evolves, learns, and matures. Adequate resources must be built in early on for the high up-front costs of creating collaborative systems and for continuous joint learning.

Implications for OD Practitioners

Clearly, the requirements for being an effective OD practitioner in multiorganizational social change settings go well beyond what most practitioners are initially trained for. Some of the requirements have to do with personal attributes and approaches to the work, and some requirements have to do with specific skills and competencies. Both kinds of requirements are summarized here.

Attributes and Approaches

• *Needed attributes for personal credibility, impact, and survival.* One's personal values, ideological commitments, and professional focus on social change can be critical to being accepted in many systems. In an ideologically charged setting, a history of previous work with some actors can either disqualify a practitioner from consideration for a piece of work or ensure it. Also, previous experience actually *doing* work (for example, organizing, funding, doing policy analysis, and so on) similar to that of key actors in the client system contributes both to credibility and competence as an OD practitioner. At a personal level, this work is very demanding and extraordinarily rewarding. Unless a practitioner really believes in the missions of one's clients, it is unlikely that he or she will be able to sustain the level of attention these systems require, or be able to challenge one's clients in the service of the mission, as is frequently required. If the OD practitioner is not ready to fire the client for the sake of the mission, this work may not be appropriate for the practitioner.

• *Ability and interest in intervening at multiple levels.* Many social change systems cannot afford multiple external consultants, so being able to function competently across levels—individual, group, intergroup, organizational, and interorganizational—of analysis and intervention is a real asset.

• *Ability and interest in juggling many balls.* Providing change agent services to most social change organizations is not as profitable as offering similar services to the private sector. The practitioner wishing to serve this market can do so by some combination of these strategies: accept a lower level of income, work more billable days per year than private sector colleagues, have a mixed portfolio of lower-paying social change clients and higher-paying private sector ones, or obtain grant funding to subsidize what clients themselves can afford.

• *Balancing appreciative and critical approaches to diagnosis and planning.* In potentially high conflict, multigroup, and social change settings, one can often help build momentum and trust by highlighting organizations' strengths and accomplishments and identifying areas of shared understanding and successes. However, as inherently political systems, participants are keenly aware that conflicts of ideology and interest (as well as of skills, resources, and potential contribution) do exist. These conflicts *must* be discussible if multiparty OD interventions are to have any credibility or power.

Skills and Competencies

Apart from these attitudes and approaches to the work, the OD practitioner working in multiorganization social change settings also needs to be competent in other areas:

• *Political skill and sensibilities.* Analysis of power relationships and stakeholder interests and having an accurate theory of social change for the field in which one is working are fundamental to competent practice in social change consulting and making change in the world from the outside.

• *Conscious escalation or reduction of conflict as part of mediation.* A combination of interest-based negotiation and the ability to create shared understandings (of interests, visions, contributions, and limitations of social change actors, of goals and outcomes, and so on) is a powerful approach to reducing unproductive conflict in social change systems. A competent practitioner in this arena must also know when there is *too little* expressed conflict, leading to suppression of ideas and approaches critical to pursuing the systems' mission. Raising these conflicts so that they are discussible and can be dealt with constructively is a big contribution the OD practitioner can make in multiparty work. Ignoring inevitable conflict is not an option.

• *Redefining organizations' role in social issues.* This includes conceptualizing social change initiatives, mediating and synthesizing differing values within and among organizations, helping articulate shared visions and goals, and designing effective multiparty systems. The OD practitioner should be able to help organizations determine their own best contribution (including owning up to their own shortcomings) and find their appropriate place, with others, in making changes no one organization can succeed at alone.

- *Facilitator of multiparty dialogues and decision-making processes.* This requires techniques, skills, and familiarity with information technology needed for working with multiple parties and with groups ranging in size from dozens to many hundreds of people. A particularly tricky balancing act is knowing how and when to enact the role of content expert and that of facilitator, and knowing when one should not attempt to combine the roles.
- *Ability to take on system leadership.* Making social change from the outside in multiorganizational, shared-power settings requires the OD practitioner to shift among varying roles—from technical consultant (for example, on organizational design), to temporary leader in an underorganized system (providing entrepreneurial leadership to launch a collaboration of groups that come with high ideals but low trust), to activist for social change, to catalyst for network learning. Taking such leadership also may require practitioners to shift from the individual consultant model to being just one of several members of a team of change agents.

A Cautionary Conclusion

Social change agents, be they individuals or organizations, are usually very clear about their vision of how the world should be different and about how *others* should change to help achieve that vision. However, individual and organizational change agents are frequently unprepared for the personal and collective changes they themselves must go through to be effective agents of change in the external world. At the individual level, this may mean confronting one's own limitations and blind spots—such as areas of weak but needed skills; the ability to work effectively with people from other racial, religious, or national groups; or unwillingness to take up or relinquish leadership and control when needed.

Many organizational representatives in collaborative social change have said that one of the biggest impacts of their work with others has been to significantly alter key aspects of their own organization—missions and roles in society are clarified, new organizational strengths are discovered, organizational weaknesses are unmasked and challenged by outsiders, definitions of success can drastically change, and so on. One cannot make change from the outside without also changing on the inside.

Reference

Brown, D., Leach, M., & Covey, J. (2005). Organization development for social change. In T. G. Cummings (Ed.), *Handbook of Organizational Development*. Thousand Oaks, CA: Sage.

CHAPTER NINETEEN

BUILDING A SUSTAINABLE WORLD: A CHALLENGING OD OPPORTUNITY

John D. Adams

Even though many OD professionals are excellent practitioners, they are all operating under the influence of society's prevailing shared mental models. This means they may be contributing to the collapse of a sustainable human presence on the planet. Those mental models generally produce incremental change approaches, which are short-term, reactive, local, either-or, blaming, and doing-and-having-oriented. If OD is practiced within the milieu of these mental models, it will largely be stuck in first-order change efforts. Even the most successful OD practitioners will unwittingly contribute to the growing list of global environmental pressures and economic inequities (Adams, 1992).

The OD profession is in a perfect position to ask questions in order to generate increased versatility in thinking, and to create more long-term, creative, global, and systems-level change efforts that are focused relatively more toward learning and being, all essential qualities for building a sustainable world. It is difficult to change deeply held, habitual patterns of thought, including the prevailing shared mental models as reflected in one's culture. This chapter describes research about these models that necessarily guide individual and collective behaviors within organizations. It is a hypothesis of this chapter that as OD practitioners and their clients learn to think more consciously, and in more versatile (which is to say, appropriately flexible) ways, they are more able to contribute to the growth of sustainable organizational practices.

Twelve change "success factors" are described that can support and facilitate this outcome (Adams, 2003). The second part of this chapter summarizes research into these success factors promoting successful deep-pattern change. This chapter describes an opportunity for organization development professionals to participate in establishing a viable and sustainable world that is rich in life choices, more thoughtful about the use of nonrenewable resources, more careful about the impact of human activity on the environment, and more generative of economic and social justice.

Environmental, social quality of life, and economic processes are rapidly approaching critical interrelated challenges. The pathways society uses now are likely to lead to severely reduced options for an acceptable quality of life in the next one or two generations. It is clear that human activity has a profound effect on the future. What an individual or a group thinks about a situation has a profound influence on behavior. The big question is, Will societies choose to have a conscious effect, or an unconscious one, on the future?

Opportunities and Challenges

The twentieth century was filled with remarkable progress. Humans traveled into space and made every part of the globe accessible. Computers evolved from large, room-filling, stand-alone units to extremely powerful handheld devices with wireless connections to a global network of other such devices—in less than forty years. Diseases have been eradicated, and agricultural advances have kept up with continued population growth (see Adams, 2000; and Meadows, Meadows, and Randers, 1992).

Many severe challenges have also emerged alongside this progress. Thousands of species are being eliminated at a rate unprecedented in history. Pollution of the air, water, and earth is a critical issue everywhere. Grain and fishing production, which peaked in the 1980s, are in steady decline. The climate has warmed significantly, causing rapid loss of polar ice and ever-more-extreme weather events. Civil wars rage continuously, and terrorism has gone "mainstream." The global economic system continues to make the rich richer and the poor poorer. The population now exceeds six billion and will double every forty to fifty years, with most new births occurring in devastatingly poor (in a Western economic sense) circumstances. Only 15 percent of the world's population makes ends meet with at least a minimal degree of what people in developed countries consider comfortable.

How can practitioners in OD work more effectively with these challenges and still preserve the many beneficial advances? A first step is for people to pay attention to their prevailing shared mental models. Albert Einstein expressed the idea on many occasions that "you cannot expect to be able to solve a complex problem using the same manner of thinking that caused the problem" (1933). Learning to think more versatilely and consciously makes it possible to treat more than symptoms and allows people to come face-to-face with the underlying problems.

Journalist Marilyn Ferguson, in her talks and seminars, frequently made this statement: "If I continue to believe as I have always believed, I will continue to act as I have always acted. If I continue to act as I have always acted, I will continue to get what I have always gotten" (1980). The self-fulfilling prophecy is always at work and is always in a self-reinforcing mode. For example, someone who is seen to be a good problem solver will always be finding problems to solve. The more problems solved, the more strongly others will believe he or she is a good problem solver, and the more new problems he or she will find.

The late Scottish psychiatrist R. D. Laing suggested that the self-reinforcing and self-fulfilling nature of one's prevailing mental models occurs mostly in autopilot—outside of a person's awareness and consciousness—and it is this unaware autopilot that is often the real source of limitation: "The range of what we think and do is limited by what we fail to notice. And because we fail to notice that we fail to notice, there is little we can do to change; until we notice [become conscious of] how failing to notice shapes our thoughts and deeds" (cited in Abrams and Zweig, 1991).

The Brighter the Light, the Darker the Shadow

Selected OD practitioners and corporate managers were asked to identify where their organizations or clients fall, as an average default position, on each of six dimensions (Adams, 2001). The percentages in Figure 19.1 indicate their responses to this question. The largest percentage on each of the six dimensions was in the left third of the continua: short-term, reactive, local, either-or, blaming, and doing-having. On four of the six dimensions, the smallest percentage was in the right third of the continua: long-term, creative, systems, and learning.

Regarding the perceived zones of comfort, or degree of versatility (appropriate flexibility) in thinking along these dimensions, most indicated "narrow," a few indicated "moderate," and only three or four indicated "broad." There is more "left-side" thinking (see Figure 19.1); and regardless of where placed along the six dimensions, the range or versatility of thinking is rather narrow. To summarize the findings, the present shared default mind-set in U.S. businesses is seen to be most often located at or toward the left end of these dimensions, with a rather narrow "zone of comfort" (little variability in thinking) around each.

FIGURE 19.1.　CLIENT MENTAL MODELS.

	Left third	Middle third	Right third	
Short-term: Focus on deadlines, immediate priorities, sense of urgency	72	46 *Time orientation*	10	**Long-term:** Vision and strategies, potentials, opportunities
Reactive: External drives, prevailing rules and procedures	79	33 *Focus of responsiveness*	16	**Creative:** Taking initiative, new approaches, internal drives
Local: Focus on self or immediate group, competition	67	28 *Focus of attention*	33	**Global:** Whole organization, inclusive, ecumenical, larger community
Separation: Either-or, specialization	64	35 *Prevailing logic*	29	**Systems:** Both/and, holistic, interrelationships
Blaming: Self-protection, it's not my fault (don't get caught)	57	43 *Problem consideration*	28	**Learning:** Understanding, building on all types of experience
Doing-Having: Materialism, greed, cost effectiveness, financial performance, quantitative growth	62	32 *Life orientation*	34	**Being:** Having enough, self-realization, "greater good," intangibles valued, qualitative growth

Note: Responses ($N = 128$) of OD practitioners' assessment of their clients' (externals) and organizations' (internals) prevailing autopilot mental models.

When groups of managers are asked to describe scenarios for the future if organizations collectively continue to reflect these left-side mental models (and the behaviors these mental models generate) into the future, the responses have always resulted in gloomy scenarios. There is unanimous agreement when the manager groups are asked if these default mind-sets are driving the major ecological, social, and economic challenges around the world.

What can one expect from the OD profession if practitioners do an impeccable job and are successful, while operating in environments in which these mental models prevail? If an OD practitioner's daily efforts are focused on short cycles and working ever faster to do more with less, is not that person's effort primarily going to add pressure to the growing systems of challenges? Thus the title of this section: the brighter the OD work, when carried out from within the prevailing mental models, the darker the results, when viewed from a big-picture, long-time-frame perspective.

What would happen if a critical mass of the population shifted their mental model defaults significantly toward the right side of the scale and generated wider zones of comfort? Would society create the kind of future people say they really want? Would individuals bring their lives into better balance? This scenario represents a tremendous opportunity for OD professionals to help people become more aware of prevailing mental models and then facilitate culture change, knowing that shared prevailing mental models are a core part of an organization's culture and thus the collective behavior.

Mental models are able to protect themselves from change and usually operate on a kind of autopilot. Humans are presumably the only species with the capacity to think about how they think. Most of the time, however, people don't engage this capacity and instead reinforce their outlook on life by repeating the same thoughts day after day (Harman, 1988). To become responsible, a person must develop conscious, versatile thought processes and move from autopilot to awareness to choice. Society has done a reasonably good job of preparing for the future technologically. It still has a long way to go to prepare psychologically and emotionally for a better future.

Autopilot Consequences

In the workplace, extensive business plans are created regularly; but they are frequently given little further attention and often remain unimplemented. In addition, there are many contemporary and historic examples of low-integrity, questionable ethics in the areas of business, finance, government, and even child care. When it comes to the environment, relatively few organizations voluntarily restrict themselves in toxic emissions and solid waste disposal, and where regulations do exist minimum compliance (or finding loopholes) are often the norm. It is still the exceptional organization that engages in developing quality of life in the community in which it operates.

At the individual level, relatively few people feel they are personally responsible for their situation in life. Taking personal responsibility for other than personal

economic gain, though increasing, is still not widespread. It seems few people realize how small and endangered the world has "become," and even fewer recognize the things each person can do daily to alleviate, in a small way, some of the
larger challenges to the earth. (The word *world* is used here to designate the so-
cial-economic-political systems of humanity, and *earth* to designate the natural
ecological system in which the world resides.)

Are people by nature self-destructive? Do people generally not care if the environment continues to be degraded until vast tracts become uninhabitable? Are
people unconcerned about the legacy that society appears to be leaving its grandchildren? Do people really think that their lifestyle habits won't have any consequences? For most people, the answer is no to each question; yet the pressures
continue to grow. The reason for this contradiction lies in the fundamental
processes of thinking—in the mental models learned early in life and reinforced
by everyday activities throughout life. With continuous, totally normal repetition
and reinforcement, each person gradually develops an outlook that is persistent
and operates (generates predictable behaviors) for the most part outside his or her
awareness.

However, it is only through conscious choice that a person can develop a
mind-set that is more versatile and flexible. Developing a set of mental models
that is broad and versatile is a key ingredient if society in general, and OD in particular, are to address the growing worldwide environmental and social challenges
effectively. Teaching conscious choice at all levels of education is a critical component of this solution (Adams, 2000). Meanwhile, OD professionals can promote
versatility in thought in their practices in the workplace. Years of experience have
demonstrated that versatility in consciousness is essential for ongoing individual
learning and that the only sustainable consciousness is a continuously learning
consciousness.

Reprogramming an autopilot set of mental models requires the same processes
that established them in the first place: repeating messages and experiences (Adams,
2003). Left to itself, the human mind will attempt to maintain its present state; repetition of new ideas and intentions must be carried out consciously. New structures
or mechanisms that guarantee a sufficient number of new repetitions may be necessary to get beyond the status quo protection efforts of the old autopilot.

It is easiest to change one default message at a time. A wholesale change of
one's consciousness, a complete personal transformation, is possible and sometimes happens; but step-by-step change is probably going to be a lot easier for
most people to assimilate. Tables 19.1 and 19.2 (from Adams, 2001) offer guidance on how to increase versatility in mental models through raised awareness of
them and use of questions to broaden perspectives and increase versatility of
thought. These tables can be helpful in strategy-planning and coaching sessions.

TABLE 19.1. WORKING WITH LEFT-SIDE FOCUSES.

Focus	Messages That Reinforce This Focus	Questions to Bring Focus Here	The Positive Value of Focusing Here	The Result of Overuse of This Focus
Short-term	• Don't fix it if it ain't broke. • Just do it.	• What needs attention now? • What are your immediate priorities?	• Establishing priorities • Acting with efficiency	• Lose the big picture. • Overlook long-term consequences. • Put bandages on symptoms.
Reactive	• Do as you're told. • If it feels good, do it. • Life's a bitch and then you die.	• What is the established policy, procedure, or practice? • What has been done before in this kind of situation?	• Consistency • Responsiveness • Loyalty	• Stuck in a rut • Unable to flow with change
Local	• Look out for Number One. • You've got to expect that from a _____!	• What makes you different or unique? • What is special about this situation?	• Survival • Protection • Maintaining position	• Loss of perspective • Ethnocentrism • Loss of diversity
Separation	• The best way to understand it is to take it apart. • A place for everything, and everything in its place.	• What are the relevant facts in this situation? • What do you get when you crunch the numbers?	• Convergence • Specialization • Rationality	• Fragmentation • Low synergy • Get lost in minutiae
Blaming	• It's not my fault! • All right, who's to blame here?	• What are your reasons for your actions? • What's wrong with this picture?	• Judgment, law, and rule enforcement	• Win-lose polarization • Risk aversion
Doing-Having	• What's in it for me? • Faster, cheaper, better!	• What is the most cost-effective thing to do? • What's the bottom line?	• Financial performance and material comforts	• Attachment to possessions • Loss of human sensitivity • Burnout

TABLE 19.2. WORKING WITH RIGHT-SIDE FOCUSES.

Focus	Messages That Reinforce This Focus	Questions to Bring Focus Here	The Positive Value of Focusing Here	The Result of Overuse of This Focus
Long-term	• Create a vision. • Plan ahead.	• What do you anticipate? • Where are we headed? • Where do we want to go?	• Anticipation • Prediction • Possibilities • Contingencies	• Lose timely responsiveness • Ignore pressing realities
Creative	• Take responsibility for yourself. • You can be anything you want to be.	• Is there a different or better approach? • What would you do about this situation if you had a magic wand?	• Innovation • New ideas • New directions	• Overlook proven processes • Reinvent the wheel
Global	• Look at the big picture. • Let's think about the consequences of this decision.	• What's best for the organization as a whole? • How can you make a difference in the world?	• Comprehensive view • Inclusiveness • Value of diversity	• Idealism • Loss of initiative or drive • Inattention to detail
Systems	• Solving one problem almost always creates others. • The whole is more than the sum of its parts.	• Who are the key stakeholders? • If we take this action, what consequences can we predict?	• Divergent • Holistic • Finding key interrelationships	• Equate models to reality • Get lost in the clouds of complexity or theory
Learning	• Let one who is without sin cast the first stone. • Here's another learning and growth opportunity.	• What can you learn from this experience? • How might you benefit from letting go of that grudge?	• Ease of exploration • Seeking growth and learning	• May be taken advantage of • Self-sacrificing • Loss of discipline
Being	• You'll never walk alone. • Trust the process. • As ye sow, so shall ye reap.	• What really matters in your life? • What does your "higher self" say about this?	• Self-realization • "Greater good" point of view	• Become ungrounded • Lose touch with main stream

The Responsibilities of the Dominant Institution

Until about four hundred years ago, before the days of Galileo, Copernicus, and Newton, the church was the dominant institution in Western society and took responsibility for all aspects of human experience within its sphere of influence. The Holy Roman Empire ruled most of what we know as Europe, and the pope was more or less responsible for everything within the realm.

Mythologist Joseph Campbell has taught that the dominant institution in a society tends to build the tallest buildings; the churches' cathedral spires towered over the landscape in those days. After the "Copernican revolution," however, national governments rapidly became the dominant institutions in the West, and government buildings defined the peaks in the urban skyline. Government leaders (first genealogically determined and then elected) took responsibility for all aspects of the human experience. Federal government buildings were soon taller than the church steeples.

Today it is obvious which institution has the tallest buildings. The financial system now defines the urban skyline worldwide, and the practice of business has become the dominant activity just about everywhere. To date, however, business has taken responsibility first for its own short-term profitability (shareholder interest) and only a little energy, if any, is invested into the larger concerns of the community. The current practice of business, with its focus on short-cycle profitability, calls into question whether or not it is even possible for business to assume this wider responsibility (Daly and Cobb, 1991; Hawken, 1993).

However, business still expects government to be responsible for human activities and experiences that do not directly flow to their bottom line. Business also expects government to keep up the infrastructure and ensure that all supportive nonbusiness systems are functioning well. Governments maintain military forces in large part to protect economic activities. But when the government tries to protect the environment, sometimes causing businesses increased costs, many business leaders look for loopholes or attempt to have the laws changed in ways that will be more favorable to short-term corporate net profits.

The business section of every U.S. newspaper these days is a review of companies' stock market performance. More than 95 percent of all financial transactions now involve speculation, with the equivalent of the annual GDP of the entire planet (a measure of the sale of goods and services) passing through Wall Street every three weeks. Financial security is dependent on the collective psyche of those who are playing the market and living out the last days of the doing-and-having "greed paradigm." The rich are getting richer at an alarming rate. In the early 1990s, the average discrepancy between the annual income of a *Fortune 500* CEO and an entry-level employee in the same organization was estimated at 157 to 1.

Now, ten years later, figures of more than 500 to 1 appear regularly in business magazines and newspaper business sections. In 2003, for example, average CEO compensation in the United States increased dramatically—while the country was still recovering from a recession.

> Despite last year's loud cries for reform, plenty of boards are still paying their CEOs like it's 1999. That's the message from our analysis of 2003 CEO pay, conducted with the help of Equilar, an independent provider of compensation data in San Mateo, Calif. The median CEO compensation at the 363 Fortune 500 companies that had filed their proxies by April 7 was $7.1 million—2.6% higher than last year's median. Among the very biggest companies—those in the Fortune 100—median pay was nearly twice that: $12.2 million. Granted, Fortune 500 profits were five times larger in 2003 than in 2002. But let's not forget how high 2002 pay was. That year the average U.S. CEO earned 282 times what the average worker did, a survey shows. In 1982 the ratio was 42 to 1 [Boyle, 2004].

Senior executives of publicly traded companies are awarded huge bonuses and are often able to buy shares of company stock at a reduced rate. It is not unusual for key corporate decisions to be made solely on the basis of the likely impact on share price (and therefore on the immediate net worth of the executive making the decision), rather than giving first consideration to longer-term concerns such as the likely impact of the decision on the environment.

To be fair, many large business organizations around the world now recognize the need for environmental restraint and so maintain compliance with regulations intended to protect the environment. This, however, frequently does not go far enough, because the regulations themselves are rooted in some unsustainable and as yet largely untested assumptions: that they can somehow find a way to go on growing indefinitely, and that doing a little better than we have in the past will be sufficient. Most businesses won't, or can't, go beyond compliance unless there is a "business case" for doing so—that is, steps taken to prevent or mitigate environmental issues must also lead to increased profitability.

Evidence of Progress

A growing number of companies have already demonstrated that caring for the environment as a corporate policy can indeed be supported by a "business case" for doing so. Interface Carpets (http://www.interfacesustainability.com/) has become a benchmark company in the carpeting industry in this regard. Energy companies have formed the International Petroleum Industry Environmental Conservation Association, which in turn has produced a report of energy company accomplishments to date on a dozen dimensions of sustainability (www.ipieca.org/downloads/WSSD.pdf). The number of corporations choosing to engage in sustainable business practices is growing rapidly worldwide (www.ftse4good.com/./ftse4good/index.jsp).

The emerging paradigm is now leading to businesses that naturally move beyond compliance to anticipation and prevention of ecological and social degradations, and then even further to ecological and social "capacity building," as their natural modes of operating. The challenge everyone faces ultimately is whether or not this evolutionary development of perspective (or consciousness) will occur rapidly enough to create the kind of future people would describe as ideal for their own grandchildren. There are increasing signs that fundamental transformations are under way. Among the presumed positive trends are the emergence of a single, global economy and marketplace, enormous technological advancement, and instantaneous global communications.

Additional signs that change is coming appear to be less positive: ongoing degradation of the natural environment; a rapidly widening gap between rich and poor as wealth concentrates among fewer and fewer people; and increasing worldwide unemployment, underemployment, and homelessness (for details and research reports, see the Worldwatch Institute's annually published *State of the World* books).

The future state of the world (and the earth) will depend on how these trends unfold, along with the likely emergence of new trends and unexpected surprises. Whatever the future, business practices will have a strong influence on quality of life everywhere in the world in the twenty-first century. Decline into chaos is in no way ensured, nor is a smooth slide into some utopian state.

One opportunity for OD is to evolve a larger focus for its application. Before too many more years, a "transorganizational, transformational" community of practice will emerge drawing on the fundamental skills and knowledge developed by OD practitioners in the past four or five decades (Adams, 2000). The perspectives will shift from internal "organizational behavior" to the interface between organizations and the larger community; and from relatively short-term focused improvement strategies to long-term realization of worthy societal outcomes.

Will OD people be in the vanguard of this emerging practice area? To date there is relatively little evidence on which to base such a prediction (Adams, 1992, 1994). There are relatively few OD practitioners involved in the sustainability programs that are currently under way, and people not trained in OD are reinventing the field to address the needs they are finding as they implement their sustainability programs.

Building Critical Mass for Change

When attempting to influence a group or an organization, it is often better to influence the "easiest" people first, rather than following the more natural tendency to focus on the biggest resisters. When 25 percent or so of a population is steadfastly committed to a change, the change is likely to occur. If change efforts are focused instead on the hard-core resisters, the less obvious resisters may well join forces with them, creating a vocal critical mass against the change.

As portrayed in Figure 19.2 (Adams, 1988), this chapter recommends that our work on raising awareness about the larger concerns voiced here be focused on those who are ready to listen, and that these people receive lots of attention and support. At the same time, OD practitioners should avoid alienating those who think there is nothing to worry about—or that it isn't their organization's responsibility—in terms of environmental degradation and social and economic injustice. In other words, preach to the choir, call frequent choir practice, and recruit people to join the choir when they start humming along! An important role for OD is placing a priority on helping the early adopters become aware of their prevailing mental models, and then on facilitating the emergence of more versatile ways of thinking.

FIGURE 19.2. BUILDING CRITICAL MASS FOR CHANGE.

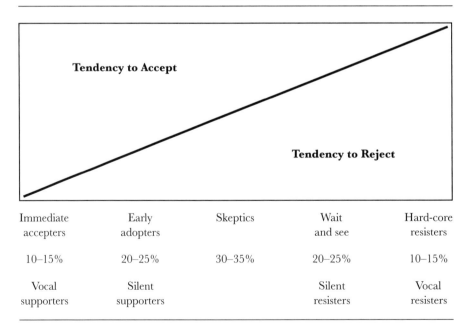

Immediate accepters	Early adopters	Skeptics	Wait and see	Hard-core resisters
10–15%	20–25%	30–35%	20–25%	10–15%
Vocal supporters	Silent supporters		Silent resisters	Vocal resisters

Leaders of change efforts on all levels, from stimulating individual lifestyle or habit changes to implementing large-scale organizational changes, know that the percentage of completely successful change projects is low. Similarly, Beer (Beer and Nohria, 2000) and Maurer (1996) have found that most change efforts either fall short or fail altogether. Maurer suggests that a majority of organizational change efforts fail in their early stages because of insufficient buy-in.

Why this low incidence of full success? What does it take to achieve successful change? Those who have been successful can offer some clues to their success. A series of interviews with individuals and organizational groups that have successfully completed change projects reveals themes that recur in every story. This research has found eight qualities that are almost invariably present when individuals make successful habit pattern changes, and four additional qualities (all twelve are essential) once organizational groups have completed successful changes. Stories about individual and organizational failures were also collected, and they led to the conclusion that most or all of the twelve change success factors were missing if the change results fell short of the original goals (see Adams, 2003, for a more complete description of this study).

Individual Change Success Factors

1. *Understanding and acceptance of the need for change.* A person must understand a recommended change and think there's a need for it. Without this understanding and acceptance, a person won't be enthusiastic about making the change, whether individually or organizationally. Without enthusiasm, change is not a priority.

2. *Belief that the change is both desirable and possible.* If the change is seen as impossible to undertake, or not the right thing to do, then it will not get full attention. If this judgment prevails, the person resists attempts to engage with the change process.

3. *Sufficient passionate commitment.* Changing habits—especially habits of thinking (mental models)—is difficult. To stay the course requires a strong commitment to being successful. In organizations, there seems to be a need for a critical mass (conventional wisdom suggests 25 percent) of people to hold a heartfelt commitment to making the change a success (see nine and eleven below).

4. *A specific deliverable or goal and a few first steps.* Even when change is seen as necessary, desirable, and possible and there is commitment to it, a person needs a clear picture of the goal and a doable first step to build momentum. Though no one mentioned following a plan, everyone in a successful effort knew the outcomes they were committed to and what they were going to do next.

5. *Structures or mechanisms that require repetition of the new pattern.* Habits reach autopilot status through repetition. When a new habit is needed, there are few

repetitions of this new behavior in the new habit's memory account and a great many repetitions of the old behavior in the outgoing habit's memory account. To reinforce repetition of the new behavior, mechanisms or structures need to be created that require practicing the new behavior. An example of a reinforcing mechanism is regular use of a set of provocative questions such as those in Exhibit 19.1 (at the end of this list), in individual reflection or as a part of a dialogue group. These questions may also be used in coaching situations.

6. *Feeling supported and safe.* Many argue that people do not resist change *per se*; people resist the unknown. Those intent on making change are more willing to dive into the unknown if they feel they are in a safe environment. Having a support network with unconditional acceptance is important to successful deep personal change. Culture (shared mental model habits) change in the workplace is more difficult when job security is in doubt.

7. *Versatility of mental models.* If your only tool is a hammer, then everything becomes a nail! Because autopilot mental models are most often limited in scope and flexibility, deep pattern change becomes very difficult. Successful significant change, individually and organizationally, is more likely to happen if the scope of thinking reflects long-range, deep, and self-reflective perspectives. Versatility means an appropriate amount of flexibility in how one mentally holds a situation (see Tables 19.1 and 19.2).

8. *Patience and perseverance.* Establishing change takes time and effort. Most often there is progress and then there is backsliding. To hang in there, a sense of patience and a drive to be persistent are essential. As has already been noted, many repetitions of the new habit must be added to the account. Patience and perseverance ensure frequent repetition of the required new behaviors.

Additional Change Success Factors for Organizational Changes

The eight factors just listed are almost always present in both successful individual habit changes and organizational culture changes; the next four are almost always *additionally* present in successful organizational changes that include significant organizational culture change (shared mental models and shared behaviors).

9. *Clear accountability—visible, vocal, consistent, persistent sponsors and stakeholders.* The absence of clear accountabilities for implementing and sustaining organizational change was a frequent reason for falling short of change goals. When employees see sponsors and stakeholders engaged and accountable in no uncertain terms, then there is greater success. This is related to sufficient passionate commitment (factor three above). Do key change leaders regularly demonstrate their unambiguous commitment to the success of the change?

10. *Explicit "boundary management" regarding the role of other people.* Every change has identifiable boundaries around it. People at the boundary line of a significant change need to be considered carefully. Are they resources to be engaged? Might they become stakeholders in the foreseeable future? Do they need to be kept informed? Is it advisable to keep them out of the way? Open systems analysis and planning appear to be highly important to key relationships at the boundary of the change.

11. *Critical mass in alignment.* Conventional wisdom is that when 25–30 percent of the members of a system overtly support an idea (visibly, vocally, consistently, and persistently), success is inevitable. If this percentage is valid, then there is a race of sorts involved here. To be successful in complex organizational change requires developing an aligned support base of 25–30 percent of those affected, faster than developing a critical mass of those in opposition to the desired change. Early-adopter models (Adams, 1988) tell us that for any significant change we can count on starting out with 10–15 percent of the affected population being supportive and another 10–15 percent being equally antagonistic toward it. Whichever end of the new idea adoption continuum doubles in size first is likely to win out. This suggests that it is important to focus primary attention on those in favor and encourage the next level of accepters to join in, rather than trying to fix the hard-core resisters' "erroneous stance"—which may only drive the skeptics into more vocal resistance.

12. *Reward the new behavior and withdraw rewards for the old behavior.* This factor should be self-evident, but it is often overlooked by change leaders. "You get what you pay for" is true. If a change goal includes enhancing teamwork but annual bonuses continue to reward "individual heroics," then teamwork will suffer when opportunities for individual achievement are present.

EXHIBIT 19.1. SAMPLE QUESTIONS FOR BUILDING VERSATILITY

Questions for Dialogue and Contemplation
- What can I do today to further positive change? Am I currently doing the right things to help build a sustainable tomorrow?
- What would be better terms than *growth* and *sustainability*?
- How do we learn to shift from "us versus them" to "we're all in this together"?
- How can organizations learn to incorporate more long-term, big-picture thinking?
- How do I maintain my awareness of the growing global challenges and not get so overwhelmed that I turn off and go back to business as usual?
- How do we overcome widespread greediness and belief in scarcity?
- If the corporations in my community grow at an average annual rate of 3 percent (or 5 percent, 10 percent, 15 percent), what will be the impact on resources, waste, community life, and the local environment?

(Continued)

EXHIBIT 19.1. SAMPLE QUESTIONS FOR
BUILDING VERSATILITY, Cont'd

- How can we reconcile short-term needs of having jobs that help businesses grow, when this does not appear to be sustainable in the long run?
- How can I help my organization take a more global, long-term view?
- How can we influence organizations to consider questions of future impact?
- How can we bring more attention to emerging external challenges into the everyday operations of organizations?
- How can we better reward integrity and ethical practice at work?
- What support systems are needed for organizations of all kinds to find meaning beyond the bottom line?
- How do we get the attention of the CEOs and other key decision makers?
- How can we help business leaders connect directly with people outside their direct business sphere—especially children or the elderly?
- Is sustainable consciousness even possible in an organization in crisis? Is survival possible without sustainable consciousness?
- How can we link organizational incentives to activities that promote sustainable consciousness?
- How do we distinguish between "good people" and "bad systems"?
- What can I do to remember the physical environment in every decision I make?
- How can we speak for the poor if we don't know any poor people?
- Will I ever be able to feel secure in my work life again?
- What is the maximum population the earth can sustain—for centuries and centuries—at a decent standard of living?
- How can we make more conscious connections between global challenges and local actions?

Summary

Most people, most of the time, in U.S. organizations, operate from a set of shared prevailing mental models that encourage only first-order changes and focus on fast results and financial priorities. If OD is practiced under the influence of these shared prevailing mental models, successful practitioners will unwittingly contribute to an unsustainable situation for society and the environment. The better the OD work, the greater influence it has and the greater the challenges when viewed from a long-range systems perspective. The field of OD has an opportunity to face these challenges of sustainability; but practitioners of OD must be aware of their own prevailing mental models and take steps to increase their versatility of thinking. They need to make working with the mental models of their clients (awareness and then choice for greater versatility) a priority whenever possible, especially in the coaching, mentoring, and strategy-planning arenas. This newly emerging community of practice will draw on OD skills and knowledge, but it will have transorganizational and transformational perspectives.

At present, there are a rapidly growing number of companies making commitments to environmental sustainability and increased social responsibility. These programs, by and large, are being implemented with little or no OD involvement—and the implementation and planning skills that are second-nature to OD practitioners are being reinvented by others in the absence of OD presence. This represents a huge opportunity for OD practitioners to get involved, and also an opportunity for professional development and academic programs to provide the education and training that is needed to support these programs.

The difficult task of changing mental models requires changing deeply held habitual patterns. Research reveals twelve success factors for changing individual and collective habit patterns, which can serve as a checklist for making successful and enduring changes in how OD practitioners think and in how their clients think.

Using the dialogue and meditation questions in Exhibit 19.1 can facilitate emergence of more versatile thinking processes. Attempting to hold significant positive conversation among people who hold differing worldviews is extremely difficult. Another huge opportunity for OD practitioners is to facilitate dialogues for groups with differing worldviews (for example, the economic paradigm and the ecological paradigm), intended to promote mutual understanding and to prevent win-lose or right-wrong discussions.

References

Abrams, J., & Zweig, C. (1991). *Meeting the shadow.* Los Angeles: Tarcher.

Adams, J. D. (1988). Creating critical mass for change. *OD Practitioner, 20*(2).

Adams, J. D. (1992, June). The brighter the light, the darker the shadow. *Vision/Action,* 8–11.

Adams, J. D. (1994). Working today as if tomorrow mattered. *OD practitioner, 26*(3), 2–10.

Adams, J. D. (2000). *Thinking today as if tomorrow mattered: The rise of a sustainable consciousness.* San Francisco: Eartheart Enterprises.

Adams, J. D. (2001). Six dimensions of a sustainable consciousness. *Perspectives on Business and Global Change, 14*(2), 41–52.

Adams, J. D. (2003). Successful change: Paying attention to the intangibles. *OD Practitioner, 35*(4), 22–26.

Beer, M., & Nohria, N. (Eds.). (2000). *Breaking the code of change.* Cambridge, MA: Harvard Business School.

Boyle, M. (2004). When will they stop? *Fortune,* May 3, 2004 (http://www.fortune.com/fortune/subs/article/0,15114,612495,00.html).

Daly, H. E., & Cobb, J. B. (1991). *For the common good.* Boston: Beacon Press.

Einstein, A. (1933). *Essays in science.* New York: Wisdom Library.

Ferguson, M. (1980). *The Aquarian conspiracy.* Los Angeles: Tarcher.

Harman, W. (1988). *Global mind change: The promise of the last years of the twentieth century.* Indianapolis, IN: Knowledge Systems.

Hawken, P. (1993). *The ecology of commerce.* New York: HarperBusiness.

Maurer, R. (1996). *Beyond the wall of resistance: Unconventional strategies that build support for change.* Austin, TX: Bard.

Meadows, D. H., Meadows, D. L., & Randers, J. (1992). *Beyond the limits: Confronting global collapse, envisioning a sustainable future.* Post Mills, VT: Chelsea Green.

Worldwatch Institute. (Annually). *State of the world.* New York: Norton.

PART FIVE

ORGANIZATION DEVELOPMENT IN AN INTERNATIONAL AND WORLD SETTING

CHAPTER TWENTY

BORDERS AND BOUNDARIES: CROSS-CULTURAL PERSPECTIVES FOR OD PRACTITIONERS

Seán Gaffney

This chapter explores some core constructs in cross-cultural studies, both well known and lesser known, and applies them to the work of international organization development (OD) practitioners. The implications of national culture, individual identity, and boundaries for cross-cultural work of OD practitioners are examined. The chapter begins with a minicase study to set the scene and exemplify the work. The minicase is adapted from my experiences as an international OD practitioner and is intended to highlight some of the issues involved in cross-cultural OD work, as well as possible resolutions. Throughout the chapter are references, where appropriate, to other aspects of cross-cultural OD work. The chapter concludes with a brief exploration of national culture and racial identity, as well as implications for OD practitioners doing cross-cultural work.

An Introductory Minicase

This minicase is based on the author's experiences as an international OD practitioner. For case story purposes, the OD practitioner is named Liam Quinn.

Liam was contacted by a former client, Adam Svensson. Adam had been headhunted by a U.S. multinational and competitor to his previous company. Liam first met Adam as technical director of a major Swedish multinational corporation and worked with him as OD consultant to his division, coach to his senior managers, and trainer in cross-cultural business and management. During this time, Adam played a leading role in the acquisition and integration of an Italian company, which was a challenging and complex process, successfully completed. The U.S. company recently acquired an Italian subsidiary and pinpointed Adam for his proven experience both in the business itself and with Italian production facilities.

Adam was now located in Northern Italy as technical director at a major production facility, and living nearby with his wife and daughter. He knew Liam worked regularly in Milan and arranged for him to visit his office during his next trip to Milan. Liam presented himself at reception, asked for Direttore Svensson, and was led by a receptionist down a long corridor to a door with a brass plate on the wall beside it. On it was his client's title and name. There was a smaller and simpler plate on the door, with an initial and a surname; he took this (rightly) to be the female secretary's name. The receptionist knocked, and the secretary came and took him into her room. She asked him to be seated and then went and knocked on an inner door, stepped into the adjoining room, and announced his arrival to Adam. Adam came immediately to the door, and soon all three were somewhat awkwardly sharing the threshold. The secretary moved back into her room, and Adam and Liam stepped into his large, comfortable office.

One of the first things Adam did was take him to another inner door at the far end of his room. This led into another corridor, parallel with the first one Liam was in. This corridor was the private entrance to the senior executive offices—and one of Adam's small problems. He felt uncomfortable using it and preferred to come into his office through his secretary's room, greeting her on his way. He sensed that she seemed uncomfortable with his doing this, which became one specific part of the general dilemma: the distance he was expected to keep from his staff, and especially from the factory floor. In Sweden, Adam just loved visiting the factories, whipping off his jacket, and getting into the nitty-gritty of production. Now, he felt he did not know his staff, could not distinguish between those under his management and any others. This was new to him. Liam's task was to support Adam in dealing with this dilemma.

We will return to the minicase later. First, some background to the main themes of this chapter.

Border Crossings

The notion of cultural differences has moved from exotic tales of far-flung countries and exciting travel books to an academic subject that combines aspects of anthropology, history, sociology, social psychology, and (increasingly) organization, management, and business. Indeed, Hofstede (1980) has declared that "the business of international business is culture." OD practitioners are more and more working at the interface of cross-cultural interactions. Those who work with multinational companies are working within the same organization, but in varying sociocultural contexts as they move from subsidiary to subsidiary. In this regard, Hofstede's work began as a study of corporate culture, only to discover that local and national culture was more a significant characteristic of local subsidiaries than corporate culture was; indeed, it thrived in creative ways despite the lip service generally being paid to the notion of a corporate culture.

Sometimes success in one context leads to work in totally different cultures, and OD practitioners find themselves challenged by the insight that what works in one's home culture does not necessarily work everywhere—or even anywhere—else. The very competence that led to the new contract may turn out to be a barrier to best OD practice in this new cultural context.

The clearest sign of a move from one sociocultural context to another is when a physical national border is crossed. In most cases, this means a change in language as well as social and business behaviors. Indeed, on arrival at an airport there are already distinctive behaviors. As an Irishman with an Irish/European Union passport and a resident of Sweden for twenty-nine years, I can compare quick and painless border-crossings into Denmark or Italy, for example, with those into the United States, Canada, Israel, Iran, and Latvia or Estonia in the immediate aftermath of the Soviet era. There is the additional experience of getting into Iran with fifteen (they counted!) stamps in my passport from Tel Aviv airport in Israel—and then into Israel with a visa to Iran in my passport. Not to mention the U.S immigration!

Then there are the local variations in signposting at Arrivals—not to forget the taxi queue (or lack of it) as well as the negotiation options, which may or may not arise as one finally gets seated in a taxi. Then hotels *do* differ! For example, checking in at my regular hotel in Milan is now a long series of handshakes and mutual assurances on how delighted we all are to meet again. So it is often in these early encounters that OD practitioners can begin sensing that the environment is not what they are used to; a cultural and behavioral border has indeed been crossed. All of this can happen *before* starting work with the actual client!

There are important additional issues that have an impact on border crossings. First, this is a postcolonial world, with former colonies struggling still to emerge from years of submission into a new era of self-sufficiency and cultural identity. The notion that "the West knows best" carries with it many undertones of an old and new colonialism. Those of us who are in any way representative of a form of dominance—be it racial, gender, political, historical, financial, organizational or management approach, linguistic, or other—have to be aware of and sensitive to how this may affect our cross-cultural relations. This is especially relevant as we move in areas of the world where fundamentalism of any kind has created sharply divisive attitudes based on the fuzziest of generalizations ("All Americans are evil." "All Muslims are aggressive." "All Catholics in the North of Ireland are Republican terrorists." "Globalization is a Western plot."). Such notions are impossible to calmly discuss or lightly dismiss.

The second issue is related to the first: anyone who opposes Western political or business ideals can now be branded a terrorist. This is enough to justify a coalition of Western powers invading another country and imposing democracy—a truly paradoxical contradiction in terms. For many people in the Middle East, this is the new face of twenty-first-century colonialism. Working recently in Tehran, I was given a clear perspective on local perceptions. I was shown a map of the region and had it pointed out to me that Iran is surrounded on each side by "America": to the east in Afghanistan and to the west in Iraq. Then they mentioned the threat also posed by America's ally, Israel. The English-language newspapers make regular references to "the American devil" and "the Zionist plot."

Whatever one thinks of the validity or realism of these perceptions, they are to be reckoned with if OD practitioners choose to work in these cultures. Preparing for a border crossing into Iran, for example, it is necessary to be mindful and respectful of the important distinction that Iranians are not Arabs, that Iran is an Islamic Republic, and that one can be arriving in the middle of Ramadan. In my own case, it could be added that I am an Irish Catholic by tradition, white, Western, comparatively well off, and living comfortably and to a high standard in Sweden. I needed to be aware and sensitive that such aspects of my background would color my perceptions of Iranian culture, and equally aware of and sensitive to how these characteristics may be perceived in the context of Iranian culture.

Generally speaking, border crossings are the focus of research in cross-cultural business. Hofstede (1991, 2001), Adler (1991), Trompenaars (1993), and Zander (1997), for example, have thoroughly researched and explored aspects of culture related to organization, management, and business, thus establishing a foundation for the work of OD practitioners. Of the authors mentioned here, Geert Hofstede of the Netherlands is recognized as having produced major work on culture and business. He began his research in the 1970s and now covers some fifty countries and regions in his work, thus covering the broadest spectrum in the field. Hofstede currently explores and compares cultures through the five dimensions described in Exhibit 20.1.

EXHIBIT 20.1. HOFSTEDE'S FIVE DIMENSIONS OF CULTURE.

1. Power distance (large, small): issues and attitudes around the use and acceptability of formal power
2. Uncertainty avoidance (strong, weak): the tendency toward fixed or flexible structures
3. Individualism–collectivism: individual choice versus collective norms
4. Masculinity–femininity: assertive performance versus modest contribution
5. Long-term and short-term orientation: perseverance versus speed

Source: Hofstede (2001).

Hofstede's dimensions are useful as a guide to issues at the border of another culture and helpful in explaining the experience as one works in other cultures. For example, applying the dimensions to the minicase that opened this chapter yields relevant and interesting information about Sweden (Adam's home culture) and Italy. Italy is toward the *large power distance* end of the scale, indicating acceptance of hierarchy, inequality, and privilege. Sweden is at the *small power distance* end, indicating equality, interdependence, democratic management values, and avoidance of privilege. Italy scores on *strong uncertainty avoidance,* indicating such attitudes as "what is different is dangerous" and an emotional need for structures and rules, even if they do not work. Sweden, on the other hand, scores for *weak uncertainty avoidance*; what is different is curious, and there is a minimum of readily changed rules. Both cultures score high on *individualism,* which would indicate an equal amount of energy in defending a position. Italy is high on the *masculinity* index while Sweden tops the *femininity* index—thus pitching, for example, assertive performance against intuition and consensus.

So Hofstede certainly offers much food for thought. Using his dimensions, both explanations and background can be found for the kinds of difficulty that arise when OD practitioners move from their cultural context to another, or to support clients across cultural borders. For travel to work in a new culture, Hofstede's simplest book, *Cultures and Organizations* (1991), is an indispensable guide to general attitudes and behavioral tendencies in a new culture. It also serves as a reminder that OD practitioners are themselves a cultural product, carrying attitudes and behavioral preferences that are not necessarily the result of deliberate individual choice and rational, tactical value, but rather acquired as naturally as the language one uses (and also deeply embedded in that language).

At the same time as Hofstede's work is supportive, it explains and somehow justifies cultural differences without offering solutions to such dilemmas as those

Liam's client Adam faced. Using only Hofstede would leave Adam in some sort of so-what situation. When in Italy, do as the Italians do. But then Adam is not Italian, and changing cultural values and behaviors is no easy task.

Indeed, a useful cross-cultural exercise when training Swedish managers is to ask them to try a thirty-minute experiment: "For the next half hour, make statements that are not honest, boast about your professional achievements, and make flattering remarks to and about your colleagues." Groups of Swedish managers get to about five minutes before the whole experiment is called off. The requested behaviors are so alien to generally accepted Swedish values that they are beyond the capacity of a group, even as a fun exercise. This despite the fact that these same managers, a few minutes earlier, were claiming that "business is business" and beyond such abstractions as "culture"; that employees are morally bound to espouse the work ethic of their employers, no matter what; and other such rationalizations. Values such as honesty, modesty, and moderation are so deeply embedded in Swedishness that it becomes impossible to devalue them.

So even though knowledge and understanding of the other culture supports orientation to what is new and different, it does not naturally follow that OD practitioners can—or will want to—adapt their behavior. Knowing that traders in the Old City of Jerusalem, or the Carpet Market in Jaffa, for example, all like to haggle over prices (and expect to) does not necessarily mean that the visitor simply adapts and does the same. It will *never* be "the same." Many foreigners in this situation become so focused on haggling and not being conned that they could spend all day negotiating and walk away without the object they so wanted to have. In other words, changing the behaviors of a lifetime, embedded in our primary cultural context, is no easy task. Even if we try it, we may simply find ourselves second-class members of the new culture, functioning below our capacity.

This leads to the concept of boundaries.

Boundaries

For Gestalt-trained OD practitioners, the concept of boundary is a central theoretical and methodological frame of reference. The contact boundary is where organism and environment meet and exchange influence on each other. Change occurs at this boundary as influence is exchanged, responded to, rejected, or integrated. A practitioner is an organism with the client as environment and at the same time is environment for the client as organism. OD practitioners must attend very carefully and with as much awareness as possible to the exchanges at the boundary of practitioner and client, to the flow of influences, and to what supports an appropriately permeable or rigid boundary. Discussion of other boundary issues follows, but first, a brief diversion.

Other Cultural Dimensions: The Issue of Identity

Hofstede—and to a lesser extent Trompenaars—have explored culture and applied their findings to organization and management, but there is still much to be learned from the social psychology perspective. Both Hofstede and Trompenaars include the continuum individualism–collectivism in their conceptual structures. In his more recent work, Hofstede now includes "the family" as a metaphor for a specific combination of scores on his dimensions. This reflects work done from a more anthropological or social psychology perspective, which generally emphasizes three perspectives, all connected to finding and maintaining a sense of identity (Sedikides and Brewer, 2001; Smith and Bond, 1993; Lonner and Malpass, 1994). These perspectives are individualism, familism, and collectivism. Two of them, individualism and collectivism, are also well established cultural constructs. Familism was introduced by Annick Sjögren (1990), a French ethnologist resident, who has conducted research in Sweden for many years. This construct is also used by Marin (1994), though named "familialism." These identity constructs, a brief description of core issues in each construct, and examples taken from the literature of where they apply are shown in Exhibit 20.2.

EXHIBIT 20.2. DIMENSIONS OF CULTURE AND CORE ISSUES OF IDENTITY.

Individualism: identity is self-defined, also interpersonally defined. Membership of any sort is largely voluntary, and often strategically chosen. (United States, Australia, United Kingdom, Northern Continental Europe)

Familism: identity is defined by family membership, family status, sibling position, and responsibilities. Other memberships are usually in the context of family. (Jewish tradition, Mediterranean area, Arab cultures, Iran)

Collectivism: identity is in group membership, which becomes a given. Group is embedded in the larger social collective. (Japan, Korea)

Embedded familism: the family is embedded in other social structures (for example, clan, tribe, ethnic group), which are in turn embedded in the collective of an ethnic group in a defined geographical area. Or the family is embedded in segregated social strata. (West, South, and East Africa, China, India)

These macro-level constructs are a solid ground for distinctions in cross-cultural attitudes and behaviors in organizations. It is immediately noticeable that the OD industry, both theoretically and through countless publications and training programs, originates in individualistic cultures. People from embedded familistic and collectivistic cultures have, for example, little or no need for training in group membership and leadership along individualistic lines. They behave in cultures where much about groups is given and accepted as the cultural norm. Personal suboptimization in a group setting is also normal, rather than an individual choice in a strategic context as it can be in more individualistic cultures.

Consequently models of, say, group development and dynamics, grounded in one cultural context, may not necessarily be equally valid in others. For example, in working with a multicultural student group, the variety of reactions and competencies displayed when students are assigned project groups is fascinating—and culturally congruent. Any attempt to indiscriminately apply Anglo-Saxon or Western developmental and leadership models fails dismally—and I have tried them all! As a result, I now work from the constructs of individualism, familism, and collectivism and find that most students are more able and willing to relate to them.

Identity as a Boundary Issue

The "environmental other"—and therefore the shared boundary—varies in subtle and meaningful ways across the constructs of individualism, familism, and collectivism as applied to cultures. It is common in U.S. OD literature to talk of "levels of system" (see, for example, Huckabay, 1992). They are usually given as individual, interpersonal, subgroup, and group as a whole, and interventions are aimed at a specific level in the context of the work. In familistic and collectivistic cultures, the individual or interpersonal level is not always appropriate. Similarly, in strongly individualistic cultures, subgroup and group-as-a-whole interventions are often quickly individualized. In Denmark, for example, just about all group and organizational issues are quickly focused on interpersonal-level exchanges. People from Denmark can cognitively grasp systemic concepts, but their natural tendency is to personalize and individualize systemic issues.

Clearly, if identity is self-chosen and interpersonally developed, as in individualistic cultures, then the preferred contact boundary is individual and other individual or individuals. In the cultures of familism, there is a private, individual-family boundary. The social and work-related boundary is more likely to be family (member)-environment. The Irish are a culture of strong familism, tinged with colorful shades of individualism. Irish people—especially perhaps men—can therefore find themselves quite at home in Italy, and even more so in Israel.

I have already mentioned my homecoming twice a year to a Milan hotel, where the same staff has been there now for at least seven years. Being part of the hotel family, as a regular visitor with a two-to-three-week stay, confers some privileges (the occasional complimentary brandy in the bar). It also brings obligations not to have too many troublesome requests, and absolutely no demands (a small price to pay for feeling at home!). In Italy there is also a difference between what is said in an office and what is said at the dinner table in someone's home—in a family context. Luigi Barzini writes that anything said in public in Italy is probably not true (Barzini, 1983). However, since all Italians know this, no one is fooled—except perhaps some honest Northern Europeans who are more used to believing and trusting in everything they hear in a business and organizational context.

With embedded familism, then, we may be meeting the family as clan members, the clan as tribal members, and so forth. In discussing work with a Ghanaian colleague, I was reminded of the need to see the family and clan context of any decisions or proposals I wished to make. Similarly, in Iran the family is the primary environmental other, embedded in the rich ethnic tapestry of being Iranian. For example, I was asked out by one of my clients there to have dinner with him, his wife, and their daughter, aged fourteen. My client specifically asked me to speak English with his daughter and help her with her grammar. As we passed a music store, and I asked the daughter to help me choose a CD by an Iranian musician who was popular with Iranians of her age. My client insisted on making the purchase, and from that moment on our relationship became open and sound.

The cultures of collectivism have the group as the core organism or environment. I well remember a Japanese CEO who asked me to work with his management team. I asked him what he wanted to get from the consultancy. He replied: "We need. . . . What we want is. . . ." His identity lay not in having a distinct, individual opinion; as a CEO it lay in responsibly representing his group.

Before applying this boundary concept to the minicase, there is one more ingredient to this recipe for cross-cultural OD: context.

Context and Communication

Edward Hall (1973, 1976, and 1990) introduced the concept of "high context" and "low context" cultures, specifically in relation to communication. By high-context he means cultures where most of the meaning of a communication is in the cultural context; the participants respond to a shared meaning making. In low-context cultures, each speaker needs to be explicit about the intended meaning of a communication. This is highly relevant to international OD work and facilitation in both homogeneous and heterogeneous cultural settings.

In other words, when facilitators work with homogeneous groups from a high-context culture other than their own, they can expect that much of what is happening will be beyond their comprehension. This certainly reflects my experience in Italy, and more so in Finland. Who knows when *yes* actually means *yes* and not *maybe, who knows, not on your life*, or even *if I feel like it at the time*? In Finland, silence is almost a norm. Anything spoken is expected to be meaningful, accurate, and necessary. In the research mentioned earlier by Zander, Finnish leadership style was characterised as "silent coaching": if your boss says nothing to you, then you are doing fine!

As OD practitioners, we need to remember that our discipline is grounded in low-context cultures of individualism, where being explicit is the cultural norm. Let us not apply this as a universal norm.

Borders, Boundaries, Context, and the Minicase

We now return to the beginning and explore the case of Adam Svensson in Italy from all of the perspectives brought up in this chapter. The border issue is clear: Adam is in Italy, and this is an Italian company, located in an Italian township.

Boundary issues can now be added to the information previously derived from Hofstede. Adam is individually oriented, tending toward good interpersonal interactions (for example, with his secretary, and—as he tells Liam—with his assistant, an Italian and long-time employee). There is also the boundary of managing up through a somewhat symbolic Italian former owner to a U.S.-based headquarters. This latter boundary would be satisfactorily interpersonal for both Adam and his U.S. manager. Both can also handle low-context communication, though Adam may not be as used to it as his U.S. manager. With his Italian CEO, Adam is a little lost. Strongly paternalistic, very high-context (and the context is Italy), mildly hierarchical—all of these things add up to confuse Adam. He can see them, he is not surprised by them, and he does not know what to say or do in a way that will influence any change.

Adam and Liam had a good relationship. Liam had, at this time, lived in Sweden for more than twenty years, lectured and consulted in fluent though accented Swedish, and worked in Adam's former company for many years as a consultant and trainer. Liam had also previously worked for two Italian companies and was lecturing in master's programs at an Italian business school. These factors combined to give them great permeability at their shared boundary. They could pool their resources and experience and look for creative solutions.

They reached a quick agreement around the fact that, yes, this is Italy, and they both know that this is how Italian organizations tend to be. Likewise, they both know that Adam is used to—and prefers—a more egalitarian, democratic, and personal leadership style. He needs to know "his people." He desires casual and flexible access to the factory floor. He requires the sense of hands-on leadership that this gives him. He also knows that this is his Swedishness talking, in an Italian context.

Switching from the border to the boundaries: the border between Sweden and Italy is as it is; the crossing has its difficulties. What boundaries were there for Adam to explore, where influence could be exercised and change could occur?

Liam went for family. His proposal was that Adam, his wife, and their daughter could begin frequenting the restaurants and cafés of the town at weekends. Adam could involve his secretary, and also his assistant, in selecting a choice of places "where ordinary Italian families eat." Adam and his wife wanted to practice their Italian, and get to know the customs of the area. Adam and Liam were both well aware that Adam's secretary and assistant would probably recommend establishments run by their relations (at the same time, they would not short-change him). After all, he was formally their superior in a hierarchical structure. Liam's thinking was this: as Adam and family moved around the town, they would inevitably be seen, noticed, and greeted, however briefly and informally, by "his people." He would get to know their faces, recognize them at work, and find it easy to make contact with particular people on the factory floor if he had, just the Sunday before, sat at a table adjoining them and their family for lunch.

In terms of communication, Adam now moved to a form that was nonverbal and very high-context: his family was communicating with the environment, in a language (family) that the Italian environment could understand. Adam moved from being a distant figure on the executive floor to a man in the family out for lunch.

Needless to say, the restaurants recommended included one that was frequented by the CEO and family, and another by the assistant and family. Within three months, Adam found that he was well on the way to resolving his dilemma, as well as establishing an easier social relationship with his CEO.

So Adam was apparently out of the woods. But probably heading into the trees! Liam's work was not finished. Since Liam already knew Adam's family well from having met socially in Sweden, he arranged to meet them all at their home in Italy.

Liam's concerns were around two main issues. One is that Swedes in general do not easily nor readily mix their private lives with their work. He expected that Birgitta, Adam's wife, had a threshold for how much she would be willing to use family lunches for Adam's business purposes. Adam would support her in this matter. The second was around Adam's capacity, from the ground of his Swedishness, to maintain and develop a delicate balance between social and managerial relationships, which comes so naturally to an Italian.

Liam discussed these issues with Adam, Birgitta, and Cecilia, their daughter. They also discussed the qualitative difference between Adam being a senior executive in the Swedish parent company coming on regular visits to the Italian subsidiary and his current position as a senior executive in a U.S-owned though otherwise very Italian company, where he was the only non-Italian. They agreed that there was a limit to the extent of the whole family's involvement in his work-related relationships, and that this limit was not far off.

Liam looked at contact boundaries from another perspective with them. He used a simple concept that looks at the various levels or themes of contact in an international context (see Exhibit 20.3).

EXHIBIT 20.3. CONTACT LEVELS AND THEMES.

- Culture
- Organization
- Function
- Social
- Personal
- Private

They looked at their experience of Italians (and Liam's experience of Swedes). Italians move early and easily to talking about "in Italy," so the cultural level or theme is a natural boundary at which to establish contact. Adam was clear that Sweden would not readily be available to him as a theme, though he could sense his curiosity and insatiable thirst for knowledge about Italy. Sweden would be both too abstract and too subjective. Subjective opinions are not highly regarded in a Swedish context. He would feel more at ease at the levels of organization and function, much more "factual" and "objective" themes. They then looked at how Adam could combine these with his experience, rather than his opinions. In other words, he could interact around the themes of organization and function, in the "language" of culture (for example, "This is how I would structure my division in Sweden; how would that be done in Italy?") and similarly for function.

They could all agree that what was—and probably would remain—most unclear for them was where the distinctions lay between the social and the personal. The private was clear for them, and they shared the view that this is a level of contact that takes time to develop in an Italian context and is often best left to the Italian party to initiate. So their shared view was that the family would pay careful attention to the whole process of contacts at these particular boundaries (the social and the personal)—in other words, everyday public contacts and possible personal friendships.

Liam's interventions supported Adam and his family in being proactive in their exchange of influence at a number of specific and permeable boundaries, as well being aware of alternatives in reacting to their environment. They were now engaged with their environment, rather than confused onlookers or detached observers.

Borders, Boundaries, and Race

This chapter has explored implications of the dimensions of national cultural, individual identity, and boundaries for OD practitioners engaged in cross-cultural work. The issue of racial identity and culture is often present in cross-cultural work, generally avoided by cultural theorists, and subsumed under the generic descriptors of national cultures. The people in many nations have experienced centuries of direct colonial oppression by whites and the dehumanization of the oppressed by the oppressor. Added to this are the twin violations of the patronizing and the condescending attitudes of traditionally "well-meaning" whites toward indigenous peoples and the mutually binding relational consequences that can arise. These interracial experiences have ramifications for the international OD practitioner that cannot be ignored.

Returning for a moment to the earlier references to working in Iran: the borders were clear and mostly explicit—I was Western in the context of Iranian, Christian in the general context of Islam and the particular context of Ramadan, and white in the multiethnic context of the variety of ethnic origins contained within "being Iranian." What I found was that placing myself as a representative of a cultural collective and raising my feelings as an Irishman against British colonialism cocreated a permeable boundary and a cultural bridge on which my Iranian clients and I could meet. This permeable shared boundary—shared criticism and bad experience of British colonialism—allowed both parties to move beyond the more rigid borders of our differences; we could meet as we explored their cultural values in the context of international business.

On the sensitive subject of race, it is otherwise only in Cuba that I have met such a variety of ethnicity, giving true meaning to the phrase "people of color." My sense in both countries is that the issue is not so much that I am white but rather that I am non-Cuban or non-Iranian, evident through my comparative whiteness. In Havana, being Irish in the bars and restaurants of O'Reilly Street is certainly more important than my color; in Iran, being Irish rather than British or American is certainly more important than that I am white. In both countries, the sense of a shared, historical cultural identity is important, as is the cultural identity of the other. Not being a representative of the old colonialism (Britain), nor of the new version (United States) creates the possibility of finding areas of contact.

Incidentally, people from more individualistic cultures may see all this in terms of an interpersonal interaction; that is, that the Cubans and Iranians had gotten to know the individual, Seán. Another perspective is more likely: I had become subsumed into another postcolonial culture. Being Irish, I must clearly share the environments' view of colonial oppressors. Even as I write this, I am supporting four Ghanaian colleagues in dealing with visa refusals into Ireland. I am ashamed to say that the Irish have moved from the oppressed to the casually oppressive and to institutionalized racism in less than a century.

My point here in all of this is that the issue of racial cultures is deeply enmeshed in interracial perceptions and confounded with descriptors of national cultures. Perhaps the only path for the OD practitioner to tread is to continuously work to be aware of his or her own racial (and, yes, racist) attitudes and perceptions; constantly question, explore, and honestly acknowledge any evidence of their existence in the practitioner; and examine and own the possible impact of these perceptions and attitudes on interactions with people of other races.

Conclusion

International OD practitioners can apply the approach, mentioned earlier, of engaging with the environment at chosen permeable boundaries, to become not just proactive or reactive but rather more fully interactive with clients, more fully in a cocreated and shared learning experience.

Along with OD training, OD skills, and OD competence, OD practitioners need knowledge of their own culture and awareness about its impact on thinking and behavior; knowledge of the other culture, respect for its impact on clients and their behavior, and awareness about how it may affect us; and knowledge, awareness, and sensitivity to the boundaries where shared themes and mutual influencing are found.

References

Adler, N. (1991). *Organizational behavior* (2nd ed.). Belmont, CA: Wadsworth.
Barzini, L. (1983). *The Europeans.* Harmondsworth: Penguin Books.
Hall, E. T. (1973). *The silent language.* New York: Anchor Books.

Hall, E. T. (1976). *Beyond culture.* New York: Anchor Books.

Hall, E. T. (1990). *Understanding cultural differences.* Yarmouth, ME: Intercultural Press.

Hofstede, G. (1980, Summer). Motivation, leadership, and organization: Do American theories apply abroad? *Organizational Dynamics,* 42–63.

Hofstede, G. (1991). *Cultures and organizations: Software of the mind.* London: McGraw-Hill.

Hofstede, G. (2001). *Culture's consequences* (2nd ed.). London: Sage.

Huckabay, M. A. (1992). An overview of the theory and practice of Gestalt group process. In E. Nevis (Ed.), *Gestalt therapy: Perspectives and applications.* Cleveland: GIC Press.

Lonner, W. J., & Malpass, R. S. (Eds.). (1994). *Psychology and culture.* Needham Heights, MA: Allyn and Bacon.

Marin, G. (1994). The experience of being a Hispanic in the United States. In W. J. Lonner & R. S. Malpass (Eds.), (1994), *Psychology and culture.* Needham Heights, MA: Allyn and Bacon.

Sedikides, C., & Brewer, M. B. (2001). *Individual self, relational self, collective self.* Philadelphia: Psychology Press.

Sjögren, A. (1990). Doctoral seminar notes, Stockholm School of Economics.

Smith, P. B., & Bond, M. H. (1993). *Social psychology across cultures.* London: Harvester Wheatsheaf.

Trompenaars, F. (1993). *Riding the waves of culture.* London: Brealey.

Zander, L. (1997). *The licence to lead.* Stockholm: Institute of International Business.

CHAPTER TWENTY-ONE

WORKING EFFECTIVELY AS A GLOBAL OD PRACTITIONER: THE WHOLE WORLD IN ONE ROOM

Rebecca Chan Allen

This whole world is a sacred space, an open circle, whose center is everywhere and whose circumference is nowhere.
ADAPTED FROM NICOLAUS CUSANUS, 1401–1464, AS QUOTED IN CAMPBELL (1964), P. 522

T his chapter presents a "whole world in one room" approach to practicing global organization development (OD). This approach involves (1) adopting a whole-world perspective and ethics, (2) using systems matrices to map and design change strategies, and (3) practicing four global leadership competencies to effect structural, cultural, systemic, and experiential change. The array of challenges facing global organizations can be overwhelming. By using whole-world perspectives, tools, and competencies, global OD practitioners can feel more empowered to make a difference. The challenges facing practitioners are explored, and then the whole-world approach and applications are described.

Challenges in Working with the Whole World in One Room

The interlinking of the world's economies and communities has made the twenty-first-century global village a daily reality—whatever the work setting, wherever the locale. By interconnecting disparate and hitherto separated peoples and cultures into one virtual community, globalization is creating a whole-world-in-one-room reality. Wherever one is, the whole world seems to be there too, virtually or actually. Whether the OD practitioner works on the far side of the world or in her or his office at home, the ubiquitous influence and challenges of the whole have to be taken into consideration. The practitioner's work affects the whole, and the whole is reflected in the practitioner.

The twenty-first-century global village is a place of diversities and inequities. According to figures assembled by James L. Cash of Harvard Business School, using World Development Forum data, if the whole world is viewed as a global village of one thousand inhabitants, the demographics of the twenty-first century global village would be about 50 percent Asian, 21 percent European, 9 percent African, 8 percent South American, and 6 percent North American. By the year 2020, Africans will make up about 19 percent of the population, outnumbering Europeans' 11 percent. This global village is about 30 percent Christians, 18 percent Moslems, 13 percent Hindus, 6 percent Buddhists, 5 percent animists, 0.4 percent Jews, 21 percent other religions, and 21 percent no religion. Significantly, 6 percent of the global villagers control half of the resources, 50 percent are hungry, and 60 percent live in a shantytown (Lodge, 1995). The global village is burdened by a legacy of racism, sexism, ageism, homophobia, and other prejudicial and discriminatory barriers. This legacy hampers collaboration and wastes talent and resources.

The diversities and inequities of the global village bring an array of challenges to practicing global OD. Key among the challenges are expanding perspective, practicing global competencies, and centering in an ethic of responsibility.

Expand Perspective

The first challenge to working effectively with the whole world in one room is shifting from a partial ethnocentric perspective. Such a perspective can create many gaps and block connecting actions with the whole. A perspective of multiple realities is needed to appreciate the rich capabilities of the whole. This chapter presents a whole-world perspective to frame global OD practice.

Practice Global Competencies

The second challenge to working with the whole world in one room is applying competencies that address the diversities and inequities in many human systems. To make a positive difference, OD practitioners have to be able to intervene in a system's structure, culture, processes, and policies, as well as the knowledge, skills, and attitude of systems participants. This means adding four critical OD competencies to a global repertoire: structural, systemic, cultural, and experiential leadership.

Centering Ethics and Responsibility

The third challenge to working with the whole world in one room is how to center the purpose, ethics, and responsibility of a global practice. Given the multiple challenges in global human systems, having a clear sense of responsibility and purpose is vital to sustaining energy and motivation. The whole-world perspective and competencies help center a global OD practice in an inclusive vision and an ethic of wholeness and responsibility. The perspectives, tools, and practices that can help meet the challenges of working more effectively with the whole world in one room are described in the next sections.

Adopting a Whole-World Perspective and Ethics

A perspective is the vantage point for viewing an entity and evaluating the relationship of its constituent parts. The perspective one chooses affects what is seen, ethical positions, and actions taken. Integral to practicing global OD is adopting a perspective that can bring the whole world into focus and consideration.

The whole-world perspective envisions the global community in an image of a living circle. Ever-changing and self-renewing, the circle is a versatile vessel and safe container for differences and similarities. The circle is an archetype of inclusion, acceptance, and perfection. People in diverse cultures and times have used the attributes of a circle to form communities, self-organize, and find life-enhancing solutions. Using the living circle as an image supports more inclusive and creative thinking about work with global human systems.

Imagine the center of a human system as an open space, a shared commons. The open space holds the riches and potential of the whole community. The center represents the inexhaustible resources and gifts available to address individual and collective problems. Imagine this world circle as formed by the unique presence of everyone in the global village. There is a place for all people, no matter what their race, gender, class, ethnicity, sexual orientation, age, abilities, or culture. People from any background can form a circle. A community circle can link with an organization circle. A work unit circle in one part of the organization can link with one across the globe. By holding the image that the center of the circle is the same center everywhere, OD practitioners inspire themselves and others to care for and contribute their best to the whole (Allen, 2001).

By imaging a whole system as a living, self-renewing circle, global OD practitioners can center their work with organizations in a vision of inclusion and inspiration. The circle-centered, whole-world perspective can reveal the hidden, open the closed off, connect the isolated, and harness untapped talents and potential. The whole-world vision can empower practitioners to exercise their leadership and practice beyond their parochial comfort zone. Here are the key ideas of the whole-world perspective:

• Practitioners and their client organizations are part of the whole-world circle. The center of their circle is an open space, a receptacle for the talents, ideas, and aspirations of the people who make up the circle. The shared common is cocreated, and cosustained by everyone. Everyone can draw on the rich resources of the center for support and self-renewal.

• A whole-world circle is created by the unique presences of all the global villagers. There is a place in the circle for everyone. When newcomers arrive, everyone shifts a little to include them in the growing circle. Shifting a little to open physical space for others is easy. Shifting a little mentally to include others' thoughts is easy.

• The center of the whole-world circle is everywhere—whenever a group of people comes together to work, play, and form community. The center is not a fixed place. It is ever-changing and ever-opening to new people and ideas.

• The circumference of this circle is nowhere; there is no limit to the number of people who can come together to form a community. The boundary of the whole-world community does not stop along lines of race, gender, religion, nationality, abilities, sexual orientation, geography, culture, language, or other socially constructed categorization.

• The whole-world perspective calls for everyone to take and claim a place around the community circle. It calls everyone to journey to new competencies and discoveries. No one person, group, nation, or culture has all the answers. This new world circle is emergent. Everyone is a new immigrant to this new world environment. Individuals hold the integrity and viability of the whole circle in their hand.

• Whatever the project or enterprise, individual work affects the shared common. Individual work is interwoven into the whole. Whether or not OD practitioners see the impact of their work directly, their work is important and their contribution counts. Practitioners are accountable for the quality of the whole.

Impasse, dilemma, and frustration are often part of global OD work and life. The whole-world perspective keeps practitioners focused on the work at hand and sustains their motivation and energy, as they face uncertainty and ambiguity. Having a perspective is important, but it is not enough. Practitioners also want to translate this perspective into practical use by employing systems tools.

Systems Matrix

A system is a whole composed of connected and interacting parts. A system is dynamic and self-organizing; it can produce predictable and unpredictable behavior. A systems perspective focuses on the essence of the whole and the uniqueness of the parts. By viewing individuals, cultures, organizations, work units, and communities as living systems, practitioners can join with other systems participants to map and design transformation strategies.

Inspired by Buchmann (1989), the Systems Matrix (Allen, 2001) is made up of four interrelated quadrants or fields: structural, cultural, systemic, and experiential (Table 21.1). These four quadrants capture key aspects of a human system as well as the interaction of global factors and microprocesses. The human system under focus can be the world, organization, team, community, individual, or family. The matrix can be used as a quick method to map, assess, and redesign any human system under focus. In the next sections the four quadrants of the Systems Matrix are described, and the sample applications and global OD competencies associated with each quadrant are discussed.

TABLE 21.1. SYSTEMS MATRIX.

Structural	Systemic
• What is the form of the system? • How does authority flow? • What are the demographics of the ranks? • What sustains the system's economy? • What are the physical facilities?	• What are the policies, practices, procedures, and processes that make up the employment and business systems?
Cultural	**Experiential**
• What are the central beliefs? • What visions and values guide priorities? • What norms shape behavior? • What languages, symbols, and rituals are used in communication?	• Which competencies are mission-critical? • What attitudes motivate participants? • How do participants experience the system?

Structural

The structural field refers to the configuration of power, role, and status arrangements. A hierarchy is one type of status-role-power structure; a circle is another type. Like pillars and beams, structures hold up a system, facilitating or obstructing interaction and exchange in prescribed ways. As containers, structures can include and exclude people, as well as open and close interaction possibilities.

A system's structure includes power and authority distribution, the flow of decision making and communication, and the ranking distribution of demographic and social groups in the organization chart. The structures of many organizations reveal that individuals' location in the authority and decision-making flow may be associated with their group memberships. People of a certain race, gender, age, sexual orientation, nationality, or class may be found at the top of the structure, and people of other groups may be at the bottom, or even outside the structure. The structure of a system, whether hierarchical or otherwise, requires corresponding cultural beliefs and norms for perpetuation.

Cultural

The cultural field refers to the vision, values, beliefs, norms, customs, rituals, language, and material artifacts. Culture is the invisible operating software that guides the mental and physical action and interaction of systems participants. Through cultural socialization and programming, system participants learn beliefs, assumptions, principles, and recipes and use them as tools to think, perceive, value, question reality, and rationalize existing social structures. To perpetuate itself, the culture of a system is enacted and replicated through systemic policies, processes, and practices.

Systemic

The systemic field refers to the policies, practices, procedures, and processes that form the institutionalized ways of getting high-priority tasks done. Using cultural values and beliefs, systems participants create institutions such as family, education, and religion to make available specialized best practices to accomplish certain cultural goals: economic survival and child rearing in a family system; marketing, production, customer service, recruitment, compensation, and training in an organization system. The systemic dimension of a work unit includes work processes, scheduling, and feedback processes. The best practices of a particular time, once institutionalized, become covert operating procedures and processes. Systems participants use these procedures and practices to sustain the existing structures and cultures.

Experiential

The experiential field refers to a set of competencies: knowledge, skills, attitudes, and experiences that systems participants develop and use in their system. These competencies help them fit into and perpetuate a particular status quo. Participants use their competencies to shape the structural, cultural, and systemic operations to reflect who they are and what they want themselves and their world to be. In turn, a system's structural, cultural, and systemic features shape individual competencies.

Systems matrices are self-organizing, self-perpetuating, and self-renewing. For a particular human system to sustain itself, all four fields—structural, cultural, systemic, and experiential—must work together. This means that OD practitioners as systems agents are all implicated in the continuance and change of any system. If individuals decide they will stop using their competencies to support existing policies, practices, values, norms, ranking structures, and decision flow, the system will become unsustainable and change. The interconnectedness of the matrix means that change can be initiated in any quadrant of the system; provided that there is follow through to the other quadrants, the system can be reshaped. Conversely, for example, if behavior is changed but the same structure, culture, and systemic processes are maintained, very soon the new behavior will be overwhelmed.

Tables 21.2 and 21.3 are applications of the Systems Matrix. Table 21.2 shows a matrix highlighting the strengths and weaknesses of the global human system. Table 21.3 shows a systems approach to developing cultural competencies, an organization's capabilities in furnishing solutions to a diverse population. Note the variations of the quadrant headings; they give an idea of how the matrix can be customized.

TABLE 21.2. MAPPING A GLOBAL HUMAN SYSTEM.

Structural	**Systemic**
• Strength: interlinked communities • Weakness: stratification by race, gender, education, age, and other characteristics, creating hierarchical access to life resources	• Strength: shared best practices for addressing challenges facing humanity • Weakness: covert policies, practices, and processes perpetuating structural barriers
Cultural	**Experiential**
• Strength: cultural diversity and opportunity for synergy • Weakness: Culture clash through cultural domination and subordination	• Strength: increased opportunities to learn new perspectives, skills, and attitudes • Weakness: replicating ethnocentric knowledge, skills, and attitudes

TABLE 21.3. WHOLE-WORLD COMPETENCIES MATRIX.

Structural Leadership	Systemic Leadership
• Interrupt default power structures • Open up off-limit space to excluded groups	• Actualize hidden potential by reducing blind spots and barriers • Involve participants in system audit and redesign
Cultural Leadership	Experiential Leadership
• Create cultural spaciousness • Facilitate cultural synergy	• Venture into the unknown in yourself and your cultural system • Lead journeys to new competencies

Whole-World Competencies

In this section, four OD competencies for working with the whole world in one room are examined. They are derived from the four fields of the Systems Matrix. Practitioners can use these competencies to intervene in a human system mindfully and strategically.

Structural Leadership

Structural leadership refers to taking a lead role in transforming existing status and role rankings to include more systems participants in the use of power, decision making, and problem solving. Leadership often means taking very small actions:

• Opening up structural spaces that have been off-limits to certain peoples, groups, and individuals; supporting those who are new to previously off-limit spaces; showing them how to occupy and use the space.
• Including others when the whole world gathers in one room, shifting a little to make physical space; not blocking others with one's body; using inclusive gathering processes by introducing people, formally welcoming them, and informing the whole group who the people are in the room; sharing air time and floor space, so that others can join the conversation.

The legacy of our world system abounds in structural inequalities created through racism, sexism, and other limiting patterns. Consequently, when the whole world is in one room, these legacies of dominant and subordinated group dynamics come into play, covertly or openly. Instead of working synergistically, systems participants often enact historical inequities, playing out roles and differences unconsciously and destructively. Instead of developing inclusive relationships, the whole world can mire itself in replaying old grievances—bogging down in indifference, mistrust, hatred, or violence. People with unearned privileges associated with skin color, class, gender, age, nationality, and other socially constructed categorizations can continue to act with those privileges taken for granted. Those who have been long oppressed may play out oppressed roles; or they may try to gain the upper hand and subjugate their oppressors. These systems roles—oppressed and oppressor—though unsatisfying are nonetheless familiar or habitual. In short, the structural legacy is such that we perpetuate and co-construct a world of physical and mental impoverishment.

Habitual structural dynamics are default patterns. The default is the taken-for-granted way of functioning and relating. A common default pattern is to let newcomers sink or swim. The default patterns kick in automatically whenever a group of people come together, unless the autopilot response is overridden with new intentions and practices. Structural leadership has to be an intentional act, because without intentional shift the default structure will play itself out, replicating through cultural, systemic, and experiential practices. One way of altering default dynamics is to use circle practices: ways of restructuring inspired by the circle archetype. Circle practices gently balance autonomy with interdependence, the unique with the universal, differences with similarities. Here are some simple steps that can be used to create open structure and new structural space.

Form a Circle. Gather people in the room into a circle, actually or virtually. There is a place for everyone in the circle. Invite people to take and claim their space. When newcomers arrive, everyone shifts a little to include them into the expanding circle. The circumference of this inclusive circle is as limitless as the whole world. When some people leave, close the space to reform a new circle. The circle is always complete for the people there. The center of the circle is everywhere the individual participants are.

Decentering. When people gather in a circle, an open space is created. This center can be filled with imported ideas and legacy rules that are irrelevant to the participants there. Decenter the shared space by eliminating outdated ideas. Open up the center by declaring its emptiness and openness.

Recentering. Recentering is a process of choosing governing principles and norms appropriate to the circle of participants. Invite participants to fill the center with ideas important to them and appropriate to the tasks at hand. Recenter the circle with the ideas. Speak them into the circle.

Give and Take. Each participant can give a gift to the center and take a gift from it.

Abundant Roles. Each participant has the chance and responsibility to play multiple roles: teacher, learner, facilitator, participant, resource person, researcher, advisor, and decision maker. No one can monopolize. When it comes to working with the whole world in one room, everyone is a novice and all are interdependent.

Dancing Organization. The circle is a living system. It dances as it responds to emergent needs and circumstances. In a circle organization, there are no fixed core and noncore business units. Depending on the situation, certain people step up to the front, moving into an inner circle to lead. Others step back and forth as required. As the situation changes, other people step forward and lead for a while. Circles create dancing organizations. By using simple structural practices, OD practitioners can transform the flow of power, roles, and status, and open up cultural, systemic, and experiential spaces for change.

Cultural Leadership

When there are multiple cultures in one room, which culture should prevail? Commonly, the culture of the dominant group kicks in, in an autopilot fashion; systems participants play out the wasteful default of domination and subordination ("Follow my way, or you are out"), unless we intervene through cultural leadership.

Cultural leadership refers to intentional facilitation of cultural interaction and exchange to create innovation or synergy. Cultural leadership creates cultural spaciousness and new possibilities. There are fewer blind spots when issues are addressed from differing cultural perspectives. Ideas and solutions can multiply spectacularly as cultural assumptions and strategies are shared. Cultural leadership can help system participants:

- Increase understanding of the power of hidden cultural diversity in shaping how we think, talk, and work with each other
- Gain deeper appreciation of the silent drivers of our views, opinions, and ideas
- Enhance the ability to collaborate with others in finding creative solutions for improved performance and breakthrough results

Many cultural differences are invisible. They influence and direct mind and actions, silently and covertly. Cultural participants are like fish in separate ponds.

The challenge is to become conscious of the medium that forms and limits awareness. To facilitate coming to awareness and synergy with clients' systems, one can use a learning laboratory called "Whole World in One Room" (WWIOR; Allen, 2002). In a WWIOR workshop, participants role-play an assigned culture and job role, and work with others to find solutions to case scenarios mirroring issues they face in real life. Participants work in same-culture groups and diverse-culture groups. After debriefing and dialogue, they apply simulation insights to real-life issues. The simulation laboratory is an effective learning methodology in raising cultural consciousness. Through hands-on role-play activities, participants can engage in learning and discovery about invisible diversity and inequality. A cultural simulation program can be created by using these steps:

1. Create four or five cultural profiles, on the basis of the demographics in the client system. Create job roles that mirror client authority structures. Create case scenarios, using research data about client issues.
2. Assign cultures and job roles for participants to role-play. Divide participants into groups to work on solutions for the case scenarios, while role-playing their assigned culture and role.

Synergy Steps is another tool that can be used to facilitate synergy (Allen, 2001; Adler, 1997). Here is a brief description of these steps.

Gather Solitudes. Within the whole world in one room, there can be multiple "solitudes"—peoples, groups, and individuals who are culturally isolated, disconnected, or oblivious to their cultural blind spots. They may be in the same physical space, but not necessarily in community. Use cultural leadership to open up cultural space by bringing cultural solitudes together.

Create Common Ground. When disparate peoples are brought into the same room, there is a need to find common ground for meaningful interaction. Create common ground by discovering similarities and shared purpose.

Accentuate Distinctiveness. Being in the one room with the whole world can create anxiety over identity and individuality. Help systems participants give voice to their uniqueness.

Reconfigure Boundaries. When people gather in one room, they bring along old boundaries: rank distinctions, us-and-them attitudes. To decenter these boundary notions, create a new cultural container by defining a boundary around the whole group as one community, however temporary. Invite the participants to hold the container of newly shared cultural space.

Proliferate Resources. Within the new cultural container, participants can freely exchange their gifts and talents—knowledge, skills, experiences, visions, aspirations, imagination, and stories—to generate resources that come into existence only when people come together in one room.

Journey into the Unknown. When the whole world gets together in one room, unusual dynamics and unknown patterns are created. Within the unknown lie new destinies for the group. Recognize, embrace, and traverse the unknown together. Lead this journey with care and daring. Help folks live with the ambiguity that inevitably accompanies the birth of synergy.

Champion New Possibilities. Through journeying to the unknown, system participants create new possibilities for themselves as a community and individuals. The new solutions are the cultural synergy of coming together. Because of their newness, the synergistic solutions may not be recognized, accepted, or valued. OD practitioners can act as champions for the emergent, the unheard of, the newly voiced, and the just-born cultural possibilities. By exercising cultural leadership, practitioners help prepare organizations for systemic change.

Systemic Leadership

Systemic leadership can be defined as intentional intervention in uncovering hidden potential by removing systemic barriers. When the whole world is in one room, the potential for high performance is greatly increased. Unfortunately, the barriers to high performance also multiply. The goal of systemic leadership is to help unleash potential by removing systemic barriers to high performance, the business and employment policies, processes, procedures, and practices that inadvertently exclude certain groups. For example, some organizations value "arrow style" communication—direct, up-front, and to the point—and depreciate the diplomatic, subtle and contextual approach of the "spiral style" (Allen, 2001).

Unintentionally, arrow values are built into recruitment, training, coaching, and compensation. The effect of this practice for a culturally diverse workplace is that groups and individuals who have different definitions of good communication are viewed as underperformers. This effect is referred to as cultural adverse impact, the statistically measurable result of a business or employment practice, process, or decision that disproportionately excludes certain racial, ethnic, gender, and abilities groups (Allen, 1990). The major cause of cultural adverse impact is pervasive and unconscious use of dominant cultural processes and practices.

To remove hidden barriers, OD practitioners can use participatory systems audits to involve systems participants in auditing their business and employment practices, rather than relying on consultant audits. A participatory systems audit includes these steps:

1. Brainstorm written and unwritten policies practices, norms, processes, and procedures used by systems participants. List them one by one. For each policy, practice, or procedure, identify the underlying cultural belief or assumption.
2. Assess the impact of each policy, practice, process, or procedure, using these or other agreed-on criteria (Canadian Human Rights Commission, 2002):

   Legality. Is the practice legal according to human rights codes?

   Consistency. Is the same practice applied to all system participants? Is there a bona fide business reason for applying varying practices?

   Cultural adverse impact. Will the practice unintentionally but disproportionately exclude a cultural, racial, gender, or other social group?

   Validity. Is the practice a valid measure of performance?

   Job relatedness. Is the practice related to doing the actual job?

   Business necessity. Is the practice essential to conducting organization business?

3. Create an alternative policy, practice, procedure, or process. Identify specific actions to remove barriers and implement alternatives.

A participatory systems audit is useful in freeing up trapped energies in the system. The emphasis is on participants themselves understanding and evaluating the processes they use every day to replicate their own system. Table 21.4 shows a matrix of strategies for developing cultural competency in a community agency.

TABLE 21.4. STRATEGIES FOR DEVELOPING CULTURAL COMPETENCY WITH A SERVICE AGENCY IN A MULTICULTURAL COMMUNITY.

Structures	Systemic Policies and Procedures
• Represent diverse demographics at all decision-making levels • Institute stakeholder consultation and feedback	• Integrate hiring and promotion goals into organization effectiveness strategy • Regularly audit and redesign business systems and employment systems
Organization Culture	**Individual Competencies**
• Integrate cultural competency into organization beliefs, vision, values, norms, and customs	• Expand cultural knowledge and skills • Disclose cultural assumptions • Gather feedback on own cultural behavior

Experiential Leadership

Experiential leadership refers to intentional acquisition of competencies that are essential to working effectively with the whole world in one room. Because these competencies are new, a key experiential practice is to undertake a learning journey. Practitioners are only beginning to appreciate the challenges associated with working with the whole world in one room. To meet these challenges, they need new perspectives, knowledge, skills, and attitudes to help them traverse, interpret, and discover the unknown territory in the whole-world community. Specifically, OD practitioners need competencies to:

- Interrupt default dominant and subordinated group dynamics
- Open up structural spaces to include previously excluded groups and individuals
- Create new cultural space for creative exchange
- Facilitate cultural synergy
- Remove systemic barriers
- Lead participatory audit and redesign
- Lead learning journeys

To acquire these competencies, global OD practitioners have to be willing to learn from each other, give and receive feedback on cultural blind spots, and shift from an ethnocentric worldview to a global one. To be successful at interrupting the default pattern of domination and subordination, practitioners have to give up internalized privileges and oppression, and reconceive their identity as self and community. This call to learning and change can be scary. Letting go of habitual prejudices and mind-sets can create disorientation. Shifting from a comfort zone of ignorance and denial can disturb peace of mind.

OD practitioners can explore their own areas of discovery, discomfort, and uncertainty by using Journey Mapping, a tool based on transformation insights from diverse cultures (Allen, 2001). The Journey Map is described in Exhibit 21.1. It shows eight archetypal change cycles that learners go through to discover the power and competencies for actualizing individual and organization potential.

EXHIBIT 21.1. JOURNEY MAP QUESTIONNAIRE.

System under focus: _____

  1. Inertia: What status quo is immobilizing the system?

  2. Call: What new directions will be explored?

  3. Jump: What risks will be taken?

(Continued)

EXHIBIT 21.1. JOURNEY MAP QUESTIONNAIRE, Cont'd.

4. Trials: What fears and fantasies are distracting the system's creative energies?

5. Dissolution: What default patterns will be let go?

6. Discovery: What new competencies will be developed?

7. Integration: How will synergy be created out of the diversity in the system?

8. Actualization: How will new competencies and patterns be supported and sustained?

Source: Adapted from Allen (2001).

According to the Journey Map, a journey to global discovery begins with awareness of being stuck in inertia, immobilized by a familiar status quo of domination and subordination. The unused potential in the system is calling for creative attention. Answering the call, global OD practitioners commit themselves by jumping into the unknown, embracing the uncertainty and disorientation that come with global change. On traversing the unknown, practitioners are met with trials—coming face to face with frightful dragons. These dragons are really the shadows of untapped energies and unacknowledged fears and desires about money, status, and power. Practitioners may try to preserve the status quo by wrestling with these dragons. Exhausted, they fall further into a metaphorical pit of dissolution, where fears of impoverishment, abandonment, and inadequacy finally have to be let go. Letting go of old default patterns opens up discovery of new resources (money), relationships (status), and competencies (power). There are now new resources and skills to integrate the gifts of the learning journey and actualize the true potential of the whole-world community.

The wisdom traditions of the world teach us that the more we ourselves venture into paths of learning and discovery, the better able we are to guide others in exploring the unknown. The Journey Map can be used to map retrospective, current, and prospective journeys by changing the tenses in the Journey Map questions. See the Journey Map Questionnaire in Exhibit 21.1 for the eight cycles and the mapping questions.

The four global OD competencies associated with the Systems Matrix—structural leadership, cultural leadership, systemic leadership, and experiential leadership—complement each other. They enable practitioners to translate the whole-world perspective into action and address the challenges of global OD practice.

Benefits of Using Whole-World Perspective and Practices

The perspective, tools, and competencies described in this chapter yield specific benefits:

- A holistic perspective that keeps the focus on the capabilities and potential of the whole versus being disoriented by the myriad distractions of the whole world in one room.
- An empowering vision that sustains motivation and energy against the over-whelming complexity and uncertainty that are part of global work. The vision motivates practitioners to provide leadership in addressing diversities and in-equalities, and it supports change agents to take action where they are and when they can.
- An inclusive process that enrolls all system participants in developing change strategies that integrate, involve, and connect the effort of disparate groups and initiatives.
- Realistic and affirming assessments of the strengths and areas of growth of the current system. The matrix assessments identify change strategies and actions that enhance the whole system. The journey map offers signposts and helps organizations anticipate trials and rewards in the journey to global effectiveness.

Conclusion: Meeting the Challenges of Global OD

Globalization brings the challenges of perspective, competencies, and ethics to the practice of OD. To meet these challenges, OD practitioners want to adopt whole-world perspectives, practice whole-world competencies, and center in an ethic of wholeness and responsibility.

Adopting Whole-World Perspectives

The complexity of a global environment requires OD practitioners to view and expand partial perspectives in the context of the larger whole. A partial world-view can create biased policies and actions and in turn lead to inadvertent adverse consequences. The more practitioners work with the whole world in one room, the more biases they encounter, in themselves and in others. Adopting a whole-world perspective is vital to opening one's mind to see the whole picture of the global village. The whole-world perspective images the global community as an open circle, living, changing, and self-renewing. This inclusive and inspiring image connects practitioners to the whole wherever they work.

Practicing Whole-World Competencies

Global diversities and inequalities invite organizations and practitioners to be-come agents of change. In global OD, practitioners have the opportunity to make a world of difference. Through their work, they can open up organizational spaces that have been off-limits to men and women from diverse backgrounds. They can show people how to create cultural synergy out of conflict and difference. Through systemic leadership, they can unleash trapped potential by removing hidden barriers. Through their courage to lead learning journeys, they can guide organizations to perform beyond the familiar comfort zone. By practicing structural, cultural, systemic, and experiential leadership, global OD practitioners facilitate positive organization change.

Centering in an Ethic of Wholeness and Responsibility

The world is a two-tiered global village. More than half of the world population has poor access to the basic necessities for life. The challenges of the global village can overwhelm the mind and immobilize action. To make a difference, global OD practitioners can center their perspective and action in an ethic of wholeness and integrity. By holding their client organizations as part of an open global circle, OD practitioners can be more mindful of their presence, their thoughts, and the impact of their actions. Ambiguity, uncertainty, dilemma, and confusion are part of global OD work and global life. By seeing themselves as part of the living circle, global OD practitioners can empower themselves to journey even though they are uncertain about the road ahead.

References

Adler, N. J. (1997). *International dimensions of organization behavior.* Cincinnati, OH: South-Western.

Allen, R. C. (1990). *Recognizing cultural adverse impact training manual.* Calgary, AB: Delta Learning.

Allen, R. C. (2001). *Guiding change journeys: A synergistic approach to organization transformation.* San Francisco: Jossey-Bass/Pfeiffer.

Allen, R. C. (2002). *Whole world in one room* (programs pamphlet). Vancouver, BC: Delta Learning.

Buchmann, M. (1989). *The script of life in modern society: Entry into adulthood in a changing world.* Chicago: University of Chicago Press.

Campbell, J. (1964). *Occidental mythology: The masks of God.* New York: Penguin Books.

Canadian Human Rights Commission. (2002). *Employment systems review: Guide to the audit process* (http://www.chrc-ccdp.ca/pdf/ESR2002.pdf).

Lodge, G. (1995). *Managing globalization in the age of interdependence.* Toronto: Pfeiffer.

CHAPTER TWENTY-TWO

ORGANIZATION DEVELOPMENT IN ASIA: GLOBALIZATION, HOMOGENIZATION, AND THE END OF CULTURE-SPECIFIC PRACTICES

Tojo Thatchenkery

Heterogeneity across cultures and markets is widely acknowledged by academics and practitioners alike operating in the international domain (Adler, 2001; Boyacigiller and Adler, 1991; Hofstede, 1980, 1993, 2003). Ignoring such heterogeneity can lead to financial disaster for any company operating in global markets. Jim Mann shares a fascinating story of one such mishap. In his book *Beijing Jeep* (1989), Mann traces the history of the stormy relationship between U.S. business and Chinese communism through the experience of American Motors and its operation in China. Mann shows how some of the world's savviest executives completely miscalculated the organizational culture of Chinese businesses and made poor decisions one after another. In the end, the Chinese acquired valuable new technology at virtually no cost by outgunning the U.S. executives through deception and manipulations.

However, in dealing with heterogeneity across cultures and markets, going to the other extreme of paying too much attention to cultural uniqueness can lead to equally severe disasters. As Percy Barnevik, the first chief executive officer of ABB, a global leader in power and automation technologies, observed: "Global managers have exceptionally open minds. They respect how different countries do things, and they have the imagination to appreciate why they do them that way. But, they are also incisive; they push the limits of the culture. Global managers don't passively accept it when someone says, 'You can't do that in Italy or Spain because of the unions,' or 'You can't do that in Japan because of the Ministry of

Finance.' They sort through the debris of cultural excuses and find opportunities to innovate" (quoted in Taylor, 1991, p. 93).

Organization development (OD) practitioners have not been that decisive. To the contrary, the nearly complete globalization of organizations has led many OD practitioners to reiterate the call for a radical redefinition of organization development in the international context. The underlying notion here is that when OD practitioners are in various countries, they should stay away from a "U.S.-centric" view of OD and instead customize their offerings to suit the local culture. For example, as early as 1986 Jaeger claimed that cultural and value differences were constraints in the use of intervention technologies in Asia. Three years later, Kirkbride, Tang, and Shae (1989) pointed out that culture was a barrier to introducing Western management training and organization development techniques into the Chinese community.

Others have suggested that the applicability of OD in the international context may depend on the congruence of national cultural values and OD values (Fagenson-Eland, Ensher, and Burke, 2004; Golembiewski, 1993). For example, Hofstede (1993) described overseas Chinese firms as extremely cost-conscious, applying Confucian virtues of thrift and persistence and thereby less likely to make use of OD practitioners. Kirkbride, Tang, and Westwood (1991) examined Chinese conflict behavior and suggested that open disclosure and critical reflection might be perceived as a threat to authority and hierarchy. Therefore, OD intervention tools such as confrontation meetings (Beckhard, 1967) and role negotiation might be inappropriate. Lau, McMahan, and Woodman (1996) compared the organization development practices in the United States and Hong Kong and pointed out differences, such as that the Hong Kong firms spent a quarter of their time on strategic planning in lieu of 16.3 percent for the U.S. firms.

Other studies have looked at the kind of OD practiced in Eastern European countries (McManus, 1979) or the former Soviet Union (Walck, 1993.) The latter study found that the Russians were interested in a technology called gaming (*igoprakitika*), which resembled the typical OD retreat in the United States. Regarding another country, Singh and Krishnan (2004) studied the transformational aspect of organization development in India by conceptually separating its leadership dimension into universal and culture-specific leadership. Their results implied a 56 percent weight for various culture-specific factors in the corporate sector, such as nurturing, personal touch, expertise, simple living, loyalty, and sacrifice. The most recent study was by Fagenson-Eland, Ensher, and Burke (2004), who compared differences in OD intervention in seven countries: Finland, Ireland, the Netherlands, New Zealand, South Africa, and the UK.

In summary, if these studies are any indication, most OD researchers and practitioners are of the view that OD as practiced in the West or the United States should be used only for Asian organizations with appropriate customization to accommodate the local cultures. However, as shown in this chapter such views are at odds with the more visible and powerful trends of globalization and its accompanying homogenization of cultures and organization development.

The focus of this chapter is on OD practices in Asia within these polarities of views. It is written primarily for a U.S. or European OD practitioner who might be interested in Asian organizations, though the ideas here can be used by anyone. Asia is chosen for two reasons. One, the author is familiar with the Asian culture, having grown up in India and continuing to have long-term research and consulting experience in the region. The second is that Asia is thought to be the textbook case for cultural heterogeneity in comparison to the West. Rooted in everyday metaphors such as "East versus West" or "the East meets the West," Asian culture is typically framed as distinctly different from the West. Likewise, Eastern philosophy is perceived in popular culture as being in direct contrast to Western philosophy.

Is the Asian corporate or organizational culture distinctly different from Western or U.S. organizational cultures, such that OD practitioners need to customize their offerings to suit the Asian culture? It is true there are differences between Asian and Western organizational cultures, but they are exaggerated and often based on a Western view of the East as exotic or "oriental." Although the urban middle and upper class of most Asian countries can often seem Americanized or Westernized, U.S. and European OD practitioners often propose an espoused value about the need to "Asianize" or customize their offerings. The outcome is a self-fulfilling prophecy of finding what one is looking for (cultural differentiation) and juxtaposition of the resultant conflicting worldviews and confusion. Understanding this difference helps OD practitioners avoid such stereotypical traps about their understanding of Asian organizations and people.

Asian Stereotypes and OD Practice

Despite the globalization of economies and organizations, widespread myths exist about Asian cultures. Hollywood movies are one source for identifying cultural stereotypes of Asians. For example, Hollywood typically pushes a stereotype of Asian men as asexual machines and Asian women as submissive. In other instances, the Asian woman is depicted as sexually available, exotic, overly feminine, and eager to please, creating the character of "China doll." When Asian males are given roles, they are primarily for the purpose of comic relief, such as the Japanese man in *Breakfast at Tiffany's*. Also, Hollywood typically lumps Asians—the Chinese, Koreans, Taiwanese, Vietnamese, Indian, and Indonesian—all together and gives them one identity. Regardless of the race of the person in the script, any person from an Asian country will fit the role, whether Korean, Japanese, or Chinese.

In a scholarly work titled *Global Culture/Individual Identity: Searching for Home in the Cultural Supermarket,* anthropologist Gordon Mathews (2000) shows that the traditional anthropological definition of culture—the way of life of a people—should be updated to include the identities available to people through what he termed the "cultural supermarket." According to him, national identities are eroded by the global material and cultural supermarkets that saturate the global marketplace with products and identities well in excess of anyone's capacity to consume or comprehend. Mathews shows that even though state-led cultural identity evolved over several centuries and involved coercion through the law, cultural identity through the market has taken a mere twenty years to evolve and has become a more powerful force in influencing people's behavior.

According to Mathews (2000), culture shapes the self at three levels of consciousness, as shown in Figure 22.1. The first is the *taken-for-granted* level, where people are shaped by language and various social practices. The second is the *shikata ga nai* level, which involves the external force of the nation-state that requires people to act in a given way. *Shikata ga nai* is illustrated by *ga nai* (it cannot be helped) and *gaman* (persevere), two concepts that are synonymous with the Japanese American spirit. During World War II, when more than 110,000 Americans of Japanese ancestry were incarcerated in the United States, Japanese Americans are thought to have said *shikata ga nai* and *gaman* to one another to make sense of the events.

FIGURE 22.1. THREE LEVELS OF CULTURAL CONSCIOUSNESS.

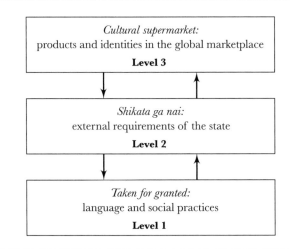

Source: Adapted from Mathews (2000).

These two levels of cultural consciousness make up the traditional anthropological definition of culture (as a way of life of a people), and it is here that national identity is cultivated. Citizens do not have much control in changing these two levels, but the third level—the cultural supermarkets—allows people to freely choose the identities that they want to live by. The self has full control and comprehension at this level. Cultural identity can be viewed as a social performance embedded in our social world, which censors our choices within the cultural supermarket (Mathews, 2000).

Most of the discourses on OD practices in the multicultural global environment are focused on understanding culture at the first two levels. When OD practitioners talk of culture in India or China in order to sort out which OD interventions might be appropriate, most of the available descriptions are derived from the taken-for-granted and *shikata ga nai* levels of consciousness. Yet the lived experiences of the participants of Indian or Chinese organizations come from the cultural supermarket level of consciousness. This is a subtle but important distinction.

The cultural supermarket is what is most readily available to the majority of employees of Asian organizations. It is their perceived reality and lived experience. The "aisles" of the supermarket—the media, Hollywood, MTV, books, and fashion—have flooded them with cultural products well in excess of their capacity for consumption. The result is a workforce that has become reflexively unaware of the first two levels of cultural identity and is engaged more intensely with the third. The challenge for OD practitioners is therefore to go past their own likely preoccupation with the first two levels. OD practitioners need to relate to participants through understanding and appreciation of the third level. This is understandably a challenging task since most of the writing on OD in the international area is focused on the first two levels.

The Homogenization of OD

There are differences between the Asian and Western organizational cultures, but cross-cultural researchers caution that lumping all Asian countries into one is a gross error. Not only are there cultural differences between organizations in China and India; equally significant differences exist among organizations across geographical regions within the same country. For example, business organizations in the Western (Mumbai) region of India are culturally different from those in the Northern (Delhi) region, which in turn differ from those in the Southern areas (Bangalore, Chennai, and Hyderabad). Bangalore, dubbed the "Silicon Valley of India," has a culture similar to the one in San Jose, California, from where the term originated. The culture in the capital city of New Delhi and its suburbs is not so different from culture in the U.S. capital city of Washington, D.C., and its suburbs.

Despite various cultural differences, organization development practices worldwide are growing more homogenized because of two trends: (1) the commodification of OD as a cultural product of late modernity, and (2) assimilation of U.S. and Western organizational values into the cultures of Asian organizations as a result of globalization. Both these trends are discussed here.

OD as a Project of Modernity

The umbrella terms modernism and postmodernism describe a collage of social trends and philosophical developments. The concepts are used to explore the implications of globalization and provide a radically different framework for understanding organization development. The concept of postmodernism is used here as a way of talking about modernism. By contrasting modern science and modernism with postmodernism, the attributes of modern science and modernism are used to demonstrate the need to understand the inevitability of global OD practices.

The common denominator for modernity may be the concept of *social change*, or to a finer level, *change*, a core term in the field of organization development. Modernization, and its accompanying notion of progress, has brought a series of seemingly indisputable benefits to people. Lower infant mortality rate, a drop in poverty, eradication of some fatal diseases such as smallpox, overall improvement in living standards, and rising gender equality are some of the examples of this progress. Lyotard (1984) points out that modernity is legitimated by two kinds of meta-narratives of progress, the meta-narrative of emancipation and the meta-narrative of *unified knowledge*. Examples for emancipation include the enlightenment narrative of liberation from serfdom through knowledge and equality, the capitalist narrative of escape from poverty through industrial development, and the Marxist narrative of emancipation from exploitation and alienation through socialization of labor.

Modernity resulted out of the collapse of religious authority and the rise of a rationalized, bureaucratic social order (Lyotard, 1984). Separate groups of professionals, each with their own expertise and technical abilities, were granted responsibility for independent areas of activity. Scientists oversee nature, critics determine taste, lawyers administer justice, physicians maintain health, therapists and the clergy foster psychological well-being, and so on. It is in this social, historical, and cultural context that the field of organization development emerged as yet another specialized area of knowledge. The central assumption of this era was that specialization and rationalization "would promote not only the control of natural forces, but would also further understanding of the world and of the self, would promote moral progress, the justice of institutions, and even the happiness of human beings" (Habermas, 1984, p. 116). In that vein, OD, mostly spearheaded by scholars and practitioners of the National Training Laboratories (NTL), sought to eradicate social oppression and promote justice and equality in organizations and communities through its original and creative OD interventions, based on the T-group methodology (Greiner and Cummings, 2004).

Just as modernity sought to achieve progress through *managed* transformation of social institutions (Cheal, 1990), the NTL sought to transform organizations through empowerment and participative methodologies. In modernity, the industrial organization came to be seen as the source of human unity and progress. Bell's celebrated thesis of modern (postindustrial) society was that it was "organized around knowledge for the purpose of social control and the directing of innovation and change" (Bell, 1973, p. 20). Intellectual technologies available for this purpose, according to Bell, were information theory, cybernetics, decision theory, game theory, and utility theory. Their function was definition of rational action and identification of means to achieve the goals. Finally, the urge to certainty or determinacy was a basic drive in modernity.

Organization development, as developed by NTL and other practitioners, bears a significant resemblance to the modernist discourse, even though the values that NTL and others sought to propagate were more humanistic in nature.

Postmodernity and Local Narratives in OD

Modernity's influence was later challenged by postmodernity, which rejected modernity's totalizing perspectives of progress and rationality. Postmodernists longed for small stories from heterogeneous subject positions of individuals and plural social groups, rather than large stories about the world. Accordingly, postmodernist culture demanded and showed pluralism, absence of a universally binding authority, and an overabundance of meaning and diversity. For example, they pointed out that the body of objectively available cultural products today is well in excess of the assimilating capacity of any member of society.

Could and should OD have embraced postmodernism? After all, organization development is a reflective discipline, thought to be populated by reflective practitioners, as envisaged by Schön (1983). The core task of the field—helping people in organizations deal with change—calls for a certain amount of "thinking about the thinking" or "double loop learning," as Chris Argyris and Don Schön (1978) would argue. Thus, when Boje, Gephart, and Thatchenkery (1996) coedited the first book on *Postmodern Management and Organization Theory,* their hope was that the powerful ideas of postmodernism would transform organization development too, making it more reflective and proactive.

Specifically, there was strong optimism and anticipation that more refreshing and humanizing local knowledge and practices would counter the influence of totalizing narratives of modernist organization development. It was also thought that in postmodern organization development stakeholders would have the freedom to develop their own ideas using local knowledge and practices against the hegemony of the totalizing theories. During the height of the popularity of postmodernism (1985–1999), many OD theorists and practitioners believed that the growing globalization of organizations would prompt cultures to interact more intensely and create a mosaic of new knowledge, innovation, and practices. Accordingly, Boje, Gephart, and Thatchenkery (1996) hoped that the output of the interaction between universal and local knowledge, or grand narratives and local narratives in the field of organization development, would be new insights, theories, models, and practices, uniquely crafted for each cultural and geographic region. OD for China or India would be different from OD in North America.

A decade later the hope has given way to gradual realization that organization development has been completely co-opted and assimilated into the modernist system. Instead of showing reflexivity and innovativeness, the field has adopted the modernist values of performativity, commodification, and instrumentality. Despite Asia being a best-case scenario for a unique line of culture-specific practices, organization development's values and practices have become indistinguishable from its more mainstream, modernist sister disciplines: organizational behavior, strategy, knowledge management, human resource development, and industrial psychology. Though most OD theorists and practitioners were comfortable holding on to a dichotomy of cultural experiences spread between Western and Eastern values, the reality on the ground seems to be near complete homogeneity.

OD as a Cultural Product

Having explained how OD's growth has been facilitated by the trends and forces of late modernity, it is time to turn attention to how OD is a cultural product. Neilsen and Rao, in an insightful article, traced the institutional genesis of organization development by showing that OD was a form of etiquette designed to help individuals manage their emotions in difficult interpersonal situations: "OD blossomed after World War II as the by-product of a long term trend in modern society toward increasing interdependence and heterogeneity. Those conditions rendered every-day social etiquettes obsolete and required new procedures for guiding human interaction in order to enable groups of intelligent and interdependent strangers to work together" (Neilsen and Rao, 1990, p. 67).

In other words, OD emerged when Tayloristic management in the modern factory created conditions ripe for social conflict. Neilsen and Rao (1990) offered a sophisticated analysis of the development of OD inspired by Weber's theory of rationalization in capitalist societies (1947) and Elias's treatise (1978) on the development of civilized behavior in Western Europe. The Neilsen and Rao (1990) conclusion that OD has historically played an organizational harmony-creation role is highly relevant to how OD has been applied in the United States and elsewhere.

Following the social etiquette role of OD, most OD theories and models have a modernist flavor, synonymous with the Western worldview of science, society, and organizations. The economic and political forces of globalization have led OD to a constant move toward homogeneity. OD theories of the person, group, and organization are all based on modernist assumptions of rationality and universalism. The rich heterogeneity that existed across the various nations of Asia has given way to a form of homogeneity supported by a global capitalist system based on efficiency, optimization, and commodification. For the field of organization development, the accompanying trend has been an uncritical export of traditional OD values and an equally uncritical acceptance of them by local OD practitioners, except for a few lonely dissenters.

Globalization and OD

One of the most profound changes in the world of organizations is their almost total globalization. In the 1980s "going global" was a catchword as evidenced by its appearance in media, academic conferences, and political debates. Research on globalization was fast becoming a topic in itself during that time. For example, a search of articles published in business journals under the term *globalization* yielded 1,406 entries for the period from December 1986 to November 1991 (according to University Microfilms International's Abstracted Business Information). A similar search for the period until October 2004 yielded 34,277 articles, which was an increase of 2,337 percent or twenty-four times over. The general theme in these business journal articles is that business organizations are becoming more global and hence managers need to pay attention to this process.

Today, the effect of globalization is felt in almost every aspect of social, cultural, and organizational lives. Globalization is the reality in front of OD practitioners. Indian physicist and activist Vandana Shiva calls it "monoculture of the mind." Driven by a consumer-based, free-market ideology, the global monoculture is strongly felt in Asian countries. In China and India, for example, young people wear Nike sneakers, Gap and Abercrombie & Fitch clothes, listen to music on their iPods, and watch the latest-release U.S. movies, MTV, and the most current television series. This is in marked contrast to what most people think of as the Asian culture. It is true that there are differences between Western and Asian culture at the national level, but the differences diminish quickly when one looks at the organizational level catered by the cultural supermarket mentioned earlier. Therefore, it is only natural to ask, How has globalization affected the field of organization development?

This author recently made three field visits with several global corporations operating in India both as subsidiaries and as back-end operations. Some were Indian companies that have become global corporations, while the rest were firms from the United States with a strong global presence. The culture of cities such as Bangalore, Mumbai, Pune, Chennai, and Delhi in India has changed so dramatically during the last five years that only a visit to the area would help one comprehend its magnitude. In interviews with senior human resource and organization development executives, geopolitical distinctions became more diffused. Interview results from Bangalore were indistinguishable from what would have been experienced in the heart of Silicon Valley, California. Some call this experience "hyperglobalization," a stage of development where geographical boundaries feel irrelevant.

Indian OD practitioners were no longer able to describe anything that would be "the Indian way of doing an OD intervention." More significant, attempting to identify local OD approaches is not a good question to ask anymore. The driving forces behind OD approaches are elements of the global capitalist system: profits, efficiency, best quality at the lowest cost, and strategic advantage. Culture-specific OD practices have become more of a politically correct term to use at the espoused level among OD practitioners and clients than a conceptual or operational necessity.

It is useful to explore what globalization is and how it has contributed to this redefinition of OD practices. According to prominent social theorist Anthony Giddens (2004), globalization is the intensification of worldwide social relationships, which link distant localities in such a way that local happenings are shaped by distant events and in turn distant events are shaped by local happenings. Globalization has led to reduction of geographical, spatial, and temporal factors as constraints, resulting in the perception of the world as a whole, and a readjustment of societal thought and action away from national to global spheres.

A decade ago, in *Global Dreams: Imperial Corporations and the New World Order*, Richard Barnet portrayed the rise of a "standardized culture" across the world propelled by the products of PepsiCo, Madonna, Bertelsmann, American Express, Sony, Citibank, and the like. He showed how the global corporate power structure and financial markets were detached from accountability to the human interest (Barnet, 1995). David Korten, in his best-seller *When Corporations Rule the World*, shows how the concept of the nation-state itself is questioned by the transnational relationships that powerful global corporations have created. He explains how economic globalization has concentrated the power to govern in global corporations (Korten, 2001). Even those critical of the antiglobalization views of Barnet and Korten would agree that the growing consolidation and rise of global corporations has created an overwhelming array of homogeneous and standardized cultural products.

There are at least five broad definitions of globalization (Scholte, 2000, pp. 15–17), and they all have relevance to OD and its practices in the global context:

1. Globalization as internationalization
2. Globalization as liberalization
3. Globalization as universalization
4. Globalization as Westernization or modernization
5. Globalization as deterritorialization

Globalization as Internationalization

In the first view, globalization is cross-border relations between countries. It describes the growth in international exchange and interdependence. In this case, the OD practices prevalent in different nations are exchanged just as in international trade and commerce. However, it turns out that because OD as a field of practice emerged primarily in the United States, the direction of traffic has been from that nation to the rest of the world.

Globalization as Liberalization

In the second case, the focus of globalization is on the processes of removing government-imposed restrictions on movement between countries in order to create an "open," "borderless" world economy (Scholte, 2000, p. 16). Although the term *liberalization* is used in an economic or trade sense, it can be applied to OD as well. Many of the OD practices in the West were initially seen as too "liberal" or "bold" in the East; examples are authenticity, T-group, direct feedback, and individual initiative. Each of these practices broke some local norm in Asia, especially around authority and hierarchy; yet they stuck almost as in liberalization.

Globalization as Universalization

In the third instance, globalization is seen as the process of spreading various objects and experiences to people in all corners of the globe. A classic example of this would be the spread of computing and television. In the same vein, globalization of OD refers to the process of transmitting dominant OD practices to the rest of the world.

Globalization as Westernization or Modernization

Globalization is seen in a U.S.-based form whereby the social structures of modernity such as capitalism, rationalism, industrialism, and commodification are spread the world over. This is the strongest form of globalization that OD has experienced during the last ten years and a source of much criticism from OD practitioners.

Globalization as Deterritorialization

Globalization in the last case entails a reconfiguration of geography, so that social space is no longer wholly mapped in terms of territorial places, distances, and borders. This is an equally valid point for OD. The significant growth of outsourcing by U.S. corporations has created a culture of "twenty-four, seven" in many cities of India, leading to a reconfiguration of geography and time. With thousands of employees working in this mode, OD interventions are no longer limited to a nine-to-five day format but may have to operate in three shifts, just like all other operations.

All these categories support the contention that globalization is the driving force of change for organization development. None of them has a focus on local theories or practices. However, this does not mean OD in the international arena is merely implementing Western concepts without regard to local customs and practices. OD practices do incorporate local traditions and practices in several interventions. Yet they are not meant to replace core OD offerings, which are still U.S.-based.

OD Mind-Sets and OD Practice

Because of the gradual emergence of homogeneity for organization development in the world, it is time to abandon the romantic or idealized notion of a culture-specific or culture-unique organization development. As globalization becomes omnipotent and omnipresent, OD tools and practices too will become homogeneous. Grand narratives will replace local narratives of OD. The natural question in such a scenario is "What should OD practitioners do?" under those circumstances.

One of the best options for OD practitioners is to cultivate a global mind-set. Two noted management theorists, Anil Gupta and Vijay Govindarajan, describe a model, shown in Figure 22.2, that makes use of the metaphor of mind-sets as knowledge structures. They describe three mind-sets that can be applied to use of OD in international and world settings: the parochial, diffused, and global (Gupta and Govindarajan, 2002). This author adds a fourth mind-set, laissez-faire. The concepts of integration and differentiation must be described to fully articulate what these mind-sets are.

FIGURE 22.2. OD PRACTICE MODELS.

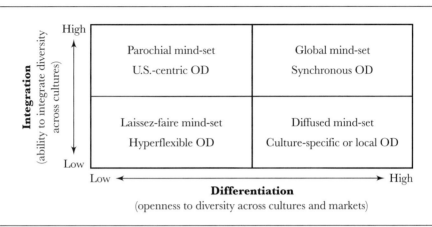

Source: Adapted from Gupta and Govindarajan (2002), p. 18.

The Gupta and Govindarajan (2002) model, supported by evidence from cognitive psychology, shows that mind-sets exist in the form of knowledge structures. The two primary attributes of any knowledge structure are differentiation and integration. When the Gupta and Govindarajan model is applied to organization development, differentiation in knowledge structures signifies the narrowness versus breadth of knowledge that OD practitioners bring to a particular engagement. For example, consider an OD practitioner who wants to use a specific team-development model in most projects. This person may have "tunnel vision," an example of low differentiation in knowledge structures. The second attribute, integration in knowledge structures, denotes the capacity of the OD practitioner to comprehend and synthesize disparate knowledge elements received from client interviews and other sources. Integration is the capacity to make sense of diverse and highly differentiated knowledge in an embodied, assimilated, fused, or synthesized format. Using high- and low-end possibilities in differentiation and integration, there are four mind-sets and corresponding OD styles.

Laissez-Faire Mind-Set: Hyperflexible OD

A low-differentiation and low-integration state may lead to a laissez-faire mind-set and hyperflexible OD. For an OD practitioner with low differentiation, integration would not be an issue since there is no need to integrate if the knowledge itself is not differentiated. This is what one might call "casual OD," a form of OD practice in which anything goes. Whatever the client wants is provided, without much re-flection on the appropriateness of the tools or the interventions recommended.

Parochial Mind-Set: U.S.-Centric OD

The parochial mind-set is evidenced with high-integration and low-differentia-tion knowledge structure. According to Gupta and Govindarajan (2002), "an or-ganization would be termed as having a parochial mindset when it is blind to diversity across cultures and markets. Such an organization makes little, if any, effort to adapt its products and processes to local conditions in foreign markets" (p. 126). They explain this quadrant using the story of IKEA, the world's largest furniture retailer, based in Sweden. Until the early 1990s, Swedish nationals who spoke fluent Swedish constituted most of the top management. Whenever IKEA entered foreign markets it replicated its traditional Swedish concepts, such as no home delivery and a Swedish cafeteria. Their entry into the U.S. market suffered heavy losses because it did not customize its products to the U.S. consumer's buy-ing behavior. Eventually, IKEA shifted from a parochial to a more global mind-set (Gupta and Govindarajan, 2002).

When it comes to going from their home turf to a global arena, many OD practitioners may do what IKEA did in its early globalization practices. Since the focus of this chapter is on OD in Asia, the most appropriate comparison might be North American OD practitioners in China, Singapore, or India. The paro-chial mind-set emerges when OD practitioners based in the United States see Asian organizational cultures and practices mostly through the perspectives and mental models they are used to in North America.

Diffused Mind-Set: Culture-Specific or Local OD

Most OD practices are rooted in the low-integration and high-differentiation quad-rant, leading to a diffused mind-set: "An organization would be termed as having a diffused mindset when it behaves as a loose federation of geographic units such that each local unit has a deep understanding of the local culture and market, yet the organization as a whole lacks the ability to synthesize across this" (Gupta and Govindarajan, 2002, p. 126). Diffused mind-sets are found in professional service firms such as accounting, advertising, and consulting. According to Gupta and Govindarajan (2002), these firms behave like networks of local partner-owned or-ganizations where the power of the CEO is constrained. Even if one or two top executives have a global mind-set, the firm as a whole behaves as if it has a diffused mind-set. The appreciation for and understanding of local issues and local differ-ences is great, but the ability to see the bigger global picture is limited.

OD practitioners who are heavily influenced by client inputs and change their diagnosis of the situation frequently on the basis of the intensity of such feedback have the high-differentiation and low-integration knowledge structure. This structure applies as well to the OD practitioner who is overly influenced by the desire to be culturally responsive and so adapts tools and interventions at the slightest indication of cultural sensitivity.

Global Mind-Set: Synchronous OD

What is needed is a global mind-set, grounded in the high-integration and high-differentiation quadrants. A high-global-mind-set organization demonstrates deep knowledge of diverse cultures and markets as well as ability to synthesize across this diversity (Gupta and Govindarajan, 2002). An OD practitioner with a global mind-set has a high-differentiation and high-integration knowledge structure accompanied by openness to and awareness of diversity across cultures and markets and the ability to synthesize across this diversity. Such a person understands and accurately judges the local cultural subtleties and at the same time is aware of the overall picture to create the necessary long-lasting changes in the organization. The global mind-set allows the OD practitioner to go beyond the traditional views of OD interventions in Asia and integrate a plurality of views and perspectives before deciding on intervention strategies. Such a practitioner is an avid reader of global politics and willing to engage in double-loop learning by continuously questioning her or his assumptions.

Synchronous OD describes the OD practitioner using the global mind-set. The word *synchronous* refers to the process of simultaneously differentiating and integrating. When faced with a decision to consider which intervention to use or what approach to adopt, the OD practitioner with a global mind-set is able to differentiate the cultural contour of client systems and yet come to actions that integrate the diverse perspectives emerging out of the differentiation.

Conclusion

This chapter has presented a counterintuitive position regarding the strategies available to OD practitioners operating in the Asia region. Thanks to the gradual emergence of homogeneity of OD at the global level, the idealized notion of a culture-specific or culture-unique OD has become almost impossible to realize in practice. Most of the taken-for-granted assumptions about cross-cultural management have become untenable thanks to the rapid acceleration of globalization and the rise of the twenty-four, seven culture. The global corporation has come to assert a significant influence on organizational practices worldwide, leading to more sameness than uniqueness among OD practices. As a result, OD as practiced in Asia is no longer significantly different from the way it is in North America or Western Europe.

Globalization is a double-edged sword. It has forced OD practitioners and management consultants to think about the impact of globalization no matter whether they are in the United States or Asia. The rise of the global corporation has created a circulation of managers leading to movement of key executives among all its operations. As a result, a multinational corporation in the United States would have a much higher number of executives from overseas than ever before. International experience has become a prerequisite for senior leadership positions in most blue-chip global corporations headquartered in the United States. In the same vein, a good number of North American or European managers can be found in corporations in Asia.

As the trend of global circulation of talent across geographical boundaries accelerates, OD practitioners have a new opportunity to adopt a global mind-set as a way to resolve the cultural contradictions of late modernity and global capitalism. Presented with the challenge of having to walk a fine line between differentiation and integration as presented in the model, this chapter suggests a new model of OD, *synchronous OD,* as the most suitable for the future. Synchronous OD represents a fusion and embodiment of the simultaneous demands placed on the OD practitioner to see both the trees and the forest at once. Metaphorically, the OD consultant must not only appreciate the uniqueness and diversity of the trees but also have the knowledge to appreciate the ecological system of the forest.

F. Scott Fitzgerald once said that the test of a first-class mind is the ability to hold two opposing ideas in the head at the same time and still retain the ability to function. Synchronous OD is not a compromise between the opposing forces of differentiation and integration. Instead, it is derived from a unique competence called the global mind-set, which requires the OD practitioner to hold both integration and differentiation in *practice* at the same time.

References

Adler, N. (2001). *International dimensions of organizational behavior.* Cincinnati, OH: Southern-Western.

Argyris, C., & Schön, D. (1978). *Organizational learning: A theory of action perspective.* Reading, MA: Addison-Wesley.

Barnet, R. (1995). *Global dreams: Imperial corporations and the new world order.* New York: Touchstone Books.

Beckhard, R. (1967). The confrontation meeting. *Harvard Business Review, 45*(2), 149–155.

Bell, D. (1973). *The coming of post-industrial society: A venture in social forecasting.* New York: Basic Books.

Boje, D., Gephart, R., & Thatchenkery, T. (Eds.). (1996). *Postmodern management and organization theory.* Thousand Oaks: CA: Sage.

Boyacigiller, N. A., & Adler, N. J. (1991). The parochial dinosaur: Organizational science in a global context. *Academy of Management Review, 16*(2), 262–290.

Cheal, D. (1990). Social construction of consumption. *International Sociology, 5*(3), 305–306.

Elias, N. (1978). *The history of manners: A study of civilizing process* (Vol. 1). New York: Pantheon.

Fagenson-Eland, E., Ensher, E. A., & Burke, W. W. (2004). Organization development and change interventions: A seven nation comparison. *Journal of Applied Behavioral Science, 40*(4), 432–464.

Giddens, A. (2004). *Defining globalization* (http://www.lse.ac.uk/Giddens/FAQs.htm#GQ1), accessed Nov. 23, 2004.

Golembiewski, R. T. (1993). Organizational development in the Third World: Values, closeness of fit and cultural boundness. *International Journal of Public Administration, 16*(11), 1667–1691.

Greiner, L., & Cummings, T. (2004). Wanted: OD more alive than dead! *Journal of Applied Behavioral Science, 40*(4), 374–391.

Gupta, A., & Govindarajan, V. (2002). Cultivating a global mind-set. *Academy of Management Executive, 16*(1), 116–127.

Habermas, J. (1984). *The theory of communicative action* (T. McCarthy, Trans.). Boston: Beacon Press.

Hofstede, G. (1980). Motivation, leadership and organization: Do American theories apply abroad? *Organizational Dynamics, 9*(1), 42–63.

Hofstede, G. (1993). Cultural constraints in management theories. *Academy of Management Executive, 7*(1), 81–94.

Hofstede, G. (2003). *Culture's consequences: Comparing values, behaviors, institutions and organizations across nations.* Thousand Oaks, CA: Sage.

Jaeger, A. (1986). Organization development and national culture: Where's the fit? *Academy of Management Review, 11*(1), 178–190.

Kirkbride, P., Tang, S., & Westwood, R. (1991). Chinese conflict preferences and negotiating behaviour: Cultural and psychological influences. *Organization Studies, 12*(3), 365–387.

Kirkbride, P. S., Tang, S.F.Y., & Shae, W. C. (1989). The transferability of management training and development: The case of Hong Kong. *Asia Pacific Human Resource Management, 27*(1), 7–19.

Korten, D. (2001). *When corporations rule the world.* San Francisco: Berrett-Koehler.

Lau, C. M., McMahan, G. C., & Woodman, R. (1996). An international comparison of organization development practices: The U.S.A. and Hong Kong. *Journal of Organizational Change Management, 9*(2), 4–14.

Lyotard, J. F. (1984). *The post-modern condition: A report on knowledge* (G. Bennington & B. Massumi, Trans.). Minneapolis: University of Minnesota Press. (Original work published 1979).

Mann, J. (1989). *Beijing Jeep: The short, unhappy romance of American business in China.* New York: Simon and Schuster.

Mathews, G. (2000). *Global culture/individual identity: Searching for home in the cultural supermarket.* New York: Routledge.

McManus, M. (1979). Two worlds of OD. Contrasting practices and values in an East-West "organizational intervention" perspective. *Academy of Management Proceedings,* 309–313.

Neilsen, E. H., & Rao, H. (1990). Strangers and social order: The institutional genesis of organization development. *Research in Organizational Change and Development, 4*, 67–99.

Scholte, J. A. (2000). *Globalization: A critical introduction.* London: Palgrave.

Schön, D. (1983). The reflective practitioner: How professionals think in action. New York: Basic Books.

Singh, N., & Krishnan, V. (2004). *Towards understanding transformational leadership in India: Grounded theory approach.* Jamshedpur, India: Xavier Labor Relations Institute.

Taylor, W. E. (1991). The logic of global business: An interview with ABB's Percy Barnevik. *Harvard Business Review, 69*(1), 93–105.

Walck, C. (1993). Organization development in the USSR: An overview and a case example. *Journal of Managerial Psychology, 8*(2), 10–18.

Weber, M. (1947). *The theory of social and economic organization* (A. M. Henderson and T. Parsons, Trans.). New York: Oxford University Press.

PART SIX

ORGANIZATION
DEVELOPMENT
APPLICATIONS
AND PRACTICES

CHAPTER TWENTY-THREE

THE IMPACT AND OPPORTUNITY OF EMOTION IN ORGANIZATIONS

Annie McKee and Frances Johnston

You know it when you feel it: the subtle, powerful undercurrent that seems to guide people and their behavior in organizations. It is not culture—though norms, habits, myths, rituals, and taboos are related. It is not just "the shadow of the leader" (Senn and Childress, 1999), though leaders certainly have something to do with it. It is not just situational; it is pervasive. This powerful, invisible, energetic force is the *emotional reality* of organizations. Consider these brief examples of organizations (described with pseudonyms).

Walking into the headquarters of a moderate size telecommunications company, which we'll call Connexis, the first thing you notice is the light. Somehow, there seems to be more sunlight here than in most buildings, and despite the fact that it is in the northeastern United States the warmth and brilliance are noticeable and unusual. People are walking about, a bounce in their step and a smile—yes, a smile—on their face. The receptionist engages you in conversation, and it is clear that she is really interested in talking with you. Her eyes tell the story: she actually cares about you. This behavior was not learned in a customer service course!

Note: We would like to thank Gretchen Schmelzer for her editorial assistance in the preparation of this chapter.

Nearby, small groups are chatting; people look energized and calm at the same time. There is a pleasant hum in the air, and all of a sudden you begin to feel excited and energized yourself. Something is happening here, and you want to be part of it. You make your way to your meeting, noticing the hundreds of "family" pictures on the walls. Every spare inch is covered—photos of people at parties, laughing together, group shots of teams working hard and having fun at the same time, then proudly displaying the results of their efforts. Then there are the letters, hundreds of them, all from happy, grateful customers.

Arriving at the designated conference room, there is an easy, welcoming serve-yourself set-up with coffee, sodas, and snacks. Your Connexis colleagues join, effortlessly engaging you in conversation. Talk moves fluidly from personal greetings to how everyone is doing, including brief but authentic discussion of people's lives. There is a sense of real concern and interest, and time is given to simply connecting. The group moves naturally to discussion of the day's agenda; there is work to be done, and everyone seems so ready to begin. . . . What a fantastic way to start a meeting.

By the way, Connexis is doing just fine, despite industry competition and volatile technology markets. They continue to meet targets, grow, and move toward a positive, profitable future.

Then, by contrast, there is a key division of XYZ Company (obviously, we cannot name this institution; it would be too embarrassing for them). Spending two hours in this division's cafeteria is an exhausting experience. People are rushing, almost pushing to get to the food. Trays are clattering; people are talking in short bursts. There is some laughter, but listening closely you notice that it is usually derisive—the food, the weather, the fact that it is "only Monday" are all sources of somewhat bitter jokes. As you join your colleagues at a table, the welcome is polite, but distant. You have to remind yourself that you know these people well, have been working with them for a long time. It surely does not feel that way.

People are busy talking with no small level of frustration and anger about the latest issue—from what you can tell, it has something to do with the leadership team failing yet again to communicate adequately about some changes that will occur over the next few months. Again, you almost pinch yourself as you listen; most of the members of the much-maligned leadership team are *at the table*. The conversation continues down a path that by now you know well. It starts with finger pointing and blaming, then moves into ten or twenty minutes of cynical comments about individuals, the organization, the work, and even each other. It is at this point that the conversation always gets tense: veiled criticism, minor slights, and even contempt for so-called colleagues and friends, all camouflaged as jokes. Defensiveness is in the air. Finally, you can almost feel every one sigh and slump; resignation sets in, the table falls silent, and one by one people pick up their trays and head back to work.

This division, it seems, could have been at the top of its industry. It is not. Though it has been in existence for some twenty years and is likely to limp along because of its association with a brand name company, this division has not and most likely will not achieve greatness. This despite the fact that the vision, the services, and at least initially the talent was there and the market *wants* to respond. Something is very wrong.

These two organizations have many differences, obviously. One is successful, one is not. One is guided by inspired, brilliant leaders; the other is caught in the grip of a clueless and arrogant manager. One company is an exciting, vibrant place to work, and the other is just plain depressing.

The stories of these organizations support recent research indicating that the degree to which leadership demonstrates emotional intelligence (Goleman, Boyatzis, and McKee, 2001, 2002) and the degree to which the environment is grounded in positive emotions affect performance and results significantly (Ashkanasy and Tse, 2000; George, 1995; Spencer, 2001). In *Primal Leadership*, Goleman and coauthors (2002) integrated significant research on the links between organizational results and the emotional intelligence of the leader to create a breakthrough model of primal leadership, where the leader inspires and motivates others through resonance—and can leverage this resonance to impact results in the organization.

In fact, in our work as organization development (OD) practitioners, we have become convinced that the success of our work with our clients is largely dependent on deciphering and working with *emotion:* both the individual's emotions and emotional intelligence (especially that of the leaders) as well as the collective emotional state present in any group or organization.

This chapter reviews the existing knowledge about the power of emotions in driving individual behavior, focusing on the impact of emotional intelligence on effective leadership. Then it explores the power of constructive and destructive emotional states on group and organizational functioning and discusses how practitioners and change agents can discern the emotional reality of the organizations in which they work. Finally, we discuss how practitioners can apply the current knowledge and wisdom about the "use" of emotions, their own and others', to their professional development and refinement of their craft.

Emotion and Leadership Effectiveness

Leadership behavior is a key to an organization's health. Of particular importance is the relationship of competencies, especially those related to emotional intelligence, leadership styles, climate, and results (Boyatzis, McKee, and Goleman,

2002; Goleman, Boyatzis, and McKee, 2002; Wolff, Pescosolido, and Druskat, 2002). In addition, the role of emotions in determining member leadership must also be considered (Wheelan and Johnston, 1996). Specifically, it seems that emotional intelligence is directly linked to leadership effectiveness, which affects the overall climate of a group or an organization. The climate, in turn, has an impact on results (Goleman, Boyatzis, and McKee, 2002; Spencer, 2001).

Emotional Reality

Current research and writing indicates that another important component of a group or organization's climate (and hence results) is emotion—how it "feels" to be a part of the group, and how those feelings drive individual and group behavior (Boyatzis and McKee, 2005). This experience is the *emotional reality* of the organization. Emotional reality comprises feelings, aspirations, sensations, and experiences such as hope, excitement, creativity, and compassion, as well as trauma, loss, disappointment, frustration, and sadness. A group's emotional reality is more dynamic, ethereal, and, frankly, more emotional than organizational culture as it has been described in traditional management literature. Emotional reality is an atmospheric state. It is a term that is inclusive of both the macro environment as well as microclimates within the whole.

There is an emotional reality that is shared among people in an organization. Individuals' emotions are contagious from one person to the next, and it seems even from one group to another; they come to influence the extent to which the environment is *resonant* or *dissonant* (Bartel and Saavedra, 2000; Forgas, 2003; Goleman, Boyatzis, & McKee, 2002). Attending to, interpreting, and shifting emotional intelligence and the collective emotions of a group or system can be a powerful force for change.

Resonance and Dissonance in Organizations

In a resonant environment, people are attuned to one another and to a shared vision and goals. They are oriented toward positive collective action, they weather trials and challenges with hope and resiliency, and they generally operate with collective efficacy and optimism. Dissonant environments, on the other hand, are characterized by hostility or resignation, disappointment, pessimism, and a general sense of hopelessness. Energy for work is depleted or diverted, and for the most part people operate as if they are under duress and in need of protecting themselves.

The research based on the relationship of emotional intelligence to effective leadership continues to expand (Boyatzis and McKee, 2005; Cherniss, 2001). Uncovering and working intentionally with the relationship among emotion, cognition, and behavior as well as the emotional reality of organizations—including the extent to which they are resonant or dissonant—affords a means for developing both individuals and the systems they are in, simultaneously (Isen, 2002). In looking at the emotional reality of an organization, we are interested in the subjective life of the system manifested through the sensations, experiences, thoughts, and feelings of the individuals within that system (Wilber, 2000). Historically, the study of organizations and systems has relied on observable data and descriptors of the external, outside, objective reality. Ken Wilber and other postmodern theorists have convincingly demonstrated the limitations of this worldview, arguing that we must add an appreciation for and interest in the power of subjective reality if we are to truly experience and understand the totality of human existence.

Exploring and working with the emotional reality of a system illuminates this aspect of organizational life. Lasting change occurs only when core values, beliefs, mind-sets, and emotions guide us to appreciate the subjective as at least equal in importance to the more traditional organizational development lenses of structure, marketplace dynamics, and work efficiency processes. We are interested in the latter being understood and changed in light of the former.

Leading with Emotional Intelligence

With Daniel Goleman's seminal work in 1995, the term *emotional intelligence* became an exciting addition to the language explaining human behavior (Goleman, 1995). Building on the work of previous scholars, he articulated an essential truth: emotions matter in human behavior, and in fact they have a profound impact on individual effectiveness and relationships, especially for people in leadership roles (Salovey, Mayer, and Caruso, 2002).

Some research supports the assertion that the most important set of competencies for effective management and leadership are those associated with emotional intelligence (Goleman, Boyatzis, and McKee, 2002; Kelner, Rivers, and O'Connell, 1996). Studies indicate that in our increasingly complex and fast-paced world, EI is twice as important as the combination of technical knowledge and IQ in determining successful leaders. EI is proving to be as much as four times as important in terms of overall organizational success, and a study of fifteen global companies attributes 85–90 percent of leadership success to emotional intelligence (Goleman, 1998).

A Definition of Emotional Intelligence

What is emotional intelligence? EI enables leaders to understand and deal with their own internal responses, feelings, and moods. Emotional intelligence also yields the insight and skills for relating to and with other people. Specifically, emotionally intelligent leaders are self-aware, manage their own and others' emotions, are highly attuned to and skillful in managing the social environment, and have highly developed relationship skills. Emotionally intelligent leaders:

- Attend *mindfully* to self, others, and the environment
- Stay intensely in touch with what the people they lead are thinking and feeling to motivate and energize them
- Act in ways that leave the people around them (partners, team members, employees, community members, and so on) feeling stronger and more capable
- Manage themselves effectively under stress or when dealing with ambiguous circumstances, remaining calm and staying focused
- Cultivate positive emotions, engaging *hope and compassion* in themselves and with others to counter the natural stress of leadership and to engage people in moving energetically toward a positive vision of the future (Boyatzis and McKee, 2005)

Leaders Affect the Emotional Reality

Return to the examples from the beginning of this chapter. At Connexis, the CEO, "Pat," has been central to the establishment of both the culture and the emotional reality of the company. Pat is known as the architect of the culture at Connexis, which is touted as one of the most vibrant and successful customer service cultures in the industry. It is no coincidence that Pat also epitomizes emotional intelligence in the workplace through these behaviors and practices: a deep, understanding of self, grounded in values and beliefs, which creates a confident presence, even under stress; good emotional management that usually stays on the positive end of the emotional continuum; a strong empathic connection with as many employees and customers as possible through early morning e-mails and a series of daily phone calls; and a continuous interest in being grounded in the daily lives and experiences of employees so as to be able to respond directly and appropriately to them. In addition to managing personal energy and time carefully to avoid depletion or burnout, Pat puts "Pat" on the daily agenda with some part of each day dedicated to activities that engage the heart as well as the mind.

On the other hand, the CEO at the struggling division of XYZ, "Chris," simply chooses to use a managerial style that ignores the emotional intelligence of everyone in the workplace. Chris considers any time spent developing self-awareness as time wasted and consequently charts a superficial daily course based on either short-term performance needs or personal issues. Even when challenged, Chris does not see how destructive this is and is shocked and offended when questioned about managerial philosophy. This philosophy includes the belief that keeping people unsure and off balance is a good tactic to "get people moving." To accomplish this end, Chris will even stage "blow ups" to upset people and jumpstart the process. This CEO has created a negative, critical, and generally unstable environment in which to work. Beyond shocking people from time to time, Chris has no interest in what employees think about leadership or the organization. Chris does not believe that this personal behavior and leadership style contributes to a distressingly negative emotional reality and a dysfunctional organization.

Suffice it to say that emotional intelligence enhances leadership effectiveness significantly, and the lack of it has a profound effect on followers *and* the organization. For organizational development practitioners, the implications are obvious: part of the work is to engage leaders in assessing and developing their EI. In fact, a virtual industry has grown up around coaching for emotional intelligence.

But there is a catch: effective leadership is necessary but not sufficient for creating vibrant, resonant, and healthy organizational environments. Even the best leadership cannot ensure health and wholeness in a group, especially a large, complex, multinational, mixed functional and geographically dispersed group! To accelerate change and support creation and maintenance of healthy climates, we need informal, as well as formal, leaders who can tap into the emotional reality of the group, shift it in the direction of resonance, and articulate a compelling vision for moving forward.

Demystifying Emotion and Bringing It Back to Work

Over the past few years, several streams of research have come together to paint a compelling picture of how emotions affect individual behavior, leadership, relationships and group dynamics, and behavior.

The Science and Wisdom of Emotion

Specifically, in the field of neuroscience the study of affect (emotion) and its relationship to human behavior has advanced substantially in recent years. Research led by such notable scientists as Richard Davidson of the University of Wisconsin advanced understanding of the physiology of emotion, as well as its relationship to personality, health, cognitive functioning, and social interaction (Davidson and Irwin, 1999). In psychology, the movement toward what is now called "positive psychology" has created both theory and research data that support our hypotheses regarding the impact of positive and negative emotions on psychological well-being, attitudes, and relationships at work (Seligman, 2002). Furthermore, current thinking in these two fields supports recent findings in the field of management education and learning: positive emotions support the growth and development of human beings, and the groups to which they belong (Davidson, 2004).

What's New Is Very Old

The fields of neuroscience and psychology come together in a fascinating way when juxtaposed against some of the ancient and modern teachings of the greatest philosophers. For example, indigenous peoples all over the world have "models" to explain the interaction of the various aspects of our humanity (Brown, 1992; Lewis, 1990; Markus and Kitayama, 1991). In North America, the model used by Native Americans is akin to a compass and called a Medicine Wheel (Niehardt, 1932/2000). On the wheel, each point on the compass is associated with an aspect of our human experience: heart, mind, body, and spirit. At the center of the wheel there is balance (Sidle, in press).

The study of the holistic experience has also been a foundation of Buddhism, as well as several other great religious and philosophical traditions. For most of Western history, however, religious leaders and philosophers have been far removed from the scientists. Happily, this is beginning to change. Recently, His Holiness the Dalai Lama led a meeting of the Mind and Life Institute, in which neuroscientists, psychologists, educators, monks, and leaders came together to articulate their various viewpoints on the impact of emotion on humans and humanity. Of course there were differences in approach and definitions, but this "conversation" uncovered more similarity of thought than difference, more shared understanding than disagreement (Goleman, 2003).

Whatever course of study one pursues, the argument that emotion has no place at work is fast losing credibility. Whether one leans toward research on neurophysiology, psychology, or management, or chooses to follow the teachings of the great philosophers, the message is clear. Emotions drive our behavior, both individually and collectively. Learning to work with emotions, rather than attempting to ignore them (impossible) or underestimate them (foolhardy), is now mandated by science and philosophy, as well as common sense.

Contagious Emotions: Resonance and Dissonance and the Emotional Reality of Groups

Practitioners of organizational development are working at the intersection of neuroscience, psychology, philosophy, and management. One particular point at this intersection holds great interest for us, and is important to the study of organizational development and change. This particular point is related to a current finding in all fields noted here: *emotions are contagious.* Colleagues have coined the phrase *limbic resonance* (Lewis, Amini, and Lannon, 2000), which basically means that feelings are transmitted through extremely subtle and sophisticated means, from one person to the next, one group to another. Our moods really do matter, and whether we intend to or not we share our feelings constantly with the people around us.

Recent research on emotional contagion and how emotions pass from one person to another, and between leaders and followers, has very interesting implications for the practice of organizational development (Goleman, Boyatzis, and McKee, 2002; Boyatzis and McKee, 2005). In our work, we take this study quite seriously, coining the words *resonance* and *dissonance* to describe the condition of groups and organizations when they fall into a positive, engaged, and optimistic state or a negative, cynical, destructive state, respectively.

A Shift in Emotional Reality

Depression, fragmentation, and lack of confidence characterized the mood of the top leadership group of one of the largest divisions of a global leader in sporting goods. These achievement-oriented individuals were not used to losing; they did not act like a team and felt beaten up and misunderstood by headquarters. Targets had been negotiated and adjusted, new marketing strategies attempted, innovative structures tried, all with limited impact in shifting the performance of the organization. As a result of poor performance and marketplace dynamics, multiple reorganizations resulted in many layoffs. The organization was in pain and hope was hard to find. The leaders had lost their way.

An intervention was planned to address the senior team's ambition, aspiration, and ability to get results. Coaching of individuals ensued, as did intensive "group self-awareness" sessions where important collective conversations were held. Over a period of six months, the group's emotional reality was explored in an environment that was both challenging and supportive. Both individual and group performance, emotion, and aspiration were explicitly addressed. Team members also explored the interaction of their feelings and behavior as individuals with the functioning of their collective as a group.

Nothing was off limits, and they explored powerful emotions such as guilt, blame, and embarrassment. They also looked at interpersonal conflicts; there were just a few, but they had paralyzed the group. Slowly, through frank dialogue, relationships were rebuilt, and hope and a sense of efficacy returned to the team.

Decisions are now made faster; information is shared proactively; and inspirational, resonant leadership is offered to the organization. The leadership team members have stopped blaming each other and learned how to support one another (and their functions). Because the relationships now feel more authentic, conflict can be more proactively addressed, and support genuinely offered and accepted.

This team was stuck in contagious and intractable dissonance. Individual leaders were negatively affected by each other and the climate, making positive team functioning impossible. The organization that surrounded the leadership team, both at headquarters and within the division, caught the group's mood and began to lose hope and perceive the group as dysfunctional and depressing.

Inherent Optimism

People and groups want to function at their best, and emotions can both help and inhibit doing so. By addressing performance, mood, and how moods and feelings affect behavior, this team was able to pull itself out of a dissonant cycle. They recaptured a feeling of hope and a workable plan of action that everyone was committed to, powered by dialogue and authentic relationships.

Addressing emotional reality allowed this team to:

- Reveal key areas of interdependency, independence, and dependence
- Develop a shared language of leadership, which comes to be a bond that keeps people focused
- Deepen and strengthen key relationships
- Renew or release positive energy and direct it toward change
- Develop new collective norms of behavior of adaptability, collaborative action, and goal attainment

Discovering the Emotional Reality of an Organization

Before attempting to change the emotional reality of an organization, an accurate diagnosis must be made. One of the most effective tools for discovering the emotional reality of an organization is to notice and use your own sensations and emotional responses. Edgar Schein (1987), Edwin Nevis (DiBella and Nevis, 1998), and Sonia Nevis (personal communication, 1998) articulated the importance of using one's "self" as an instrument of diagnosis; they demonstrate this core element of organizational development practice. The theory of limbic resonance states that your emotions mirror the emotions in the people and groups with whom you work. As you mindfully attend to your sensations, thoughts, and feelings, you pick up truths about the individual and collective emotional reality of the people and groups in the environment. Knowing and managing yourself well enables you to decipher what is yours, what is theirs, and what is idiosyncratic and located only within individuals. In a diagnostic mode, you can pick up information from your own experience about the organization's expression of emotions, how authority is taken up and received, and about the expression of power, inclusion and exclusion, dependence and independence.

The use of self as a diagnostic instrument is essential. But it is not enough and can be quite misleading and limiting. When seeking the emotional reality of a group, do not rely only on experience or on data from "people surveys" and the like. Organizational surveys and diagnostic instruments can offer a picture, but they are limited by the questions they ask. More important, they cannot plumb the depths of human emotion—which is essential. To truly discern the emotional reality of a complex system requires engaging in relationships with individuals within it and hearing from them what their subjective experience is. This can be done with an approach called *dynamic inquiry* (McKee and McMillen, 1992).

As discussed in *Primal Leadership* (Goleman, Boyatzis, and McKee, 2002), dynamic inquiry is a process born of action research, co-inquiry, and a humanistic approach to studying the underlying reality of a group or groups. It has been used in businesses as large as 250,000 employees and companies with barely twenty people, in not-for-profits, with boards, religious organizations, rural communities, and even countries. In all cases several basic principles are followed.

The Truth Is in the System

Assume that the individuals who live in the system *do* know the truth about it. They may, however, have lost (or never had) either the ability or the permission to discuss the underlying truths of the emotional reality and therefore may have some difficulty articulating it. It takes safe space and intimacy to move past this barrier. It is the organizational practitioner's job to create this kind of relationship—respectfully, humbly, and with openness, care, and compassion. These conversations must be approached seriously, with respect, compassion, and integrity. The dynamic inquiry conversations are framed to be inclusive of the positive and negative aspects of peoples' experience of the organization. People approach the task of expressing themselves from both ends of the emotional continuum, and this approach creates space for the totality of their experience. When people can actually speak their truth, they have the chance to say "Yes, that's us, and that's working for us" or "Yes, that's what it's like around here, and it is awful. We must change."

Authentic Dialogue Is the Key

Authentic *dialogue* is necessary to surface and explore individual's experiences, thoughts, perceptions, and feelings. However, no one person's description of the group's emotional reality can fully reveal the emotional profile of a group. It is the practitioner's job to ensure an honest accounting of the collective, rather than focusing on that which is most focal (for example, the loudest voice, the leader's voice, or issues that resonate with the practitioner's point of view). This means the practitioner must walk a fine line; authentic connection is a must, and real dialogue that includes the practitioner's own emotion is important. On the other hand, the practitioner can not dominate, guide, or collude with the experience of the other; this is about their experience, not yours.

Handle the Data with Extreme Care

The data collected through this type of interview must be treated with care. The interviewer enters into an *intimate* and very real conversation with each person. Confidentiality on the individual level must be adhered to, without any exceptions. Especially in a dissonant environment, the quickest, surest way to get bad data (superficial, partial, or just plain erroneous) is to sidestep confidentiality.

Conduct a Rigorous Analysis

Analyze the data rigorously. We hold ourselves to the highest academic standards: no lone individual analyzes data, and it is coded and double-checked by colleagues. In a relational, iterative process, themes that appear to emerge from the data are checked with organizational members for accuracy and meaningfulness, thus promoting another opportunity for deepening the dialogue.

Involve the Leader

Finally, the most senior leader and his or her team need to be actively involved in the process. Talking openly about emotions, strengths, and challenges is generally not the typical manner of discourse in an organization. Leadership support and articulated interest allow participants to speak their truth. Senior team members need to be *part of the inquiry process.* Given the effects of emotional contagion, it is important to understand the leaders' subjective experience of the organization since it is potentially a critical point of intervention. It is unacceptable to include the leaders in a perfunctory manner.

In summary, the dynamic inquiry process is intentionally designed to emotionally engage clients in an intimate conversation about their organization's emotional reality. The interviews explore both positive and negative emotions and the full range of human experience within organizational life. In a dynamic inquiry process the emotional reality is uncovered, while people have a positive and sometimes transformative experience. In fact, the experience of truly being listened to and empathized with is transformational for many people, giving them hope and inspiring commitment for organizational change. The organization members, OD practitioners, and the organization are all positively affected by this process of discovering the emotional reality of individuals and the system within which they work.

Doing Sacred Work

Exploring and influencing emotional states is sacred work, involving a holistic view and approach, and a grounded sense of self. It requires openness, compassion, and hopeful views of individuals and groups. Emotions are powerful, and to choose to work with them implies responsibility. To do this work responsibly, we prepare in a number of ways.

Invest in Self-Development

Do not attempt to teach emotional intelligence (or guide others in developing it) if you are deficient in it (or worse, have underdeveloped emotional intelligence and may not realize it). You can not teach self-awareness, self-management, and social awareness if you are not actively and consistently engaged in personal growth and development—a practice of lifelong learning. Do your own work first. If you choose to engage leaders and their organizations in this kind of personal, professional, and organizational development, then continuously develop *your* emotional intelligence. Seek to deepen your self-awareness, understanding how your emotions (and your experience) have an impact on your behavior. Cultivate self-management, including emotional self-control, managing your achievement drive, and acting consistently and optimistically. Work to deepen your capacity for empathy and self awareness. In the words of a friend and colleague, Lechesa Tsenoli of South Africa, you must "never, ever, confuse your beliefs for those of another person."

As an instrument of another's development, be authentically, wholly yourself, and yet manage the boundaries of the professional relationship. This calls for the practice of mindfulness: being awake, aware, and attentive to self and others and the environment (Boyatzis and McKee, 2005). Cultivate the capacity for generative thought and emotional renewal. Discovering and working with emotion is difficult and draining, as well as exhilarating and seductive. Try to be grounded, hopeful, open, nonjudgmental, and compassionate. Living this way takes practice, and possibly even *practices* such as meditation as part of ongoing personal growth. A final word: this kind of personal and professional development cannot be done in a vacuum or simply by reading and reflecting. Have contact with people, get feedback, and seek opportunities to explore some of the underlying issues that help, or hinder, your capacity for emotional intelligence.

Immerse Yourself in the Research

The link between EI and leadership does make sense—common sense. But for many people in organizations, long-standing habits of attempting to decouple emotions from work life are powerful. It is simply not enough to use the phrase *emotional intelligence* and assume that (1) people will understand what you mean or (2) they will pay attention to what you have to say. Read the literature. Do your own research. If you use tools (for example, 360 degree feedback instruments such as the Emotional Competence Inventory), be absolutely sure they have been rigorously studied for reliability and validity. Use a research-based instrument such as the Emotional Competence Inventory (Boyatzis and Goleman, 2002).

Remember that other than a starting point for a conversation, self-assessment of EI is an oxymoron for those people who need to develop it in the first place. Clients who lack self-awareness obviously cannot assess themselves, and they would likely stop a process of exploring emotional reality as soon as emotions are stirred up.

Work Courageously and Respectfully with Groups

The growing body of literature in psychology and neuroscience indicates the true power of emotion in groups. In fact, the research supports what we know about ourselves as human beings: we attune to others emotionally to ensure smooth social functioning, maximize predictability, or protect ourselves. But the process of limbic resonance is subtle and almost invisible. Most people have not been trained to read emotions consciously. In many organizations, people have been actively encouraged to ignore both individual and collective emotions. So if you intend to raise emotion to the level of consciousness in individuals or groups, you must have an understanding of neuroscience and psychology. Then (and as important) you need to be able to talk about it in plain language. Speak knowledgeably and simply. Drop the jargon. It is the curse of many fields, including organizational development.

Conclusion

In short, to work effectively with individual leaders on issues related to their emotional intelligence, develop yourself, and be humbly involved in a practice of self-discovery over the course of your life. Be your own expert; do the research, study the academic world, and know current best practices. This enables you to build a solid, research-based, and business-relevant argument for engaging leaders in developing their own, and others', emotional intelligence.

Advancing the strategic initiatives of the organization is as important as individual growth, and the motivation for change of both entities—the individual and the system—originates from, and is inspired by, the other. In its highest form, intentionally and lovingly working with emotions can result in a state where the individual's interests and the collective's interests are experienced as synergistic and reinforcing. This is a state of collective emotional intelligence and can yield transformational insights and actions that could not be imagined by individuals working alone, or together with intellect alone. Emotional resonance in groups facilitates the emergence of a group mind and heart that sometimes is able to vibrate and "think" in extraordinary ways and inspire change in aspiration and behavior.

Emotions are a source of energy at both the individual and collective levels. Our emotional states can be a source of inspiration and forward-moving energy, or they can constrict or drain our energy and hope. Manifestation of negative emotions and habits can be particularly destructive to group and organizational functioning. Cynicism, pessimism, fear, anxiety, false busy-ness, and arrogance are a few key emotional states that create dissonance and have a significantly negative impact on performance.

On the other hand, compassion, hope, flexibility, contentment, and happiness are emotions that create resonance within the self and in groups and organizations and positively influence performance. Groups and organizations characterized by resonance have greater capacity to be more creative, innovative, and generous of spirit toward people.

Leaders and leadership teams are exceptionally influential mood setters. Helping leaders and leadership teams live more in the positive register of emotions—hope, optimism, happiness, benevolence—is exceedingly important work, leading to better business outcomes. Supporting the development and discernment of emotions on the part of leaders can be a potent way to support effective change in an organization.

This chapter attempts to introduce the powerful research that supports the validity and opportunity presented by explicitly, unapologetically, and ethically addressing emotions in organization development. Emotions have impact, negative and positive, and OD practitioners can use them to help create more inspiring and effective environments. As change agents, we need to discern emotional states in a disciplined way, and this chapter has offered two means of doing so. There is an emerging interest in addressing the impact, and opportunity, that emotions hold for organizational development. Finally, we have presented a few principles to live by when working with emotions in organization development, including implications for OD practitioners. We hope that you will be inspired to open your heart and mind to an approach to working with change in organizations that is holistic and authentic, and that nourishes both the client system and the OD practitioner.

References

Ashkanasy, N., & Tse, B. (2000). Transformational leadership as management of emotion: A conceptual review. In N. Ashkanasy, C. Hartel, & W. Zerbe (Eds.), *Emotions in the workplace: Research, theory and practice* (pp. 221–235). Westport, CT: Quorum Books.

Bartel, C., & Saavedra, R. (2000). The collective construction of work group moods. *Administrative Science Quarterly, 45,* 187–231.

Boyatzis, R., & Goleman, D. (2002). *The Emotional Competence Inventory* (Hay Group, www.eisglobal.com).

Boyatzis, R., & McKee, A. (2005) Resonant leadership. Cambridge, MA: Harvard Business School Press.

Boyatzis, R., McKee, A., & Goleman, D. (2002, April). Reawakening your passion for work. *Harvard Business Review,* 86–94.

Brown, I. (1992). *The spiritual legacy of the American Indian.* New York: Crossroad.

Cherniss, C. (2001). Emotional intelligence and organizational effectiveness. In C. Cherniss & D. Goleman (Eds.), *Emotionally intelligent workplace: How to select for, measure and improve emotional intelligence in individuals, groups and organizations.* San Francisco: Jossey-Bass.

Davidson, R. (2004). Well-being and affective style: Neural substrates and biobehavioral correlates. *Philosophical Transactions of the Royal Society: Biological Sciences, 359,* 1395–1411.

Davidson, R. J., & Irwin, W. (1999). Functional neuroanatomy of emotion and affective style. *Trends in Cognitive Science, 3,* 11–21.

DiBella, A., & Nevis, E. (1998). *How organizations learn.* San Francisco: Jossey-Bass.

Forgas, J. (2003). Affective influences on attitudes and judgments. In R. Davidson, K. Sherer, & H. Goldsmith (Eds.), *Handbook of Affective Sciences.* Oxford: Oxford University Press.

George, J. (1995). Leader positive mood and group performance: The case of customer service. *Journal of Applied Psychology, 25*(9), 778–794.

Goleman, D. (1995). *Emotional intelligence.* New York: Bantam.

Goleman, D. (1998). *Working with emotional intelligence.* New York: Bantam.

Goleman, D. (2003). *Destructive emotions: A scientific dialogue with the Dalai Lama.* New York: Bantam.

Goleman, D., Boyatzis, R., & McKee, A. (2001, December). Primal leadership: The hidden driver of great performance. *Harvard Business Review,* 44–51.

Goleman, D., Boyatzis, R., & McKee, A. (2002). *Primal leadership: Realizing the power of emotional intelligence.* Cambridge, MA: Harvard Business School Press.

Isen, A. (2002). A role for neuropsychology in understanding the facilitating influence of positive affect on social behavior and cognitive processes. In C. Snyder & S. Lopez (Eds.), *The handbook of positive emotion.* Oxford: Oxford University Press.

Kelner, S. P., Rivers, C. A., & O'Connell, K. H. (1996). *Managerial style as a behavioral predictor of organizational climate.* Boston: McBer.

Lewis, T. (1990). *The medicine men: Oglala Sioux ceremony and healing.* Lincoln: University of Nebraska Press.

Lewis, T., Amini, F., & Lannon, R. (2000). *A general theory of love.* New York: Random House.

Markus, H., & Kitayama, S. (1991). Culture and the self: Implications for cognition, emotion, and motivation. *Psychological Review, 98,* 224–253.

McKee, A., & McMillen, C. (1992). Discovering social issues: Organizational development in a multicultural community. *Journal of Applied Behavioral Sciences, 28,* 445–460.

Niehardt, J. (2000). *Black Elk speaks.* Lincoln: University of Nebraska Press. (Originally published 1932)

Salovey, P., Mayer, J. D., & Caruso, D. (2002). The positive psychology of emotional intelligence. In C. R. Snyder and S. J. Lopez (Eds.), *The handbook of positive psychology* (pp. 159–171). New York: Oxford University Press.

Schein, E. (1987). *Process consultation: Its role in organization development* (2nd ed.). New York: Wiley.

Seligman, M. (2002). *Authentic happiness: Using the new positive psychology to realize your potential for lasting fulfillment.* New York: Free Press.

Senn, L., & Childress, J. (1999). *The secret of a winning culture: Building high performance teams.* New York: Senn-Delaney.

Sidle, C. (in press). *Five archetypes of leadership.* New York: Palgrave Macmillan.

Spencer, L. (2001, April). *Improvement in service climate drives increase in revenue.* Paper presented at meeting of Consortium for Research on Emotional Intelligence in Organizations, Cambridge, MA.

Wheelan, S., & Johnston, F. (1996). The role of informal leaders in a system containing formal leaders. *Small Group Research, 27,* 33–55.

Wilber, K. (2000). *A theory of everything.* Boston: Shambhala.

Wolff, S., Pescosolido, A., & Druskat, V. (2002). Emotional intelligence as the basis of leadership emergence in self-managing teams. *Leadership Quarterly, 13,* 505–522.

CHAPTER TWENTY-FOUR

WORKING WITH ENERGY
IN ORGANIZATIONS

Juliann Spoth

Energy . . . the word is omnipresent in popular organization development (OD) literature. Frequent references are made to generating, depleting, sustaining, or renewing energy (Ackerman-Anderson and Anderson, 2001; Goleman, Boyatzis, and McKee, 2002; Olson and Eoyang, 2001). Although the frequency of references in the OD literature underscores the importance of energy in organizational life, there is little guidance for practitioners on using this information. This chapter attempts to fill that gap by offering a model, principles, and interventions to help the practitioner be more intentional when working with energy.

This application to organizational life lies at the edge of discovery. Some scientific information and research is available, but it is incomplete; therefore some of the information here is extrapolated from related research and experience. Translating this information, which is often abstract and esoteric, into concrete, practical terms is both exciting and daunting. The chapter begins by reviewing basic knowledge about energy, continues with a review of an energy cycle and how to use it to guide interventions, and finally examines the implications of the practitioner as an energetic being.

An Energy Primer

Everything literally pulsates with energy. It is the vital force that enables every complex system—whether at the level of the individual, subgroup, group, orga-

424

nization, community, or even beyond—to do its work and fulfill its purpose. In the case of living beings, this energy is defined as the potential force for action.

This force takes many forms. In human systems, it can be physical, mental, emotional, psychological, or social. Within these forms, energy manifests as gross or subtle energy. Gross energy, the most easily perceived and experienced, is the energy embodied in and acted out through physical behavior. Subtle energy, which is created by molecular, cellular, tissue, and system oscillations; thoughts; feelings; and a separate energy system, also contributes to the bioenergetic field that surrounds an individual. Even though it is easy to associate energy with biological processes, subtle energy is also created by feelings and thoughts as they alter biological reactions and emit vibrations of their own; for example, thoughts create a "T-field" (see Wilber, 2003).

Individuals also have a subtle energetic system that is separate from the biological body. Although not yet widely accepted in the Western world, it has been a vital part of Eastern belief and medicine for at least four thousand years (Judith, 1987). It consists of seven major energy plexuses, called *chakras,* distributed along the spinal axis, and thousands of additional minor ones distributed throughout the body. Each has specific characteristics and qualities that have been well described by many authors (Judith, 1987; Bruyere, 1991; Johari, 2000).

These chakras organize a form of subtle energy that is then distributed though various channels in the body, which generally correlate with the meridians used in acupuncture. Like acupuncture meridians, these channels do not replicate the physical layout of the nervous system in the body but nonetheless have an impact on every function in the body.

Energy Fields

The sources of subtle energy in an individual generate vibrations that are propagated outward and create a surrounding energy field. This field is dynamic, having its own properties of intensity, density, color, rhythms and fluctuations, and others, on the basis of the unique characteristics of the person and the environment (Oschman, 1997b). Because the characteristics of sources vary, each person has a unique field and hence a unique energetic signature. This field is normally interactive, exerting a force upon everything in its proximal environment much as a magnet organizes all filings within its field.

Researchers report that the alterations or perturbations in these fields are more accurate in identifying what is going on in the body than pulsations detected by an electrocardiogram (EKG) or electroencephalogram (EEG), which detect the heart and brain's electric signals (Oschman, 1997a). These disturbances reflect changes or problems in the source from which they emanate. Research also suggests that disturbances detected in the energy field precede physical changes in the body (Oschman, 1997a). It seems to follow that detecting changes in a field coupled with prompt intervention could prevent the occurrence or decrease the intensity of problems when they do occur. Unfortunately, most people are not able to perceive this subtle energy field unless technology such as a magnetometer (Oschman, 1997a) is used for detection. Research at University of California at Los Angeles (Hunt, Massey, Bruyere, and Hahn, 1977) has confirmed that some people, however, have the ability to accurately detect the presence of and changes in subtle energy.

Interacting Fields

Neither organizations nor groups have biophysical processes or energetic (chakra) systems per se; nonetheless, they have subtle fields. These fields are formed by a combination of the interaction of individual fields, including nonhuman biological fields such as animals and plants, and even fields from inanimate objects (Oschman, 1997c). For instance, lighting and equipment such as computers create fields from their atomic pulsations, electrical components, and other radiant materials. Decorations, colors, and physical materials also emit vibrations. All these various emanations and attenuations create a large pulsating field that can alter individuals' fields. Biological systems, in fact, are very responsive to external energy fields and changes within them (Bialek, 1987, as cited in Oschman, 1997a). Even weak electromagnetic fields equivalent to a light bulb ten feet away can change the firing rate of human brain cells (Becker and Selden, 1985).

The totality of these interacting human and inanimate fields creates an energetic signature unique to a group or organization. An energetic signature can become imprinted in a physical space and remain even after people depart, just as radioactive materials leave invisible residue on objects that were in their field. The interaction of these imprinted energy signatures with individual fields is one reason some people can walk into an empty room and immediately have a discernible reaction such as anxiety or peacefulness. Also, this is the reason it behooves the practitioner to attend to the feel and arrangement of the physical space used for a gathering.

Characteristics of Interacting Energy Fields. No one would contest that others' moods, appearance, actions, and words affect us, yet even when two people are confronted by the same individual the degree to which they are affected may differ markedly. This is commonly explained by variances in past experience, perception, and meaning making, but another possibility is that these differences are also a function of the variance in field transference between and among people.

People react to one another's subtle energy field, but variably in the extent to which their field oscillation actually resonates or entrains another's.

Resonance results from a sympathetic vibration between fields. The profound effect of empathy may, in part, be explained by an individual's changing his or her vibrations to literally join the vibration of another's field; we say they have "connected."

Entrainment, on the other hand, occurs when the rhythms of one field are captured by the rhythms of another field. When, for example, brainwaves are not entrained by the thalamus and run free, they can be captured by external forces such as another person's biological rhythms or geomagnetic oscillations (Oschman, 1997b). This and other findings from research at UCLA suggest that humans have times when they are more "programmable" by others' energy fields (Bruyere, 1991). Conditions such as stress, trauma, meditation, and illness can trigger this programmable state.

On the other hand, when people's vibrations differ, this creates conflicting wave patterns. This field energy is relatively chaotic, and the people may experience negative reactions such as disorientation or irritation.

Implications of Interacting Fields in Organizational Development. The larger the field, the more it tends to entrain a smaller field, especially if it is coherent or vibrates in a unified manner and the two fields have similar oscillations. Thus a group's field is more likely to influence an individual's field than the other way around; likewise, an organization field usually has more impact on a group than vice versa. An example of this large coherent field is the strong organizational culture typically seen in not-for-profit organizations that are ideological and altruistically driven. The commitment of their employees is often disproportionate to their material rewards, but they stay because they literally "resonate" with the organizational field as it offers a profound connection they would have difficulty getting elsewhere.

Some individuals, however, can change a group field through resonance. For example, a charismatic leader typically has a larger, coherent field that can strike a sympathetic resonance in others' fields. Once a critical number of fields start resonating, then an energetic tipping point is reached in the group's field.

The emotional contagion that can occur in groups is yet another example of resonance and entrainment. A powerful example of this occurred in a group of black South Africans during the Apartheid period. In this case, a member started crying as she recounted her violent and painful experience. Within minutes, all thirteen group members were sobbing or moaning, and one fainted. The suddenness and depth of the contagion was startling. Each individual field, however, was easily entrained because it already contained a similar resonance based on his or her own painful experiences. The group field cohered rapidly, amplifying and precipitating similar emotions. On a smaller scale, emotional contagion also explains why a person who radiates calmness can have an apparent effect on others without saying a word.

These phenomena are important because a skilled practitioner can use field transference to understand and shape a group. Thinking of oneself as a tuning fork and attending to what is being evoked in one's body or field may give some information about what is happening within the group or organization. In addition, a practitioner can tune others' fields by changing the resonance in her own field. Research demonstrates that biofields can be attuned using the heart's electromagnetic field, which is the largest and "most powerful generator of rhythmic information patterns in the body" (McCraty, Atkinson, and Tomasino, 2001). Focusing on specific feelings, such as compassion, gratitude, or appreciation, causes the rhythms of the heart, brain, and nervous system to oscillate similarly. This creates a physiological coherence that, besides improving individual well-being, creates a field effect able to cause other nearby fields to resonate with it. Additional research found that even in cases where people were separated by at least five feet from a very weak coherent signal, such entrainment was possible and caused a significant effect on another's biological system (McCraty, 2003b).

Besides applying the principles of interacting fields in organizational work, a practitioner can intentionally build and release energy at a gross or subtle level. Before describing these interventions, an overview of energy dynamics is needed.

The Cycle of Energy

Every field pulsates with its own rhythm of contraction and expansion. In a healthy state, this cyclical pattern creates a fluid, continuous flow of energy between the polarities of building or restoring energy and releasing or using it. Familiarity with this cycle can enable a practitioner to track in which mode or phase the energy of an individual, group, or organization is and identify specific interventions that may be needed. This cycle can be applied to either gross or subtle energy. Interventions that work on the gross energy level can have the secondary impact of changing or repatterning a field. An aid for diagnosing and intervening in this energy cycle is the infinity loop, shown in Figure 24.1. Energy does not actually flow in an infinity loop but moves in waveforms; nonetheless, it is a useful illustration of the components and principles of working with energy and possible intervention points.

FIGURE 24.1. THE ENERGY CYCLE.

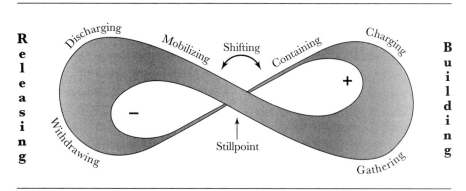

This infinity loop embraces four important energy principles. The first is that energy flows through an endless cycle of transformation, where it is neither created nor destroyed but merely gathered and released into other forms. The second principle is that energy flows within a dynamic open system where it is continuously affected by the nature and type of energetic environment surrounding it. The third principle is that some balance between expenditure and renewal of energy needs to be maintained; otherwise energy in the cycle cannot be sustained. The final principle is that regardless of the overt behavior and focus of any individual, group, or organization, there is a covert, underlying energy cycle affecting that manifestation.

Understanding the cycle dynamics and what may go wrong offers the practitioner more specific options for intervening. To facilitate this understanding, the cycle is explored in more detail.

Modes and Phases of the Cycle

In the cycle of Figure 24.1, the two polarities of building and releasing energy represent active (kinetic) energy states. On the right side, the positive pole, energy is built, whereas on the left side, the negative pole of the cycle, energy is released. Energy typically flows from the positive pole to the negative.

Energy builds by containing, charging, and gathering. It is contained by creating an energetic net, or boundaries, wherein the energy can be held much as a cup holds water. During charging, a positive energetic attractor is identified or created, which then attracts additional energy to it. Energy continues to gather until the capacity of the person or entity is reached or prematurely ends. In either case the cycle then shifts into the destructuring of the release mode, where energy is mobilized, discharged, and withdrawn. If the shift does not occur, the energy recycles again through the building mode, possibly resulting in an overenergized system. Once the release mode begins, the discharge needs to be sustained long enough for the energy to be converted into a usable or meaningful physical, mental, psychological, emotional, social, or spiritual form. If a form emerges, this mode is literally transformational. The discharge ends when the energy is sufficiently expended or prematurely stopped.

In either case, whatever energy is still available is used to assist for the purpose of withdrawing. During withdrawal, energy is used to clear, let go of the form, and create space (L. Gutierrez, personal communication, Jan. 20, 2004), so that there can be a shift into the restructuring of energy that occurs in the building mode. If there is no restructuring shift, the cycle may remain in the release mode and the entity may become underenergized.

As energy goes through destructuring and restructuring shifts, it may pass through or linger in a state of potential energy, or a stillpoint (Figure 24.1). This is a neutral place; as with zero point energy in quantum physics (McTaggart, 2002), all possibilities exist here. It is the great velvet void, a place of rest, of no effort, of no mind, of no knowing. Though there may be a pause at any point in the energy cycle as a result of dysfunction, or a need to rest, this is not the same as the stillpoint. The stillpoint offers a more profound experience, which has been described as "being at the Source." In this place the seeds of both energy generation and release are present in equal measure, and from this place energy can move in either direction.

Energy can flow through this cycle in myriad ways. It can move quickly, slowly, steadily, or erratically. The shifts from one mode to another may be dramatic or gradual, or the energy may not shift at all but be recycled through the same mode. It also can pause at any point or linger at the stillpoint for awhile. Any of these or additional patterns can be adaptive to what is required at the time—but they also can be dysfunctional, if the pattern interferes with the person's or system's health, needs, or ability to perform.

Using the Cycle to Guide Interventions

This cycle can be used to guide the intervener through an assessment and selection of interventions. If the system is in a state of health, the interventions selected support what is occurring naturally or a part of the cycle that is under the most strain. Dysfunction, however, requires that the practitioner understand where the cycle is off and why and then target the source of the problem. The first consideration in this assessment is whether the amount of energy available is enough to fuel the current needs.

An Over- or Underenergized System.

When considering the amount of energy available, the two most extreme possibilities are either too much or too little energy. Between these two polarities is a continuum of other possibilities, including the right match.

One frequent assessment mistake practitioners make is not differentiating between internalized energy and low energy. Energy is temporarily internalized, for instance, when people are processing information or an experience. This does not require any intervention other than waiting until the processing is completed and inviting a report out.

From an energetic viewpoint, the capacity of the individual, group, or organization to generate the energy needed to get the desired outcomes should be assessed. No intervention should require more energy than what can be replenished, as people and systems do not easily recover from energy debts. Thus, when energy is low the type and timing of interventions may be more critical. For example, although an individual or group may need to process a traumatic experience, the catharsis has to be monitored and possibly contained because of the extreme depletion of energy that can result.

A dilemma is that if there is a mismatch, the presenting symptoms do not necessarily indicate the source of the problem in the cycle. When there is not enough energy for work, for instance, there can be a dysfunction in any of the phases within releasing, building, or shift modes. Identifying the source is important, as the intervention(s) may differ considerably depending on where the problem is in the cycle.

Specific Interventions.

Examples of specific interventions that can alter each phase of the energy cycle are in Table 24.1. Some of the interventions mentioned, such as movement, ceremony, and appreciation, can affect either the releasing or the building mode, depending on how they are designed. The intention, timing, and pace of the intervention are not addressed here, but these factors do have an impact on the energetic effectiveness. The rationale for several of these interventions is explained next.

Building Interventions.

Before the energy field can be built, the cycle may have to be shifted from the release mode or stillpoint. Energy can be shifted by offering reflections, reframing, holding space, appreciating the "what was" and the "what is," voicing what is coming, and helping people express their resistance.

TABLE 24.1. EXAMPLES OF INTERVENTIONS.

Cycle Components		Examples of Interventions		
Building mode		Individual	Group	Organization
	Containing	• Personal vision, goals, plans, identifying needs and wants	• Charter, agenda, guidelines, project plans, identifying needs and wants	• Vision, strategy, strategic plans, budgets
	Charging	• Ceremony or ritual • Quick vigorous movement • Laughter • Pressing select acupuncture points • Music • Dancing • Identifying desired future, interests, or passions • Celebrations • Short episodes of rapid abdominal breathing • Providing desired opportunities	• Ceremony or ritual • Fun or interesting icebreakers • Laughter • Rhythmic repetitive movement • Changing seating arrangements • Music • Acting on voiced needs or wants • Celebrations • Reframing	• Ritual, ceremony, symbols • Giving resources that are being asked for • Celebrations
	Gathering	• Ceremony • Anything that generates positive emotions or acts on areas of interest or passion • Rest • Yoga, Tai Chi exercises • Gratitude	• Ceremony and ritual • Identifying commitment in complaints (Kegan and Lahey, 2001) • Breaking into subgroups • Showing gratitude • Appreciative feedback • Increasing physical proximity • Breaks	• Appreciative inquiry • Large system interventions • Open Space technology • Future Search

Releasing mode			
Mobilizing	• Identifying and testing assumptions • Grading experiments • Empathy	• Testing assumptions • Testing and breaking norms • Grading experiments • Empathy	• Creating a "burning platform" or urgency • Pilots
Discharging	• Breathing • Expressive movement • Empathy • Drawing self • Problem solving • Slow deep breathing	• Ceremony, ritual • Storytelling • Team process checks • Focus groups • Drawings of the group • Wailing wall exercise	• Ceremony, ritual • Storytelling • Providing feedback or suggestion opportunities • Drawings of the organization • Conflict resolution activities between conflicting groups or departments
Withdrawing	• Giving opportunities to be alone, quiet, reflective • Breaks • Decreasing environmental stimuli	• Giving reflection time • Summaries • Closing units of work • Decreasing environmental stimuli	• Reviewing what has been learned • Celebrating completion of organizationwide or intergroup projects
Stillpoint	• Experiment with just "being" • Normalize not knowing, no effort • Practicing stillness of mind and body	• Group visualizations • Create times of no blame, no judgment • Normalize not knowing, no effort • Group meditation	

Once the shift begins, the intention is to contain the energy or energy field and prevent energy from dissipating. Establishing energetic boundaries or a focus is a way to limit dissipation of energy; creating a vision, guidelines, goals, and plans is how this is typically done. If boundaries are set too rigidly, however, they may actually overconstrain the field and prevent energy from gathering to the degree needed.

Another aspect of building energy is charging the field. One principle way a positive valence can be established is by framing something so as to attract interest—for instance, identifying a theme or figure, reframing, or providing analogies or provocative language. Martin Luther King illustrated this when he repeated the phrase "I have a dream" over and over, electrifying his audience.

Paradoxically, negative emotional states—for example, the hatred that fuels misogyny or racism—can have a positive valence for some people or groups who use them to feel superior, worthier, or justified in acting to promote self-interest. Unfortunately, fields made up largely of negative emotional states can entrain the fields of otherwise positive individuals, who may then be swept along by the power of the group field. A negative field can be transformed into a more positive one through interventions that promote a kind of energetic alchemy, as in using Kegan and Lahey's process (2001) for identifying the positive commitments embedded in complaints. Another intervention is to challenge norms that encourage negative behavior, such as telling jokes that target ethnic groups.

Gathering energy happens by keeping the focus on the energetic attractor long enough to generate or attract even more energy. Interventions that promote being fully present, and activities which hold the interest or are regenerative, facilitate this. Open Space technology and appreciative inquiry are methodologies that encourage the person to fully engage in a topic of interest. Creating or encouraging heartfelt positive emotional states such as sincere acknowledgment, appreciation, gratitude, and compassion create a resonate frequency that builds emotional and physical regeneration for oneself or among individuals (McCraty, 2003). Encouraging playfulness—for example, using humor, kinesthetic toys such as "Kush," or stress balls—can be regenerating and also help externalize energy. Other types of physical activity, whether they take the form of energizing exercises or working at a wall to create affinity groupings with Post-it notes, can also gather energy. They stimulate both physical energy and the chakra system. Movement is especially useful when people have been mentally engaged for a period of time.

Since entrainment and synchronization happen faster within a shorter distance and within a smaller field, energy also can be gathered by attending to the arrangement of a group. Breaking larger groups into dyads or subgroups, sitting in a circle, moving people closer together, and ensuring that they can see one another are all ways energy can be heightened. Having a space that is neither too large nor too small also supports building energy.

Given the interaction of inanimate and biological fields, the environment and its configuration also influence the gathering of energy. Providing harmonious sounds, natural lighting, plants, and select colors and decorations create vibrations in the room that are more supportive of building a field.

Rituals, ceremonies, and celebrations can be powerful energetic interventions as they combine many of the elements discussed so far; there is a common purpose, attention is given to the space and its arrangement, and everyone engages in common activities such as singing or dancing, which usually incorporate meaningful symbols. All these factors have a synergistic effect.

What is least efficient in building others' energy is for the practitioner to pump out more and more of his energy. The more difficult or toxic an individual or group field is, the more this is true. Even if a practitioner has a large field or can generate one, his field will deplete quickly if he is constantly feeding a person or group with his own energy. If he has the skill of pulling additional energy into or through his field, he may prevail, but a better strategy is engaging the individual or group in activities that accomplish the same end.

Releasing Interventions. Depending on the problem, releasing energy in the field may be the first intervention needed. The field may be filled with the wrong type of energy, or it may be overenergized. The intent of a releasing intervention is to initiate release of energy only as fast or slow as needed, without depleting the system. A release starts with a destructuring and mobilizing of energy, much as the bonds in atoms break in order to release the energy contained within a molecule. This shift may start naturally, just as the sensation of pressure in the bladder prompts a release (passive shift), or it may be triggered (activated shift).

Interventions such as reframing, provocation, and increasing awareness can activate energy. Encouraging breathing as someone enters an emotional state is a common technique used with individuals to facilitate further emotional release. Sympathetic touch and empathy can also help mobilize energy.

Once the release begins, interventions are aimed at shaping the type and pace of the discharge. For instance, if the release is in the form of impulsive behavior (an explosion of energy) interventions may focus on slowing down the group or individual by using cognitive or reflective techniques to support more considered action.

There are many interventions that can be used to discharge energy. Ceremony and ritual, legitimizing or normalizing what is happening, playing devil's advocate, naming the known but unexpressed "elephant" in the room, breaking confining taboos, identifying operating assumptions, and movement are ways of breaking the bonds preventing energy from being expressed. Drawings, music, and storytelling also have been used successfully in OD to release the energy suppressed by covert or unrealized organizational dynamics (Marshak and Katz, 1994).

Once this energy is activated, the discharge continues until a natural diminution or truncated process leads to withdrawal. In this phase, energy is used to pave the way for the next restructuring shift. The release slows as energy is cleared from the field and a space is created for shifting into a new cycle. Interventions in withdrawal assist the individual or group to let go of what was. This creates a space to assimilate what needs to be held onto and prepare to move on. In this phase, energy is not used solely for externalized expression but also for internalized reflection; therefore interventions that decrease the pace, create an opportunity for reflection, and encourage letting go of striving or effort are useful. Breaking field interactions, and reestablishing strong individual boundaries through closing activities or rituals, can also facilitate withdrawal.

Many useful interventions for building and releasing energy are less traditional than the more common cognitive interventions such as problem solving and planning. Practitioners may be uncomfortable at first in offering this type of intervention, but it can be a more powerful source of energy generation and release than a more cognitive intervention. These interventions may as a result be more immediately effective and lead to better cognitive functioning in the long run. Until some of these modalities become more acceptable in organizations, practitioners may face constraints on choice of intervention.

Interventions at the Stillpoint. The stillpoint may be thought of as an energetic state of being rather than doing. There is no form, only possibility. The experience of oneness with the universe and being totally free of any attachment to outcomes are examples of this state. Although we can recognize this state when we are in it, it is difficult to create and is often entered by accident rather than by intent. Interventions that can help induce, but not necessarily create, this state are refraining from judgment or blame, compassion, being receptive, staying open, inviting wonder, cultivating mental calm or stillness, and experiencing unconditional love or acceptance.

So far the interventions have focused on using the energy cycle. The most potent intervention of all, however, is how the practitioner uses self as an energetic being.

The Practitioner as an Energetic Being

It is well accepted in the OD field that knowledge about oneself and one's impact is critical to being successful. This is equally true in the energy arena. Working with energy requires a certain level of energetic health, as well as knowledge about and skill in dealing with energetic phenomena.

Energetic Health

Energy systems that are functioning optimally foster vitality. There is enough energy to propel one through life as well as a reserve, which can be called on when needed. For a practitioner, the greater the energetic health, the larger and more powerful the energy field; hence the more it can influence other fields. Unfortunately, almost everyone's energy system suffers from the onslaught of one or more types of abuse by personal habits such as not getting enough rest, exercise, or healthy food; social behaviors such as unhealthy relationships, violence, and the like; and environmental stresses such as noise, toxins, and other factors. In addition, OD practitioners usually deal with problematic situations; thus they are often in disrupted or toxic energy fields. All these factors can lead to loss, disruption, blockage, or accumulation of energy in a part of the body (Wright, 1991).

To recharge the energy system, one must invest in the physical, emotional, social, mental, spiritual, and psychological conditions or activities that are renewing; and, when possible, avoid people, events, or activities that needlessly deplete energy. For instance, there are many treatments (acupuncture and polarity therapy are examples) that directly deal with these systems by redirecting areas of accumulated energy, reestablishing flow, and directing energy to depleted areas. All of these efforts help repattern the field so that it regains its healthy state.

The Practitioner's Energy Profile: Knowledge and Skills

Each practitioner also has a unique energetic signature that is based on her biological and energy patterns. The knowledge of one's signature and how it typically manifests and is managed is critical to working with others. But knowledge is not enough, as the practitioner also needs to be able to intentionally alter his energy and field in different ways. This energetic self-knowledge and skills make up the practitioner's energy profile.

Self-Knowledge. The chakra system can be used as an assessment (metaphoric or literal) to give the practitioner another way of understanding his energy profile. Each chakra has a unique energetic characteristic that correlates with aspects of the self, such as the physical, emotional, intellectual, heart, creative, and spiritual realms. Insight can be gained by determining when and how each is used and manifested, and if there is any type being overused or underused. Correlating physical problems with the chakra regulating that part of the body is a way to trace energy sources that may be operating less than optimally.

Another aspect of the profile is how the practitioner depletes or revitalizes his energy. One factor to consider is the degree of introversion or extroversion.

Introverts prefer expending more energy on their inner world than on the outer world and regenerate through solitary activities. Extroverts, on the other hand, prefer expending their energy in transactions with the outer world and are renewed by doing so.

The energy cycle can also be used as a prompt for self-exploration by identifying strengths and limitations in the modes and phases of the cycle. Determining which interventions are favored can also indicate a bias toward a mode or select phase.

All this knowledge offers the practitioner insight on the energetic self, but the ability to use one's energy states and apply tools skillfully is equally important.

Skills. The ability to alter one's field is quite useful and necessary if one wants to have an energetic impact on another. This includes expanding or contracting it, gathering or releasing energy from it, and changing the type and frequency of vibrations within it. Changing the characteristics and boundaries of one's field requires less skill than one might think. Focusing on emitting the vibrations of particular chakras or modulating the breath illustrates how field characteristics can be changed. Influencing the fields of a group or organization is more difficult because these fields are usually larger and more complex than an individual's. It is axiomatic that the larger field always wins, so there is always the danger of a practitioner's field being entrained by a larger field. Of course, if the larger field is basically healthy, it may actually positively affect the practitioner's field. If it is unhealthy, it can deplete or otherwise negatively affect the field of the practitioner, who may become exhausted, confused, fragmented, or otherwise impaired.

Using a cofacilitator or even a team of facilitators may sometimes be advisable when fields are particularly toxic, even though the size of the group or project may not seem to warrant it. This also assumes that the facilitators can create a coherent field between or among themselves and have similar intentions; otherwise additional facilitators may disrupt the field even more.

Other skills include sensing and tracking energy and energetic fields (one's own and others'), identifying strengths and limitations in the energy cycle, designing interventions to accomplish energetic intention, and translating what is energetically known or needed into common language.

Conclusion

From the earliest times, OD has sought to understand the interconnectedness among people, systems, and the environment. This interconnectedness has been explored in many ways: through social networks, group dynamics, and systems thinking, to name a few. Energetic fields represent one more way in which humans share profound connections with one another, their environment, and even the universe. Increasing understanding of energetic forces and how to alter them gives the practitioner more options for shaping interventions. OD started as a field on the margins, offering new ways of thinking about and intervening in organizations. It is time to be nonnormative again and embrace the fascinating world of energy, understanding its impact on all levels of systems and how to effectively intervene. This chapter offers one possibility of what that understanding and intervention could look like.

References

Ackerman-Anderson, L., & Anderson, D. (2001). *The change leader's roadmap*. San Francisco: Jossey-Bass.

Becker, R., & Selden, G. (1985). *Body electric*. New York: Quill.

Bialeck, W. (1987). Physical limits to sensation and perception. *Annual Review of Biophysics and Biophysical Chemistry, 16,* 455–478.

Bruyere, R. (1991). *Wheels of light*. Sierra Madre, CA: Bon Productions.

Goleman, D., Boyatzis, R., & McKee, A. (2002). *Primal leadership*. Boston: Harvard Business School.

Hunt, V., Massey, W., Bruyere, R., & Hahn, P. (1977). *A study of structural integration from neuromuscular, energy field, and emotional approaches*. Los Angeles: Rolf Institute, UCLA.

Johari, H. (2000). *Chakras*. Rochester, VT: Destiny Books.

Judith, A. (1987). *Wheels of life*. St. Paul, MN: Llewellyn.

Kegan, R., & Lahey, L. (2001). *How the way we talk can change the way we work*. San Francisco: Jossey-Bass.

Marshak, R., & Katz, J. (1994). *The covert processes workshop*. San Diego: National Training Laboratories.

McCraty, R. (2003a). *The appreciative heart*. Boulder Creek, CA: Institute of HeartMath.

McCraty, R. (2003b). The energetic heart: Bioelectromagnetic interactions within and between people. Boulder Creek, CA: Institute of HeartMath.

McCraty, R., Atkinson, M., & Tomasino, D. (2001). *Science of the heart* (no. 01–001). Boulder Creek, CA: Institute of HeartMath.

McTaggart, L. (2002). *The field*. New York: HarperCollins.

Olson, E., & Eoyang, G. (2001). *Facilitating organizational change: Lessons from complexity science*. San Francisco: Jossey-Bass.

Oschman, J. (1997a, January). What is healing energy? Part 2: Measuring the fields of life. *Journal of Bodywork and Movement Therapies, 1,* 117–128.

Oschman, J. (1997b, April). What is healing energy? Part 3: Silent pulses. *Journal of Bodywork and Movement Therapies, 1,* 179–194.

Oschman, J. (1997c, July). What is healing energy? Part 4B: Vibrational medicine. *Journal of Bodywork and Movement Therapies, 1,* 239–250.

Wilber, K. (2003). *Toward a comprehensive theory of subtle energies*. Boston: Shambhala.

Wright, S. (1991). Validity of the human energy field assessment form. *Western Journal of Nursing Research, 13,* 635–647.

CHAPTER TWENTY-FIVE

APPRECIATIVE INQUIRY AS AN ORGANIZATION DEVELOPMENT AND DIVERSITY PROCESS

Cathy L. Royal

Appreciative Inquiry (AI) is a change process that begins with affirmation and creates opportunity for growth and change by identifying what is working in a system. Characteristics and themes from personal stories and appreciative interviews of individuals involved in this process are used to design total system dialogue and activities that guide the organization's path toward change and its future. Appreciative Inquiry seeks to discover the characteristics and actions that make successful organizations and vibrant, desirable communities. A basic assumption of AI is that organizations and individuals respond to success and affirmation.

AI holds that the first questions are fateful. Energy follows the inquiry; what is inquired about will be found. Language creates images that are powerful forces. These images stimulate and guide the actions and behaviors of individuals and organizations. The theory and process of AI affirms the power of story and individual experience in organizations. It is designed to focus on and facilitate creative conversations between people, and to identify and capture when people have been at their best and what they value about work and themselves. At its best, Appreciative Inquiry brings all voices into the inquiry conversation. It involves all levels of an organization (or any system), bringing its members together in real time and common space to imagine and design a desired future.

This chapter examines AI as an organization development (OD) change process and a diversity intervention. Emphasis is placed on what is needed to create an environment where the inquiry is organization-driven and the OD practitioner is the inquiry guide. The underlying assumptions of Appreciative Inquiry, the mechanics of the 4D model, the philosophy of AI, and how this philosophy is important to the work of the OD practitioner using it are described. The process of conducting an Appreciative Inquiry is explored, along with how the principles of AI speak to diversity, inclusion, equitable systems, and to work in international settings. The chapter includes information that the OD practitioner needs when using AI as an OD and diversity change process in systems, communities, and organizations.

Appreciative Inquiry Pillars

Appreciative Inquiry and its effectiveness as an OD change process is supported by four pillars: appreciation, application, provocative possibilities, and coconstruction.

Begin with Appreciation

Every system works to some degree, and a primary task of management and members in organizations is to discover, describe, and explain those exceptional moments that give life to the system and activate members' imagination and energy. The appreciative approach takes its inspiration from what is and builds toward *what is possible*. It is an inquiry into the organization's life-giving forces and collective history. The aims of the appreciative spirit are affirmation, discovery, and inspired understanding.

Application

Application is the development of new behaviors, policies, and attitudes that are rooted in the reality of the experiences and desires of employees in an organization. Application of new (or improved) action is possible because it is based in the ideas of employees at all levels. Affirmative and effective organizational study leads to generation of knowledge that can be used, applied, and validated in action.

Provocative Possibilities

An organization is an open-ended, indeterminate system capable of becoming more than it is at any moment, and capable of learning how to actively take part in guiding its own evolution. Appreciative knowledge of "what is" becomes provocative when the learning takes on a normative value for members. In this way, AI permits using systematic inquiry and analysis to help the organization's members shape an effective future according to their own imaginative and moral purposes. Possibilities generated for the future are provocative in the sense that they inspire the organization to creative action.

Coconstructed Inclusive Action

The fourth pillar assumes an inseparable relationship between the process of inquiry and its content. A multilateral approach to the study of social innovation is a direct result of AI inclusion and interaction. Coconstruction as a collaborative action is integral to every aspect of the Appreciative Inquiry process: collaboration between the OD practitioner and the organization, collaboration among participants in the AI process, and collaboration throughout the organization all occur through coconstructing each phase and decision in AI. This pillar creates an atmosphere where every voice counts and every voice is heard.

Setting the Stage for Appreciative Inquiry

The nature of AI emphasizes a participatory action research process that involves the whole organization in learning through coconstructed affirmative inquiry and research. The OD practitioner role is central to helping the organization carry out the AI principles in selecting a design and planning team; creating a collaborative, diagonal slice of the organization for participation in the AI effort; and identifying the inquiry topic. Organization leaders put the word out early about an appreciative process and then engage in a dialogue with the community about what it means to be committed to an AI change initiative. The intentional act of open communication at every phase of Appreciative Inquiry integrates every voice into the design and implementation of the AI process.

AI Design and Planning Team

AI involves participatory action research, which begins with the initial step of creating the AI design and planning team. The OD practitioner is centrally positioned to ask the organization or community to design a team that reflects equal voice and equal commitment and represents all divisions of the organization. This intentional design of the planning team also begins the shift in access for many organization members who are excluded from decisions about the life of the organization.

In a very real sense, AI is an organization intervention that supports inclusion, equity, and diversity. Selection of the AI planning team is a first step in using

AI as a diversity intervention, and it is quite necessary and valuable when working in any culture where caste and class hierarchies are present. In large systems, it is possible to have representation of all voices and all parts of the system by developing a design and planning team that is representative of gender, race, age, ability, sexual orientation, and other key factors of human diversity. Organizational diversity in terms of status and level in the institution is also reflected by representation on the diagonal slice. All stakeholders have equal access to the information necessary to participate in the inquiry.

Choice of the AI Topic

In selecting a topic or focus of inquiry, the organization uses a process that includes all voices and perspectives. For example, organization leaders might begin the AI process with the conclusion that team building will be its focus. After an opportunity to talk with the AI design and planning team and through them the organization members with whom they are in contact, organization leaders might discover, for example, that the AI focus will be most significant if the topic choice is trust or flexibility. In this case, the practitioner helps the organization craft an AI protocol to discover what the organization knows about trust or flexibility in teams.

Environmental Scanning

In environmental scanning, the OD practitioner joins the client in identifying factors present in the organizational environment that need to be considered as the AI begins, for example, employee, stakeholder, and vendor profiles; work climate; geography; community population; and so on. The environmental scanning process is critical in ensuring that the AI is collaborative and participatory. It affects the composition of the design and planning team, the choice of AI topic, and whose voices and perspectives are included in the outcomes of the AI process. The fuller the scanning process, the higher the probability that the topic chosen for the AI change process will truly reflect the perspectives of organization members.

The OD practitioner supports the organization with an environmental scanning process that guarantees full participation, flat (equal) status, and diagonal representation. This scanning process includes the voices of women; people of color; gay, lesbian, and bisexual people; and people with disabilities. The AI environment scan also addresses inclusion of all levels of the organization flowchart. Stakeholders from the executive suite to the custodial staff all have a unique perspective and value to add to creating the shared future. In community interventions, this diagonal fosters inclusion by religion, class, economic status, and age. In international settings, it is important to bring multicultural members and historical adversaries to the dialogue with equal voice. Each setting broadens the scan of human dimensions for equal voice and inclusion.

Phases of the Appreciative Inquiry Process

The Appreciative Inquiry process has four phases, as described in the Four-D Appreciative Inquiry Model (Mann and Cooperrider, 1993). The four phases are *discover, dream, design, and deliver* (Figure 25.1). They can be conducted over a period of time, beginning with individual interviews in the discover phase; and in small-group, large-group, and organizationwide meetings in subsequent phases. Or all the phases can be carried out in a conference of the diagonal slice of the organization, or an organizationwide conference. The AI process can also be implemented in parts of a system; for example, a division or a department of an organization can conduct the AI process with an intact team or group. In this chapter, the AI process is described in terms of a conference of a diagonal slice of the organization or an organizationwide conference, referred to as "the great gathering" and "the organizational grand dialogue."

FIGURE 25.1. FOUR-D APPRECIATIVE INQUIRY MODEL.

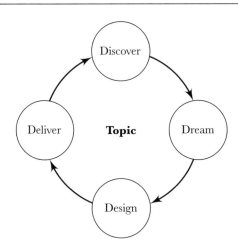

Source: Mann and Cooperrider (1993).

The Discover Phase of the AI Process

The Appreciative Inquiry process begins with the discover phase. The purpose of this phase is to identify, appreciate, and value the best of "what is" about the organization—that is, to inquire into the life-giving properties of the organization. The first step in the AI discovery phase is appreciative interviews. The interview process is an inquiry into the AI topic through sharing of personal stories and focused dialogue. Themes and data points from one-on-one conversations, small group interviews, or organizationwide meetings are summarized and reviewed. Themes of success and inspiration are shared to become the inspirational sparks used to move the organization to the dream phase. If the AI process is a large conference, interviews are conducted in the great gathering, which is also the beginning of the organizational grand dialogue. The OD practitioner helps to create an environment where people engage with each other on the spot with spontaneity. The session design ensures adequate time for reflection and opportunity for people to gather and organize their thoughts and tell their stories.

Interviews follow an "interview protocol" template, in which questions have a set sequence. See Exhibit 25.1 for a sample set of AI interview questions. Additional examples of AI interview questions and interview protocols are listed in Royal and Hammond (1998). Interviews begin with questions about the person and then move to the organization, to a peak experience focused on the topic, and finally questions about the gifts or wishes that the person has for the organization.

EXHIBIT 25.1. EXAMPLE OF AN AI INTERVIEW PROTOCOL.

1. What do you value about yourself, and the nature of your work? What makes this work exciting for you?

2. Looking at your entire experience in your organization, and without being humble, recall a time when you felt most alive, most excited, or most fulfilled about your involvement in the organization.

   - What made it a peak experience?

   - Who are some significant others? Why were they significant?

   - What was it about you that made it a peak experience?

   - What were the most important situational or organizational factors helping to make it an important experience? (For example, type of work, leadership, structure, climate, relationship, rewards, and so on)

3. As you think about your organization (or about the AI topic), what are the life-giving forces of the organization?

4. If you could develop or transform your organization, what three wishes or gifts would you give or grant to heighten its vitality and health?

(Continued)

EXHIBIT 25.1. EXAMPLE OF AN AI INTERVIEW PROTOCOL, Cont'd.

Comments for the Interview

AI interviews are conducted in the affirmative. Encourage the speaker to talk about what is good and exciting for her or him. The conversation is open-ended and can flow without structured intervention from the listener. Remember: it is done in the narrative to create a space for sharing and affirmative memories about inspirational and successful times in the organization. The focus is on the storyteller; the listener is acting as guide, asking questions only to stimulate the speaker.

AI seeks to discover what is in the speaker's thoughts and feelings about the topic when it is at its best. If the speaker is unable to find such times, ask her or him to talk about a time in another organization or another period of time in the same organization. Another way to tap the positive is to encourage the speaker to talk about "what it would be like *if* you were excited and inspired by work or the topic of inquiry."

The protocol includes questions about what members of the organization value about themselves, the nature of their work, the mission of the organization, and two or three key things that give life to the organization. The final question is one that identifies what each person wishes to see in the preferred future. What would people give the organization if they had "the gift to give or the wish to grant" for vitality and health in that system?

Interviews are held at the beginning of the conference between two people who have limited day-to-day contact with each other in the diagonal relationships of the organization. Conducting the interviews between two people is intentional. It can represent a philosophical shift in an organization's values about individual pride and attribution. Sharing in pairs about one's part in creating a positive experience in the organization moves individuals and the organization toward a norm of disclosure about success and about creating positive, life-giving experiences. Sharing one's personal story and revealing things about which one has passion and pride helps to create a connection with another person in the organization beyond relationships founded in job descriptions and titles.

Each person shares his or her story, while the other person listens. This is an opportunity to create community and organization intimacy. The appreciative interview is a shared personal experience, a time when one person is singularly focused in sharing and valuing experience and the other person is listening with intention. The protocol does not ask people to retell someone else's story. The sharing of stories is personal. The story is confidential. The themes, characteristics, and actions become data for the grand dialogue. Discovering what people value is phase one of the four-D model.

The Dream Phase of the AI Process

In the dream phase of the AI process, the grand organizational dialogue becomes the innovative process that lifts themes and actions from the interviews and shared stories. The dream phase invites creative reflection and stimulates ideas for co-constructed action. Each person has an opportunity to dream publicly about what should be present for the preferred future. Every person can engage, and all are asked to listen for common ground while honoring past experiences.

Shared stories of actions (remembered as positive, successful, and worth repeating) support change for a healthy and affirming workplace. This generates hope and promotes healing. The dream phase is rooted in reality as people report their experiences. The process is flexible, people-driven, and designed to facilitate connections in the moment and in the environment.

The OD practitioner guides the process and "suggests the gift of patience" for the work in this stage (Royal, 1997). Each person deserves to be heard, and working for consensus requires a flexible environment. Introducing the language of flexibility and patience is part of the OD practitioner's role as a model for the AI change philosophy. The AI dream process is conducted as a whole system intervention, engaging everyone in the process. The people assembled in the room cocreate the change they prefer to see.

The purpose of the dream phase is to vision the ideal for "what might be" by creating provocative possibility propositions developed from the interview themes and best stories or quotes about the AI topic. They are propositions that move the organization to action—for example, a statement that describes "teams that maximize trust throughout this organization."

Provocative possibility statements emerge from the grand dialogue. Organization members write five to seven statements about the key themes that emerge as being vital for their future. The role of the OD practitioner is to keep the discussion focused on the topic choice for the inquiry and ask questions that guide the focus. Do the themes speak to the topic choice? When "it" (the topic) is at its best, what key factors are present? Have all voices been heard? Has everyone spoken? A key methodology tip here is to remember the gift of patience and flexibility. It is often in this phase that AI participants want to rush to completion and close the dialogue too quickly.

Many things will emerge in the dream phase. All the emerging possibilities are available for the design phase, which follows the dream phase. What the participants are asked to do is keep focused on the possibilities that create the best future for the current topic. All dream topics stay in the organizational memory and in the documents of the AI. These topics are available for future inquiries, or as possibilities that support or affirm items in the design phase.

The dream phase allows sufficient time for "dreaming out loud" and reflection to take place. The OD practitioner is the system guide who encourages each participant to actively hear colleagues' ideas and dreams before moving to the design stage. At this stage, the OD practitioner inserts AI references and holds the AI framework while the organization integrates new language, new policies, and new behaviors. Every new innovation of society is the manifestation of someone's dream (Royal, 1996). Things that are attributed to the wonder of science began as a creative dream or wish for what could be and an exploration of the horizon of the possible. It is helpful to remind AI participants of the value of dreaming.

The Design Phase of the AI Process

In the design phase participants conduct a dialogue about what should be. Here the importance of the possibility propositions as an ideal for the organization is contrasted with the current reality of the propositions as seen in organizational practice. Attitudes and behaviors that are inclusive become the model for the future of the organization. The parallel histories of all participants in the inquiry are respected. The voices of targeted groups, in terms of cultural dimension of diversity and organizational level of status, come to the table with the voices of privilege. The parallel experiences of the multicultural lives that exist in any section of the organization move into dialogue with each other. The dialogue creates "compassionate meaning" for the multiple experiences present in the system (Royal, 2000). Compassionate meaning creates the path forward toward a shared meaning of a preferred future. This evolved in the dream phase and is crafted in the design phase.

In the design phase, every policy, behavior, norm, rule, action, or assumption is open to change. The OD practitioner guides this phase by asking questions such as "Who should be in the room for the creation of the training, policy shifts, or behavior changes?" "What do you want to have happen as a result of the design phase?" "Have you done a second series of interviews to reach as many people as possible, and are external stakeholders included?"

In the dream phase a new set of "attitudes, behaviors, and circumstances of inclusion" (ABCs) was created (Royal, 2003) These new ABCs from the dream phase show up again in the design phase. In diversity work or social justice change work, awareness training and policy shifts often occur through preplanned intervention. Awareness training and policy shifts are cocreated in AI as a part of the design phase process.

Participants dialogue in this phase about what will be present in the preferred future. Voices of the other come forward during the process to speak about the significance of their histories and experience in the organization's culture, the systems, the organization, and their work environment. At this time, the norms of the organization, the attitudes and behaviors of the participants, and the circumstances of the environment are open to design revision.

Training to develop competencies for work in an antiracist, gender-fair, multicultural, and inclusive environment is an important part of the actions and activities of the design phase. Hurt and exclusion are part of the stories. If people have shared these stories and requested training and policy changes, their experiences and desires must be addressed in the design phase. Otherwise, increased burden has been created instead of hope and joy. Inaction pushes the organization out of the philosophy of Appreciative Inquiry, from supporting life-giving experiences to supporting life-diminishing ones.

The design phase of the AI methodology also creates "How will we know we are there?" instruments. What will be present in the preferred future? Ethical and committed members of any organization want to contribute to its growth and history from wherever they sit in the organization. What are the compelling ideas and actions that will drive each participant to work for the new possibilities?

The Deliver Phase of the AI Process

In the deliver phase of the AI process, participants commit to actions they design. They speak publicly about their desire to work for the preferred future. Their ability to work from strength and passion generates a deep pocket of potential, where the possibilities are endless. Once a basic level of competency is achieved and passion is ignited, people want to do more of that activity. They build on their efficacy. Commitment comes from full participation in cocreating the deliver items and from participants' areas of passion and experience. This creates energy that sustains the change over time. In AI there is a higher success rate and a self-reported higher level of satisfaction from employees at all levels. Every member of the inquiry is asked to speak his or her preferred future and what this person can be counted on to deliver. Participants agree to support each other. Each participant is encouraged to say what they need, to be at their best.

In the deliver phase, the timeline and the manifestation of the dream unfold. The OD practitioner reminds the organization's members that the attitudes, behaviors, and circumstances of inclusion must be embedded in every action that takes the system toward its preferred future. This is a time as well to scan and ensure that all voices are included, and that every person in the inquiry feels she or he is still part of the AI process.

The deliver phase allows listing things that can be done, now, today. The "now things" are changes at the group and individual levels, emphasizing how each person will embrace the provocative possibility statements from where he or she is in the organization. People in organizations know what is wrong. They also hold in their head and heart a vision of what it will look like when things are right. Each area that the inquiry elevates as an area of change includes behaviors that organization members can use as a method to check where we are now on the journey. These are factors that individuals can change immediately to facilitate their preferred future.

Leaders, policy makers, directors, and organization members declare how they will anchor and support the deliver items over time. The details of funding allocations, training opportunities and schedules, policy shifts, and expectations about the organization's climate are reviewed in a published time frame. The now things at the organization level focus on how leaders, managers, and officials with power will shift the use of norms, mores, and policies in support of the provocative possibility statements from the dream phase and the areas of attention identified in the design phase.

Implications for OD Practitioners

OD practitioners must understand AI well enough to be able to support organizations as they go through the four phases of the AI process. Understanding the AI process in a toolbox way is not enough. Practitioners must have an understanding of AI that goes beyond the procedural steps of facilitating the four AI phases, or stopping after the dream phase! AI is a diversity intervention, as well as an OD intervention, and as such it requires the OD practitioner's ability to incorporate and support diversity, inclusion, and equity as an integral part of the AI process. Supporting the AI process entails an understanding by OD practitioners of the philosophical, methodological, and process aspect of AI; how multiple levels of system are involved (individual, group, organization, and society); and the language and power of stories.

Diversity, Inclusion, and Equity

Appreciative Inquiry is an intervention that supports diversity, inclusion, and equity in organizations. Three aspects of AI are important in sustaining affirmative intervention and change, for supporting life-giving rather than life-diminishing experiences:

1. Every voice counts. Each individual has value and merit.
2. Every voice deserves to be heard. Each individual has a unique contribution to make.
3. Every voice is included in AI conversations in the room.

These principles position AI as an OD change process that speaks directly to the subject of social justice and diversity. It is also a valuable intervention when working with international clients and nation-states. AI has great value where nations are affected by colonial histories and hurts. AI is uniquely intended to discover, understand, and foster change toward affirmation, inclusion, and open dialogue. It diminishes the hierarchy in systems and places equal value on every voice and individual. Appreciative Inquiry is the "people's process," making it possible for citizens of all classes and status in the organization or community to have their voice heard in creating a preferred future (Royal, 2000).

In the AI process a diagonal slice is created. It is a cross-section of a system, any system, and it gathers all voices of the system into the room for an inquiry into "What is good here?" The OD practitioner supports the community by voicing AI principles at every opportunity as the diagonal cross-section of the organization is assembled for the grand dialogue and the beginning of the discover phase. The OD practitioner must have solid knowledge of the philosophy that AI is based on, use of participatory action research, and the steps in the four-D process. The OD practitioner educates all members about the process and makes available to everyone the information needed if one is to be a full participant in the AI intervention and change initiative.

Organizational status and class attributes are collapsed for the inquiry. Every person in the system is valued and has a story to tell, regardless of rank, responsibility, or tenure. Working on the diagonal of the organization minimizes power and privileged behaviors. The AI intervention illuminates the power of story and the positive effect of including all voices in the grand dialogue.

Levels of AI Understanding

Sustainable and continuous change in organization culture occurs through AI at three levels of paradigm shift and understanding: the philosophical, the methodological, and the process. Viewing AI alone as a four-D process or as an organizational tool misses the significance of assisting an organization through a paradigm shift in its culture.

The first shift toward affirmative change is in philosophy. AI is a shift from critical to affirming, and from critical analysis at every level of system to affirmative inquiry and curiosity as a method of discovery. This requires an intentional shift in language, metaphors, and mental models, which begins with affirmation and solution-focused dialogue. Such a philosophical change opens the organization and the OD practitioner to the impact of the positive principle of AI (Cooperrider, Srivastva, and Associates, 1990). The skill for the practitioner is to hold the philosophy container and continuously ask the AI question, "What do you (the organization) want to have happen here?"

The second shift is toward the AI methodology of inquiry and participation, which shifts behavior on the part of the OD practitioner and the organization from investigating and reporting to participatory action research. In the AI context, this is research that continuously inquires into and discovers what is working "in service to creating the best change process possible" through active participation by all voices in the organization. The inquiry becomes organization-driven; people are engaged because they are heard and included.

With diagonal representation and AI principles in practice, AI becomes an organizational process in which all members are involved and engaged. AI shifts the intervention from top down to the people's process (Royal, 2000); the OD practitioner is the organization's coach and inquiry guide. Each employee wants the organization to thrive and has ideas that will contribute to the best future possible.

The third shift is the four-D process of Appreciative Inquiry. Most OD practitioners use the four-D model to shape inquiry and dialogue about any topic or situation facing a system. This is the toolbox process. The OD practitioner who brings the philosophy of affirmation and inclusion and use of participatory action research into an AI intervention is capable of a more in-depth and sustainable intervention. Having this awareness at a deep, knowing level equips the practitioner with skills that embed inclusion and diversity into any AI topic choice. The four-D model is the road map for identifying a topic choice, gathering data, and constructing an AI interview protocol. The model guides the organization through the appreciative interviews and the grand dialogue. It helps structure a communication model that is intentional about providing enough time for dialogue, reflection, and information among all participants and organization members. This use of time and information is an inclusive philosophical shift and creates a renaissance in the organization's development.

The methodology, the philosophy, and the 4D process of AI shift communities, organizations, and personal behavior from hierarchical, militaristic, command-and-control, and need-to-know to collaborative, open, and inclusive behavior. For people who have been historically excluded or are currently victims of discrimination or structural inequality, this method opens up closed systems. It is important to recognize the power of stories and shared participation.

Working at Multiple Levels of System

AI can create a shift in an organization's norms. It is important to view this shift from the perspective of four levels of system: societal, organization, group, and individual. The AI principles shake the "cultural membrane" of society at all levels of systems (Royal, 2003). This membrane is the environment in which all organized activity in a culture takes shape and meaning. For the AI intervention in an organization to be as in-depth as possible, the OD practitioner must be able to scan and diagnose the environment on multiple levels. This allows the organization and participants the gift of multilevel inquiry. To have this multilevel information early in the dream phase is significant for guiding creation of activities and policies in this phase and later ones of the change process.

At the macro level, AI initiates a philosophical shift in the culture membrane that surrounds each society—values, norms, assumptions, and mores that influence all societal facets. The values and norms of the membrane vary with the culture, and each culture has a surrounding membrane. The cultural membrane, which includes systemic norms and rules, guides the behavior of all institutions that are part of the larger national culture. Institutions that make up the legal, financial, educational, religious, and medical framework of the larger culture reflect, support, and enforce the membrane. Assuming that AI change creates a positive outcome for every voice, an Appreciative Inquiry is about change that starts at the large cultural level.

To bring change and create a diverse and productive environment for all participants and organization members, organizations and other systems must inquire about behavior changes for both leaders and average citizens. They must inquire about macro-level change and systems change. This redirection of inquiry toward a cocreated and shared vision of a preferred future supports change at the micro and institutional levels. At the micro level, the culture membrane affects the behavior of groups and individuals in organizations. The shift to a set of ABCs (attitudes, behaviors, and circumstances of inclusion) happens when the choice is made to think and image a new set of norms and values and to stay committed to this change and to the AI principles (Royal, 2003). The key in the inquiry is to be curious at every level of system. Therefore the overarching cultural membrane must be explored.

Language and the Power of Story

OD practitioners need to incorporate into their AI practice the understanding and belief that language and the use of words to image others and oneself are central to Appreciative Inquiry. Language and the use of words are a major factor in shaping the shared vision of a preferred future. To work appreciatively at all levels, thinking must shift. How people image the future, themselves, and other groups or individuals has great applicability and implications for how they can see the future. Language and images guide how cultures and systems see the inclusion of targeted or excluded groups in their preferred futures.

Appreciative Inquiry avoids using critical analysis to explain AI change efforts. Language that speaks in the negative or the critical confuses the inquiry and the inquirer. The use of language that speaks of the critical, joined with negative

The NTL Handbook of Organization Development and Change

images, places the inquiry outside the framework of the positive and outside the framework of AI.

Defining the AI topic as a problem or a detriment also reinforces mental images of the difficult, painful, or troublesome, and the energy in the system as blocked and constricted. The language that the OD practitioner uses to explain, contract, or implement any phase of Appreciative Inquiry is central to the shift in an organization resulting from AI interventions. Language images the preferred future. A central point of creating a preferred future is being intentional and clear about the language used to describe this future and the importance of compassionate dialogue.

The images that OD practitioners speak about and the beliefs they hold in mind also determine how each member of the organization holds and maintains the image of the future. In turn, when OD practitioners work in organizations, they are also affected by how the organizations engage with them. Words create the world where we live and work. Powerful, positive stories generate energy to fuel the inquiry and cocreate the future.

Appreciative Inquiry affirms the power of story and experience in systems and personal lives. The significant images and feelings that emerge throughout the process are stored in the personal stories of organization members. It is vital for people to remember the positive experiences in their lives. Beginning the AI process with stories of when people were at their best informs the listener and the speaker about the times when things did work. These stories set a standard, a place to work from, that has hope and possibility integrated in the telling.

AI asks people to tell their stories about their peak experiences with an organization when individuals and the organization are at their best. Through a guided and structured interview dialogue, AI enables people to speak from the personal, one-to-one. Through personal interviews and sharing of positive experiences, people dialogue about their success and their personal peak experiences. AI assists all organization members to envision policies, practices, and behaviors that promote organizational and personal vitality. AI seeks out the "best of what is" to ignite the collective imagination toward "what might be" (Cooperrider, Srivastva, and Associates, 1990). The goal is to discover and expand the realm of the possible, to think beyond the current horizon. People envision a collectively desired future. They carry these innovative ideas in ways that translate intention into reality. The OD practitioner is there as the guide during the Appreciative Inquiry journey.

Conclusion

The AI philosophy is uniquely equipped to assist any system through inquiry and discovery. Practitioners who shift their own beliefs and behaviors toward AI concepts are most capable of seeing the possibility of a shift in a client system.

AI methodology is at its best when the OD practitioner uses the model and embraces the principles of inclusion at each level of consultation, facilitation, and inquiry. AI as an intervention is not an appropriate fit if the practitioner feels that the system is not ready or able to make a shift in its norms and behaviors. The choice between AI and another OD intervention is a collaborative decision of the client and the OD practitioner. It is rare to find a situation concerned with improving the human side of organizational dynamics where one would choose other OD interventions.

Appreciative Inquiry is a change process that creates space for all the people in an organization to share commitment and pride. It is a chance to tell their story, remember their contributions, speak their dreams, and connect to the future health and wellness of the system. AI has emerged as a process that locates joy in systems and offers a pathway for hope, as well as reconciliation between groups and cultures where painful histories and experiences exist. Hope, reconciliation, and joys are vital components of sustainable organizational change.

References

Cooperrider, D., Srivastva, S., & Associates. (Eds.). (1990). *Appreciative management and leadership.* San Francisco: Jossey-Bass.

Mann, A. J., & Cooperrider, D. (1993). *Global excellence in management project.* Cleveland, OH: USAID/Case Western Reserve.

Royal, C. L. (1996, April). *The fractal initiative.* Tonoloway women's workshop, Wolfordsburg, PA.

Royal, C. L. (1997). *The fractal initiative.* Doctoral dissertation, Fielding Institute, Santa Barbara, CA.

Royal, C. L. (2000, March). *Conference on diversity: Conference proceedings.* Department of Health and Human Services, Washington, DC.

Royal, C. L. (2003). *Quadrant-behavior theory: A social justice and diversity practitioner's handbook.* Unpublished manuscript.

Royal, C. L., & Hammond, S. (1998). *Lessons from the field: The appreciative inquiry handbook.* Plano, TX: Thinbook.

CHAPTER TWENTY-SIX

CULTURE ASSESSMENT AS AN OD INTERVENTION

Edgar H. Schein

M ost culture-related interventions do not involve culture change. Instead, they are interventions into some aspect of how the organization works that can actually be changed *using* the culture rather than changing it. Most clients do not understand the nature of culture and therefore often label something as cultural that may not be cultural at all. This chapter explores how OD practitioners can work with organizations on cultural issues in such a way as to enable members of the organization to identify important cultural assumptions and evaluate the degree to which those assumptions aid or hinder changes the organization is trying to make. A cultural assessment process is examined that can assist an organization describe and understand its culture as part of a specific organization change initiative. This assessment draws mostly on the ten-step process described in *The Corporate Culture Survival Guide* (Schein, 1999a).

Organization Culture and Cultural Assessment

The cultural assessment process described in this chapter is based on a model of culture that differentiates observed, but undecipherable, artifacts from espoused values and the tacit shared assumptions that are the essence of the culture (Schein, 1992/2004). These three levels of culture—artifacts, espoused values, and shared tacit assumptions—are shown in Figure 26.1. For example, the observed artifact might be that the senior management team is constantly arguing and fighting among themselves. When queried, their espoused value is "That's the way we get our work done; we debate until we get consensus." The tacit underlying assumption is that they are making decisions—say, on a new technology where no one person is smart enough to know the answer, but collectively by debating alternatives, the truth gradually emerges. This process was in fact one of the essences of the culture of Digital Equipment Corporation (Schein, 2003).

FIGURE 26.1. LEVELS OF CULTURE.

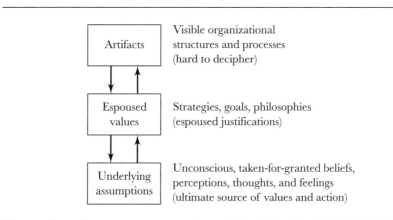

Artifacts — Visible organizational structures and processes (hard to decipher)

Espoused values — Strategies, goals, philosophies (espoused justifications)

Underlying assumptions — Unconscious, taken-for-granted beliefs, perceptions, thoughts, and feelings (ultimate source of values and action)

Focus on the "Business Problem," Not the Culture

Many organizations think that a general cultural assessment would be of value to them. Unless the culture assessment is tied to a change initiative, however, it is fairly useless because culture is vast and covers all aspects of an organization's functioning. The OD practitioner should not offer to do a culture assessment unless the organizational clients know what they are trying to achieve. If the client says they want to "assess the culture" or "change the culture," that is not specific enough to proceed. The practitioner should probe what the organizational client means by culture and why he or she thinks a culture assessment would be useful. The answers typically reveal some change agenda that the client has, what he or she defines as the business problem; it is important to specify clearly what that change agenda is.

Focus on How the Culture Will Help "the New Way of Working"

The OD practitioner functioning as a process consultant must help the client be specific, avoid general comments such as "We want to change the culture," and keep probing for what is wrong that is motivating a change in the first place (Schein, 1999b). Once the client has identified in concrete terms what the desired *new* way of working is, the culture assessment can then be done in order to identify which elements of the culture will aid the change program and which will hinder it (Schein, 1999a).

For example, in the case of Alpha Power, a large urban utility, the organization was required by the court to become more environmentally responsible. The court-appointed monitor defined the problem as being "Alpha's culture," which launched a culture change program. A culture assessment was not relevant, however, until it was determined that a new way of working was required. This new way of working involved (1) more sense of responsibility on the part of the hourly employees for identifying, reporting, and remediating environmental spills and other environmental health and safety (EH&S) problems; (2) more openness in reporting EH&S problems rather than go on tending to cover up to protect the workgroup from embarrassment or disciplinary action; and (3) more teamwork in dealing with EH&S problems.

The culture *change* portion of this larger agenda then concerned primarily (1) the change in the self-image of the hourly workers, (2) a change in the role of their immediate supervisors toward delegating more responsibility, and (3) changes in such supporting structures as the discipline system and reward system. The Alpha Power culture was built on traditions of technical excellence, reliability of performance, a strong but highly paternalistic hierarchy, and a commitment to extensive and detailed training and development of the workforce. These cultural elements enabled Alpha to retrain workers and supervisors, and to institute reward and control systems that supported the new way of working. The bulk of the Alpha culture did not change and indeed should not have. Actually, it was this culture that enabled the specific environmental changes to be made efficiently. The bulk of the culture was used to make significant changes in one portion of the culture and was in fact essential to achieving the changes that were made in how work was done at the front line and how supervisors restructured their role.

The Culture Assessment Process

Once the purpose of the assessment is clear, the essence of the assessment process is to bring together one or more representative groups in the organization; give them a model of how to think about organizational culture and subcultures; and then ask them to identify the main artifacts, the espoused values, and the shared tacit assumptions. An outside OD practitioner plays the role of consultant, documenter, gadfly when necessary, and question asker.

Assumptions Underlying the Assessment

Several important assumptions lie behind this approach:

- Culture is a set of *shared* assumptions; hence obtaining the initial data in a *group* setting is more appropriate and valid than conducting individual interviews. Surveys are useless because one does not know what to ask about in the first place, and the survey methodology does not elicit the deeper assumptions that form the essence of culture.
- The contextual meaning of cultural assumptions can be fully understood only by members of the culture; therefore creating a vehicle for *their understanding* is more important than it is for the consultant to obtain that understanding.
- Not all parts of a culture are relevant to a given issue the organization may be facing, so attempting to study an entire culture in all of its facets is not only impractical but also usually inappropriate.
- Insiders are capable of understanding and making explicit the shared tacit assumptions that make up the culture, but they need outsider help in this process. The helper/consultant should therefore operate primarily from a process consulting model and avoid as much as possible being an expert on the content of any group's culture (Schein, 1999b).
- Some cultural assumptions will be perceived as helping the organization achieve its strategic goals or resolve its current issues. Others will be perceived as constraints or barriers. It is important for the group members to have a process that allows them to sort cultural assumptions into these categories.
- Changes in organizational practices to solve the problems that initiated the culture analysis can usually be achieved by building on existing assumptions. That is, the culture deciphering process often reveals that new practices can and should be derived from the existing culture, as the Alpha Power example shows.
- If changes in the culture are discovered to be necessary, those changes will rarely involve the entire culture. It is always a matter of changing one or two assumptions. Only rarely does the basic paradigm have to change, but if it does then the organization faces a multiyear major change process (Schein, 1992/2004, 1999a).

The Ten-Step Culture Assessment Process

Implementation of a culture deciphering process that is based on these assumptions can now be described in terms of a number of steps (see Exhibit 26.1).

EXHIBIT 26.1. CULTURE ASSESSMENT: A TEN-STEP PROCESS.

1. Obtain leadership commitment.
2. Select groups for interviews.
3. Select an appropriate setting for the group interviews.
4. Explain the purpose of the meeting.
5. Explain the culture model.
6. Elicit descriptions of artifacts.
7. Identify espoused values.
8. Identify shared tacit assumptions.
9. Identify cultural aids and hindrances.
10. Do joint analysis and next steps.

Step One: Obtain Leadership Commitment. Deciphering cultural assumptions and evaluating their relevance to some organizational purpose needs to be viewed as a major intervention in the organization's life and must therefore be undertaken only with the full understanding and consent of the leaders of the organization. In practical terms, this means that if someone from an organization calls or writes to ask for help to figure out their organization's culture, the first question is always some form of "Why do you want to do this?" or "What problem are you having that makes you think a cultural analysis is relevant?" When a group analyzes its own culture without a problem or issue to motivate the process, the analysis usually fails for lack of interest on the part of the group.

Step Two: Select Groups for Interviews. The next step is for the consultant to work with the leaders and executives to determine how best to select some groups representative of the culture. The criteria for selection usually depend on the concrete nature of the problem to be solved. Groups can be homogeneous with respect to a given department or rank level, or deliberately heterogeneous by way of selecting diagonal slices from the organization. The group can be as small as three or as large as thirty. If important subcultures are believed to be operating, one can repeat the process in other groups, or deliberately bring in samples of members from various groups to test in the meetings whether the assumed differences exist.

The composition of the group is further determined by the client's perception of the level of trust and openness in the group, especially in regard to the decision of whether senior people who might inhibit the discussion should be present. On the one hand, it is desirable to have a fairly open discussion, which might mean keeping higher-levels out. On the other hand, it is critical to determine to what extent the assumptions that eventually come out in the group meetings are shared by the leaders, which argues for their presence. Because the level of trust and openness across various boundaries is itself likely to be a cultural issue, it is best to start with a heterogeneous group and let the group experience reveal the extent to which certain areas of communication are or are not inhibited by the presence of others.

Once groups have been chosen, it should be the leaders or executives who inform the groups of the purpose of the meetings. Just coming to a meeting to do a culture assessment is too vague. The participants must know what change problems are being worked on that motivate the culture assessment in the first place.

Step Three: Select an Appropriate Setting for the Group Interviews. An appropriate locale and setting for doing the assessment is usually a large, comfortable room with lots of wall space for hanging flipchart pages and a set of breakout rooms in which subgroups can meet.

Step Four: Explain the Purpose of the Group Meeting. The large group meeting should start with a restatement (by someone from the organization who is perceived to be in a leadership or authority role) of what the purpose of the meeting is so that openness of response is encouraged. The process consultant is then introduced as being the outsider who will help the group conduct an analysis of how the organization's culture is either an aid or a constraint to solving the problem or resolving the issue. The consultant can be an outsider or a member of the organization who is part of a staff group devoted to providing internal consulting services.

Step Five: Explain the Culture Model. It is essential for the group to understand that culture manifests itself at the level of artifacts and espoused values, but the goal is to try to decipher the shared tacit assumptions that lie underneath. The consultant should therefore present the three-level model (Figure 26.1) and ensure that everyone understands the distinctions among the three levels and that culture is a learned set of assumptions that are based on a group's shared history. It is important for the group to understand that what they are about to assess is a product of their own history; the culture's stability rests on the organization's past success.

Step Six: Elicit Descriptions of Artifacts. The process consultant then tells the group that they are going to start by describing the culture through its artifacts. A useful way to begin is to find out who joined the group most recently, and ask that person what it felt like to enter the organization, and what he or she noticed most upon entering it. Everything that is mentioned is written down on a flipchart, and as the pages are filled they are torn off and hung on the wall so that everything remains visible.

If group members are active in supplying information, the process consultant can stay relatively quiet. If the group needs priming, the consultant should suggest categories, such as dress code, desired mode of behavior in addressing the boss, the physical layout of the workplace, how time and space are used, what kind of emotions one would notice, how people are rewarded and punished, how one gets ahead in the organization, and so forth. The consultant should not decide ahead of time which content categories to use but instead let the group develop them in order to determine what is central in their thinking.

This process should continue for about one hour, or until the well clearly runs dry; it should produce a long list of artifacts covering all sorts of areas of the group's life. Being visually surrounded by the description of their own artifacts is a necessary condition for the group to begin stimulating its own deeper layers of thinking about what assumptions the members share.

Step Seven: Identify Espoused Values. The question that elicits artifacts is, "*What is going on here?*" By contrast, the question that elicits espoused values is, "*Why are you doing what you are doing?*" The process consultant should pick an artifactual area that is clearly of interest to the group and ask people to articulate the reasons they do what they do. For example, if they have said that the place is very informal and that there are few status symbols, ask "Why?" This usually elicits value statements such as, "We value problem solving more than formal authority" or "We think that a lot of communication is a good thing" or even "We don't believe that bosses should have more rights than subordinates."

As values or beliefs are stated, the consultant should check for consensus and, if there appears to be consensus, write down the values or beliefs on a new chart pad. If members disagree, explore why by asking whether this is a matter of subgroups having their own values or whether there is genuine lack of consensus, in which case the item goes on the list with a question mark to remind the group to revisit it. The group should be encouraged to look at all the artifacts they have identified and figure out as best they can what values seem to be implied. If there are some obvious values that the group has not named, the process consultant should suggest them as possibilities—in the spirit of joint inquiry, *not* as an expert conducting a content analysis of their data. The list of values is usually completed within another hour or so. At that point, the group is ready to push on to shared tacit assumptions.

Step Eight: Identify Shared Tacit Assumptions. The key to getting at the underlying assumptions is to check whether the espoused values that have been identified really explain all the artifacts. Some of the things described as going on may not have been clearly explained or may be in conflict with some of the articulated values. For example, the members of a group from a computer company lived by the espoused values of "cooperation and team work." They discovered that decisions made by consensus did not stick; the real underlying assumption was "individual competition," and the only way to get things done was by making various kinds of deals with people on whom one was dependent.

Important and salient assumptions are ones that trigger a whole new set of insights and begin to make sense of a range of things that had previously not made sense. These salient assumptions often reconcile what the group may have perceived as value conflict. For example, a group of human resource professionals at an insurance company doing this exercise identified as an important value "becoming more innovative and taking more risks as the environment changed." The members could not reconcile this goal with the fact that very little actual innovation was taking place. In pushing to the assumption level, they realized that throughout its history the company had operated on two central assumptions about human behavior: (1) people work best when they are given clear rules to cover all situations (among the artifacts the group listed was a "mile-long shelf of procedure manuals"), and (2) they like immediate feedback and will not obey rules unless rule violation is immediately punished. Once the group stated these tacit assumptions, they realized that the assumptions were driving the behavior far more than the espoused value of innovation and risk taking was. There was no real positive incentive for innovating. In fact, innovation was risky because any false steps would immediately be punished.

This phase of the exercise is finished when the group and the consultant feel they have identified most of the critical assumption areas and participants are now clear on what an assumption is. As a time estimate, these steps should take three to four hours.

Step Nine: Identify Cultural Aids and Hindrances. If the group is larger than ten or so people, this step is conducted in smaller breakout groups. The task for subgroups depends in part on what the presenting problems were, whether or not subcultures were identified in the large group exercise, and how much time is available. For example, if there was evidence in the large group meeting that there are functional, geographical, occupational, or hierarchical subcultures, the consultant may wish to send off subgroups that reflect those presumed differences and have each subgroup further explore its own assumption set. Or if the consultant finds there is reasonable consensus in the large group on the assumptions identified, the subgroups can be composed randomly, by business unit or any other criterion that makes sense given the larger problem or issue being addressed.

In any case, the task for the subgroups consists of two parts: (1) spending some time (an hour or so) refining assumptions and identifying other assumptions that may have been missed in the large group meeting, and (2) categorizing the assumptions according to whether they will aid or hinder the solution of the problem that is being addressed.

The groups need to review what the new way of working is and how the assumptions identified help or hinder in getting there. The subgroups report back to the total group about the two or three main assumptions that will aid and the two or three that will hinder the desired changes.

It is highly important to require the participants to look at assumptions from this dual point of view because of a tendency to see culture only as a constraint, and thus put too much emphasis on the assumptions that hinder. In fact, successful organizational change probably arises more from identifying assumptions that aid than from changing assumptions that hinder, but groups initially have a harder time seeing how the culture can be a source of positive help.

Step Ten: Joint Analysis and Next Steps. The purpose of this step of the exercise is to reach some kind of consensus on what the important shared assumptions are and the implications of those assumptions for what the organization wants to do. The process starts with the subgroups reporting their own separate analyses to the full group. If there is a high degree of consensus, the consultant can go straight into a discussion of implications. More likely, there are some variations, possibly disagreements, which require some further inquiry by the total group with the help of the process consultant.

For example, the group may agree that there are strong subculture differences that must be taken into account. Or some of the assumptions may have to be reexamined to determine whether they reflect an even deeper level that would resolve disagreements. Or the group may come to recognize that for various reasons it does not have many shared assumptions. In each case, the role of the consultant is to raise questions, force clarification, test perceptions, and in other ways help the group achieve as clear a picture as possible of the assumption set that is driving the group's day-to-day perceptions, feelings, thoughts, and ultimately behavior.

Once there is some consensus on what the shared assumptions are, the discussion proceeds to the role of those assumptions in aiding or hindering what the group wants to do. At this point, the process consultant must be careful to ensure balanced discussion because of the tendency to quickly identify a constraining assumption and put all the energy into figuring out what to do about it. As previously stated, one of the biggest insights for the group comes from seeing how some of the assumptions will aid them, creating the possibility that their energy should go into strengthening those positive assumptions instead of worrying about overcoming the constraining ones.

Following step ten, if real constraints are identified the group discussion then has to shift to an analysis of how culture can be managed and what it will take to overcome the identified constraints. At this point, a brief further lecture on change theory and on the mechanisms by which culture changes is useful, and a new set of subgroups may be formed to develop a change strategy. Typically, this entails an additional half-day at a minimum. Thus, if culture *change* is now to be undertaken, additional time beyond the original one-day meeting is required. Note, however, how much can be accomplished in a day if this group self-diagnostic intervention is used.

Summary and Conclusions

The main point of this approach is *not* to get involved with culture assessment or change until the client has clearly specified what problems are being addressed, what new ways of working have been identified, and how much commitment to the change program there is at the top of the organization. Senior management must have a clear sense of what culture is, what it means to even contemplate changes in culture, and the likelihood that the culture will be a positive force in making some of the changes.

A ten-step process using the culture model of artifacts, espoused values, and shared tacit assumptions with groups from inside the organization working with the OD practitioner as the process consultant can then assess the culture within a day's program. The organization can now decide how the strengths of its culture are to be used to make the desired changes. If elements of the culture have to be changed, a culture change program can be launched using general change models that emphasize transformative change (Schein, 1999b).

References

Schein, E. H. (1992). *Organizational culture and leadership* (2nd ed.). San Francisco: Jossey-Bass. (3rd ed. 2004)

Schein, E. H. (1999a). *The corporate culture survival guide.* San Francisco: Jossey-Bass.

Schein, E. H. (1999b). *Process consultation revisited: Building the helping relationship.* Reading, MA: Addison-Wesley-Longman.

Schein, E. H. (2003). *DEC is dead; long live DEC: The lasting legacy of Digital Equipment Corporation.* San Francisco: Berrett-Koehler.

CHAPTER TWENTY-SEVEN

A COMPLEXITY SCIENCE APPROACH TO ORGANIZATION DEVELOPMENT

Edwin E. Olson

In a stable environment with predictable cause-and-effect relationships, organization development (OD) practitioners can be successful with social engineering methods that are essentially logical and linear. OD methods can be helpful in closing the gap between the organization's current situation and a more hopeful future. Increasingly, however, OD practitioners are finding that problems remain unsolved; other parts come unraveled as one part is solved; or new problems and dilemmas arise that they have not seen before. The desired future remains elusive and unrealistic. These are indicators that the organization is in an unpredictable environment.

In such an environment, planned change that focuses on cause-and-effect analysis and rational solutions does not work. In an unpredictable environment, organizations—just like bacteria, ant colonies, and other living entities—must adapt to survive, guided only by a few simple rules or principles that describe how parts of the entity have learned to interact. This is the opposite of the traditional OD approach of top-down change, which assumes that prediction and control is possible and that the wisdom at or near the top of the organization will trickle down the organization in an orchestrated process of buy-in (Pascale, 2004). In unpredictable environments, unintended consequences are the norm.

Richard Pascale says: "Stated plainly, when societies, communities and organizations encounter the need for adaptive change (that is, change that departs from the trajectory of "business as usual"), social engineering doesn't work. And it never has" (Pascale, 2004, p. 3).

In unpredictable environments, OD practitioners must focus on the micro level where the most powerful processes of change occur and where relationships, interactions, small experiments, and simple rules shape emerging patterns. When an organization is ready for change, small beginnings can morph into large-scale change, much like an avalanche where small beginnings escalate into dramatic and powerful forces. Especially with the connectivity of the Internet and the media, small disturbances can wipe out a company's competitive advantage.

Organizational change occurs as small changes are integrated and scaled throughout the organization. OD practitioners face the challenge of identifying small successes and replicating them, rather than imposing "best practices" on the organization that will evoke an immune defense response of "Not invented here" (Pascale, 2004).

The approach to OD presented in this chapter applies a complexity science perspective to current OD diagnostic and intervention methods in unpredictable environments. A complexity science approach for intervening in organizations and the roles of OD practitioners in this approach are examined. The use of this complexity science approach is explored for two OD processes: team building and diversity interventions.

Complexity Science and OD

Complexity science challenges our expectations about how the world works and how individuals and groups respond to their environments. Pascale, Millemann, and Gioja describe complexity science this way: "We are entering another scientific renaissance. . . . Also known as 'complexity science,' this work grapples with the mysteries of life itself, and is propelled forward by the confluence of three streams of inquiry: (1) breakthrough discoveries in the life sciences (for example, biology, medicine, and ecology); (2) insights of the social sciences (for example, sociology, psychology, and economics); and (3) new developments in the hard sciences (for example, physics, mathematics, and information technology). The resulting work has revealed exciting insights into life and has opened up new avenues for management" (2000, pp. 1–2).

Complexity science helps us make sense of what happens in organizations. OD practitioners can use the perspectives of complexity science to assess the environments inside and outside the organization and then choose appropriate concepts, tools, and techniques to intervene (see Eoyang, 1999; Goldstein, 1994; Kelly and Allison, 1998; Olson and Eoyang, 2001; Petzinger, 1999; Stacey, Griffin, and Shaw, 2000; Zimmerman, Lindberg, and Plsek, 1998). These authors use concepts and methods from theories of chaos, complex adaptive systems, nonlinear dynamics, and quantum theory to develop innovative models for change in organizations. The approach applied in this chapter is taken from Olson and Eoyang (2001).

Although the field of OD is diverse and constantly changing, there are some well-known traditional OD approaches and assumptions that can be contrasted with a complexity perspective. Warner Burke (2004) has recently identified what is known about the practice of OD. Three of the current OD practice areas Burke identified—process, content, and change leadership—are described in Table 27.1. A complexity science perspective of the three areas is outlined in the table and contrasted with the current practice and underlying assumptions of traditional OD. The key aspects of a complexity approach to OD involve working with complex responsive processes, helping organizations and leaders find a balance between order and disorder, and fostering the conditions of self-organizing.

TABLE 27.1. DIFFERENCES BETWEEN TRADITIONAL OD AND OD FROM A COMPLEXITY SCIENCE PERSPECTIVE.

Practice Area	Current OD Practice	Assumptions of OD	OD from a Complexity Perspective
Process	Lewin's three stages of unfreeze, change, and refreeze and Beckhard and Harris's three-step process of planned change (present state, transition state, future state) describe the process most OD practitioners follow, using such specific consulting steps as entry, contracting, data collection, diagnosis, feedback, intervention, and evaluation.	These approaches assume that change can be planned and orchestrated, that outcomes can be predicted and controlled, and that the process can manage unintended consequences. The approaches are used without much regard to the degree of uncertainty or agreement in the organization or in the task environment.	A complexity perspective uses methods that are appropriate for the degree of uncertainty and agreement in the situation. The outcomes of the process cannot be predicted, but a new pattern that is responsive and adapted to the environment will arise if the conditions of self-organizing are met. In uncertain environments, unintended consequences are expected and incorporated.

TABLE 27.1. DIFFERENCES BETWEEN TRADITIONAL OD AND OD FROM A COMPLEXITY SCIENCE PERSPECTIVE, Cont'd.

Practice Area	Current OD Practice	Assumptions of OD	OD from a Complexity Perspective
Content	OD practitioners work with the organization's vision, mission, strategy, climate and culture, and leadership selection. OD practitioners identify management behaviors and practices that reflect organizational values and attitudes. They focus on clarity, recognition, standards, participation, mutual support, and performance management.	The emphasis is on facilitating consensus. Identifying and working with the norms and values that guide behavior in the organization and intervening with rational, planned strategies will contribute to an organization's development.	A complexity perspective assumes that by amplifying differences new and more adaptive patterns will emerge. The emphasis is on identifying the simple rules that create self-organizing processes. Interventions focus on experiments to affect the conditions of self-organizing.
Change leadership	OD looks for competent leadership to develop the future state, vision, and direction for the organization. Leaders are expected to develop a clear value base, especially in establishing change goals. Effective leaders are very participative and involving in the implementation of the change goals and match their words to their actions.	OD practitioners see the organization as a system where inputs are transformed into outputs; they identify and intervene at key leverage points to bring about change and development (e.g., strategic planning). They trust that designated or elected leadership will move the organization forward and so help managers maintain control of the change process and create goals, plans, and structures.	A complexity approach focuses on the micro level and encourages connections and interactions to help the organization evolve. An organization is a combination of many complex responsive processes and continuously changing networks and iterative relationships, which produce surprising outcomes and consequences. Effective leadership emerges from the interactions. A balance between excessive order and disorder in the organizational processes creates the conditions for self-organizing. Interventions occur at all levels. Leaders are encouraged to recognize emerging goals, plans, and structures.

Source: The discussion of current OD practice is from Burke (2004).

Working with Complex Responsive Processes

Any organization that is trying to thrive in an unpredictable and changing environment uses complex responsive processes. Stacey, Griffin, and Shaw (2000) believe that organizing is best described not as a system but as "highly complex, ongoing processes of people relating to each other," which they refer to as complex responsive processes. They use the term *system* to describe information and control tools devised to speed up communication of a standardized, repetitive nature. "The organization" is not a system or a tool; rather, systems are some of the tools of communication employed by people in their relational processes of organizing joint action. An organization is a combination of complex responsive processes.

It is useful to think of an organization as a combination of processes rather than a "complex adaptive system" (CAS), which is pervasive in the complexity literature. Complex adaptive processes better describes the evolution and adaptation that occurs at many levels—individual, group, and organizationwide. Order emerges, rather than developing according to a predetermined structure such as a hierarchy. The basic building blocks of these complex responsive processes are semiautonomous individuals, ideas, or groups that follow simple rules to maximize some measure of performance as they self-organize over time.

The interactions in complex responsive processes are very rich, a combination of nonlinear, competitive, collaborative, and power-oriented interactions where even a small interaction can have multiplying effects. The interactions are primarily between those elements close at hand, or with those elements in one of many connected networks. The influence of one upon another is enhanced, altered, or suppressed in various ways. The feedback loops in the process are many and varied, bringing both positive and negative feedback that is essential for adapting to changes in the environment. These environmental changes push the processes into conditions far from equilibrium. The transactions with the environment also furnish energy and resources to maintain the processes. As the processes constantly respond to the information that is available to them, complexity is produced from the interactions between the elements (Cilliers, 1998).

Since meaning is derived from the relationships in the processes and since complex structures emerge from fairly small, unstructured beginnings, an OD practitioner mainly needs to focus on the relationships and the small events. Orchestrating elaborate events such as strategic planning is likely to have only a small effect on what actually happens.

Self-Organizing

Self-organizing is the term used to describe the tendency of complex responsive processes to generate new patterns spontaneously. For example, an organization will generate new structures and patterns on the basis of the interaction of its managers, employees, customers, and other stakeholders—even evolving its own mission and leadership. Any member of a self-organizing process can be a change agent to influence the patterns that emerge from the interaction of these internal and external forces.

OD practitioners and leaders who come into an unpredictable situation with detailed plans and expectations of predictable behavior and outcomes will be disappointed by what happens in the self-organizing process. Rather than requiring conformance to a preconceived plan, OD practitioners and leaders need to observe the patterns that form and then influence the interactions, if the emerging patterns are not acceptable to them. The outcomes of self-organizing, besides being unpredictable, are not necessarily good or bad. They are outcomes that the OD practitioner and organization leaders must deal with, whatever they are.

Fostering Self-Organizing Processes

When attending to complexity processes, the goal for the OD practitioner is to foster self-organizing. This is done by helping to create a balance in organizational functions between order and disorder, between being too constrained and too unconstrained. If organizational functions are too *tightly controlled*, then:

- Members do not have the flexibility they need
- Individuals and organizational units (teams, departments, functions) do not engage in meaningful contacts or dialogue
- The focus is on matters that are not vital for the organization

If organizational functions are too *loosely controlled*, then:

- Individuals and groups engage in meaningless activities
- Support structures are absent
- The work is diffuse

In either extreme, self-organizing processes are thwarted. Pascale, Millemann, and Gioja describe the Goldilocks Principle: "Neither too many rules or too few rules. The key to self-organizing resides in a field of tension between discipline and freedom. Nature achieves this tension through selection pressures (which impose discipline) and by upending occurrences (such as chance mutations and environmental disruptions). In organization, rules provide discipline" (2000, p. 6).

The challenge for OD practitioners is to identify aspects in the organization that are too ordered and those that are too disordered. An organization is most creative and adaptable to environmental changes when there is a balance between order and disorder.

If a leader, with the support of the OD practitioner, understands what aspect is keeping the organization from self-organizing because that aspect is either too controlled or uncontrolled, the leader can take action to adjust the situation. For example, a franchise operation such as McDonald's that imposes strict requirements and uniformity on its branches may not satisfy customers if it does not allow creative adaptation to local customer needs. On the other hand, if the franchise headquarters is too flexible in its requirements, the customer will not be able to depend on the level of service, quality, or product uniformity that they desire.

Conditions of Self-Organizing

Three processes create the conditions for a self-organizing process: (1) containing, (2) differentiating, and (3) transforming exchanges. By understanding these three conditions, a leader or OD practitioner can support self-organizing by intervening to tighten or loosen the degree of control and order (see Olson and Eoyang, 2001; Olson and Townsend, n.d.).

Containing. Containing defines what is "in" and what is "outside" the organization. A containing process establishes the semipermeable boundary within which the change occurs. With this process, new relationships and structures form over time. Many aspects of an organization can serve as a containing process:

- *Magnet:* one strong force pulls parts of the process together. People who work in the same building may develop norms that strain relationships between them and others who work in remote locations.
- *Fence:* an external boundary holds things together. Departmental loyalties facilitate teamwork within a department but may also foster suspicion and rivalry between departments.
- *Affinities:* connections between and among individuals hold them together. Professional, personal, psychological, social, and cultural affinities shape the behavior of people in the organization.

Differentiating. Differentiating works as an engine for change, fostering potential for individual and organizationwide evolution. Significant differences establish the shape of the emerging patterns.

- By mixing people with differing backgrounds and work histories, the potential of self-organizing is increased.
- The existence of contradiction and conflict suggests the possibilities of a new emerging pattern.
- What is deemed a significant difference depends on what is figural. If, for example, an organization places high value on expertise, the patterns that emerge will feature the areas of knowledge and experience of the most powerful organization members.

Transforming Exchanges. Transforming contacts connect across significant differences and create changes in the organization by connecting employees, managers, ideas, departments, customers, suppliers, and other stakeholders. The exchanges between these entities create chains of responses.

- Any transfer of information, energy, or material can be part of a transforming exchange.
- Not all exchanges are transforming. If contact is superficial or insufficient, people work as disjointed and independent parts; coherent, organizationwide patterns fail to emerge. Individuals experience a sense of isolation and confusion. When contacts are too strong or too numerous, people have few degrees of freedom and their behavior is limited.
- The more nodes and connections in an organization, the more likely individual members are to contribute to self-organizing.

Intervening in Complex Responsive Processes

Intervening in complex responsive processes is experimental and iterative. Interventions help to create a balance in organizational functions between being too constrained and too unconstrained in order to foster self-organizing. To influence the pattern, paths, and products of the self-organizing process, OD practitioners can:

- Continuously evaluate the conditions of self-organizing (containing, differentiating, transforming exchange)
- Notice if one or more of the conditions are too controlled or too uncontrolled

- If so, identify the condition where change is likely to have the greatest impact and is also easiest to affect
- Make the intervention and evaluate the impact, including the impact on the other two conditions
- Repeat the process until the organization reaches a state that the practitioner and the client can accept
- If the organization wishes to stay in the process of self-organizing, the conditions need to be continuously monitored

OD Practitioner Roles

In this section we look at roles the OD practitioner can play from a complexity sciences perspective in order to intervene in complex responsive processes and foster self-organizing to be effective with organizations that are trying to thrive in an unpredictable and changing environment.

Change Through Connection

Facilitating organization change depends on individual and immediate connections. OD practitioners can make the case for building interactive networks to foster self-organizing processes that will enhance trust and cooperation. Opening information channels and creating transforming contacts helps the organization evolve in ways no one could have predicted.

Adapt to Uncertainty

In complex responsive processes, the practitioner must expect the unexpected. Anticipating and responding quickly, but not too quickly, gives the self-organizing dynamics time to work within any guidelines the OD practitioner needs to establish.

Emerging Goals, Plans, and Structures

A practitioner must know when a group has achieved "good enough" results—that is, results that further the self-organizing process, make a contribution, or are a worthy experiment. Practitioners must watch multiple horizons and not hesitate to encourage leaders to plan again, as plans become outdated. Practitioners help identify paths that leaders can follow.

Amplify Difference

Rather than focus on achieving consensus, which may suppress significant differences, OD practitioners must allow differences to be generative and integrated in the new patterns that emerge. Practitioners can amplify communications from clients to reveal hidden differences. They can encourage inclusion of new ideas and perspectives. They can see opportunities for learning in unexpected events.

Self-Similarity

Practitioners can observe the inherent similarities between changes that are occurring at various levels and parts of the organization. By highlighting these similar patterns, a practitioner can bring coherence to a change effort. Parts of an organization may be stuck in a culture and patterns of behavior that were helpful for survival but are detrimental to succeeding in a new and changed environment. By shifting attention to what is working well in other parts of the organization, the practitioner can give an impetus for change to the dysfunctional parts of the organization.

Success as Fit with the Environment

Since the organizational environment is unstable and unpredictable, it is not possible to develop a long-term organizational vision that is a basis for action. OD practitioners need to focus on shorter-term measures of success at the individual, local level where each person tries to close the gap between oneself and one's environment. The process of building fitness adapts the organization to work productively in a changing environment.

Using a Complexity Approach for OD Processes

A complexity approach to organization development is described in this chapter. It is an approach that includes the concepts of complex responsive processes and self-organizing. OD interventions are designed to support a balance in organization functions between order and disorder, being neither too constrained nor too unconstrained. OD practitioners are concerned with fostering the process of self-organizing. This complexity approach is explored in further detail in the next sections through examination of two OD processes: team building and diversity initiatives.

Using a Complexity Approach with Team Building

The OD practitioner aids a team by helping it achieve the three conditions of self-organizing: containing, differentiating, and transforming exchange. All three conditions are important in building a productive team. Too much focus on one or another of the conditions can result in frustration. Since some team leaders and team members like certain conditions best, the OD practitioner can be helpful in balancing their attention on all three.

The practitioner should watch out for colluding with restrictive practices, rigid procedures, and required best practices. By tracking the team's readiness for change and championing variation and experimentation, the OD practitioner increases the team's resiliency and capability for continual adaptation.

In the process of team building, all three of the conditions for self-organizing are linked. A change in one shifts the behavior of the team, which results in changes in the other two conditions. An intervention in one condition is likely to generate new learning and productive patterns in the other two.

- All three conditions are important to building a lasting and productive team.
- Too much focus on one or another of the conditions can result in frustration.
- Teams move from focus on one of the conditions to another over time.
- A team must spend shared time talking about and practicing each condition.
- When a team is in trouble, it is because one or two conditions are neglected.
- Each condition requires its own set of skills and sensitivities.

Containing Processes. The containing processes establish boundaries, center points, and connections. How a team frames its purpose, its culture, and its processes yields multiple ways of containing its self-organizing activities. If too strong or constricting, the team will not be able to self-organize. If too weak or loose, the team also will not be able to self-organize. Self-organizing occurs only when the containing processes allow the members to freely interact and new patterns to form. For example, a team that schedules its meetings at a time and in a place with constant interruption has insufficient boundaries. A team that tolerates individual functional "stovepipes" does not foster organizational coherence. A team with cultural norms that suppress dissent and adhere to rigid work processes has containing processes that are too strong.

Without a common, stated reason for working together, a relationship can turn from being generative to being competitive. Without a focus, the group loses energy and thinks more about itself than about its goals. In this case, the OD practitioner can help the team establish ground rules for team interaction, which can shape coherent self-organization.

Significant Differences. Differences such as level of expertise, functional specialty, culture, alternative views about quality, contrasting views about use of resources, and decision making are the engine for change. If each member focuses on a difference that is significant to him or her, but the group as a whole has no shared significant difference around which to build a generative interaction, the team will stagnate. One function of the OD practitioner is to discover or articulate the important differences hidden or unacknowledged among the many that exist in the team. By focusing the group on the most significant ones, the consultant helps the group move to self-organizing.

An effective group must have similarities to bring them together and differences to introduce new ideas. If a group is too much the same, it gets stuck in old ways of thinking. If the group is too different, members find it difficult to build relationships. To build and sustain productive work, a group must learn to establish its similarities and identify and work with the significant differences. The OD practitioner can help bring out the hidden or avoided difference that will move the team to adaptive self-organizing.

Transforming Exchange. A team with an autocratic leader may be so constrained that it cannot self-organize. At the other extreme, when team members exchange only minimal task information, they find it difficult to support each other as individual workloads increase. The OD practitioner has the opportunity to see if the feedback mechanisms are adequate and if the available channels are used. If not, the practitioner can identify and intervene on the aspects of the team that are blocking the flow of quality information. Without meaningful exchanges and appreciative discussions, team members work as disjointed or independent parts and fail to come together into a pattern than spans the entire team.

Communication across differences constitutes the glue that holds a generative relationship together. Talking and listening among members of the group creates opportunities to learn and grow. Communication beyond the group allows sharing and learning. If a group does not have contacts that are transformative, it gets stuck in misunderstandings and irreconcilable differences. In this case, the OD practitioner can help maximize the number and quality of interactions among team members and note the self-organizing patterns of connections.

Strategies for Intervening in Self-Organizing Teams. To determine which condition of self-organizing may afford the most leverage for change, the OD practitioner can diagnose the level of constraint in the three conditions and intervene in one of them, knowing that the other conditions will also be affected. Observe how newly formed conditions affect the new patterns that emerge. Begin the cycle again, assessing, intervening, and observing the conditions and the patterns of self-organization that result from the constant interaction of the team members and its internal and external customers. Evaluate the impact of the interventions, and adapt practitioner interactions with the team to increase the opportunity for self-organizing. Depending on the client, teach the model of self-organizing as a tool for the team to use in its day-to-day work.

Using a Complexity Approach with Diversity Initiatives

In complex responsive processes, diversity is an asset and a requirement, not the liability often seen by top management. Diversity pushes an organization into that middle ground between order and disorder, a place far enough from equilibrium for self-organizing to take place. In organizations, diversity can mean a range of ideas, thoughts, and projects as well as difference in age, gender, race or ethnicity, group identity, physical ability, cultural background, nationality, sexual orientation, job experience, job function, values, skills, communication styles, and educational and professional background.

The OD practitioner's role in diversity initiatives is examined in this section from a complexity perspective, along with the three conditions that affect the likelihood that a diversity initiative can self-organize.

OD Practitioner Role. OD practitioners are often called on to sustain and institutionalize workforce diversity initiatives. Because everything in a self-organizing organization is interconnected, large-scale change evolves from the interaction of the parts of the system (if the OD practitioner can help create the right conditions). The targets of an OD intervention in a diversity initiative are the conditions that create self-organizing.

The processes of change fostered by diversity occur at the micro level, where relationships, interactions, small experiments, and simple rules shape emerging patterns. OD practitioners can facilitate development of inclusive norms, interactions across demographic boundaries, and cross-cultural structures. They can look for unrecognized diversity in the system and set the context of issues so the diversity dialogue does not happen in a vacuum. They need to be willing to confront behaviors that diminish diversity, and be willing to be "wrong" when engaging with difference.

Creating the Appropriate Degree of Order. To enhance self-organizing, OD interventions in a diversity initiative are designed to maintain a balance both within and between the three conditions of self-organizing. If the dominant group is exerting strong pressure to assimilate to dominant-group norms, the OD practitioner may choose to explore the consequences of those norms. However, the degree of imposed order is always situational. It might be appropriate to impose strict recruiting protocols when dealing with a legacy of discrimination, but appropriate to reduce diversity requirements on recruiting for a department that has demonstrated a high commitment to diversity. In a strongly religious culture, self-organizing may be limited if there are prohibitions about contact with people from another religious tradition.

Figure 27.1 shows the relationship between the degree of order in a system and the likelihood that a diversity initiative will be self-organizing. A high degree of self-organizing is only possible if there is a balance between order and disorder in the organization.

FIGURE 27.1. RELATIONSHIP OF ORDER AND SELF-ORGANIZING IN DIVERSITY INITIATIVES.

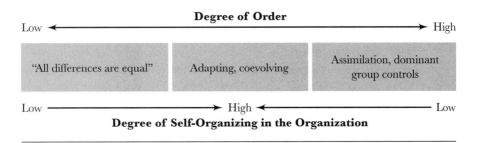

Containing. The existing culture or legacy, the organization's mission, the business case for diversity, the diversity program itself, and current policies and procedures are examples of the containing processes that hold the diversity initiative together as change occurs. Within any of these containing processes, various perspectives are shared, and group identity emerges. If the containing processes are too strong or constricting, the initiative will not be able to self-organize. If the containing process is too weak or loose, the initiative also will not be able to self-organize. Self-organizing is supported only when the diversity initiative's boundaries are permeable, but not too permeable. For example:

• A program that schedules diversity meetings at times and places that make it difficult to attend has a *physical* containing process that is too weak.

• An initiative without support from the top of the organization has an overall *organizational* containing process that is too loose. Functional divisions (research, finance, manufacturing, distribution) have their own more cohesive containing processes that will thwart the overall effort.

• An organization with cultural norms that suppress dissent has *behavioral* containing processes that are too strong or tight. A diversity dimension such as sexual orientation is a strong containing process. For example, heterosexism frames reality in a way that excludes those who are gay, lesbian, bisexual, and transgender.

• An organization that has recruitment and promotion policies fostering unearned privilege has *conceptual* containing processes that are too strong.

An OD practitioner may identify one of these containing processes for an intervention. For example, it is appropriate to have affirmative action policies and strict rules regarding recruitment if the organization is systemically discriminating against whole classes of people on the basis of the color of their skin or gender. It may be appropriate, though, for a subunit to have wide discretion within minimum procedures if it has a history of recruiting a diverse and capable workforce. OD practitioners are uniquely positioned to point out these differences.

Differentiating. Even though a diversity initiative is all about difference, it may not focus on the underlying differences that block the initiative. These could include differences in the strategic importance of various organizational units, perhaps determining which management voices about diversity are heard.

Organizational members may be aware of the unresolved difference that is blocking the initiative but be unwilling to engage with each other. This is sometimes referred to as ignoring the "dead elephant" in the middle of the room. When this happens, the organization locks in to destructive behavior that exaggerates difference without using its potential for learning and growth.

To move the organization to self-organizing, an OD practitioner can discover or articulate the important differences that are hidden or unacknowledged among the many differences that exist in the organization. Some differences may not emerge until trust is built within a diversity initiative and the participants have time to reflect on their new learning.

Transforming Exchange. Transforming contacts in a diversity initiative link the members of the organization into a meaningful and adaptive whole as they have cross-cultural experiences. An OD practitioner can intervene to develop adequate feedback mechanisms. If the mechanisms for communication are not used, the OD person can focus on the factors or individuals that are blocking the flow of information.

Interventions to Move an Initiative to Self-Organizing. In the examples given here the containers are permeable, contacts are encouraged to achieve mutual influence, and important differences are recognized and used for creative solutions.

Containing Interventions

- A multicultural environment is developed with ongoing checks to ensure that diversity is present in all endeavors.
- Allow quiet time for personal reflection, journaling, or intentional pauses in the conversation to create opportunities for individuals to reflect and clarify their own points of view. In this instance the transforming exchange is within the individual's own psyche.
- Establish overarching objectives; reinforce shared values and visions. Articulate the common ground that holds the group together.
- Establish a single diversity leadership group for the whole institution, and define new organizational and committee structures.
- Introduce concepts and activities that set a unique context for the interaction. Norms, structured practices, and rituals lend coherence to interaction.
- Invite the system into times of quiet and reflection, so the differences that are significant to individuals and to the group have an opportunity to emerge.
- Recognize the potential for turbulence, and help keep a group safe during the storm that necessarily comes with engagement.
- Hold regular cross-functional meetings where inclusion is the highest value.

Differentiating Interventions

- Introduce a conflict resolution intervention to focus on differences that can be negotiated if the system becomes stalled over a significant difference and new patterns do not emerge. For example, if there is anger about perceived special treatment, develop indicators of fair treatment for everyone and negotiate behavioral guidelines.
- Deconstruct differences to reveal the meaningful distinctions between the categories. For example, one person might be labeled an engineer and another an artist, but both are interested in creating new physical objects although they take their inspiration from differing sources and use dissimilar materials.
- Differences are presented as an essential condition for continued creativity, productivity, and sustainability for the organization.
- Do not let a single difference predominate. A small number of significant differences help a group focus, but when just one predominates the conversation tends to collapse into an argument.

• Frame differences so people can see that within them there are other important ones—for example, those that can exist between white women and women of color.

• Identify the systemic policies and procedures that maintain inequity.

• Introduce questions or possibilities that multiply the significant differences and open up the decision space to new possibilities.

• Provide power and system workshops to discover or articulate the small number of differences that are significant (for example, who holds power in the system), and keep the system focused on them.

Transforming Exchange Interventions

• Establish cross-functional learning teams to focus on specific issues of shared, systemic interest.

• Improve exchanges between the top and bottom of the organization.

• Offer mentoring programs that are readily available to all.

• Encourage transformation of the dominant culture through a high degree of interaction and inclusion across lines of difference. If the dominant group denies its unearned privilege, identify the similarities and differences in daily concerns experienced by the dominant and nondominant groups. The dominant group will see the many things they take for granted.

Conclusion

When an OD practitioner is working with an organization in an unpredictable environment or with organizational parts where there is a profound lack of agreement or certainty about how to function, using rational social engineering approaches is not likely to be successful. In this instance, an OD approach that encourages interactions and small experiments, and that identifies small successes, is likely to help clients make sense of what is trying to emerge as an adaptive response to the uncertainty the organization is facing.

The processes that can be influenced by the actions of a change agent are the "complex responsive processes" described by Stacey, Griffin, and Shaw (2000). These processes are ongoing, rich interactions and relationships of semiautonomous individuals, ideas, or groups. Small interactions of people in close proximity and those in networks have multiplying effects that produce the complexity we experience.

Interventions in these interactions and small events can aid self-organizing, the tendency of complex responsive processes to spontaneously generate new patterns by following simple rules that maximize some measure of performance over time.

An OD practitioner can foster self-organizing by keeping the processes from being too tightly controlled or too loosely controlled, thus creating a balance between order and disorder. The three processes that bring about the phenomenon of self-organizing are containing, differentiating, and transforming exchange. OD interventions in containing help establish semipermeable boundaries within which change can occur. Interventions in differentiating establish what kinds of outcomes will emerge. Intervening in transforming exchange ensures that the interactions and relationships are filled with contact and meaningful.

By focusing on any one of these three conditions of self-organizing, which are all connected, the OD practitioner contributes to emergent change by the interaction of all stakeholders rather than through top-down directives. The practitioners help the organization leaders adapt to uncertainty and avoid premature solutions (so-called) that have unintended consequences. By intervening in one of the conditions, the practitioner can keep the organization from being complacent and continuing with outdated plans and functions. OD practitioners can also amplify differences that are being ignored in the organization but that hold the promise to help the organization adapt to changes in the environment. At the same time, the OD practitioner can help the organization members see similarities across the organization that can bring some necessary coherence amid change. To respond to organization needs for performance measures, the OD practitioner can identify some short-term successes that are consistent with what is required by the organization's environment.

In this chapter, two examples of applying this complexity science approach were given: team building and diversity initiatives. In both of these areas of organization change (and others), it is essential that self-organizing processes be created to avoid locking into norms, practices, or procedures that make the team or organization unresponsive to the continuing changes that are happening elsewhere in the organization, or in the task environment served by the organization.

References

Burke, W. W. (2004). Organization development: What we know and what we need to know going forward. *OD Practitioner, 36*(3), 4–8.

Cilliers, P. (1998). *Complexity and postmodernism: Understanding complex systems.* London: Routledge.

Eoyang, G. (1999). *Coping with chaos: Seven simple tools.* Cheyenne, WY: Lagumo.

Goldstein, J. (1994). *The unshackled organization.* New York: Productivity Press.

Kelly, S., & Allison, M. A. (1998). *The complexity advantage: How the science of complexity can help your business achieve peak performance.* New York: McGraw-Hill.

Olson, E. E., & Eoyang, G. H. (2001). *Facilitating organization change: Lessons from complexity science.* San Francisco: Jossey-Bass/Pfeiffer.

Olson, E. E., & Townsend, M. (n.d.). *Leading in organizations: Tapping the energy of self-organizing.* Manuscript in process.

Pascale, R. T. (2004). Spotlight on Richard T. Pascale. In *Emerald now* (http://www.emerald insight.com).

Pascale, R. T., Millemann, M., & Gioja, L. (2000). *Surfing the edge of chaos: The laws of nature and the new laws of business.* New York: Crown Business.

Petzinger, T. (1999). *The new pioneers.* New York: Simon and Schuster.

Stacey, R., Griffin, D., & Shaw, P. (2000). *Complexity and management: Fad or radical challenge to systems thinking?* London: Routledge.

Zimmerman, B., Lindberg, C., & Plsek, P. (1998). *Edgeware: Insights from complexity science or health care leaders.* Irving TX: VHA.

CHAPTER TWENTY-EIGHT

DEVELOPING ORGANIZATIONS AS LEARNING SYSTEMS

Anthony J. DiBella

The field of organization development (OD) is fundamentally about the processes and products of change. To develop an organization means taking it from one level or stage of performance to another, presumably in some positive direction. OD practitioners are not bound by or required to recite the Hippocratic oath ("First, do no harm"), yet that remark or affirmation is consistent with the beliefs and values of the profession. In OD, there is a presumption that change or development represents positive improvement in one or more key indicators that are of concern to clients. The practitioner's role is to help clients move along that path in as fast, safe, and harmless a way as possible.

In OD, the focal or reference point for improvement is some organizational context or system. But organizational systems don't change by themselves. They change through and because of individuals. This is not to say individual well-being is not a concern. Indeed, a hallmark of traditional OD is appreciation and respect for every individual. The challenge is how to make organizational systems more productive without placing the burden of the improvement on the shoulders (or shrinking paychecks) of individual employees.

In today's competitive, global marketplace, performance improvement as promoted through OD is more critical than ever to organizational survival. In fact, one might argue that within the dominant paradigm of positivism, progress and improvement are not only inevitable but at the core of American (if not all of

Western or industrialized) culture. A key issue in OD is not whether change will occur but rather what role the OD practitioner plays in determining the pace, direction, and outcome of change.

The practice of OD is based on intimacy and activism with change, as opposed to alienation and fatalism. Consultants, whether based inside or outside their client organizations, have a direct impact on the welfare and effectiveness of their clients, and it is not an inconsequential one. When practitioners behave in accordance with a belief that their actions can change the world, then directed and meaningful action is bound to ensue, which promotes a self-fulfilling cycle.

OD is not the indiscriminate practice of applying some fixed solution from afar. In developing and taking action with or for their clients, practitioners create intimate relationships. From the anxieties and uncertainties of the initial diagnostic stage to the joy of celebrating outcomes, feelings are shared, thus making the experiences more organic and vibrant than mechanistic. There is a belief within OD that when our body and spirit, mind and soul, thoughts and feelings are all engaged, clients benefit far more than if consultants merely function as dispassionate, tinkering intellectuals or engineers (with no offense to that profession).

Through the course of their careers, OD practitioners may help clients learn from their own experience and that of others to more effectively and more efficiently realize their missions and stated goals. This chapter explains the overlap and relationship between OD and learning. In so doing, it covers various issues that parallel the coverage of other topics and themes in this book. For practitioners, this chapter offers a framework to intervene in organizational systems in order to promote learning in a manner that is consistent with traditional OD principles. For scholars and researchers, this chapter lays out ideas for framing new research questions that challenge the dominant, normative paradigm of "the learning organization."

This chapter presents perspectives regarding the link between the development of organizations and the domain of team and organizational learning. Indeed, you cannot have one without the other. Unless change is institutionalized or embedded by manifest or latent learning processes, organizations are bound to return to old ways or habits; but this insight gets ahead of the story. First, here are a few observations regarding OD and learning.

Learning and Change, Learning and OD

It is impossible to promote change without generating learning as well. Successfully altering how people work together entails learning new skills and new patterns of communication. To change an organization's culture, employees must learn new values or assumptions. For staff to effectively work in a newly designed organization or structure, they must learn new roles and forms of social interaction.

Learning a new skill or way of perceiving the world enhances the capability of better realizing goals and aspirations. This is the fundamental objective of OD: developing capacity to realize and achieve our aims. Perhaps at some point in history, developing capacity in and of organizations was optional, but now in a world that is constantly changing it is not; this demands constant learning. Even maintaining the same, relative capability demands learning. Symbolic of this requirement is the burgeoning presence of internal, corporate positions that combine learning and organization development, as in the job title vice president for learning and OD.

Fundamental Assumptions of Learning Systems

Developing organizations as learning systems is based on three fundamental assumptions and principles. These principles, acquired through applied research and practical experience, exhibit how interwoven OD and learning really are. They apply equally to public or private, profit or nonprofit organizations.

Cybernetic (Self-Regulating) Systems. First, all living or social systems are cybernetic (self-regulating) systems. The essence of living is the capacity to monitor or be aware of oneself or one's environment through various forms and mechanisms of feedback. Whether our clients monitor their costs, profits, social benefits, or how much paper needs to be ordered for the copy machines, information about current and desired performance is always being processed. Performance feedback systems generate and percolate the lifelines of learning so organizations may adjust or alter their actions, tactics, and strategies.

Relevant here is a fundamental definition of *organizational learning.* Organizational learning comprises a set of processes to maintain or improve performance on the basis of experience. Performance feedback systems generate and disseminate the information and knowledge that is necessary for organizations to learn. Some performance feedback is automatic, as with monthly accounting or daily inventory; or it can be intermittent, as in learning histories (Roth, 2000, Roth and Kleiner, 1998). In some cases feedback is linear; in others it is chaotic or stochastic. Either way, what living systems do is process their experience (and that of others) through cybernetics. The insight or information that is generated is available to help an organization better achieve its mission or vision.

Living Systems Are Reactive Systems. A second principle that should guide work in OD and learning is that all living systems are reactive systems. All forms of engagement with a system promote change. This principle stems from the seminal work of Kurt Lewin, an OD pioneer (Lewin, 1951). It is the antithesis of an oft-cited article "Why Change Programs Don't Promote Change" (Beer, Eisenstat, and Spector, 1990). All change programs produce change and generate after-effects; some are intentional, others unintentional.

You cannot merely touch, interact, or intervene in something that is living or organic without having an effect or prompting a response. Consistent with a fundamental principle in physics, to every action there is a reaction. As suggested by the uncertainty principle, even measuring a phenomenon produces an impact.

Capability Is a Form of Engagement with an OD Orientation. The third principle builds on the first and second. Developing learning capability is a form of engagement; to be successful, it requires an OD orientation. Organizations, as cybernetic systems, have embedded learning processes. When we try to develop learning in an organization, we must acknowledge what already exists and expect some reaction from it. Efforts to build learning organizations have failed because they did not follow this principle.

When working with clients in a manner consistent with these principles, always keep in mind a corollary that reflects the context in which a practitioner works. Every living system contains the seeds of its own growth and its own decay. One interpretation of autopoeisis, as articulated by Maturana (2000), is that living systems have the capacity to become what they are. In essence, systems grow and develop in an ongoing manner through a maturation process. Conversely, even as systems grow and develop they are countered by the forces of entropy that promote decline and decay. As systems mature and acquire learning (some might call this wisdom), some abilities are, in parallel, decaying through the aging process. Change agents need to tap into the forces of growth while being cognizant of the coexisting forces or processes of decline.

Learning and Levels of Analysis and Engagement

Learning as a process of development can be promoted at a number of levels of analysis or identity. OD engagements may be oriented or focused on these levels. At a primary level, OD practitioners help individuals learn the skills or competencies they need to be successful in their own career and for their own organization. Whether the practitioner's role is that of coach, facilitator, teacher, or trainer, the focus is on the competence of an individual. Through feedback and encouragement, clients come to learn new behaviors or see new possibilities.

Learning and development is much more complex on a social level of engagement, the simplest of which is the workgroup or team. Behaviors, competencies, and lessons of experience are shared or acquired together. In some cases, learning occurs through one-to-one mentoring or role modeling. In other cases, it is a collective process as promoted through communities of practice (Wenger, 1998).

When the client is an entire organization or institution, practitioners function on another level of complexity. This requires awareness of the dynamics that occur not only within groups or teams but between them as well (Schein, 1996). Learning on an organizational, divisional, or business unit level is more challenging and rewarding but has some distinctive properties.

As organizations grow, mature, and change, they confront new situations and circumstances. In responding to them, new skills, values, or behaviors are created or acquired. What is learned in the process becomes the property of some collective unit and remains there even as certain members leave. Otherwise, if what has been learned is lost as individuals leave, then one cannot say that the organization per se has learned.

Some claim there is a fourth level of learning (beyond individual, group, and organizational): societal. How do entire societies learn and develop? Can such learning be directed or facilitated in any way? It is difficult to conceive of such a movement in a free or market-driven society. One example may be the collective experience of the Union of South Africa after Apartheid to learn from the past to ensure a more prosperous and emotionally satisfying future. In this case, led by Desmond Tutu and Nelson Mandela, South African officials conducted open reconciliation hearings to encourage people to admit their actions during the era of Apartheid so others could know what had happened and why. The resulting catharsis was aimed at helping South Africans learn from their experience in a collective manner to promote a more informed and accepting society.

Learning in Response to Notable Events

Learning and change are problematic to managers, executives, and organizations because of the costs and disruption they entail. It is much easier to go along as if in some productive mode (seemingly or otherwise) without having to cope with the changes that learning generates, or having to make the investment learning requires. Make no mistake about it: both change and learning require a commitment of time and other resources.

The values of a market economy demand that companies and their executives focus on activities that are immediately productive or contribute directly to profitability. Investing in change efforts, such as learning, to make worklife or organizations better in the future is time taken from activities that can be regarded or measured as worthwhile in the present. Even though some learning and change occurs simply through a process of maturation or serendipity, it takes an investment to learn from experience. Learning that contributes to the development of an organization's human and social capital can be costly, with an uncertain or immeasurable return.

So what *does* spur an investment in learning, if it is not part of one's values? Two simple answers are considered here: first, a change in one's external environment, and second, an unexpected and undesirable event. If some change occurs in the external environment, organizations must learn how to cope with the change or the new conditions it fosters. An excellent example of this phenomenon on a societal level was the occasion of the launch of the satellite *Sputnik* by the Soviet Union in 1957. This event, which took place in the middle of the Cold War, demonstrated the superiority of the Russians in space flight and caused the United States to invest heavily in educational programs focused on engineering and the physical sciences to make up the gap.

A more common way to spur change these days is through benchmarking. By comparing their business practices with others, companies learn about what works and what doesn't. In the 1980s Motorola thought their production techniques were state-of-the-art, until they compared themselves to Japanese manufacturers and found how lacking they really were. That spurred a gigantic investment in learning and establishment of Motorola's Six Sigma program, which has become a trademark process for change and business improvement (Eckes and Derickson, 2002).

Change is also inevitable as organizations learn about rules or regulations that govern their industry. When governments pass new laws or change existing ones, businesses must often alter their practices to remain in compliance. During the years 2003–04, a major concern in the U.S. beef industry was the prevalence of mad cow disease. One likely outcome is new regulations that ranchers and beef processing companies must learn to implement. In 2003, a tragic nightclub fire in Rhode Island that killed one hundred people led to widespread changes in fire laws governing public places and venues. Nightclub and theater owners now have to learn how they can stay in business given their higher costs.

As external change requires us to learn, sometimes our own experience prompts learning. Operational errors, mistakes, or accidents highlight failures or problems that, if left uncorrected, will cause further harm to private property or personal lives. For example, whenever there is a crash of a civilian airplane in the United States, the owner, builder, and designer of the aircraft come together to understand the cause of the crash and what might be done to avoid similar incidents in the future. Under the auspices of the National Transportation Safety Board (NTSB), a panel of experts investigates the crash and makes a series of recommendations. The outcome may lead to changes in pilot training, communication protocols between flight staff and air traffic controllers, or equipment maintenance procedures.

To learn from experience means that we have made some change in our attitudes, behaviors, or the world we live in. Sometimes those changes are generated from within, sometimes from without. In effect, change prompts learning, which in turn promotes further change.

Learning and Diversity

Over the past forty years, a significant amount of research has been done on the benefits of diverse workforces. Journal articles that have become classics (Maier, 1967; Schachter, Ellertson, McBride, and Gregory, 1951) point out how differences between people affect workplace dynamics and can be used for competitive advantage. The same principle applies to the learning that takes place in and of organizations.

Would you expect a group (or department) of mechanical engineers to learn together the same way that a group of accountants or graphic designers would? Of course not. In promoting change in organizations, we need to recognize the learning capabilities and styles of individuals and groups. The work of Howard Gardner (1993) on multiple intelligences and Daniel Goleman (1995) on emotional intelligence has shown that understanding competence requires more than just testing for IQ. Competence, intelligence, and learning are all multidimensional concepts that cannot be determined with a single measure. Reliance on one kind of assessment simplifies reality and devalues forms that deviate from social norms. For example, in his theory of multiple intelligences Gardner identifies seven types, among them spatial, musical, and mathematical intelligence. In his book *A Mind at a Time*, Mel Levine explains the functioning of eight systems of learning, such as attention control, memory, and sequential ordering (Levine, 2003).

Much as individuals learn in different ways, so too do organizations. To some extent these differences are a function of the diverse environments in which organizations operate. For example, what and how an organization in a stable environment with established products (ketchup, or cement) learns is different from what happens in an industry that is volatile and involves new products or evolving technologies (such as computer software or nanotechnology).

Diverse learning styles also occur as a result of an organization's history, culture, size, and age. New, entrepreneurial firms are apt to learn differently from larger, established corporations. The former learn through knowledge created about leading-edge products or technologies, while the latter focus on improving existing ones. Learning styles do not reflect how well an organization is learning, or how valuable those learnings are, but they do shape *what* the organization is learning and *how* that learning is taking place.

Learning Orientations

Research studies have identified seven learning orientations or processes whereby knowledge in organizations is acquired or developed, shared, and used (DiBella, 1998, 2001; DiBella, Nevis, and Gould, 1996). These learning dimensions, shown in Table 28.1, can be juxtaposed to recognize distinctive learning styles in organizations. Acknowledging the presence of multiple styles within a company can explain some intergroup conflicts and barriers to learning. If parts of a company learn in contrasting ways, then it is highly unlikely that knowledge will be efficiently transferred across functional or group boundaries. Once we recognize such barriers, we can manage them as a potential source of diversity and competitive advantage.

TABLE 28.1. LEARNING ORIENTATIONS.

Orientation	Description
Knowledge source	Preference for developing knowledge internally as opposed to acquiring knowledge developed externally
Content-process focus	Emphasis on knowledge about what products and services are as compared to emphasis on knowledge about how those products and services are developed or delivered
Knowledge reserve	Knowledge is possessed by individuals, compared to knowledge that is publicly available
Dissemination mode	Knowledge is shared in formal, prescribed methods, compared to knowledge shared through informal methods such as role modeling and casual interaction
Learning scope	Preference for knowledge related to improving existing capabilities, products, or services, compared to preference for knowledge related to developing new ones
Value-chain focus	Emphasis on learning investments in engineering or production activities ("design and make" functions) as opposed to sales or service ("market and deliver" functions)
Learning focus	Development of knowledge pertaining to individual performance, compared to development of knowledge pertaining to group performance

Learning Portfolio

Learning practices and styles constitute the raw elements of an organization's "learning portfolio."

The idea of an organization as a learning portfolio reflects a capability that has evolved and grown as the organization's culture has matured. To use that capability for competitive advantage, organizational members must first recognize the elements that shape and compose it. Identifying current capabilities is a starting point for strategic action to change, augment, or enhance a style or portfolio of styles. Rather than presume no existing competence and the need to build it from the bottom up, managers work with and from what already exists. By focusing on the positive, this approach is consistent with techniques of appreciative inquiry (Watkins and Mohr, 2001). It contrasts with prescriptive techniques wherein organizations that do not have specific competencies are regarded as failing. A learning portfolio reveals how learning practices, styles, and profiles form a complete organizationwide system of learning and change.

Companies with a large portfolio of learning practices are apt to have multiple competencies and a greater capacity to adapt to change than are companies relying on a single approach to learning. By focusing on a company's learning portfolio in its entirety, learning advocates can reorient themselves from wondering whether the company has the *right* set of learning practices or styles to considering their *complementarity*. Instead of focusing on individual activities, they can take a systemic view to consider synergistic possibilities between elements in the learning portfolio.

For example, many learning advocates suggest that double-loop or transformative learning is preferable to single or corrective, incremental learning (Argyris and Schön, 1978). Yet in the control room of a nuclear power plant, a transformative learning style is apt to lead to disastrous consequences (as was the case with the nuclear accident at Chernobyl). However, it would be entirely appropriate and strategically advantageous for a company that runs a nuclear power plant to operate an equipment R&D lab where employees practiced transformative learning. In the context of the entire firm, the styles are complementary.

Learning and OD Practitioner Skills

OD practitioners should engage with clients in diverse ways to develop their learning capability. Their role may be to coach a plant manager, help a technically oriented professional acquire the skills demanded of a managerial position, or facilitate a workteam's ability to process some learning opportunity. To perform in these roles requires process skills that are generic to OD, such as the ability to offer feedback, facilitate conversations, prompt dialogue, resolve conflict, and offer encouragement. However, to promote learning in organizations requires content knowledge as well.

First, an OD professional must have an understanding of the complex social processes whereby organizations are constituted and function. Whichever metaphor is used to understand some organization (Morgan, 1993), it's critical that OD practitioners recognize their own working theory about organizations and learning and what it means to juxtapose these two concepts (organization learning, learning organization). In-depth knowledge of organization theory and learning theory, including historical and contemporary perspectives, establishes an essential foundation.

With that, practitioners may assess specific models and techniques that claim to promote learning organizations. A key focus in developing learning capability is establishing the conditions that enable learning to take place. Research studies have identified ten factors, as shown in Exhibit 28.1, that facilitate learning (DiBella, 1998, 2001). Two of these factors are particularly aligned with the work and perspective that OD practitioners offer a client: climate of openness, and systems perspective.

EXHIBIT 28.1. FACTORS THAT PROMOTE LEARNING.

1. *Scanning imperative* Gather information about conditions and practices outside one's own unit; seek out information about the external environment.

2. *Performance gap* Shared perception of gap between current and desired performance.

3. *Concern for measurement* Considerable effort is spent defining and measuring key factors. Discourse over metrics is regarded as a learning activity.

4. *Organizational curiosity* Curiosity about conditions and practices; interest in creative ideas and new technologies; support for experimentation.

5. *Climate of openness* Open communication among organizational members; problems, errors, or lessons are shared, not hidden.

6. *Continuous education* Commitment of quality resources for learning.

7. *Operational variety* Value different methods, procedures, and competencies; appreciate diversity.

8. *Multiple advocates* New ideas and methods can be advanced by employees at all organizational levels. Multiple advocates or champions exist.

9. *Involved leadership* Leaders are personally and actively involved in learning initiatives and in ensuring that a learning environment is maintained.

10. *Systems perspective* Recognition of interdependence among organizational units and groups; awareness of time delay between actions and their outcomes.

Climate of openness refers to a feeling employees have that encourages them to share perceptions and offer feedback about organizational or team performance. This means an ability to speak out without fear of retribution and with confidence that feedback will not be avoided or ignored but used in some constructive manner. Learning requires dissemination and processing of feedback and information. If information about operational mistakes, errors, or poor performance is hidden rather than shared, an organization will not learn. Promoting a climate of openness may sound Pollyanna, but it requires traditional OD work to encourage employee participation and reduce defensiveness. OD practitioners should encourage organizational leaders to reward rather than penalize those who speak out and act as messengers. In establishing a climate of openness, an organization also promotes creativity and innovation, which is so dependent on the sharing of information and knowledge (Mauzy and Harriman, 2003).

In large companies, sharing information means crossing organizational, business unit, or departmental boundaries. Doing so successfully requires the ability to think in terms of whole systems and the interdependence of parts. Working cross-organizationally can encourage learning in one part of a company to be transferred to another. In some situations, as when NTSB investigates a plane crash as described earlier, learning must take place across or between entire industries. OD practitioners help clients develop a systems perspective when the relationships between organizational units are understood and time lags between action and consequence are acknowledged.

Finally, professionals who promote learning in others must model the behavior. It is said that there is no more dangerous or vulnerable a position to be in than one held by someone who thinks he is fully knowledgeable about a topic or fully prepared for some event. Consistent with Maturana's view of autopoeisis, the day we stop learning is the day we start dying. Professionals need to keep up with the methods and ideas of their field, the challenges faced by their clients, and their own personal needs and wants. Attending professional conferences and workshops, reading the latest books and essays of colleagues, writing down personal experiences and insights, and maintaining healthy self-awareness can help us stay current with our inner self and the world around us. Through constant upgrading of skills, we can be better positioned to enhance the skills and competencies of others.

Developing Organizations as Learning Systems

Promoting and building learning capability in an organization means promoting change. To do so within an OD framework requires three basic steps:

1. Recognizing and appreciating current learning processes
2. Establishing a gap between existing learning and strategic learning needs
3. Identifying actions to enhance desired learning capability

To survive, any social system requires learning processes, whether overt or covert, if only to acculturate newcomers to preexisting values and assumptions. To promote learning in a system, we need first to acknowledge what those existing learning processes are; then we can work with a client to improve or change them. By surfacing existing (although perhaps transparent) processes, an OD approach empowers individuals to focus on present capabilities and use their awareness as a take-off point for desired competencies. The key question is not whether an organization is a learning organization, but does the organization's learning portfolio help realize its mission in the most effective manner? By framing the issue in this manner, the OD practitioner is less apt to impose a fixed or canned solution.

To improve learning processes, we need to ask what must employees learn for an organization to realize its mission or implement its strategy, and how well are they currently learning. In organizations, learning is valued because it helps realize desirable outcomes. However, learning can only contribute in this way if our clients know what those outcomes are. Once an organization's mission is established and a strategy designed, then the learning implications become clear. For example, if a company wants to be customer-focused, what do employees need to learn to be that way, and how will they learn those competencies? In this way a gap can be established between what employees currently learn and how they learn on the one hand and the learning that needs to take place on the other. Various assessment tools have been developed to help OD practitioners with this step in the process (DiBella, 2001).

Once existing and desired capabilities are identified, a client needs to develop an action plan to eliminate any gaps and produce change. Some actions may be designed for the individual level, others at a collective or social level. For example, to become more customer-oriented, managers and professionals may need some additional training in marketing or listening skills. On a collective level, workteams may need to learn how to better process customer feedback and use customer complaints as learning opportunities. Encouraging communities of practice could be another element of an action plan.

This basic, three-step process to develop learning capability is a traditional one in OD: recognize the present, develop a consensus about the future, and then create a plan to get there. It sounds simple, and certainly the theory of it is; but people and the systems they formulate and occupy are far more complex than imagined. Resistance to change lurks in many physical and virtual spaces. However, over time OD practitioners can become aware of where to look and how to avoid, cope with, or overcome the dynamics of change and learning.

Summary

It's preferable that OD practitioners not promote just-in-case learning, learning that might someday be useful. Rather, we need to promote learning and learning capability that contributes to specific outcomes. The question is therefore what outcomes we are seeking to affect or perpetuate through our (or our client's) efforts and investments in learning.

The answer involves, and certainly would reflect, our value system. When we ask "Why learn?" our honest answer demonstrates what we consider important. *Honest* because certain answers may not be socially or politically acceptable. For example, if a hospital wants to learn in order to reduce medical error, its intent could be better patient care or greater profits. The latter answer is inconsistent with the perceived (or at least oft-stated) values of health care practitioners.

OD practitioners must promote win-win scenarios and avoid exploitation of people or the environment. To learn in order to do better or to do good is what the OD profession is all about. To help organizations such as Amtrak learn to make its trains run on time, or the airlines and nuclear power plants to avoid accidents, helps them become more profitable while concurrently increasing social benefits. Who could say that isn't worth the effort?

References

Argyris, C., & Schön, D. A. (1978). *Organizational learning.* Reading, MA: Addison-Wesley.

Beer, M., Eisenstat, R. A., & Spector, B. (1990, November–December). Why change programs don't produce change. *Harvard Business Review,* 158–166.

DiBella, A. J. (1998). *How organizations learn: An integrated strategy for building learning capability.* San Francisco: Jossey-Bass.

DiBella, A. J. (2001). *Learning practices: Assessment and action for organizational improvement.* Upper Saddle River, NJ: Prentice Hall.

DiBella, A. J., Nevis, E. C., & Gould, J. M. (1996). Understanding organizational learning capability. *Journal of Management Studies, 33,* 361–379.

Eckes, G., & Derickson, S. (2002). *Six Sigma dynamics: The elusive key to project success.* San Francisco: Wiley.

Gardner, H. (1993). *Multiple intelligences: Theory in practice.* New York: Basic Books.

Goleman, D. (1995). *Emotional intelligence.* New York: Bantam Books.

Levine, M. (2003). *A mind at a time.* Carmichael, CA: Touchstone Books.

Lewin, K. (1951). *Field theory in social science.* New York: HarperCollins.

Maier, N. (1967, July). Assets and liabilities in group decision-making. *Psychological Review, 74*(4), 239–249.

Maturana, H. (2000). *Steps to an ecology of mind: Collected essays in anthropology, psychiatry, evolution, and epistemology.* Chicago: University of Chicago Press.

Mauzy, J., and Harriman, R. (2003). *Creativity, Inc.: Building an inventive organization.* Boston: Harvard Business School Press.

Morgan, G. (1993). *Imaginization.* Thousand Oaks, CA: Sage.

Roth, G. (2000). Constructing conversations: Lessons from learning from experience. *Organizational Development Journal, 18*(4), 69–78.

Roth, G., & Kleiner, A. (1998, Autumn). Developing organizational memory through learning histories. *Organizational Dynamics, 27,* 43–60.

Schachter, S., Ellertson, N., McBride, D., and Gregory, D. (1951). An experimental study of cohesiveness and productivity. *Human Relations, 4,* 229–238.

Schein, E. (1996). The three cultures of management: Implications for organizational learning. *Sloan Management Review, 38,* 9–20.

Watkins, J. M., & Mohr, B. (2001). *Appreciative inquiry: Change at the speed of imagination.* San Francisco: Jossey-Bass/Pfeiffer.

Wenger, E. (1998). *Communities of practice: Learning, meaning, and identity.* Cambridge, England: Cambridge University Press.

PART SEVEN

THE FUTURE OF ORGANIZATION DEVELOPMENT

CHAPTER TWENTY-NINE

A POSITIVE VISION OF OD'S FUTURE

Christopher G. Worley and Ann McCloskey

The field of organization development (OD) is facing serious questions about its future (Burke, 1976, 2002; Cummings and Worley, 2005). Several observers have described the current situation as an important crossroads in the field's history (Freedman, 1999; Farias and Johnson, 2000; Worren, Ruddle, and Moore, 1999; Hornstein, 2001; Worley and Feyerherm, 2003). On the one hand, OD is a powerful and institutionalized activity in many large and small companies, and it significantly influences how organizations are managed (Kleiner, 1996). On the other hand, OD is struggling with its own identity. It is often confused with change management and other forms of organizational change, its professional associations are grappling with their image, and many question the value of OD.

A critical question facing the field at this crossroads is, What does the future of OD look like, and how will it get there? This chapter proposes one answer by describing a positive, possible, and hopefully provocative future scenario. Other scenarios are certainly possible, and good practice supports articulation of several

Note: We extend a warm and special thanks to Scott Sherman for helping us keep the voices in our heads straight; to our MSOD colleagues—Terri Egan, Ann Feyerherm, and Miriam Lacey—for their commitment to the ongoing conversation; and to Beth Waitkus, Laura Jackson, and the Greenhouse gang for their inputs on messaging and the future of OD. In addition, we gratefully acknowledge the careful reviews of earlier drafts by Foster Mobley, Ken Murrell, Daphne Deporres, and the editors.

alternative scenarios (Porter, 1985; Klein and Linneman, 1981; Wack, 1985). However, our approach was to generate a positive and integrative scenario.

Any view of what is positive is biased, and every effort will be made to be transparent about the choices. The scenario draws from likely economic, social, technical, cultural, and organizational trends (Cummings and Worley, 2005), other views of the future (Murrell, 2003; International Forum on Globalization, 2002), and a variety of alternative future scenarios found on the Internet (examples: www.gsg.org/scenario_descriptions.html, http://mars3.gps.caltech.edu/which world/explore/scenarios_top.html, and http://www.futurestudies.co.uk/predic tions/083.pdf, all accessed in October 2004).

This chapter stands in that future, to recount the historical role a rejuvenated OD played in creating this positive scenario. OD strongly influenced the future because OD practitioners (1) formed and leveraged an alliance among the field's professional associations and (2) supported implementation of the responsible progress doctrine.

A Positive Future Scenario

The world of 2025 is a culturally diverse, mostly safe, and increasingly connected society. A complementary and aligned set of governmental, technological, organizational, and workforce trends and policies enable an overwhelming majority of the world's people to benefit from globalization. North America shares the economic leadership with other economies. Shifts in the cultural identity of the United States from unconscious imperialism to conscious capitalism between 2005 and 2010 hastened this more collaborative approach to global governance. The U.S. movement was similar to the more community-oriented, connected, and sustainable vision that emerged in the European Union during the early 2000s (Rifkin, 2004). The move clearly changed the conversation among governments, religions, and other interests. A revamped United Nations is making progress to resolve centuries-old conflicts around the world and to slow the spread of AIDS/ HIV considerably. Terrorism remains a global threat, but its impact has been greatly reduced.

A tacit global industrial policy emerged following facilitated and coordinated action among the financial markets, organizations, governments, and other stakeholders in the early 2010s. A key element in development of this policy was an agreement among these groups to pursue moderate growth that allowed environmental issues to be addressed alongside economic performance concerns. Moderated growth rates radically slowed greenhouse effects and created opportunities for sustainable economies. Tax policies were shifted through unprecedented governmental coordination to encourage ecologically responsible behavior. Investors from New York's Wall Street to Hong Kong's Hang Seng have been swifter in rewarding companies that "do the right thing" and equally swift in punishing organizations that fail to balance long-term development against short-term profit maximization.

Technology has helped and is helping to address a variety of environmental, health, hunger, and education issues in 2025. The demise of fossil fuels as the basis of most economies followed major viable breakthroughs in alternative energy sources. Alternative energy sources—fuel cells, solar and wind power—and their development have become new economic opportunities. Remaining efforts to explore and extract natural resources are coordinated with environmental concerns in a truly sustainable fashion. Information technologies also are used to empower extensive participation by all vested groups in governance, protect individual privacy, and secure communication. Broad-based information availability and access have created an environment where organizations and governments are expected to act responsibly and are rewarded for it. The 2025 media have detailed many accounts of how individuals and organizations use the Internet to promote public responsibility. The adaptable nongovernmental organizations are one notable example. The NGOs and others have used the truly World Wide Web of 2025 to monitor organizations and governments, and to alert the media about unsafe or environmentally unsound activities and violations of basic human rights.

The economics of collaboration replaced traditional notions of competition at the organizational level around 2018. Revised definitions of *wealth* and new methods of accumulation lowered wealth concentration and closed the gap between the haves and the have nots. Network structures that enable small systems to be part of large wholes have proliferated. These structures were, ironically, what made the early terrorist movement so effective. Large and small organizations, governments, and public infrastructure systems are less vulnerable to attack and disruption as a result. The triumph of loose over tight systems integration without loss of efficiency was enabled by advances in security and privacy software. The advanced software technologies obviated concerns over Big Brother and allowed more effective monitoring of terrorist communications and planning.

Organization networks also support the policy of sustainability by decreasing the size of most organizations. Organizations in a network specialize in specific products or services across a variety of countries and cultures. The only constraint these organizations operate under is to provide what was agreed to. They are free to operate according to local custom, use local resources, and organize according to principles of sustainability.

OD's Role in Creating A Positive Future

The field of OD is broadly regarded as making a substantive contribution to this scenario. The keynote speaker at the 2025 World OD Alliance (WODA) Conference in Baghdad, Wangari Muta Maathai, recounted OD's amazing rejuvenation as the most influential service offering the world has ever known. She proposed that the alliance among professional OD associations and enactment of the responsible progress doctrine were the two key events that energized OD influence.

An Orchestrated Alliance: From Fragmented to Coordinated Action

Maathai, now more than eighty years old, suggested that OD's rejuvenation began with the 2007 announcement of the World OD Alliance, a network of professional OD associations. The alliance signaled the field's commitment to move from fragmented to coordinated action, and to discard what had been unproductive promulgation of distracting and competing voices. The alliance committed almost immediately to a conversation about its values. "Learning" emerged as a cornerstone of practice. The alliance created an integrated marketing and education program as its next step. Maathai detailed for the conference the alliance's initial rationale, subsequent creation of an integrative and cornerstone value, and the alliance activities that promoted OD practice.

Alliance Rationale. The alliance announcement symbolized the field's intention to coordinate its efforts toward an integrative view of OD's potential. It sought to end the sometimes subtle and frequently distracting competition among three OD views or voices of the past. The traditional, pragmatic, and scholarly voices each believed that one form of OD was better than another, more aligned with certain values, or more supportive of certain outcomes (Alderfer, 2003; Cummings and Worley, 2005; Worley and Feyerherm, 2003). One example is that the traditional OD voice believed OD's primary goal was to create organizational processes that were transparent, treated people with dignity, and served diversity. The traditional voice relied on humanistic values of democracy, trust, and human integrity. Traditionalists saw the key to improving organization effectiveness as transformation of the relationship between the individual and the organization (Friedlander, 1998).

A pragmatic voice believed that developing the organization created an environment where people could become healthy. The pragmatic voice relied on instrumental values of relevance, utility, and professionalism to increase effectiveness by managing changes in the relationship between the organization and its environment (Friedlander, 1998). The pragmatic approach to change was seen as more helpful, less likely to address the distracting emotional aspects of change, and more concerned with implementation than traditional approaches.

The third voice was the scholarly, which focused on creating valid knowledge and on generalizing conclusions about how change occurs, how it is triggered, under what conditions it works well, and so on (Pettigrew, Woodman, and Cameron, 2001). The scholarly voice was not concerned about how OD was defined, what its values were, how it was practiced, or whether an OD practitioner was involved except as a potential explanation for change success. OD was just one of several ways organizations could be changed.

Twentieth-century OD practitioners had hoped that such diverse voices would strengthen and grow the field by encouraging innovation, exploration, and knowledge creation. However, the professional associations were ineffective at expanding the influence and reputation of the field despite considerable new interventions, processes, and philosophies. The reality was that professional associations did not spend much time together, no infrastructure was available to orchestrate their efforts, and each group created and defended its own version of what OD should be.

The World OD Alliance that brought these divergent groups together did what the individual associations could not. The alliance increased the field's capacity for influence by leveraging members' unique resources and perspectives. Examples are recognizing that the National Training Laboratories (NTL) and university OD programs were a natural choice to lead the field in building OD practitioner process skills, and that the Academy of Management's ODC division, the Society of Industrial and Organizational Psychology (SIOP), and other groups were an equally natural choice to generate knowledge on the empirical relationship between change and performance and the moderating effects of commitment, participation, communication, and organization capability. Additional capacity and leverage was created by setting and resetting the research agenda for the field each year in collaboration with the OD Network, the American Society for Training and Development, and other practice-oriented associations to address both long-term issues and pressing business concerns.

The World OD Alliance succeeded because its members recognized the powerful and pervasive trend toward organizational networks. The advantages of organizational networks included smallness, agility, support for local culture and diversity, and global reach. These advantages were offset by a weak and impractical knowledge base that afforded OD an incredible opportunity. OD would be a microcosm (Alderfer, 1987) of an important organizational trend if it could resolve the voice and value conflicts fragmenting the field into an integrative belief and intervention system, and if it could implement the alliance with an eye on watching the alliance itself evolve. Practitioners then could develop powerful tools, concepts, interventions, and processes for facilitating globalization of the economy. The emerging networks of business, government, and nongovernmental organizations were paralleled by an alliance among the professional OD associations.

Learning: From Fuzzy Values to Clear Priorities. Creation of the alliance was a watershed event in OD's rejuvenation. A three-day strategy conference shortly after the alliance was announced resulted in commitment by all parties to a conversation about values. Conference participants recount that it was clear to everyone that the field possessed a "fuzzy logic" with respect to values. The group was in 100 percent agreement that what made OD unique was "its values." However, little or no consensus existed on what the values were. Each voice prioritized its own set of values (Davis, 1999) and claimed to be speaking for the field. The conference resulted in a commitment to begin a conversation on OD's cornerstone values. A process crafted and started by Gellermann, Frankel, and Ladenson (1990) was used. Participants in this process were not asked to agree or commit to particular values. They were asked only to agree to being involved in the process of discussing and debating the values.

The conversation unfolded in articles, online messages, and informal exchanges among researchers and practitioners. One issue was that many traditional OD values were seen as hypocritical, judgmental, and often dogmatic, especially in the context of a globalized economy and cross-cultural practice. Examples were honesty and integrity seen as culturally determined values. What was open and honest in one country was very different in another. Another example of culturally determined values is an unequivocal commitment to participation that leads to democratic change designs in highly autocratic or power distant cultures and colludes with an unmindful capitalism to reduce cultural diversity.

The value of learning emerged as a means to reconcile differing voices and gave OD a stake in the outcomes of economic and social activity. A change design focused around learning would decrease the chance of judgment and increase the chance of appreciating diversity in thought. For example, by incorporating periods of reflection and review during the change process, organization members could inquire into what worked and did not work in producing change. Such learning could then be factored into subsequent intervention designs.

Learning was also a value with a long tradition in OD. Educational interventions, for example, were one of the early change strategies (Bennis, Benne, Chin, and Corey, 1976) and remain an important element in many organization, management, and leadership development efforts. Moreover, learning was a long-held element of good OD practice in terms of transfer of skills and knowledge to the client system or the increased capacity of the client system to manage change in the future (Worley and Varney, 1998; Worley, Rothwell, and Sullivan, 2005).

The traditionalists saw learning as an important part of OD because it differentiated OD from change management. It was a legitimate answer to the question, "Why is OD different?" Pragmatists favored learning as a value because a strong economic argument existed for building the learning and knowledge management capabilities of organizations. Successful innovation relied heavily on learning as new technologies were applied over time and in varied contexts (Sahal, 1981). Organizations in rapidly changing environments and growing industries had to either increase their capacity to learn in proportion to their growth rate or suffer a competitive disadvantage in adapting. The capability to learn and change became a central part of the discourse in strategic management as a result.

Alliance Contributions to Practice: Knowledge Management and Marketing.
OD practitioners operating under the umbrella of the alliance and the emerging consensus of learning modeled the new economics of collaboration through a knowledge management portal and a marketing Website. A knowledge management portal was developed first to create a central location where OD practice knowledge was stored, develop best practices in emerging areas quickly, and improve the quality of change interventions and OD practice. The portal was a place where new ideas could be posted, practice experiences shared and searched, and conversations about practice maintained. A variety of tools, concepts, interventions, exercises, frameworks, and experiences were captured, including practical tips about how to understand and work with power and politics, when to intervene and when to be patient, how to resolve ethical and value dilemmas, and how to make choices about the speed of the process.

The portal was successful in increasing practice effectiveness. OD was better able to influence organizational effectiveness because OD provided valuable information for both beginning and seasoned practitioners; refreshed practice with new intervention ideas; recognized the contributions of practitioners to the portal through citation, references, and business referrals; and was easy to work with.

A second alliance effort was a marketing Website to educate the public and potential client systems about OD. OD's reputation was in flux at the start of the millennium because many people simply did not know what it was, and many others were claiming to practice OD without any preparation, knowledge, education, skill, or experience. The Website responded by describing the purpose, philosophy, and processes associated with organization development. It also described practitioner competencies, likely outcomes, and key differences between OD and other forms of change. The Website was tremendously helpful in articulating differences among autocratic, fast, and directed change; facilitated change management; and organization development. OD's focus on learning, building capacity in the system, and attending to improved effectiveness was seen as an increasingly relevant option for organizations. Educated clients were better able to make decisions about staffing an internal OD organization or hiring external consulting help. The Website encouraged clients to seek out internal and external help that matched their particular needs and offered the opportunity to recommend good practice. The site also presented a broad set of resources related to the specialties within OD.

Individual alliance members included the address for the World OD Alliance Website on their business cards, e-mail signatures, and their own Websites. This helped to build a community of practitioners and create an OD brand, but it did not homogenize OD practice. Practitioners retained their own unique skill sets, approaches, and value-add propositions, and they did so within the boundaries of the field as explained on the Website. The upshot of including the site address on client communications was creation and communication of a de facto method of quality control. Practitioners unwilling to live by the generic guidelines described on the Website were not forced to comply. The voluntary participation to support the site and its overview of the field effectively controlled the supply side of the consulting equation. The increasing sophistication of the client systems controlled the demand side. Some practitioners were successful despite resistance to the idea. However, many who were not qualified to deliver OD services found it increasingly difficult to find work.

Summary

The World OD Alliance came together and signaled the OD field's commitment to resolving differences generating more harm than good and preventing the OD field from being a positive and substantive force in organization and social change. The alliance's first two orders of business were a conversation about valuing learning as an integrative and overarching principle and acting on that value by educating the marketplace about what OD should do, how it works, and what it can offer. Two key events in this process were the knowledge management portal and the marketing Website.

The Responsible Progress Doctrine

The alliance's early activities were an important step in OD's rejuvenation and established a broader infrastructure for influence on organizations. But Maathai stressed that OD's ability to shape the globalization process required articulation of a set of goals and strategies. To actualize OD's potential for organizational and social change, a strategic planning process was initiated that leveraged learning from the processes that created the alliance, developed the conversation on values, and promoted the field. The planning process resulted in creation of the *responsible progress doctrine*.

This doctrine called on the field to support governments, nongovernmental organizations, corporations, and other stakeholders to jointly optimize the four elements of global success: technological innovation, economic development, ecological sustainability, and cultural diversity. The doctrine was influenced by the joint optimization principle from sociotechnical systems theory and recognized that each element alone was insufficient to produce responsible progress; pursuit of each element's goal had to be achieved within the bounds of the other three. The doctrine was also influenced by Murrell's proposal (2002, 2003) to (1) treat people as ends, (2) drive for performance as an important outcome, (3) address the balance and tension between trying to achieve both people and performance outcomes, and (4) design for sustainability. Finally, responsible progress doctrine was influenced by the "triple bottom line," which focused on the economic, social, and ecological value added or destroyed by governments, organizations, and individuals.

Technological innovation supported the goal of new and better ideas for progress. It was the economic drive train of responsible progress guided by the principles of sustainability. Investment prior to the responsible progress doctrine often favored incremental innovation with a higher likelihood of generating incremental profits over riskier innovation with great potential (Mensch, 1978; Sahal, 1981). Too often, these incremental investments increased commitment to fossil-fuel–based paradigms. The progress achieved was fleeting and in the wrong direction. In contrast, the responsible progress doctrine encouraged OD practitioners to ensure that organizations included a broader set of criteria when choosing technologies to support, pursue, develop, or deploy. Organizations were recognized whenever practicable by media accounts and the financial markets for pursuing development of clean technologies, substitution of clean technology for fossil-fuel–based business models, and use of technology to preserve cultural diversity. Development of communications technologies that protected security and privacy was also encouraged. These technological trajectories supported learning as a core organizational value, as the World OD Alliance founding had proposed.

Economic development supported the goal of organizations and countries to grow and operate effectively, guided by the principles of cultural diversity and sustainability. It specifically recognized the importance of profit, productivity, and growth at all levels. Technological innovations were deployed to create effective organizations, productive countries, and a vigorous global economy. A variety of policy and tax incentive changes were needed to support the technological investments, look carefully at the distribution of wealth (specifically the gap between the haves and the have nots), pursue growth not at the expense of cultural diversity but because of it, and promote business models that examine the return on living capital.

Ecological sustainability supported the goal of living within the environment's ability to support life over the long run and contribute to diversity and growth. It was a link-pin value in the responsible progress doctrine and suggested that business strategies built around productive use of natural resources could solve environmental problems at a profit (Lovins, Lovins, and Hawken, 1999). These frameworks began with a simple premise: the economic models based on growth that were current in the early 2000s could not reconcile the increasing demand for finite and fundamental natural resources with the decreasing supply of those resources. Recognizing and addressing this incompatibility as part of the responsible progress doctrine created a larger number of available and socially acceptable solutions (Natrass and Altomare, 1999).

Cultural diversity supported the goal of human and cultural dignity and its key role in innovation and long-term adaptability. The models of globalization that emerged in the late 1900s consciously or unconsciously sought predictability and control over operations through standardization. Standardized operating procedures and technological platforms were not optimized within cultural norms that varied across global subsidiaries. Adopting a standard culture was preferred and encouraged in a variety of subtle and gross ways as a result.

Although cultural diversity was important in its own right, it clearly supported other elements of the responsible progress doctrine. For example, cultural diversity was and is a real source of creativity and innovation. The cultural diversity principle raised into saliency what had been happening unconsciously and asked decisions makers to commit to the health of the long-term source of growth, development, and innovation.

The responsible progress doctrine reflected an updated view of industrial-organization economics (Scherer, 1980). An economic system's performance traditionally was judged by the extent to which (1) scarce resources were efficiently used to maximize real income, (2) a broader and higher-quality set of goods and services were produced over time, (3) employment was being maximized, and (4) outputs and outcomes were distributed such that people's needs were being met and productive effort rewarded. However, market conditions that evolved in the late twentieth century warped those criteria. Globalization was less about economic equality than about standardization and the dominance of a certain view of capitalism. The globalization that resulted maximized short-term profitability at the expense of long-term viability, unintentionally homogenized national cultures, and failed to account for the ecology in its calculation of profits and return (Korten, 1995; International Forum on Globalization, 2002; Lovins, Lovins, and Hawken, 1999).

Elaboration, discussion, and implementation of the responsible progress doctrine gave OD a voice in shaping and influencing significant social and organizational change. Because it embraced and integrated the traditional and pragmatic voices and leveraged the strengths of alliance partners and members, OD was not marginalized as it was during the reengineering, downsizing, and total quality management crazes.

Maathai concluded her recounting of OD's rejuvenation by noting that members of the OD community around the world began adapting and promulgating the responsible progress doctrine in publications, conversations, and practice. The field began shaping organizational strategies, structures, and processes both internally and externally according to the policies of responsible progress. The changes were imperceptible at first and began occurring with faster momentum as time went on. The World OD Alliance sponsored large multigovernmental, multiorganizational, and multicountry conferences on cultural contributions to innovation, alternative energy integration, government-business coordination, sustainability, network structures, and other transorganizational problems in line with the responsibility doctrine (Cummings, 1984; Huxham and Vangen, 2004). OD practitioners were called on with increasing frequency and at ever higher levels of influence to facilitate changes. These changes were intended to move globalization in a valued direction, where more and more people became involved and benefited from diversity, innovation, development, and sustainability.

Summary and Conclusions

Returning to the present, we conclude by saying this chapter presented a vision of the future and OD's role in it. The future of OD is very bright. But a bright future for OD does not mean the field is now a coherent and singular voice for responsible progress and the organization changes that are necessary. OD is currently fragmented, and the voices in the field have strong beliefs about how it should evolve. A bright future for OD does not mean it is now a vibrant community of practitioners and researchers developing new interventions and exploring the impact of the work. Understanding of the relationship between change and organization effectiveness remains primitive. The task of conveying OD's credibility is not easy. A bright future for OD does not mean it is now growing. Depending on how the field is defined, OD's reputation is quite weak and the trajectory of the field's development is not clear.

But dedicated members of the field do not view these challenges as reasons to give up or give in. The world is changing in positive as well as horrific ways, and OD practitioners believe they have the knowledge and the skill to influence the trajectory of change. This is their passion and their calling. There is, in fact, considerable common ground among the voices within OD, and the emergence of a more integrated view of the field is not a pipe dream. As an example, the traditional, pragmatic, and academic voices agree that applying behavioral science to organizations can improve effectiveness and increase member satisfaction. The traditional and pragmatic voices believe that knowledge and skill should be transferred to a client system, and all three voices believe that a body of theory and practice underlies the process of change in organizations. The trends in the economic, social, political, and technological environments—and trends within OD itself—all contain the seeds of an integrative and influential force that is capable of shaping the positive future of our world.

References

Alderfer, C. (1987). An intergroup perspective on group dynamics. In J. Lorsch (Ed.), *Handbook of organization behavior* (pp. 190–222). Upper Saddle River, NJ: Prentice Hall.

Alderfer, C. (2003). Letter from the editor. *Journal of Applied Behavioral Science, 39,* 357–359.

Bennis, W., Benne, K., Chin, R., & Corey, K. (1976). *The planning of change* (3rd ed.). Austin, TX: Holt, Rinehart, and Winston.

Burke, W. (1976). Organization development in transition. *Journal of Applied Behavioral Science, 12,* 22–43.

Burke, W. (2002). *Organization change: Theory and practice.* Thousand Oaks, CA: Sage.

Cummings, T. (1984). Transorganization development. In B. Staw and L. Cummings (Eds.), *Research in organization behavior* (pp. 367–422). Greenwich, CT: JAI Press.

Cummings, T., & Worley, C. (2005). *Organization development and change* (8th ed.). Cincinnati: South-Western.

Davis, M. (1999). *As a child grows: An examination of influences on OD's assumptions and values.* (Working paper). Winchester, VA: Shenandoah University, Department of Management.

Farias, G., & Johnson, H. (2000). Organizational development and change management: Setting the record straight. *Journal of Applied Behavioral Science, 36,* 376–379.

Freedman, A. (1999). The history of organization development and the NTL Institute: What we have learned, forgotten, and rewritten. *Psychologist-Manager Journal, 3*(2), 125–141.

Friedlander, F. (1998, Spring). The evolution of organization development: 1960s to 1990s. *Vision/Action, 17,* 10–12.

Gellermann, W., Frankel, M., & Ladenson, R. (1990). *Values and ethics in organization and human systems development.* San Francisco: Jossey-Bass.

Hornstein, H. (2001). Organizational development and change management: Don't throw the baby out with the bath water. *Journal of Applied Behavioral Science, 37*(2), 223–226.

Huxham, C., & Vangen, S. (2004). *Managing to collaborate.* London: Routledge.

International Forum on Globalization. (2002). *Alternatives to economic globalization.* San Francisco: Berrett-Koehler.

Klein, H., & Linneman, R. (1981). The use of scenarios in corporate planning: Eight case histories. *Long Range Planning, 14,* 69–77.

Kleiner, A. (1996). *The age of heretics.* New York: Doubleday.

Korten, D. (1995). *When corporations rule the world.* San Francisco: Berrett-Koehler.

Lovins, A., Lovins, L., & Hawken, P. (1999, May–June). A roadmap for natural capitalism. *Harvard Business Review,* 145–158.

Mensch, G. (1978). *Stalemate in technology: Innovations overcome the depression.* New York: Ballinger.

Murrell, K. (2002). The new century for global organization development: Responding to the challenges of the day. *OD Practitioner, 34*(1), 24–30.

Murrell, K. (2003). Hope: Our intended legacy for 2050. *Organization Development Journal, 22*(2), 21–28.

Natrass, B., & Altomare, M. (1999). *The natural step for business: Wealth, ecology and the evolutionary corporation.* Gabriola Island, BC, Canada: New Society.

Pettigrew, A., Woodman, R., & Cameron, K. (2001). Studying organizational change and development: Challenges for future research. *Academy of Management Journal, 44,* 697–713.

Porter, M. (1985). *Competitive advantage.* New York: Free Press.

Rifkin, J. (2004, August 17). Worlds apart on the vision thing. *Globe and Mail,* A15.

Sahal, D. (1981). *Patterns of technological innovation.* Reading, MA: Addison-Wesley.

Scherer, F. (1980). *Industrial market structure and economic performance* (2nd ed.). Boston: Houghton Mifflin.

Wack, P. (1985, September–October). Scenarios: Uncharted waters ahead. *Harvard Business Review,* 89.

Worley, C., & Feyerherm, A. (2003). Reflections on the future of organization development. *Journal of Applied Behavioral Science, 39*(1), 97–115.

Worley, C., Rothwell, W., & Sullivan, R. (2005). Competencies of OD practitioners. In W. Rothwell & R. Sullivan (Eds.), *Practicing organization development: A guide for consultants* (2nd ed.). San Francisco: Jossey-Bass/Pfeiffer.

Worley, C., & Varney, G. (1998, Winter). A search for a common body of knowledge for master's level organization development and change programs. *Academy of Management ODC Newsletter,* 1–4.

Worren, N., Ruddle, K., & Moore, K. (1999). From organizational development to change management: The emergence of a new profession. *Journal of Applied Behavioral Science, 35*(3), 273–286.

ABOUT THE EDITORS

Brenda B. Jones is an organizational consultant with a focus on organization strategy and change, leadership, diversity initiatives, and developing consultants. She consults internationally; is on the faculty of the American University/NTL OD Master's Program and the Gestalt Institute of Cleveland; is a past chair of the OD Network Board; and is a member of the NTL Institute, OD Network, Academy of Management, and the International Organization Development Association (IODA). She lives in Columbia, Maryland, and can be reached at bjones@ntl.org.

Michael Brazzel is an organization development and diversity/social justice practitioner, economist, former manager in U.S. government agencies, and university educator-researcher. He is a member of the NTL Institute and cofounder of the NTL Diversity Practitioner Certificate Program. His life's work is based in values: respect for human differences, racial and social justice, and lifelong learning. He lives in Columbia, Maryland, and can be reached at mbrazzel@ntl.org.

ABOUT THE CONTRIBUTORS

John D. Adams has been at the forefront of organization development for more than thirty-five years. He is an author, speaker, consultant, and academician and is chair of the organizational systems Ph.D. program at Saybrook Graduate School. He began his professional career as a lecturer at the University of Leeds in 1969 and also served as director of professional development at NTL.

Billie T. Alban is president and senior partner of Alban and Williams, Consultants to Organizations. She is a national and international management consultant who teaches regularly in executive development programs at Columbia University. She works with organizations and communities on large-scale change efforts, using highly participative methods.

Rebecca Chan Allen is an organization facilitator specializing in diversity and transformation. Clients include transnational corporations, governments, professional associations, and community agencies. She is on the *OD Practitioner*'s editorial board, a member of NTL Institute, and a faculty member of NTL's Diversity Practitioner Certificate Program. Rebecca has taught in several universities, including Simon Fraser, Calgary, and Keio in Tokyo.

Barbara Benedict Bunker is an organizational social psychologist and professor of psychology emeritus at the University at Buffalo. She is also an independent consultant and coauthor (with Billie Alban) of *Large Group Interventions* (Jossey-Bass, 1997) and articles on large group methods.

Anthony J. DiBella is an associate professor of National Security Affairs at the Naval Ware College in Newport, Rhode Island. As an educator and scholar-practitioner, his research interests include team and organizational learning, leadership and organization development. He has a Ph.D. from the MIT Sloan School of Management and is author of *How Organizations Learn* (Jossey-Bass, 1998) and *Learning Practices* (Prentice-Hall, 2001).

Katherine Farquhar teaches in the American University/NTL MSOD program, having been on American University's faculty since 1989. Her research focuses on the dynamics of executive transitions and on women's tennis. Her Ph.D. is in social psychology from Boston University, where she studied OD with Robert Chin. She serves on private and educational boards and consults to nonprofits. She is an NTL member.

Arthur M. Freedman is a consulting psychologist specializing in organization development and change. He is director of the AU/NTL Master's Program, School of Public Affairs, American University. He is a Fellow of the Society of Consulting Psychology and past president of the Society of Psychologists in Management. He is a well-known author and longtime member of the NTL Institute.

Seán Gaffney was born and raised in Ireland and is a resident of Sweden. He works internationally as a Gestalt therapist/OSD consultant and trainer, university lecturer in cross-cultural management, and faculty member with the Gestalt Institute of Cleveland, Gestalt International Study Center, and the Gestalt Academy of Scandinavia. He is completing his Ph.D. at the University of Derby, United Kingdom.

Susan M. Gallant is a consultant, coach, teacher, and speaker with more than twenty-five years of experience in the OD field. She specializes in developing cultures where caring is genuine, competence is the norm, and wisdom is honored. She enjoys working with leaders to help them create organizations that flourish in complex and diverse environments.

William Gellermann is an OD/HSD consultant and teacher with more than forty years of experience. He is coauthor of *Values and Ethics in Organization and Human Systems Development* (Jossey-Bass, 1990). He holds a Ph.D. in behavioral science for management from UCLA and has been on the faculty of several universities, among them Cornell, State University of New York, and City University of New York.

Jonno Hanafin is principal of Jonno Hanafin Associates, a strategic resource to executives and organizations, based in Long Valley, New Jersey. He is chair of the Gestalt Institute of Cleveland's Organization and System Development International program. He has been an international organizational practitioner for thirty years.

Stanley R. Hinckley Jr., established his OD consulting-training firm in 1978 after ten years as OD manager and twenty years in international engineering at Procter & Gamble. He was an NTL member, a Certified Consultants International charter member, and chairman of the CCI board of trustees. He is now a member of the OD Network, International OD Association, and Academy of Management.

Bailey W. Jackson is professor of education, University of Massachusetts, Amherst, and former dean of the School of Education. He has published articles and edited a book on racial identity development, social oppression and liberation, managing diversity in the workplace, multicultural organization development, and large systems change. Jackson is a frequent keynote speaker at conferences and seminars.

David Jamieson is president of the Jamieson Consulting Group and adjunct professor of management, Pepperdine University. He consults to organizations on change, strategy, design, leadership, and human resources. He was president of ASTD and Consultation Division chair, Academy of Management. He is coauthor of *Managing Workforce 2000: Gaining the Diversity Advantage* (Jossey-Bass, 1991) and *The Complete Guide to Facilitation: Enabling Groups to Succeed.*

Frances Johnston is cochair of the Teleos Leadership Institute. Her expertise includes leadership development and transformation, emotional intelligence, group dynamics, and organizational renewal. Working with top management teams, she helps clients use development-oriented programs and practices, as well as build effective structures for ongoing development and growth. Johnston also serves on the faculty of the Gestalt Institute of Cleveland.

Mark Leach is a consultant and researcher with twenty-five years of experience working on equality and social justice issues with nonprofit, private, and government organizations. He has expertise in organization change, nonprofit strategy and governance, and creating inclusive systems. He holds a doctorate in organizational behavior from Boston University. He is a senior consultant with Management Assistance Group.

Roland E. Livingston is a consultant, human resource executive, and educational leader specializing in organizational change processes, senior-level team effectiveness, and executive coaching. His research interest is the effectiveness of leadership development training in organizations and organizational change. He uses the Leadership Effectiveness Analysis, the Emotional Competency Inventory, and the MBTI in his work and teaching in colleges and universities.

Carolyn J. Lukensmeyer is president and founder of America*Speaks.* She served in the White House and was chief of staff to the governor of Ohio. She has run her own OD firm, consulting to corporate and public sector organizations. Lukensmeyer holds a doctorate in organizational behavior from Case Western Reserve University.

Robert J. Marshak has a global consulting practice, teaches in the AU/NTL MSOD program, and has authored more than forty publications on organizational consulting and change. He has been a member of the NTL board of directors and is currently a trustee of the OD Network. He received the OD Network's Lifetime Achievement Award in 2000.

Rick Maurer is a consultant specializing in change who serves on the faculty of the OSD program at the Gestalt Institute of Cleveland. He is author of *Beyond the Wall of Resistance, Why Don't You Want What I Want?, Building Capacity for Change Sourcebook,* and the Change Without Migraines System.

Ed Mayhew was educated at Dartmouth College and the Amos Tuck School of Business Administration. He was an executive with a major telecommunications company and now consults with public and private organizations in the United States, Asia, and Europe in the areas of complex systems change, executive education, team development, and leadership development. He is a member of NTL Institute.

Ann McCloskey is senior vice president of learning and development for Wells Fargo Bank—California Business Banking. She has more than fifteen years of management, strategy, change management, and training experience in the financial services industry. McCloskey earned her bachelor's in finance from Northern Illinois University and her master's of science in organization development from Pepperdine University.

Annie McKee is cochair of the Teleos Leadership Institute, where she advises and works collaboratively with senior executives to design and create innovative approaches to leadership development and organizational transformation. She serves on the faculty of the University of Pennsylvania's Graduate School of Education. McKee coauthored the book *Primal Leadership: Realizing the Power of Emotional Intelligence* with Daniel Goleman and Richard Boyatzis.

Matt Minahan is a member of NTL Institute and president of MM & Associates, specializing in strategic planning, organization design and development, and leadership development. His clients are in the private and public sectors, implementing enterprisewide change programs, including business strategy, mission, business process simplification, new structures, and communications. He also teaches in the business school at Johns Hopkins University.

Edwin C. Nevis is president of the Gestalt International Study Center, Cape Cod, and a founder of the OSD and International OSD programs of the Gestalt Institute of Cleveland. He was a faculty member and administrator at MIT Sloan School of Management. He is a member of NTL and author of *Organizational Consulting: A Gestalt Approach* and coauthor of *Intentional Revolutions* (Jossey-Bass, 1996).

Julie A. C. Noolan is an international OD practitioner focusing on organization assessment, facilitating strategic planning, institutional capacity building, board development, and cross-cultural diversity. She teaches in the AU/NTL MSOD program at American University in Washington, D.C., and currently serves as chair of the board of the NTL Institute for Applied Behavioral Science.

Edwin E. Olson is collegiate professor, MBA program, University of Maryland and adjunct professor, Executive Leadership Program, George Washington University. He has applied complexity science to organizations in *Facilitating Organization Change: Lessons from Complexity Science* (with Glenda Eoyang) and *Organization Leadership: Tapping the Energy of Self-Organizing* (with Maya Townsend). He has been a member of NTL Institute since 1978.

Daisy Ríos is an OD practitioner who works independently and in collaboration with OD firms to design and deliver organization development strategies and interventions in a variety of settings. She earned a Ph.D. in education from Temple University and an M.S. in education from the University of Pennsylvania. She is bilingual, fluent in English and Spanish.

Cathy L. Royal is a system and human development professional with specialties in diversity, structural equality, appreciative inquiry, and organizational transformation. She is a member, trainer, and Ken Benne Scholar for NTL Institute. The U.S. Congress has recognized Royal for her work on gender and empowerment, and she is a recipient of the Fielding Institute Social Justice award.

Edgar H. Schein has taught at the MIT Sloan School of Management since 1956, where he is professor emeritus and senior lecturer. His most recent books are *Process Consultation Revisited* (1999), *The Corporate Culture Survival Guide* (Jossey-Bass, 1999), and *DEC Is Dead: Long Live DEC* (2003). He consults with organizations on organizational culture, organization development, process consultation, and career dynamics.

Charles Seashore is a faculty member of the doctoral program in human and organization development of the Fielding Graduate Institute and the American University/NTL Institute Master's Program in organization development in Washington, D.C. He received the Organization Development Network's Lifetime Achievement Award in 2004. He is a coauthor of *What Did You Say? The Art of Giving and Receiving Feedback.*

Edith Whitfield Seashore is a consultant in organization development and past president of the NTL Institute. She is the cofounder of the American University/NTL Institute Master's Program in organization development. Edie received the Organization Development Network's Lifetime Achievement Award in 2001. She co-edited *The Promise of Diversity* and co-authored *What Did You Say? The Art of Giving and Receiving Feedback.*

Juliann Spoth is a consultant, coach, and educator with twenty-five years of experience in organizational and cultural change, strategic planning, conflict mediation, creating high-performing teams, and leadership development. For more than fifteen years she has explored the role of energy in promoting health and change in individuals, groups, and organizations.

Daniel Stone is head of WholeSystem Consulting, helping organizations create genuine and sustainable change in what they do and how they go about doing it. He has consulted for more than twenty-five years to organizations in corporate, government, health care, education, and nonprofit sectors. As senior associate with America*Speaks,* he has produced and facilitated numerous 21st Century Town Meetings.

Tojo Thatchenkery is professor of organizational learning and knowledge management at George Mason University. He has written extensively on change and knowledge management and is a consultant to corporations and international organizations. His most recent book is *Appreciative Sharing of Knowledge: Leveraging Knowledge Management for Strategic Change.* His Ph.D. is in organizational behavior from Case Western Reserve University.

Mary Ann Rainey Tolbert is an external practitioner specializing in executive coaching, management development, and group effectiveness. She was a vice president for Exelon. She holds a Ph.D. in organizational behavior, cochairs the Gestalt Institute of Cleveland's International OSD program, teaches at Benedictine University, and is a member of NTL.

Ted Tschudy is a member and past board chair of NTL. He has more than thirty years' experience as an internal and external OD practitioner and serves on the adjunct faculty of the American University/NTL Master's Program in organization change and development.

Christopher G. Worley is director of the MSOD program and associate professor of organization theory, Pepperdine University. He is coauthor of *Integrated Strategic Change* and *Organization Development and Change* and a member of NTL, the Academy of Management, and OD Network. Consulting clients include Microsoft, American Healthways, and BP.

NAME INDEX

A

Abrams, J., 337
Ackerman-Anderson, L., 424
Adams, J. D., 110, 164, 335, 336, 337, 340, 345, 346
Adler, N., 42, 358, 387
Ahlstrand, B., 195
Alban, B. T., 38, 43, 165, 167, 174, 218, 287, 290, 291, 293
Alda, A., 138
Alderfer, C. P., 109, 504, 505
Allen, R. C., 370, 372, 374, 380, 381
Allison, M. A., 468
Aloni, R., 37
Alper, S. W., 208
Altomare, M., 510
Amini, F., 415
Anderson, D., 424
Argyris, C., 19, 51, 54, 86, 90, 94, 168, 213, 226, 393, 493
Ashkanasy, N., 409
Atkinson, M., 428
Axelrod, D., 43, 290, 297

B

Backman, S., 249

Bamford, K., 54, 85
Banet, A., Jr., 271, 272
Barnet, R., 396
Barnevik, P., 387
Bartel, C., 410
Barzini, L., 363
Bateson, G., 273
Becker, R., 426
Beckhard, R., 13, 33, 34, 38, 55, 107, 113, 114, 164, 165, 202
Beer, M., 347, 488
Beisser, A., 135–136
Bell, C., 51, 84, 86, 163
Bell, D., 393
Bellman, G. M., 244
Benne, K. D., 30, 54, 70, 84, 266, 506
Bennis, W. G., 33, 51, 55, 62, 269–272, 506
Bialek, W., 426
Bion, W., 266–267
Blake, R. R., 32
Block, P., 90, 94, 169, 208, 209, 240, 242
Bohm, D., 273
Boje, D., 393, 394
Bolman, L. G., 165, 200, 201
Bond, M. H., 361

Boyacigiller, N. A., 387
Boyatzis, R., 409, 410, 411, 412, 415, 420, 424
Boyle, M., 344
Braaten, L. J., 271
Brache, A. P., 199
Bradbury, H., 86, 94
Bradford, D. L., 266, 273
Bradford, L. P., 30, 54
Brannick, T., 86, 90, 91
Brewer, M. B., 361
Bridger, H., 39, 106
Bridges, W., 134–135
Broadhead, J. L., 241
Brown, D., 317
Brown, I., 414
Brown, J., 299
Brown, L. D., 321
Bruyere, R., 425, 426
Buchmann, M., 374
Bunker, B. B., 38, 43, 165, 167, 174, 218, 287, 290, 291, 293, 300
Burke, W. W., 14, 37, 39, 57, 195, 198, 206, 388, 468, 501
Burns, F., 38
Burns, T., 54
Burrell, G., 70
Byham, W. C., 193

SUBJECT INDEX

A

ABCs (attitudes, behaviors, and circumstances of inclusion), 448

Abstracted Business Information (University Microfilms International), 395

Academy of Management, 39, 505

Academy of Management conference (1982), 36

ACC (Association for Creative Change), 35, 36

ACCORD (Association for Creative Change in Organizational Renewal and Development), 36

Accountability issues, 305–306

Action planning phase, 88, 169–170

Action research: context of the consultation, 88–90; as core of ODC (organization development and change), 83; described, 29, 83–84, 161*fig*–162*fig*; ERP project example of, 94–100; four steps of, 86–88, 87*fig*; Lewin's concept of, 85*fig*; operational values of, 100–102; origins of, 84–86; planning and implementation processes, 88, 169–170; purposes of, 86; as reiterative cyclical process, 84, 85*fig*; relationship to consultation process phases, 90–94

Action research project: Lewin's concept of, 85*fig*; single cycle in, 87*fig*

Action taking phase, 170

Actual values, 47

Adaptation to uncertainty, 474

Addison-Wesley OD series, 38

Affirming organization, 145

Alpha Power, 458, 459

American Association for the Advancement of Science, 36

American Society for Training and Development OD Division, 36

American University, 3, 40

America*Speaks*, 295–296, 311

Amplifying differences, 475

Apartheid (South Africa), 427, 489

Appreciative Inquiry (AI): change using, 43, 440–441; described, 440; example of interview protocol, 445*e*–446*e*; Four-D Appreciative Inquiry Model of, 444*fig*–450; implications for OD practitioners, 450–454; large groups using, 297, 298–299; pillars of, 441–442; setting the stage for, 442–444

Appreciative Inquiry (AI) phases: deliver phase, 449–450; described, 444*fig*; design phase, 448–449; discover phase, 445–446; dream phase, 447–448

The Appreciative Inquiry (Ludema and others), 298

ARABS (Association for Religion and Applied Behavioral Science), 35

Artifacts (organization culture), 461–462

Asian stereotypes: OD practice and, 389–391; three levels of cultural consciousness and, 390*fig*

Assessment: cultural, 456–465, 460*e*; MCOD process and, 151–152. *See also* Evaluation

Audit data (MCOD), 152

Authentic commitment, 226

Authentic dialogue, 418

Awareness expert role, 172

high and low cultural context related to, 363–364; power of language and story in, 454–455; sustaining commitment through, 132. *See also* Dialogue; Feedback; Transforming exchanges

Competence-eccentricity continuum, 79

Competencies. *See* OD practitioner competencies

Complex responsive processes: conditions of self-organizing, 472–473; fostering self-organizing, 471–472; intervening in, 473–474; overview of system and organization, 470; self-organizing, 471

Complexity approach: described, 475; used with diversity initiatives, 478–482; used with team building, 476–478

Complexity science: OD practitioner roles in, 474–475; overview of, 467–468; working with complex responsive processes in, 470–474

Compliance organization, 145

Conference Model, 290

Confidence/trust issues, 126–127

Confidentiality: breaches of, 227; feedback and, 208; of interview data, 418

Conflict (group), 281–282

Congruence Model, 195, 196*fig*–197

Connecticut State Inter-Racial Commission, 30

Connections: OD practitioner role in change through, 474; transforming exchanges to build, 473, 477, 480–481

Consultant competencies: attending to parallel processes, 189–190; boundary management, 188; dialogue and communication skills, 190; managing diversity, 189; managing polarities, 189; managing resistance to change, 29, 121–128, 188; use of presence, 72–81, 190–191; use of self, 71–72, 171–173, 190–191. *See also* OD practitioner competencies

Consulting: action research and context of, 88–90; competencies required for, 29, 71–81, 121–128, 171–173, 187–191; early history of OD, 34–35. *See also* OD practitioners

Consulting phases: application of the AR cycle to each, 92*fig*; illustrated diagram of, 91*fig*; reiterative AR cycles applied to implementation of, 93*fig*; relationship of action research to, 90–94

Containing self-organizing processes: described, 472; implementing diversity initiatives and, 479–480; team building and, 476

Contracting. *See* Entry and contracting phase

The Corporate Culture Survival (Schein), 456

Countertransference, 260

CoVision (San Francisco), 296

Credibility: perceptions required for, 182; 21st Century Town Meeting, 308

Cross-cultural perspectives: border crossings over cultural differences, 356–360; borders, boundaries, and race, 367–368; boundaries in context of, 360–361; on high and low context and communication, 363–364; issue of identity, 361*e*–362; minicase on, 355–356, 364–367. *See also* Cultural differences

Cultivating presence, 76–77*fig*

Cultural assessment: assumptions underlying, 459; described, 458–459; organization culture and, 456–458; ten-step process of, 459–465, 460*e*

Cultural assessment steps: 1: obtain leadership commitment, 460; 2: select groups for interviews, 460–461; 3: select appropriate setting for group interviews, 461; 4: explain purpose of group meeting, 461; 5: explain the culture model, 461; 6: elicit descriptions of artifacts, 461–462; 7: identify espoused values,

462; 8: identify shared tacit assumptions, 462–463; 9: identify cultural aids and hindrances, 463–464; 10: join analysis and next steps, 464–465; listed, 460*e*

Cultural competency development, 382*t*

Cultural differences: border crossings over, 356–360; diminishing due to globalization, 395–398; homogenization of OD and, 391–395. *See also* Cross-cultural perspectives; Differences

Cultural field: mapping global human system, 376*t*; Systems Matrix, 374*t*, 375; whole-world competencies matrix, 377*t*, 379–381

Culture: border crossings between differences in, 356–360; dealing with heterogeneity across, 387–388; high and low context of, 363–364; Hofstede's five dimensions of, 359*e*; identity issues and, 361*e*–362; OD focus on issues of globalization and, 42, 388–389, 395–398; OD as product of, 394–395; rise of "standardized," 396–397; stereotypes regarding, 389–391, 390*fig*. *See also* Diversity; Multicultural organizations

Culture (organization): Alpha Power, 458, 459; focusing on "business problem" instead of, 457; levels of, 457*fig*; process of assessing, 458–465, 460*e*

Culture-specific OD mind-set, 400–401

Cybernetic (self-regulating) systems, 497

Cyclical and pendular models, 271, 273

D

Dannemiller Tyson Associates, 289

Data analysis: of cultural assessment, 464–465; OD process of, 169; of organization emotional reality, 418; process and presentation of, 205–206

Pfeiffer Publications Guide

This guide is designed to familiarize you with the various types of Pfeiffer publications. The formats section describes the various types of products that we publish; the methodologies section describes the many different ways that content might be provided within a product. We also provide a list of the topic areas in which we publish.

FORMATS

In addition to its extensive book-publishing program, Pfeiffer offers content in an array of formats, from fieldbooks for the practitioner to complete, ready-to-use training packages that support group learning.

FIELDBOOK Designed to provide information and guidance to practitioners in the midst of action. Most fieldbooks are companions to another, sometimes earlier, work, from which its ideas are derived; the fieldbook makes practical what was theoretical in the original text. Fieldbooks can certainly be read from cover to cover. More likely, though, you'll find yourself bouncing around following a particular theme, or dipping in as the mood, and the situation, dictate.

HANDBOOK A contributed volume of work on a single topic, comprising an eclectic mix of ideas, case studies, and best practices sourced by practitioners and experts in the field.

An editor or team of editors usually is appointed to seek out contributors and to evaluate content for relevance to the topic. Think of a handbook not as a ready-to-eat meal, but as a cookbook of ingredients that enables you to create the most fitting experience for the occasion.

RESOURCE Materials designed to support group learning. They come in many forms: a complete, ready-to-use exercise (such as a game); a comprehensive resource on one topic (such as conflict management) containing a variety of methods and approaches; or a collection of like-minded activities (such as icebreakers) on multiple subjects and situations.

TRAINING PACKAGE An entire, ready-to-use learning program that focuses on a particular topic or skill. All packages comprise a guide for the facilitator/trainer and a workbook for the participants. Some packages are supported with additional media—such as video—or learning aids, instruments, or other devices to help participants understand concepts or practice and develop skills.

- *Facilitator/trainer's guide* Contains an introduction to the program, advice on how to organize and facilitate the learning event, and step-by-step instructor notes. The guide also contains copies of presentation materials—handouts, presentations, and overhead designs, for example—used in the program.

- *Participant's workbook* Contains exercises and reading materials that support the learning goal and serves as a valuable reference and support guide for participants in the weeks and months that follow the learning event. Typically, each participant will require his or her own workbook.

ELECTRONIC CD-ROMs and Web-based products transform static Pfeiffer content into dynamic, interactive experiences. Designed to take advantage of the searchability, automation, and ease-of-use that technology provides, our e-products bring convenience and immediate accessibility to your workspace.

METHODOLOGIES

CASE STUDY A presentation, in narrative form, of an actual event that has occurred inside an organization. Case studies are not prescriptive, nor are they used to prove a point; they are designed to develop critical analysis and decision-making skills. A case study has a specific time frame, specifies a sequence of events, is narrative in structure, and contains a plot structure—an issue (what should be/have been done?). Use case studies when the goal is to enable participants to apply previously learned theories to the circumstances in the case, decide what is pertinent, identify the real issues, decide what should have been done, and develop a plan of action.

ENERGIZER A short activity that develops readiness for the next session or learning event. Energizers are most commonly used after a break or lunch to stimulate or refocus the group. Many involve some form of physical activity, so they are a useful way to counter post-lunch lethargy. Other uses include transitioning from one topic to another, where "mental" distancing is important.

EXPERIENTIAL LEARNING ACTIVITY (ELA) A facilitator-led intervention that moves participants through the learning cycle from experience to application (also known as a Structured Experience). ELAs are carefully thought-out designs in which there is a definite learning purpose and intended outcome. Each step—everything that participants do during the activity—facilitates the accomplishment of the stated goal. Each ELA includes complete instructions for facilitating the intervention and a clear statement of goals, suggested group size and timing, materials required, an explanation of the process, and, where appropriate, possible variations to the activity. (For more detail on Experiential Learning Activities, see the Introduction to the *Reference Guide to Handbooks and Annuals*, 1999 edition, Pfeiffer, San Francisco.)

GAME A group activity that has the purpose of fostering team spirit and togetherness in addition to the achievement of a pre-stated goal. Usually contrived—undertaking a desert expedition, for example—this type of learning method offers an engaging means for participants to demonstrate and practice business and interpersonal skills. Games are effective for team building and personal development mainly because the goal is subordinate to the process—the means through which participants reach decisions, collaborate, communicate, and generate trust and understanding. Games often engage teams in "friendly" competition.

ICEBREAKER A (usually) short activity designed to help participants overcome initial anxiety in a training session and/or to acquaint the participants with one another. An icebreaker can be a fun activity or can be tied to specific topics or training goals. While a useful tool in itself, the icebreaker comes into its own in situations where tension or resistance exists within a group.

INSTRUMENT A device used to assess, appraise, evaluate, describe, classify, and summarize various aspects of human behavior. The term used to describe an instrument depends primarily on its format and purpose. These terms include survey, questionnaire, inventory, diagnostic, survey, and poll. Some uses of instruments include providing instrumental feedback to group members, studying here-and-now processes or functioning within a group, manipulating group composition, and evaluating outcomes of training and other interventions.

Instruments are popular in the training and HR field because, in general, more growth can occur if an individual is provided with a method for focusing specifically on his or her own behavior. Instruments also are used to obtain information that will serve as a basis for change and to assist in workforce planning efforts.

Paper-and-pencil tests still dominate the instrument landscape with a typical package comprising a facilitator's guide, which offers advice on administering the instrument and interpreting the collected data, and an initial set of instruments. Additional instruments are available separately. Pfeiffer, though, is investing heavily in e-instruments. Electronic instrumentation provides effortless distribution and, for larger groups particularly, offers advantages over paper-and-pencil tests in the time it takes to analyze data and provide feedback.

LECTURETTE A short talk that provides an explanation of a principle, model, or process that is pertinent to the participants' current learning needs. A lecturette is intended to establish a common language bond between the trainer and the participants by providing a mutual frame of reference. Use a lecturette as an introduction to a group activity or event, as an interjection during an event, or as a handout.

MODEL A graphic depiction of a system or process and the relationship among its elements. Models provide a frame of reference and something more tangible, and more easily remembered, than a verbal explanation. They also give participants something to "go on," enabling them to track their own progress as they experience the dynamics, processes, and relationships being depicted in the model.

ROLE PLAY A technique in which people assume a role in a situation/scenario: a customer service rep in an angry-customer exchange, for example. The way in which the role is approached is then discussed and feedback is offered. The role play is often repeated using a different approach and/or incorporating changes made based on feedback received. In other words, role playing is a spontaneous interaction involving realistic behavior under artificial (and safe) conditions.

SIMULATION A methodology for understanding the interrelationships among components of a system or process. Simulations differ from games in that they test or use a model that depicts or mirrors some aspect of reality in form, if not necessarily in content. Learning occurs by studying the effects of change on one or more factors of the model. Simulations are commonly used to test hypotheses about what happens in a system—often referred to as "what if?" analysis—or to examine best-case/worst-case scenarios.

THEORY A presentation of an idea from a conjectural perspective. Theories are useful because they encourage us to examine behavior and phenomena through a different lens.

TOPICS

The twin goals of providing effective and practical solutions for workforce training and organization development and meeting the educational needs of training and human resource professionals shape Pfeiffer's publishing program. Core topics include the following:

Leadership & Management

Communication & Presentation

Coaching & Mentoring

Training & Development

e-Learning

Teams & Collaboration

OD & Strategic Planning

Human Resources

Consulting

What will you find on pfeiffer.com?

- The best in workplace performance solutions for training and HR professionals

- Downloadable training tools, exercises, and content

- Web-exclusive offers

- Training tips, articles, and news

- Seamless online ordering

- Author guidelines, information on becoming a Pfeiffer Affiliate, and much more

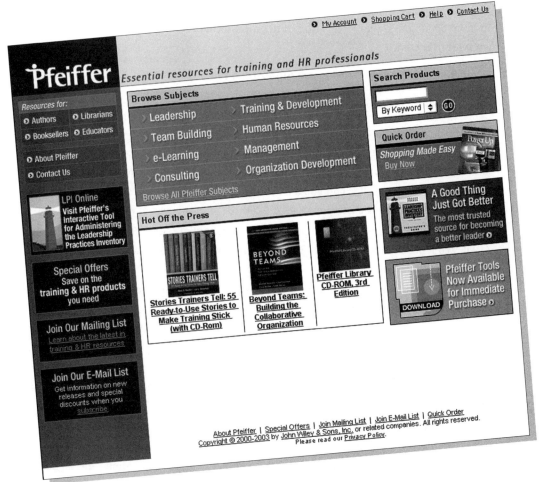

Discover more at www.pfeiffer.com

Customer Care

Have a question, comment, or suggestion? Contact us! We value your feedback and we want to hear from you.

For questions about this or other Pfeiffer products, you may contact us by:

E-mail: **customer@wiley.com**

Mail: **Customer Care Wiley/Pfeiffer**
10475 Crosspoint Blvd.
Indianapolis, IN 46256

Phone: **(US) 800-274-4434** (Outside the US: 317-572-3985)

Fax: **(US) 800-569-0443** (Outside the US: 317-572-4002)

To order additional copies of this title or to browse other Pfeiffer products, visit us online at **www.pfeiffer.com**.

For **Technical Support** questions, call **800-274-4434.**

For authors guidelines, log on to www.pfeiffer.com and click on "Resources for Authors."

If you are . . .

A **college bookstore, a professor, an instructor, or work in higher education** and you'd like to place an order or request an exam copy, please contact jbreview@wiley.com.

A **general retail bookseller** and you'd like to establish an account or speak to a local sales representative, contact Melissa Grecco at 201-748-6267 or mgrecco@wiley.com.

An **exclusively online bookseller**, contact Amy Blanchard at 530-756-9456 or ablanchard @wiley.com or Jennifer Johnson at 206-568-3883 or jjohnson@wiley.com, both in our Online Sales department.

A **librarian or library representative**, contact John Chambers in our Library Sales department at 201-748-6291 or jchamber@wiley.com.

A **reseller, training company/consultant, or corporate trainer**, contact Charles Regan in our Special Sales department at 201-748-6553 or cregan@wiley.com.

A **specialty retail distributor** (includes specialty gift stores, museum shops, and corporate bulk sales), contact Kim Hendrickson in our Special Sales department at 201-748-6037 or khendric@wiley.com.

Purchasing for the **Federal government**, contact Ron Cunningham in our Special Sales department at 317-572-3053 or rcunning@wiley.com.

Purchasing for a **State or Local government**, contact Charles Regan in our Special Sales department at 201-748-6553 or cregan@wiley.com.